G.S.

THE CANADIAN BORN
IN THE UNITED STATES

THE RELATIONS OF
CANADA AND THE UNITED STATES

———

A SERIES OF STUDIES
PREPARED UNDER THE DIRECTION OF THE
CARNEGIE ENDOWMENT FOR INTERNATIONAL PEACE
DIVISION OF ECONOMICS AND HISTORY

JAMES T. SHOTWELL, *Director*

THE CANADIAN BORN
IN
THE UNITED STATES

An Analysis of the Statistics of the Canadian Element
in the Population of the United States
1850 to 1930

BY

LEON E. TRUESDELL

CHIEF STATISTICIAN FOR POPULATION
UNITED STATES BUREAU OF THE CENSUS

NEW HAVEN : YALE UNIVERSITY PRESS
TORONTO : THE RYERSON PRESS
LONDON : HUMPHREY MILFORD : OXFORD UNIVERSITY PRESS
FOR THE CARNEGIE ENDOWMENT FOR INTERNATIONAL
PEACE : DIVISION OF ECONOMICS AND HISTORY
1943

INTRODUCTION

THIS volume is one of three, in this series of studies of Canadian-American relations, which deal with a hitherto missing chapter in one of the most important sections of the history of the New World, that of the migration of the European peoples and the long story of how they settled, moved, and settled again as they took possession of the North American continent. The volume by the late Professor Marcus Lee Hansen, entitled *The Mingling of the Canadian and American Peoples*, dealt with the theme as the historian sees it, an inspiring epic of achievement by those who laid the basis of a new society, seeking homes either in the wilderness or among the children of the pioneers who had conquered it. But most of those who wove the rich fabric of American life left little or no personal record, living and dying unconscious of the fact that they were making history. The result is that the data of that history are most elusive and that the historian must fall back upon sources other than the scant documentary material which has come down from an earlier day. Social history may well be supplemented by the impersonal records of statistics in which many otherwise forgotten movements and attitudes of the people are reflected. It is fortunate, therefore, that in this case we have authoritative statistical studies of the "mingling of the American and Canadian peoples" in two extensive surveys, of which this volume, summarizing the decennial census data on *The Canadian Born in the United States*, is one. The other, *The American Born in Canada*, by Dr. R. H. Coats and the late M. L. MacLean offers the parallel data from the Canadian sources in the Dominion Bureau of Statistics. In these two volumes are presented, so to speak, statistical cross-sections of the intermingling populations of Canada and the United States, spaced at ten-year intervals, from 1850 to 1930, and picturing in some fashion the net results of the movements and changes which took place during the successive decades.

In this vast and confused story of migration, an important factor was the movement into the United States of persons from various European countries who came to the United States by way of Canada. Considerable numbers of persons who had previously come to Canada from the Old World then moved from Canada into the United States in much the same way as the Americans of the Atlantic seaboard moved over the Alleghenies and up the Erie Canal. Some of these Europeans who came to the United States through Canada were hardly more than transients there and therefore cannot properly be counted among the Canadian immigrants, because they had not stayed long enough in Canada to become Canadians. They should not be overlooked, however, in any consideration of the sum total of migration from Canada into the United States merely because there is no way of telling just how long it takes to make a European over into either a Canadian or an American. The length of time naturally varies not only with the individual but with the European homeland from which the immigrant first came. The task of discriminating between the various degrees of cultural adaptability is not that of the statistician but that of the historian, and it has been adequately dealt with in the historical volume by Professor Hansen. It may, however, be recalled here that among all the immigrants into the two countries, those whose amalgamation and absorption was quickest and easiest were the Canadians in the United States and the Americans in Canada. The Canadian born share the common heritage of their birthright—America—with the American-born citizens of the United States.

The present volume, however, deals only in general terms with these intimate social factors in the history of migration. It is a contribution to the scientific study of the movement of population, a subject which has only recently, and only in a limited degree, received the attention it deserves. To most people the statistical apparatus upon which it is based is technical and forbidding, a register of abstractions furnishing raw material for specialists, or even, when reduced to the simplest terms and presented in graphic form, a quantitative measure in one or two dimensions applied to personal characteristics and social movements whose actual interrelations are manifold. But these columns of figures and the variously shaded bars and maps are also the record of human lives, not merely of the bare fact of living but of the interests and friends, the homely contacts and social and economic factors which affect them. It is the task of the historian to detect these influences on the outlook and movement of peoples; but the horizon is so wide and the movement so slow that no single observer can fully appreciate, still less measure, the total extent of any of these tidal drifts in human affairs. Fortunately, the statistical record fairly well covers the period during which the social movements of our own time have developed. The taking of the census in such fashion as to show the numbers of the Canadian born in the United States and the American born in Canada began in 1850 and in 1851, respectively; and in later decades additional details have been added, until the census reports both in Canada and in the United States have become extensive national repositories of material for the use of social scientists in the analysis of complex social and economic data. The contribution which is here offered is therefore doubly important, both by reason of the subject-matter and of the high competence of the author, who presides over that division of the Bureau of the Census of the United States which deals with its major problem, that of population. No one can write with greater authority on so important a subject. It is to be hoped that in the planning for a post-war world the significance of these movements of free and freedom-loving people may be more widely recognized than it has been in the past.

JAMES T. SHOTWELL

CONTENTS

TABLES

CHAPTER VIII. AGE OF THE CANADIAN STOCK

MAPS AND DIAGRAMS

THE CANADIAN BORN IN THE
UNITED STATES

CHAPTER I

INTRODUCTION AND SUMMARY

THE major part of the North American Continent is occupied by two nations whose peoples, if not homogeneous, are at least heterogeneous in like fashion. These two nations had their origins in contemporaneous colonial enterprises starting on the Atlantic Coast; in both there was a considerable period during which settlement was mainly limited to the Atlantic Seaboard and the valleys of the rivers emptying into the Atlantic; and in the westward movement of population which finally swept across the continent to the Pacific, one kept pace with the other except that the settlement of the Great Canadian Northwest had to await the development of varieties of wheat suited to its rigorous climate. Their governments are similar in form; their business enterprises follow the same pattern, with many concerns having interests in both countries;[1] their monetary unit is the same, and under normal conditions exchange is close to par, the two peoples read the same magazines, buy the same brands of packaged goods, and see the same moving pictures; and thus, while each retains its own distinguishing characteristics, they have more customs and habits in common than otherwise. There are no physical barriers separating the territory of one nation from that of the other and few artificial restrictions to hamper free passage back and forth across the established line, north of which is Canada and south of which is the United States. Thus one need not be surprised to learn that 14.9 per cent of the immigrant population of Canada is made up of persons born in the United States and that 9.1 per cent of the foreign-born population of the United States are of Canadian birth. Further, the American-born element in the Canadian population is more like the native Canadian population in many ways than is the immigrant population from other countries, even that from the British Isles; and the Canadian born in the United States are more like the native population of the United States than are the foreign born from any European country.

The historical aspects of the movements of population between the two countries are set forth in the volume entitled *The Mingling of the Canadian and American Peoples.* In two other volumes, the first one devoted

1. See *Canadian-American Industry,* by Marshall, Southard, and Taylor, which was the first volume in the present series.

primarily to the American born in Canada, and the second (the present volume) to the Canadian born in the United States, are presented the current statistics of the two peoples, with some series running back to 1850. These volumes seek to apply to the population growth and interchange the relatively exact measurements of statistics. In comparison with the historian, it may be noted, the statistician must work within rather narrow limitations. His material is primarily quantitative and secures even the appearance of qualitative significance only through the use of relatively small numbers of rigid categories, in contrast with the wide range of infinite gradation available in a treatment which is mainly descriptive, without claim to nicety of measurement. These limitations are perchance the price which the statistician pays for the seeming exactness of his findings.

Many phases of the interrelations between Canada and the United States are covered by the volumes in the series of which these three volumes dealing primarily with the population are only a small part—relations which are mainly economic or political. Into every phase of these relations, however, population enters as a significant factor. If there were no Americans in Canada or no Canadians in the United States, their joint business ventures would never have reached their present extent; and the history and outcome of such political controversies as have occurred might have been altogether different. A detailed study of the interchange of population between the two countries and its results in the form of Canadian-born persons resident in the United States and American-born persons resident in Canada seems therefore well justified as a contribution to an adequate understanding of the whole complicated subject, as well as for its own interest as an exposition of one separable (but by no means independent) aspect of the national life of Canada and the United States.

The statistics of total population, including both the American born in Canada and the Canadian born in the United States, go back to 1850 or 1851, and a number of significant classifications of these population groups, one or both, can be traced back over several decades. The main sources of statistical material are of course the census reports of the two countries, supplemented in many instances by unpublished data from the records of the United States Bureau of the Census in Washington or from the Dominion Bureau of Statistics in Ottawa. Comparisons between the statistics of the two countries are facilitated by the fact that their censuses of population follow in many respects a similar plan, with tabulations and published reports running parallel one to the other.

One might assume that the records of the immigration officials of the two countries would provide additional material to supplement the decennial counts of the census. After a careful examination of the figures available from these sources, however, it was decided that they could not be used in connection with the census figures, since they appeared to indicate more migration than that which could be accounted for by the census increases in the numbers of persons from either country living in the other.[2]

METHOD OF PRESENTATION

THE statistical tables which occupy most of the space in this volume are arranged somewhat as follows: Each new topic is presented so far as possible in a simple form, then in combination with one after another of those classifications previously introduced which are pertinent. For example, the Canadian born as a whole are presented in one table, the Canadian born classified by color in another table, and the Canadian born classified by color and sex in still another.

Summary tables are presented giving the available material in all practicable detail for the United States as a whole; then tables giving somewhat less detail for the decidedly significant subdivision of the country into urban, rural-nonfarm, and rural-farm areas; and finally there are many detailed tables giving figures for States and cities, and one table showing the Canadian-born population in those counties in which it is most important. These detailed tables serve two purposes: First, they supply local figures for those interested in specific localities, and second, they afford material for a more intensive analysis of various population relationships than can be made on the basis of the United States totals, which represent in too many cases the averaging of a wide range of differing conditions existing in different parts of the country.

The text discussion presents first the necessary definitions and explanations of terms or classifications. This is accompanied by comment on the more outstanding of the relations shown by the figures. This comment is designed to be mainly suggestive—especially the comment that is presented with respect to the figures for States or cities, for the complete discussion of which hundreds of pages would be required. In the text are also presented historical reasons or probable explanations for some of the relationships. It is hoped that persons having time for more than a cursory reading of this volume will take time to locate in the tables themselves those figures mentioned in the text paragraphs, and to observe

2. This situation may perhaps be explained, without too much criticism of the immigration records, by the fact that there are literally millions of persons crossing the Canadian boundary in either direction every year, so that the task of separating out from this large number of persons crossing the border those persons who intend to make permanent settlement in the new country (only a few thousands in any one year) is one which presents tremendous difficulties.

other similar relations there. For a statistical table is a device for presenting in small space a large number of relations between numbers, some of them definitely represented by percentages or ratios, others to be inferred from inspection and comparison of the basic figures themselves.

Scattered throughout the text are a considerable number of charts or diagrams presenting in graphic form some of the outstanding features of the various subjects, including in particular two maps on which are indicated the location of the total Canadian-born population of the United States and of the French Canadian born in New England and New York.

Brief Summary of Findings

THE growth of the population of Canada and the growth of the population of the United States since 1850 have been roughly parallel, as indicated by Figure 1 on page 11. The population of the United States increased from 23,000,000 in round numbers in 1850 to 123,000,000, or 5.3 times as much, in 1930, while the population of Canada increased between 1851 and 1931 from 2,400,000 to 10,400,000, or 4.3 times as much. In 1850 there were 147,711 Canadian born in the United States, where they formed 0.64 per cent of the population, while in 1851 there were about 63,000 American born in Canada, where they formed 2.6 per cent of the population. By 1930 the number of Canadian born in the United States had increased to 1,286,389, or 1.05 per cent of the total population, and the American born in Canada in 1931 numbered 344,574 and formed 3.3 per cent of the total population. The most rapid increase in the number of Canadian born in the United States was between 1850 and 1870, while the most rapid increase in the number of American born in Canada was between 1891 and 1911. The number of Canadian born in the United States in 1930 was almost one-sixth as great as the entire native population of Canada, that is, the number of Canadian born living in Canada, while the number of American born in Canada, though forming a fairly large percentage of the population of that country, represented only a small fraction of one per cent of the native population remaining in the United States.

The number of Canadian born in the United States increased rather rapidly from 1850 to 1900, but its increase since that date has been less rapid, and the characteristics of the group as a whole have become those of a relatively static population rather than those of an immigrant group constantly being recruited from outside. The age distribution of the Canadian born, for example, shows considerably larger percentages of persons in the older ages in 1930 than in 1910.

As compared with the foreign born who have come to the United States from other countries, particularly from the European continent, the Canadian born are more like the native population of the United States. This is particularly true of the Canadian born of English stock, who differ very little except in age and sex distribution from the native population of the States in which they are found. In the matter of age the Canadian-born population contains more persons in the adult ages and fewer children than the native population—but decidedly more children than the foreign born from most other countries. In the matter of sex distribution the Canadian-born population in general contains an appreciable excess of females, while there is still an excess of males in the native population of the United States. This excess of females is especially evident in the industrial centers of New England and Michigan and represents a progressive development, the number of males per 100 females showing a continuous decrease from one census to the next.

Of the Canadian born in the United States, 77.3 per cent were living in urban areas in 1930. This figure may be compared with 79.2 per cent for all foreign born in the United States, on the one hand, and with 56.2 per cent for the entire population, on the other. A more significant comparison than the last, however, might be a comparison with the total population of those Northern and Western States in which most of the Canadian born are found. In the 16 States having one per cent or more of their population Canadian born, 71.8 per cent of the population was classified as urban, or slightly less than the percentage shown for the Canadian born.

While the American born in Canada are distributed rather widely over the whole area of the Dominion, the Canadian born in the United States are rather closely concentrated in the New England States, along the northern border from New York westward, and in the Pacific Coast States, as indicated by the map on page 31. More than half of all the Canadian born in the United States in 1930 were found in 23 counties, and more than three-quarters in 91 counties, out of the 3,100 counties making up the entire area of the United States. Concentration of the French Canadian born in the northeastern corner of the United States is especially marked.

Nearly three-tenths of the Canadian born in the United States in 1930 were of French mother tongue, this being practically the same as the percentage returned as of French origin in the 1931 census of Canada.

Statistics are given in many of the chapters of this volume not only for the Canadian born but also for the children of the Canadian born, that is, for persons born in the United States but having one or both parents born in Canada, and for the two groups combined under the designation, "population of Canadian stock." The second generation of this Canadian stock is in general even more like the native population of the States in which it is found than are the Canadian born, though in its age distribution it shows appreciably fewer children than the general native white population.

The classification of the Canadian born enumerated in the United States in 1930 by year of immigration is especially significant as indicating their different periods of arrival in different parts of the United States—especially their early arrival in the agricultural States of the Middle West and their recent arrival in some of the eastern manufacturing centers and in the Pacific Coast States.

There is considerable evidence, both statistical and otherwise, of a rather extensive movement of both the Canadian born and the children of the Canadian born back and forth between Canada and the United States. For example, nearly one-third of the American born in Canada in 1931 were enumerated as having one or both parents Canadian born. The same conditions which offer encouragement to the permanent migration of the natives of one country to the other of course facilitate this back-and-forth movement.

A comparison of the occupational classification of the Canadian born with that of the population of the 16 Northern and Western States in which most of the Canadian born are found indicates that appreciably larger proportions of the Canadian born are found in skilled and semi-skilled occupations than of the total number of gainful workers in the 16 States, with correspondingly smaller proportions in unskilled occupations and domestic service. The percentage of the Canadian workers returned as farm laborers, in particular, was only about half that shown for all workers in the 16 States (3.8 per cent as compared with 7.4 per cent). On the other hand, the percentage of the Canadian workers, especially the French Canadian, employed as factory operatives, was much higher than in the larger group (French Canadian born, 35.4 per cent; all workers in 16 States, 14.9 per cent).

A Canadian family is defined as a family having a Canadian-born person as its head. From the classification by tenure of home it appears that 43.4 per cent of the French Canadian families in 1930 were living in homes which they owned, and 50.4 per cent of the English Canadian families, as compared with 46.8 per cent of all families in the United States, the percentage of home owners being much higher, for all three groups, in rural areas, especially on farms, than in urban areas. The median value of the urban homes occupied by Canadian families was $6,081, and of the rural-nonfarm homes, $2,958—both of these figures being appreciably higher than the average for all families in the urban and rural-nonfarm areas in the United States as a whole, though in many of the individual

States in which Canadians are numerous this relation was reversed, especially in the urban areas. The median monthly rental of urban homes rented by Canadian families was $34.39 and of the rented rural-nonfarm homes, $16.12, these figures being likewise higher than the national averages.

In average or median size, the French Canadian families were appreciably larger than families in the entire population of the United States, and the English Canadian families somewhat smaller. The percentage of both French and English Canadian families without children under 10 years old was larger than the corresponding percentage of all families in the United States—partly, at least, because of the higher age of the Canadian heads of families.

The classifications thus briefly summarized are presented in fuller detail in the chapters which follow, together with many additional classifications and comparisons—all directed toward the setting forth of an adequate picture of the Canadian element in the population of the United States, with sufficient information about the American population as a whole to provide the necessary background.

CHAPTER II

BASIC POPULATION RELATIONSHIPS BETWEEN THE UNITED STATES AND CANADA

For a period of 80 years, beginning in 1850 and 1851, there are available in the census reports of the United States and Canada, statistics measuring the growth of the populations of the respective countries and some of their interrelations, including the number of Canadian born living in the United States and the number of American born (that is, persons born in the United States) living in Canada.

With the aid of some estimates for marginal areas in Canada it is possible to get figures representing the total population of the two countries for a much longer period. It is estimated, for example, that in 1791 there were in Canada 233,000 persons of European origin,[1] which may be compared with the population of 3,929,214 shown by the First Census of the United States in 1790. On the basis of these figures it appears that the population of the United States, 140 years prior to the date of the 1930 and 1931 censuses, was nearly 17 times that of Canada.

The population of Canada in 1851, at the beginning of the period covered by the present series of decennial censuses, was 2,436,297, and the population of the United States on its corresponding census date in 1850 was 23,191,876, or a little less than 10 times the Canadian population. The major part of the population of Canada at that time was in the five provinces from Ontario eastward, and the major part of the population of the United States was in the States east of the Great Plains. There were therefore in each country large areas of land farther west still to be settled; and the settlement of this western land was an important factor, both in the later growth of the population of the two countries and in the intermingling of their peoples.

By 1901 the Canadian population had grown to 5,371,315 and had spread over all the western provinces, though in many areas the people were widely scattered. In the United States, by 1900, there were no extensive areas of good farming land left unoccupied in any of the States (unless one might except the Indian lands in what is now Oklahoma), but much of the West still had room for many more people, as evidenced by the more rapid growth of the Western States as compared with the eastern in the decades immediately following.

In the United States the growth of the population from 1850 to 1930

---

1. Census of Canada: 1931, Vol. I, p. 100.

was continuous and spread evenly over the period, with a gradually falling rate of increase. In Canada, after a single decade of rapid increase from 1851 to 1861, the population growth was relatively slow, with a slight general downward trend in the rate until 1901. In the next decade, as a result of the opening up of the Prairie Provinces, there was an increase of 34.2 per cent, amounting in numbers to more than the combined increase of the three preceding decades. While this rate of increase was not maintained in the following decades, the period from 1911 to 1921 showed an increase of 21.9 per cent, and the decade ending in 1931, an increase of 18.1 per cent, even this last being appreciably higher than the rate of increase in the United States during the corresponding period.

The population data for the United States and Canada for the 80-year period under discussion are presented in Table 1, together with the increase in each decade and the gradually changing ratio between the populations of the two countries.

TABLE 1. POPULATION OF THE UNITED STATES AND CANADA: 1850 TO 1930

CENSUS YEAR	UNITED STATES			CANADA*			Ratio, United States to Canada	Ratio, Canada to United States
	Number	Increase		Number	Increase			
		Amount	Per cent		Amount	Per cent		
1930.......	122,775,046	17,064,426	16.1†	10,376,786	1,588,837	18.1	11.83	0.085
1920.......	105,710,620	13,738,354	14.9†	8,787,949	1,581,306	21.9	12.03	0.083
1910.......	91,972,266	15,977,691	21.0	7,206,643	1,835,328	34.2	12.76	0.078
1900.......	75,994,575	13,046,861	20.7	5,371,315	538,076	11.1	14.15	0.071
1890.......	62,947,714	12,791,931	25.5	4,833,239	508,429	11.8	13.02	0.077
1880.......	50,155,783	10,337,334	26.0	4,324,810	635,553	17.2	11.60	0.086
1870‡......	39,818,449	8,375,128	26.6	3,689,257	459,624	14.2	10.45	0.096
1860.......	31,443,321	8,251,445	35.6	3,229,633	793,336	32.6	9.74	0.103
1850.......	23,191,876	....	....	2,436,297	......	....	9.52	0.105

*Canadian census in each case 1 year later than date indicated; that is, 1931, 1921, etc.
†An increase of 16.1 per cent for the period from January 1, 1920, to April 1, 1930, is equivalent to an increase of 15.7 per cent for an exact decade. Likewise, an increase of 14.9 per cent for the period from April 15, 1910, to January 1, 1920, is equivalent to an increase of 15.4 per cent for an exact decade.
‡Figures corrected for under-enumeration in certain southern States. This under-enumeration did not affect any areas in which there were appreciable numbers of Canadian born.

Between 1850 and 1900, by reason of the more rapid increase in the population of the United States already referred to, the ratio between its population and that of Canada increased from 9.52 to 14.15. During the 30-year period ending in 1930, however, the population of Canada increased 93.2 per cent while that of the United States increased only 61.6 per cent, as a result of which the ratio dropped to 11.83. This was the period during which there were only small increases in the number of Canadian born in the United States, so it may perhaps be assumed that the normal increase of the Canadian population found places for settlement within the borders of the Dominion. As a matter of fact, the increase in the population of Canada was 1,600,000 in excess of what would have been necessary to maintain the 1900 ratio with the United States, whereas only about 600,000 more net additions to the Canadian born in the United States would have been needed to maintain the same percentage of the total population of the United States as in 1900 (1.55 per cent). It may be assumed, therefore, that expanding opportunities for settlement in Canada during this period not only diverted the natural increase of the Canadian population from migrating to the United States, but attracted to Canada increasing immigration both from the United States and from European sources. This assumption is supported by the figures given below, in Tables 3 and 4, which show that both the number of American born in Canada and that country's whole foreign-born population more than doubled between 1901 and 1911.

Table 2 presents the number of Canadian-born persons in the United States at the time of each census from 1850 to 1930, with decennial increases and various significant percentages and ratios.

In 1930 there were 1,286,389 persons of Canadian birth in the United States, forming 1.05 per cent of that country's entire population of 122,775,046, and 9.1 per cent of the whole number of foreign born in the United States (14,204,149). In 1850, the first census year for which data on the foreign born by country of birth are available, there were 147,711 Canadian born in the United States, forming 0.64 per cent of the total population of that country and 6.6 per cent of all foreign born.

TABLE **2**. CANADIAN-BORN* POPULATION IN THE UNITED STATES: 1850 TO 1930

(A minus sign (—) denotes decrease)

CENSUS YEAR	Number	INCREASE		Per cent of total population of United States	Per cent of foreign born in United States	Per cent of total population of Canada	Per cent of native population of Canada	Per cent of foreign-born population of Canada
		Amount	Per cent					
1930.........	1,286,389	161,464	14.4	1.05	9.1	12.4	15.9	55.7
1920.........	1,124,925	—79,712	—6.6	1.06	8.1	12.8	16.5	57.5
1910.........	1,204,637	24,715†	2.1	1.31	8.9	16.7	21.4	75.9
1900.........	1,179,922	198,984	20.3	1.55	11.4	22.0	25.3	168.7
1890.........	980,938	263,781	36.8	1.56	10.6	20.3	23.4	152.4
1880.........	717,157	223,693	45.3	1.43	10.7	16.6	19.3	118.9
1870.........	493,464	243,494	97.4	1.28	8.9	13.4	16.4	82.0
1860.........	249,970	102,259	69.2	0.79	6.0	7.9	10.3	36.6
1850.........	147,711	......	....	0.64	6.6	6.2	9.8	32.1

*All Canadian born, including white, Negro, and other races. Beginning with Table 17, the tables give white population only (1,278,421 in 1930), for reasons explained in the text, page 56. Figures for years prior to 1910 include persons born in Newfoundland. These numbered 3,423 in 1870 and 4,789 in 1880. Separate data are not available for 1890 or 1900, but since the number of Newfoundland born in the United States in 1910 was only 5,080, their number in 1890 or 1900 was probably less than 5,000.
†This increase would be greater by around 5,000, if allowance were made for the fact that Newfoundland born were included in 1900 but not in 1910.

The growth of population in the United States and Canada and the increase in the numbers of Canadian born in the United States and of American born in Canada are presented graphically in Figure 1. Since the curves in this graph are drawn on a semi-logarithmic scale, they show the rate of increase from one census date to another, but do not show the relative magnitude of the items represented. Compare especially the curve representing the growth of the population of the United States, with its even sweep over the whole period, with that representing the growth of the Canadian population, which runs evenly up to 1900 or 1901 and then takes a sharp turn upward, which is fairly well maintained to the end of the period.

FIGURE 1. POPULATION OF THE UNITED STATES AND CANADA: 1850/51 TO 1930/31

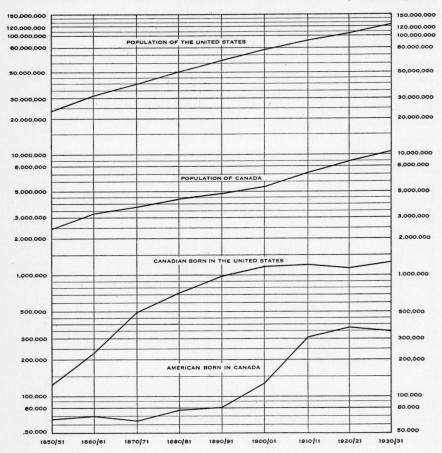

The growth of the Canadian-born element in the population of the United States up to 1890 was much more rapid than the growth of the country as a whole. Between 1850 and 1860 the Canadian born increased 69.2 per cent, and in the decade ending in 1870 they nearly doubled in number, while the total population of the United States increased only 35.6 per cent and 26.6 per cent, respectively, in these two decades. As a result, the Canadian born in 1870 formed 1.28 per cent of the total population, or almost exactly twice the percentage in 1850. This percentage continued to increase until it reached its maximum in 1890 at 1.56, though this was practically maintained (at 1.55) in 1900. Since 1900 the Canadian born in the United States have increased relatively little; in fact the number reported in the census of 1920 was actually less than in 1910, and the percentage they represented of the total population declined to 1.31 in 1910, to 1.06 in 1920, and to 1.05 in 1930.

The population of Canadian birth in the United States in 1930 was equivalent to 12.4 per cent of the total population of Canada, or 15.9 per cent of the native population of Canada. In 1850 the Canadian born in the United States were equivalent to 6.2 per cent of the whole Canadian population, or 9.8 per cent of the Canadian born living in Canada, while in 1900, the year of the relative maximum, the Canadian born in the United States were equal to 22.0 per cent of the whole Canadian population and 25.3 per cent of the native population of Canada.

The Canadian born in the United States are represented graphically by one of the curves in Figure 1. This curve indicates very effectively the rapid increase in the number of Canadian born in the United States, as compared with the increase in the population of either country, from 1850 to 1900, and its almost stationary position since that date.

A discussion of the growth and relationships of the Canadian born in the United States would hardly be complete without some reference to the American born in Canada, who represent another measurable factor in the interchange of population which has been going on between the two countries over the whole period covered by the records. A summary of these figures is presented in Table 3.

In 1931 there were in Canada 344,574 persons born in the United States, representing 3.3 per cent of the population of Canada. This percentage is three times as high as the percentage of Canadian born in the population of the United States in 1930, though if one considers the fact that there were large areas of the United States in which there were practically no Canadian born, while the American born were spread rather evenly over the whole of Canada, the difference between these two specific percentages becomes of less importance.

As compared with the total population of the United States, the Ameri-

can born in Canada represented a very small fraction—only 0.3 per cent.
They were equivalent in number, however, to more than one-fourth (26.8
per cent) of the number of Canadian born in the United States, and represented an appreciable fraction of the immigration to Canada from other
countries which is sometimes referred to as a partial compensation for
the Canadian contributions of population to the United States.

TABLE **3**. AMERICAN-BORN POPULATION IN CANADA: 1851 TO 1931

(A minus sign (—) denotes decrease)

| CENSUS YEAR | Number | INCREASE | | Per cent of total population of Canada | Per cent of total population of United States | Per cent of total Canadian born in United States |
		Amount	Per cent			
1931...............	344,574	—29,448	—7.9	3.3	0.3	26.8
1921...............	374,022	70,342	23.2	4.3	0.4	33.2
1911...............	303,680	175,781	137.4	4.2	0.3	25.2
1901...............	127,899	46,984	58.1	2.4	0.2	10.8
1891...............	80,915	3,162	4.1	1.7	0.1	8.2
1881...............	77,753	13,140	20.3	1.8	0.2	10.8
1871...............	64,613	—5,387	—7.7	1.8	0.2	13.1
1861...............	70,000*	7,000	11.1	2.2	0.2	28.0
1851...............	63,000*	.....	....	2.6	0.3	42.7

*Estimate obtained from Dominion Bureau of Statistics.

In Figure 2 the numbers of the Canadian born in the United States and
the American born in Canada, respectively, are shown graphically for
the censuses from 1850/51 to 1930/31.

Another item of importance in any attempt to analyze population relationships between Canada and the United States is the total foreign-
born population of Canada. This is given, with some classification by
source, in Table 4. These figures provide, among other things, the base for
the ratios between the Canadian born in the United States and the total
foreign-born population of Canada, which ratios are given in the last column of Table 2. The purpose of these ratios is to show the relation between the Canadian contribution (that is, the contribution of Canadian-
born persons) to the population of the United States, and the foreign
born or immigrant population of Canada itself.

In 1931 the population of Canada included 2,307,525 foreign born,
that is, persons born outside the Dominion (including 344,574 persons
born in the United States). Against this number may be set 1,286,389
Canadian-born persons in the United States. This number is equivalent to
55.7 per cent of the foreign-born population of Canada, and one may
figure that in some fashion the Canadian contribution to the population
of the United States has been more than repaid by contributions to her
own population from other countries, mainly from the British Isles and

from the United States itself (which last item might be considered in the light of partial exchange).

Figure **2**. Canadian Born in the United States and American Born in Canada: 1850/51 to 1930/31

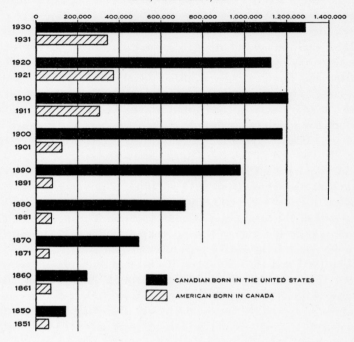

Table **4**. Foreign-Born Population of Canada by Place of Birth: 1851 to 1931

(A minus sign (—) denotes decrease)

CENSUS YEAR	TOTAL			NUMBER BORN IN—		
	Number	Increase		United States	British Isles	Other countries
		Amount	Per cent			
1931................	2,307,525	351,800	18.0	344,574	1,138,942	824,009
1921................	1,955,725	368,764	23.2	374,022	1,025,119	556,584
1911................	1,586,961	887,461	126.9	303,680	804,234	479,047
1901................	699,500	55,629	8.6	127,899	404,848	166,753
1891................	643,871	40,887	6.8	80,915	477,735	85,221
1881................	602,984	1,009	0.2	77,753	470,906	54,325
1871................	601,975	—84,318	—12.3	64,613	496,595	40,767
1861*...............	686,293	219,507	47.0	70,000	616,293	
1851*...............	466,786	......	....	63,000	403,786	

*Figures for 1851 and 1861 are partly estimated.

Going back a few decades into the statistical history of the two countries, however, we find the situation quite different. In 1901 the entire foreign-born population of Canada was only 699,500 (including 127,899 from the United States) while the number of Canadian born in the United States (in 1900) was 1,179,922, or more than one and two-thirds times as many as the entire foreign-born or immigrant population of Canada. At this time, then, and likewise (though to a less extent) in 1890 and 1880, the Canadian contribution to the population of the United States was considerably more than the entire contribution which the Canadian population had received from all other countries. In 1871, however, the foreign-born population of Canada was 601,975, as compared with 493,464 Canadian born in the United States, and at the two earlier census periods for which figures are available, the excess of foreign born in Canada over Canadian born in the United States was considerably greater.

Considering by itself the growth of the immigrant population of Canada, one may note that, from 1871 to 1901, it increased rather slowly, being 601,975 in 1871 and 699,500 in 1901, in which latter year it formed 13.0 per cent of the total population of Canada. The increase in the foreign-born population during this 30-year period was materially slower than the increase in the native population.

Between 1901 and 1911, however, the foreign-born population of Canada more than doubled, the addition through immigration from the United States alone amounting to more than twice the total increase from all countries in any of the four immediately preceding decades; and during this decade the increase in the foreign born was far more rapid on a percentage basis than the increase in the native population of Canada (126.9 per cent, as compared with 20.3 per cent) and amounted to almost as much in absolute amount (887,461, as compared with 947,867). The main reason for this influx of population into Canada was doubtless the opening up of the Prairie Provinces, which in turn was to some extent the result of the development of new varieties of wheat which could be successfully and profitably grown in those northern latitudes.

It may be noted that during this decade the Canadian-born population of the United States increased by only 24,715, as compared with an increase of around 200,000 or more during each of the four preceding decades. This change was doubtless the result of the diversion of the surplus population of the older communities toward the Canadian Northwest.

The increase in the foreign-born population of Canada between 1901 and 1911 was made up of 175,781 from the United States; 399,386 from the British Isles; and 312,294 from other countries, mainly from continental Europe.

From 1911 to 1931 the foreign-born population of Canada increased at approximately the same rate as the native population, forming, in 1911, 22.0 per cent of the total population; in 1921, 22.3 per cent; and in 1931, 22.2 per cent.

Comparisons have already been made between the number of Canadians in the United States and the total population of Canada. It is perhaps even more significant to compare the number of Canadian born in the United States with the whole number of Canadian born both in the United States and in Canada. Theoretically, it would be desirable to make the comparison with the whole number of Canadian born, including those who have migrated to all parts of the world. Since this theoretically desirable total, however, even if it were available, would be very little larger than the sum of the two figures representing the Canadian-born resident in Canada and in the United States, we may proceed on the assumption that this latter figure represents a satisfactory approximation.

In 1930/31 the whole number of Canadian born, obtained by adding to the number returned in the 1931 census of Canada the number returned in the 1930 census of the United States, was 9,355,650. Of these, 1,286,389, or 13.7 per cent, were living in the United States. On the basis of similar figures for 1850/51 (involving some estimates) it would appear that 7.0 per cent of the Canadian born at that time were living in the United States. The percentage increased gradually to a maximum of 20.2 in 1900/01, and decreased rather rapidly (to 13.7) in 1930/31. The data for the 80-year period are summarized in Table 5, and shown

TABLE 5. POPULATION BORN IN CANADA AND RESIDENT IN CANADA OR THE UNITED STATES: 1850/51 TO 1930/31

(A minus sign (—) denotes decrease)

CENSUS YEAR	ALL CANADIAN BORN LIVING IN CANADA OR UNITED STATES			LIVING IN CANADA			LIVING IN UNITED STATES*			
	Number	Increase		Number	Increase		Number	Per cent of total	Increase	
		Amount	Per cent		Amount	Per cent			Amount	Per cent
1931......	9,355,650	1,398,512	17.6	8,069,261	1,237,048	18.1	1,286,389	13.7	161,464	14.4
1921......	7,957,138	1,132,819	16.6	6,832,213	1,212,531	21.6	1,124,925	14.1	—79,712	—6.6
1911......	6,824,319	972,582	16.6	5,619,682	947,867	20.3	1,204,637	17.7	24,715	2.1
1901......	5,851,737	681,431	13.2	4,671,815	482,447	11.5	1,179,922	20.2	198,984	20.3
1891......	5,170,306	731,323	16.5	4,189,368	467,542	12.6	980,938	19.0	263,781	36.8
1881......	4,438,983	847,837	23.6	3,721,826	624,144	20.1	717,157	16.2	223,693	45.3
1871......	3,591,146	794,192	28.4	3,097,682	550,698	21.6	493,464	13.7	243,494	97.4
1861......	2,796,954	672,946	31.7	2,546,984	570,687	28.9	249,970	8.9	102,259	69.2
1851......	2,124,008	......	....	1,976,297	......	....	147,711	7.0	......	....

*United States census in each case 1 year earlier than date indicated; that is, 1930, 1920, etc. Persons born in Newfoundland included with Canadian born in the United States for years prior to 1910.

graphically in Figures 3 and 4. Figure 3 represents the numerical growth of the Canadian-born population in the two countries, while Figure 4 pictures the increase (and decline) in the proportion of the total who were in the United States, as expressed in the form of a percentage.

FIGURE 3. CANADIAN BORN IN CANADA AND IN THE UNITED STATES: 1850/51 TO 1930/31

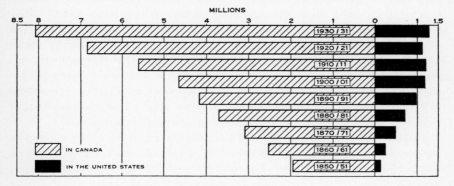

FIGURE 4. PERCENTAGE OF ALL CANADIAN BORN WHO WERE IN THE UNITED STATES: 1850 TO 1930

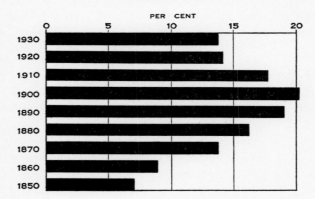

It may be noted that the percentages of increase shown for the total Canadian born from one census to another are more regular than the percentages for either the Canadian born who were in the United States or the Canadian born who remained in Canada. The increase in the whole number of Canadian born, for example, ranged gradually downward from 31.7 per cent in the decade 1851 to 1861 to 13.2 per cent in the decade ending in 1901, while the range for the native population living in Canada between the same periods was from 28.9 per cent to 11.5 per cent. In the decade ending in 1911, the total Canadian born increased 16.6 per cent, as compared with 13.2 in the previous decade, this higher figure resulting, without doubt, from the inclusion of appreciable numbers of children of the new immigrants who arrived in large numbers between 1901 and 1911. Further, of the persons representing the increase in all Canadian born during this decade, a larger fraction remained in Canada, with the result that the native population of Canada increased 20.3 per cent during this 10-year period (as compared with 11.5 per cent during the preceding decade), while the number of Canadian born in the United States increased only 2.1 per cent. During the next decade, from 1911 to 1921, the increase in the total Canadian born remained about the same, while the increase in the Canadian born living in Canada was slightly greater by reason of a further decline in the extent of migration to the United States, the number of Canadian born in the United States showing an actual decrease of 6.6 per cent during this decade. Finally, for the decade from 1921 to 1931, there was an increase of 17.6 per cent in the whole number of Canadian born, made up of an increase of 18.1 per cent in those remaining in Canada, and an increase of 14.4 per cent in those living in the United States.

By way of explanation of the general trend of these figures, one may note that the conditions affecting the natural increase in the whole number of Canadian born during the 80-year period have been much more regular than the conditions resulting in migration which have determined the relation between the two groups distinguished on the basis of residence. Even the increase in the total Canadian born, however, cannot be explained entirely as representing the normal course of increase in a self-contained population group, since the whole number of Canadian born includes the children of the immigrant population—as witness, for example, the break in the downward trend in the percentages of increase shown for 1911, immediately following considerable additions to this immigrant population.

FOREIGN BORN FROM CANADA AND OTHER COUNTRIES

BY way of background for the consideration of the place which the Canadian born occupy in the population of the United States, it may be well to compare the numbers of Canadian born with the numbers of persons in the United States who were born in other countries which have contributed heavily to the population of the United States. Such figures are presented for the census years from 1850 to 1930, with various significant percentages, in Tables 6 and 7.

TABLE **6**. FOREIGN-BORN POPULATION OF THE UNITED STATES FROM SELECTED COUNTRIES: 1850 TO 1930

COUNTRY OF BIRTH	1930	1920	1910	1900	1890	1880	1870	1860	1850
All foreign born...	**14,204,149**	**13,920,692**	**13,515,886**	**10,341,276**	**9,249,560**	**6,679,943**	**5,567,229**	**4,138,697**	**2,244,602**
PERSONS BORN IN—									
Canada*.........	1,286,389	1,124,925	1,204,637	1,179,922	980,938	717,157	493,464	249,970	147,711
England.........	809,563	813,853	877,719	840,513	909,092	664,160	555,046	433,494	278,675
Scotland.........	354,323	254,570	261,076	233,524	242,231	170,136	140,835	108,518	70,550
Wales...........	60,205	67,066	82,488	93,586	100,079	83,302	74,533	45,763	29,868
Ireland†.........	923,642	1,037,234	1,352,251	1,615,459	1,871,509	1,854,571	1,855,827	1,611,304	961,719
Norway.........	347,852	363,863	403,877	336,388	322,665	181,729	114,246	43,995	12,678
Sweden.........	595,250	625,585	665,207	582,014	478,041	194,337	97,332	18,625	3,559
Denmark‡........	182,238	189,154	181,649	153,690	132,543	64,196	30,107	9,962	1,838
Germany.........	1,608,814	1,686,108	2,311,237	2,663,418	2,784,894	1,966,742	1,690,533	1,276,075	583,774
Poland§.........	1,268,583	1,139,979	937,884	383,407	147,440	48,557	14,436	7,298	.....
Italy...........	1,790,429	1,610,113	1,343,125	484,027	182,580	44,230	17,157	11,677	3,679
Greece...........	174,526	175,976	101,282	8,515	1,887	776	390	328	86
Mexico..........	641,462	486,418	221,915	103,393	77,853	68,399	42,435	27,466	13,317
All other countries..	4,160,873	4,345,848	3,571,539	1,663,420	1,017,808	621,651	440,888	294,222	137,148

*Figures for years prior to 1910 include persons born in Newfoundland.
†Includes, for 1930, both Northern Ireland and Irish Free State.
‡Iceland included with Denmark.
§Persons reported in 1910 as of Polish mother tongue born in Germany (190,096), Austria (329,418), and Russia (418,370) have been deducted from the respective countries and combined as "Poland," for comparison with the number reported in other years as born in Poland.

TABLE **7**. PERCENTAGES BASED ON NUMBER OF FOREIGN BORN FROM SELECTED COUNTRIES: 1890, 1910, AND 1930

(Per cent not shown where less than 0.1)

COUNTRY OF BIRTH	PER CENT OF TOTAL POPULATION OF THE UNITED STATES			PER CENT OF ALL FOREIGN BORN IN UNITED STATES			PER CENT OF POPULATION OF COUNTRY OF BIRTH			Population of country of birth at census nearest to 1930
	1930	1910	1890	1930	1910	1890	1930	1910	1890	
Canada.......	1.05	1.31	1.56	9.1	8.9	10.6	12.4	16.7	20.3	10,376,786
England.......	0.66	0.95	1.44	5.7	6.5	9.8	2.1	2.6	3.3	37,794,003
Scotland.......	0.29	0.28	0.38	2.5	1.9	2.6	7.3	5.5	6.0	4,842,980
Wales.........	0.05	0.09	0.16	0.4	0.6	1.1	2.8	4.1	6.6	2,158,374
Ireland........	0.75	1.47	2.97	6.5	10.0	20.2	21.7	30.8	39.8	4,258,854
Norway.......	0.28	0.44	0.51	2.4	3.0	3.5	12.4	16.9	21.2	2,814,194
Sweden........	0.48	0.72	0.76	4.2	4.9	5.2	9.7	12.0	10.0	6,142,191
Denmark......	0.22	0.20	0.21	1.3	1.3	1.4	5.1	6.5	6.1	3,550,656
Germany......	1.31	2.51	4.42	11.3	17.1	30.1	2.4	3.6	5.6	66,030,491
Poland........	1.03	1.02	0.23	8.9	6.9	1.6	3.9	(*)	(*)	32,133,500
Italy..........	1.46	1.46	0.29	12.6	9.9	2.0	4.3	3.9	0.6	41,176,671
Greece........	0.14	0.11	....	1.2	0.7	....	2.8	3.8	0.1	6,204,684

*Satisfactory base figures not available.

In 1930 there were two other countries whose representation in the foreign-born population of the United States was greater than that of Canada, namely, Germany, with 1,608,814 (in comparison with Canada's 1,286,389), and Italy, with 1,790,429; while Poland, with 1,268,583, was a close fourth. Next in order were Ireland, with 923,642; England, with 809,563; Mexico, with 641,462; and Sweden, with 595,250. In 1850, however, Ireland and England, as well as Germany, had a larger representation in the foreign-born population of the United States than Canada.

There were more Canadian born in the United States in 1930, as already noted, than on any previous census date, though the increase since 1900 had been relatively slow. For several of the countries shown in Table 6, however, the date of maximum representation among the foreign born in the United States was some decades earlier. For the Irish born it was 1890, at which time they numbered 1,871,509, forming 2.97 per cent of the total population of the United States and 20.2 per cent of all foreign born. For persons from Germany, England, and Wales, likewise, the maximum number was reported in 1890, when they formed, respectively, 30.1 per cent, 9.8 per cent, and 1.1 per cent of all foreign born in the United States. For the Norwegians and Swedes, the maximum was in 1910, when they formed 3.0 per cent and 4.9 per cent, respectively, of the total foreign-born population.

In 1860, when there were more than 1,600,000 Irish, and nearly 1,300,000 Germans in the United States, there were only 7,298 Poles, 11,677 Italians, and 27,466 persons of Mexican birth. The increase in the number of foreign born in the United States from Poland, Italy, and Mexico has been continuous, however, and the maximum number was recorded in 1930.

The comparison between the Canadian born and the immigrant population in the United States from other countries may be made on another basis. It has already been noted that the Canadian born in the United States in 1930 were equivalent to 12.4 per cent of the population of Canada at the nearest census date (and to 20.3 per cent in 1890). The Irish born in the United States in 1930, however, were equivalent to 21.7 per cent of the population of Ireland (Northern Ireland and the Irish Free State combined); and on the same date the Norwegian born in the United States formed 12.4 per cent of the population of the country of origin, or practically the same as the Canadian born, while in 1890 the percentages for both of these countries were above that for Canada on the higher level then prevailing—39.8 for Ireland and 21.2 for Norway.

Other countries where the number of immigrants living in the United States in 1930 was equivalent to a considerable fraction of the home country's population included Sweden, with 9.7 per cent; Scotland, with 7.3 per cent; Denmark, with 5.1 per cent; and Italy, with 4.3 per cent.

The circumstance of having contributed a considerable part of the natural growth of its own population to the settlement and the urban growth of the United States is therefore not peculiar to Canada, though in no other case has there been anything at all like the free interchange of population between the two countries concerned which is evidenced by the fact that in proportion to the population of the receiving country, there are far more persons born in the United States living in Canada than there are Canadian born living in the United States.

Some of the most significant percentage relations between the various immigrant groups and the population of the United States and the population of the countries from which the immigrants came are presented in graphic form in Figure 5.

FIGURE 5. FOREIGN BORN IN THE UNITED STATES FROM SELECTED COUNTRIES: PERCENTAGE OF ALL FOREIGN BORN IN THE UNITED STATES AND PERCENTAGE OF POPULATION OF HOME COUNTRY: 1930 AND 1890

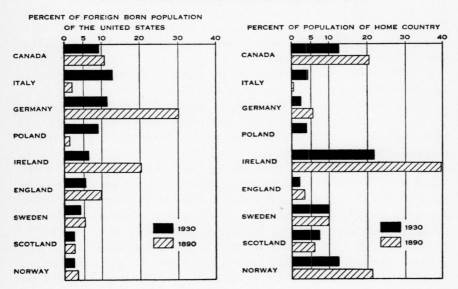

URBAN AND RURAL AREAS

URBAN population, as defined by the United States Bureau of the Census, is in general that residing in cities and other incorporated places having 2,500 inhabitants or more, the remainder of the population being classified as rural.[2] This basis of classification differs from that employed in the Canadian census, where all persons living in incorporated places are included in the urban population without regard to the size of the place.

The percentage of the entire population of the United States classified as urban has shown a continuous increase since the first census in 1790, this increase being especially rapid since about 1880. In 1790 only 5.1 per cent of the inhabitants lived in urban areas; in 1820, 7.2 per cent; in 1850, 15.3 per cent; in 1880, 28.2 per cent; in 1900, 39.7 per cent; and in 1930, 56.2 per cent. Since the excess of births over deaths in the cities is almost always materially smaller than in the surrounding country, the more rapid growth of the cities has been obviously the result of migration from the rural areas, and especially from the farms, to the cities. The existence of this internal migration even among the American born should be considered in any analysis of the data with respect to the urban-rural classification of those who have come into the United States from Canada (or of their children). It may appear, for example, that the reason why such a large part of the population coming into the United States, both from Canada and from other countries, finds its way to the cities is primarily to be found in the existence of this general city-ward movement among the entire population of the United States.

The farm population, as shown in the United States Census Reports for 1930, comprises all persons living on farms, without regard to occupation. To a slight extent this classification cuts across the urban-rural classification, in that 287,837, or about 0.4 per cent, out of a total urban population of 68,954,823, were living on farms—for the most part on the edge of cities which included within their boundaries considerable areas of vacant land, and in the urban towns of Massachusetts. In order to simplify the classification, the urban-farm population was omitted (that is, simply counted as a part of the urban) in most of the detailed tabulations, including that from which the data for Canadians are obtained, and only the rural group subdivided as farm and nonfarm. Thus the data are presented in three classes, namely, urban, rural-nonfarm, and rural-farm, instead of the possible four.

2. There are two minor variations from the general rule for urban classification. In 3 of the New England States, New Hampshire, Massachusetts, and Rhode Island, where the compactly built portions of the towns (townships) are not separately incorporated until they reach a population of 10,000 or more, the entire town is counted as urban if there is in it a village of 2,500 or more which contains more than one-half of the population of the entire town. In 5 other States (Connecticut, New York, New Jersey, Pennsylvania, and California) where the practice of incorporation is somewhat irregular, townships having a population in excess of 10,000 and a population density of 1,000 or more per square mile are classified as urban even though not specifically incorporated as municipalities. This second special rule affected 28 places in all in 1930.

While the farm classification is made without direct regard for occupation, it naturally happens that a very large fraction of the workers who live on farms are engaged in agricultural occupations, that is, either as farmers or as farm laborers.[3]

The urban-rural classification of the Canadian-born population of the United States is presented for 1930, 1920, and 1910, in Table 8, with parallel data for the total and the foreign-born population of the United States, and the principal items are shown graphically in Figure 6. The total rural population of the United States, as shown in the fifth column of this table, includes 9,183,453 persons living in small incorporated places—that is, places having less than 2,500 inhabitants. If this number be added to the official urban population, the resulting total is 78,138,-276, or 63.6 per cent of the population (as compared with the official 56.2 per cent) which may be considered roughly to represent the urban population of the United States classified on the Canadian basis. At the same time the number remaining as rural would be correspondingly reduced to 44,636,770, or 36.4 per cent, instead of 43.8 per cent. It is evident, then, that the urban population of the United States census classification is more strictly urban than the Canadian, and the rural less strictly rural.

FIGURE **6**. URBAN-RURAL CLASSIFICATION OF CANADIAN BORN, ALL FOREIGN BORN, AND TOTAL POPULATION: 1910 TO 1930

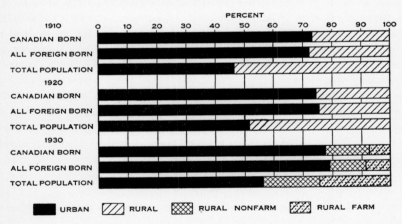

3. Out of a total of 9,318,959 male gainful workers in the rural-farm population of the United States in 1930, 8,308,530, or 89.2 per cent, were engaged in agriculture; and of 1,326,130 female workers, 832,832, or 62.8 per cent, were in agriculture. When a large proportion of any group of Canadian origin is found in the farm population, therefore, it may be assumed that they are mainly engaged in farming.

TABLE **8**. CANADIAN-BORN POPULATION OF THE UNITED STATES IN URBAN AND RURAL AREAS: 1910 TO 1930

CENSUS YEAR AND AREA	CANADIAN BORN IN UNITED STATES				TOTAL POPULATION OF UNITED STATES		ALL FOREIGN BORN IN UNITED STATES	
	Number	Per cent distri-bution	Per cent of total popula-tion	Per cent of all foreign born	Number	Per cent distri-bution	Number	Per cent distri-bution
1930, total	**1,286,389**	**100.0**	**1.0**	**9.1**	**122,775,046**	**100.0**	**14,204,149**	**100.0**
Urban	994,800	77.3	1.4	8.8	68,954,823	56.2	11,250,815	79.2
Rural	291,589	22.7	0.5	9.9	53,820,223	43.8	2,953,334	20.8
Rural—nonfarm	191,192	14.9	0.8	11.1	23,662,710	19.3	1,728,449	12.2
Rural—farm	100,397	7.8	0.3	8.2	30,157,513	24.6	1,224,885	8.6
1920, total	**1,124,925**	**100.0**	**1.1**	**8.1**	**105,710,620**	**100.0**	**13,920,692**	**100.0**
Urban	835,562	74.3	1.5	8.0	54,304,603	51.4	10,500,942	75.4
Rural	289,363	25.7	0.6	8.5	51,406,017	48.6	3,419,750	24.6
1910, total	**1,204,637**	**100.0**	**1.3**	**8.9**	**91,972,266**	**100.0**	**13,515,886**	**100.0**
Urban*	880,985	73.1	2.0	9.0	42,623,383	46.3	9,745,697	72.1
Rural*	323,652	26.9	0.7	8.6	49,348,883	53.7	3,770,189	27.9

*Figures are for urban and rural as established in 1910.

Of the Canadian-born population in the United States in 1930, 77.3 per cent were in urban areas, as compared with 56.2 per cent of the total population of the country. Since, however, there are many areas in the United States, in particular the entire South, in which there are practically no Canadians and in which the percentage urban is relatively low, it may be more significant to compare the percentage urban among the Canadian born with the percentage urban in those States in which the Canadian born are located. Taking as a group the 16 States in which the Canadian born form 1 per cent or more of the population, we find the percentage urban to be 71.9. The percentage urban among the Canadian born is still appreciably higher than this figure, but the difference is less extreme.

It may be noted that the urban-rural distribution of the Canadian born is very similar to that of the total foreign-born population, the percentage urban and the percentage rural-farm being slightly smaller in the Canadian born than in the total, and the percentage rural-nonfarm a little higher. The excess of the percentage urban among the Canadian born over that in the total population of the United States was greater in 1910 (73.1 − 46.3 = 26.8) than in 1930 (77.3 − 56.2 = 21.1), which would indicate that the tendency toward greater urban concentration had not affected the Canadian born—nor the total foreign born either, for that matter—as much as the remainder of the American population. The ratio of the percentage urban in the Canadian born to the percentage urban in the total population in 1930 was 1.38, as compared with 1.45 in 1920, and 1.58 in 1910.

Considering the relation of the Canadian born to the total population in the several urban-rural areas, it may be noted that while they formed almost exactly 1 per cent of the total population in 1930, they constituted 1.4 per cent of the urban population, and only 0.8 per cent of the rural-nonfarm and 0.3 per cent of the rural farm. In relation to the total foreign-born population in the United States, the Canadian born formed 9.1 per cent of this class in 1930 in the United States as a whole, but only 8.8 per cent in urban areas, and 8.2 per cent in rural-farm areas, making up for these smaller figures by a larger percentage (11.1) in the rural-nonfarm areas.

CANADIAN BORN BY STATES AND COUNTIES

EVEN more significant than the distribution of the Canadian-born population in the United States as between cities and farms is its geographic distribution within the area of the United States. While there are some Canadians in every State in the Union, more than seven-eighths of the whole number of Canadian born returned in the 1930 census were living in the States along the Canadian border, plus Massachusetts, Rhode Island, and Connecticut in the East, and Oregon and California on the Pacific Coast. The maximum number of Canadian born found in any one State in 1930 was 289,496 in Massachusetts, where they formed 6.81 per cent of the whole population. In New Hampshire there were 50,992 Canadian born, who formed 10.96 per cent of the State's population, this being the highest percentage in any State.

The Canadian-born population is shown by States for the censuses from 1850 to 1930 in Table 9, while Table 10 shows in corresponding form the percentage of the population represented by the Canadian born. In these tables the figures representing the maximum number or the maximum percentage in any census year are printed in bold-face type. The percentages are also shown in graphic form in Figure 7 for the 16 States having 1 per cent or more of their population Canadian born.

One outstanding fact indicated by these tables is that in many States the number of Canadian born, and in particular the percentage of the total population represented by Canadian born, was much larger at some earlier census date than in 1930. In fact, there are 4 States (Wisconsin, Minnesota, Utah, and Oregon) in which the maximum percentage Canadian born is shown for 1850, and 16 other States in which the maximum percentage is shown for 1860 or 1870, these including New York, Indiana, Illinois, Iowa, Missouri, Dakota Territory, Nebraska, and Kansas. The maximum percentage Canadian born in any State in any census year shown in the table was 23.32 in Minnesota in 1850, this figure representing, however, only 1,417 Canadian born in a total population of 6,077.

TABLE **9**. CANADIAN BORN IN THE UNITED STATES, BY STATES: 1850 TO 1930

(Figures for years prior to 1910 include persons born in Newfoundland. Figures indicating the largest number at any census are printed in bold face type)

DIVISION AND STATE	1930	1920	1910	1900	1890	1880	1870	1860	1850
United States........	**1,286,389**	1,124,925	1,204,637	1,179,922	980,938	717,157	493,464	249,970	147,711
NEW ENGLAND:									
Maine................	73,995	74,420	**76,223**	67,077	52,076	37,114	26,788	17,540	14,181
New Hampshire.......	50,992	52,312	57,878	**58,967**	46,321	27,142	12,955	4,468	2,501
Vermont.............	27,194	24,885	26,058	25,655	25,004	24,620	**28,544**	15,776	14,470
Massachusetts........	289,496	263,478	**297,369**	293,169	207,601	119,302	70,055	27,069	15,862
Rhode Island.........	39,325	36,482	**41,954**	39,277	27,934	18,306	10,242	2,830	1,024
Connecticut.........	**37,863**	24,679	26,757	27,045	21,231	16,444	10,861	3,145	970
MIDDLE ATLANTIC:									
New York...........	**149,148**	112,804	123,551	117,535	93,193	84,182	79,042	55,273	47,200
New Jersey..........	**16,665**	10,396	9,135	7,132	4,698	3,536	2,474	1,144	581
Pennsylvania.........	**16,617**	15,100	15,683	14,760	12,171	12,376	10,022	3,484	2,500
E. NORTH CENTRAL:									
Ohio................	**27,345**	24,670	23,692	22,767	16,515	16,146	12,988	7,082	5,880
Indiana.............	**6,267**	5,147	5,838	5,934	4,954	5,569	4,765	3,166	1,878
Illinois.............	43,988	38,773	45,751	**50,595**	39,525	34,043	32,550	20,132	10,699
Michigan............	**203,783**	165,902	172,863	184,398	181,416	148,866	89,590	36,482	14,008
Wisconsin...........	15,613	19,400	24,996	**33,951**	33,163	28,965	25,666	18,146	8,277
W. NORTH CENTRAL:									
Minnesota...........	27,216	33,862	41,121	**47,578**	43,580	29,631	16,698	8,023	1,417
Iowa...............	6,353	8,944	11,619	15,687	17,465	**21,097**	17,907	8,313	1,756
Missouri............	5,460	6,562	8,069	8,616	8,525	**8,685**	8,448	2,814	1,053
North Dakota........	12,509	15,743	21,507	**28,166**	23,045 }	10,678	906	1,458	...
South Dakota........	3,414	4,462	6,010	7,044	**9,493** }				...
Nebraska............	4,410	5,780	7,335	9,049	**12,105**	8,622	2,635	438	...
Kansas.............	4,068	5,352	7,188	8,538	11,874	**12,536**	5,324	986	...
SOUTH ATLANTIC:									
Delaware............	479	453	**504**	298	309	246	112	39	21
Maryland............	**2,307**	1,894	1,430	1,230	1,020	988	644	333	215
Dist. of Columbia......	**1,729**	1,726	1,161	906	655	452	290	59	32
Virginia.............	1,647	**1,947**	1,360	1,130	780	585	327	389	235
West Virginia........	980	**981**	872	711	374	295	207	...	...
North Carolina.......	**948**	663	543	480	355	425	171	48	30
South Carolina.......	280	271	**282**	204	159	141	77	86	57
Georgia.............	**1,104**	965	801	759	609	348	247	178	108
Florida.............	**8,189**	4,141	1,728	1,202	1,151	446	174	77	97
E. SOUTH CENTRAL:									
Kentucky............	934	903	1,070	**1,208**	1,173	1,070	1,082	618	275
Tennessee...........	949	988	**1,156**	1,045	1,020	545	587	387	76
Alabama............	**919**	904	833	706	620	271	183	239	49
Mississippi..........	365	406	**450**	420	345	309	375	184	79
W. SOUTH CENTRAL:									
Arkansas............	715	893	1,074	**1,093**	947	787	342	154	41
Louisiana............	1,009	1,186	**1,191**	1,034	762	726	714	830	499
Oklahoma...........	2,146	2,489	**2,871**	1,807	420	...	...	...	...
Texas...............	**4,563**	4,200	3,534	2,949	2,866	2,472	597	458	137
MOUNTAIN:									
Montana............	11,193	**14,700**	13,842	13,826	9,040	2,481	1,172	...	...
Idaho...............	4,529	4,961	**5,371**	2,923	1,791	584	334	...	...
Wyoming............	1,144	**1,440**	1,431	1,248	1,314	542	329	...	...
Colorado............	5,845	7,642	9,581	**9,797**	9,142	5,785	753	684	...
New Mexico..........	618	738	**1,023**	764	681	280	125	76	38
Arizona.............	**2,037**	1,964	1,827	1,269	732	571	142	...	...
Utah................	1,192	1,471	**1,690**	1,331	1,222	1,036	687	647	338
Nevada.............	955	1,181	1,847	1,032	1,662	**3,147**	2,365	208	...
PACIFIC:									
Washington..........	**48,269**	43,179	39,482	20,284	17,412	2,857	1,121	407	...
Oregon.............	**17,946**	13,800	12,409	7,508	6,460	3,019	1,187	663	293
California...........	**101,677**	59,686	44,677	29,818	26,028	18,889	10,660	5,437	834

TABLE **10**. PERCENTAGE OF TOTAL POPULATION CANADIAN BORN, BY STATES: 1850 TO 1930

(Per cent not shown when less than 0.01. Figures indicating the highest percentage at any census are printed in bold face type)

DIVISION AND STATE	1930	1920	1910	1900	1890	1880	1870	1860	1850
United States.....	1.05	1.06	1.31	1.55	1.56	1.43	1.28	0.79	**0.64**
NEW ENGLAND:									
Maine...............	9.28	9.69	**10.27**	9.66	7.88	5.72	4.27	2.79	2.43
New Hampshire......	10.96	11.81	13.44	**14.33**	12.30	7.82	4.07	1.37	0.79
Vermont.............	7.56	7.06	7.32	7.47	7.52	7.41	**8.64**	5.01	4.61
Massachusetts........	6.81	6.84	8.83	**10.45**	9.27	6.69	4.81	2.20	1.59
Rhode Island.........	5.72	6.04	7.73	**9.16**	8.08	6.62	4.71	1.62	0.69
Connecticut..........	2.36	1.79	2.40	**2.98**	2.84	2.64	2.02	0.68	0.26
MIDDLE ATLANTIC:									
New York............	1.18	1.09	1.36	1.62	1.55	1.66	**1.80**	1.42	1.52
New Jersey..........	**0.41**	0.33	0.36	0.38	0.33	0.31	0.27	0.17	0.12
Pennsylvania........	0.17	0.17	0.20	0.23	0.23	**0.29**	0.28	0.12	0.11
EAST NORTH CENTRAL:									
Ohio................	0.41	0.43	0.50	**0.55**	0.45	0.50	0.49	0.30	0.30
Indiana.............	0.19	0.18	0.22	0.24	0.23	0.28	**0.28**	0.23	0.19
Illinois.............	0.58	0.60	0.81	1.05	1.03	1.11	**1.28**	1.18	1.26
Michigan............	4.21	4.52	6.15	7.62	8.66	**9.09**	7.57	4.87	3.52
Wisconsin...........	0.53	0.74	1.07	1.64	1.96	2.20	2.43	2.34	**2.71**
WEST NORTH CENTRAL:									
Minnesota...........	1.06	1.42	1.98	2.72	3.33	3.80	3.80	4.66	**23.32**
Iowa................	0.26	0.37	0.52	0.70	0.91	1.30	**1.50**	1.23	0.91
Missouri............	0.15	0.19	0.25	0.28	0.32	0.40	**0.49**	0.24	0.15
North Dakota........	1.84	2.43	3.73	8.83	12.07 }	7.90	6.39	**30.14**	....
South Dakota........	0.49	0.70	1.03	1.75	2.72 }				....
Nebraska............	0.32	0.45	0.62	0.85	1.14	1.91	**2.14**	1.52	....
Kansas..............	0.22	0.30	0.43	0.58	0.83	1.26	**1.46**	0.92	....
SOUTH ATLANTIC:									
Delaware............	0.20	0.20	**0.25**	0.16	0.18	0.17	0.09	0.03	0.02
Maryland............	**0.14**	0.13	0.11	0.10	0.10	0.11	0.08	0.05	0.04
Dist. of Columbia.....	0.36	**0.39**	0.35	0.33	0.28	0.25	0.22	0.08	0.06
Virginia.............	0.07	**0.08**	0.07	0.06	0.05	0.04	0.03	0.02	0.02
West Virginia........	0.06	0.07	0.07	**0.07**	0.05	0.05	0.05	....	....
North Carolina......	0.03	0.03	0.02	0.03	0.02	**0.03**	0.02	....	....
South Carolina.......	0.02	0.02	**0.02**	0.02	0.01	0.01	0.01	0.01	0.01
Georgia.............	**0.04**	0.03	0.03	0.03	0.03	0.02	0.02	0.02	0.01
Florida.............	**0.56**	0.43	0.23	0.23	0.29	0.17	0.09	0.05	0.11
EAST SOUTH CENTRAL:									
Kentucky............	0.04	0.04	0.05	0.06	0.06	0.06	**0.08**	0.05	0.03
Tennessee...........	0.04	0.04	0.05	0.05	**0.06**	0.04	0.05	0.03	0.01
Alabama.............	0.03	0.04	0.04	0.04	**0.04**	0.02	0.02	0.02	0.01
Mississippi..........	0.02	0.02	0.03	0.03	0.03	0.03	**0.05**	0.02	0.01
WEST SOUTH CENTRAL:									
Arkansas............	0.04	0.05	0.07	0.08	0.08	**0.10**	0.07	0.04	0.02
Louisiana............	0.05	0.07	0.07	0.07	0.07	0.08	0.10	**0.12**	0.10
Oklahoma...........	0.09	0.12	0.17	**0.23**	0.16	....	....	....	....
Texas...............	0.08	0.09	0.09	0.10	0.13	**0.16**	0.07	0.08	0.06
MOUNTAIN:									
Montana............	2.08	2.68	3.68	5.68	6.33	**6.34**	5.69	....	....
Idaho...............	1.02	1.15	1.65	1.81	2.02	1.79	**2.23**	....	....
Wyoming............	0.51	0.74	0.98	1.35	2.10	2.61	**3.61**	....	....
Colorado............	0.56	0.81	1.20	1.82	2.21	**2.98**	1.89	2.00	....
New Mexico..........	0.15	0.20	0.31	0.39	**0.42**	0.23	0.14	0.08	0.06
Arizona.............	0.47	0.59	0.89	1.03	0.83	1.41	**1.47**	....	....
Utah................	0.23	0.33	0.45	0.48	0.58	0.72	0.79	1.61	**2.97**
Nevada..............	1.05	1.53	2.26	2.44	3.51	5.05	**5.57**	3.03	....
PACIFIC:									
Washington..........	3.09	3.18	3.46	3.92	**4.87**	3.80	4.68	3.51	....
Oregon..............	1.88	1.76	1.84	1.82	2.03	1.73	1.31	1.26	**2.20**
California............	1.79	1.74	1.88	2.01	2.15	**2.18**	1.90	1.43	0.90

FIGURE 7. PERCENTAGE OF POPULATION CANADIAN BORN, BY STATES: 1930

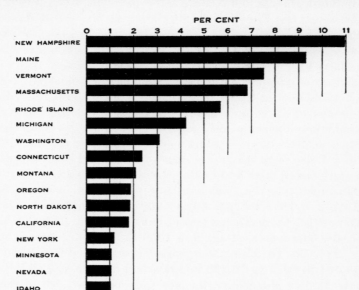

In the earlier days of the settlement of Canada there was much more commerce and much more interchange of population between the Canadian settlements and the New England colonies than with the colonies farther south. This was mainly because of convenient access to the New England ports by water, though another important element was the common interest in fishing on the Banks off Newfoundland. At the time of the northward migration of the United Empire Loyalists during the revolutionary period, however, there were well-established routes for land travel, and we find in 1850 a larger number of Canadian born in the State of New York than in any other State, with large numbers likewise in Michigan, Illinois, and Wisconsin, as well as in the four northern New England States.

The Canadian-born population of New York continued to grow rather slowly, but continuously, from 1850 to 1930, increasing from 47,200 in 1850 to 149,148 in 1930. In Michigan the growth was somewhat more rapid up to 1900, the Canadian-born population in this State increasing from 14,008 in 1850 to 184,398 in 1900, and finally to 203,783 in 1930. In Illinois and Wisconsin, however, while the growth was fairly rapid from 1850 to 1900, there has been an appreciable decline since that date in Illinois, and a rapid decline in Wisconsin. In Minnesota and North

Dakota likewise the maximum number of Canadian born was reported in 1900; in South Dakota and Nebraska the maximum was in 1890; and in Iowa, Missouri, and Kansas, in 1880, the decline in some of these States since the maximum having been very considerable. In Iowa, for example, there were 21,097 Canadian born in 1880 and only 6,353 in 1930; in Kansas there were 12,536 in 1880 and only 4,068 in 1930.

This situation would indicate that persons of Canadian birth had taken a considerable part in the settling of these areas but that they had not been followed by large numbers of other Canadians after the pioneer stages in the development of the country were over; and perhaps that even some of the settlers themselves had moved on to newer regions, either because of a desire to be still on the edge of the settled area or because of opportunity to sell their first holdings at attractive prices.

In Massachusetts the Canadian-born population increased rapidly from 15,862 in 1850 to 293,169 in 1900; again increased slightly to 297,369 in 1910 (the maximum year); decreased about 34,000 during the next decade, and increased again in 1930 to the figure already quoted, namely, 289,496. In Maine, the Canadian-born population increased from 14,181 in 1850 to 76,223 in 1910, and has declined slightly since that date. In New Hampshire, the increase was from 2,501 in 1850 to a maximum of 58,967 in 1900, with a small decline in each decade since that date. In Vermont the increase was from 14,470 in 1850 to a maximum of 28,544 in 1870, with the Canadian-born population remaining approximately at this level in subsequent decades. In Rhode Island the Canadian-born population increased from a little over 1,000 in 1850 to 41,954 in 1910, with a decrease of more than 5,000 in 1920, only partly made up by an increase in the next decade. In Connecticut there was an almost continuous increase from a little less than 1,000 in 1850 to 37,863 in 1930.

The increase in the Canadian-born population of the Pacific Coast States has been continuous from the beginning, though somewhat more rapid in recent decades than in the early part of the period. In all of the Mountain States the date of the maximum percentage of Canadian born in the total population was in 1890 or earlier; the date of the maximum absolute number of Canadian born in most of these States was in 1910 or 1920, with a smaller population in 1930, except in Arizona, where the increase was less than 100.

In the Southern States, where the present Canadian population is relatively unimportant, there is no indication of any tendency for an appreciable increase, about half of the States showing an actual decrease over several decades prior to 1930, and more of them showing a decrease in the percentage represented by the Canadian born.

In general, it would seem that the most important single reason for the location of the Canadian born in the United States in the areas where they were found in the census of 1930 was that of convenience of access from Canada. If Massachusetts is included with the border States by reason of its close connection by water, these States account for three-fourths of the Canadian-born population in the United States. The Pacific Coast States, and particularly California, have drawn very heavily in recent decades upon population from outside their borders—from other States to the eastward as well as from foreign countries. Only 34.1 per cent of the 1930 population of California was born in California, 45.4 per cent having come in from other States and 18.9 per cent from foreign countries, including 1.8 per cent from Canada.

If the distribution of the Canadian born in the United States is examined on the basis of figures for counties, rather than for entire States, it appears that in some of the contiguous States, especially in Vermont, New York, and Michigan, the Canadian born have settled mainly in those counties near the Canadian border, while in other States they are found in clusters in and around certain urban centers; and that in addition there are small numbers of Canadian born scattered widely over most of the States outside the South. These details are brought out clearly by Figure 8, which is a map of the United States on which the approximate location of the Canadian born is indicated by dots, each dot representing 250 Canadian-born persons.[4]

On this map the numbers of Canadian born are shown in relation to the area of the various States and counties. To a large extent the areas where the dots are thickest on the map, indicating the presence of large numbers of Canadian born, are areas of very dense total population. Conversely many of the areas where the dots on the map are relatively few are areas where the total population per square mile is very low, and where the Canadian born, while not constituting large absolute numbers, nevertheless form a considerable percentage of the total population. In the State of Montana, for example, with an area of 146,316 square miles

4. For certain of the areas shown in solid black on the map, especially those in eastern Massachusetts, northern Rhode Island, and the Detroit area, the density of Canadian-born population is considerably greater than what a strict interpretation of the 250-persons-per-dot relationship would indicate. It seemed best, however, to adopt a scale of representation which would give a good picture of the approximate location of the Canadian born outside these few areas of concentration, since the very fact that the areas just mentioned appear in solid black on the map gives correctly the impression that they represent the outstanding centers of Canadian-born population in the United States. The dots have been placed on the map county by county, with due regard for the location of cities in which there were many Canadian born, but with only approximate representation of other irregularities of distribution within the county. Further, where an entire State has less than 2,000 or 3,000 Canadian born, the dots can hardly do more than indicate that these are scattered through the State.

FIGURE 8. DISTRIBUTION OF CANADIAN BORN IN THE UNITED STATES: 1930
(Each dot represents 250 Canadian-born persons)

and a population in 1930 of 537,606, or 3.7 per square mile, there were 11,193 Canadian born. These Canadian born formed 2.08 per cent of the total population of Montana, a percentage which is exceeded in only two States outside New England, but because of the large area of the State the 41 dots on the map (Fig. 8) do not provide an adequate indication of their relative importance in the population of the State. This is because the dot map, as a graphic device for showing the distribution of a particular class of the population, does not take account of the very wide variations within the United States in the density of the total population.

The relationship between the total population and the number of Canadian born, that is, the percentage of the population Canadian born, may be depicted on a map by an entirely different method, namely, by a series of shadings representing the percentages. Such a map taken by itself would tend to exaggerate the importance of the Canadian born in the thinly populated areas, since in many cases a large county would be given a heavy shading to represent a very small number of Canadian born. By way of supplement to the dot map, however, a shaded map may be of value, especially as setting forth in more readily discernible form the relationship referred to just above. Such a map covering the State of Montana, which is typical of those areas where small absolute numbers of Canadian born represent relatively high percentages of the total population, is presented in Figure 9. The shadings on this map represent the percentages Canadian born in the population of each county and the figure under each county name represents the number of Canadian born living in that county in 1930. In Daniels County, near the northeast corner of the State, for example, there were 276 Canadian born, representing nearly 5 per cent of the total population of the county. This county receives the heaviest shading on the shaded percentage map (Fig. 9), on the basis of this percentage, but shows only a single dot on the dot map (Fig. 8), on the basis of the absolute number of Canadian born. Again, Liberty County, near the center of the northern edge of the State, had only 45 Canadian born in 1930, but these represented more than 2 per cent of the total population. In fact, there were only 3 counties in Montana which had as many as 500 Canadian born, these 3 being counties which contain fairly large cities, but in 7 of the 56 counties in the State more than 3 per cent of the population were Canadian born; in 15 additional counties, more than 2 per cent; and in another 21 counties, more than 1 per cent.

The concentration of the Canadian born in a relatively small number of the 3,100 counties in the United States may be indicated in another way through the use of the following figures, based in part on Table 20, which appears in Chapter IV and gives the Canadian-born (white) popu-

lation of all counties and cities having 1,000 or more Canadian born in
1930. There were 23 counties in which there were 10,000 or more Canadian born in 1930, these containing 52.5 per cent, or more than one-half,
of the United States total; in 19 counties reporting from 5,000 to 10,000
were found another 11.3 per cent, making 63.8 per cent in 42 counties; in
35 counties reporting 3,000 to 5,000 Canadian born there were 10.6 per
cent of the total; in 14 with 2,000 to 3,000, 2.6 per cent; and in 58 counties with 1,000 to 2,000, 6.2 per cent, making an aggregate of 83.3 per
cent of all Canadian born in the United States in the 149 counties reporting 1,000 or more.

FIGURE **9**. PERCENTAGE OF POPULATION CANADIAN BORN, FOR MONTANA,
BY COUNTIES: 1930
(Figures under each county name represent number of Canadian born in that county)

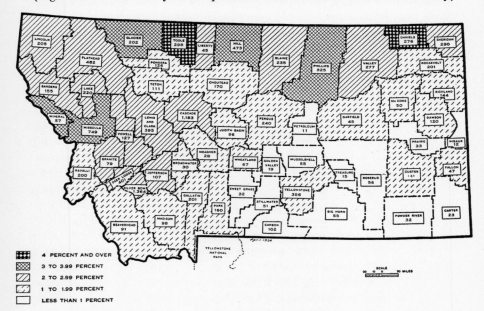

The remaining area of the country comprises 103 counties having from
500 to 1,000 Canadian born, 399 counties with 100 to 500; 651 with 25
to 100; 1,457 with 1 to 24, and 343 with none at all, the last group being
mainly in the Southern States. The 502 counties with from 100 to 1,000
Canadian born contained 12.7 per cent of the whole number; and the
2,108 with from 1 to 100, comprising more than two-thirds of all the
counties in the United States, contained only 4.0 per cent of all the Canadian born.

The counties of the various States differ widely in area and population and are therefore not ideal statistical units for a classification such as that just presented. They are the units for which data are available, however, and these figures do add something, by way of supplement to the map, to the picture of the rather sparse and irregular distribution of the Canadian born in the United States outside the two or three hundred counties in which their numbers are considerable.

CANADIAN BORN IN PRINCIPAL CITIES

TABLE 11 shows the number of Canadian born in 36 of the principal cities of the United States (these being the cities of 100,000 or more in 1930 which had more than 2,500 Canadian born), with comparative figures for earlier censuses running back in many cases as far as 1860. Table 12 shows the percentage which these Canadian born formed of the total population of the city in each case. The percentages are also shown graphically in Figure 10 for those cities having the largest proportions of Canadian born.

FIGURE **10**. PERCENTAGE OF POPULATION CANADIAN BORN, FOR PRINCIPAL CITIES: 1930

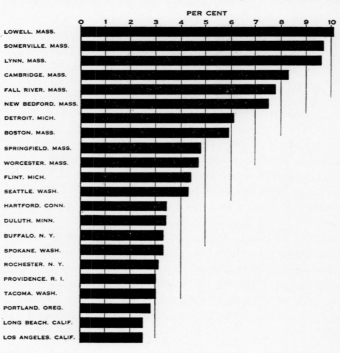

TABLE **11**. CANADIAN BORN IN THE PRINCIPAL CITIES OF THE UNITED STATES:
1860 TO 1930

(Figures given for each city as far back as data are available; for years prior to 1910 persons born in
Newfoundland are included. Figures indicating the largest number at any census are printed
in bold face type)

CITY	1930	1920	1910	1900	1890	1880	1870	1860
Boston, Mass................	46,222	42,611	**50,900**	50,282	38,294	5,729	2,420	6,813
Cambridge, Mass.............	9,488	7,908	10,172	**11,096**	7,497	1,346	939	554
Fall River, Mass.............	8,974	11,596	16,240	**22,501**	15,154	6,748	1,142	....
Lowell, Mass.............	10,172	13,790	16,342	**19,159**	15,742	7,779	2,628	1,082
Lynn, Mass................	9,848	9,695	**10,181**	7,889	5,869	426	199	....
New Bedford, Mass...........	8,475	11,004	**13,205**	9,361	4,121	....	....	....
Somerville, Mass.............	**10,090**	8,020	8,196	7,010	4,163	....	....	....
Springfield, Mass.............	**7,203**	5,806	4,551	3,618	2,735	....	....	....
Worcester, Mass.............	**9,169**	8,143	8,415	8,367	5,567	2,742	1,688	406
Providence, R. I.............	7,623	7,057	**8,835**	7,732	4,487	1,228	350	574
Hartford, Conn...............	**5,776**	2,389	2,124	2,090	815	379	300	179
Buffalo, N. Y...............	**19,038**	15,916	17,434	17,242	10,610	5,951	4,119	2,464
New York, N. Y.*...........	**40,118**	25,582	26,320	21,926	14,295	8,998	5,557	5,572
Rochester, N. Y..............	**10,150**	9,526	9,718	8,299	5,818	3,843	2,616	1,619
Syracuse, N. Y..............	**4,739**	3,499	3,257	2,955	2,222	1,182	1,166	401
Philadelphia, Pa.............	**4,337**	4,244	4,036	3,283	2,584	1,891	1,130	940
Cleveland, Ohio..............	8,496	8,724	**9,365**	8,611	5,157	4,224	2,588	747
Toledo, Ohio................	3,094	3,214	3,180	**3,295**	1,845	1,398	1,011	....
Chicago, Ill.................	30,172	26,392	31,321	**34,779**	24,297	13,352	9,045	1,867
Detroit, Mich...............	**94,973**	59,702	42,814	28,944	18,791	10,576	7,625	3,088
Flint, Mich.................	**6,881**	5,001	3,463	....	....	....	....	....
Grand Rapids, Mich..........	2,548	2,858	3,226	**3,487**	2,968	....	....	....
Milwaukee, Wis..............	**2,677**	2,062	1,889	1,904	1,249	913	706	510
Duluth, Minn................	3,483	4,711	5,863	**6,384**	3,728	....	....	....
Minneapolis, Minn............	6,752	7,471	7,542	7,343	**7,773**	2,374	....	....
St. Paul, Minn..............	3,492	3,917	4,435	4,572	**4,828**	1,474	....	....
Denver, Colo................	2,560	3,112	**3,492**	2,868	2,672	867	....	....
Seattle, Wash...............	**15,785**	13,887	10,708	3,786	2,714	....	....	....
Spokane, Wash..............	3,860	3,845	**4,350**	1,821	....	....	....	....
Tacoma, Wash...............	**3,165**	2,987	2,896	1,651	2,066	....	....	....
Portland, Oreg..............	**8,365**	6,458	5,211	2,209	1,238	....	....	....
Long Beach, Calif............	**3,590**	1,864	437	....	....	....	....	....
Los Angeles, Calif............	**30,815**	13,777	8,278	2,897	1,382	....	....	....
Oakland, Calif...............	**5,246**	3,800	3,150	1,769	1,274	....	....	....
San Diego, Calif.............	**3,012**	1,903	998	....	....	....	....	....
San Francisco, Calif..........	**9,633**	7,103	6,175	5,199	4,371	2,359	1,195	694

*Figures for years prior to 1900 are totals of New York and Brooklyn.

For a majority of the cities the increase in the number of Canadian
born has been continuous from the date of the earliest records, and the
maximum number is shown for 1930. For a number of them, however, the
increase since 1900 has been relatively slow, and for 16 cities the maximum number of Canadians was reported in 1910 or earlier. In Minneapolis and St. Paul the maximum numbers were reported in 1890, and
there has been relatively little change since that date. (In this connection
it may be noted that the whole number of Canadian born in the United
States has increased relatively little since 1900, and actually decreased
between 1910 and 1920.) In 7 other cities, namely, Cambridge, Fall
River, Lowell, Toledo, Chicago, Grand Rapids, and Duluth, the maximum was reported in 1900, with considerable decreases in most cases since
that date.

TABLE **12**. PERCENTAGE OF TOTAL POPULATION CANADIAN BORN, FOR THE PRINCIPAL
CITIES OF THE UNITED STATES: 1860 TO 1930

(Figures indicating the largest percentage at any census are printed in bold face type)

CITY	PER CENT OF TOTAL POPULATION							
	1930	1920	1910	1900	1890	1880	1870	1860
Boston, Mass............	5.9	5.7	7.6	**9.0**	8.5	1.6	1.0	3.8
Cambridge, Mass........	8.3	7.2	9.7	**12.1**	10.7	2.6	2.4	2.1
Fall River, Mass.........	7.8	9.6	13.6	**21.5**	20.4	13.8	4.3	...
Lowell, Mass............	10.1	12.2	15.4	20.2	**20.3**	13.1	6.4	2.9
Lynn, Mass.............	9.6	9.8	11.4	**11.5**	10.5	1.1	0.7	...
New Bedford, Mass.......	7.5	9.1	13.7	**15.0**	10.1	...	...	...
Somerville, Mass.........	9.7	8.6	10.6	**11.4**	10.4	...	...	...
Springfield, Mass........	4.8	4.5	5.1	5.8	**6.2**	...	...	...
Worcester, Mass.........	4.7	4.5	5.8	**7.1**	6.6	4.7	4.1	1.6
Providence, R. I.........	3.0	3.0	3.9	4.4	3.4	1.2	0.5	1.1
Hartford, Conn..........	**3.5**	1.7	2.1	2.6	1.5	0.9	0.8	0.6
Buffalo, N. Y...........	3.3	3.1	4.1	**4.9**	4.1	3.8	3.5	3.0
New York, N. Y.........	0.6	0.5	0.6	**0.6**	0.6	0.5	0.4	0.5
Rochester, N. Y.........	3.1	3.2	4.5	**5.1**	4.3	4.3	4.2	3.4
Syracuse, N. Y..........	2.3	2.0	2.4	**2.7**	2.5	2.3	2.7	1.4
Philadelphia, Pa.........	0.2	0.2	**0.3**	0.3	0.2	0.2	0.2	0.2
Cleveland, Ohio.........	0.9	1.1	1.7	2.3	2.0	**4.0**	2.8	1.7
Toledo, Ohio............	1.1	1.3	1.9	2.5	2.3	2.8	**3.2**	...
Chicago, Ill.............	0.9	1.0	1.4	2.0	2.2	2.7	**3.0**	1.7
Detroit, Mich...........	6.1	6.0	9.2	**10.1**	9.1	9.1	9.6	6.8
Flint, Mich.............	4.4	5.5	**9.0**	...	...	...	...	...
Grand Rapids, Mich......	1.5	2.1	2.9	4.0	**4.9**	...	...	...
Milwaukee, Wis..........	0.5	0.5	0.5	0.7	0.6	0.8	1.0	**1.1**
Duluth, Minn...........	3.4	4.8	7.5	**12.1**	11.3	...	...	...
Minneapolis, Minn.......	1.5	2.0	2.5	3.6	4.7	**5.1**	...	...
St. Paul, Minn..........	1.3	1.7	2.1	2.8	**3.6**	3.6	...	...
Denver, Colo............	0.9	1.2	1.6	2.1	**2.5**	2.4	...	...
Seattle, Wash...........	4.3	4.4	4.5	4.7	**6.3**	...	...	...
Spokane, Wash..........	3.3	3.7	4.2	**4.9**	...	...	...	...
Tacoma, Wash...........	3.0	3.1	3.5	4.4	**5.7**	...	...	...
Portland, Oreg..........	**2.8**	2.5	2.5	2.4	2.7	...	...	...
Long Beach, Calif........	2.5	**3.4**	2.5	...	...	...	...	...
Los Angeles, Calif........	2.5	2.4	2.6	**2.8**	2.7	...	...	...
Oakland, Calif..........	1.8	1.8	2.1	**2.6**	2.6	...	...	...
San Diego, Calif.........	2.0	**2.6**	2.5	...	...	...	...	...
San Francisco, Calif......	**1.5**	1.4	1.5	1.5	1.5	1.0	0.8	1.2

Comparing individual cities, by far the largest Canadian-born population is found in Detroit, which happens to be the only city on the list—
and the only very large American city—which is situated on the Canadian
border. The Canadian-born population of Detroit has increased rapidly
and consistently, starting with 3,088 in 1860 and standing at 94,973 in
1930. The city with the next largest Canadian-born population in 1930
was Boston, which reported 46,222, this figure representing a decrease
from somewhat over 50,000 reported both in 1900 and 1910. The third
on the list was New York, with 40,118, followed by Los Angeles, with
30,815, and Chicago, with 30,172. The trend of Canadian-born population in Chicago has been somewhat similar to that in Boston, the maximum figure, 34,779, having been reported in 1900.

On the basis of percentage of total population represented, the Canadian-born element in most of the 36 cities under consideration reached its maximum in 1900 or earlier.

In Milwaukee, the maximum percentage Canadian born was in 1860; in Toledo and Chicago, in 1870; in Cleveland and Minneapolis in 1880; and in St. Paul in 1890. In a number of important cities having a larger absolute number of Canadian born in 1930 than in any earlier year, the maximum percentage represented by the Canadian born is shown for a much earlier year. In Detroit, for example, the maximum percentage, 10.1, is shown for 1900, while the percentage in 1870 (9.6) was almost as high. In Los Angeles, though the number of Canadians reported in 1930 was more than twice as great as in any earlier census year, the maximum percentage Canadian born is shown for 1900, this indicating that while Canadians have been going to Los Angeles in rather large numbers, the growth of the city from other sources has been even more rapid. In Buffalo, though the number of Canadian born reported in 1930 was somewhat higher than in any previous census year, the increase since 1900, the date of the maximum percentage, has not been very great. In Chicago, as already noted, the maximum number of Canadian born was reported in 1900, though the decrease since that date has not been very great. The maximum percentage of Canadian born in Chicago appeared, however, in 1870.

CHAPTER III

CANADIAN BORN IN THE UNITED STATES
BY COLOR AND SEX

Color or Race

Practically all of the Canadian born in the United States are of the white race, as indicated by the figures in Table 13, which shows the distribution by color or race for the years from 1900 to 1930. The nonwhite element in 1930 amounted to only 7,968, comprising 5,817 Negroes, 1,969 Indians, small numbers of Chinese, Japanese, and Mexicans,[1] and a few others.

Table **13**. Canadian Born in the United States, by Color or Race: 1900 to 1930

(Per cent not shown when less than 0.01)

COLOR OR RACE	1930		1920		1910		1900*		1890*	
	Number	Per cent	Number	Per cent	Number	Per cent	Number	Per cent	Number	Per cent
Total..	1,286,389	100.00	1,124,925	100.00	1,204,637	100.00	1,179,922	100.00	980,938	100.00
White†...	1,278,421	99.38	1,117,878	99.37	1,196,070	99.29	1,172,860	99.40	975,496	99.45
Nonwhite †	7,968	0.62	7,047	0.63	8,567	0.71	7,062	0.60	5,442	0.55
Negro...	5,817	0.45	5,651	0.50	6,772	0.56	....	....	....	....
Indian...	1,969	0.15	1,329	0.12	1,756	0.15	....	....	....	....
Chinese..	38	....	41		38	....	....	....	....	....
Japanese.	45	....	23	....	1	....	....	....	....	....
Mexican ‡	91	0.01	....	....	....	....	....	....	....	....
All other.	8	....	3	....	....	....	....	....	....	....

*Includes persons born in Newfoundland.
†Figures for 1890 partly estimated; see note (‡) on Table 17.
‡Included with white prior to 1930—and again in 1940.

The percentage of the total number of Canadian born in the United States which is represented by nonwhite persons has changed but little since 1900, the first year for which the data are available (except for an estimate for 1890), being 0.60 in 1900 and 0.62 in 1930; and because of the small numbers of Canadian born other than white, the color classification is of little importance. Figures are presented, however, for the Cana-

1. Mexicans were shown separately in the reports of the United States Census for the first time in 1930, having been previously included with the whites; and since this classification was discontinued in 1940 (for reasons not reflecting at all on its statistical usefulness) and Mexicans were again counted as white, the Mexicans have been added to the 1930 white population of the United States in all cases where figures for all native white or all foreign-born white are presented for comparison with the Canadian born. It is not practicable to consolidate the Mexicans in the Canadian-born population with the whites, since they are not tabulated in the same detail; but their number is so small (only 91) as to be negligible.

dian born classified by color in the two or three tables following; but beginning with Table 17 the data for persons of Canadian birth or parentage are limited to those of the white race—not primarily because the data in this form are considered more significant, but because most of the detailed tabulations of data relating to Canadians made in recent censuses of the United States have been made for white persons alone.

SEX CLASSIFICATION

THE Canadian-born population in the United States in 1930 comprised 620,762 males and 665,627 females, or only 93.3 males per 100 females. The sex ratio (that is, the number of males per 100 females) for the white population alone, as indicated by the figures in Table 14, was exactly the same (to the nearest tenth) as that for the total.[2]

TABLE **14**. CANADIAN BORN IN THE UNITED STATES, BY COLOR AND SEX, WITH COMPARATIVE DATA FOR TOTAL POPULATION, ETC.: 1900 TO 1930

(Figures for sex in 1890 not available)

CLASS AND CENSUS YEAR	Total	Male	Female	Males per 100 females
All Canadian born:				
1930	1,286,389	620,762	665,627	93.3
1920	1,124,925	550,679	574,246	95.9
1910	1,204,637	605,956	598,681	101.2
1900*	1,179,922	610,121	569,801	107.1
White Canadian born:				
1930	1,278,421	617,090	661,331	93.3
1920	1,117,878	547,357	570,521	95.9
1910	1,196,070	601,833	594,237	101.3
1900*	1,172,860	606,666	566,194	107.1
Nonwhite Canadian born:				
1930	7,968	3,672	4,296	85.5
Negro	5,817	2,554	3,263	78.3
Indian	1,969	1,001	968	103.4
Other races	182	117	65	180.0
All foreign-born white:				
1930	13,983,405	7,502,491	6,480,914	115.8
1920	13,712,754	7,528,322	6,184,432	121.7
1910	13,345,545	7,523,788	5,821,757	129.2
1900	10,213,817	5,515,285	4,698,532	117.4
Total population of United States:				
1930	122,775,046	62,137,080	60,637,966	102.5
1920	105,710,620	53,900,431	51,810,189	104.0
1910	91,972,266	47,332,277	44,639,989	106.0
1900	75,994,575	38,816,448	37,178,127	104.4

*Includes persons born in Newfoundland.

Since 1900, the first year for which data for the Canadian-born population are available by sex, the sex ratio has declined rapidly. In 1900

2. The sex ratio for the nonwhite element alone was only 85.5, but the number of the nonwhite was so small that this difference does not change the ratio computed only to tenths. Carrying the computation further, we find that the sex ratio for the total was 93.26, and for the white alone, 93.31.

there were 107.1 males per 100 females; in 1910, 101.2; in 1920, 95.9; and in 1930, as already noted, 93.3. Some of the reasons for this change will be discussed later.

The sex ratio of the Canadian born is in marked contrast with that shown for the whole number of foreign-born white in the United States, which has stood at a high level throughout the period under consideration, being 117.4 in 1900, rising to 129.2 in 1910, as a result of heavy immigration, predominantly male, and then declining to 121.7 in 1920 and 115.8 in 1930. It likewise differs materially, especially in its rapid change, from the sex distribution of the total population of the United States.

The excess of males or females represented by the various sex ratios under consideration is shown graphically in Figure 11.

FIGURE **11**. EXCESS OF MALES OR FEMALES IN THE CANADIAN-BORN POPULATION, IN THE TOTAL POPULATION, AND IN THE TOTAL FOREIGN-BORN WHITE: 1900 TO 1930

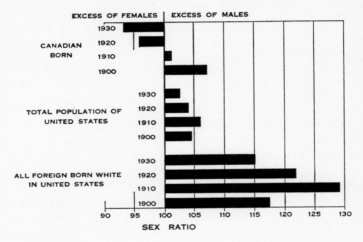

URBAN AND RURAL AREAS

TABLE 15 shows the Canadian-born population in urban and rural areas by sex and color or race for 1930. All classes of the Canadian born in the United States except the small number of Indians are predominantly urban. Of the white Canadian born in the United States, 77.3 per cent were in urban areas; of the Negroes, 90.4 per cent, and of the "Other races" (mainly Chinese and Japanese), 80.2 per cent. The Indians, on the other hand, were predominantly rural, only 33.5 per cent of them be-

ing found in urban places. The percentage urban among the females was
79.3, as compared with 75.2 among the males.

TABLE **15**. CANADIAN BORN IN THE UNITED STATES, BY COLOR AND SEX, FOR URBAN
AND RURAL AREAS: 1930

(Per cent or sex ratio not shown where base is less than 100)

SEX AND COLOR	Total	URBAN		RURAL-NONFARM		RURAL-FARM	
		Number	Per cent of total	Number	Per cent of total	Number	Per cent of total
Total..................	**1,286,389**	**994,800**	**77.3**	**191,192**	**14.9**	**100,397**	**7.8**
White........................	1,278,421	988,738	77.3	189,946	14.9	99,737	7.8
Negro........................	5,817	5,257	90.4	429	7.4	131	2.3
Indian.......................	1,969	659	33.5	795	40.4	515	26.2
Other races..................	182	146	80.2	22	12.1	14	7.7
Male..................	**620,762**	**466,726**	**75.2**	**98,577**	**15.9**	**55,459**	**8.9**
White........................	617,090	464,065	75.2	97,927	15.9	55,098	8.9
Negro........................	2,554	2,248	88.0	227	8.9	79	3.1
Indian.......................	1,001	314	31.4	412	41.2	275	27.5
Other races..................	117	99	84.6	11	9.4	7	6.0
Female..................	**665,627**	**528,074**	**79.3**	**92,615**	**13.9**	**44,938**	**6.8**
White........................	661,331	524,673	79.3	92,019	13.9	44,639	6.7
Negro........................	3,263	3,009	92.2	202	6.2	52	1.6
Indian.......................	968	345	35.6	383	39.6	240	24.8
Other races..................	65	47	....	11	....	7	....
Males per 100 females							
Total..................	**93.3**	**88.4**	....	**106.4**	....	**123.4**	....
White........................	93.3	88.4	....	106.4	....	123.4	....
Negro........................	78.3	74.7	....	112.4	....	....	....
Indian.......................	103.4	91.0	....	107.6	....	114.6	....

The differences in the distribution of males and females in the various
areas may perhaps be best brought out by comparing the sex ratios,
though it should be kept in mind that the sex ratio is a statistical device
which magnifies somewhat (at least as compared with a percentage distribution) the differences which it represents.

The sex ratio for all Canadian born in urban areas was only 88.4, as
compared with 106.4 in rural-nonfarm areas and 123.4 in rural-farm
areas. The low sex ratios for urban areas indicate a considerable excess
of females in the Canadian-born population of American cities, a condition which, without doubt, grows out of the fact that there are more opportunities for employment for women in the cities than elsewhere. The
relatively high sex ratios shown for the rural-farm areas likewise reflect
the opportunity for employment for men on the farms.

CANADIAN-BORN NEGROES, BY STATES

IT may be noted incidentally that there were 19,456 Negroes in the population of Canada in 1931, of whom 15,487 were born in Canada and

2,211, or 11.4 per cent, were born in the United States; and that the number of Canadian-born Negroes in the United States (5,817) was equal to more than one-third of the number of Canadian-born Negroes in Canada.

The Canadian-born Negroes in the United States in 1930, male and female, are shown by States in Table 16. Except in Maine, where the whole number of Negroes was very small, and in Massachusetts, Negroes born in Canada formed a negligible proportion (less than 1 per cent) of the Negro population of the State in which they were living; and it may be noted that the States having appreciable numbers of Canadian-born Negroes are all States in which the whole Negro population was relatively unimportant. It seems probable that most of the Canadian-born Negroes now in the United States are descendants of American Negroes who went to Canada at an earlier date—perhaps in the days of the "underground railway" before the Civil War.

The number of males per 100 females in the entire Canadian-born Negro group in 1930 was only 78.3; and in some States it was considerably lower, being only 62.0 in Massachusetts, from which State about one-fourth of the Canadian-born Negroes were reported. It seems probable that a relatively large proportion of the Canadian Negroes in this State may be employed in domestic service, which is an occupation dominantly female.

TABLE **16**. CANADIAN-BORN NEGROES IN THE UNITED STATES, BY SEX, BY STATES: 1930

STATE	CANADIAN-BORN NEGROES					TOTAL NEGRO POPULATION	
	Total	Per cent of all Negroes	Male	Female	Males per 100 females	Number	Males per 100 females
United States.....	5,817	0.05	2,554	3,263	78.3	11,891,143	97.0
Maine.................	153	14.00	80	73	109.6	1,096	119.6
Massachusetts..........	1,408	2.68	539	869	62.0	52,365	99.3
New York.............	866	0.21	363	503	72.2	412,814	93.5
New Jersey............	130	0.06	66	64	103.1	208,828	97.2
Pennsylvania..........	237	0.05	103	134	76.9	431,257	102.6
Ohio.................	459	0.15	213	246	86.6	309,304	106.0
Indiana...............	61	0.05	27	34	79.4	111,982	103.9
Illinois...............	376	0.11	165	211	78.2	328,972	99.9
Michigan.............	1,199	0.71	501	698	71.8	169,453	110.5
Minnesota............	63	0.67	23	40	57.5	9,445	112.7
California.............	145	0.18	72	73	98.6	81,048	97.7
Other States..........	720	0.01	402	318	126.4	9,774,579	96.2

CHAPTER IV

CANADIAN-BORN WHITE POPULATION, FRENCH AND ENGLISH

THE first permanent settlements in what is now Canada were made by the French shortly after 1600, at about the same time as the first English settlements in Virginia; and for a century and a half there were recurrent struggles between the French and the English for the possession of Canada (or of such settlements as there were then in the territory of the eastern provinces of the present Dominion). These struggles were for the most part concurrent with war between the two nations in Europe.

The growth of the early settlements in Canada was rather slow, and it is estimated that by 1660 there were no more than 2,000 or 3,000 white persons, practically all French, in Canada. In 1666 a census of the settled area, then called New France, was taken, which showed a population of 3,215. This was presumably the first census ever taken anywhere in which were recorded the names and characteristics of all individuals in the population.

In 1763, at the end of the Seven Years' War, Canada was officially ceded to England. At this time there were in the territory probably 90,000 French and not more than 2,000 English; and from this time on there was practically no further immigration from France. In fact, in 1871 there were only 2,908 persons born in France in all Canada, with a French population at that time of 1,089,040; and even in 1931, out of a total French population of nearly 3,000,000 in Canada, there were only 15,361 persons who had been born in France.

It is evident, therefore, that the increase of the French Canadian population from 90,000 to nearly 3,000,000 has been almost entirely the result of excess of births over deaths within the population group itself. This means that the French population must in effect have doubled every 33 years for the entire period of 168 years from 1763 to 1931.

In 1775, at the beginning of the American Revolution, the population of Canada was still practically all French. The English speaking population was rapidly increased, however, by the immigration of loyalists from the colonies which were engaged in war with England. This immigration continued throughout the period of the war and for some years afterwards, and these United Empire Loyalists formed the first considerable element of English speaking people in the Canadian population. This immigration was supplemented by immigration from Europe, mainly from the British Isles in the early days, so that the English element in the population was being continuously augmented by immigration as well as by its own natural increase.

The French in Canada at the present time are to a large extent segregated in their own distinctive communities rather than being scattered freely over the wide territory which now constitutes the Dominion of Canada. Nearly four-fifths of them were, at the time of the 1931 census, in the Province of Quebec, where they formed about four-fifths of the population. In the much smaller Province of New Brunswick they formed one-third of the population; in the Province of Prince Edward Island, nearly fifteen per cent; in Nova Scotia, 11 per cent; and in the other provinces materially less than 10 per cent. Of the whole number of French in Canada, nearly 85 per cent were in Quebec and the provinces to the eastward, and 10 per cent more were in Ontario, leaving only 5 per cent for the western provinces. In contrast, the English Canadians are scattered throughout the whole range of provinces from the Atlantic to the Pacific, forming a large majority of the population in all provinces except Quebec.

Considerable numbers of French Canadians have emigrated to the United States, where they have settled rather thickly in relatively small areas—in contrast with the English Canadians in the United States, who are found in considerable numbers in almost all parts of the country except the South. The whole number of French Canadian born in the United States in 1930 was 370,852, or about one-eighth as many as there were at the same time in Canada. Of this number, 264,261, or 71.3 per cent, were in the six New England States, including 115,241, or 31.1 per cent, in the single State of Massachusetts. In New York there were 28,955; and in Michigan, another border State, 28,539. In no other State were there as many as 8,000.

Between the areas of French Canadian settlement in the United States and the dominantly French areas in Canada there has been a considerable interchange of population from year to year. There were in Canada in 1931, for example, 55,632 persons of the French race born in the United States, these representing mainly children of French Canadians who had earlier gone to the United States.

Their distinctive language is one characteristic which has made it natural for the French Canadians to congregate in areas of their own, rather than to mix with other elements of the population or to spread freely into the newer areas either in Canada or in the United States, as these have been opened up for settlement. One of the privileges granted the French population by the Quebec Act in 1764 was that of maintaining their own language and their own religion. This maintenance has been effectively continued until the present time, as is evidenced by the fact, among other things, that many of the Canadian public documents, including the census reports, are printed both in French and in English. The Roman Catholic Church has also, without doubt, contributed both to the maintenance of the French language and traditions and to the continuance of the segregation of the French population into specified areas. In the Canadian census of 1931, 97.3 per cent of the French in Canada were returned as members of the Roman Catholic Church. In the Province of Quebec, where the French formed such a great majority of the population, 99.4 per cent were Catholic, while most of the non-Catholic French were in the Province of Ontario, where they are more extensively intermingled with the English Canadians, and among the small numbers of French in the western provinces.

The English-speaking element in the population of Canada, in contrast with the French, has been continuously recruited, as already noted, by new immigration from the British Isles and from various parts of the United States. This element has contributed mainly to the settlement of the newer western provinces of Canada and has likewise furnished the major part of the Canadian born who have settled in the United States, especially those who have settled outside New England and a few eastern centers. If only by reason of the fact that it has been made up rather largely of the children and grandchildren of immigrants from other countries, this element in the Canadian population, with its wider range of experience, might be expected to be more venturesome and to have a greater inclination for pioneering and for settlement of such new territory as the Prairie Provinces. Further, if only by reason of language, the English Canadians would be much more readily assimilated with the population of the United States in such movements as the settlement of the western States. This explains in part why we now find scattered widely throughout the northwestern part of the United States many English Canadians and few French Canadians.

The classification which separates French Canadians from other Canadians is one of the most important and fundamental classifications embodied in the census statistics of both the United States and Canada. In the Canadian census reports the classification is based on a direct question with respect to racial origin. In the census of the United States the classification is based on mother tongue, that is, language of customary speech in the home prior to immigration. By reason of the fact, however, that practically all of the Canadians of the French race continue to use the French language, the two classifications are practically identical, in spite of the difference in the statistical technique through which they are obtained.

In the classification by mother tongue, the Canadian born in the United States in 1930 were divided as follows: French, 29.0 per cent; English, 68.9 per cent; and other languages, 2.1 per cent.[1] In the tables that follow, data are presented in general for two classes, termed, respectively, "French" and "English," the latter class including the small numbers of persons reporting as mother tongue languages other than French or English. In the reports of the United States census this second class is designated "Other," or "Other than French," but in view of the fact that English is actually the mother tongue in almost all of the cases, it seems not worth while to employ these cumbersome terms in the present discussion.

This "English" group is primarily based on language, and in this case the language does not, as with the French, coincide with the racial origin of the Canadian census, in which the group would be divided among several classifications, including in particular Scotch and Irish, as well as English.

The classification is important, not only because it gives representation to the two principal European stocks which had a part in the earlier settlement of Canada, but also because there are consistent differences between the two classes both in their characteristics and in their location within the United States. The French stock is more closely unified in its racial characteristics and more consistent in its behavior as a contributor to the population of the United States, making its settlements for the most part in the eastern States near the border, and in Michigan and Minnesota. The English stock, on the other hand, is scattered over a much wider area, and has manifested many characteristics in common with the pioneer families which have gone from eastern States of the United States to help people the West.

Data for the Canadian-born white population of the United States, classified as French and English (the latter including, as already noted, a small miscellaneous group) are presented in Table 17 for the censuses from 1890, the year in which the classification was first made, to 1930.

There were in the United States, in 1930, 370,852 French persons of Canadian birth, these forming 29.0 per cent of the whole number of white persons of Canadian birth (1,278,421). These percentages have changed but little during the 40-year period for which the statistics are available. In 1890, 31.0 per cent of the white Canadian-born population in the

1. The whole number of Canadian born in 1930 with mother tongue other than French or English was 26,815. The principal groups represented, on the basis of mother tongue, were as follows: German, 9,818; Yiddish, 5,146; Polish, 2,141; Italian, 1,754; Russian, 1,245; Ukrainian, 1,097; and Swedish, Norwegian, Danish, and Icelandic together, 2,166.

United States spoke French; in 1900, 33.6 per cent; in 1910, 32.2 per cent; and in 1920, 27.5 per cent.

TABLE **17**. CANADIAN-BORN WHITE POPULATION IN THE UNITED STATES, CLASSIFIED AS FRENCH AND ENGLISH, BY SEX: 1890 TO 1930

CLASS AND SEX	1930	1920	1910	1900*	1890*
Total..................	1,278,421	1,117,878	1,196,070	1,172,860	975,496
French..................	370,852	307,786	385,083	394,461	302,496
English†	907,569	810,092	810,987	778,399	673,000‡
Per cent French.......	29.0	27.5	32.2	33.6	31.0
Male..................	617,090	547,357	601,833	606,666	.....
French..................	187,523	157,748	201,164	210,204	.....
English†	429,567	389,609	400,669	396,462	.....
Per cent French.......	30.4	28.8	33.4	34.6	.....
Female..................	661,331	570,521	594,237	566,194	.....
French..................	183,329	150,038	183,919	184,257	.....
English†	478,002	420,483	410,318	381,937	.....
Per cent French.......	27.7	26.3	31.0	32.5	.....
Males per 100 females:					
Total..................	93.3	95.9	101.3	107.1	.....
French..................	102.3	105.1	109.4	114.1	.....
English†	89.9	92.7	97.6	103.8	.....

*Includes persons born in Newfoundland.
†The designation "English" covers all Canadian born who were not of French race or mother tongue, including a small number—about 2 per cent of the total—with mother tongue other than English. See discussion in text, p. 46.
‡Partly estimated; total reported for "Canada–Other" was 678,442, of whom eight-tenths of 1 per cent were estimated to be nonwhite, this proportion being based on the returns of later censuses.

Incidentally, it may be noted that 28.2 per cent of the population of Canada were of French origin, according to the Canadian census of 1931, which indicates that the racial distribution of the Canadian born in the United States in 1930 was approximately the same as that of the population of Canada itself.

The distribution of the Canadian born as between French and English at each of the five censuses for which statistics are available is shown graphically in Figure 12.

FIGURE **12**. CANADIAN BORN IN THE UNITED STATES, FRENCH AND ENGLISH: 1890 TO 1930

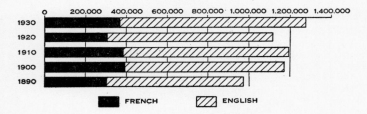

SEX DISTRIBUTION

THE French element in the Canadian-born population of the United States in 1930 comprised 187,523 males and 183,329 females, or 102.3 males per 100 females. The English element comprised 429,567 males, and 478,002 females, or only 89.9 males per 100 females. The sex ratio, that is, the number of males per 100 females, has been gradually declining since the census of 1900. At that census there were shown for the French Canadian born in the United States, 114.1 males per 100 females. In 1910 the ratio had declined to 109.4; in 1920, to 105.1; and in 1930, as already noted, to 102.3. The corresponding ratios for the English Canadian born were: 103.8 in 1900; 97.6 in 1910; 92.7 in 1920; and 89.9 in 1930. The extent of the decline in the ratios for the two classes was therefore approximately the same, except that the French started with a relatively high ratio in 1900 and reached what might be considered a normal ratio in 1930, while the English started with a normal ratio in 1900 and reached, in 1930, a ratio unusually low except for small groups of highly urbanized population.

The decline in the sex ratio of the French and English Canadian born is shown graphically in Figure 13.

FIGURE **13**. EXCESS OF MALES OR FEMALES IN THE CANADIAN-BORN POPULATION OF THE UNITED STATES, FRENCH AND ENGLISH: 1900 TO 1930

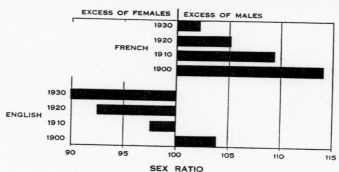

SEX RATIO FOR SELECTED COUNTRIES

IN Table 18 are presented data for the foreign-born white in the United States from the principal European countries classified by sex, in comparison with similar figures for the Canadian born.

TABLE **18**. FOREIGN-BORN WHITE POPULATION OF THE UNITED STATES FROM SELECTED COUNTRIES, BY SEX: 1910 TO 1930

COUNTRY OF BIRTH	1930		Males per 100 females	1920		Males per 100 females	1910		Males per 100 females
	Male	Female		Male	Female		Male	Female	
Canada...	617,090	661,331	93.3	547,357	570,521	95.9	601,833	594,237	101.3
French..	187,523	183,329	102.3	157,748	150,038	105.1	201,164	183,919	109.4
English..	429,567	478,002	89.9	389,609	420,483	92.7	400,669	410,318	97.6
England...	412,065	396,607	103.9	425,038	387,790	109.6	476,531	399,924	119.2
Scotland...	181,654	172,669	105.2	133,955	120,612	111.1	144,637	116,397	124.3
Wales.....	32,189	28,016	114.9	36,184	30,882	117.2	45,388	37,091	122.4
Ireland*...	405,929	517,713	78.4	455,571	581,662	78.3	611,515	740,640	82.6
Norway...	196,349	151,503	129.6	202,757	161,105	125.9	230,143	173,715	132.5
Sweden....	333,623	261,627	127.5	344,933	280,647	122.9	369,938	295,245	125.3
Denmark..	109,975	69,499	158.2	114,063	75,091	151.9	109,105	72,516	150.5
Germany..	843,136	765,678	110.1	891,289	794,813	112.1	1,239,516	1,071,569	115.7
Poland....	681,425	587,158	116.1	646,387	493,591	131.0	568,030	369,854	153.6
Italy......	1,042,621	747,803	139.4	958,274	651,835	147.0	880,857	462,213	190.6
Greece....	129,101	45,425	284.2	143,602	32,370	443.6	93,430	7,834	1192.6

*Includes both Northern Ireland and Irish Free State.

In general, the figures for the other countries show a considerable decline in the sex ratio between 1910 and 1930, running parallel in this respect with the figures for the Canadian born, both French and English. The only country which shows a lower sex ratio than Canada in 1930 is Ireland. Among the foreign-born white from Ireland there were only 78.4 males per 100 females, this ratio being materially lower than that for the English Canadians (89.9) upon which comment has already been made. One reason for the low ratio shown by the Irish lies in the fact that Irish immigration began at a very early date, and that the present Irish-born population includes large numbers of very old persons, with the usual excess of females.

Some of the countries from which there has been more recent immigration, on the other hand, show sex ratios much higher than either the 1930 ratios of the Canadian born, or even their 1910 ratios. In the very large foreign-born white population from Italy, for example, there were, in 1930, 139.4 males per 100 females; and among the foreign-born whites from Greece, 284.2 males per 100 females.

URBAN AND RURAL AREAS

THE data for French and English Canadian born, classified by sex, are presented in Table 19 for urban and rural areas. The percentage of the French Canadian born living in urban areas in 1930 was slightly higher than that of the English Canadian born, 78.9 as compared with 76.7, and the percentage living in rural-farm areas was correspondingly smaller, 6.1, as compared with 8.5. The percentage urban for both French and English females was considerably higher than the percentage urban for males and the percentage rural-farm much lower, reflecting the differences in opportunity for employment which have already been noted.

The excess of males or of females, as the case may be, in the French and English Canadian born in the United States, is shown graphically in Figure 14. There is about the same range between urban areas and

TABLE **19**. CANADIAN-BORN WHITE POPULATION, FRENCH AND ENGLISH, BY SEX, FOR URBAN AND RURAL AREAS: 1930

CLASS AND AREA	TOTAL		MALE		FEMALE		Males per 100 females
	Number	Per cent	Number	Per cent	Number	Per cent	
Total............	**1,278,421**	**100.0**	**617,090**	**100.0**	**661,331**	**100.0**	**93.3**
Urban..................	988,738	77.3	464,065	75.2	524,673	79.3	88.4
Rural-nonfarm...........	189,946	14.9	97,927	15.9	92,019	13.9	106.4
Rural-farm...............	99,737	7.8	55,098	8.9	44,639	6.7	123.4
French...........	**370,852**	**100.0**	**187,523**	**100.0**	**183,329**	**100.0**	**102.3**
Urban..................	292,564	78.9	144,357	77.0	148,207	80.8	97.4
Rural-nonfarm...........	55,620	15.0	30,018	16.0	25,602	14.0	117.2
Rural-farm...............	22,668	6.1	13,148	7.0	9,520	5.2	138.1
English...........	**907,569**	**100.0**	**429,567**	**100.0**	**478,002**	**100.0**	**89.9**
Urban..................	696,174	76.7	319,708	74.4	376,466	78.8	84.9
Rural-nonfarm...........	134,326	14.8	67,909	15.8	66,417	13.9	102.2
Rural-farm...............	77,069	8.5	41,950	9.8	35,119	7.3	119.5

FIGURE **14**. EXCESS OF MALES OR FEMALES IN THE CANADIAN-BORN POPULATION, FRENCH AND ENGLISH, IN URBAN AND RURAL AREAS: 1930

(First [black] bar in each group represents urban; second [cross-hatched], rural-nonfarm; and third [diagonals], rural-farm)

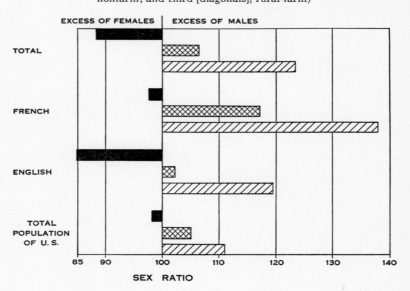

rural-farm areas for the French Canadians as for the English, but the
former start at a relatively high level, ranging from 97.4 in urban areas
to 138.1 in rural-farm areas, while the latter run from 84.9 in urban
areas to 119.5 in rural-farm areas.

DATA FOR STATES, COUNTIES, AND CITIES

FIGURES for the Canadian born classified as French and English are presented by States in Chapter V, where they appear as one element in the
population of Canadian stock. (See especially Tables 28 to 34.) The
numbers in each of the 13 States reporting 25,000 or more Canadian
born are presented in graphic form in Figure 15.

FIGURE **15**. CANADIAN BORN, FRENCH AND ENGLISH, FOR 13 SELECTED STATES: 1930

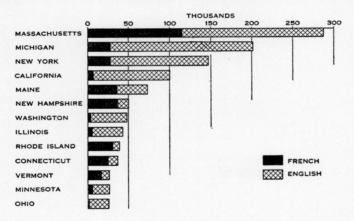

Figures for the Canadian born, French and English, are presented in
Table 20 for each county and each city in which there were 1,000 or more
Canadian born in 1930. The counties are arranged alphabetically by
States, and the cities are arranged alphabetically under the counties.
The 149 counties for which figures are presented in this table contain,
as already indicated above, 83.3 per cent of all the Canadian born in the
United States in 1930. The French Canadian born living in these coun-
ties in 1930 represented an even larger proportion of the United States
total, namely, 90.4 per cent.

The 9 counties in which there were more than 10,000 French Canadian born in 1930 contained 45.6 per cent of the United States total. The 16 counties in which there were from 3,000 to 10,000 French Canadians contained an additional 19.8 per cent, making a total of 65.4 per cent in 25 counties. An additional 33 of the 149 counties had as many as 1,000 French Canadian born in 1930, making a total of only 58 counties having as many as 1,000 French Canadian born.

In like manner we may note that the 15 counties in which there were in 1930, 10,000 or more English Canadian born contained 46.8 per cent of the United States total. The 32 counties in which there were from 3,000 to 10,000 English Canadians contained an additional 18.4 per cent, making a total of 65.1 per cent in 47 counties. There were an additional 69 counties in which there were as many as 1,000 English Canadian born, making a total of 116 counties containing 1,000 or more English Canadian born, which may be compared with the 58 counties indicated above as containing 1,000 or more French Canadians.

On the basis of data for all of the 3,100 counties in the United States, it may be further noted that, while there are 343 counties in which there were no Canadian born, either French or English, there were 1,217 counties with no French Canadian born and 374 with no English Canadian born. These figures give further support to the general statement already made to the effect that the geographic distribution of the French Canadian born was much more restricted than that of the English Canadian born.

The distribution of the French Canadian born in the six New England States and New York (seven States in which were found nearly 80 per cent of all French Canadian born in the United States) is indicated by the position of the dots on the map designated Figure 16. This map shows in particular the concentration of the French Canadian born in a few urban areas in Massachusetts, New Hampshire, and Rhode Island. It may be compared with Figure 8, which is a similar map of the United States indicating the location of all Canadian born (including, of course, the French Canadian born) in the country as a whole.

TABLE **20**. CANADIAN-BORN WHITE POPULATION, FRENCH AND ENGLISH, IN COUNTIES AND CITIES REPORTING 1,000 OR MORE: 1930

STATE, COUNTY, AND CITY	Canadian born Total	French	Eng-lish	Per cent of population Canadian born	STATE, COUNTY, AND CITY	Canadian born Total	French	Eng-lish	Per cent of population Canadian born
MAINE					**MASS.—Continued**				
Androscoggin	12,185	10,551	1,634	17.1	Hampshire	3,783	3,158	625	5.2
Auburn	2,044	1,505	539	11.0	Northampton	1,166	905	261	4.8
Lewiston	8,884	8,276	608	25.4	Middlesex	79,277	19,418	59,859	8.5
Aroostook	10,573	2,560	8,013	12.0	Cambridge	9,254	1,672	7,582	8.1
Cumberland	9,856	3,252	6,604	7.3	Everett	4,141	366	3,775	8.6
Portland	4,917	687	4,230	6.9	Lowell	10,169	7,763	2,406	10.1
Westbrook	1,558	1,170	388	14.4	Malden	4,917	506	4,411	8.5
Franklin	1,290	702	588	6.5	Marlborough	1,230	662	568	7.9
Kennebec	7,036	4,756	2,280	10.0	Medford	4,609	394	4,215	7.7
Augusta	2,190	1,638	552	12.7	Melrose	2,010	179	1,831	8.7
Waterville	2,361	1,847	514	15.3	Newton	4,619	733	3,886	7.1
Oxford	4,495	2,618	1,877	10.8	Somerville	10,069	905	9,164	9.7
Penobscot	7,304	1,919	5,385	7.9	Waltham	4,867	1,636	3,231	12.4
Bangor	2,301	384	1,917	8.0	Norfolk	18,951	2,117	16,834	6.3
Piscataquis	1,582	322	1,260	8.7	Quincy	4,631	551	4,080	6.4
Sagadahoc	1,018	387	631	6.0	Plymouth	7,665	1,730	5,935	4.7
Somerset	3,525	1,671	1,854	9.0	Brockton	2,946	720	2,226	4.6
Washington	3,440	117	3,323	9.1	Suffolk	50,606	4,985	45,621	5.8
York	9,173	7,772	1,401	12.6	Boston	45,558	4,083	41,475	5.8
Biddeford	4,013	3,889	124	22.8	Chelsea	2,403	582	1,821	5.2
					Revere	1,613	261	1,352	4.5
NEW HAMPSHIRE					Worcester	33,751	23,142	10,609	6.9
Belknap	2,288	1,655	633	10.1	Fitchburg	4,178	3,491	687	10.3
Laconia	1,673	1,324	349	13.4	Gardner	2,438	2,121	317	12.6
Cheshire	1,913	1,377	536	5.7	Leominster	2,793	2,127	666	12.8
Coös	7,873	5,459	2,414	20.2	Worcester	9,146	4,947	4,199	4.7
Berlin	5,381	4,434	947	26.9					
Grafton	3,496	1,652	1,844	8.2	**RHODE ISLAND**				
Hillsborough	20,138	17,246	2,892	14.4					
Manchester	12,118	10,696	1,422	15.8	Kent	3,284	2,802	482	6.4
Nashua	5,482	4,895	587	17.4	Providence	33,824	27,434	6,390	6.3
Merrimack	4,994	3,509	1,485	8.9	Central Falls	4,009	3,938	71	15.5
Concord	1,870	1,098	772	7.4	Cranston	1,148	491	657	2.7
Rockingham	3,339	1,518	1,821	6.2	Pawtucket	5,561	4,898	663	7.2
Strafford	3,957	3,298	659	10.3	Providence	7,594	3,837	3,757	3.0
Rochester	1,178	1,032	146	11.5	Woonsocket	10,256	9,990	266	20.8
Sullivan	2,309	1,777	532	9.5					
					CONNECTICUT				
VERMONT					Fairfield	4,502	1,837	2,665	1.2
Caledonia	3,396	1,637	1,759	12.5	Bridgeport	1,909	935	974	1.3
Chittenden	3,941	3,345	596	8.3	Hartford	12,137	7,890	4,247	2.9
Burlington	1,962	1,581	381	7.9	Bristol	2,118	1,671	447	7.4
Essex	1,224	684	540	17.3	Hartford	5,771	3,739	2,032	3.5
Franklin	3,853	2,741	1,112	12.9	New Britain	1,280	952	328	1.9
Orleans	4,691	2,862	1,829	20.4	Litchfield	1,564	1,108	456	1.9
Rutland	1,077	596	481	2.2	New Haven	8,222	5,348	2,874	1.8
Washington	3,215	2,067	1,148	7.7	Meriden	1,006	790	216	2.6
Windsor	1,352	590	762	3.6	New Haven	1,495	581	914	0.9
					Waterbury	3,917	3,276	641	3.9
MASSACHUSETTS					New London	4,342	3,174	1,168	3.6
Berkshire	4,013	3,186	827	3.3	Windham	5,868	5,549	319	10.8
North Adams	1,266	1,126	140	5.9	Willimantic	1,403	1,350	53	11.6
Pittsfield	1,348	963	385	2.7					
Bristol	25,793	21,283	4,510	7.1	**NEW YORK**				
Attleboro	2,011	1,115	896	9.2					
Fall River	8,973	8,477	496	7.8	Albany	3,900	2,740	1,160	1.8
New Bedford	8,462	7,643	819	7.5	Albany	1,400	572	828	1.1
Taunton	1,996	1,159	837	5.3	Cohoes	1,948	1,873	75	8.4
Essex	40,938	18,633	22,305	8.2	Bronx*	5,270	890	4,380	0.4
Beverly	1,816	365	1,451	7.2	Clinton	2,187	1,491	696	4.7
Gloucester	2,827	473	2,354	11.7	Erie	23,433	1,130	22,303	3.1
Haverhill	3,637	1,907	1,730	7.5	Buffalo	18,735	851	17,884	3.3
Lawrence	6,318	5,280	1,038	7.4	Kenmore	1,117	40	1,077	6.8
Lynn	9,727	2,930	6,797	9.5	Franklin	3,331	2,146	1,185	7.3
Salem	4,613	3,365	1,248	10.6	Jefferson	6,317	762	5,555	7.6
Franklin	1,649	953	696	3.3	Watertown	2,899	361	2,538	9.0
Hampden	20,248	16,385	3,863	6.0	Kings*	12,264	1,798	10,466	0.5
Chicopee	4,908	4,663	245	11.2	Monroe	12,930	888	12,042	3.1
Holyoke	5,355	4,939	416	9.5	Rochester	10,113	693	9,420	3.1
Springfield	7,194	4,918	2,276	4.8	Nassau	2,389	304	2,085	0.8

*New York City: Total, 39,622, French, 6,863, English, 32,759; per cent of population Canadian born, 0.6.

TABLE **20**. CANADIAN-BORN WHITE POPULATION, FRENCH AND ENGLISH, IN COUNTIES AND CITIES REPORTING 1,000 OR MORE: 1930—Continued

STATE, COUNTY, AND CITY	CANADIAN BORN			Per cent of population Canadian born	STATE, COUNTY, AND CITY	CANADIAN BORN			Per cent of population Canadian born
	Total	French	English			Total	French	English	
NEW YORK—Cont.					**MICHIGAN**—Cont.				
New York*	14,271	2,732	11,539	0.8	Kent	3,496	269	3,227	1.5
Niagara	10,032	805	9,227	6.7	Grand Rapids	2,529	214	2,315	1.5
Niagara Falls	7,635	580	7,055	10.1	Lapeer	1,292	39	1,253	4.6
Oneida	2,529	732	1,797	1.3	Macomb	3,516	510	3,006	4.6
Utica	1,156	315	841	1.1	Marquette	1,312	745	567	3.0
Onondaga	6,003	1,257	4,746	2.1	Muskegon	1,300	404	896	1.5
Syracuse	4,693	1,026	3,667	2.2	Oakland	13,485	1,255	12,230	6.4
Oswego	1,461	370	1,091	2.1	Ferndale	2,056	359	1,697	9.9
Queens*	6,670	1,336	5,334	0.6	Pontiac	3,530	325	3,205	5.4
Rensselaer	1,133	598	535	0.9	Royal Oak	2,068	123	1,945	9.0
Richmond*	1,147	107	1,040	0.7	Saginaw	3,631	551	3,080	3.0
St. Lawrence	8,424	2,822	5,602	9.3	Saginaw	2,624	415	2,209	3.3
Massena village	2,179	1,075	1,104	20.5	St. Clair	6,261	220	6,041	9.3
Ogdensburg	1,951	585	1,366	11.5	Port Huron	3,856	92	3,764	12.3
Schenectady	1,522	613	909	1.2	Sanilac	2,865	53	2,812	10.3
Schenectady	1,214	499	715	1.3	Shiawassee	1,181	55	1,126	3.0
Suffolk	1,291	334	957	0.8	Tuscola	1,827	53	1,774	5.5
Westchester	4,996	874	4,122	1.0	Washtenaw	1,553	84	1,469	2.4
					Wayne	110,130	14,894	95,236	5.8
NEW JERSEY					Dearborn	2,723	354	2,369	5.4
Bergen	1,904	250	1,654	0.5	Detroit	94,284	12,477	81,807	6.0
Essex	4,702	798	3,904	0.6	Highland Park	4,376	333	4,043	8.3
Newark	1,946	498	1,448	0.4	River Rouge	1,314	711	603	7.6
Hudson	2,487	407	2,080	0.4					
Jersey City	1,227	184	1,043	0.4	**WISCONSIN**				
Union	1,661	202	1,459	0.5	Douglas	1,199	259	940	2.6
					Superior	1,002	213	789	2.8
PENNSYLVANIA					Milwaukee	3,367	583	2,784	0.5
Allegheny	3,077	280	2,797	0.2	Milwaukee	2,662	456	2,206	0.5
Pittsburgh	1,683	154	1,529	0.3					
Erie	1,264	96	1,168	0.7	**MINNESOTA**				
Philadelphia	4,229	636	3,593	0.2	Hennepin	7,343	1,517	5,826	1.4
Philadelphia	4,229	636	3,593	0.2	Minneapolis	6,731	1,373	5,358	1.4
					Ramsey	3,694	795	2,899	1.3
OHIO					St. Paul	3,461	720	2,741	1.3
Cuyahoga	12,627	971	11,656	1.1	St. Louis	4,901	1,224	3,677	2.4
Cleveland	8,265	674	7,591	0.9	Duluth	3,479	872	2,607	3.4
Lakewood	1,309	73	1,236	1.9					
Hamilton	1,013	84	929	0.2	**MISSOURI**				
Lucas	3,502	615	2,887	1.0	Jackson	1,776	181	1,595	0.4
Toledo	3,031	534	2,497	1.0	Kansas City	1,424	...	...	0.4
Summit	1,445	149	1,296	0.4	St. Louis city	1,374	172	1,202	0.2
Akron	1,043	104	939	0.4					
					NORTH DAKOTA				
INDIANA					Cass	1,077	149	928	2.2
Lake	1,869	193	1,676	0.7	Cavalier	1,221	118	1,103	8.4
					Grand Forks	1,161	77	1,084	3.6
ILLINOIS					Pembina	1,596	166	1,430	10.8
Cook	35,153	4,889	30,264	0.9					
Chicago	29,831	4,211	25,620	0.9	**NEBRASKA**				
Oak Park village	1,077	133	944	1.7	Douglas	1,001	111	890	0.4
Lake	1,101	92	1,009	1.1					
					MARYLAND				
MICHIGAN					Baltimore city	1,211	176	1,035	0.2
Alpena	1,277	401	876	6.9					
Bay	3,003	1,011	1,992	4.3	**DIST. OF COLUMBIA**				
Bay City	2,270	704	1,566	4.8	Washington	1,681	223	1,458	0.3
Calhoun	1,442	59	1,383	1.7					
Chippewa	3,616	428	3,188	14.4	**FLORIDA**				
Sault Ste. Marie	2,073	241	1,832	15.1	Dade	1,788	222	1,566	1.3
Delta	1,728	1,273	455	5.4	Miami	1,301	...	...	1.2
Genesee	8,682	942	7,740	4.1					
Flint	6,837	798	6,039	4.4	**MONTANA**				
Houghton	1,233	807	426	2.3	Cascade	1,163	140	1,023	2.8
Huron	2,450	112	2,338	7.9	Silver Bow	1,361	341	1,020	2.4
Ingham	2,255	149	2,106	1.9	Butte	1,047	244	803	2.6
Lansing	1,666	107	1,559	2.1					
Jackson	1,454	133	1,321	1.6					

*New York City: Total, 39,622, French, 6,863, English, 32,759; per cent of population Canadian born, 0.6.

TABLE **20**. CANADIAN-BORN WHITE POPULATION, FRENCH AND ENGLISH, IN COUNTIES AND CITIES REPORTING 1,000 OR MORE: 1930—Continued

STATE, COUNTY, AND CITY	CANADIAN BORN			Per cent of population Canadian born	STATE, COUNTY, AND CITY	CANADIAN BORN			Per cent of population Canadian born
	Total	French	English			Total	French	English	
COLORADO					**CALIFORNIA**				
Denver..............	2,546	243	2,303	0.9	Alameda.............	8,572	559	8,013	1.8
Denver.............	2,546	...	...	0.9	Berkeley...........	1,612	61	1,551	2.0
					Oakland............	5,227	404	4,823	1.8
					Contra Costa........	1,057	63	994	1.3
WASHINGTON					Fresno..............	1,193	84	1,109	0.8
Grays Harbor........	1,651	174	1,477	2.8	Humboldt...........	1,118	67	1,051	2.6
King................	18,981	1,347	17,634	4.1	Los Angeles.........	53,453	3,999	49,454	2.4
Seattle.............	15,745	1,116	14,629	4.3	Glendale...........	1,794	84	1,710	2.9
Pierce..............	4,471	335	4,136	2.7	Long Beach.........	3,589	235	3,354	2.5
Tacoma............	3,155	238	2,917	3.0	Los Angeles.........	30,740	2,439	28,301	2.5
Skagit..............	1,058	101	957	3.0	Pasadena...........	2,216	91	2,125	2.9
Snohomish...........	2,801	380	2,421	3.6	Santa Monica.......	1,475	104	1,371	4.0
Everett............	1,295	185	1,110	4.2	Orange..............	1,565	61	1,504	1.3
Spokane.............	4,755	453	4,302	3.2	Riverside...........	1,263	88	1,175	1.6
Spokane............	3,855	391	3,464	3.3	Sacramento..........	1,723	119	1,604	1.2
Whatcom............	2,782	133	2,649	4.7	Sacramento.........	1,182	75	1,107	1.3
Bellingham.........	1,525	75	1,450	4.9	San Bernardino.......	2,105	128	1,977	1.6
Yakima.............	1,879	533	1,346	2.4	San Diego...........	4,123	302	3,821	2.0
					San Diego..........	3,004	230	2,774	2.0
					San Francisco........	9,601	909	8,692	1.5
OREGON					San Francisco.......	9,601	909	8,692	1.5
Marion..............	1,048	67	981	1.7	San Joaquin.........	1,116	102	1,014	1.1
Multnomah...........	9,180	584	8,596	2.7	San Mateo...........	1,490	124	1,366	1.9
Portland...........	8,351	537	7,814	2.8	Santa Barbara........	1,044	71	973	1.6
					Santa Clara..........	2,007	139	1,868	1.4

FIGURE **16**. DISTRIBUTION OF FRENCH CANADIAN BORN IN NEW ENGLAND AND NEW YORK: 1930

(Each dot represents 250 French Canadian born)

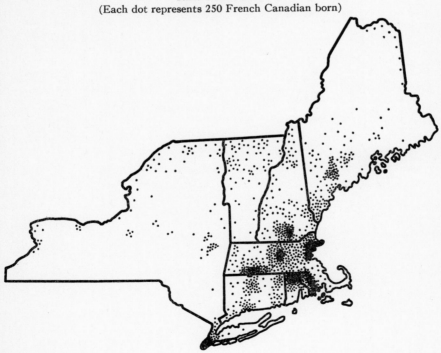

CHAPTER V

WHITE POPULATION OF CANADIAN STOCK IN THE UNITED STATES

THE discussion has so far been limited to the Canadian born, that is, to those persons in the population of the United States who were born in Canada. Except for the last four tables (Tables 17, 18, 19, and 20) the figures under discussion have included the small number of nonwhite persons of Canadian birth resident in the United States, though separate figures have been shown in some of the tables for the Canadian-born white population.

Statistics are also available in the census reports of the United States, limited in this case to persons of the white race, for the children of the Canadian born, that is, for those persons having one or both parents born in Canada. This group may be combined with the Canadian-born white to make up what has been termed the population of Canadian stock. This Canadian stock forms a part of the "foreign white stock" for which extensive data are presented in the United States census reports.

With relation to the population of immediate European origin, the figures for the foreign white stock in the reports of the census of the United States serve somewhat the same purpose as the statistics of racial origin in the reports of the Canadian census, though unlike the latter, they are limited in their coverage to the immigrants and their children. This limitation has been justified on the assumption that the grandchildren of the immigrants have become so largely assimilated with the general population that there is little need for counting them separately. Be that as it may, these figures for the first and second generations of population of foreign origin represent the material which is available. Further, the figures for the Canadian stock at least provide a more nearly complete quantitative measure of the Canadian element in the population of the United States than do the statistics of the Canadian born alone—though the second generation of the Canadian stock differs even less from the native white population of native parentage in the United States in most of its characteristics than do the Canadian born.

Wherever statistics are presented in this volume for the population of Canadian stock, figures are also given for its two constituent parts—the Canadian born (white) and those natives of the United States who are of Canadian parentage. In these presentations the few thousand nonwhites of Canadian birth in the United States are omitted altogether. The group comprising the Canadian born is in some respects the more important, and the statistical material relating to it is more extensive in point of time, since the Canadian born are shown separately in the reports of every decennial census of the United States beginning with 1850, while the group comprising native white persons of Canadian parentage was first distinguished in the census of 1890.

The figures representing the Canadian stock for the five censuses from 1890 to 1930 are presented in Tables 21 and 22, with various significant ratios and percentages.

TABLE **21**. WHITE POPULATION OF CANADIAN STOCK (CANADIAN BIRTH AND PARENTAGE) IN THE UNITED STATES, WITH COMPARATIVE DATA FOR TOTAL POPULATION, ETC.: 1890 TO 1930

CLASS	1930	1920	1910	1900*	1890*
All Canadian stock................	3,337,345	2,959,483	2,846,891	2,562,330	1,845,032
Per cent of total population........	2.7	2.8	3.1	3.4	2.9
Canadian born†......................	1,278,421	1,117,878	1,196,070	1,172,860	975,496
Per cent of total population..........	1.0	1.1	1.3	1.5	1.5
Per cent of all foreign-born white.....	9.1	8.2	9.0	11.5	10.7
Canadian parentage‡..................	2,058,924	1,841,605	1,650,821	1,389,470	869,536
Per cent of total population..........	1.7	1.7	1.8	1.8	1.4
Per cent of all native white.........	2.1	2.3	2.4	2.5	1.9
Per cent of native white of foreign or mixed parentage...................	7.9	8.1	8.7	8.9	7.6
Ratio to Canadian born.............	1.61	1.65	1.38	1.18	0.89
Total population of United States....	122,775,046	105,710,620	91,972,266	75,994,575	62,947,714
Foreign-born white§....................	13,983,405	13,712,754	13,345,545	10,213,817	9,121,867
Native white§.......................	96,303,335	81,108,161	68,386,412	56,595,379	45,979,391
Native white of foreign or mixed parentage§	25,902,383	22,686,204	18,897,837	15,646,017	11,503,675

*Canadian figures include persons born in Newfoundland or with parents born in Newfoundland.
†The 1920 figures for Canadian born are taken from the tabulation by place of birth of person, whereas the data for foreign born presented in the 1920 report on foreign white stock are based on country of birth of father. The number of persons born in Canada was considerably larger than the number of foreign-born white persons with father born in Canada, by reason of the considerable foreign-born element in the population of Canada itself. The present figures for Canadian stock therefore exceed by a considerable amount the figures published in the 1920 Census report. The 1890 figures involve a slight element of estimate, in that they are obtained by subtracting from the reported number of all Canadian born, an estimate of the small number of nonwhite persons included.
‡For 1920, 1910, and 1900, the figures for Canadian parentage have been revised to conform to the 1930 classification, in which the assignment of persons of mixed foreign parentage was made on the basis of the country of birth of father. The 1890 figures include an estimate, based on the relations shown in the later censuses, of the number of persons having a Canadian-born father and mother born in some other foreign country—the equivalent of the addition from the original classification of mixed foreign parentage made for the three succeeding censuses on the basis of actual tabulations by country of birth of father and mother. This estimate is based on the relations shown in the later censuses.
§Includes Mexicans, who were shown separately in the 1930 Census reports.

TABLE **22**. INCREASE IN THE WHITE POPULATION OF CANADIAN STOCK, TOTAL POPULATION, ETC.: 1890 TO 1930

[A minus sign (—) denotes decrease]

CLASS	INCREASE, 1920–1930		INCREASE, 1910–1920		INCREASE, 1900–1910		INCREASE, 1890–1900	
	Number	Per cent	Number	Per cent	Number	Per cent	Number	Per cent
All Canadian stock.......	377,862	12.8	112,592	4.0	284,561	11.1	717,298	38.9
Canadian-born........	160,543	14.4	—78,192	—6.5	23,210	2.0	197,364	20.2
Canadian parentage....	217,319	11.8	190,784	11.6	261,351	18.8	519,934	59.8
Total population of the United States......	17,064,426	16.1	13,738,354	14.9	15,977,691	21.0	13,046,861	20.7
Foreign-born white*........	270,651	2.0	367,209	2.8	3,131,728	30.7	1,091,950	12.0
Native white*.............	15,195,174	18.7	12,721,749	18.6	11,791,033	20.8	10,615,988	23.1
Native white, foreign or mixed parentage*......	3,216,179	14.2	3,788,367	20.0	3,251,820	20.8	4,142,342	36.0

*Includes Mexicans.

There is some historical significance in the relation between the two elements of the Canadian stock. In certain parts of the United States there was a considerable immigration from Canada two or three generations ago, perhaps in connection with the original settling of the territory. Into some of these areas there have come very few persons from Canada in recent years, with the result that while there are relatively few Canadian born to be found in the present population, the number of persons of Canadian parentage is considerable. On the other hand, there are areas in which the immigration from Canada is of fairly recent date, and where the number of Canadian born still exceeds the number of native persons of Canadian parentage.

The total Canadian stock in 1930 amounted to 3,337,345 persons, or 2.7 per cent of the whole population of the United States, and 8.4 per cent of the foreign white stock from all countries.

The Canadian born formed 9.1 per cent of the foreign-born white, and the natives of Canadian parentage formed 7.9 per cent of the whole number of native whites of foreign or mixed parentage.

The relation of the Canadian stock to the entire population of the United States and to some of its general classifications is shown graphically in Figure 17, in which the areas of the several shaded sections are proportional to the population groups which they represent.

FIGURE **17.** RELATION OF CANADIAN STOCK TO POPULATION OF THE UNITED STATES: 1930

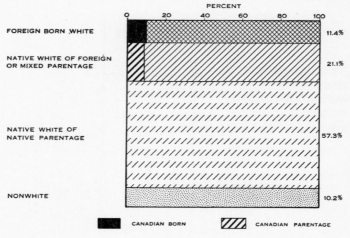

The relative importance of the Canadian stock in the United States changed considerably during the 40 years covered by the available statistics. From 1890 to 1900 the percentage of the total population of the United States represented by the Canadian stock increased from 2.9 to 3.4 by virtue of an increase of 38.9 per cent during a decade in which the population of the United States increased only 20.7 per cent. During the next three decades, though the Canadian stock continued to increase, it increased less rapidly than the total population, with the result that the percentage which it represented declined to 3.1 in 1910, to 2.8 in 1920, and to 2.7 in 1930. These changes are mainly the result of the declining relative importance of the Canadian born, since there was little change in the percentage represented by native persons of Canadian parentage.

In 1890, the Canadian stock, numbering 1,845,032 in all, comprised 975,496 Canadian born and 869,536 persons born in the United States of Canadian parentage, there being 89 of the latter for each 100 of the former. The Canadian-parentage group increased much faster than the Canadian born up to 1920, when there were 165 of this class for each 100 Canadian born ; and not quite so fast during the last decade, with the result that the ratio was 161 to 100 in 1930.

The Canadian stock as a whole increased during the 40-year period from 1890 to 1930 from 1,845,032 to 3,337,345, or 80.9 per cent. This was made up of an increase of 31.1 per cent in the Canadian born, most of which took place between 1890 and 1900, and an increase of 136.8 per cent in the second-generation group. These figures are shown graphically in Figure 18, which indicates clearly the relative increase from 1890 to 1930 in the Canadian born and the second generation of the Canadian stock.

FIGURE 18. CANADIAN STOCK IN THE UNITED STATES: 1890 TO 1930

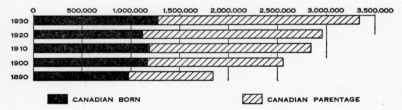

CANADIAN STOCK, FRENCH AND ENGLISH

In Table 23 the data for the French and English elements in the Canadian stock are presented separately for the censuses from 1890 to 1930. Of the total population of Canadian stock—that is, persons of Canadian birth or parentage—in 1930 (amounting to 3,337,345), 1,106,159, or 33.1 per cent, were French, as indicated by the mother tongue reported, and 2,231,186 were mainly English, the latter figure including, as already noted in the discussion of the corresponding classifications of the Canadian born, a small number of persons whose native tongue was neither French nor English. Of the Canadian born, 29.0 per cent were French; of the natives of the United States having one or both parents born in Canada, 35.7 per cent were French. These relationships are shown in graphic form in Figure 19, in which the several shaded blocks are proportional in area to the elements of the Canadian stock which they represent.

TABLE **23**. WHITE POPULATION OF CANADIAN STOCK IN THE UNITED STATES, FRENCH AND ENGLISH: 1890 TO 1930

[A minus sign (—) denotes decrease]

CLASS	1930	1920	1910	1900*	1890*	PER CENT INCREASE			
						1920 to 1930	1910 to 1920	1900 to 1910	1890 to 1900
All Canadian stock....	3,337,345	2,959,483	2,846,891	2,562,330	1,845,032	12.8	4.0	11.1	38.9
French............	1,106,159	870,146	947,792	850,491	535,501	27.1	—8.2	11.4	58.8
English...........	2,231,186	2,089,337	1,899,099	1,711,839	1,309,531	6.8	10.0	10.9	30.7
Canadian born...	1,278,421	1,117,878	1,196,070	1,172,860	975,496	14.4	—6.5	2.0	20.2
French.......	370,852	307,786	385,083	394,461	302,496	20.5	—20.1	—2.4	30.4
English.......	907,569	810,092	810,987	778,399	673,000	12.0	—0.1	4.2	15.7
Canadian parentage........	2,058,924	1,841,605	1,650,821	1,389,470	869,536	11.8	11.6	18.8	59.8
French.......	735,307	562,360	562,709	456,030	233,005	30.8	—0.1	23.4	95.7
English.......	1,323,617	1,279,245	1,088,112	933,440	636,531	3.5	17.6	16.6	46.6
Per cent French:									
All Canadian stock.	33.1	29.4	33.3	33.2	29.0	....	....	....	....
Canadian-born.....	29.0	27.5	32.2	33.6	31.0	....	....	....	....
Canadian parentage	35.7	30.5	34.1	32.8	26.8	....	....	....	....
Ratio of Canadian parentage to Canadian born:									
Total............	1.61	1.65	1.38	1.18	0.89	....	....	....	....
French..........	1.98	1.83	1.46	1.16	0.77	....	....	....	....
English..........	1.46	1.58	1.34	1.20	0.95	....	....	....	....

*Figures for 1900 and 1890 include persons born in Newfoundland or with parents born in Newfoundland. The 1890 figures for Canadian parentage include an estimate for persons having father born in Canada and mother born in some other foreign country.

During the 40-year period covered by the available statistics, the French Canadian born gained only 22.6 per cent, as compared with 34.9 per cent for the English Canadian born. The second generation of the French stock, however, gained 215.6 per cent, increasing from 233,005 in 1890 to 735,307 in 1930, as compared with 107.9 per cent for the second generation of the English stock.

These increases were not spread evenly over the 40-year period, as the percentages for the four constituent decades shown in Table 23 clearly indicate. The Canadian born, both French and English, increased materially from 1890 to 1900, and again from 1920 to 1930; the French

Canadian born actually decreased during the two middle decades of the period (from 1900 to 1920) ; the English Canadian born gained 4.2 per cent from 1900 to 1910, and lost very slightly from 1910 to 1920.

FIGURE **19.** COMPOSITION OF CANADIAN STOCK, FRENCH AND ENGLISH: 1930

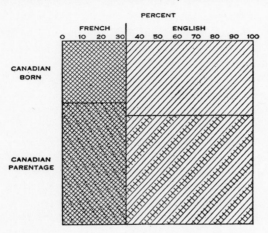

So far as concerns the English Canadian born in the United States, the counter-attraction of the opening up of the Canadian Northwest may explain why there was so little increase in their numbers between 1900 and 1910 as compared with the period from 1890 to 1900—and with earlier decades, in which increase in English Canadian born may be inferred from the increase in all Canadian born in States where there have never been many French. (See Table 2.) It should be noted, however, that even an increase of 32,588, or 4.2 per cent, in the census count would require a considerable amount of immigration to the United States, since even maintenance of the same number during this decade would necessitate replacements of more than 120,000 to offset the effects of mortality.[1]

Because relatively few French Canadians settled in the new Prairie Provinces, this explanation cannot be considered to any great extent in connection with the French Canadian born, whose numbers actually decreased between 1900 and 1910 (though not enough to indicate cessation

1. It is roughly estimated on the basis of the age distribution of the Canadian born and life-table rates that the deaths in this decade would amount to about 16 per cent of the number at the beginning of the decade. See Table 39, page 99, and the accompanying discussion, but note that the estimated mortality rate for the decade 1900–1910 is somewhat lower than that used for the decade 1920–1930, by reason of the more favorable age distribution in the earlier period.

of immigration to the United States during this decade) and decreased so much between 1910 and 1920 as to make certain that there was some net repatriation, in addition to a failure to replace the losses by death among those who were in the United States in 1910. In general, the decline in the number of Canadian born in the United States, both French and English, between 1910 and 1920 can be attributed to war conditions, since Canada entered the war more than two and one-half years earlier than the United States. Many Canadian born actually returned to their home country to enlist in the Canadian army ; and many more, who under other conditions might have emigrated to the United States, doubtless either joined the army or remained at home to man the war industries and to take the places in agriculture and industry left vacant by men who had joined the colors.

The increases in the second generation of Canadian stock might well be expected to follow rather closely, with a lag of one or two decades, the increases in the Canadian born. Only in a general way, however, does this seem to have been the case. The increase of 59.8 per cent in the Canadian-parentage group between 1890 and 1900 finds some explanation in the increase of 97.4 per cent in the Canadian born between 1860 and 1870, this being the maximum percentage increase in any decade since 1850 (see Table 2 and Fig. 1) ; but the relation between an increase of only 18.8 per cent in the Canadian-parentage group from 1900 to 1910, and increases of 45.3 per cent and 36.8 per cent, respectively, in the Canadian born during the decades 20 and 10 years earlier, indicates that there were other factors which disturbed the normal relations between the numbers of Canadian born in the United States and the numbers of the children of Canadian born appearing at later dates. One important factor of this kind is without doubt the movement of the children of Canadians back to Canada. The numerical increase in second-generation Canadians between 1900 and 1910, however, was less, by 258,583, than the increase (starting from a much smaller base) between 1890 and 1900, while the entire increase in the number of American born in Canada between 1901 and 1911 was only 175,781, which number was not by any means all made up of returning sons and daughters of Canadians in the United States. Even with due allowance for mortality,[2] then, the possibility of return to Canada does not altogether explain why the increase in the second generation of Canadian stock did not reach the full extent which might have been forecast on the basis of the earlier increase in the number of Canadian born in the United States.

The increase in the second generation of French Canadian stock fell

2. Mortality among the second generation of Canadians would be at a lower rate than among the Canadian born, by reason of their lower age.

off so rapidly—from 223,025, or 95.7 per cent, in the decade ending in 1900, to 106,679, or 23.4 per cent, in the decade ending in 1910, and then to a decrease of 349, or 0.1 per cent, in the war decade—as to make it certain that large numbers of second-generation French Canadians, as well as of French Canadian born, must have returned to Canada between 1910 and 1920. There was, however, a net increase of only 70,342 American born in Canada during the decade ending in 1921, which offers scant explanation for the failure to maintain during this decade at least the reduced rate of increase in the second generation of French Canadian stock established between 1900 and 1910. Between 1920 and 1930, however, there was an increase in this class amounting to 172,947, or 30.8 per cent.

The rate of increase in the second generation of English Canadian stock was maintained more evenly from 1890 to 1920, being, respectively, 46.6 per cent, 16.6 per cent, and 17.6 per cent, for the three decades, but fell off suddenly to 3.5 per cent during the decade ending in 1930—a decade during which there was a substantial decrease, almost equal in number to the probable mortality,[3] in the number of American born in Canada, so that little return migration can be assumed.

The changes just outlined are presented in graphic form in Figure 20, which indicates more effectively than any verbal statement the somewhat inconsistent movements of these classes of the population of the United States.

The increase in the ratio of the second generation to the Canadian born between 1890 and 1930 has already been noted. Here it may be added that this increase was more pronounced in the French stock than in the English. In 1890 there were only 77 native persons of French Canadian parentage in the United States for each 100 French Canadian born. This ratio increased to 116 in 1900, to 146 in 1910, to 183 in 1920, and finally to 198 in 1930. Reasons which may account for this include the tendency of the French to have larger families; their greater stability, that is, less movement from one place in the United States to another; and their much greater concentration in certain cities and localities.

The ratio of the second generation to the first in the English stock increased less regularly and less rapidly, from 95 in the second generation per 100 in the first in 1890 to 158 in 1920, and then declined to 146 in 1930, as a result of the very meager increase in the second generation between 1920 and 1930 already noted.

The percentage French in the total Canadian stock increased from 29.0 in 1890 to 33.2 and 33.3, respectively, in 1900 and 1910, then

3. The mortality among the American born in Canada might be computed at the rate of about 10 per cent in a decade, since their average age was much lower than that of the Canadian born in the United States.

dropped to 29.4 in 1920, with the assumed return of many Canadian French to Canada during the war decade, and rose again to 33.1 in 1930. During the 40-year period, however, the percentage French among the Canadian born declined from 31.0 to 29.0, so the general increase just noted is chargeable entirely to the more rapid growth of the French element in the second generation, where the percentage French increased from 26.8 in 1890 to 35.7 in 1930.

FIGURE **20**. PERSONS OF CANADIAN BIRTH AND PARENTAGE, FRENCH AND ENGLISH: 1890 TO 1930

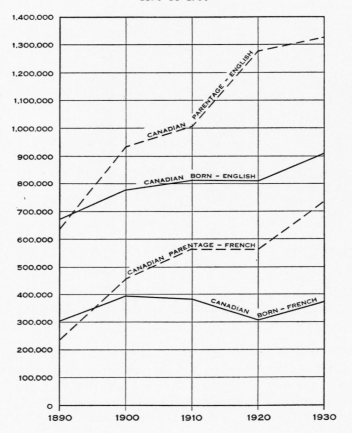

PARENTAGE OF SECOND GENERATION

THE Canadian-parentage group which is presented in the accompanying tables is a part of a larger class shown in the reports of the United States census under the designation "Native white persons of foreign or mixed parentage." This group includes persons born in the United States, with either one or both parents born in Canada, and represents a consolidation of 3 or 4 separate subclasses shown in the basic tabulations. These different subdivisions of the Canadian-parentage group are shown for the censuses from 1910 to 1930 in Table 24.

TABLE 24. NATIVE WHITE POPULATION OF CANADIAN PARENTAGE IN THE UNITED STATES, FRENCH AND ENGLISH, WITH PARENTAGE OF SUBCLASSES: 1910 TO 1930

CLASS	1930		1920		1910	
	Number	Per cent	Number	Per cent	Number	Per cent
TOTAL						
Canadian parentage.............	2,058,924	100.0	1,841,605	100.0	1,650,821	100.0
Both parents Canadian born.............	805,801	39.1	670,030	36.4	638,267	38.7
Father born in Canada, mother in other foreign country.......................			99,227	5.4	92,276	5.6
Father born in Canada, mother in United States.........................	678,181	32.9	596,409	32.4	521,616	31.6
Mother born in Canada, father in United States.............................	574,942	27.9	475,939	25.8	398,662	24.1
FRENCH						
Canadian parentage.............	735,307	100.0	562,360	100.0	562,709	100.0
Both parents Canadian born.............	389,131	52.9	326,435	58.0	330,976	58.8
Father born in Canada, mother in other foreign country.......................			16,726	3.0	15,554	2.8
Father born in Canada, mother in United States.........................	198,512	27.0	129,203	23.0	133,999	23.8
Mother born in Canada, father in United States.............................	147,664	20.1	89,996	16.0	82,180	14.6
ENGLISH						
Canadian parentage.............	1,323,617	100.0	1,279,245	100.0	1,088,112	100.0
Both parents Canadian born.............	416,670	31.5	343,595	26.9	307,291	28.2
Father born in Canada, mother in other foreign country.......................			82,501	6.4	76,722	7.1
Father born in Canada, mother in United States.........................	479,669	36.2	467,206	36.5	387,617	35.6
Mother born in Canada, father in United States.............................	427,278	32.3	385,943	30.2	316,482	29.1

In 1930 there were three subclasses: (1) Persons with father born in Canada and mother born in a foreign country, usually Canada, who formed 39.1 per cent of the entire Canadian-parentage group; (2) persons with father born in Canada and mother born in the United States, who formed 32.9 per cent; and (3) persons with mother born in Canada and father born in the United States, who formed 27.9 per cent of the Canadian-parentage group.

In 1920 the first group was subdivided, separating (a) persons with both parents born in Canada, who formed 36.4 per cent of the Canadian-parentage total, and (b) persons with father born in Canada and mother in some other foreign country, who formed 5.4 per cent.[4] The other two groups were the same in 1920 as in 1930. In 1910 the same four groups were shown separately as in 1920.

There are considerable differences in the distribution among these various subclasses of the French and English stock. In the first place, in 1930, 40.7 per cent of the whole English Canadian stock was born in Canada, as compared with 33.5 per cent of the French. This difference was considerably more marked in 1930 than in 1920 or in 1910. In the second place, a much larger percentage of the French Canadian-parentage group was represented by persons with both parents born in Canada, and correspondingly smaller percentages by persons of mixed Canadian parentage. This difference appears both in the 1930 figures for persons with one parent born in Canada and the other in the United States, and in the 1920 and 1910 figures for persons with one parent born in Canada and the other in some other foreign country.

CANADIAN STOCK BY SEX

In all of the elements of the Canadian stock there has been a continuous decline in the relative number of males as compared with females since 1910, the first census date for which the figures are available by sex. In the total Canadian stock the number of males per 100 females in 1910 was 99.7, this ratio representing 1,421,487 males and 1,425,404 females, or an excess of only 3,917 females. In 1920, the ratio was 97.0, and by 1930 it had fallen to 95.2 with corresponding increases in the excess of females, to 44,523 and 81,585, respectively. The statistics of the Canadian stock are summarized by sex in Table 25.

The most rapid change in the sex ratio took place in the Canadian born, on which comment has already been made. (See page 48.) Among the French Canadian born there were 109.4 males per 100 females in 1910, but only 102.3 in 1930. Among the English Canadian born the change was even more rapid—from 97.6 in 1910 to 89.9 in 1930, this latter figure

4. Subclass (b) is a part of the class designated in the reports of the 1910 and 1920 censuses as "Mixed foreign parentage." This class was tabulated by country of birth of father in combination with country of birth of mother, but was shown as a distinct class in the general tables showing the second-generation population by country of birth of parents, so that none of it was credited to either the country of birth of father or the country of birth of mother. In 1930 it was decided to include this group in the general distribution by country of birth of parents on the basis of country of birth of father, and these combinations were made in the 1910 and 1920 figures for the comparative tables. In the tabulations for 1930 itself, however, the mixed foreign parentage cases were all directly assigned to the country of birth of father, so that there are only three parentage classes in 1930, instead of the four shown for 1910 and 1920.

representing an unusual situation in any population group, especially as
the excess of females was well distributed over the normal age range (see
Table 51), and did not represent the accumulation of women in the older
ages which might be characteristic of a group which was dying out—for
example, the Irish born.

TABLE **25**. WHITE POPULATION OF CANADIAN STOCK IN THE UNITED STATES,
FRENCH AND ENGLISH, BY SEX: 1910 TO 1930

CENSUS YEAR AND CLASS	ALL CANADIAN STOCK			CANADIAN BORN			CANADIAN PARENTAGE		
	Male	Female	Males per 100 females	Male	Female	Males per 100 females	Male	Female	Males per 100 females
TOTAL									
1930.........	1,627,880	1,709,465	95.2	617,090	661,331	93.3	1,010,790	1,048,134	96.4
1920.........	1,457,480	1,502,003	97.0	547,357	570,521	95.9	910,123	931,482	97.7
1910.........	1,421,488	1,425,403	99.7	601,833	594,237	101.3	819,655	831,166	98.6
FRENCH									
1930.........	553,345	552,814	100.1	187,523	183,329	102.3	365,822	369,485	99.0
1920.........	438,413	431,733	101.5	157,748	150,038	105.1	280,665	281,695	99.6
1910.........	482,291	465,501	103.6	201,164	183,919	109.4	281,127	281,582	99.8
ENGLISH									
1930.........	1,074,535	1,156,651	92.9	429,567	478,002	89.9	644,968	678,649	95.0
1920.........	1,019,067	1,070,270	95.2	389,609	420,483	92.7	629,458	649,787	96.9
1910.........	939,197	959,902	97.8	400,669	410,318	97.6	538,528	549,584	98.0

The sex ratios for American-born persons of Canadian parentage show
less variation from the even distribution which would be represented by
100, but even here there was an appreciable decline in the relative number
of males from 1910 to 1930. Among the English Canadians of the second
generation the ratio had fallen from 98.0 in 1910 to 95.0 in 1930, the latter figure representing 644,968 males and 678,649 females, or an excess
of 33,681 females. Since the number of males and females in the American
born of Canadian parentage must have been originally about equal (with
a slight excess of males), one must assume the departure from the United
States of approximately 34,000 males[5]—presumably for Canada, since
there is no indication of any considerable emigration of persons of Canadian origin from the United States to countries other than Canada.

5. The only alternative would seem to be the assumption of the misclassification of
something like this number as of American parentage. Such misclassification might be
more likely for males living in boarding houses, etc., than for females; but it would *not*
be likely to happen more extensively in 1930 than in 1920 or in 1910, except as longer
residence with population of native parentage might increase the tendency to consider
oneself of native parentage.

URBAN AND RURAL AREAS

TABLE 26 shows the population of Canadian stock, French and English, in urban and rural areas from 1910 to 1930, with the rural for 1930 subdivided into farm and nonfarm.

TABLE **26**. WHITE POPULATION OF CANADIAN STOCK, FRENCH AND ENGLISH, IN URBAN AND RURAL AREAS: 1910 TO 1930

CENSUS YEAR AND AREA	ALL CANADIAN STOCK			CANADIAN BORN			CANADIAN PARENTAGE		
	Total	French	English	Total	French	English	Total	French	English
1930									
Total........	3,337,345	1,106,159	2,231,186	1,278,421	370,852	907,569	2,058,924	735,307	1,323,617
Urban........	2,450,541	847,518	1,603,023	988,738	292,564	696,174	1,461,803	554,954	906,849
Rural-nonfarm	555,867	178,908	376,959	189,946	55,620	134,326	365,921	123,288	242,633
Rural-farm...	330,937	79,733	251,204	99,737	22,668	77,069	231,200	57,065	174,135
Per cent......	100.0	100.0	100.0	100.0	100.0	100.0	100.0	100.0	100.0
Urban........	73.4	76.6	71.8	77.3	78.9	76.7	71.0	75.5	68.5
Rural-nonfarm	16.7	16.2	16.9	14.9	15.0	14.8	17.8	16.8	18.3
Rural-farm...	9.9	7.2	11.3	7.8	6.1	8.5	11.2	7.8	13.2
1920									
Total........	2,959,483	870,146	2,089,337	1,117,878	307,786	810,092	1,841,605	562,360	1,279,245
Urban........	2,084,927	667,295	1,417,632	830,115	243,750	586,365	1,254,812	423,545	831,267
Rural........	874,556	202,851	671,705	287,763	64,036	223,727	586,793	138,815	447,978
Per cent......	100.0	100.0	100.0	100.0	100.0	100.0	100.0	100.0	100.0
Urban........	70.4	76.7	67.9	74.3	79.2	72.4	68.1	75.3	65.0
Rural........	29.6	23.3	32.1	25.7	20.8	27.6	31.9	24.7	35.0
1910									
Total........	2,846,891	947,792	1,899,099	1,196,070	385,083	810,987	1,650,821	562,709	1,088,112
Urban........	1,933,895	724,993	1,208,902	874,750	313,184	561,566	1,059,145	411,809	647,336
Rural........	912,996	222,799	690,197	321,320	71,899	249,421	591,676	150,900	440,776
Per cent......	100.0	100.0	100.0	100.0	100.0	100.0	100.0	100.0	100.0
Urban........	67.9	76.5	63.7	73.1	81.3	69.2	64.2	73.2	59.5
Rural........	32.1	23.5	36.3	26.9	18.7	30.8	35.8	26.8	40.5

Of the total Canadian stock in 1930 (amounting to 3,337,345) 2,450,541, or 73.4 per cent, were urban, that is, living in cities and other incorporated places having 2,500 inhabitants or more. The percentage urban in the total population of the United States in 1930 was 56.2, and in the entire foreign white stock, 75.8; but if we take only the 16 States having more than 1 per cent of their population Canadian born, which contained 85.2 per cent of all the Canadian born in the United States in 1930, we find that 71.9 per cent of their population was urban. The Canadian stock, therefore, shows a lower percentage urban than either the entire foreign white stock in the United States (of which it is a part), or of the total population of the States in which most of the persons of Canadian origin reside.

In general, the French stock shows an appreciably higher percentage urban than does the English; and the Canadian born show a higher percentage urban than the American born of Canadian parentage. One might expect, then, that the French Canadian born would be the most highly urbanized of the four subclasses into which the Canadian stock is divided in the present analysis. This was actually the case; its percentage urban was 78.9, as compared with 76.7 for the English Canadian born, and with 75.5 and 68.5, respectively, for the French and English of the second generation.

The higher urban percentage of the French stock is doubtless mainly to be explained on the basis of the occupations which they follow in the United States,[6] and further by the fact that they have tended to settle in one place and remain there—except when they have gone back to their original homes in Canada—while the English Canadians have been more inclined to try first one locality and then another, with the result that they are now much more widely distributed in the United States than are the French Canadians, both in cities and in rural areas. Another reason is to be found in the fact that the French Canadians are mainly settled in States which are primarily urban and industrial, while the English Canadians are found in much larger numbers in States where farming is an important occupation. Many English Canadians, for example, took part in the initial settlement of the Western States where farming is a dominant occupation, and where their children still remain.

The higher percentage urban in the Canadian born as compared with the American born of Canadian parentage is partly due to the fact that the former group includes many unattached single persons who have come to the cities to find employment, while the latter group contains more families with considerable numbers of children and relatively long residence in the United States, which families have tended to spread out from the industrial cities into the rural areas.

In the Canadian stock as a whole, the percentage urban has increased materially since 1910, being 67.9 in that year, 70.4 in 1920, and 73.4 in 1930. This increase was not so rapid as the increase in the percentage urban in the entire population of the United States, which was, respectively, 45.8, 51.4, and 56.2 in the same three census years, but follows rather closely the increase in the percentage urban in the 16 States referred to above, which percentage was 65.2 in 1910, 69.5 in 1920, and 71.9 in 1930.

For the French Canadian born taken alone the trend was in the opposite direction, the percentages urban being 81.3 in 1910, 79.2 in 1920, and

6. In the census of 1910, which is the latest for which occupation statistics are available for the Canadian born in the United States (and these have never before been published), 35.4 per cent of the French Canadian-born gainful workers were returned as semiskilled workers in manufacturing, as compared with 11.0 per cent of the English Canadian workers. For further differences in the occupational distribution, see Table 101.

78.9 in 1930, but the other three subclasses show continuous, though not by any means uniform, increases in urbanization from census to census.

A subdivision of the rural population into farm and nonfarm is available for 1930. Of the 886,804 persons in the rural Canadian stock, 330,937, or 37.3 per cent, were living on farms. This rural-farm population formed 9.9 per cent of the total Canadian stock. Of the rural French Canadian born, 29.0 per cent were on farms, and of their children, 31.6; of the rural English Canadian born, 36.5 per cent were living on farms, and of their children, 41.8. The same general conditions that explain the higher percentage rural (or the lower percentage urban) among the English Canadians will help to explain the higher proportion on farms. The higher percentage on farms in the second generation than among the Canadian born is partly the result of the fact that the second-generation group contains far more children than the group made up of persons born in Canada, and that children are more numerous in the farm families than elsewhere.

In Table 27 the various groups making up the Canadian stock are shown by sex for urban and rural areas.

TABLE **27**. WHITE POPULATION OF CANADIAN STOCK, FRENCH AND ENGLISH, BY SEX, FOR URBAN AND RURAL AREAS: 1930

AREA AND SEX	ALL CANADIAN STOCK			CANADIAN BORN			CANADIAN PARENTAGE		
	Total	French	English	Total	French	English	Total	French	English
Total......	**3,337,345**	**1,106,159**	**2,231,186**	**1,278,421**	**370,852**	**907,569**	**2,058,924**	**735,307**	**1,323,617**
Male...	1,627,880	553,345	1,074,535	617,090	187,523	429,567	1,010,790	365,822	644,968
Female .	1,709,465	552,814	1,156,651	661,331	183,329	478,002	1,048,134	369,485	678,649
Urban........	**2,450,541**	**847,518**	**1,603,023**	**988,738**	**292,564**	**696,174**	**1,461,803**	**554,954**	**906,849**
Male.....	1,165,837	415,052	750,785	464,065	144,357	319,708	701,772	270,695	431,077
Female ...	1,284,704	432,466	852,238	524,673	148,207	376,466	760,031	284,259	475,772
Rural- **nonfarm**...	**555,867**	**178,908**	**376,959**	**189,946**	**55,620**	**134,326**	**365,921**	**123,288**	**242,633**
Male.....	282,349	93,579	188,770	97,927	30,018	67,909	184,422	63,561	120,861
Female...	273,518	85,329	188,189	92,019	25,602	66,417	181,499	59,727	121,772
Rural-farm..	**330,937**	**79,733**	**251,204**	**99,737**	**22,668**	**77,069**	**231,200**	**57,065**	**174,135**
Male.....	179,694	44,714	134,980	55,098	13,148	41,950	124,596	31,566	93,030
Female...	151,243	35,019	116,224	44,639	9,520	35,119	106,604	25,499	81,105
Males per 100 **females**									
Total.....	95.2	100.1	92.9	93.3	102.3	89.9	96.4	99.0	95.0
Urban........	90.7	96.0	88.1	88.4	97.4	84.9	92.3	95.2	90.6
Rural-nonfarm.	103.2	109.7	100.3	106.4	117.2	102.2	101.6	106.4	99.3
Rural-farm....	118.8	127.7	116.1	123.4	138.1	119.5	116.9	123.8	114.7

With respect to the urban-rural classification, it is true in general that in any population class the proportion of males will be highest in the rural-farm areas and lowest in the urban areas—usually the very lowest in the largest cities, with the smaller cities intermediate between the urban average and the rural-nonfarm. This relationship results from the fact that the farms offer many opportunities for employment for males, but relatively few for females, so that the latter are impelled to go to the towns and cities in search of employment—going for the most part at a relatively early age.

This excess of females in the urban areas and the correlative excess of males on farms appear in the statistics for all four of the constituent groups making up the Canadian stock. The widest range is shown for the French Canadian born, with 138.1 males per 100 females in the rural-farm areas, 117.2 in the rural-nonfarm, and only 97.4 in the urban. The English Canadian born are next, with a range from 119.5 in the rural-farm to 84.9 in the urban, followed by the French of the second generation, with a range from 123.8 to 95.2; and finally by the English of the second generation, with a range from 114.7 to 90.6. The differences shown by any one of the constituent groups between one and another of the urban-rural areas are generally greater than the differences shown in any one area between or among the various constituent groups. To some extent the basic differences among the groups may result from differences in their urban-rural distribution, but the effects of this cannot be very great, since all of the groups (Canadian born, French and English; Canadian parentage, French and English) are dominantly urban, with little inclination to settle on farms.

DATA FOR STATES AND CITIES

DATA for the Canadian stock in the United States are presented by States in Tables 28 to 32 and for selected cities in Tables 33 and 34. In all cases figures are given both for the Canadian born and for persons born in the United States of Canadian parentage (that is, with one or both parents born in Canada); and in all cases both the Canadian stock and its two main elements are further subdivided into French and English—the latter including, as already indicated, the small number of persons whose mother tongue is neither French nor English.

Table 28 provides a compact summary of the 1930 figures for all the States in the United States, and Table 29 presents four significant sets of percentages or ratios based on the figures in Table 28, namely, the percentage of the total population of each State represented by the Canadian stock and its two main elements; the percentage French; the ratio of persons of Canadian parentage to Canadian born, both in the French stock and in the English; and the percentage distribution of the Canadian born, French and English, among the States.

TABLE 28. WHITE POPULATION OF CANADIAN STOCK, FRENCH AND ENGLISH, BY STATES: 1930

DIVISION AND STATE	ALL CANADIAN STOCK			CANADIAN BORN			CANADIAN PARENTAGE		
	Total	French	English	Total	French	English	Total	French	English
United States....	**3,337,345**	**1,106,159**	**2,231,186**	**1,278,421**	**370,852**	**907,569**	**2,058,924**	**735,307**	**1,323,617**
NEW ENGLAND:									
Maine.............	201,748	99,765	101,983	73,743	36,947	36,796	128,005	62,818	65,187
New Hampshire.....	137,418	101,324	36,094	50,959	37,682	13,277	86,459	63,642	22,817
Vermont..........	74,023	46,956	27,067	27,182	17,320	9,862	46,841	29,636	17,205
Massachusetts......	724,800	336,871	387,929	288,051	115,241	172,810	436,749	221,630	215,119
Rhode Island.......	110,551	91,173	19,378	39,278	31,501	7,777	71,273	59,672	11,601
Connecticut........	97,015	67,130	29,885	37,808	25,570	12,238	59,207	41,560	17,647
MIDDLE ATLANTIC:									
New York.........	340,644	83,057	257,587	147,874	28,955	118,919	192,770	54,102	138,668
New Jersey........	40,348	7,423	32,925	16,521	2,470	14,051	23,827	4,953	18,874
Pennsylvania.......	43,903	6,141	37,762	16,352	1,911	14,441	27,551	4,230	23,321
E. N. CENTRAL:									
Ohio..............	70,006	9,428	60,578	26,847	2,606	24,241	43,159	6,822	36,337
Indiana...........	19,254	3,120	16,134	6,201	682	5,519	13,053	2,438	10,615
Illinois.	121,777	24,250	97,527	43,589	6,189	37,400	78,188	18,061	60,127
Michigan..........	499,002	87,911	411,091	202,316	28,539	173,777	296,686	59,372	237,314
Wisconsin.........	64,718	22,043	42,675	15,572	4,292	11,280	49,146	17,751	31,395
W. N. CENTRAL:									
Minnesota.........	95,935	29,384	66,551	27,102	6,484	20,618	68,833	22,900	45,933
Iowa.............	30,622	4,233	26,389	6,333	608	5,725	24,289	3,625	20,664
Missouri...........	20,259	2,701	17,558	5,412	588	4,824	14,847	2,113	12,734
North Dakota......	40,177	6,084	34,093	12,241	1,354	10,887	27,936	4,730	23,206
South Dakota......	14,736	2,773	11,963	3,351	492	2,859	11,385	2,281	9,104
Nebraska..........	19,068	2,591	16,477	4,378	436	3,942	14,690	2,155	12,535
Kansas............	19,229	3,588	15,641	4,037	569	3,468	15,192	3,019	12,173
SOUTH ATLANTIC:									
Delaware..........	1,146	177	969	460	61	399	686	116	570
Maryland..........	6,067	908	5,159	2,266	291	1,975	3,801	617	3,184
Dist. of Columbia...	4,864	745	4,119	1,681	223	1,458	3,183	522	2,661
Virginia...........	4,671	574	4,097	1,617	157	1,460	3,054	417	2,637
West Virginia.......	2,658	371	2,287	957	118	839	1,701	253	1,448
North Carolina.....	2,491	227	2,264	930	80	850	1,561	147	1,414
South Carolina.....	896	132	764	278	31	247	618	101	517
Georgia...........	2,901	343	2,558	1,094	109	985	1,807	234	1,573
Florida............	17,194	2,358	14,836	8,156	985	7,171	9,038	1,373	7,665
E. S. CENTRAL:									
Kentucky..........	2,962	373	2,589	918	96	822	2,044	277	1,767
Tennessee.........	2,957	350	2,607	939	92	847	2,018	258	1,760
Alabama..........	2,667	342	2,325	902	117	785	1,765	225	1,540
Mississippi........	1,222	196	1,026	351	42	309	871	154	717
W. S. CENTRAL:									
Arkansas..........	2,582	380	2,202	695	77	618	1,887	303	1,584
Louisiana..........	3,583	895	2,688	981	222	759	2,602	673	1,929
Oklahoma.........	9,757	1,372	8,385	2,119	243	1,876	7,638	1,129	6,509
Texas.............	14,766	1,797	12,969	4,525	452	4,073	10,241	1,345	8,896
MOUNTAIN:									
Montana..........	31,585	6,788	24,797	10,753	1,966	8,787	20,832	4,822	16,010
Idaho.............	13,715	2,075	11,640	4,502	571	3,931	9,213	1,504	7,709
Wyoming..........	4,271	570	3,701	1,136	118	1,018	3,135	452	2,683
Colorado..........	19,256	2,568	16,688	5,816	572	5,244	13,440	1,996	11,444
New Mexico.......	2,117	282	1,835	613	62	551	1,504	220	1,284
Arizona...........	5,872	652	5,220	2,018	158	1,860	3,854	494	3,360
Utah..............	4,851	545	4,306	1,190	97	1,093	3,661	448	3,213
Nevada...........	2,869	483	2,386	952	134	818	1,917	349	1,568
PACIFIC:									
Washington........	113,206	14,137	99,069	48,064	4,340	43,724	65,142	9,797	55,345
Oregon...........	45,659	4,930	40,729	17,916	1,345	16,571	27,743	3,585	24,158
California..........	225,327	23,643	201,684	101,445	7,657	93,788	123,882	15,986	107,896

TABLE **29.** PERCENTAGES AND RATIOS BASED ON WHITE CANADIAN STOCK, FRENCH AND ENGLISH, BY STATES: 1930

[Per cent not shown where less than 0.1]

DIVISION AND STATE	PER CENT OF TOTAL POPULATION			PER CENT FRENCH			RATIO OF CANADIAN PARENTAGE TO CANADIAN BORN			PER CENT DISTRIBUTION OF CANADIAN BORN BY STATES		
	All Canadian stock	Canadian born	Canadian parentage	All Canadian stock	Canadian born	Canadian parentage	Total	French	English	Total	French	English
United States..	2.7	1.0	1.7	33.1	29.0	35.7	1.61	1.98	1.46	100.00	100.00	100.00
NEW ENGLAND:												
Maine.............	25.3	9.2	16.1	49.5	50.1	49.1	1.74	1.70	1.77	5.77	9.96	4.05
New Hampshire...	29.5	11.0	18.6	73.7	73.9	73.6	1.70	1.69	1.72	3.99	10.16	1.46
Vermont.........	20.6	7.6	13.0	63.4	63.7	63.3	1.72	1.71	1.74	2.13	4.67	1.09
Massachusetts....	17.1	6.8	10.3	46.5	40.0	50.7	1.52	1.92	1.24	22.53	31.07	19.04
Rhode Island.....	16.1	5.7	10.4	82.5	80.2	83.7	1.81	1.89	1.49	3.07	8.49	0.86
Connecticut......	6.0	2.4	3.7	69.2	67.6	70.2	1.57	1.63	1.44	2.96	6.89	1.35
MIDDLE ATLANTIC:												
New York........	2.7	1.2	1.5	24.4	19.6	28.1	1.30	1.87	1.17	11.57	7.81	13.10
New Jersey.......	1.0	0.4	0.6	18.4	15.0	20.8	1.44	2.01	1.34	1.29	0.67	1.55
Pennsylvania.....	0.5	0.2	0.3	14.0	11.7	15.4	1.68	2.21	1.61	1.28	0.52	1.59
E. N. CENTRAL:												
Ohio.............	1.1	0.4	0.6	13.5	9.7	15.8	1.61	2.62	1.50	2.10	0.70	2.67
Indiana..........	0.6	0.2	0.4	16.2	11.0	18.7	2.10	3.57	1.92	0.49	0.18	0.61
Illinois...........	1.6	0.6	1.0	19.9	14.2	23.1	1.79	2.92	1.61	3.41	1.67	4.12
Michigan.........	10.3	4.2	6.1	17.6	14.1	20.0	1.47	2.08	1.37	15.83	7.70	19.15
Wisconsin........	2.2	0.5	1.7	34.1	27.6	36.1	3.16	4.14	2.78	1.22	1.16	1.24
W. N. CENTRAL:												
Minnesota........	3.7	1.1	2.7	30.6	23.9	33.3	2.54	3.53	2.23	2.12	1.75	2.21
Iowa............	1.2	0.3	1.0	13.8	9.6	14.9	3.84	5.96	3.61	0.50	0.16	0.63
Missouri.........	0.6	0.1	0.4	13.3	10.9	14.2	2.74	3.59	2.64	0.42	0.16	0.53
North Dakota.....	5.9	1.8	4.1	15.1	11.1	16.9	2.28	3.49	2.13	0.96	0.37	1.20
South Dakota.....	2.1	0.5	1.6	18.8	14.7	20.0	3.40	4.64	3.18	0.26	0.13	0.32
Nebraska.........	1.4	0.3	1.1	13.6	10.0	14.7	3.36	4.94	3.18	0.34	0.12	0.43
Kansas...........	1.0	0.2	0.8	18.7	14.1	19.9	3.76	5.31	3.51	0.32	0.15	0.38
SOUTH ATLANTIC:												
Delaware........	0.5	0.2	0.3	15.4	13.3	16.9	1.49	1.90	1.43	0.04	0.02	0.04
Maryland........	0.4	0.1	0.2	15.0	12.8	16.2	1.68	2.12	1.61	0.18	0.08	0.22
Dist. Columbia...	1.0	0.3	0.7	15.3	13.3	16.4	1.89	2.34	1.83	0.13	0.06	0.16
Virginia..........	0.2	0.1	0.1	12.3	9.7	13.7	1.89	2.66	1.81	0.13	0.04	0.16
West Virginia.....	0.2	0.1	0.1	14.0	12.3	14.9	1.78	2.14	1.73	0.07	0.03	0.09
North Carolina....	0.1	...	...	9.1	8.6	9.4	1.68	1.84	1.66	0.07	0.02	0.09
South Carolina....	0.1	...	...	14.7	11.2	16.3	2.22	3.26	2.09	0.02	0.01	0.03
Georgia..........	0.1	...	0.1	11.8	10.0	12.9	1.65	2.15	1.60	0.09	0.03	0.11
Florida..........	1.2	0.6	0.6	13.7	12.1	15.2	1.11	1.39	1.07	0.64	0.27	0.79
E. S. CENTRAL:												
Kentucky.........	0.1	...	0.1	12.6	10.5	13.6	2.23	2.89	2.15	0.07	0.03	0.09
Tennessee........	0.1	...	0.1	11.8	9.8	12.8	2.15	2.80	2.08	0.07	0.02	0.09
Alabama.........	0.1	...	0.1	12.8	13.0	12.7	1.96	1.92	1.96	0.07	0.03	0.09
Mississippi.......	0.1	...	...	16.0	12.0	17.7	2.48	3.67	2.32	0.03	0.01	0.03
W. S. CENTRAL:												
Arkansas.........	0.1	...	0.1	14.7	11.1	16.1	2.72	3.94	2.56	0.05	0.02	0.07
Louisiana........	0.2	...	0.1	25.0	22.6	25.9	2.65	3.03	2.54	0.08	0.06	0.08
Oklahoma........	0.4	0.1	0.3	14.1	11.5	14.8	3.60	4.65	3.47	0.17	0.07	0.21
Texas............	0.3	0.1	0.2	12.2	10.0	13.1	2.26	2.98	2.18	0.35	0.12	0.45
MOUNTAIN:												
Montana.........	5.9	2.0	3.9	21.5	18.3	23.1	1.94	2.45	1.82	0.84	0.53	0.97
Idaho...........	3.1	1.0	2.1	15.1	12.7	16.3	2.05	2.63	1.96	0.35	0.15	0.43
Wyoming.........	1.9	0.5	1.4	13.3	10.4	14.4	2.76	3.83	2.64	0.09	0.03	0.11
Colorado........	1.9	0.6	1.3	13.3	9.8	14.9	2.31	3.49	2.18	0.45	0.15	0.58
New Mexico......	0.5	0.1	0.4	13.3	10.1	14.6	2.45	3.55	2.33	0.05	0.02	0.06
Arizona..........	1.3	0.5	0.9	11.1	7.8	12.8	1.91	3.13	1.81	0.16	0.04	0.20
Utah............	1.0	0.2	0.7	11.2	8.2	12.2	3.08	4.62	2.94	0.09	0.03	0.12
Nevada..........	3.2	1.0	2.1	16.8	14.1	18.2	2.01	2.60	1.92	0.07	0.04	0.09
PACIFIC:												
Washington......	7.2	3.1	4.2	12.5	9.0	15.0	1.36	2.26	1.27	3.76	1.17	4.82
Oregon..........	4.8	1.9	2.9	10.8	7.5	12.9	1.55	2.67	1.46	1.40	0.36	1.83
California........	4.0	1.8	2.2	10.5	7.5	12.9	1.22	2.09	1.15	7.94	2.06	10.33

These tables are significant among other things as indicating the decided concentration of the Canadian stock, and especially of the Canadian French, in a small number of States, for the most part along or near the Canadian border. More than half the entire Canadian stock (52.9 per cent) were found in four States, namely, Massachusetts, Michigan, New York, and Maine. About half of the Canadian born as a whole and more than half of the French and English Canadian born each taken separately were found in three States (Massachusetts, Michigan, and New York for the total and the English, and Massachusetts, Michigan, and Maine for the French). Further, more than 90 per cent of the Canadian born were found in sixteen States and 98 per cent in twenty-eight States, while 90 per cent of the French Canadian born were found in ten States, including only New York, Michigan, Minnesota, and California, in addition to the six New England States.

The figures in the second and third columns of Table 29 indicate that the Canadian stock (or more specifically the second generation of the Canadian stock) was somewhat more widely distributed than the Canadian born. For example, while only 0.5 per cent of the population of Wisconsin was of Canadian birth, persons of Canadian parentage represented 1.7 per cent; likewise in Minnesota, Iowa, Missouri, North Dakota, South Dakota, Nebraska, and Kansas the percentage (and of course the number also) of second-generation Canadians was from 2 to 4 times the percentage of Canadian born. These are States, as already mentioned above,[7] to which considerable numbers of Canadians migrated several decades ago but which have received relatively few Canadians in recent years. A somewhat similar situation is found in the Mountain States, but on the Pacific Coast the percentages (and numbers) of the two elements of the Canadian stock are more nearly equal—betokening more extensive recent immigration from Canada.

The outstanding importance of the French stock in the New England States is clearly indicated by the percentages shown in the second section of Table 29, ranging from 46.5 per cent French in Massachusetts to 82.5 per cent in Rhode Island, as compared with 18.2 per cent French in the Canadian stock outside New England. The areas in which the French form an important part of the Canadian stock outside New England are perhaps shown most clearly by the absolute numbers presented in Table 28, since many of the percentages in Table 29 are based on rather small numbers. New England alone had more than two-thirds of the entire French Canadian stock, namely, 743,219 out of 1,106,159, leaving 362,940 for all other States; and of this last number Michigan

7. See page 25 (discussion of Canadian-born population from 1850 to 1930). See also the discussion of the statistics on year of immigration, page 92.

had 87,911 (mainly in Detroit) ; New York had 83,057 (mainly along
the northern border) ; Minnesota, 29,384 ; Illinois, 24,250 (more than
half in Chicago) ; California, 23,643 ; and Wisconsin, 22,043.

The percentage French in the Canadian stock was lower in California
(10.5) than any other State having a considerable number of Canadians ; and the percentage French among the Canadian born in California and Oregon (7.5) was lower than any other State whatever.

Table 30, which shows the Canadian stock and its various elements by
States back to 1890, is presented primarily as a matter of historical interest and as a basis for the study of the movements of the Canadian
born and their children in individual States or groups of States. It shows,
for example, a rather rapid decline in the number of Canadian born in
many of the midwestern farming States, coupled with a much smaller
decline in the second generation of Canadians, as in Iowa and Arkansas,
or an increase in the latter for at least two or three decades of the 40-year
period, as in Minnesota and New Hampshire. In other States, however,
the decennial additions to the number of Canadian born seem to have
been accompanied by proportional additions to the second generation,
as, for example, in Ohio or in the Pacific Coast States.

Table 31 presents for 29 selected States (those States with Canadian
stock of 10,000 or more) the numbers of males and females among the
Canadian born and in the native population of Canadian parentage,
French and English, with sex ratios for each. The points made in the discussion of sex ratios for the United States as a whole in connection with
Tables 25 and 26, above, may offer suggestions for the interpretation of
these figures for individual States—among which will be found, of course,
rather wide variations. The ratio of 102.3 per 100 females shown for all
French Canadian born in the United States as a whole is an average of
figures ranging from 92.9 (representing a considerable excess of females)
in Rhode Island and 93.4 in New Jersey to 133.6 in Wisconsin and 145.4
in Montana. Likewise the very low ratio of 89.9 males per 100 females
which is shown for the English Canadian born in the United States as a
whole is made up of State figures ranging from 68.6 in Rhode Island and
70.4 in Massachusetts to 131.3 in Montana and 144.5 in Idaho.

The range among the States in the sex distribution of the second-generation Canadian stock is not so wide, but even here the United States
average of 99.0 males per 100 females in the second generation of the
French Canadian stock represents the merging of ratios running from
91.9 in California and Iowa, and 94.4 in the important State of Rhode
Island to something like 104 in Michigan and Vermont (with 90,000 persons of French Canadian parentage) and to an extreme of 114.2 in
Idaho. The second generation of the English stock, with a United States

average of 95.0, likewise presents a fairly wide range of constituent State figures, namely, from 89.1 in Rhode Island to 108.6 in Idaho.

The urban-rural distribution of the Canadian stock is shown in Table 32 for the 29 selected States, the percentage urban being indicated in each case for the several elements of the Canadian stock. In the three northern New England States, Maine, New Hampshire, and Vermont, the percentage urban among the Canadian French is much higher than among the English Canadians, though in most of the other States the differences are less marked and sometimes in one direction and sometimes in the other. The main purpose of this table, as in the case of Table 31, is to provide a basis for localized studies, since limitations of space make it impracticable to comment here on the significant relationships shown by individual States or to make comparisons between different States where the variations are obviously the result of differences in dominant occupation or other related factors.

In Table 33 are presented statistics of the Canadian stock and its various elements for those cities of 100,000 or more which had 2,500 or more Canadian born in 1930. Figures are given for earlier censuses back to 1900—or as far back as the data are available. Similar figures are given for 1930 alone in Table 34 for all cities of 25,000 or more which had either 3 per cent of their population of Canadian stock or 3,000 persons of Canadian stock. The 1930 figures for the cities shown in Table 33 are repeated in this table in order to make the list complete for convenience in reference. These figures will be of special interest in any detailed study of the Canadian stock in those States where it forms a relatively large fraction of the total population, since the Canadians in these States are found rather largely in the cities.

TABLE **30**. WHITE POPULATION OF CANADIAN STOCK, FRENCH AND ENGLISH, BY STATES: 1890 TO 1930

(Figures for 1900 and 1890 include persons born in Newfoundland or with parents born in Newfoundland. See footnotes on Table 21 for explanation of changes in published figures for Canadian parentage in 1900 and 1890, and for Canadian born in 1920.)

DIVISION AND STATE	ALL CANADIAN STOCK			CANADIAN BORN			CANADIAN PARENTAGE		
	Total	French	English	Total	French	English	Total	French	English
United States									
1930	3,337,345	1,106,159	2,231,186	1,278,421	370,852	907,569	2,058,924	735,307	1,323,617
1920	2,959,483	870,146	2,089,337	1,117,878	307,786	810,092	1,841,605	562,360	1,279,245
1910	2,846,891	947,792	1,899,099	1,196,070	385,083	810,987	1,650,821	562,709	1,088,112
1900	2,562,330	850,491	1,711,839	1,172,860	394,461	778,399	1,389,470	456,030	933,440
1890	1,845,032	535,501	1,309,531	975,496	302,496	673,000	869,536	233,005	636,531
New England									
Maine:									
1930	201,748	99,765	101,983	73,743	36,947	36,796	128,005	62,818	65,187
1920	185,894	86,397	99,497	74,150	35,580	38,570	111,744	50,817	60,927
1910	167,664	75,678	91,986	75,918	35,013	40,905	91,746	40,665	51,081
1900	135,234	58,683	76,551	66,828	30,895	35,933	68,406	27,788	40,618
1890	93,184	38,727	54,457	51,875	23,882	27,993	41,309	14,845	26,464
New Hampshire:									
1930	137,418	101,324	36,094	50,959	37,682	13,277	86,459	63,642	22,817
1920	126,379	90,709	35,670	52,274	38,277	13,997	74,105	52,432	21,673
1910	119,263	81,630	37,633	57,846	40,865	16,981	61,417	40,765	20,652
1900	103,655	74,598	29,057	58,937	44,416	14,521	44,718	30,182	14,536
1890	70,598	48,757	21,841	46,299	34,107	12,192	24,299	14,650	9,649
Vermont:									
1930	74,023	46,956	27,067	27,182	17,320	9,862	46,841	29,636	17,205
1920	68,607	39,846	28,761	24,868	14,181	10,687	43,739	25,665	18,074
1910	68,790	40,782	28,008	26,040	14,643	11,397	42,750	26,139	16,611
1900	67,515	41,286	26,229	25,646	14,982	10,664	41,869	26,304	15,565
1890	59,959	32,889	27,070	24,998	13,650	11,348	34,961	19,239	15,722
Massachusetts:									
1930	724,800	336,871	387,929	288,051	115,241	172,810	436,749	221,630	215,119
1920	645,839	292,109	353,730	262,021	108,691	153,330	383,818	183,418	200,400
1910	619,280	298,258	321,022	295,631	134,659	160,972	323,649	163,599	160,050
1900	528,433	250,024	278,409	291,285	134,387	156,898	237,148	115,637	121,511
1890	328,045	153,553	174,492	206,023	96,286	109,737	122,022	57,267	64,755
Rhode Island:									
1930	110,551	91,173	19,378	39,278	31,501	7,777	71,273	59,672	11,601
1920	95,523	76,381	19,142	36,412	28,887	7,525	59,111	47,494	11,617
1910	89,844	73,682	16,162	41,894	34,087	7,807	47,950	39,595	8,355
1900	70,973	56,382	14,591	39,220	31,530	7,690	31,753	24,852	6,901
1890	44,064	34,778	9,286	27,888	22,591	5,297	16,176	12,187	3,989
Connecticut:									
1930	97,015	67,130	29,885	37,808	25,570	12,238	59,207	41,560	17,647
1920	67,000	41,712	25,288	24,631	14,769	9,862	42,369	26,943	15,426
1910	61,028	43,966	17,062	26,686	18,889	7,797	34,342	25,077	9,265
1900	54,136	37,914	16,222	27,003	19,167	7,836	27,133	18,747	8,386
1890	36,046	25,071	10,975	21,201	15,245	5,956	14,845	9,826	5,019
Middle Atlantic									
New York:									
1930	340,644	83,057	257,587	147,874	28,955	118,919	192,770	54,102	138,668
1920	277,858	52,105	225,753	111,974	15,560	96,414	165,884	36,545	129,339
1910	279,240	71,300	207,940	122,642	24,563	98,079	156,598	46,737	109,861
1900	257,499	74,326	183,173	116,768	27,150	89,618	140,731	47,176	93,555
1890	193,620	52,826	140,794	92,582	22,597	69,985	101,038	30,229	70,809
New Jersey:									
1930	40,348	7,423	32,925	16,521	2,470	14,051	23,827	4,953	18,874
1920	26,316	2,330	23,986	10,292	772	9,520	16,024	1,558	14,466
1910	20,887	2,983	17,904	9,051	1,203	7,848	11,836	1,780	10,056
1900	15,101	2,582	12,519	7,052	1,105	5,947	8,049	1,477	6,572
1890	8,591	733	7,858	4,641	395	4,246	3,950	338	3,612
Pennsylvania:									
1930	43,903	6,141	37,762	16,352	1,911	14,441	27,551	4,230	23,321
1920	39,762	2,352	37,410	14,828	713	14,115	24,934	1,639	23,295
1910	38,248	3,926	34,322	15,278	1,246	14,032	22,970	2,680	20,290
1900	35,585	4,388	31,197	14,564	1,450	13,114	21,021	2,938	18,083
1890	24,847	1,378	23,469	12,020	601	11,419	12,827	777	12,050

TABLE **30**. WHITE POPULATION OF CANADIAN STOCK, FRENCH AND ENGLISH, BY STATES: 1890 TO 1930—Continued

DIVISION AND STATE	ALL CANADIAN STOCK			CANADIAN BORN			CANADIAN PARENTAGE		
	Total	French	English	Total	French	English	Total	French	English
East North Central									
Ohio:									
1930	70,006	9,428	60,578	26,847	2,606	24,241	43,159	6,822	36,337
1920	62,904	4,508	58,396	24,176	1,277	22,899	38,728	3,231	35,497
1910	57,102	7,693	49,409	23,191	2,310	20,881	33,911	5,383	28,528
1900	54,542	8,220	46,322	22,421	2,870	19,551	32,121	5,350	26,771
1890	34,654	2,892	31,762	16,249	1,291	14,958	18,405	1,601	16,804
Indiana:									
1930	19,254	3,120	16,134	6,201	682	5,519	13,053	2,438	10,615
1920	16,847	1,911	14,936	5,096	406	4,690	11,751	1,505	10,246
1910	17,203	3,099	14,104	5,784	789	4,995	11,419	2,310	9,109
1900	18,135	3,678	14,457	5,893	947	4,946	12,242	2,731	9,511
1890	13,267	1,100	12,167	4,920	360	4,560	8,347	740	7,607
Illinois:									
1930	121,777	24,250	97,527	43,589	6,189	37,400	78,188	18,061	60,127
1920	110,351	15,512	94,839	38,375	4,032	34,343	71,976	11,480	60,496
1910	116,137	24,484	91,653	45,233	7,440	37,793	70,904	17,044	53,860
1900	120,021	27,109	92,912	50,230	9,102	41,128	69,791	18,007	51,784
1890	81,605	13,795	67,810	39,237	5,944	33,293	42,368	7,851	34,517
Michigan:									
1930	499,002	87,911	411,091	202,316	28,539	173,777	296,686	59,372	237,314
1920	441,673	64,613	377,060	164,502	18,635	145,867	277,171	45,978	231,193
1910	432,633	84,759	347,874	171,157	28,083	143,074	261,476	56,676	204,800
1900	423,024	82,420	340,604	183,220	32,422	150,798	239,804	49,998	189,806
1890	342,494	56,840	285,654	180,466	30,446	150,020	162,028	26,394	135,634
Wisconsin:									
1930	64,718	22,043	42,675	15,572	4,292	11,280	49,146	17,751	31,395
1920	72,888	21,786	51,102	19,331	4,917	14,414	53,557	16,869	36,688
1910	83,038	29,738	53,300	24,921	7,992	16,929	58,117	21,746	36,371
1900	97,272	30,398	66,874	33,911	10,079	23,832	63,361	20,319	43,042
1890	77,451	18,586	58,865	33,139	8,748	24,391	44,312	9,838	34,474
West North Central									
Minnesota:									
1930	95,935	29,384	66,551	27,102	6,484	20,618	68,833	22,900	45,933
1920	110,635	27,786	82,849	33,732	6,796	26,936	76,903	20,990	55,913
1910	115,565	36,319	79,246	40,918	11,062	29,856	74,647	25,257	49,390
1900	120,313	34,644	85,669	47,427	12,047	35,380	72,886	22,597	50,289
1890	89,303	23,136	66,167	43,465	10,910	32,555	45,838	12,226	33,612
Iowa:									
1930	30,622	4,233	26,389	6,333	608	5,725	24,289	3,625	20,664
1920	37,239	2,298	34,941	8,929	401	8,528	28,310	1,897	26,413
1910	42,458	4,354	38,104	11,596	944	10,652	30,862	3,410	27,452
1900	55,408	6,553	48,855	15,671	1,515	14,156	39,737	5,038	34,699
1890	49,453	2,428	47,025	17,455	886	16,569	31,998	1,542	30,456
Missouri:									
1930	20,259	2,701	17,558	5,412	588	4,824	14,847	2,113	12,734
1920	21,906	1,493	20,413	6,503	299	6,204	15,403	1,194	14,209
1910	24,649	3,164	21,485	7,961	779	7,182	16,688	2,385	14,303
1900	26,919	4,230	22,689	8,559	1,049	7,510	18,360	3,181	15,179
1890	20,960	1,410	19,550	8,485	559	7,926	12,475	851	11,624
North Dakota:									
1930	40,177	6,084	34,093	12,241	1,354	10,887	27,936	4,730	23,206
1920	47,501	5,957	41,544	15,550	1,533	14,017	31,951	4,424	27,527
1910	53,837	7,271	46,566	21,097	2,376	18,721	32,740	4,895	27,845
1900	53,131	7,062	46,069	27,843	3,105	24,738	25,288	3,957	21,331
1890	34,167	5,202	28,965	22,819	3,009	19,810	11,348	2,193	9,155
South Dakota:									
1930	14,736	2,773	11,963	3,351	492	2,859	11,385	2,281	9,104
1920	17,706	2,262	15,444	4,453	508	3,945	13,253	1,754	11,499
1910	21,079	4,022	17,057	5,992	998	4,994	15,087	3,024	12,063
1900	20,788	3,813	16,975	7,029	1,135	5,894	13,759	2,678	11,081
1890	20,924	2,481	18,443	9,483	1,061	8,422	11,441	1,420	10,021
Nebraska:									
1930	19,068	2,591	16,477	4,378	436	3,942	14,690	2,155	12,535
1920	22,289	1,570	20,719	5,758	351	5,407	16,531	1,219	15,312
1910	25,658	2,929	22,729	7,271	674	6,597	18,387	2,255	16,132
1900	28,794	3,584	25,210	9,021	1,035	7,986	19,773	2,549	17,224
1890	28,848	1,808	27,040	12,085	838	11,247	16,763	970	15,793
Kansas:									
1930	19,229	3,588	15,641	4,037	569	3,468	15,192	3,019	12,173
1920	22,470	3,160	19,310	5,319	571	4,748	17,151	2,589	14,562
1910	26,836	5,076	21,760	7,140	1,087	6,053	19,696	3,989	15,707
1900	30,382	6,083	24,299	8,515	1,480	7,035	21,867	4,603	17,264
1890	32,231	4,843	27,388	11,859	1,661	10,198	20,372	3,182	17,190

TABLE **30**. WHITE POPULATION OF CANADIAN STOCK, FRENCH AND ENGLISH, BY STATES: 1890 TO 1930—Continued

DIVISION AND STATE	ALL CANADIAN STOCK			CANADIAN BORN			CANADIAN PARENTAGE		
	Total	French	English	Total	French	English	Total	French	English
South Atlantic									
Delaware:									
1930	1,146	177	969	460	61	399	686	116	570
1920	1,075	58	1,017	446	23	423	629	35	594
1910	961	133	828	495	63	432	466	70	396
1900	619	106	513	293	41	252	326	65	261
1890	477	19	458	305	14	291	172	5	167
Maryland:									
1930	6,067	908	5,159	2,266	291	1,975	3,801	617	3,184
1920	4,870	372	4,498	1,864	117	1,747	3,006	255	2,751
1910	3,299	294	3,005	1,393	110	1,283	1,906	184	1,722
1900	2,887	244	2,643	1,201	87	1,114	1,686	157	1,529
1890	2,040	146	1,894	995	68	927	1,045	78	967
District of Columbia:									
1930	4,864	745	4,119	1,681	223	1,458	3,183	522	2,661
1920	4,944	505	4,439	1,688	147	1,541	3,256	358	2,898
1910	2,829	306	2,523	1,123	109	1,014	1,706	197	1,509
1900	2,070	281	1,789	866	93	773	1,204	188	1,016
1890	1,221	82	1,139	624	32	592	597	50	547
Virginia:									
1930	4,671	574	4,097	1,617	157	1,460	3,054	417	2,637
1920	4,760	349	4,411	1,923	106	1,817	2,837	243	2,594
1910	3,055	325	2,730	1,337	104	1,233	1,718	221	1,497
1900	2,402	258	2,144	1,117	103	1,014	1,285	155	1,130
1890	1,361	47	1,314	770	19	751	591	28	563
West Virginia:									
1930	2,658	371	2,287	957	118	839	1,701	253	1,448
1920	2,512	157	2,355	957	54	903	1,555	103	1,452
1910	2,302	283	2,019	854	88	766	1,448	195	1,253
1900	1,753	191	1,562	703	71	632	1,050	120	930
1890	886	61	825	368	25	343	518	36	482
North Carolina:									
1930	2,491	227	2,264	930	80	850	1,561	147	1,414
1920	1,535	51	1,484	650	15	635	885	36	849
1910	1,227	98	1,129	534	29	505	693	69	624
1900	1,062	81	981	472	36	436	590	45	545
1890	665	18	647	348	16	332	317	2	315
South Carolina:									
1930	896	132	764	278	31	247	618	101	517
1920	747	71	676	268	24	244	479	47	432
1910	639	75	564	273	39	234	366	36	330
1900	435	64	371	199	30	169	236	34	202
1890	286	25	261	156	12	144	130	13	117
Georgia:									
1930	2,901	343	2,558	1,094	109	985	1,807	234	1,573
1920	2,492	188	2,304	955	50	905	1,537	138	1,399
1910	1,936	206	1,730	781	70	711	1,155	136	1,019
1900	1,855	246	1,609	751	79	672	1,104	167	937
1890	1,175	72	1,103	603	47	556	572	25	547
Florida:									
1930	17,194	2,358	14,836	8,156	985	7,171	9,038	1,373	7,665
1920	8,692	568	8,124	4,121	277	3,844	4,571	291	4,280
1910	3,655	347	3,308	1,698	151	1,547	1,957	196	1,761
1900	2,667	239	2,428	1,189	87	1,102	1,478	152	1,326
1890	1,862	75	1,787	1,141	51	1,090	721	24	697
East South Central									
Kentucky:									
1930	2,962	373	2,589	918	96	822	2,044	277	1,767
1920	2,879	192	2,687	885	50	835	1,994	142	1,852
1910	2,944	333	2,611	1,037	98	939	1,907	235	1,672
1900	3,327	496	2,831	1,184	134	1,050	2,143	362	1,781
1890	2,605	119	2,486	1,154	50	1,104	1,451	69	1,382
Tennessee:									
1930	2,957	350	2,607	939	92	847	2,018	258	1,760
1920	2,765	170	2,595	972	47	925	1,793	123	1,670
1910	2,912	327	2,585	1,141	91	1,050	1,771	236	1,535
1900	2,749	362	2,387	1,027	119	908	1,722	243	1,479
1890	2,137	49	2,088	1,005	25	980	1,132	24	1,108

TABLE **30**. WHITE POPULATION OF CANADIAN STOCK, FRENCH AND ENGLISH, BY STATES:
1890 TO 1930—Continued

DIVISION AND STATE	ALL CANADIAN STOCK			CANADIAN BORN			CANADIAN PARENTAGE		
	Total	French	English	Total	French	English	Total	French	English
E. S. Central—Con.									
Alabama:									
1930..............	2,667	342	2,325	902	117	785	1,765	225	1,540
1920..............	2,468	154	2,314	892	52	840	1,576	102	1,474
1910..............	2,082	270	1,812	814	96	718	1,268	174	1,094
1900..............	1,698	240	1,458	688	89	599	1,010	151	859
1890..............	1,107	54	1,053	605	35	570	502	19	483
Mississippi:									
1930..............	1,222	196	1,026	351	42	309	871	154	717
1920..............	1,210	84	1,126	397	30	367	813	54	759
1910..............	1,143	151	992	435	46	389	708	105	603
1900..............	1,058	175	883	401	70	331	657	105	552
1890..............	766	22	744	333	14	319	433	8	425
West South Central									
Arkansas:									
1930..............	2,582	380	2,202	695	77	618	1,887	303	1,584
1920..............	3,025	242	2,783	880	58	822	2,145	184	1,961
1910..............	3,120	444	2,676	1,066	119	947	2,054	325	1,729
1900..............	3,214	476	2,738	1,081	159	922	2,133	317	1,816
1890..............	2,108	71	2,037	938	36	902	1,170	35	1,135
Louisiana:									
1930..............	3,583	895	2,688	981	222	759	2,602	673	1,929
1920..............	3,482	520	2,962	1,165	157	1,008	2,317	363	1,954
1910..............	3,390	779	2,611	1,159	250	909	2,231	529	1,702
1900..............	3,068	888	2,180	1,014	247	767	2,054	641	1,413
1890..............	1,940	275	1,665	750	95	655	1,190	180	1,010
Oklahoma:									
1930..............	9,757	1,372	8,385	2,119	243	1,876	7,638	1,129	6,509
1920..............	9,733	787	8,946	2,475	126	2,349	7,258	661	6,597
1910..............	10,296	1,403	8,893	2,831	320	2,511	7,465	1,083	6,382
1900*.............	6,507	985	5,522	1,778	224	1,554	4,729	761	3,968
1890†.............	963	18	945	398	11	387	565	7	558
Texas:									
1930..............	14,766	1,797	12,969	4,525	452	4,073	10,241	1,345	8,896
1920..............	13,087	920	12,167	4,175	249	3,926	8,912	671	8,241
1910..............	10,066	1,130	8,936	3,498	356	3,142	6,568	774	5,794
1900..............	8,397	1,238	7,159	2,930	397	2,533	5,467	841	4,626
1890..............	6,249	290	5,959	2,852	128	2,724	3,397	162	3,235
Mountain									
Montana:									
1930..............	31,585	6,788	24,797	10,753	1,966	8,787	20,832	4,822	16,010
1920..............	37,828	6,393	31,435	14,316	2,211	12,105	23,512	4,182	19,330
1910..............	30,895	6,813	24,082	13,501	2,874	10,627	17,394	3,939	13,455
1900..............	25,132	6,292	18,840	13,254	3,266	9,988	11,878	3,026	8,852
1890..............	13,220	3,079	10,141	8,766	2,213	6,553	4,454	866	3,588
Idaho:									
1930..............	13,715	2,075	11,640	4,502	571	3,931	9,213	1,504	7,709
1920..............	14,772	1,527	13,245	4,954	476	4,478	9,818	1,051	8,767
1910..............	14,008	2,117	11,891	5,361	796	4,565	8,647	1,321	7,326
1900..............	7,056	978	6,078	2,917	395	2,522	4,139	583	3,556
1890..............	3,347	194	3,153	1,786	124	1,662	1,561	70	1,491
Wyoming:									
1930..............	4,271	570	3,701	1,136	118	1,018	3,135	452	2,683
1920..............	4,706	341	4,365	1,438	92	1,346	3,268	249	3,019
1910..............	4,070	486	3,584	1,419	143	1,276	2,651	343	2,308
1900..............	3,262	460	2,802	1,236	150	1,086	2,026	310	1,716
1890..............	2,602	161	2,441	1,304	96	1,208	1,298	65	1,233
Colorado:									
1930..............	19,256	2,568	16,688	5,816	572	5,244	13,440	1,996	11,444
1920..............	22,382	1,587	20,795	7,621	418	7,203	14,761	1,169	13,592
1910..............	25,163	2,692	22,471	9,533	789	8,744	15,630	1,903	13,727
1900..............	22,507	2,673	19,834	9,777	959	8,818	12,730	1,714	11,016
1890..............	16,218	1,002	15,216	9,126	575	8,551	7,092	427	6,665
New Mexico:									
1930..............	2,117	282	1,835	613	62	551	1,504	220	1,284
1920..............	2,210	196	2,014	732	42	690	1,478	154	1,324
1910..............	2,729	424	2,305	1,009	111	898	1,720	313	1,407
1900..............	1,874	295	1,579	759	84	675	1,115	211	904
1890..............	1,333	54	1,279	677	25	652	656	29	627

*Figures for Oklahoma include Indian Territory.
†Exclusive of Indian Territory, not separately reported in 1890.

TABLE **30**. WHITE POPULATION OF CANADIAN STOCK, FRENCH AND ENGLISH, BY STATES: 1890 TO 1930—Continued

DIVISION AND STATE	ALL CANADIAN STOCK			CANADIAN BORN			CANADIAN PARENTAGE		
	Total	French	English	Total	French	English	Total	French	English
Mountain—Con.									
Arizona:									
1930	5,872	652	5,220	2,018	158	1,860	3,854	494	3,360
1920	5,139	320	4,819	1,962	90	1,872	3,177	230	2,947
1910	4,111	433	3,678	1,818	177	1,641	2,293	256	2,037
1900	2,839	347	2,492	1,259	152	1,107	1,580	195	1,385
1890	1,257	50	1,207	724	27	697	533	23	510
Utah:									
1930	4,851	545	4,306	1,190	97	1,093	3,661	448	3,213
1920	5,632	273	5,359	1,466	45	1,421	4,166	228	3,938
1910	5,724	525	5,199	1,687	114	1,573	4,037	411	3,626
1900	4,808	634	4,174	1,329	128	1,201	3,479	506	2,973
1890	3,355	109	3,246	1,220	38	1,182	2,135	71	2,064
Nevada:									
1930	2,869	483	2,386	952	134	818	1,917	349	1,568
1920	3,194	283	2,911	1,178	108	1,070	2,016	175	1,841
1910	4,286	654	3,632	1,844	272	1,572	2,442	382	2,060
1900	2,522	546	1,976	1,030	222	808	1,492	324	1,168
1890	2,905	352	2,553	1,660	263	1,397	1,245	89	1,156
Pacific									
Washington:									
1930	113,206	14,137	99,069	48,064	4,340	43,724	65,142	9,797	55,345
1920	101,078	7,863	93,215	42,988	2,581	40,407	58,090	5,282	52,808
1910	87,223	9,790	77,433	39,263	3,711	35,552	47,960	6,079	41,881
1900	42,545	4,532	38,013	20,108	1,892	18,216	22,437	2,640	19,797
1890	28,081	2,695	25,386	17,268	1,607	15,661	10,813	1,088	9,725
Oregon:									
1930	45,659	4,930	40,729	17,916	1,345	16,571	27,743	3,585	24,158
1920	36,499	2,160	34,339	13,774	679	13,095	22,725	1,481	21,244
1910	30,676	3,149	27,527	12,365	1,146	11,219	18,311	2,003	16,308
1900	18,430	2,469	15,961	7,484	872	6,612	10,946	1,597	9,349
1890	12,353	760	11,593	6,441	431	6,010	5,912	329	5,583
California:									
1930	225,327	23,643	201,684	101,445	7,657	93,788	123,882	15,986	107,896
1920	138,180	7,018	131,162	59,562	2,306	57,256	78,618	4,712	73,906
1910	101,711	8,692	93,019	44,554	3,109	41,445	57,157	5,583	51,574
1900	68,727	6,718	62,009	29,770	2,407	27,363	38,957	4,311	34,646
1890	48,202	2,369	45,833	25,990	1,352	24,638	22,212	1,017	21,195

TABLE **31**. WHITE POPULATION OF CANADIAN BIRTH AND PARENTAGE, FRENCH AND ENGLISH, BY SEX, FOR 29 SELECTED STATES: 1930

(Selected States are those having Canadian stock of 10,000 or more, including the 10 border States, which are indicated by italics)

CLASS AND STATE	TOTAL			FRENCH			ENGLISH		
	Male	Female	Males per 100 females	Male	Female	Males per 100 females	Male	Female	Males per 100 females
CANADIAN BORN United States.....	617,090	661,331	93.3	187,523	183,329	102.3	429,567	478,002	89.9
Maine................	35,990	37,753	95.3	18,413	18,534	99.3	17,577	19,219	91.5
New Hampshire........	24,775	26,184	94.6	18,724	18,958	98.8	6,051	7,226	83.7
Vermont..............	14,174	13,008	109.0	9,367	7,953	117.8	4,807	5,055	95.1
Massachusetts.........	127,586	160,465	79.5	56,192	59,049	95.2	71,394	101,416	70.4
Rhode Island.........	18,337	20,941	87.6	15,173	16,328	92.9	3,164	4,613	68.6
Connecticut..........	18,782	19,026	98.7	13,070	12,500	104.6	5,712	6,526	87.5
New York............	68,332	79,542	85.9	14,780	14,175	104.3	53,552	65,367	81.9
New Jersey...........	7,624	8,897	85.7	1,193	1,277	93.4	6,431	7,620	84.4
Pennsylvania.........	7,826	8,526	91.8	965	946	102.0	6,861	7,580	90.5
Ohio................	12,952	13,895	93.2	1,297	1,309	99.1	11,655	12,586	92.6
Indiana..............	3,285	2,916	112.7	366	316	115.8	2,919	2,600	112.3
Illinois..............	21,844	21,745	100.5	3,142	3,047	103.1	18,702	18,698	100.0
Michigan.............	101,756	100,560	101.2	15,434	13,105	117.8	86,322	87,455	98.7
Wisconsin............	8,572	7,000	122.5	2,455	1,837	133.6	6,117	5,163	118.5
Minnesota............	14,295	12,807	111.6	3,591	2,893	124.1	10,704	9,914	108.0
Iowa................	3,174	3,159	100.5	304	304	100.0	2,870	2,855	100.5
Missouri.............	2,783	2,629	105.9	317	271	117.0	2,466	2,358	104.6
North Dakota.........	6,441	5,800	111.1	745	609	122.3	5,696	5,191	109.7
South Dakota.........	1,808	1,543	117.2	273	219	124.7	1,535	1,324	115.9
Nebraska............	2,190	2,188	100.1	228	208	109.6	1,962	1,980	99.1
Kansas..............	2,071	1,966	105.3	299	270	110.7	1,772	1,696	104.5
Florida..............	3,796	4,360	87.1	508	477	106.5	3,288	3,883	84.7
Texas...............	2,497	2,028	123.1	263	189	139.2	2,234	1,839	121.5
Montana.............	6,153	4,600	133.8	1,165	801	145.4	4,988	3,799	131.3
Idaho...............	2,689	1,813	148.3	366	205	178.5	2,323	1,608	144.5
Colorado.............	2,926	2,890	101.2	310	262	118.3	2,616	2,628	99.5
Washington...........	24,666	23,398	105.4	2,363	1,977	119.5	22,303	21,421	104.1
Oregon..............	9,192	8,724	105.4	727	618	117.6	8,465	8,106	104.4
California............	48,942	52,503	93.2	4,048	3,609	112.2	44,894	48,894	91.8
CANADIAN PARENTAGE United States.....	1,010,790	1,048,134	96.4	365,822	369,485	99.0	644,968	678,649	95.0
Maine................	64,098	63,907	100.3	31,554	31,264	100.9	32,544	32,643	99.7
New Hampshire........	42,698	43,761	97.6	31,658	31,984	99.0	11,040	11,777	93.7
Vermont..............	23,664	23,177	102.1	15,171	14,465	104.9	8,493	8,712	97.5
Massachusetts.........	212,037	224,712	94.4	108,899	112,731	96.6	103,138	111,981	92.1
Rhode Island.........	34,449	36,824	93.6	28,983	30,689	94.4	5,466	6,135	89.1
Connecticut..........	29,092	30,115	96.6	20,691	20,869	99.1	8,401	9,246	90.9
New York............	94,560	98,210	96.3	27,222	26,880	101.3	67,338	71,330	94.4
New Jersey...........	11,653	12,174	95.7	2,511	2,442	102.8	9,142	9,732	93.9
Pennsylvania.........	13,403	14,148	94.7	2,148	2,082	103.2	11,255	12,066	93.3
Ohio................	20,641	22,518	91.7	3,306	3,516	94.0	17,335	19,002	91.2
Indiana..............	6,292	6,761	93.1	1,210	1,228	98.5	5,082	5,533	91.8
Illinois..............	37,565	40,623	92.5	8,835	9,226	95.8	28,730	31,397	91.5
Michigan.............	147,473	149,213	98.8	30,298	29,074	104.2	117,175	120,139	97.5
Wisconsin............	24,308	24,838	97.9	9,094	8,657	105.0	15,214	16,181	94.0
Minnesota............	33,347	35,486	94.0	11,200	11,700	95.7	22,147	23,786	93.1
Iowa................	11,666	12,623	92.4	1,736	1,889	91.9	9,930	10,734	92.5
Missouri.............	7,059	7,788	90.6	1,030	1,083	95.1	6,029	6,705	89.9
North Dakota.........	14,359	13,577	105.8	2,495	2,235	111.6	11,864	11,342	104.6
South Dakota.........	5,830	5,555	105.0	1,174	1,107	106.1	4,656	4,448	104.7
Nebraska............	7,092	7,598	93.3	1,046	1,109	94.3	6,046	6,489	93.2
Kansas..............	7,485	7,707	97.1	1,537	1,482	103.7	5,948	6,225	95.6
Florida..............	4,161	4,877	85.3	643	730	88.1	3,518	4,147	84.8
Texas...............	5,266	4,975	105.8	711	634	112.1	4,555	4,341	104.9
Montana.............	10,704	10,128	105.7	2,515	2,307	109.0	8,189	7,821	104.7
Idaho...............	4,815	4,398	109.5	802	702	114.2	4,013	3,696	108.6
Colorado.............	6,457	6,983	92.5	984	1,012	97.2	5,473	5,971	91.7
Washington...........	32,340	32,802	98.6	4,989	4,808	103.8	27,351	27,994	97.7
Oregon..............	13,754	13,989	98.3	1,830	1,755	104.3	11,924	12,234	97.5
California............	59,865	64,017	93.5	7,656	8,330	91.9	52,209	55,687	93.8

TABLE **32**. WHITE POPULATION OF CANADIAN STOCK, FRENCH AND ENGLISH, IN URBAN AND RURAL AREAS, FOR 29 SELECTED STATES: 1930

STATE AND AREA	ALL CANADIAN STOCK			CANADIAN BORN			CANADIAN PARENTAGE		
	Total	French	English	Total	French	English	Total	French	English
United States...	**3,337,345**	**1,106,159**	**2,231,186**	**1,278,421**	**370,852**	**907,569**	**2,058,924**	**735,307**	**1,323,617**
Urban..............	2,450,541	847,518	1,603,023	988,738	292,564	696,174	1,461,803	554,954	906,849
Rural-nonfarm.......	555,867	178,908	376,959	189,946	55,620	134,326	365,921	123,288	242,633
Rural-farm..........	330,937	79,733	251,204	99,737	22,668	77,069	231,200	57,065	174,135
Per cent urban.....	73.4	76.6	71.8	77.3	78.9	76.7	71.0	75.5	68.5
Maine........	**201,748**	**99,765**	**101,983**	**73,743**	**36,947**	**36,796**	**128,005**	**62,818**	**65,187**
Urban..............	104,124	63,597	40,527	39,762	24,123	15,639	64,362	39,474	24,888
Rural-nonfarm.......	69,592	29,141	40,451	25,052	10,700	14,352	44,540	18,441	26,099
Rural-farm..........	28,032	7,027	21,005	8,929	2,124	6,805	19,103	4,903	14,200
Per cent urban.....	51.6	63.7	39.7	53.9	65.3	42.3	50.3	62.8	38.2
New Hampshire	**137,418**	**101,324**	**36,094**	**50,959**	**37,682**	**13,277**	**86,459**	**63,642**	**22,817**
Urban..............	96,515	78,553	17,962	36,610	29,885	6,725	59,905	48,668	11,237
Rural-nonfarm.......	31,931	18,961	12,970	11,160	6,537	4,623	20,771	12,424	8,347
Rural-farm..........	8,972	3,810	5,162	3,189	1,260	1,929	5,783	2,550	3,233
Per cent urban.....	70.2	77.5	49.8	71.8	79.3	50.7	69.3	76.5	49.2
Vermont.......	**74,023**	**46,956**	**27,067**	**27,182**	**17,320**	**9,862**	**46,841**	**29,636**	**17,205**
Urban..............	26,330	18,100	8,230	9,319	6,217	3,102	17,011	11,883	5,128
Rural-nonfarm.......	23,523	12,968	10,555	8,261	4,389	3,872	15,262	8,579	6,683
Rural-farm..........	24,170	15,888	8,282	9,602	6,714	2,888	14,568	9,174	5,394
Per cent urban.....	35.6	38.5	30.4	34.3	35.9	31.5	36.3	40.1	29.8
Massachusetts.	**724,800**	**336,871**	**387,929**	**288,051**	**115,241**	**172,810**	**436,749**	**221,630**	**215,119**
Urban..............	660,245	306,893	353,352	264,918	106,053	158,865	395,327	200,840	194,487
Rural-nonfarm.......	55,769	25,960	29,809	19,789	7,916	11,873	35,980	18,044	17,936
Rural-farm..........	8,786	4,018	4,768	3,344	1,272	2,072	5,442	2,746	2,696
Per cent urban.....	91.1	91.1	91.1	92.0	92.0	91.9	90.5	90.6	90.4
Rhode Island...	**110,551**	**91,173**	**19,378**	**39,278**	**31,501**	**7,777**	**71,273**	**59,672**	**11,601**
Urban..............	104,194	86,063	18,131	37,202	29,863	7,339	66,992	56,200	10,792
Rural-nonfarm.......	5,622	4,584	1,038	1,812	1,462	350	3,810	3,122	688
Rural-farm..........	735	526	209	264	176	88	471	350	121
Per cent urban.....	94.2	94.4	93.6	94.7	94.8	94.4	94.0	94.2	93.0
Connecticut...	**97,015**	**67,130**	**29,885**	**37,808**	**25,570**	**12,238**	**59,207**	**41,560**	**17,647**
Urban..............	67,124	46,082	21,042	27,208	18,426	8,782	39,916	27,656	12,260
Rural-nonfarm.......	27,119	19,333	7,786	9,553	6,540	3,013	17,566	12,793	4,773
Rural-farm..........	2,772	1,715	1,057	1,047	604	443	1,725	1,111	614
Per cent urban.....	69.2	68.6	70.4	72.0	72.1	71.8	67.4	66.5	69.5
New York......	**340,644**	**83,057**	**257,587**	**147,874**	**28,955**	**118,919**	**192,770**	**54,102**	**138,668**
Urban..............	257,196	57,960	199,236	117,588	21,345	96,243	139,608	36,615	102,993
Rural-nonfarm.......	53,787	16,534	37,253	19,962	5,230	14,732	33,825	11,304	22,521
Rural-farm..........	29,661	8,563	21,098	10,324	2,380	7,944	19,337	6,183	13,154
Per cent urban.....	75.5	69.8	77.3	79.5	73.7	80.9	72.4	67.7	74.3
New Jersey.....	**40,348**	**7,423**	**32,925**	**16,521**	**2,470**	**14,051**	**23,827**	**4,953**	**18,874**
Urban..............	34,230	6,414	27,816	14,066	2,162	11,904	20,164	4,252	15,912
Rural-nonfarm.......	5,407	909	4,498	2,107	277	1,830	3,300	632	2,668
Rural-farm..........	711	100	611	348	31	317	363	69	294
Per cent urban.....	84.8	86.4	84.5	85.1	87.5	84.7	84.6	85.8	84.3
Pennsylvania...	**43,903**	**6,141**	**37,762**	**16,352**	**1,911**	**14,441**	**27,551**	**4,230**	**23,321**
Urban..............	34,099	4,793	29,306	13,076	1,557	11,519	21,023	3,236	17,787
Rural-nonfarm.......	7,570	1,131	6,439	2,551	312	2,239	5,019	819	4,200
Rural-farm..........	2,234	217	2,017	725	42	683	1,509	175	1,334
Per cent urban.....	77.7	78.0	77.6	80.0	81.5	79.8	76.3	76.5	76.3
Ohio.........	**70,006**	**9,428**	**60,578**	**26,847**	**2,606**	**24,241**	**43,159**	**6,822**	**36,337**
Urban..............	58,726	7,765	50,961	23,270	2,246	21,024	35,456	5,519	29,937
Rural-nonfarm.......	8,149	1,264	6,885	2,708	288	2,420	5,441	976	4,465
Rural-farm..........	3,131	399	2,732	869	72	797	2,262	327	1,935
Per cent urban.....	83.9	82.4	84.1	86.7	86.2	86.7	82.2	80.9	82.4
Indiana........	**19,254**	**3,120**	**16,134**	**6,201**	**682**	**5,519**	**13,053**	**2,438**	**10,615**
Urban..............	14,487	2,236	12,251	5,045	537	4,508	9,442	1,699	7,743
Rural-nonfarm.......	2,794	551	2,243	797	113	684	1,997	438	1,559
Rural-farm..........	1,973	333	1,640	359	32	327	1,614	301	1,313
Per cent urban.....	75.2	71.7	75.9	81.4	78.7	81.7	72.3	69.7	72.9

TABLE **32**. WHITE POPULATION OF CANADIAN STOCK, FRENCH AND ENGLISH, IN URBAN AND RURAL AREAS, FOR 29 SELECTED STATES: 1930—Continued

STATE AND AREA	ALL CANADIAN STOCK			CANADIAN BORN			CANADIAN PARENTAGE		
	Total	French	English	Total	French	English	Total	French	English
Illinois	**121,777**	**24,250**	**97,527**	**43,589**	**6,189**	**37,400**	**78,188**	**18,061**	**60,127**
Urban	108,110	20,775	87,335	40,329	5,635	34,694	67,781	15,140	52,641
Rural-nonfarm	9,338	2,384	6,954	2,528	446	2,082	6,810	1,938	4,872
Rural-farm	4,329	1,091	3,238	732	108	624	3,597	983	2,614
Per cent urban	88.8	85.7	89.5	92.5	91.0	92.8	86.7	83.8	87.5
Michigan	**499,002**	**87,911**	**411,091**	**202,316**	**28,539**	**173,777**	**296,686**	**59,372**	**237,314**
Urban	350,179	62,558	287,621	157,477	22,278	135,199	192,702	40,280	152,422
Rural-nonfarm	78,826	15,753	63,073	25,031	3,885	21,146	53,795	11,868	41,927
Rural-farm	69,997	9,600	60,397	19,808	2,376	17,432	50,189	7,224	42,965
Per cent urban	70.2	71.2	70.0	77.8	78.1	77.8	65.0	67.8	64.2
Wisconsin	**64,718**	**22,043**	**42,675**	**15,572**	**4,292**	**11,280**	**49,146**	**17,751**	**31,395**
Urban	38,853	13,811	25,042	9,906	2,693	7,213	28,947	11,118	17,829
Rural-nonfarm	13,426	4,313	9,113	3,155	868	2,287	10,271	3,445	6,826
Rural-farm	12,439	3,919	8,520	2,511	731	1,780	9,928	3,188	6,740
Per cent urban	60.0	62.7	58.7	63.6	62.7	63.9	58.9	62.6	56.8
Minnesota	**95,935**	**29,384**	**66,551**	**27,102**	**6,484**	**20,618**	**68,833**	**22,900**	**45,933**
Urban	62,966	18,964	44,002	18,785	4,319	14,466	44,181	14,645	29,536
Rural-nonfarm	14,908	4,478	10,430	4,110	1,060	3,050	10,798	3,418	7,380
Rural-farm	18,061	5,942	12,119	4,207	1,105	3,102	13,854	4,837	9,017
Per cent urban	65.6	64.5	66.1	69.3	66.6	70.2	64.2	64.0	64.3
Iowa	**30,622**	**4,233**	**26,389**	**6,333**	**608**	**5,725**	**24,289**	**3,625**	**20,664**
Urban	15,375	2,468	12,907	3,451	360	3,091	11,924	2,108	9,816
Rural-nonfarm	7,361	892	6,469	1,707	133	1,574	5,654	759	4,895
Rural-farm	7,886	873	7,013	1,175	115	1,060	6,711	758	5,953
Per cent urban	50.2	58.3	48.9	54.5	59.2	54.0	49.1	58.2	47.5
Missouri	**20,259**	**2,701**	**17,558**	**5,412**	**588**	**4,824**	**14,847**	**2,113**	**12,734**
Urban	14,344	1,968	12,376	4,023	432	3,591	10,321	1,536	8,785
Rural-nonfarm	3,080	431	2,649	807	106	701	2,273	325	1,948
Rural-farm	2,835	302	2,533	582	50	532	2,253	252	2,001
Per cent urban	70.8	72.9	70.5	74.3	73.5	74.4	69.5	72.7	69.0
North Dakota	**40,177**	**6,084**	**34,093**	**12,241**	**1,354**	**10,887**	**27,936**	**4,730**	**23,206**
Urban	8,450	1,301	7,149	2,527	267	2,260	5,923	1,034	4,889
Rural-nonfarm	12,646	1,661	10,985	4,342	443	3,899	8,304	1,218	7,086
Rural-farm	19,081	3,122	15,959	5,372	644	4,728	13,709	2,478	11,231
Per cent urban	21.0	21.4	21.0	20.6	19.7	20.8	21.2	21.9	21.1
South Dakota	**14,736**	**2,773**	**11,963**	**3,351**	**492**	**2,859**	**11,385**	**2,281**	**9,104**
Urban	4,437	648	3,789	1,088	114	974	3,349	534	2,815
Rural-nonfarm	4,545	902	3,643	1,132	199	933	3,413	703	2,710
Rural-farm	5,754	1,223	4,531	1,131	179	952	4,623	1,044	3,579
Per cent urban	30.1	23.4	31.7	32.5	23.2	34.1	29.4	23.4	30.9
Nebraska	**19,068**	**2,591**	**16,477**	**4,378**	**436**	**3,942**	**14,690**	**2,155**	**12,535**
Urban	8,306	1,209	7,097	2,090	209	1,881	6,216	1,000	5,216
Rural-nonfarm	5,067	607	4,460	1,282	113	1,169	3,785	494	3,291
Rural-farm	5,695	775	4,920	1,006	114	892	4,689	661	4,028
Per cent urban	43.6	46.7	43.1	47.7	47.9	47.7	42.3	46.4	41.6
Kansas	**19,229**	**3,588**	**15,641**	**4,037**	**569**	**3,468**	**15,192**	**3,019**	**12,173**
Urban	7,467	1,273	6,194	1,609	201	1,408	5,858	1,072	4,786
Rural-nonfarm	5,015	974	4,041	1,228	195	1,033	3,787	779	3,008
Rural-farm	6,747	1,341	5,406	1,200	173	1,027	5,547	1,168	4,379
Per cent urban	38.8	35.5	39.6	39.9	35.3	40.6	38.6	35.5	39.3
Florida	**17,194**	**2,358**	**14,836**	**8,156**	**985**	**7,171**	**9,038**	**1,373**	**7,665**
Urban	11,842	1,658	10,184	5,654	674	4,980	6,188	984	5,204
Rural-nonfarm	4,022	494	3,528	1,857	208	1,649	2,165	286	1,879
Rural-farm	1,330	206	1,124	645	103	542	685	103	582
Per cent urban	68.9	70.3	68.6	69.3	68.4	69.4	68.5	71.7	67.9
Texas	**14,766**	**1,797**	**12,969**	**4,525**	**452**	**4,073**	**10,241**	**1,345**	**8,896**
Urban	10,556	1,274	9,282	3,251	325	2,926	7,305	949	6,356
Rural-nonfarm	2,456	389	2,067	700	98	602	1,756	291	1,465
Rural-farm	1,754	134	1,620	574	29	545	1,180	105	1,075
Per cent urban	71.5	70.9	71.6	71.8	71.9	71.8	71.3	70.6	71.4

TABLE **32**. WHITE POPULATION OF CANADIAN STOCK, FRENCH AND ENGLISH, IN URBAN AND RURAL AREAS, FOR 29 SELECTED STATES: 1930—Continued

STATE AND AREA	ALL CANADIAN STOCK			CANADIAN BORN			CANADIAN PARENTAGE		
	Total	French	English	Total	French	English	Total	French	English
Montana.......	**31,585**	**6,788**	**24,797**	**10,753**	**1,966**	**8,787**	**20,832**	**4,822**	**16,010**
Urban..............	12,421	2,867	9,554	4,228	852	3,376	8,193	2,015	6,178
Rural-nonfarm........	9,325	1,890	7,435	3,197	570	2,627	6,128	1,320	4,808
Rural-farm...........	9,839	2,031	7,808	3,328	544	2,784	6,511	1,487	5,024
Per cent urban.....	39.3	42.2	38.5	39.3	43.3	38.4	39.3	41.8	38.6
Idaho..........	**13,715**	**2,075**	**11,640**	**4,502**	**571**	**3,931**	**9,213**	**1,504**	**7,709**
Urban..............	4,978	769	4,209	1,668	222	1,446	3,310	547	2,763
Rural-nonfarm........	5,047	799	4,248	1,789	231	1,558	3,258	568	2,690
Rural-farm...........	3,690	507	3,183	1,045	118	927	2,645	389	2,256
Per cent urban.....	36.3	37.1	36.2	37.1	38.9	36.8	35.9	36.4	35.8
Colorado.......	**19,256**	**2,568**	**16,688**	**5,816**	**572**	**5,244**	**13,440**	**1,996**	**11,444**
Urban..............	12,015	1,569	10,446	3,879	356	3,523	8,136	1,213	6,923
Rural-nonfarm........	3,826	524	3,302	1,082	118	964	2,744	406	2,338
Rural-farm...........	3,415	475	2,940	855	98	757	2,560	377	2,183
Per cent urban.....	62.4	61.1	62.6	66.7	62.2	67.2	60.5	60.8	60.5
Washington....	**113,206**	**14,137**	**99,069**	**48,064**	**4,340**	**43,724**	**65,142**	**9,797**	**55,345**
Urban..............	72,556	8,563	63,993	32,193	2,727	29,466	40,363	5,836	34,527
Rural-nonfarm........	24,860	3,375	21,485	9,605	978	8,627	15,255	2,397	12,858
Rural-farm...........	15,790	2,199	13,591	6,266	635	5,631	9,524	1,564	7,960
Per cent urban.....	64.1	60.6	64.6	67.0	62.8	67.4	62.0	59.6	62.4
Oregon.........	**45,659**	**4,930**	**40,729**	**17,916**	**1,345**	**16,571**	**27,743**	**3,585**	**24,158**
Urban..............	27,886	2,886	25,000	11,587	795	10,792	16,299	2,091	14,208
Rural-nonfarm........	10,230	1,250	8,980	3,748	337	3,411	6,482	913	5,569
Rural-farm...........	7,543	794	6,749	2,581	213	2,368	4,962	581	4,381
Per cent urban.....	61.1	58.5	61.4	64.7	59.1	65.1	58.7	58.3	58.8
California......	**225,327**	**23,643**	**201,684**	**101,445**	**7,657**	**93,788**	**123,882**	**15,986**	**107,896**
Urban..............	178,807	18,356	160,451	82,725	6,055	76,670	96,082	12,301	83,781
Rural-nonfarm........	32,479	3,897	28,582	13,364	1,234	12,130	19,115	2,663	16,452
Rural-farm...........	14,041	1,390	12,651	5,356	368	4,988	8,685	1,022	7,663
Per cent urban.....	79.4	77.6	79.6	81.5	79.1	81.7	77.6	76.9	77.6

TABLE **33**. WHITE POPULATION OF CANADIAN STOCK, FRENCH AND ENGLISH, IN THE PRINCIPAL CITIES OF THE UNITED STATES: 1900 TO 1930

[Figures given for each city as far back as data are available; for 1900 persons born in Newfoundland are included]

CITY AND CENSUS YEAR	ALL CANADIAN STOCK				CANADIAN BORN			CANADIAN PARENTAGE		
	Total	Per cent of population	French	English	Total	French	English	Total	French	English
Boston, Mass.:										
1930................	93,994	12.0	9,774	84,220	45,558	4,083	41,475	48,436	5,691	42,745
1920................	88,252	11.8	4,253	83,999	42,008	1,743	40,265	46,244	2,510	43,734
1910................	93,587	14.0	6,292	87,295	50,195	3,098	47,097	43,392	3,194	40,198
1900................	83,736	14.9	5,133	78,603	49,551	2,895	46,656	34,185	2,238	31,947
Cambridge, Mass.:										
1930................	18,691	16.4	4,266	14,425	9,254	1,672	7,582	9,437	2,594	6,843
1920................	16,976	15.5	2,603	14,373	7,693	949	6,744	9,283	1,654	7,629
1910................	19,477	18.6	3,404	16,073	9,892	1,445	8,447	9,585	1,959	7,626
1900................	18,424	20.1	2,918	15,506	10,748	1,480	9,268	7,676	1,438	6,238
Fall River, Mass.:										
1930................	27,287	23.7	25,899	1,388	8,973	8,477	496	18,314	17,422	892
1920................	30,934	25.7	28,630	2,304	11,592	10,734	858	19,342	17,896	1,446
1910................	34,256	28.7	32,194	2,062	16,238	15,277	961	18,018	16,917	1,101
1900................	35,570	33.9	31,725	3,845	22,501	20,172	2,329	13,069	11,553	1,516
Lowell, Mass.:										
1930................	28,015	27.9	22,180	5,835	10,169	7,763	2,406	17,846	14,417	3,429
1920................	32,134	28.5	24,175	7,959	13,782	10,180	3,602	18,352	13,995	4,357
1910................	31,124	29.3	23,307	7,817	16,340	12,291	4,049	14,784	11,016	3,768
1900................	30,086	31.7	22,775	7,311	19,157	14,674	4,483	10,929	8,001	2,828
Lynn, Mass.:										
1930................	22,581	22.1	7,222	15,359	9,727	2,930	6,797	12,854	4,292	8,562
1920................	21,297	21.5	5,438	15,859	9,546	2,164	7,382	11,751	3,274	8,477
New Bedford, Mass.:										
1930................	22,412	19.9	20,384	2,028	8,462	7,643	819	13,950	12,741	1,209
1920................	25,834	21.3	23,163	2,671	10,990	9,833	1,157	14,844	13,330	1,514
Somerville, Mass.:										
1930................	20,626	19.9	2,373	18,253	10,069	905	9,164	10,557	1,468	9,089
1920................	17,943	19.3	795	17,148	7,996	317	7,679	9,947	478	9,469
Springfield, Mass.:										
1930................	20,786	13.9	14,882	5,904	7,194	4,918	2,276	13,592	9,964	3,628
1920................	16,919	13.1	11,448	5,471	5,797	3,719	2,078	11,122	7,729	3,393
Worcester, Mass.:										
1930................	26,679	13.7	17,076	9,603	9,146	4,947	4,199	17,533	12,129	5,404
1920................	23,519	13.1	14,167	9,352	8,125	4,292	3,833	15,394	9,875	5,519
1910................	21,068	14.4	14,407	6,661	8,387	5,010	3,377	12,681	9,397	3,284
1900................	18,748	15.8	12,800	5,948	8,357	5,203	3,154	10,391	7,597	2,794
Providence, R. I.:										
1930................	20,876	8.3	12,172	8,704	7,594	3,837	3,757	13,282	8,335	4,947
1920................	18,539	7.8	10,148	8,391	7,019	3,436	3,583	11,520	6,712	4,808
1910................	19,193	8.6	10,638	8,555	8,789	4,494	4,295	10,404	6,144	4,260
1900................	14,398	8.2	7,382	7,016	7,698	3,849	3,849	6,700	3,533	3,167
Hartford, Conn.:										
1930................	13,689	8.3	9,223	4,466	5,771	3,739	2,032	7,918	5,484	2,434
1920................	6,160	4.5	2,603	3,557	2,377	857	1,520	3,783	1,746	2,037
Buffalo, N. Y.:										
1930................	35,774	6.2	2,035	33,739	18,735	851	17,884	17,039	1,184	15,855
1920................	32,774	6.5	428	32,346	15,794	177	15,617	16,980	251	16,729
1910................	32,253	7.6	1,401	30,852	17,279	566	16,713	14,974	835	14,139
1900................	29,590	8.4	1,602	27,988	17,113	730	16,383	12,477	872	11,605
New York, N. Y.:										
1930................	77,497	1.1	14,923	62,574	39,622	6,863	32,759	37,875	8,060	29,815
1920................	53,436	1.0	3,995	49,441	25,271	1,757	23,514	28,165	2,238	25,927
1910................	53,161	1.1	6,673	46,488	26,072	2,844	23,228	27,089	3,829	23,260
1900................	42,088	1.2	5,625	36,463	21,759	2,511	19,248	20,329	3,114	17,215

TABLE **33**. WHITE POPULATION OF CANADIAN STOCK, FRENCH AND ENGLISH, IN THE PRINCIPAL
CITIES OF THE UNITED STATES: 1900 TO 1930—Continued

[Figures given for each city as far back as data are available; for 1900 persons born in Newfoundland are included]

CITY AND CENSUS YEAR	ALL CANADIAN STOCK				CANADIAN BORN			CANADIAN PARENTAGE		
	Total	Per cent of population	French	English	Total	French	English	Total	French	English
Rochester, N. Y.:										
1930	21,537	6.6	2,044	19,493	10,113	693	9,420	11,424	1,351	10,073
1920	20,632	7.0	535	20,097	9,505	188	9,317	11,127	347	10,780
1910	18,486	8.5	1,568	16,918	9,681	569	9,112	8,805	999	7,806
1900	15,172	9.3	1,276	13,896	8,285	552	7,733	6,887	724	6,163
Syracuse, N. Y.:										
1930	11,499	5.5	2,958	8,541	4,693	1,026	3,667	6,806	1,932	4,874
1920	8,793	5.1	1,168	7,625	3,473	357	3,116	5,320	811	4,509
1910	7,243	5.3	1,431	5,812	3,216	499	2,717	4,027	932	3,095
1900	6,164	5.7	1,522	4,642	2,936	560	2,376	3,228	962	2,266
Philadelphia, Pa.:										
1930	9,689	0.5	1,718	7,971	4,229	636	3,593	5,460	1,082	4,378
1920	9,726	0.5	562	9,164	4,136	209	3,927	5,590	353	5,237
1910	8,584	0.6	823	7,761	3,949	301	3,648	4,635	522	4,113
1900	6,703	0.5	665	6,038	3,214	289	2,925	3,489	376	3,113
Cleveland, Ohio:										
1930	17,795	2.0	1,950	15,845	8,265	674	7,591	9,530	1,276	8,254
1920	18,732	2.4	796	17,936	8,500	282	8,218	10,232	514	9,718
1910	19,000	3.4	1,539	17,461	9,107	571	8,536	9,893	968	8,925
1900	17,244	4.5	1,745	15,499	8,473	759	7,714	8,771	986	7,785
Toledo, Ohio:										
1930	8,409	2.9	1,882	6,527	3,031	534	2,497	5,378	1,348	4,030
1920	8,700	3.6	1,456	7,244	3,137	392	2,745	5,563	1,064	4,499
1910	7,950	4.7	2,245	5,705	3,116	681	2,435	4,834	1,564	3,270
1900	7,633	5.8	2,175	5,458	3,230	835	2,395	4,403	1,340	3,063
Chicago, Ill.:										
1930	73,783	2.2	14,259	59,524	29,831	4,211	25,620	43,952	10,048	33,904
1920	67,220	2.5	8,000	59,220	26,054	2,432	23,622	41,166	5,568	35,598
1910	70,901	3.2	13,451	57,450	30,946	4,633	26,313	39,955	8,818	31,137
1900	70,397	4.1	12,833	57,564	34,476	5,287	29,189	35,921	7,546	28,375
Detroit, Mich.:										
1930	174,616	11.1	26,644	147,972	94,284	12,477	81,807	80,332	14,167	66,165
1920	119,017	12.0	9,842	109,175	58,894	3,678	55,216	60,123	6,164	53,959
1910	75,956	16.3	9,807	66,149	41,945	4,166	37,779	34,011	5,641	28,370
1900	49,399	17.3	7,704	41,695	28,524	3,533	24,991	20,875	4,171	16,704
Flint, Mich.:										
1930	19,668	12.6	3,185	16,483	6,837	798	6,039	12,831	2,387	10,444
1920	14,842	16.2	1,272	13,570	4,959	301	4,658	9,883	971	8,912
Grand Rapids, Mich.:										
1930	8,618	5.1	1,022	7,596	2,529	214	2,315	6,089	808	5,281
1920	8,836	6.4	390	8,446	2,837	91	2,746	5,999	299	5,700
1910	8,477	7.5	610	7,867	3,194	197	2,997	5,283	413	4,870
1900	8,054	9.2	466	7,588	3,459	169	3,290	4,595	297	4,298
Milwaukee, Wis.:										
1930	8,742	1.5	2,384	6,358	2,662	456	2,206	6,080	1,928	4,152
1920	6,543	1.4	1,132	5,411	2,053	223	1,830	4,490	909	3,581
1910	5,170	1.4	885	4,285	1,868	218	1,650	3,302	667	2,635
1900	4,592	1.6	774	3,818	1,888	213	1,675	2,704	561	2,143
Duluth, Minn.:										
1930	10,574	10.4	3,219	7,355	3,479	872	2,607	7,095	2,347	4,748
1920	13,294	13.4	3,670	9,624	4,708	1,093	3,615	8,586	2,577	6,009
Minneapolis, Minn.:										
1930	22,128	4.8	6,182	15,946	6,731	1,373	5,358	15,397	4,809	10,588
1920	22,032	5.8	4,104	17,928	7,461	1,016	6,445	14,571	3,088	11,483
1910	19,774	6.6	5,341	14,433	7,514	1,637	5,877	12,260	3,704	8,556
1900	17,713	8.7	4,845	12,868	7,328	1,702	5,626	10,385	3,143	7,242

TABLE **33**. WHITE POPULATION OF CANADIAN STOCK, FRENCH AND ENGLISH, IN THE PRINCIPAL
CITIES OF THE UNITED STATES: 1900 TO 1930—Continued

[Figures given for each city as far back as data are available; for 1900 persons born in Newfoundland are included]

CITY AND CENSUS YEAR	ALL CANADIAN STOCK				CANADIAN BORN			CANADIAN PARENTAGE		
	Total	Per cent of popu- lation	French	English	Total	French	English	Total	French	English
St. Paul, Minn.:										
1930................	11,729	4.3	3,727	8,002	3,461	720	2,741	8,268	3,007	5,261
1920................	11,946	5.1	2,770	9,176	3,890	587	3,303	8,056	2,183	5,873
1910................	11,606	5.4	3,582	8,024	4,398	1,096	3,302	7,208	2,486	4,722
1900................	10,609	6.5	2,842	7,767	4,551	1,012	3,539	6,058	1,830	4,228
Denver, Colo.:										
1930................	7,650	2.7	1,055	6,595	2,546	243	2,303	5,104	812	4,292
1920................	8,221	3.2	483	7,738	3,102	129	2,973	5,119	354	4,765
1910................	8,436	4.0	843	7,593	3,474	232	3,242	4,962	611	4,351
1900................	6,133	4.6	667	5,466	2,858	245	2,613	3,275	422	2,853
Seattle, Wash.:										
1930................	33,011	9.0	3,359	29,652	15,745	1,116	14,629	17,266	2,243	15,023
1920................	28,619	9.1	1,616	27,003	13,854	630	13,224	14,765	986	13,779
1910................	21,039	8.9	1,916	19,123	10,686	836	9,850	10,353	1,080	9,273
1900................	7,046	8.7	555	6,491	3,772	255	3,517	3,274	300	2,974
Spokane, Wash.:										
1930................	9,227	8.0	1,097	8,130	3,855	391	3,464	5,372	706	4,666
1920................	9,086	8.7	442	8,644	3,836	144	3,692	5,250	298	4,952
1910................	9,176	8.8	756	8,420	4,339	310	4,029	4,837	446	4,391
1900................	3,416	9.3	256	3,160	1,809	138	1,671	1,607	118	1,489
Tacoma, Wash.:										
1930................	7,584	7.1	864	6,720	3,155	238	2,917	4,429	626	3,803
1920................	7,091	7.3	542	6,549	2,978	153	2,825	4,113	389	3,724
Portland, Ore.:										
1930................	18,834	6.2	1,884	16,950	8,351	537	7,814	10,483	1,347	9,136
1920................	15,486	6.0	848	14,638	6,437	285	6,152	9,049	563	8,486
1910................	11,440	5.5	1,071	10,369	5,195	442	4,753	6,245	629	5,616
1900................	4,600	5.1	586	4,014	2,198	261	1,937	2,402	325	2,077
Long Beach, Calif.:										
1930................	7,427	5.2	726	6,701	3,589	235	3,354	3,838	491	3,347
1920................	3,392	6.1	135	3,257	1,864	62	1,802	1,528	73	1,455
Los Angeles, Calif.:										
1930................	59,630	4.8	6,251	53,379	30,740	2,439	28,301	28,890	3,812	25,078
1920................	28,053	4.9	1,451	26,602	13,741	554	13,187	14,312	897	13,415
1910................	16,524	5.2	1,403	15,121	8,249	592	7,657	8,275	811	7,464
1900................	5,762	5.6	533	5,229	2,888	213	2,675	2,874	320	2,554
Oakland, Calif.:										
1930................	12,442	4.4	1,380	11,062	5,227	404	4,823	7,215	976	6,239
1920................	9,411	4.4	467	8,944	3,785	177	3,608	5,626	290	5,336
1910................	7,251	4.8	679	6,572	3,126	245	2,881	4,125	434	3,691
1900................	3,929	5.9	564	3,365	1,761	223	1,538	2,168	341	1,827
San Diego, Calif.:										
1930................	6,958	4.7	840	6,118	3,004	230	2,774	3,954	610	3,344
1920................	3,998	5.4	216	3,782	1,904	74	1,830	2,094	142	1,952
San Francisco, Calif.:										
1930................	21,297	3.4	2,506	18,791	9,601	909	8,692	11,696	1,597	10,099
1920................	16,567	3.3	910	15,657	7,083	346	6,737	9,484	564	8,920
1910................	13,824	3.3	1,220	12,604	6,161	474	5,687	7,663	746	6,917
1900................	11,587	3.4	1,235	10,352	5,190	429	4,761	6,397	806	5,591

TABLE **34**. WHITE POPULATION OF CANADIAN STOCK, FRENCH AND ENGLISH, IN SELECTED CITIES OF 25,000 OR MORE: 1930

CITY	ALL CANADIAN STOCK				CANADIAN BORN			CANADIAN PARENTAGE			Total population
	Total	Per cent of population	French	English	Total	French	English	Total	French	English	
Maine:											
Bangor.........	6,216	21.6	1,043	5,173	2,301	384	1,917	3,915	659	3,256	28,749
Lewiston........	20,629	59.0	19,253	1,376	8,884	8,276	608	11,745	10,977	768	34,948
Portland........	12,270	17.3	1,946	10,324	4,917	687	4,230	7,353	1,259	6,094	70,810
New Hampshire:											
Concord.........	5,219	20.7	3,091	2,128	1,870	1,098	772	3,349	1,993	1,356	25,228
Manchester......	30,389	39.6	26,845	3,544	12,118	10,696	1,422	18,271	16,149	2,122	76,834
Nashua..........	14,176	45.1	12,683	1,493	5,482	4,895	587	8,694	7,788	906	31,463
Massachusetts:											
Arlington........	6,733	18.7	651	6,082	2,879	217	2,662	3,854	434	3,420	36,094
Beverly.........	5,000	19.9	1,190	3,810	1,816	365	1,451	3,184	825	2,359	25,086
Boston..........	93,994	12.0	9,774	84,220	45,558	4,083	41,475	48,436	5,691	42,745	781,188
Brockton........	8,615	13.5	2,872	5,743	2,946	720	2,226	5,669	2,152	3,517	63,797
Brookline........	5,846	12.3	397	5,449	3,386	170	3,216	2,460	227	2,233	47,490
Cambridge.......	18,691	16.4	4,266	14,425	9,254	1,672	7,582	9,437	2,594	6,843	113,643
Chelsea..........	5,148	11.2	1,317	3,831	2,403	582	1,821	2,745	735	2,010	45,816
Chicopee........	13,661	31.1	13,030	631	4,908	4,663	245	8,753	8,367	386	43,930
Everett..........	9,016	18.6	918	8,098	4,141	366	3,775	4,875	552	4,323	48,424
Fall River........	27,287	23.7	25,899	1,388	8,973	8,477	496	18,314	17,422	892	115,274
Fitchburg........	11,997	29.5	10,165	1,832	4,178	3,491	687	7,819	6,674	1,145	40,692
Haverhill........	10,532	21.6	6,313	4,219	3,637	1,907	1,730	6,895	4,406	2,489	48,710
Holyoke.........	13,328	23.6	12,267	1,061	5,355	4,939	416	7,973	7,328	645	56,537
Lawrence........	16,256	19.1	13,671	2,585	6,318	5,280	1,038	9,938	8,391	1,547	85,068
Lowell...........	28,015	27.9	22,180	5,835	10,169	7,763	2,406	17,846	14,417	3,429	100,234
Lynn...........	22,581	22.1	7,222	15,359	9,727	2,930	6,797	12,854	4,292	8,562	102,320
Malden.........	10,859	18.7	1,180	9,679	4,917	506	4,411	5,942	674	5,268	58,036
Medford........	11,084	18.6	1,116	9,968	4,609	394	4,215	6,475	722	5,753	59,714
New Bedford....	22,412	19.9	20,384	2,028	8,462	7,643	819	13,950	12,741	1,209	112,597
Newton.........	9,922	15.2	1,789	8,133	4,619	733	3,886	5,303	1,056	4,247	65,276
Pittsfield........	4,382	8.8	3,218	1,164	1,348	963	385	3,034	2,255	779	49,677
Quincy..........	11,728	16.3	1,618	10,110	4,631	551	4,080	7,097	1,067	6,030	71,983
Revere..........	4,006	11.2	682	3,324	1,613	261	1,352	2,393	421	1,972	35,680
Salem...........	13,099	30.2	9,933	3,166	4,613	3,365	1,248	8,486	6,568	1,918	43,353
Somerville.......	20,626	19.9	2,373	18,253	10,069	905	9,164	10,557	1,468	9,089	103,908
Springfield.......	20,786	13.9	14,882	5,904	7,194	4,918	2,276	13,592	9,964	3,628	149,900
Taunton.........	5,631	15.1	3,754	1,877	1,996	1,159	837	3,635	2,595	1,040	37,355
Waltham........	9,915	25.3	3,413	6,502	4,867	1,636	3,231	5,048	1,777	3,271	39,247
Watertown.......	6,168	17.7	765	5,403	2,844	258	2,586	3,324	507	2,817	34,913
Worcester........	26,679	13.7	17,076	9,603	9,146	4,947	4,199	17,533	12,129	5,404	195,311
Rhode Island:											
Central Falls.....	10,728	41.4	10,534	194	4,009	3,938	71	6,719	6,596	123	25,898
Cranston........	3,313	7.7	1,618	1,695	1,148	491	657	2,165	1,127	1,038	42,911
East Providence...	2,253	7.5	866	1,387	761	214	547	1,492	652	840	29,995
Newport........	1,406	5.1	473	933	430	107	323	976	366	610	27,612
Pawtucket.......	16,285	21.1	14,591	1,694	5,561	4,898	663	10,724	9,693	1,031	77,149
Providence.......	20,876	8.3	12,172	8,704	7,594	3,837	3,757	13,282	8,335	4,947	252,981
Woonsocket......	26,442	53.6	25,743	699	10,256	9,990	266	16,186	15,753	433	49,376
Connecticut:											
Bridgeport.......	4,917	3.4	2,587	2,330	1,909	935	974	3,008	1,652	1,356	146,716
Bristol..........	4,609	16.2	3,600	1,009	2,118	1,671	447	2,491	1,929	562	28,451
Hartford........	13,689	8.3	9,223	4,466	5,771	3,739	2,032	7,918	5,484	2,434	164,072
Meriden.........	2,689	7.0	2,149	540	1,006	790	216	1,683	1,359	324	38,481
New Britain......	2,851	4.2	2,000	851	1,280	952	328	1,571	1,048	523	68,128
New Haven......	4,026	2.5	1,705	2,321	1,495	581	914	2,531	1,124	1,407	162,655
New London.....	1,671	5.6	554	1,117	631	156	475	1,040	398	642	29,640
Norwalk........	1,181	3.3	714	467	605	407	198	576	307	269	36,019
Torrington.......	898	3.4	604	294	401	271	130	497	333	164	26,040
Waterbury.......	8,377	8.4	6,803	1,574	3,917	3,276	641	4,460	3,527	933	99,902
West Haven......	1,050	4.1	455	595	348	151	197	702	304	398	25,808

TABLE **34**. WHITE POPULATION OF CANADIAN STOCK, FRENCH AND ENGLISH, IN SELECTED
CITIES OF 25,000 OR MORE: 1930—Continued

CITY	ALL CANADIAN STOCK				CANADIAN BORN			CANADIAN PARENTAGE			Total population
	Total	Per cent of population	French	English	Total	French	English	Total	French	English	
New York:											
Albany..........	3,697	2.9	1,464	2,233	1,400	572	828	2,297	892	1,405	127,412
Buffalo..........	35,774	6.2	2,035	33,739	18,735	851	17,884	17,039	1,184	15,855	573,076
New York........	77,497	1.1	14,923	62,574	39,622	6,863	32,759	37,875	8,060	29,815	6,930,446
Niagara Falls.....	13,390	17.7	919	12,471	7,635	580	7,055	5,755	339	5,416	75,460
Rochester........	21,537	6.6	2,044	19,493	10,113	693	9,420	11,424	1,351	10,073	328,132
Rome...........	1,015	3.1	260	755	414	100	314	601	160	441	32,338
Schenectady......	3,358	3.5	1,526	1,832	1,214	499	715	2,144	1,027	1,117	95,692
Syracuse.........	11,499	5.5	2,958	8,541	4,693	1,026	3,667	6,806	1,932	4,874	209,326
Troy............	2,652	3.6	1,618	1,034	711	412	299	1,941	1,206	735	72,763
Utica...........	3,185	3.1	980	2,205	1,156	315	841	2,029	665	1,364	101,740
Watertown.......	7,026	21.8	1,188	5,838	2,899	361	2,538	4,127	827	3,300	32,205
White Plains......	1,340	3.7	286	1,054	635	110	525	705	176	529	35,830
New Jersey:											
Newark..........	4,321	1.0	1,337	2,984	1,946	498	1,448	2,375	839	1,536	442,337
Pennsylvania:											
Philadelphia......	9,689	0.5	1,718	7,971	4,229	636	3,593	5,460	1,082	4,378	1,950,961
Pittsburgh.......	4,101	0.6	483	3,618	1,683	154	1,529	2,418	329	2,089	669,817
Ohio:											
Cleveland........	17,795	2.0	1,950	15,845	8,265	674	7,591	9,530	1,276	8,254	900,429
Cleveland Heights.	2,022	4.0	109	1,913	826	22	804	1,196	87	1,109	50,945
East Cleveland....	1,938	4.9	179	1,759	883	52	831	1,055	127	928	39,667
Lakewood........	3,355	4.8	245	3,110	1,309	73	1,236	2,046	172	1,874	70,509
Toledo..........	8,409	2.9	1,882	6,527	3,031	534	2,497	5,378	1,348	4,030	290,718
Illinois:											
Chicago..........	73,783	2.2	14,259	59,524	29,831	4,211	25,620	43,952	10,048	33,904	3,376,438
Evanston........	2,377	3.8	195	2,182	876	50	826	1,501	145	1,356	63,338
Maywood........	883	3.4	107	776	307	17	290	576	90	486	25,829
Oak Park........	3,124	4.9	463	2,661	1,077	133	944	2,047	330	1,717	63,982
Michigan:											
Ann Arbor.......	1,912	7.1	104	1,808	732	28	704	1,180	76	1,104	26,944
Battle Creek......	2,555	5.9	170	2,385	947	35	912	1,608	135	1,473	43,573
Bay City.........	7,814	16.5	2,858	4,956	2,270	704	1,566	5,544	2,154	3,390	47,355
Dearborn........	5,208	10.3	680	4,528	2,723	354	2,369	2,485	326	2,159	50,358
Detroit..........	174,616	11.1	26,644	147,972	94,284	12,477	81,807	80,332	14,167	66,165	1,568,662
Flint............	19,668	12.6	3,185	16,483	6,837	798	6,039	12,831	2,387	10,444	156,492
Grand Rapids.....	8,618	5.1	1,022	7,596	2,529	214	2,315	6,089	808	5,281	168,592
Highland Park....	7,548	14.3	617	6,931	4,376	333	4,043	3,172	284	2,888	52,959
Jackson..........	2,928	5.3	274	2,654	972	85	887	1,956	189	1,767	55,187
Kalamazoo.......	2,063	3.8	321	1,742	601	69	532	1,462	252	1,210	54,786
Lansing..........	5,858	7.5	551	5,307	1,666	107	1,559	4,192	444	3,748	78,397
Muskegon........	2,918	7.1	1,215	1,703	745	282	463	2,173	933	1,240	41,390
Pontiac..........	8,665	13.3	977	7,688	3,530	325	3,205	5,135	652	4,483	64,928
Port Huron.......	9,902	31.6	369	9,533	3,856	92	3,764	6,046	277	5,769	31,361
Saginaw.........	9,476	11.7	2,052	7,424	2,624	415	2,209	6,852	1,637	5,215	80,715
Wyandotte.......	2,398	8.5	596	1,802	998	180	818	1,400	416	984	28,368
Wisconsin:											
Eau Claire........	1,371	5.2	389	982	309	71	238	1,062	318	744	26,287
Fond du Lac......	849	3.2	485	364	140	57	83	709	428	281	26,449
Green Bay.......	1,583	4.2	729	854	311	137	174	1,272	592	680	37,415
Milwaukee.......	8,742	1.5	2,384	6,358	2,662	456	2,206	6,080	1,928	4,152	578,249
Superior.........	3,389	9.4	838	2,551	1,002	213	789	2,387	625	1,762	36,113
Minnesota:											
Duluth..........	10,574	10.4	3,219	7,355	3,479	872	2,607	7,095	2,347	4,748	101,463
Minneapolis......	22,128	4.8	6,182	15,946	6,731	1,373	5,358	15,397	4,809	10,588	464,356
St. Paul.........	11,729	4.3	3,727	8,002	3,461	720	2,741	8,268	3,007	5,261	271,606
Missouri:											
Kansas City......	5,215	1.3	703	4,512	1,424	159	1,265	3,791	544	3,247	399,746
St. Louis.........	4,466	0.5	736	3,730	1,374	172	1,202	3,092	564	2,528	821,960

TABLE **34**. WHITE POPULATION OF CANADIAN STOCK, FRENCH AND ENGLISH, IN SELECTED
CITIES OF 25,000 OR MORE: 1930—Continued

CITY	ALL CANADIAN STOCK				CANADIAN BORN			CANADIAN PARENTAGE			Total popula-tion
	Total	Per cent of popu-lation	French	Eng-lish	Total	French	Eng-lish	Total	French	Eng-lish	
North Dakota:											
Fargo..........	2,103	7.3	342	1,761	627	79	548	1,476	263	1,213	28,619
Nebraska:											
Omaha..........	3,686	1.7	544	3,142	948	109	839	2,738	435	2,303	214,006
Dist. of Columbia:											
Washington......	4,864	1.0	745	4,119	1,681	223	1,458	3,183	522	2,661	486,869
Florida:											
St. Petersburg....	1,507	3.7	235	1,272	701	75	626	806	160	646	40,425
Montana:											
Butte...........	2,723	6.9	755	1,968	1,047	244	803	1,676	511	1,165	39,532
Great Falls.......	2,452	8.5	369	2,083	879	111	768	1,573	258	1,315	28,822
Colorado:											
Denver..........	7,650	2.7	1,055	6,595	2,546	243	2,303	5,104	812	4,292	287,861
Washington:											
Bellingham.......	3,294	10.7	233	3,061	1,525	75	1,450	1,769	158	1,611	30,823
Everett..........	2,947	9.6	587	2,360	1,295	185	1,110	1,652	402	1,250	30,567
Seattle..........	33,011	9.0	3,359	29,652	15,745	1,116	14,629	17,266	2,243	15,023	365,583
Spokane.........	9,227	8.0	1,097	8,130	3,855	391	3,464	5,372	706	4,666	115,514
Tacoma..........	7,584	7.1	864	6,720	3,155	238	2,917	4,429	626	3,803	106,817
Oregon:											
Portland.........	18,834	6.2	1,884	16,950	8,351	537	7,814	10,483	1,347	9,136	301,815
Salem...........	1,388	5.3	112	1,276	547	28	519	841	84	757	26,266
California:											
Alameda.........	1,782	5.1	135	1,647	766	34	732	1,016	101	915	35,033
Alhambra........	1,603	5.4	127	1,476	762	35	727	841	92	749	29,472
Bakersfield......	788	3.0	92	696	262	20	242	526	72	454	26,015
Berkeley.........	3,948	4.8	271	3,677	1,612	61	1,551	2,336	210	2,126	82,109
Glendale.........	3,920	6.2	325	3,595	1,794	84	1,710	2,126	241	1,885	62,736
Long Beach.......	7,427	5.2	726	6,701	3,589	235	3,354	3,838	491	3,347	142,032
Los Angeles.......	59,630	4.8	6,251	53,379	30,740	2,439	28,301	28,890	3,812	25,078	1,238,048
Oakland.........	12,442	4.4	1,380	11,062	5,227	404	4,823	7,215	976	6,239	284,063
Pasadena........	4,270	5.6	258	4,012	2,216	91	2,125	2,054	167	1,887	76,086
Riverside........	1,378	4.6	79	1,299	659	22	637	719	57	662	29,696
Sacramento......	3,216	3.4	304	2,912	1,182	75	1,107	2,034	229	1,805	93,750
San Bernardino...	1,169	3.1	92	1,077	454	20	434	715	72	643	37,481
San Diego........	6,958	4.7	840	6,118	3,004	230	2,774	3,954	610	3,344	147,995
San Francisco.....	21,297	3.4	2,506	18,791	9,601	909	8,692	11,696	1,597	10,099	634,394
San Jose........	2,154	3.7	267	1,887	795	52	743	1,359	215	1,144	57,651
Santa Ana........	1,064	3.5	88	976	397	11	386	667	77	590	30,322
Santa Barbara....	1,507	4.5	176	1,331	728	44	684	779	132	647	33,613
Santa Monica.....	2,539	6.8	224	2,315	1,475	104	1,371	1,064	120	944	37,146
Stockton.........	1,461	3.0	190	1,271	521	43	478	940	147	793	47,963

CHAPTER VI

YEAR OF IMMIGRATION OF THE CANADIAN BORN

A QUESTION on length of residence in the United States or year of immigration (that is, of first arrival in the United States), has been asked with regard to each foreign-born person in the United States at each of the decennial censuses beginning with 1890. Prior to 1930, however, the returns from this question have been tabulated only for the total foreign born and not by country of birth. In the 1930 census this additional correlation was made, and figures representing the number of white persons of Canadian birth in the United States in 1930, classified by year of immigration, are shown in Table 35. For some of the years immediately preceding the census the data were tabulated by single years; and then in somewhat irregular groups which can be consolidated approximately into decades, back to 1900.

TABLE **35**. CANADIAN-BORN WHITE POPULATION IN THE UNITED STATES, FRENCH AND ENGLISH, BY YEAR OF IMMIGRATION AND SEX: 1930

YEAR OF IMMI-GRATION	ALL CANADIAN BORN			FRENCH			ENGLISH		
	Total	Male	Female	Total	Male	Female	Total	Male	Female
Total.....	1,278,421	617,090	661,331	370,852	187,523	183,329	907,569	429,567	478,002
Reporting year of immigration..	1,191,155	578,905	612,250	355,260	180,429	174,831	835,895	398,476	437,419
1925 to 1930...	158,992	74,831	84,161	36,096	17,616	18,480	122,896	57,215	65,681
1930, to Apr. 1	4,852	2,141	2,711	1,033	476	557	3,819	1,665	2,154
1929........	25,651	11,520	14,131	6,027	2,908	3,119	19,624	8,612	11,012
1928........	23,641	10,628	13,013	5,387	2,561	2,826	18,254	8,067	10,187
1927........	27,683	12,409	15,274	6,426	3,058	3,368	21,257	9,351	11,906
1925 and 1926	77,165	38,133	39,032	17,223	8,613	8,610	59,942	29,520	30,422
1920 to 1924....	207,015	105,409	101,606	55,352	28,615	26,737	151,663	76,794	74,869
1915 to 1919....	87,371	40,777	46,594	23,531	11,633	11,898	63,840	29,144	34,696
1911 to 1914....	57,354	26,494	30,860	16,866	8,277	8,589	40,488	18,217	22,271
1901 to 1910....	174,857	80,979	93,878	56,318	27,657	28,661	118,539	53,322	65,217
1900 and earlier.	505,566	250,415	255,151	167,097	86,631	80,466	338,469	163,784	174,685
Not reporting....	87,266	38,185	49,081	15,592	7,094	8,498	71,674	31,091	40,583
Per cent reporting.	100.0	100.0	100.0	100.0	100.0	100.0	100.0	100.0	100.0
1925 to 1930....	13.3	12.9	13.7	10.2	9.8	10.6	14.7	14.4	15.0
1920 to 1924....	17.4	18.2	16.6	15.6	15.9	15.3	18.1	19.3	17.1
1915 to 1919....	7.3	7.0	7.6	6.6	6.4	6.8	7.6	7.3	7.9
1911 to 1914....	4.8	4.6	5.0	4.7	4.6	4.9	4.8	4.6	5.1
1901 to 1910....	14.7	14.0	15.3	15.9	15.3	16.4	14.2	13.4	14.9
1900 and earlier.	42.4	43.3	41.7	47.0	48.0	46.0	40.5	41.1	39.9

Of the whole number of Canadian born enumerated in 1930 who reported year of immigration, 505,566, or 42.4 per cent, had entered prior to 1901; 174,857, or 14.7 per cent, arrived in the United States in the period from 1901 to 1910, making an average of 17,486 per year; 57,354, or 4.8 per cent, in the 4-year period from 1911 to 1914, making an average of 14,339 per year; 87,371, or 7.3 per cent, during the 5-year period from 1915 to 1919, making an average of 17,474 per year; 207,015, or 17.4 per cent, during the period from 1920 to 1924, making an average of 41,403 per year; and 158,992, or 13.3 per cent, during the period from 1925 to the time of the census in 1930, making an average of 30,284 per year. According to the figures tabulated for individual years of this last period, the numbers arriving in 1925 and 1926 were a little higher than in the later years, and the number arriving in 1930, if one may judge from the first three months of the year, was much smaller.

Those enumerated in 1930 as having arrived in the United States in the earlier years represent, of course, the survivors of the original immigrants, that is, the numbers who actually came into the United States in the period specified, minus the numbers who had died since that date and whatever numbers had gone back to Canada or emigrated to other countries. For those arriving in 1900 or earlier, in particular, these losses must have been rather large.

Of the Canadian-born French in the United States in 1930, 47.0 per cent had entered the United States before 1901, as compared with 40.5 per cent of the English Canadian born. The percentage of the French Canadians arriving in the decade 1901 to 1910 was appreciably higher also (15.9 as compared with 14.2); the percentage arriving in the period 1911 to 1919 was slightly smaller than the corresponding figure for the English Canadians, and in the period 1920 to 1930, much smaller—25.8 for the French and 32.8 for the English.

The percentages of arrival prior to 1901 are uniformly higher for males than for females, and likewise with the 5-year period from 1920 to 1924, while for all other periods shown in the table the percentage given for females is the higher. In no case, however, is there a very marked variation between the two sexes. Here again may be noted one of the differences between the Canadian immigrants to the United States and the general immigration from European countries, namely, that the Canadian immigrants have represented more nearly a normal segment of the population from which they came, rather than a group of workers predominantly male—though to some extent the balance of the sexes in the whole number of Canadian born in the United States has been maintained by the continued arrival in some of the eastern cities of an immigration with a considerable excess of females, which offset an excess of males in the newer areas of the West.

COMPARISON WITH OTHER COUNTRIES

DATA on year of immigration for the foreign-born white population from selected European countries are presented for comparison with the Canadian figures in Table 36. These data are also shown in graphic form in Figure 21.

FIGURE **21**. FOREIGN-BORN WHITE FROM SELECTED COUNTRIES BY YEAR OF IMMIGRATION: 1930

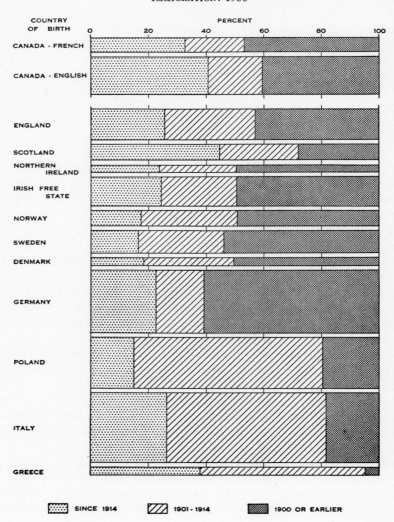

TABLE **36**. FOREIGN-BORN WHITE POPULATION OF THE UNITED STATES BY YEAR OF IMMIGRATION, FOR SELECTED COUNTRIES OF BIRTH: 1930

COUNTRY OF BIRTH	Total reporting year of immigration	1920 to 1930		1911 to 1919		1901 to 1910		1900 and earlier	
		Number	Per cent of total	Number	Per cent of total	Number	Per cent of total	Number	Per cent of total
All countries .	12,825,937	2,512,334	19.6	2,265,938	17.7	3,681,400	28.7	4,366,265	34.0
Canada.....	1,191,155	366,007	30.7	144,725	12.1	174,857	14.7	505,566	42.4
French....	355,260	91,448	25.7	40,397	11.4	56,318	15.9	167,097	47.0
English....	835,895	274,559	32.8	104,328	12.5	118,539	14.2	338,469	40.5
England....	769,383	159,672	20.8	111,252	14.5	166,553	21.6	331,906	43.1
Scotland....	340,300	139,966	41.1	42,850	12.6	62,713	18.4	94,771	27.8
Ireland.....	868,567	185,033	21.3	86,775	10.0	167,387	19.3	429,372	49.4
No. Ireland	169,650	35,269	20.8	17,601	10.4	32,819	19.3	83,961	49.5
Irish Fr. St.	698,917	149,764	21.4	69,174	9.9	134,568	19.3	345,411	49.4
Norway....	333,187	47,805	14.3	31,047	9.3	90,489	27.2	163,846	49.2
Sweden.....	575,404	77,300	13.4	55,341	9.6	133,093	23.1	309,670	53.8
Denmark...	172,512	24,693	14.3	22,357	13.0	38,787	22.5	86,675	50.2
Germany...	1,544,400	333,030	21.6	84,176	5.5	188,589	12.2	938,605	60.8
Poland.....	1,236,540	147,331	11.9	351,312	28.4	497,287	40.2	240,610	19.5
Italy.......	1,736,777	347,824	20.0	417,877	24.1	651,882	37.5	319,194	18.4
Greece.....	168,179	38,135	22.7	65,311	38.8	56,658	33.7	8,075	4.8

It has already been noted on the basis of other data that the Germans were among the earliest of the European nationalities to come into the United States in large numbers. The present classification shows that 60.8 per cent of the foreign born from Germany who were enumerated in 1930 had entered the United States prior to 1901, and only 21.6 in the decade from 1920 to 1930. The next oldest nationality group as measured by this percentage was made up of those from Sweden, 53.8 per cent of whom arrived prior to 1901; this country was followed by Denmark, with 50.2 per cent; Ireland, with 49.4 per cent; and Norway, with 49.2 per cent. In connection with the figures for Ireland, it may be noted that there was very little difference between Northern Ireland and the Irish Free State in the distribution by year of immigration.

Next in order were the French Canadians, with 47.0 per cent prior to 1901; then the group made up of persons born in England, with 43.1 per cent; and next the English Canadians, with 40.5 per cent.

At the other extreme was Greece, only 4.8 per cent of whose immigrant population as enumerated in 1930 had arrived in the United States prior to 1901, followed by Italy with 18.4 per cent, and Poland with 19.5 per cent.

The percentage of Canadian born reported as having entered the United States between 1901 and 1910 was lower than that recorded for persons from any other one of the selected countries except Germany, and only about one-half the average for all of the countries contributing to the foreign-born white population of the United States. The percentage of the Canadian born enumerated in 1930 who had entered between 1911 and 1919 was again much lower than the percentage from all countries, though it was higher than the percentage shown for several individual countries, including Ireland, Norway, Sweden, and Germany. The percentage of the Canadian born reported as having arrived in the United States between 1920 and 1930, however, was materially higher than the percentage shown for any other country with the single exception of Scotland, being 30.7 per cent (25.7 for the French and 32.8 for the English), as compared with 41.1 per cent for Scotland and 22.7 per cent for Greece, the next highest country on the list.

The general pattern shown by this classification of the 1930 Canadian born by year of immigration agrees in general with that indicated in the earlier discussion of the figures representing the change in the numbers of the Canadian born from one census to another, namely, very considerable arrivals prior to the close of the nineteenth century, and very considerable arrivals subsequent to 1920, with relatively few between 1900 and 1920.

Urban and Rural Areas

In Table 37 the data for the Canadian born classified by year of immigration are presented for urban and rural areas.

The general import of this table is to the effect that the more recent arrivals tend to be found in the cities, and those who have been longest in the United States tend to be found on farms. Thus, of the urban Canadian born only 39.9 per cent had arrived in 1900 or earlier, as compared with 48.8 per cent in the rural-nonfarm areas and 56.1 per cent in the rural-farm areas. At the other end of the scale it may be noted that of the Canadian born in urban areas, 14.4 per cent had arrived during the five years preceding the 1930 census, as compared with 10.1 per cent of those in the rural-nonfarm population, and 8.5 per cent of those in the rural-farm. These relations are shown in general for both the French and the English Canadians, and for both males and females.

In Table 38 are shown the number of males per 100 females in the Canadian-born population of the United States classified by year of immigration, including data for urban and rural areas. There were very considerable variations in the sex distribution of the Canadian born who arrived during the various periods shown by this classification, ranging for the total Canadian born from 103.7 males per 100 females for those arriving from 1920 to 1924, to 79.0 for those arriving in the first few months of 1930. The differences in sex distribution between the French

Canadian born and the English are so great, however, that it would seem better to consider these two classes separately in relation to year of immigration.

TABLE **37**. CANADIAN-BORN WHITE POPULATION, FRENCH AND ENGLISH, BY YEAR OF IMMIGRATION AND SEX, FOR URBAN AND RURAL AREAS: 1930

(For United States total see Table 36)

AREA AND YEAR OF IMMIGRATION	ALL CANADIAN BORN			FRENCH			ENGLISH		
	Total	Male	Female	Total	Male	Female	Total	Male	Female
Urban	**988,738**	**464,065**	**524,673**	**292,564**	**144,357**	**148,207**	**696,174**	**319,708**	**376,466**
Reporting year of imm.	926,443	437,862	488,581	280,954	139,267	141,687	645,489	298,595	346,894
1925 to 1930	133,673	61,825	71,848	28,794	13,743	15,051	104,879	48,082	56,797
1920 to 1924	171,337	86,604	84,733	45,025	23,052	21,973	126,312	63,552	62,760
1915 to 1919	68,874	31,488	37,386	17,996	8,713	9,283	50,878	22,775	28,103
1911 to 1914	44,712	20,127	24,585	13,073	6,270	6,803	31,639	13,857	17,782
1901 to 1910	138,098	62,314	75,784	45,593	21,974	23,619	92,505	40,340	52,165
1900 or earlier	369,749	175,504	194,245	130,473	65,515	64,958	239,276	109,989	129,287
Not reporting	62,295	26,203	36,092	11,610	5,090	6,520	50,685	21,113	29,572
Per cent (of those reptg.)	100.0	100.0	100.0	100.0	100.0	100.0	100.0	100.0	100.0
1925 to 1930	14.4	14.1	14.7	10.2	9.9	10.6	16.2	16.1	16.4
1920 to 1924	18.5	19.8	17.3	16.0	16.6	15.5	19.6	21.3	18.1
1915 to 1919	7.4	7.2	7.7	6.4	6.3	6.6	7.9	7.6	8.1
1911 to 1914	4.8	4.6	5.0	4.7	4.5	4.8	4.9	4.6	5.1
1901 to 1910	14.9	14.2	15.5	16.2	15.8	16.7	14.3	13.5	15.0
1900 or earlier	39.9	40.1	39.8	46.4	47.0	45.8	37.1	36.8	37.3
Rural-nonfarm	**189,946**	**97,927**	**92,019**	**55,620**	**30,018**	**25,602**	**134,326**	**67,909**	**66,417**
Reporting year of imm.	173,727	90,208	83,519	52,742	28,597	24,145	120,985	61,611	59,374
1925 to 1930	17,556	8,797	8,759	4,980	2,596	2,384	12,576	6,201	6,375
1920 to 1924	25,601	13,350	12,251	7,581	4,042	3,539	18,020	9,308	8,712
1915 to 1919	11,707	5,731	5,976	3,415	1,739	1,676	8,292	3,992	4,300
1911 to 1914	8,439	4,192	4,247	2,667	1,414	1,253	5,772	2,778	2,994
1901 to 1910	25,633	12,880	12,753	8,189	4,292	3,897	17,444	8,588	8,856
1900 or earlier	84,791	45,258	39,533	25,910	14,514	11,396	58,881	30,744	28,137
Not reporting	16,219	7,719	8,500	2,878	1,421	1,457	13,341	6,298	7,043
Per cent (of those reptg.)	100.0	100.0	100.0	100.0	100.0	100.0	100.0	100.0	100.0
1925 to 1930	10.1	9.8	10.5	9.4	9.1	9.9	10.4	10.1	10.7
1920 to 1924	14.7	14.8	14.7	14.4	14.1	14.7	14.9	15.1	14.7
1915 to 1919	6.7	6.4	7.2	6.5	6.1	6.9	6.9	6.5	7.2
1911 to 1914	4.9	4.6	5.1	5.1	4.9	5.2	4.8	4.5	5.0
1901 to 1910	14.8	14.3	15.3	15.5	15.0	16.1	14.4	13.9	14.9
1900 or earlier	48.8	50.2	47.3	49.1	50.8	47.2	48.7	49.9	47.4
Rural-farm	**99,737**	**55,098**	**44,639**	**22,668**	**13,148**	**9,520**	**77,069**	**41,950**	**35,119**
Reporting year of imm.	90,985	50,835	40,150	21,564	12,565	8,999	69,421	38,270	31,151
1925 to 1930	7,763	4,209	3,554	2,322	1,277	1,045	5,441	2,932	2,509
1920 to 1924	10,077	5,455	4,622	2,746	1,521	1,225	7,331	3,934	3,397
1915 to 1919	6,790	3,558	3,232	2,120	1,181	939	4,670	2,377	2,293
1911 to 1914	4,203	2,175	2,028	1,126	593	533	3,077	1,582	1,495
1901 to 1910	11,126	5,785	5,341	2,536	1,391	1,145	8,590	4,394	4,196
1900 or earlier	51,026	29,653	21,373	10,714	6,602	4,112	40,312	23,051	17,261
Not reporting	8,752	4,263	4,489	1,104	583	521	7,648	3,680	3,968
Per cent (of those reptg.)	100.0	100.0	100.0	100.0	100.0	100.0	100.0	100.0	100.0
1925 to 1930	8.5	8.3	8.9	10.8	10.2	11.6	7.8	7.7	8.1
1920 to 1924	11.1	10.7	11.5	12.7	12.1	13.6	10.6	10.3	10.9
1915 to 1919	7.5	7.0	8.0	9.8	9.4	10.4	6.7	6.2	7.4
1911 to 1914	4.6	4.3	5.1	5.2	4.7	5.9	4.4	4.1	4.8
1901 to 1910	12.2	11.4	13.3	11.8	11.1	12.7	12.4	11.5	13.5
1900 or earlier	56.1	58.3	53.2	49.7	52.5	45.7	58.1	60.2	55.4

In the whole number of French Canadian born enumerated in 1930, there were 102.3 males per 100 females; among those who had arrived prior to 1901, the sex ratio was 107.7; and among those arriving between

1920 and 1924, 107.0. Lower ratios were shown for the other periods of immigration, ranging from 96.5 to 97.8 in the period from 1901 to 1919, and materially lower for the years subsequent to 1926.

Among the English Canadian born as a whole there were only 89.9 males per 100 females. Among those who arrived in the United States prior to 1901, there were 93.8; among those who arrived between 1920 and 1924, 102.6; among those who arrived in the years 1925 and 1926, 97.0; and in the other groups classified on the basis of year of immigration, 84.0 or less.

TABLE **38**. SEX RATIOS FOR THE CANADIAN BORN, BY YEAR OF IMMIGRATION, FOR URBAN AND RURAL AREAS: 1930

(Sex ratio not shown where number of females is less than 100)

YEAR OF IMMI-GRATION	TOTAL			URBAN			RURAL-NONFARM			RURAL-FARM		
	Total	Fr.	Eng.	Total	Fr.	Eng.	Total	Fr.	Eng.	Total	Fr.	Eng.
Total......	93.3	102.3	89.9	88.4	97.4	84.9	106.4	117.2	102.2	123.4	138.1	119.5
Reporting year of imm....	94.6	103.2	91.1	89.6	98.3	86.1	108.0	118.4	103.8	126.6	139.6	122.9
1925 to 1930..	88.9	95.3	87.1	86.0	91.3	84.7	100.4	108.9	97.3	118.4	122.2	116.9
1930, to Apr.	79.0	85.5	77.3	71.2	72.3	70.9	110.6	...	104.6	142.1	...	139.8
1929......	81.5	93.2	78.2	76.5	84.4	74.4	104.0	123.0	96.1	124.8	140.1	118.0
1928......	81.7	90.6	79.2	78.3	84.9	76.7	92.3	105.9	87.4	112.6	121.1	108.3
1927......	81.2	90.8	78.5	77.4	85.6	75.2	98.5	111.3	93.4	115.7	113.3	116.8
1925, 1926..	97.7	100.0	97.0	96.4	98.9	95.6	102.0	101.6	102.1	117.5	116.1	117.9
1920 to 1924..	103.7	107.0	102.6	102.2	104.9	101.3	109.0	114.2	106.8	118.0	124.2	115.8
1915 to 1919..	87.5	97.8	84.0	84.2	93.9	81.0	95.9	103.8	92.8	110.1	125.8	103.7
1911 to 1914..	85.9	96.4	81.8	81.9	92.2	77.9	98.7	112.8	92.8	107.2	111.3	105.8
1901 to 1910..	86.3	96.5	81.8	82.2	93.0	77.3	101.0	110.1	97.0	108.3	121.5	104.7
1900 & earlier	98.1	107.7	93.8	90.4	100.9	85.1	114.5	127.4	109.3	138.7	160.6	133.5
Not reporting..	77.8	83.5	76.6	72.6	78.1	71.4	90.8	97.5	89.4	95.0	111.9	92.7

The usual differences in the sex ratio as between the urban and rural areas are somewhat accentuated in the case of some of the groups based on year of immigration. For the French Canadian born who arrived in 1900 or earlier, the sex ratio in the rural-farm areas was 160.6; in the rural-nonfarm, 127.4; and in the urban, 100.9. For the English Canadian born the corresponding ratios were 133.5, 109.3, and 85.1. For the group comprising persons who arrived from 1920 to 1924, the relations are similar, though with a smaller difference between the sex ratios of the French and the English in each area.

NET INCREASE AND YEAR OF IMMIGRATION

AN interesting study of the relation between the net increase and the number of Canadian born in the United States between 1920 and 1930 and the data for persons reported in 1930 as having arrived during this intercensal period is presented in Table 39.

TABLE **39**. RELATION BETWEEN NET INCREASE OF CANADIAN-BORN WHITE POPULATION
IN THE UNITED STATES FROM 1920 TO 1930, AND 1930 CLASSIFICATION BY YEAR
OF IMMIGRATION

ITEM	Total	French	English
1. Population 1930 (April 1).....................................	1,278,421	370,852	907,569
2. Population 1920 (January 1).................................	1,117,878	307,786	810,092
3. Net increase, 1920–1930....................................	160,543	63,066	97,477
4. Estimated mortality*.......................................	195,629	53,863	141,766
5. Total net immigration to the United States†....................	356,172	116,929	239,243
6. Number reported in 1930 as having arrived between January 1, 1920, and April 1, 1930..	366,007	91,448	274,559
7. Additional number not reporting year of immigration but estimated to have arrived between January 1, 1920, and April 1, 1930‡......	27,512	4,016	23,496
8. Estimated total number enumerated in 1930 who had arrived between January 1, 1920, and April 1, 1930.....................	393,519	95,464	298,055
9. Estimated net re-immigration§..............................	......	21,465	......
10. Estimated exchange migration ‖	37,347	.....	58,812

*Mortality estimated to be 17.5 per cent of the population at the beginning of the period; this rate obtained by applying 1920–29 life table for U. S. Registration States of 1920 to estimated 1920 age distribution of Canadian born in the United States.

†Note that loss by mortality must be made up by new immigration before there can be any net increase in the number of Canadian born in the United States.

‡Figures obtained by assigning to the period 1920–30 the same proportion of those not reporting year of immigration as of those reporting.

§Excess of net immigration to the United States (Item 5) over estimated number enumerated as having arrived in the United States for the *first time* during the intercensal period. Assumed to be persons who had been in the United States before and who returned (re-immigrated) between 1920 and 1930 but reported the time of their first arrival as year of immigration.

‖ Excess of estimated number enumerated as having arrived in the United States during the intercensal period (Item 8) over net immigration to the United States (Item 5). Assumed to represent arrivals during the decade whose coming was offset by the return to Canada of other Canadian-born persons.

The first new item in this table is Item 4, the estimated mortality among the Canadian born in the United States during the intercensal period beginning January 1, 1920, and ending April 1, 1930, which is computed on the basis of 17.5 per cent of the number at the beginning of the period. This rate was derived by applying the age-specific survival rate of the white population of the United States Registration States of 1920 taken from the life table for 1920–29 to the estimated age distribution of the Canadian-born white population of the United States in 1920. The 1920 age distribution was derived by straight-line interpolation between available age distributions for 1910 and 1930. The rates were calculated separately for males and females and the two combined as a weighted mean.

Item 4, the estimated mortality, is added to the net increase to obtain the total immigration, since a number of new immigrants equal to the mortality would be required even to maintain the number of Canadian born in the United States as it was without any increase. Thus we add to the net increase of 160,543, as shown by the census, the estimated number of deaths during the decade, amounting to 195,629, making a total of 356,172, which represents the estimated net immigration of Canadian born into the United States between 1920 and 1930, that is, the number who must have come in in order to provide replacements for deaths and produce the increase represented by the excess of the 1930 census count over that of 1920.

Item 6 represents the number of Canadian born who reported in the 1930 census, in response to the inquiry on year of immigration, that they had arrived in the United States for the first time during some year between 1920 and 1930, that is, between January 1, 1920, and April 1, 1930. Since a considerable number failed to answer this question, it seemed necessary to supplement the actual returns for the 1920–30 period by adding a portion of the number of persons (87,266) for whom the direct information on year of immigration was missing. Item 7 provides this supplement, computed by taking the same proportion of the number not reporting year of immigration that Item 6 forms of the number reporting. Item 8, which is the sum of Items 6 and 7, therefore represents an estimate of the whole number of Canadian born in the United States who would have reported arrival between 1920 and 1930 if the returns on this question had been complete.

Item 8 may now be compared with Item 5, the net immigration during the decade. From this comparison it appears that the number of Canadian born enumerated in the 1930 census as having arrived in the United States between January 1, 1920, and April 1, 1930, which amounted to 393,519, exceeded by 37,347 the net immigration of the Canadian born to the United States during the same period. In other words, the number of Canadian born in the United States in 1930 who had arrived during the decade just preceding the census was 37,347 more than the net increase in Canadian born plus the number required to replace all the Canadian born in the United States who had died during that decade.

There is a possibility of some inaccuracy in the returns for year of immigration and also of a small understatement in the estimated number of deaths of Canadian born during the decade. Both of these errors together, however, would not be likely to amount to more than a few thousand. Even after allowance for such possible errors, therefore, there would still remain a substantial number of persons reported as having arrived between 1920 and 1930 in excess of the decade's net increase plus those required to replace deaths. The explanation suggested by the heading of Item 10 in the table, namely, "exchange migration," is that 37,347 Canadian-born persons who had arrived in the United States prior to 1920 returned to Canada during the decade, and that their places were taken by additional new arrivals from Canada.[1]

1. The assumptions involved in the concept of exchange migration, both here, where an attempt is made to apply to it an approximate numerical measurement, and in other connections where it is used in a more general sense to explain changes in population groups between one census and another, are supported by figures published in the re-

It may be noted that for the French Canadians alone the balance is in the other direction; that is, the number of French Canadian born in the United States reported as having arrived between 1920 and 1930 was less by 21,465 than the net increase in French Canadian born plus the number required for replacement of mortality. This difference can perhaps be explained as representing the re-immigration of 21,465 French Canadian born who had first come to the United States at an earlier date and then gone back to Canada. (Such persons would report the date of their first arrival in response to the question on year of immigration, and would contribute to the net increase in French Canadian born without contributing to the number reporting year of immigration between 1920 and 1930.) For the English Canadian born taken alone the amount of exchange immigration required to make the figures balance is of course greater than the figure just quoted for the total Canadian born by the amount of this reverse movement of French Canadian born.

DATA FOR STATES

THE statistics of the Canadian born in the United States by year of immigration are presented by States in four tables as follows: In Table 40, the number of Canadian born; in Table 41, the percentage reporting arrival in each period, supplemented by the median year of immigration and the years in which each State had the maximum percentage of Canadian born in its population (these last based on the historical figures in Tables 9 and 10); and in Tables 42 and 43 for the French and English Canadian born, respectively, both numbers and percentages, for 29 selected States. The percentages reporting arrival in each of the periods are shown graphically for the 13 States having 25,000 or more Canadian born in Figure 22.

The medians in Table 41 are necessarily computed on the assumption that the population reported for a given period is distributed evenly over the period. The medians are given only in full years, dropping the fractional parts shown by the computation, since the concept of a fraction of an ordinal number, while theoretically valid in a situation like this, seems rather difficult to visualize.

In the interpretation of the figures in Table 40 it should be remembered that the numbers of Canadian born reporting in 1930 that they came to the United States in 1900 or earlier must represent the survivors

ports of the Canadian immigration office. During the 6 years from 1925 to 1930, for example, according to the 1936 report of the Department of Immigration and Colonization, more than 200,000 Canadian-born citizens of Canada returned from the United States to Canada.

of much larger numbers of Canadian born who were in the United States in 1900.

FIGURE 22. CANADIAN BORN BY YEAR OF IMMIGRATION, FOR 13 SELECTED STATES: 1930

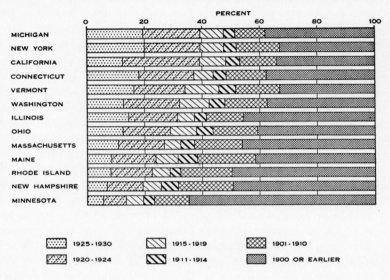

In fact, applying roughly the general method set forth for a single decade in the discussion of Table 39, above, we may compute the survivors in 1930 of the 1,172,860 Canadian-born white in the United States in 1900 at 660,000 and note that the 505,556 Canadian born who reported in 1930 that they had come to the United States in 1900 or earlier, or even this number increased by a proportionate share of the "not reporting" group, which might bring it up to 531,000, still falls short by about 129,000 of equaling the computed survivors from the 1900 Canadian-born population. It must be assumed then that considerable numbers of the Canadian born who were in the United States in 1900 had returned to Canada prior to 1930; and the 129,000 shortage just mentioned may be taken as a rough indication of the extent of this return movement.

A similar computation for 1910 shows an excess of survivors over the number enumerated in 1930 who reported arrival prior to 1920 amounting to about 94,000; and the parallel figure for 1920, as given in Table 39, is 37,347.

Against this background it may be noted that while in most States the number of Canadian born reporting arrival in 1900 or earlier represents a reasonable proportion (something less than one-half) of the Canadian-born white population of 1900, there are two States, California and Florida, in which those reported in 1930 as survivors from 1900 exceeded the number of Canadian born in the State in 1900. This was obviously the result of the migration of Canadian born from other parts of the United States into California and Florida. In a number of other States, notably Washington and Oregon, the number of Canadian born reporting arrival in 1900 or earlier considerably exceeds the expected ratio, while on the other hand there are several States in the Middle West where the 1900 survivors reported in 1930 represent not more than one-quarter or one-third of the 1900 population, thus suggesting either migration from these States to other parts of the United States or return to Canada.

Returning to a consideration of the data on year of immigration taken by themselves, without relation to other statistics, one may note that certain blocks of States can be grouped together on the basis of the percentage of Canadian born reporting arrival in the United States in 1900 or earlier. The northeastern States, running as far west as Michigan, show less than 50 per cent in this class, with several States well under 40 per cent. The Midwestern States, including Wisconsin, range from 60 to 75 per cent. The Mountain States, except Utah and Arizona, show more than 50 per cent; and the Pacific States all less than 40 per cent. Conversely, some of the eastern industrial States, notably Connecticut and New York, show nearly 40 per cent of their Canadian-born population as having arrived in the last decade, that is, between 1920 and 1930.

The French Canadian born in general reported somewhat larger proportions as having arrived in the earlier years than did the English Canadian born but this relationship is not by any means uniformly maintained in the individual States. In Maine, New Hampshire, and Vermont, in particular, the percentages of the French Canadian born reporting arrival in 1900 or earlier were considerably smaller than the corresponding percentages of the English Canadian born, while in the other eastern States they were appreciably larger and in the Pacific Coast States much larger.

TABLE **40**. CANADIAN-BORN WHITE POPULATION BY YEAR OF IMMIGRATION, BY STATES: 1930

DIVISION AND STATE	Total	REPORTING YEAR OF IMMIGRATION							Not reporting
		Total	1925 to 1930	1920 to 1924	1915 to 1919	1911 to 1914	1901 to 1910	1900 or earlier	
United States....	1,278,421	1,191,155	158,992	207,015	87,371	57,354	174,857	505,566	87,266
NEW ENGLAND:									
Maine............	73,743	69,511	5,694	10,846	5,396	4,782	13,822	28,971	4,232
New Hampshire.....	50,959	48,610	3,251	6,178	2,967	3,012	9,204	23,998	2,349
Vermont..........	27,182	26,581	4,351	4,725	3,035	1,642	3,989	8,839	601
Massachusetts......	288,051	278,394	30,242	44,297	16,239	12,944	46,888	127,784	9,657
Rhode Island......	39,278	38,501	3,088	5,544	2,398	1,482	6,887	19,102	777
Connecticut........	37,808	36,314	6,549	6,966	2,367	1,593	5,196	13,643	1,494
MIDDLE ATLANTIC:									
New York..........	147,874	136,143	27,253	26,475	10,764	6,402	19,965	45,284	11,731
New Jersey.........	16,521	14,796	2,672	2,694	1,388	787	2,308	4,947	1,725
Pennsylvania.......	16,352	14,169	1,762	2,455	1,304	801	2,231	5,616	2,183
EAST NORTH CENTRAL:									
Ohio..............	26,847	24,318	3,013	4,008	2,239	1,305	3,823	9,930	2,529
Indiana............	6,201	5,147	815	1,047	360	179	635	2,111	1,054
Illinois............	43,589	38,889	5,599	6,553	2,391	1,472	5,077	17,797	4,700
Michigan..........	202,316	192,498	37,688	38,149	15,143	7,729	20,239	73,550	9,818
Wisconsin..........	15,572	13,361	799	1,069	641	422	1,266	9,164	2,211
WEST NORTH CENTRAL:									
Minnesota..........	27,102	25,232	1,341	2,093	1,458	954	3,034	16,352	1,870
Iowa..............	6,333	5,621	233	355	229	182	503	4,119	712
Missouri...........	5,412	4,538	319	385	283	169	606	2,776	874
North Dakota.......	12,241	11,177	557	582	508	429	1,414	7,687	1,064
South Dakota.......	3,351	2,798	100	156	146	69	267	2,060	553
Nebraska..........	4,378	3,751	140	206	177	130	380	2,718	627
Kansas............	4,037	3,533	169	200	171	78	263	2,652	504
SOUTH ATLANTIC:									
Delaware..........	460	367	46	50	42	19	72	138	93
Maryland..........	2,266	1,757	264	320	173	110	279	611	509
Dist. of Columbia....	1,681	1,348	135	165	131	78	218	621	333
Virginia...........	1,617	1,275	111	130	163	106	209	556	342
West Virginia......	957	750	113	119	100	40	116	262	207
North Carolina.....	930	702	77	126	59	38	121	281	228
South Carolina.....	278	196	19	23	31	9	31	83	82
Georgia...........	1,094	858	122	108	108	54	137	329	236
Florida............	8,156	7,045	1,162	1,340	687	400	817	2,639	1,111
EAST SOUTH CENTRAL:									
Kentucky..........	918	722	77	122	51	41	104	327	196
Tennessee..........	939	657	61	84	53	27	91	341	282
Alabama..........	902	706	55	116	67	38	109	321	196
Mississippi.........	351	244	15	20	12	13	45	139	107
WEST SOUTH CENTRAL:									
Arkansas..........	695	504	35	57	25	22	70	295	191
Louisiana..........	981	753	46	91	65	41	131	379	228
Oklahoma.........	2,119	1,608	101	140	113	82	195	977	511
Texas..............	4,525	3,662	448	470	286	209	563	1,686	863
MOUNTAIN:									
Montana...........	10,753	9,563	676	705	848	841	1,575	4,918	1,190
Idaho.............	4,502	3,945	384	520	263	186	616	1,976	557
Wyoming..........	1,136	946	49	94	87	66	123	527	190
Colorado..........	5,816	4,900	177	315	334	175	668	3,231	916
New Mexico.......	613	507	31	48	35	26	79	288	106
Arizona...........	2,018	1,697	159	221	132	107	291	787	321
Utah..............	1,190	1,028	88	141	81	70	190	458	162
Nevada...........	952	868	79	77	62	40	134	476	84
PACIFIC:									
Washington.........	48,064	41,835	5,368	8,085	4,248	2,328	6,097	15,709	6,229
Oregon............	17,916	16,020	1,745	3,707	1,274	906	2,095	6,293	1,896
California..........	101,445	92,810	11,714	24,638	8,237	4,719	11,684	31,818	8,635

TABLE **41**. CANADIAN-BORN WHITE POPULATION—PER CENT DISTRIBUTION BY YEAR OF IMMIGRATION, MEDIAN YEAR OF IMMIGRATION, AND YEAR OF MAXIMUM CANADIAN BORN, BY STATES: 1930

(Percentages based on total reporting year of immigration)

DIVISION AND STATE	PER CENT ARRIVING IN SPECIFIED YEAR						MEDIAN YEAR OF IMMIGRA-TION	YEAR OF MAXIMUM CANADIAN BORN SINCE 1850	
	1925 to 1930	1920 to 1924	1915 to 1919	1911 to 1914	1901 to 1910	1900 or earlier		Maximum number	Maximum percentage
United States.	**13.3**	**17.4**	**7.3**	**4.8**	**14.7**	**42.4**	**1906**	**1930**	**1890**
NEW ENGLAND:									
Maine.........	8.2	15.6	7.8	6.9	19.9	41.7	1905	1910	1910
New Hampshire.	6.7	12.7	6.1	6.2	18.9	49.4	1901	1900	1900
Vermont.......	16.4	17.8	11.4	6.2	15.0	33.3	1912	1870	1870
Massachusetts..	10.9	15.9	5.8	4.6	16.8	45.9	1903	1910	1900
Rhode Island...	8.0	14.4	6.2	3.8	17.9	49.6	1901	1910	1900
Connecticut....	18.0	19.2	6.5	4.4	14.3	37.6	1909	1930	1900
MIDDLE ATLANTIC:									
New York......	20.0	19.4	7.9	4.7	14.7	33.3	1912	1930	1870
New Jersey.....	18.1	18.2	9.4	5.3	15.6	33.4	1911	1930	1930
Pennsylvania...	12.4	17.3	9.2	5.7	15.7	39.6	1907	1930	1880
EAST N. CENTRAL:									
Ohio..........	12.4	16.5	9.2	5.4	15.7	40.8	1906	1930	1900
Indiana........	15.8	20.3	7.0	3.5	12.3	41.0	1908	1930	1870
Illinois........	14.4	16.9	6.1	3.8	13.1	45.8	1904	1900	1870
Michigan.......	19.6	19.8	7.9	4.0	10.5	38.2	1912	1930	1880
Wisconsin......	6.0	8.0	4.8	3.2	9.5	68.6	*	1900	1850
WEST N. CENTRAL:									
Minnesota......	5.3	8.3	5.8	3.8	12.0	64.8	*	1900	1850
Iowa..........	4.1	6.3	4.1	3.2	8.9	73.3	*	1880	1870
Missouri.......	7.0	8.5	6.2	3.7	13.4	61.2	*	1880	1870
North Dakota...	5.0	5.2	4.5	3.8	12.7	68.8	*	1900	1860
South Dakota...	3.6	5.6	5.2	2.5	9.5	73.6	*	1890	1860
Nebraska......	3.7	5.5	4.7	3.5	10.1	72.5	*	1890	1870
Kansas........	4.8	5.7	4.8	2.2	7.4	75.1	*	1880	1870
SOUTH ATLANTIC:									
Delaware......	12.5	13.6	11.4	5.2	19.6	37.6	1907	1910	1910
Maryland......	15.0	18.2	9.8	6.3	15.9	34.8	1910	1930	1930
Dist. of Columbia	10.0	12.2	9.7	5.8	16.2	46.1	1903	1930	1920
Virginia........	8.7	10.2	12.8	8.3	16.4	43.6	1903	1920	1920
West Virginia...	15.1	15.9	13.3	5.3	15.5	34.9	1910	1920	1900
North Carolina..	11.0	17.9	8.4	5.4	17.2	40.0	1905	1930	1880
South Carolina..	9.7	11.7	15.8	4.6	15.8	42.3	1905	1910	1910
Georgia........	14.2	12.6	12.6	6.3	16.0	38.3	1908	1930	1930
Florida........	16.5	19.0	9.8	5.7	11.6	37.5	1911	1930	1930
EAST S. CENTRAL:									
Kentucky......	10.7	16.9	7.1	5.7	14.4	45.3	1904	1900	1870
Tennessee......	9.3	12.8	8.1	4.1	13.9	51.9	*	1910	1890
Alabama.......	7.8	16.4	9.5	5.4	15.4	45.5	1903	1930	1890
Mississippi.....	6.1	8.2	4.9	5.3	18.4	57.0	*	1910	1870
WEST S. CENTRAL:									
Arkansas.......	6.9	11.3	5.0	4.4	13.9	58.5	*	1900	1880
Louisiana......	6.1	12.1	8.6	5.4	17.4	50.3	*	1910	1860
Oklahoma......	6.3	8.7	7.0	5.1	12.1	60.8	*	1910	1900
Texas..........	12.2	12.8	7.8	5.7	15.4	46.0	1903	1930	1880
MOUNTAIN:									
Montana.......	7.1	7.4	8.9	8.8	16.5	51.4	*	1920	1880
Idaho..........	9.7	13.2	6.7	4.7	15.6	50.1	*	1910	1870
Wyoming......	5.2	9.9	9.2	7.0	13.0	55.7	*	1920	1870
Colorado.......	3.6	6.4	6.8	3.6	13.6	65.9	*	1900	1880
New Mexico....	6.1	9.5	6.9	5.1	15.6	56.8	*	1910	1890
Arizona........	9.4	13.0	7.8	6.3	17.1	46.4	1903	1930	1870
Utah..........	8.6	13.7	7.9	6.8	18.5	44.6	1903	1910	1850
Nevada........	9.1	8.9	7.1	4.6	15.4	54.8	*	1880	1870
PACIFIC:									
Washington....	12.8	19.3	10.2	5.6	14.6	37.5	1909	1930	1890
Oregon........	10.9	23.1	8.0	5.7	13.1	39.3	1909	1930	1850
California......	12.6	26.5	8.9	5.1	12.6	34.3	1913	1930	1880

*1900 or earlier.

TABLE **42**. FRENCH CANADIAN-BORN POPULATION, BY YEAR OF IMMIGRATION, FOR 29 SELECTED STATES: 1930

STATE	Total	REPORTING YEAR OF IMMIGRATION							Not reporting
		Total	1925 to 1930	1920 to 1924	1915 to 1919	1911 to 1914	1901 to 1910	1900 or earlier	
United States.........	370,852	355,260	36,096	55,352	23,531	16,866	56,318	167,097	15,592
Maine...............	36,947	35,444	2,468	6,331	3,049	2,778	6,787	14,031	1,503
New Hampshire...........	37,682	36,444	2,395	4,976	2,318	2,391	7,000	17,364	1,238
Vermont.............	17,320	16,998	3,222	3,500	2,167	1,045	2,331	4,733	322
Massachusetts...........	115,241	112,139	6,823	15,938	6,444	4,743	19,401	58,790	3,102
Rhode Island.........	31,501	30,959	2,164	4,419	1,969	1,151	5,655	15,601	542
Connecticut...........	25,570	24,825	4,345	5,040	1,529	980	3,448	9,483	745
New York...........	28,955	26,962	5,622	4,992	1,952	1,148	3,679	9,569	1,993
New Jersey.............	2,470	2,240	362	413	196	130	366	773	230
Pennsylvania.............	1,911	1,665	212	268	154	93	259	679	246
Ohio.................	2,606	2,365	222	343	196	115	363	1,126	241
Indiana...............	682	564	53	94	28	14	60	315	118
Illinois.................	6,189	5,596	647	704	294	182	660	3,109	593
Michigan.............	28,539	27,274	5,651	4,922	1,522	803	2,291	12,085	1,265
Wisconsin.............	4,292	3,850	79	111	64	67	280	3,249	442
Minnesota.............	6,484	6,143	108	282	191	156	666	4,740	341
Iowa..............	608	508	6	28	9	22	53	390	100
Missouri.............	588	515	39	40	26	25	68	317	73
North Dakota...........	1,354	1,266	55	34	34	43	183	917	88
South Dakota...........	492	411	7	18	14	7	41	324	81
Nebraska.............	436	362	6	11	17	14	49	265	74
Kansas.............	569	514	16	19	13	7	47	412	55
Florida.............	985	860	158	171	60	39	105	327	125
Texas.............	452	381	40	34	28	17	62	200	71
Montana.............	1,966	1,782	64	77	96	127	283	1,135	184
Idaho.............	571	531	40	49	22	21	80	319	40
Colorado.............	572	475	15	17	29	19	73	322	97
Washington.............	4,340	3,888	321	556	289	197	533	1,992	452
Oregon.............	1,345	1,220	85	189	71	63	205	607	125
California.............	7,657	7,020	707	1,493	600	362	948	2,910	637
Per cent:									
United States...........	...	100.0	10.2	15.6	6.6	4.7	15.9	47.0	...
Maine.............	...	100.0	7.0	17.9	8.6	7.8	19.1	39.6	...
New Hampshire...........	...	100.0	6.6	13.7	6.4	6.6	19.2	47.6	...
Vermont.............	...	100.0	19.0	20.6	12.7	6.1	13.7	27.8	...
Massachusetts...........	...	100.0	6.1	14.2	5.7	4.2	17.3	52.4	...
Rhode Island.........	...	100.0	7.0	14.3	6.4	3.7	18.3	50.4	...
Connecticut...........	...	100.0	17.5	20.3	6.2	3.9	13.9	38.2	...
New York...........	...	100.0	20.9	18.5	7.2	4.3	13.6	35.5	...
New Jersey.............	...	100.0	16.2	18.4	8.7	5.8	16.3	34.5	...
Pennsylvania.............	...	100.0	12.7	16.1	9.2	5.6	15.6	40.8	...
Ohio.................	...	100.0	9.4	14.5	8.3	4.9	15.3	47.6	...
Indiana...............	...	100.0	9.4	16.7	5.0	2.5	10.6	55.9	...
Illinois.................	...	100.0	11.6	12.6	5.3	3.3	11.8	55.6	...
Michigan.............	...	100.0	20.7	18.0	5.6	2.9	8.4	44.3	...
Wisconsin.............	...	100.0	2.1	2.9	1.7	1.7	7.3	84.4	...
Minnesota.............	...	100.0	1.8	4.6	3.1	2.5	10.8	77.2	...
Iowa.............	...	100.0	1.2	5.5	1.8	4.3	10.4	76.8	...
Missouri.............	...	100.0	7.6	7.8	5.0	4.9	13.2	61.6	...
North Dakota...........	...	100.0	4.3	2.7	2.7	3.4	14.5	72.4	...
South Dakota...........	...	100.0	1.7	4.4	3.4	1.7	10.0	78.8	...
Nebraska.............	...	100.0	1.7	3.0	4.7	3.9	13.5	73.2	...
Kansas.............	...	100.0	3.1	3.7	2.5	1.4	9.1	80.2	...
Florida.............	...	100.0	18.4	19.9	7.0	4.5	12.2	38.0	...
Texas.............	...	100.0	10.5	8.9	7.3	4.5	16.3	52.5	...
Montana.............	...	100.0	3.6	4.3	5.4	7.1	15.9	63.7	...
Idaho.............	...	100.0	7.5	9.2	4.1	4.0	15.1	60.1	...
Colorado.............	...	100.0	3.2	3.6	6.1	4.0	15.4	67.8	...
Washington.............	...	100.0	8.3	14.3	7.4	5.1	13.7	51.2	...
Oregon.............	...	100.0	7.0	15.5	5.8	5.2	16.8	49.8	...
California.............	...	100.0	10.1	21.3	8.5	5.2	13.5	41.5	...

TABLE **43**. ENGLISH CANADIAN-BORN POPULATION, BY YEAR OF IMMIGRATION, FOR 29 SELECTED STATES: 1930

STATE	Total	REPORTING YEAR OF IMMIGRATION							Not report-ing
		Total	1925 to 1930	1920 to 1924	1915 to 1919	1911 to 1914	1901 to 1910	1900 or earlier	
United States.......	907,569	835,895	122,896	151,663	63,840	40,488	118,539	338,469	71,674
Maine...............	36,796	34,067	3,226	4,515	2,347	2,004	7,035	14,940	2,729
New Hampshire........	13,277	12,166	856	1,202	649	621	2,204	6,634	1,111
Vermont.............	9,862	9,583	1,129	1,225	868	597	1,658	4,106	279
Massachusetts........	172,810	166,255	23,419	28,359	9,795	8,201	27,487	68,994	6,555
Rhode Island.........	7,777	7,542	924	1,125	429	331	1,232	3,501	235
Connecticut.........	12,238	11,489	2,204	1,926	838	613	1,748	4,160	749
New York............	118,919	109,181	21,631	21,483	8,812	5,254	16,286	35,715	9,738
New Jersey..........	14,051	12,556	2,310	2,281	1,192	657	1,942	4,174	1,495
Pennsylvania.........	14,441	12,504	1,550	2,187	1,150	708	1,972	4,937	1,937
Ohio................	24,241	21,953	2,791	3,665	2,043	1,190	3,460	8,804	2,288
Indiana.............	5,519	4,583	762	953	332	165	575	1,796	936
Illinois.............	37,400	33,293	4,952	5,849	2,097	1,290	4,417	14,688	5,107
Michigan............	173,777	165,224	32,037	33,227	13,621	6,926	17,948	61,465	8,553
Wisconsin...........	11,280	9,511	720	958	577	355	986	5,915	1,769
Minnesota...........	20,618	19,089	1,233	1,811	1,267	798	2,368	11,612	1,529
Iowa................	5,725	5,113	227	327	220	160	450	3,729	612
Missouri............	4,824	4,023	280	345	257	144	538	2,459	801
North Dakota........	10,887	9,911	502	548	474	386	1,231	6,770	976
South Dakota........	2,859	2,387	93	138	132	62	226	1,736	472
Nebraska............	3,942	3,389	134	195	160	116	331	2,453	553
Kansas..............	3,468	3,019	153	181	158	71	216	2,240	449
Florida.............	7,171	6,185	1,004	1,169	627	361	712	2,312	986
Texas...............	4,073	3,281	408	436	258	192	501	1,486	792
Montana.............	8,787	7,781	612	628	752	714	1,292	3,783	1,006
Idaho...............	3,931	3,414	344	471	241	165	536	1,657	517
Colorado............	5,244	4,425	162	298	305	156	595	2,909	819
Washington..........	43,724	37,947	5,047	7,529	3,959	2,131	5,564	13,717	5,777
Oregon..............	16,571	14,800	1,660	3,518	1,203	843	1,890	5,686	1,771
California...........	93,788	85,790	11,007	23,145	7,637	4,357	10,736	28,908	7,998
Per cent:									
United States........	...	100.0	14.7	18.1	7.6	4.8	14.2	40.5	...
Maine...............	...	100.0	9.5	13.3	6.9	5.9	20.7	43.9	...
New Hampshire........	...	100.0	7.0	9.9	5.3	5.1	18.1	54.5	...
Vermont.............	...	100.0	11.8	12.8	9.1	6.2	17.3	42.8	...
Massachusetts........	...	100.0	14.1	17.1	5.9	4.9	16.5	41.5	...
Rhode Island.........	...	100.0	12.3	14.9	5.7	4.4	16.3	46.4	...
Connecticut.........	...	100.0	19.2	16.8	7.3	5.3	15.2	36.2	...
New York............	...	100.0	19.8	19.7	8.1	4.8	14.9	32.7	...
New Jersey..........	...	100.0	18.4	18.2	9.5	5.2	15.5	33.2	...
Pennsylvania.........	...	100.0	12.4	17.5	9.2	5.7	15.8	39.5	...
Ohio................	...	100.0	12.7	16.7	9.3	5.4	15.8	40.1	...
Indiana.............	...	100.0	16.6	20.8	7.2	3.6	12.5	39.2	...
Illinois.............	...	100.0	14.9	17.6	6.3	3.9	13.3	44.1	...
Michigan............	...	100.0	19.4	20.1	8.2	4.2	10.9	37.2	...
Wisconsin...........	...	100.0	7.6	10.1	6.1	3.7	10.4	62.2	...
Minnesota...........	...	100.0	6.5	9.5	6.6	4.2	12.4	60.8	...
Iowa................	...	100.0	4.4	6.4	4.3	3.1	8.8	72.9	...
Missouri............	...	100.0	7.0	8.6	6.4	3.6	13.4	61.1	...
North Dakota........	...	100.0	5.1	5.5	4.8	3.9	12.4	68.3	...
South Dakota........	...	100.0	3.9	5.8	5.5	2.6	9.5	72.7	...
Nebraska............	...	100.0	4.0	5.8	4.7	3.4	9.8	72.4	...
Kansas..............	...	100.0	5.1	6.0	5.2	2.4	7.2	74.2	...
Florida.............	...	100.0	16.2	18.9	10.1	5.8	11.5	37.4	...
Texas...............	...	100.0	12.4	13.3	7.9	5.9	15.3	45.3	...
Montana.............	...	100.0	7.9	8.1	9.7	9.2	16.6	48.6	...
Idaho...............	...	100.0	10.1	13.8	7.1	4.8	15.7	48.5	...
Colorado............	...	100.0	3.7	6.7	6.9	3.5	13.4	65.7	...
Washington..........	...	100.0	13.3	19.8	10.4	5.6	14.7	36.1	...
Oregon..............	...	100.0	11.2	23.8	8.1	5.7	12.8	38.4	...
California...........	...	100.0	12.8	27.0	8.9	5.1	12.5	33.7	...

CHAPTER VII

CITIZENSHIP OF THE CANADIAN BORN

In the classification of the foreign born by citizenship as presented in the reports of the United States census, three specific classes are distinguished, namely, (1) naturalized; (2) having first papers; and (3) alien, the last comprising those persons who have taken no steps toward acquiring citizenship in the United States. In addition, there is a fourth group, designated "Unknown" and made up of those persons for whom the enumerator secured no report with respect to citizenship. It is the practice for many purposes to include this last group with the aliens, partly because persons not naturalized would be somewhat more likely to fail to report than those naturalized, and partly because it seems best not to include any doubtful cases in the definite classification of naturalized citizens. In general, the number and percentage naturalized may be considered the most important figures shown in the citizenship tables.

The "first papers" constitute the declaration of intention to become a citizen of the United States, which declaration may be made by any eligible alien 18 years of age or over, at any time after his or her arrival in the United States. The process of naturalization cannot ordinarily be completed, however, until at least two years have elapsed after the declaration of intention, nor until the applicant has resided at least five years continuously in the United States; except that an alien woman who married a citizen of the United States subsequent to September 22, 1922, or one whose husband became naturalized after that date, may become naturalized without declaration of intention, and after only one year of residence. Minor children ordinarily become naturalized upon the naturalization of their father.

Since the tabulations of citizenship in combination with country of birth were made in 1930 for the foreign-born white only, the data presented herewith for the citizenship of the Canadian born are limited to the Canadian-born white, omitting the small number of nonwhite Canadian born in the United States. These data are summarized, by sex and for French and English Canadians, in Table 44.

Of the total Canadian-born white population of the United States in 1930, 658,557, or 51.5 per cent, were naturalized, and 109,062, or 8.5 per cent, had taken out their first papers. The number naturalized comprised 310,145 males and 348,412 females, these figures representing 50.3 per cent and 52.7 per cent of the respective totals and indicating that an appreciably higher proportion of the females were naturalized than of the males. More than twice as many males as females had taken out first papers, however, this class forming 12.6 per cent of all Canadian-born males, as compared with 4.7 per cent of Canadian-born females. This difference is presumably the result of the provision referred to above, under which a married woman may become naturalized without the formality of taking out first papers.

TABLE **44**. CANADIAN-BORN WHITE POPULATION IN THE UNITED STATES, FRENCH AND ENGLISH, BY CITIZENSHIP AND SEX: 1930

SEX AND CITIZENSHIP	ALL CANADIAN BORN		FRENCH		ENGLISH	
	Number	Per cent	Number	Per cent	Number	Per cent
Total......................	1,278,421	100.0	370,852	100.0	907,569	100.0
Naturalized......................	658,557	51.5	173,938	46.9	484,619	53.4
Having first papers.................	109,062	8.5	29,797	8.0	79,265	8.7
Alien..........................	444,624	34.8	154,002	41.5	290,622	32.0
Unknown.......................	66,178	5.2	13,115	3.5	53,063	5.8
Male......................	617,090	100.0	187,523	100.0	429,567	100.0
Naturalized......................	310,145	50.3	89,258	47.6	220,887	51.4
Having first papers.................	77,950	12.6	22,725	12.1	55,225	12.9
Alien..........................	197,408	32.0	69,354	37.0	128,054	29.8
Unknown.......................	31,587	5.1	6,186	3.3	25,401	5.9
Female......................	661,331	100.0	183,329	100.0	478,002	100.0
Naturalized......................	348,412	52.7	84,680	46.2	263,732	55.2
Having first papers.................	31,112	4.7	7,072	3.9	24,040	5.0
Alien..........................	247,216	37.4	84,648	46.2	162,568	34.0
Unknown.......................	34,591	5.2	6,929	3.8	27,662	5.8

The French Canadian born in the United States show a much lower percentage of naturalization than the English (46.9 as compared with 53.4), in spite of the fact that on the average they have been in the United States a much longer time. This is possibly a result of the fact that very many of the French Canadians in the United States cherish the expectation of eventual return to Canada, supplemented by the fact that as compared with the English Canadians a very large proportion of them live in compact communities of their own where they are not in constant association with the English-speaking population. On the other hand, a factor which would seem likely to encourage naturalization is that the French Canadian population in a number of American cities is sufficiently large to constitute an important element in local politics. Even in these cities, however, the percentage naturalized is relatively low.

Among the French Canadian born the percentage of males naturalized was slightly larger than the percentage of females—47.6 per cent for males as compared with 46.2 per cent for females. The percentage of males having first papers, however, was three times as large as the corresponding percentage for females.

Among the English Canadian born in the United States only 51.4 per cent of the males were naturalized, as compared with 55.2 per cent of the females. This excess in the percentage naturalized among the English Canadian females is more than enough to counteract the excess shown for the males among the French Canadians, and is thus responsible for the higher percentage naturalized shown for females as compared with males in the whole Canadian-born group. In the matter of first papers, the percentage shown for males is again much higher than that for females—12.9 as compared with 5.0.

The citizenship status of the Canadian-born population, male and female, French and English, is shown graphically in Figure 23.

FIGURE **23**. CANADIAN-BORN POPULATION, FRENCH AND ENGLISH, BY CITIZENSHIP AND SEX: 1930

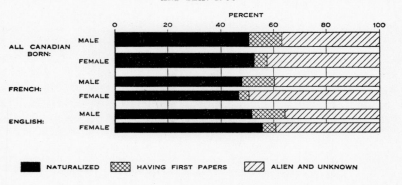

In Table 45, citizenship data are presented both for all Canadian born in the United States and for those 21 years old and over, with such comparative figures for earlier censuses as are available.

For all Canadian born in the United States the percentage naturalized decreased from 54.3 in 1920 to 51.5 in 1930. For the French Canadian born alone, however, there was an appreciable increase, from 44.8 to 46.9, while for the English Canadian born the percentage naturalized decreased from 57.9 in 1920 to 53.4 in 1930, though there was a material increase, from 6.0 to 8.7, in the percentage having first papers. Since the absolute number of English Canadians naturalized increased from 469,284 in 1920 to 484,619 in 1930, it may be assumed that the decline in the percentage was primarily the result of the arrival of additional English Canadian born in the United States; in fact, the tabulation by year of immigration indicates that 122,896 such persons arrived between 1925 and 1930, and most of these had not been in the United States long enough to become naturalized under the 5-year residence limitation.

Mainly, without doubt, because of this recent immigration, the number of English Canadian born classified as alien increased from 215,582 in 1920 to 290,622 in 1930—an increase of 34.8 per cent, as compared with an increase of only 3.3 in the number returned as naturalized. During the same period, however, there was an increase of 62.0 per cent in the number having first papers, which would indicate that these new arrivals were planning to become naturalized.

TABLE **45**. CANADIAN-BORN WHITE POPULATION, FRENCH AND ENGLISH, BY CITIZENSHIP, SEX, AND AGE (21 AND OVER): 1910 TO 1930

CENSUS YEAR, AGE, CLASS, AND SEX	Total	NATURALIZED		HAVING FIRST PAPERS		Alien	Un-known
		Number	Per cent	Number	Per cent		
ALL AGES							
1930: All Canadian born	**1,278,421**	**658,557**	**51.5**	**109,062**	**8.5**	**444,624**	**66,178**
Male	617,090	310,145	50.3	77,950	12.6	197,408	31,587
Female	661,331	348,412	52.7	31,112	4.7	247,216	34,591
French	370,852	173,938	46.9	29,797	8.0	154,002	13,115
Male	187,523	89,258	47.6	22,725	12.1	69,354	6,186
Female	183,329	84,680	46.2	7,072	3.9	84,648	6,929
English	907,569	484,619	53.4	79,265	8.7	290,622	53,063
Male	429,567	220,887	51.4	55,225	12.9	128,054	25,401
Female	478,002	263,732	55.2	24,040	5.0	162,568	27,662
1920: All Canadian born	**1,117,878**	**607,303**	**54.3**	**72,714**	**6.5**	**345,557**	**92,304**
Male	547,357	281,381	51.4	66,419	12.1	153,495	46,062
Female	570,521	325,922	57.1	6,295	1.1	192,062	46,242
French	307,786	138,019	44.8	23,777	7.7	129,975	16,015
Male	157,748	68,802	43.6	22,447	14.2	58,909	7,590
Female	150,038	69,217	46.1	1,330	0.9	71,066	8,425
English	810,092	469,284	57.9	48,937	6.0	215,582	76,289
Male	389,609	212,579	54.6	43,972	11.3	94,586	38,472
Female	420,483	256,705	61.1	4,965	1.2	120,996	37,817
21 YEARS OLD AND OVER							
1930: All Canadian born	**1,102,443**	**617,020**	**56.0**	**103,901**	**9.4**	**322,487**	**59,035**
Male	531,685	290,066	54.6	75,305	14.2	138,023	28,291
Female	570,758	326,954	57.3	28,596	5.0	184,464	30,744
French	329,153	167,196	50.8	28,842	8.8	121,142	11,973
Male	167,493	86,019	51.4	22,209	13.3	53,572	5,693
Female	161,660	81,177	50.2	6,633	4.1	67,570	6,280
English	773,290	449,824	58.2	75,059	9.7	201,345	47,062
Male	364,192	204,047	56.0	53,096	14.6	84,451	22,598
Female	409,098	245,777	60.1	21,963	5.4	116,894	24,464
1920: All Canadian born	**1,001,516**	**581,484**	**58.1**	**70,891**	**7.1**	**265,920**	**83,221**
Male	490,918	269,606	54.9	65,129	13.3	114,439	41,744
Female	510,598	311,878	61.1	5,762	1.1	151,481	41,477
French	274,176	132,981	48.5	23,176	8.5	103,573	14,446
Male	141,514	66,579	47.0	21,997	15.5	46,094	6,844
Female	132,662	66,402	50.1	1,179	0.9	57,479	7,602
English	727,340	448,503	61.7	47,715	6.6	162,347	68,775
Male	349,404	203,027	58.1	43,132	12.3	68,345	34,900
Female	377,936	245,476	65.0	4,583	1.2	94,002	33,875
1910: All Canadian-born males*	**533,359**	**271,762**	**51.0**	**26,150**	**4.9**	**150,718**	**84,729**
French	170,987	76,367	44.7	6,745	3.9	68,807	19,068
English	362,372	195,395	53.9	19,405	5.4	81,911	65,661

*Includes Newfoundland.

There was a very great difference as between 1920 and 1930 in the percentage of females classified as having first papers—an increase from 1.1 per cent in 1920 to 4.7 per cent in 1930. This is presumably the result of the change in the laws providing for naturalization of women. In 1920, married women were automatically naturalized upon the naturalization of their husbands and therefore had no occasion to take out first papers. In 1930, while married women could be naturalized without having taken out first papers, their naturalization was a separate process, and considerable numbers of them presumably did take out first papers, though the numbers, as already noted, fell far short of the numbers of males returned at the time of the census as having taken only this first step toward naturalization.

In general, citizenship figures for the population 21 years of age and over show the same relationships as those for the total population which have already been discussed, the principal difference being that because of the exclusion of persons under 21 years of age (of whom only about one-fourth are naturalized) from the base, the percentages naturalized are uniformly higher. For many purposes it may be preferable to use the figures based on the numbers of persons 21 years old and over, because these represent the population qualified, so far as concerns attained age, to exercise the rights and privileges of citizenship. For other purposes, including comparisons with other statistical presentations, most of which are not available separately for the population 21 years old and over, figures based upon the citizenship classification of the whole population may be more useful. Both series are presented in Tables 46 and 47, so that either may be used in accordance with the demands of any given situation.

While the 1910 citizenship tabulations were not so extensive as those made in 1920 or 1930, data are available for that year for males 21 years old and over. On this basis, therefore, it is possible to add one decade to the period for which comparisons can be made. The percentage of all Canadian-born males 21 years old and over in the United States in 1910 who were naturalized was 51.0, as compared with 54.9 in 1920, and 54.6 in 1930.

French Canadian-born males 21 years old and over show a steady increase in the percentage naturalized, from 44.7 per cent in 1910 to 47.0 in 1920 and 51.4 in 1930. English Canadian-born males likewise show an increase from 53.9 in 1910 to 58.1 in 1920, but a considerable decrease during the next decade, to 56.0 in 1930. The figures indicate a marked increase between 1910 and 1920 in the percentage having taken out first papers for both French and English Canadian born.

The citizenship tabulations of the 1900 census are not strictly comparable with those of later censuses, since the main item shown was the number of aliens rather than the number of persons naturalized. On the basis of these figures, however, it has been estimated that the percentage of French Canadian-born males 21 years old and over in the United States who were naturalized in 1900 was 52.3, or materially more than in 1910; and that the percentage of English Canadians naturalized was 54.2, or slightly more than in 1910.

COMPARISON WITH OTHER COUNTRIES

IN Table 46 are presented citizenship data for foreign-born white males 21 years old and over from selected foreign countries, for comparison with the Canadian data.

TABLE **46**. FOREIGN-BORN WHITE MALES 21 YEARS OLD AND OVER, BY CITIZENSHIP, FOR SELECTED COUNTRIES OF BIRTH: 1930

| COUNTRY OF BIRTH | Total | NATURALIZED | | HAVING FIRST PAPERS | | Alien | Un-known | Males, all ages, per cent naturalized |
		Number	Per cent	Number	Per cent			
All countries...	6,797,494	4,217,576	62.0	926,454	13.6	1,435,309	218,155	60.6
Canada, total........	531,685	290,066	54.6	75,305	14.2	138,023	28,291	50.3
French...........	167,493	86,019	51.4	22,209	13.3	53,572	5,693	47.6
English..........	364,192	204,047	56.0	53,096	14.6	84,451	22,598	51.4
England...........	391,838	272,566	69.6	46,307	11.8	56,671	16,294	67.8
Scotland..........	163,588	96,710	59.1	31,062	19.0	29,992	5,824	55.6
Ireland...........	394,845	278,889	70.6	48,576	12.0	47,353	19,997	69.3
Northern Ireland...	78,114	56,247	72.0	9,046	11.6	9,336	3,455	70.4
Irish Free State....	316,731	222,642	70.3	39,530	12.5	38,017	16,542	69.0
Norway...........	191,248	135,482	70.8	23,298	12.2	26,173	6,295	69.7
Sweden...........	326,663	235,680	72.1	39,475	12.1	41,881	9,627	71.1
Denmark..........	107,423	80,911	75.3	12,267	11.4	10,808	3,437	74.3
Germany..........	813,294	588,295	72.3	108,098	13.3	87,696	29,205	70.4
Poland............	656,348	363,922	55.4	110,597	16.9	169,496	12,333	55.1
Italy..............	986,531	545,729	55.3	119,191	12.1	299,015	22,596	54.6
Greece............	125,619	62,649	49.9	22,701	18.1	36,516	3,753	49.5

The citizenship status of the population 21 years old and over from the selected countries is presented in graphic form in Figure 24, in which the widths of the bars are adjusted to represent the relative numbers of persons in the United States from the several countries.

Among the countries selected for comparison, which include the principal European countries contributing to the population of the United States, there are a considerable number which show a percentage of naturalization much higher than Canada's 54.6. Denmark stands first on the list with 75.3, followed by Germany with 72.3; Sweden with 72.1; Norway with 70.8; and the Irish Free State with 70.3. All of these are countries from which the principal emigration to the United States took place at a relatively early date. This is evidenced by the year-of-immigration figures, which indicate that about 70 per cent or more of the whole number of persons from these countries who were in the United States in 1930 had arrived prior to 1911, as compared with only 57.1 per cent of those from Canada. The lower percentages naturalized which are shown for persons of Canadian birth are not, however, altogether explained by their more recent arrival. In fact, with respect to the two racial elements of the Canadian born themselves there is an inverse relation between time of arrival in the United States and percentage of naturalization. The French Canadian born, of whom 62.9 per cent had arrived before 1911, show a much lower proportion naturalized than the English Canadian born, of whom only 54.7 per cent had arrived prior to 1911.

FIGURE **24**. FOREIGN-BORN WHITE PERSONS 21 YEARS OLD AND OVER FROM SELECTED COUNTRIES, BY CITIZENSHIP: 1930

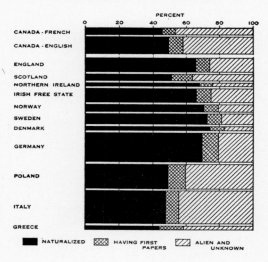

Another factor which has some bearing on the percentage naturalized is that of continued immigration, or the arrival of considerable numbers of new immigrants in recent years. A part of the explanation of the difference between the 59.1 per cent naturalized shown for persons from Scotland and the 70.3 per cent for persons from the Irish Free State may presumably lie in the fact that immigration from Scotland had continued up to 1930 on a relatively larger scale than that from Ireland. Since immigration from Canada has likewise continued on a relatively large scale, this factor would explain in part why the Canadian born should show a lower percentage naturalized than the foreign born from most European countries. It seems probable, however, that the principal reason (and one must have a very good reason in this case to offset the similarity of language and other common interests which would tend to encourage naturalization) is that very many of the Canadians come to the United States with the expectation of returning to Canada. Twenty-five or thirty years ago this was the situation also with many of the European immigrants, but under present conditions relatively few of the latter plan to return to their native countries. This factor would seem to explain also the lower percentage naturalized among the French Canadians than among the English, since there are indications that many more of the former than of the latter actually had returned to the country of their birth.

Urban and Rural Areas

Citizenship data for the Canadian born living in urban and rural areas in 1930 are presented in Table 47.

Table **47**. Canadian-Born White Population, French and English, by Citizenship and Sex, for Urban and Rural Areas: 1930

(For United States total see Table 45)

AREA, CLASS, AND SEX	ALL AGES					AGE 21 AND OVER				
	Total	Naturalized		Having first papers	Alien and un-known	Total	Naturalized		Having first papers	Alien and un-known
		Num-ber	Per cent				Num-ber	Per cent		
TOTAL										
Urban	988,738	496,382	50.2	92,152	400,204	851,722	464,645	54.6	87,803	299,274
Male	464,065	228,610	49.3	64,867	170,588	398,769	213,494	53.5	62,669	122,606
Female	524,673	267,772	51.0	27,285	229,616	452,953	251,151	55.4	25,134	176,668
Rural-nonfarm	189,946	102,073	53.7	12,096	75,777	165,633	96,230	58.1	11,559	57,844
Male	97,927	49,927	51.0	9,302	38,698	85,695	47,011	54.9	9,012	29,672
Female	92,019	52,146	56.7	2,794	37,079	79,938	49,219	61.6	2,547	28,172
Rural-farm	99,737	60,102	60.3	4,814	34,821	85,088	56,145	66.0	4,539	24,404
Male	55,098	31,608	57.4	3,781	19,709	47,221	29,561	62.6	3,624	14,036
Female	44,639	28,494	63.8	1,033	15,112	37,867	26,584	70.2	915	10,368
FRENCH										
Urban	292,564	137,728	47.1	24,789	130,047	260,445	132,479	50.9	24,003	103,963
Male	144,357	69,662	48.3	18,639	56,056	129,275	67,177	52.0	18,221	43,877
Female	148,207	68,066	45.9	6,150	73,991	131,170	65,302	49.8	5,782	60,086
Rural-nonfarm	55,620	25,269	45.4	3,583	26,768	49,523	24,251	49.0	3,488	21,784
Male	30,018	13,398	44.6	2,909	13,711	26,946	12,881	47.8	2,854	11,211
Female	25,602	11,871	46.4	674	13,057	22,577	11,370	50.4	634	10,573
Rural-farm	22,668	10,941	48.3	1,425	10,302	19,185	10,466	54.6	1,351	7,368
Male	13,148	6,198	47.1	1,177	5,773	11,272	5,961	52.9	1,134	4,177
Female	9,520	4,743	49.8	248	4,529	7,913	4,505	56.9	217	3,191
ENGLISH										
Urban	696,174	358,654	51.5	67,363	270,157	591,277	332,166	56.2	63,800	195,311
Male	319,708	158,948	49.7	46,228	114,532	269,494	146,317	54.3	44,448	78,729
Female	376,466	199,706	53.0	21,135	155,625	321,783	185,849	57.8	19,352	116,582
Rural-nonfarm	134,326	76,804	57.2	8,513	49,009	116,110	71,979	62.0	8,071	36,060
Male	67,909	36,529	53.8	6,393	24,987	58,749	34,130	58.1	6,158	18,461
Female	66,417	40,275	60.6	2,120	24,022	57,361	37,849	66.0	1,913	17,599
Rural-farm	77,069	49,161	63.8	3,389	24,519	65,903	45,679	69.3	3,188	17,036
Male	41,950	25,410	60.6	2,604	13,936	35,949	23,600	65.6	2,490	9,859
Female	35,119	23,751	67.6	785	10,583	29,954	22,079	73.7	698	7,177

With respect to the whole Canadian-born population in the United States, it may be stated that the percentage naturalized was highest in the rural-farm areas, next highest in the rural-nonfarm, and lowest in the urban areas. It may be more than a coincidence that these three areas stand in the same order and with somewhat the same margin of difference when classified on the basis of the percentage of their Canadian-born population which has been in the United States at least since 1900. (See Chapter VI, Year of Immigration.) The differences just indicated are shown even more positively by the English Canadian born who, after all, tend to dominate the total, by reason of being 2½ times as numerous as the French Canadian born.

Among the French Canadians as a whole the lowest percentage of naturalization was reported from the rural-nonfarm areas, with the urban figure almost as high as the rural-farm. For the males alone the relations were the same as for the total, but for the females the percentage naturalized in the rural-farm areas was again the highest, while the rural-nonfarm percentage was next and the urban percentage the lowest.

DATA FOR STATES

DATA on citizenship are presented by States in Table 48 for the Canadian-born population, French and English, and in graphic form for 13 States in Figure 25.

There was a very wide variation among the States in the proportion of the Canadian born returned in the 1930 census who were naturalized, the percentages ranging from 37.7 in Connecticut to 79.7 in North Dakota, an average of 51.5 for the United States as a whole. There is some correlation between the percentage naturalized in a given State and the percentage of the Canadian born in that State who had been in the United States 10 years or more, but the relationship is only a general one, with many deviations. In Connecticut, for example, with 62.8 per cent of its Canadian born reporting arrival before 1920 (see Table 41), 37.7 per cent were naturalized, while in New York, with a smaller percentage (60.6) reporting arrival before 1920, 49.2 per cent were naturalized.

As between the French and the English Canadians it may be noted that in those States where the numbers of French Canadian born were relatively large they show a decidedly lower percentage naturalized than the English Canadian born, while in the remaining States they show somewhat higher percentages naturalized. In Maine, for example, with practically the same number of French and English Canadians, 37.3 per cent of the former were naturalized as compared with 44.1 per cent of the latter; but in Washington and California, where the English Canadians

TABLE **48.** CANADIAN-BORN WHITE POPULATION, FRENCH AND ENGLISH, BY CITIZENSHIP, BY STATES: 1930

(Per cent not shown where base is less than 100)

DIVISION AND STATE	ALL CANADIAN BORN			FRENCH			ENGLISH		
	Number	Naturalized		Number	Naturalized		Number	Naturalized	
		Number	Per cent		Number	Per cent		Number	Per cent
United States...	**1,278,421**	**658,557**	**51.5**	**370,852**	**173,938**	**46.9**	**907,569**	**484,619**	**53.4**
NEW ENGLAND:									
Maine...........	73,743	30,000	40.7	36,947	13,786	37.3	36,796	16,214	44.1
New Hampshire..	50,959	24,583	48.2	37,682	16,800	44.6	13,277	7,783	58.6
Vermont........	27,182	11,625	42.8	17,320	6,319	36.5	9,862	5,306	53.8
Massachusetts ...	288,051	138,082	47.9	115,241	51,974	45.1	172,810	86,108	49.8
Rhode Island....	39,278	21,117	53.8	31,501	16,455	52.2	7,777	4,662	59.9
Connecticut.....	37,808	14,272	37.7	25,570	8,456	33.1	12,238	5,816	47.5
MIDDLE ATLANTIC:									
New York......	147,874	72,734	49.2	28,955	13,402	46.3	118,919	59,332	49.9
New Jersey......	16,521	8,752	53.0	2,470	1,279	51.8	14,051	7,473	53.2
Pennsylvania....	16,352	9,451	57.8	1,911	1,087	56.9	14,441	8,364	57.9
E. NORTH CENTRAL:									
Ohio...........	26,847	16,354	60.9	2,606	1,635	62.7	24,241	14,719	60.7
Indiana........	6,201	3,321	53.6	682	411	60.3	5,519	2,910	52.7
Illinois.........	43,589	26,329	60.4	6,189	4,053	65.5	37,400	22,276	59.6
Michigan.......	202,316	102,952	50.9	28,539	14,760	51.7	173,777	88,192	50.8
Wisconsin......	15,572	10,615	68.2	4,292	3,125	72.8	11,280	7,490	66.4
W. NORTH CENTRAL:									
Minnesota......	27,102	20,765	76.6	6,484	5,291	81.6	20,618	15,474	75.1
Iowa..........	6,333	4,917	77.6	608	446	73.4	5,725	4,471	78.1
Missouri........	5,412	3,587	66.3	588	391	66.5	4,824	3,196	66.3
North Dakota....	12,241	9,756	79.7	1,354	1,120	82.7	10,887	8,636	79.3
South Dakota....	3,351	2,567	76.6	492	371	75.4	2,859	2,196	76.8
Nebraska.......	4,378	3,172	72.5	436	316	72.5	3,942	2,856	72.5
Kansas.........	4,037	2,942	72.9	569	456	80.1	3,468	2,486	71.7
SOUTH ATLANTIC:									
Delaware.......	460	265	57.6	61	28	....	399	237	59.4
Maryland.......	2,266	1,124	49.6	291	148	50.9	1,975	976	49.4
Dist. of Columbia.	1,681	977	58.1	223	123	55.2	1,458	854	58.6
Virginia........	1,617	970	60.0	157	81	51.6	1,460	889	60.9
West Virginia....	957	478	49.9	118	65	55.1	839	413	49.2
North Carolina...	930	478	51.4	80	53	....	850	425	50.0
South Carolina...	278	149	53.6	31	20	....	247	129	52.2
Georgia.........	1,094	571	52.2	109	57	52.3	985	514	52.2
Florida.........	8,156	4,154	50.9	985	481	48.8	7,171	3,673	51.2
E. SOUTH CENTRAL:									
Kentucky.......	918	496	54.0	96	54	....	822	442	53.8
Tennessee......	939	526	56.0	92	49	....	847	477	56.3
Alabama........	902	519	57.5	117	52	44.4	785	467	59.5
Mississippi......	351	178	50.7	42	25	....	309	153	49.5
W. SOUTH CENTRAL:									
Arkansas.......	695	394	56.7	77	42	....	618	352	57.0
Louisiana.......	981	535	54.5	222	117	52.7	759	418	55.1
Oklahoma.......	2,119	1,367	64.5	243	178	73.3	1,876	1,189	63.4
Texas..........	4,525	2,595	57.3	452	278	61.5	4,073	2,317	56.9
MOUNTAIN:									
Montana........	10,753	8,010	74.5	1,966	1,503	76.4	8,787	6,507	74.1
Idaho..........	4,502	2,991	66.4	571	407	71.3	3,931	2,584	65.7
Wyoming.......	1,136	802	70.6	118	92	78.0	1,018	710	69.7
Colorado.......	5,816	4,065	69.9	572	402	70.3	5,244	3,663	69.9
New Mexico.....	613	393	64.1	62	38	....	551	355	64.4
Arizona........	2,018	1,259	62.4	158	107	67.7	1,860	1,152	61.9
Utah...........	1,190	780	65.5	97	73	....	1,093	707	64.7
Nevada.........	952	651	68.4	134	94	70.1	818	557	68.1
PACIFIC:									
Washington.....	48,064	26,401	54.9	4,340	2,529	58.3	43,724	23,872	54.6
Oregon.........	17,916	9,424	52.6	1,345	776	57.7	16,571	8,648	52.2
California.......	101,445	50,112	49.4	7,657	4,133	54.0	93,788	45,979	49.0

outnumber the French ten to one, the French show decidedly higher percentages of naturalization—58.3 and 54.0, respectively, as against 54.6 and 49.0.

FIGURE **25**. CANADIAN-BORN FRENCH AND ENGLISH—PER CENT NATURALIZED, FOR 13 SELECTED STATES: 1930

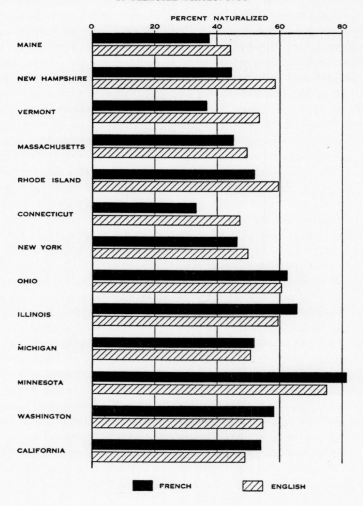

CHAPTER VIII

AGE OF THE CANADIAN STOCK

AMONG all the characteristics by which a population may be classified in a statistical presentation, there is none more important than age; and perhaps there are not more than two which might be considered at all close competitors, these being sex and color or race, taking the latter in the broad sense as illustrated by the white race, and the Negro, Indian, or Mongolian. (And since the Canadian born in the United States are practically all of the white race, this last-mentioned classification is of little significance for the present discussion.) The age classification of a population is in itself an indicator of many other attributes. For example, one expects a population comprising many young persons and few old to be a growing population; and in a population containing relatively large numbers of persons in early adult life one finds both a higher birth rate and a greater economic productivity per capita of the total population than can be maintained as the population inevitably grows older, under any conditions that are likely to obtain.

Further, age is necessary as a cross-classification with many other statistically usable characteristics, in order to bring out their full significance or perhaps even to make them significant at all. A tabulation of persons attending school and not attending school would have very little value unless the population were first separated into definite age groups; and in this case it is even necessary to fit the age groups specifically to the school-attending habits of the people. Data on marital condition, likewise, demand at least that they be limited to the population above the minimum age at marriage, and gain tremendously in value if they are tabulated for fairly small age groups, since the percentage married increases directly with increasing age over a considerable range of the normal life span—and the percentage widowed up to its very end. Occupation and the status of being a gainful worker are much more useful statistical concepts if the data are tabulated in combination with age, even a few broad age groups being very significant in this combination. Witness the social significance of the census data for gainfully employed children, or of those which show that more than one-half of the women in clerical occupations are under 30 years old.

Illiteracy appears in most of our statistics as a characteristic chiefly of the older generation, so that a population with many in the advanced ages is likely to show a high percentage of illiteracy, even though practically all of its younger members are able to read and write. The same relationship with age appears in all of the tabulations of ability to speak English among the non-English-speaking foreign born in the United States.

From the point of view of a country having a large foreign-born population the age of the immigrant group is an important measure of their value—or perchance of the seriousness of their competition if they come at a time when there is no need for more workers. For newly arrived immigrants are largely composed of workers in the younger ages, and it is only after a long period with few new arrivals that the group as a whole becomes a group of old men and old women—as will shortly be the case with the foreign born in the United States from some of those European countries which contributed extensively to its population 75 or 80 years ago.

In a group which is static or nearly static (that is, receiving no considerable additions of new immigrants), such as the Scandinavian born in the United States under present immigration practice, one can forecast the age of the people, and even the time when the group will cease to be of importance. Such forecasts for the Canadian born in the United States are hazardous, however, by reason, first, of the continued arrival of other Canadian born at rates varying widely from decade to decade; and, second, of the very considerable movement back and forth across the border, to which attention has already been called. But as an aid to the interpretation of the current statistics of the Canadian stock in the United States, the age classification is of very great importance, as will appear in some of the succeeding chapters.

Statistics of age of the population of Canadian birth in the United States are obtained from two sources, one a tabulation made in connection with the United States census of 1910, in which the Canadian-born white population, male and female, was classified into 5-year age periods, and the other a tabulation of the 1930 census data both for the Canadian born and for native persons of Canadian parentage into seven age groups (namely, under 5 years; 5 to 9; 10 to 14; 15 to 24; 25 to 44; 45 to 64; and 65 and over), in combination not only with sex, but also with literacy and ability to speak English. There was also a tabulation of the Canadian-born population of 12 States, aggregating 624,649 (or 48.9 per cent of the total number of Canadian-born white in the United States), by single years of age. By means of estimates based on this 12-State tabulation, the broad age groups used in the complete tabulation have been separated into 5-year periods for comparison with 1910.[1]

1. The process of estimating these 5-year periods has been to distribute the whole number of persons, male and female, in each of the 10 or 20-year age periods shown by the complete tabulation into 5-year periods in the proportion indicated by the figures

Because the Canadian stock in the United States is made up of two elements widely different in their age composition, namely, the Canadian born and the native population of Canadian parentage, the statistics representing its age composition are probably of less importance than those relating to the two constituent elements taken separately. Since there is much interest in the group as a whole, however, the figures are given in most cases for the Canadian stock as well as for the Canadian born and the natives of Canadian parentage, wherever data for the last-mentioned are available.

In Table 49 are summarized the age data for the Canadian stock and its two main elements, with certain parallel data for the population of the United States, which are given for comparison.

TABLE **49**. WHITE POPULATION OF CANADIAN STOCK IN THE UNITED STATES, BY AGE, WITH DATA FOR TOTAL POPULATION, ETC.: 1930

(Per cent not shown where less than 0.1)

| | CANADIAN STOCK | | | | | | POPULATION OF THE UNITED STATES, PER CENT | | |
| | Number | | | Per cent | | | | | |
AGE	Total	Cana-dian born	Cana-dian par-entage	Total	Cana-dian born	Cana-dian par-entage	Total	Foreign-born white	Native white
All ages...	3,337,345	1,278,421	2,058,924	100.0	100.0	100.0	100.0	100.0	100.0
Under 5 years	183,489	8,823	174,666	5.5	0.7	8.5	9.3	0.2	10.5
5 to 9 years	211,962	35,887	176,075	6.4	2.8	8.6	10.3	1.0	11.4
10 to 14 years	234,499	51,090	183,409	7.0	4.0	8.9	9.8	1.3	10.9
15 to 24 years	555,339	153,745	401,594	16.6	12.0	19.5	18.3	8.0	19.5
25 to 44 years	1,136,661	415,958	720,703	34.1	32.5	35.0	29.4	42.1	27.6
45 to 64 years	762,811	427,095	335,716	22.9	33.4	16.3	17.4	35.3	15.3
65 and over..	251,189	185,155	66,034	7.5	14.5	3.2	5.4	12.0	4.7
Unknown...	1,395	668	727	...	0.1	...	0.1	0.1	0.1

The age composition of the Canadian stock as a whole differs from that of the total population of the United States mainly in that it contains relatively fewer children under 15, and appreciably more persons in the several age periods beyond 25.

Of the Canadian born in the United States, 7.5 per cent were children under 15 years of age. This may be compared with 2.5 per cent under 15 years of age in the total foreign-born white population, the difference

for the 12 States. The sample was not selected with a view to being representative of the Canadian born, and in several respects it proves to be not closely representative, even though it is a very large sample, as statistical samples go. It seemed better, however, to make use of it directly for the estimated distribution rather than to make slight modifications in the ratio of distribution within the broad age periods on what would have had to be an arbitrary and rather indefinite basis. For the 12-State data see Tables 61, 62, and 63.

indicating that Canadian immigrants, far more often than those of other countries, bring their families with them; or it may be compared with 32.8 per cent under 15 years of age in the native white population, this difference indicating that after all, so far as age is concerned, the Canadian born in the United States in 1930 were more nearly like the foreign-born population in general than they were like the native population.

The percentage of the Canadian born who were found in the next age group, 15 to 24 years, was likewise considerably higher than the corresponding figure for all foreign-born white, and considerably lower than the figure shown for the native white population of the United States, the percentages being 12.0 for the Canadian born, 8.0 for the total foreign-born white, and 19.5 for the native white. The distribution of the Canadian born in the remaining age groups was as follows: 25 to 44 years, 32.5 per cent, which was about half way between the percentages shown for the two classes with which comparison has just been made; 45 to 64 years, 33.4 per cent, which was only a little lower than the percentage (35.3) shown for all foreign-born white; and 65 years and over, 14.5 per cent, which was somewhat higher than the percentage 65 and over among all foreign-born white in the United States.

The age distribution of the second generation of Canadian stock approached more nearly that of a normal resident population, though the percentage of children was much smaller than that in the entire native white population of the United States. Of the native white population of Canadian parentage in the United States in 1930, 26.0 per cent were under 15 years of age, as compared with 32.8 per cent of the total native white population; 19.5 per cent, or practically the same as in the total native white population, were 15 to 24 years of age; 35.0 per cent (as compared with 27.6 per cent in the larger group) were from 25 to 44 years of age; 16.3 per cent (as compared with 15.3 per cent in the larger group) were from 45 to 64 years of age; and only 3.2 per cent were 65 years old and over, as compared with 4.7 per cent for all native white and 14.5 per cent for the Canadian born.

In Table 50 are presented age data for the Canadian stock classified as French and English and also by sex.

Since the figures which appear in the first column of this table have already been discussed, the most important new distinctions presented are perhaps those between the French and the English elements in the Canadian stock. The French Canadian born, contrary to what one might have expected, show a smaller percentage of children under 15 than the English—5.9 as compared with 8.1; and likewise a smaller percentage of persons 15 to 24 years of age—10.9 as compared with 12.5. Conversely, 34.2 per cent of the French Canadian born were in the age period 25 to 44 years, as compared with 31.9 of the English, with a slightly higher percentage of French than of English in the period 45 to 64 years, and practically the same percentage 65 years old and over.

TABLE **50**. WHITE POPULATION OF CANADIAN STOCK, FRENCH AND ENGLISH, BY AGE AND SEX: 1930

(Per cent not shown where less than 0.1)

CLASS AND AGE	TOTAL			FRENCH			ENGLISH		
	Total	Male	Female	Total	Male	Female	Total	Male	Female
Canadian stock.	**3,337,345**	**1,627,880**	**1,709,465**	**1,106,159**	**553,345**	**552,814**	**2,231,186**	**1,074,535**	**1,156,651**
Under 5 years......	183,489	93,516	89,973	69,074	35,060	34,014	114,415	58,456	55,959
5 to 9 years......	211,962	107,174	104,788	79,435	39,979	39,456	132,527	67,195	65,332
10 to 14 years......	234,499	117,762	116,737	83,883	41,976	41,907	150,616	75,786	74,830
15 to 24 years......	555,339	269,269	286,070	191,118	93,302	97,816	364,221	175,967	188,254
25 to 44 years......	1,136,661	542,205	594,456	373,567	184,242	189,325	763,094	357,963	405,131
45 to 64 years......	762,811	373,304	389,507	234,400	119,573	114,827	528,411	253,731	274,680
65 and over........	251,189	123,983	127,206	74,356	39,060	35,296	176,833	84,923	91,910
Unknown.........	1,395	667	728	326	153	173	1,069	514	555
Per cent........	**100.0**	**100.0**	**100.0**	**100.0**	**100.0**	**100.0**	**100.0**	**100.0**	**100.0**
Under 5 years......	5.5	5.7	5.3	6.2	6.3	6.2	5.1	5.4	4.8
5 to 9 years......	6.4	6.6	6.1	7.2	7.2	7.1	5.9	6.3	5.6
10 to 14 years......	7.0	7.2	6.8	7.6	7.6	7.6	6.8	7.1	6.5
15 to 24 years......	16.6	16.5	16.7	17.3	16.9	17.7	16.3	16.4	16.3
25 to 44 years......	34.1	33.3	34.8	33.8	33.3	34.2	34.2	33.3	35.0
45 to 64 years......	22.9	22.9	22.8	21.2	21.6	20.8	23.7	23.6	23.7
65 and over........	7.5	7.6	7.4	6.7	7.1	6.4	7.9	7.9	7.9
Unknown.........	...	...	...	...	...	...	...	...	...
Canadian born..	**1,278,421**	**617,090**	**661,331**	**370,852**	**187,523**	**183,329**	**907,569**	**429,567**	**478,002**
Under 5 years......	8,823	4,396	4,427	1,913	943	970	6,910	3,453	3,457
5 to 9 years......	35,887	18,033	17,854	8,215	3,990	4,225	27,672	14,043	13,629
10 to 14 years......	51,090	25,261	25,829	11,875	5,810	6,065	39,215	19,451	19,764
15 to 24 years......	153,745	71,325	82,420	40,286	19,041	21,245	113,459	52,284	61,175
25 to 44 years......	415,958	198,124	217,834	126,874	63,656	63,218	289,084	134,468	154,616
45 to 64 years......	427,095	208,517	218,578	127,565	65,467	62,098	299,530	143,050	156,480
65 and over........	185,155	91,101	94,054	53,988	28,538	25,450	131,167	62,563	68,604
Unknown.........	668	333	335	136	78	58	532	255	277
Per cent........	**100.0**	**100.0**	**100.0**	**100.0**	**100.0**	**100.0**	**100.0**	**100.0**	**100.0**
Under 5 years......	0.7	0.7	0.7	0.5	0.5	0.5	0.8	0.8	0.7
5 to 9 years......	2.8	2.9	2.7	2.2	2.1	2.3	3.0	3.3	2.9
10 to 14 years......	4.0	4.1	3.9	3.2	3.1	3.3	4.3	4.5	4.1
15 to 24 years......	12.0	11.6	12.5	10.9	10.2	11.6	12.5	12.2	12.8
25 to 44 years......	32.5	32.1	32.9	34.2	33.9	34.5	31.9	31.3	32.3
45 to 64 years......	33.4	33.8	33.1	34.4	34.9	33.9	33.0	33.3	32.7
65 and over........	14.5	14.8	14.2	14.6	15.2	13.9	14.5	14.6	14.4
Unknown.........	0.1	0.1	0.1	....	....	....	0.1	0.1	0.1
Canadian parentage....	**2,058,924**	**1,010,790**	**1,048,134**	**735,307**	**365,822**	**369,485**	**1,323,617**	**644,968**	**678,649**
Under 5 years......	174,666	89,120	85,546	67,161	34,117	33,044	107,505	55,003	52,502
5 to 9 years......	176,075	89,141	86,934	71,220	35,989	35,231	104,855	53,152	51,703
10 to 14 years......	183,409	92,501	90,908	72,008	36,166	35,842	111,401	56,335	55,066
15 to 24 years......	401,594	197,944	203,650	150,832	74,261	76,571	250,762	123,683	127,079
25 to 44 years......	720,703	344,081	376,622	246,693	120,586	126,107	474,010	223,495	250,515
45 to 64 years......	335,716	164,787	170,929	106,835	54,106	52,729	228,881	110,681	118,200
65 and over........	66,034	32,882	33,152	20,368	10,522	9,846	45,666	22,360	23,306
Unknown.........	727	334	393	190	75	115	537	259	278
Per cent........	**100.0**	**100.0**	**100.0**	**100.0**	**100.0**	**100.0**	**100.0**	**100.0**	**100.0**
Under 5 years......	8.5	8.8	8.2	9.1	9.3	8.9	8.1	8.5	7.7
5 to 9 years......	8.6	8.8	8.3	9.7	9.8	9.5	7.9	8.2	7.6
10 to 14 years......	8.9	9.2	8.7	9.8	9.9	9.7	8.4	8.7	8.1
15 to 24 years......	19.5	19.6	19.4	20.5	20.3	20.7	18.9	19.2	18.7
25 to 44 years......	35.0	34.0	35.9	33.5	33.0	34.1	35.8	34.7	36.9
45 to 64 years......	16.3	16.3	16.3	14.5	14.8	14.3	17.3	17.2	17.4
65 and over........	3.2	3.3	3.2	2.8	2.9	2.7	3.5	3.5	3.4
Unknown.........	...	...	...	...	...	...	...	...	...

In the second generation of French Canadian stock, 28.6 per cent were under 15 years of age, as compared with 24.4 per cent of the English stock; and 20.5 per cent of the French were from 15 to 24 years old, as compared with 18.9 per cent of the English. For all the age periods covering persons 25 years old and over, the percentages shown for persons of English Canadian parentage were appreciably higher than those for the corresponding groups of French Canadian parentage.

As between the males and females in the various subdivisions of the Canadian stock there were no very significant variations in the age distribution. Among the French Canadian born, 15.2 per cent of the males, as compared with 13.9 per cent of the females, were 65 years old and over, while 10.2 per cent of the males, as compared with 11.6 per cent of the females, were between 15 and 24 years of age. The percentage of males 45 to 64 years old was slightly higher than the percentage of females, and conversely, the percentage of males 25 to 44 years of age was slightly lower than the corresponding percentage of females. Among the English Canadian born there were corresponding differences in these four age groups, though in every case much smaller.

The differences between males and females in the various age groups in the second generation of Canadian stock are likewise relatively small, and such of them as are significant can be better discussed in connection with Tables 54 and 59, which give sex ratios by age.

For the whole number of white persons born in Canada, without distinction as between French and English, the classification by age is available for 1910 as well as for 1930; in fact, as already indicated, the 1910 figures were tabulated in greater detail than those for 1930, this detail affording 5-year age periods up to age 100. A distribution of the broader age groups tabulated in 1930 into 5-year age periods has been made, however, and these figures are presented (up to age 75) in comparison with the 1910 figures, in Table 51. This table gives also for convenience in comparison the four broad age periods of the 1930 tabulation, supplemented by a consolidation of the three 5-year periods representing persons under 15 years of age.

The principal changes in the age composition of the Canadian-born population of the United States between 1910 and 1930 are marked decreases in the percentages between 20 and 49 years of age, and very considerable increases in the ages from 50 years upwards.

It has already been noted that the number of Canadian born in the United States reached nearly its 1930 level as early as 1900, that there was little increase between 1900 and about 1925; and that between 1910 and about 1925 there was probably a net decrease. For three-fourths of the 20-year period between 1910 and 1930, therefore, the Canadian born

TABLE **51**. CANADIAN-BORN WHITE POPULATION IN THE UNITED STATES BY AGE
(5-YEAR PERIODS) AND SEX: 1930 AND 1910

(Distribution of Canadian born in the United States in 1930 into 5-year age periods partly estimated.
See explanation in text, page 120)

AGE	TOTAL		MALE		FEMALE		MALES PER 100 FEMALES	
	1930	1910	1930	1910	1930	1910	1930	1910
All ages...............	1,278,421	1,196,070	617,090	601,833	661,331	594,237	93.3	101.3
Under 5 years............	8,823	14,082	4,396	7,073	4,427	7,009	99.3	100.9
5 to 9 years............	35,887	24,254	18,033	12,083	17,854	12,171	101.0	99.3
10 to 14 years...........	51,090	33,992	25,261	16,712	25,829	17,280	97.8	96.7
15 to 19 years...........	61,868	57,551	30,185	27,065	31,683	30,486	95.3	88.8
20 to 24 years...........	91,877	100,640	41,140	46,696	50,737	53,944	81.1	86.6
25 to 29 years...........	103,352	121,616	49,411	57,704	53,941	63,912	91.6	90.3
30 to 34 years...........	99,225	132,212	47,633	64,716	51,592	67,496	92.3	95.9
35 to 39 years...........	102,806	131,352	48,352	66,484	54,454	64,868	88.8	102.5
40 to 44 years...........	110,575	125,699	52,728	64,758	57,847	60,941	91.2	106.3
45 to 49 years...........	113,192	124,028	53,264	64,948	59,928	59,080	88.9	109.9
50 to 54 years...........	120,471	102,209	58,221	54,097	62,250	48,112	93.5	112.4
55 to 59 years...........	103,352	74,432	51,966	39,173	51,386	35,259	101.1	111.1
60 to 64 years...........	90,080	59,298	45,066	31,253	45,014	28,045	100.1	111.4
65 to 69 years...........	80,471	42,690	40,293	22,496	40,178	20,194	100.3	111.4
70 to 74 years...........	52,271	25,838	25,960	13,424	26,311	12,414	98.7	108.1
75 and over..............	52,413	24,900	24,848	12,432	27,565	12,468	90.1	99.7
Unknown.................	668	1,277	333	719	335	558	99.4	128.4
BROAD AGE PERIODS								
Under 15 years..........	95,800	72,328	47,690	35,868	48,110	36,460	99.1	98.4
15 to 24 years..........	153,745	158,191	71,325	73,761	82,420	84,430	86.5	87.4
25 to 44 years..........	415,958	510,879	198,124	253,662	217,834	257,217	91.0	98.6
45 to 64 years..........	427,095	359,967	208,517	189,471	218,578	170,496	95.4	111.1
65 and over.............	185,155	93,428	91,101	48,352	94,054	45,076	96.9	107.3
Per cent...........	**100.0**	**100.0**	**100.0**	**100.0**	**100.0**	**100.0**	....	....
Under 5 years...........	0.7	1.2	0.7	1.2	0.7	1.2	....	....
5 to 9 years...........	2.8	2.0	2.9	2.0	2.7	2.0	....	....
10 to 14 years..........	4.0	2.8	4.1	2.8	3.9	2.9	....	....
15 to 19 years..........	4.8	4.8	4.9	4.5	4.8	5.1	....	....
20 to 24 years..........	7.2	8.4	6.7	7.8	7.7	9.1	....	....
25 to 29 years..........	8.1	10.2	8.0	9.6	8.2	10.8	....	....
30 to 34 years..........	7.8	11.1	7.7	10.8	7.8	11.4	....	....
35 to 39 years..........	8.0	11.0	7.8	11.0	8.2	10.9	....	....
40 to 44 years..........	8.6	10.5	8.5	10.8	8.7	10.3	....	....
45 to 49 years..........	8.9	10.4	8.6	10.8	9.1	9.9	....	....
50 to 54 years..........	9.4	8.5	9.4	9.0	9.4	8.1	....	....
55 to 59 years..........	8.1	6.2	8.4	6.5	7.8	5.9	....	....
60 to 64 years..........	7.0	5.0	7.3	5.2	6.8	4.7	....	....
65 to 69 years..........	6.3	3.6	6.5	3.7	6.1	3.4	....	....
70 to 74 years..........	4.1	2.2	4.2	2.2	4.0	2.1	....	....
75 and over.............	4.1	2.1	4.0	2.1	4.2	2.1	....	....
Unknown................	0.1	0.1	0.1	0.1	0.1	0.1	....	....
BROAD AGE PERIODS								
Under 15 years..........	7.5	6.0	7.7	6.0	7.3	6.1	....	....
15 to 24 years..........	12.0	13.2	11.6	12.3	12.5	14.2	....	....
25 to 44 years..........	32.5	42.7	32.1	42.1	32.9	43.3	....	....
45 to 64 years..........	33.4	30.1	33.8	31.5	33.1	28.7	....	....
65 and over.............	14.5	7.8	14.8	8.0	14.2	7.6	....	....

in the United States might be considered a relatively static group subject
to increasing age, with hardly enough renewal through the arrival of new
immigrants in the younger ages to offset the effects of mortality. The
actual changes in the age composition shown by the census figures, however, are rather less than one might expect in a strictly self-contained
population, which fact may perhaps be explained by the assumption of a

considerable amount of movement of Canadian born back and forth between Canada and the United States. (See the discussion of Table 39,
p. 99.)

FIGURE **26**. AGE DISTRIBUTION OF THE CANADIAN BORN IN THE UNITED STATES, 1930
AND 1910, WITH DISTRIBUTION OF OTHER CLASSES FOR COMPARISON

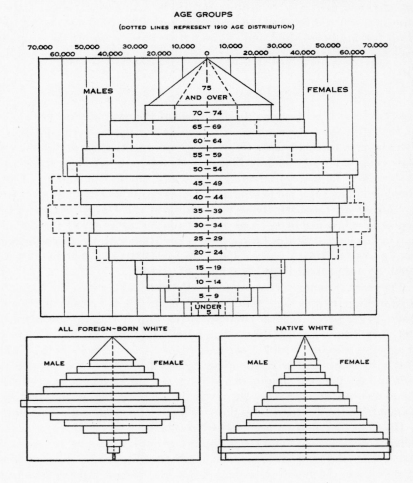

The percentage in the group 65 years old and over increased from 7.8
in 1910 to 14.5 in 1930. This would indicate that the Canadian born who
were in the United States in 1910 were growing older with the passage of
the years and were not being replaced by new immigration from Canada.

This assumption is in accord with the figures given earlier (see Table 2), representing the rather rapid increase in the number of Canadian born in the United States up to 1900 in comparison with the relatively small increase since that date.

The changes in the age distribution of the Canadian born between 1910 and 1930 are shown graphically in Figure 26, which comprises the usual age pyramid drawn in solid lines for 1930, with the 1910 distribution superimposed and represented by dotted lines. The 1930 age distribution of all foreign-born white and of the native white is shown on a smaller scale for comparison.

Canadian Born in Canada and the United States by Age

Figures have already been given in some of the comparative tables (see Table 5) for the whole number of Canadian-born persons living either in Canada or in the United States, it being assumed that since there is very little emigration of Canadian born to countries other than the United States, these figures represented practically the whole number of Canadian born. The main purpose of this presentation was to show what proportion of all Canadian born were living in the United States. These figures are classified by age and sex in Table 52 for 1930/31 (a combination of the United States census figures for 1930 with the Canadian census figures for 1931) and in Table 53 for 1910/11; and the data for 1930/31 are presented graphically in Figure 27.

The most striking difference in age distribution between the Canadian born in Canada and the Canadian born in the United States is the very much larger percentage of children in the former than in the latter. In 1931, 38.8 per cent of the Canadian born in Canada were under 15 years of age, as compared with 7.5 per cent of the Canadian born in the United States in 1930. The corresponding figures for 1910/11 were 37.9 per cent and 6.0 per cent. Beginning with age 25, the situation was reversed, the percentage in each subsequent age group being higher for the Canadian born in the United States than for those who remained in Canada.

If an age distribution be computed on the basis of the total number of persons 25 years old and over in the two groups, as has been done in the last section of Table 52, so as to eliminate the effect of the large numbers of children in the group remaining in Canada, we find higher percentages for all the age periods up to age 45 in the group residing in Canada, and higher percentages for all age periods beyond 45 in the group comprising the Canadian born living in the United States. This is simply another statistical manifestation of the fact, already mentioned in this chapter, that there was relatively little immigration from Canada to the United States

TABLE **52**. CANADIAN-BORN POPULATION RESIDENT BOTH IN CANADA AND IN THE UNITED STATES, BY AGE, SEX, AND PLACE OF RESIDENCE: 1930/31

(The figures for Canadian born living in the United States are exclusive of the 7,968 nonwhite, for whom the age distribution is not available; and the total is therefore less by this number than the total shown in Table 5. Per cent not shown where less than 0.1)

AGE (YEARS)	ALL CANADIAN BORN			MALE			FEMALE		
	Total	In Canada, 1931	In United States, 1930	Total	In Canada, 1931	In United States, 1930	Total	In Canada, 1931	In United States, 1930
All ages.......	9,347,682	8,069,261	1,278,421	4,693,091	4,076,001	617,090	4,654,591	3,993,260	661,331
Under 5..........	1,060,590	1,051,767	8,823	536,010	531,614	4,396	524,580	520,153	4,427
5 to 9..........	1,107,185	1,071,298	35,887	559,101	541,068	18,033	548,084	530,230	17,854
10 to 14..........	1,056,858	1,005,768	51,090	533,057	507,796	25,261	523,801	497,972	25,829
15 to 19..........	1,006,752	944,884	61,868	504,317	474,132	30,185	502,435	470,752	31,683
20 to 24..........	808,595	716,718	91,877	401,068	359,928	41,140	407,527	356,790	50,737
25 to 29..........	633,579	530,227	103,352	313,906	264,495	49,411	319,673	265,732	53,941
30 to 34..........	546,513	447,288	99,225	270,402	222,769	47,633	276,111	224,519	51,592
35 to 39..........	522,152	419,346	102,806	258,483	210,131	48,352	263,669	209,215	54,454
40 to 44..........	488,077	377,502	110,575	244,390	191,662	52,728	243,687	185,840	57,847
45 to 49..........	451,426	338,234	113,192	227,979	174,715	53,264	223,447	163,519	59,928
50 to 54..........	419,797	299,326	120,471	214,085	155,864	58,221	205,712	143,462	62,250
55 to 59..........	344,241	240,889	103,352	177,355	125,389	51,966	166,886	115,500	51,386
60 to 64..........	291,405	201,325	90,080	148,324	103,258	45,066	143,081	98,067	45,014
65 to 69..........	245,704	165,233	80,471	124,117	83,824	40,293	121,587	81,409	40,178
70 to 74..........	179,574	127,303	52,271	90,569	64,609	25,960	89,005	62,694	26,311
75 and over.......	181,573	129,160	52,413	87,458	62,610	24,848	94,115	66,550	27,565
Unknown.........	3,661	2,993	668	2,470	2,137	333	1,191	856	335
Under 15..........	3,224,633	3,128,833	95,800	1,628,168	1,580,478	47,690	1,596,465	1,548,355	48,110
15 to 24..........	1,815,347	1,661,602	153,745	905,385	834,060	71,325	909,962	827,542	82,420
25 to 44..........	2,190,321	1,774,363	415,958	1,087,181	889,057	198,124	1,103,140	885,306	217,834
45 to 64..........	1,506,869	1,079,774	427,095	767,743	559,226	208,517	739,126	520,548	218,578
65 and over.......	606,851	421,696	185,155	302,144	211,043	91,101	304,707	210,653	94,054
25 and over........	4,307,702	3,278,826	1,028,876	2,159,538	1,661,463	498,075	2,148,164	1,617,363	530,801
Per cent........	**100.0**	**100.0**	**100.0**	**100.0**	**100.0**	**100.0**	**100.0**	**100.0**	**100.0**
Under 5...........	11.3	13.0	0.7	11.4	13.0	0.7	11.3	13.0	0.7
5 to 9...........	11.8	13.3	2.8	11.9	13.3	2.9	11.8	13.3	2.7
10 to 14...........	11.3	12.5	4.0	11.4	12.5	4.1	11.3	12.5	3.9
15 to 19...........	10.8	11.7	4.8	10.7	11.6	4.9	10.8	11.8	4.8
20 to 24...........	8.7	8.9	7.2	8.5	8.8	6.7	8.8	8.9	7.7
25 to 29...........	6.8	6.6	8.1	6.7	6.5	8.0	6.9	6.7	8.2
30 to 34...........	5.8	5.5	7.8	5.8	5.5	7.7	5.9	5.6	7.8
35 to 39...........	5.6	5.2	8.0	5.5	5.2	7.8	5.7	5.2	8.2
40 to 44...........	5.2	4.7	8.6	5.2	4.7	8.5	5.2	4.7	8.7
45 to 49...........	4.8	4.2	8.9	4.9	4.3	8.6	4.8	4.1	9.1
50 to 54...........	4.5	3.7	9.4	4.6	3.8	9.4	4.4	3.6	9.4
55 to 59...........	3.7	3.0	8.1	3.8	3.1	8.4	3.6	2.9	7.8
60 to 64...........	3.1	2.5	7.0	3.2	2.5	7.3	3.1	2.5	6.8
65 to 69...........	2.6	2.0	6.3	2.6	2.1	6.5	2.6	2.0	6.1
70 to 74...........	1.9	1.6	4.1	1.9	1.6	4.2	1.9	1.6	4.0
75 and over.......	1.9	1.6	4.1	1.9	1.5	4.0	2.0	1.7	4.2
Unknown.........	...	...	0.1	0.1	0.1	0.1	...	...	0.1
Under 15...........	34.5	38.8	7.5	34.7	38.8	7.7	34.3	38.8	7.3
15 to 24...........	19.4	20.6	12.0	19.3	20.5	11.6	19.5	20.7	12.5
25 to 44...........	23.4	22.0	32.5	23.2	21.8	32.1	23.7	22.2	32.9
45 to 64...........	16.1	13.4	33.4	16.4	13.7	33.8	15.9	13.0	33.1
65 and over.......	6.5	5.2	14.5	6.4	5.2	14.8	6.5	5.3	14.2
25 and over........	46.1	40.6	80.5	46.0	40.8	80.7	46.2	40.5	80.3
Per cent of total 25 and over....	**100.0**	**100.0**	**100.0**	**100.0**	**100.0**	**100.0**	**100.0**	**100.0**	**100.0**
25 to 29...........	14.7	16.2	10.0	14.5	15.9	9.9	14.9	16.4	10.2
30 to 34...........	12.7	13.6	9.6	12.5	13.4	9.6	12.9	13.9	9.7
35 to 39...........	12.1	12.8	10.0	12.0	12.6	9.7	12.3	12.9	10.3
40 to 44...........	11.3	11.5	10.7	11.3	11.5	10.6	11.3	11.5	10.9
45 to 49...........	10.5	10.3	11.0	10.6	10.5	10.7	10.4	10.1	11.3
50 to 54...........	9.7	9.1	11.7	9.9	9.4	11.7	9.6	8.9	11.7
55 to 59...........	8.0	7.3	10.0	8.2	7.5	10.4	7.8	7.1	9.7
60 to 64...........	6.8	6.1	8.8	6.9	6.2	9.0	6.7	6.1	8.5
65 to 69...........	5.7	5.0	7.8	5.7	5.0	8.1	5.7	5.0	7.6
70 to 74...........	4.2	3.9	5.1	4.2	3.9	5.2	4.1	3.9	5.0
75 and over.......	4.2	3.9	5.1	4.0	3.8	5.0	4.4	4.1	5.2
Unknown.........	0.1	0.1	0.1	0.1	0.1	0.1	0.1	0.1	0.1

during the 20 or 30 years preceding the 1930 census; and that, consequently, the Canadian born in the United States increased appreciably in average age, while the Canadian born remaining in Canada were every year recruited by tens of thousands of children born during the year.

TABLE **53**. CANADIAN-BORN POPULATION RESIDENT BOTH IN CANADA AND IN THE UNITED STATES, BY AGE, SEX, AND PLACE OF RESIDENCE: 1910/11

(The figures for Canadian born living in the United States are exclusive of the 8,567 nonwhite, for whom the age distribution is not available; and the total is therefore less by this number than the total shown in Table 5)

AGE	ALL CANADIAN BORN			MALE			FEMALE		
	Total	In Canada, 1911	In United States, 1910	Total	In Canada, 1911	In United States, 1910	Total	In Canada, 1911	In United States, 1910
All ages..	6,815,752	5,619,682	1,196,070	3,451,275	2,849,442	601,833	3,364,477	2,770,240	594,237
Under 15...	2,201,925	2,129,597	72,328	1,109,571	1,073,703	35,868	1,092,354	1,055,894	36,460
15 to 19.....	614,374	556,823	57,551	307,097	280,032	27,065	307,277	276,791	30,486
20 to 24.....	612,263	511,623	100,640	303,939	257,243	46,696	308,324	254,380	53,944
25 to 29.....	554,373	432,757	121,616	277,584	219,880	57,704	276,789	212,877	63,912
30 to 34.....	501,067	368,855	132,212	254,092	189,376	64,716	246,975	179,479	67,496
35 to 39.....	454,486	323,134	131,352	232,142	165,658	66,484	222,344	157,476	64,868
40 to 44.....	402,528	276,829	125,699	206,222	141,464	64,758	196,306	135,365	60,941
45 to 49.....	370,914	246,886	124,028	191,306	126,358	64,948	179,608	120,528	59,080
50 to 54.....	319,509	217,300	102,209	165,799	111,702	54,097	153,710	105,598	48,112
55 to 59.....	238,485	164,053	74,432	123,696	84,523	39,173	114,789	79,530	35,259
60 to 64.....	194,779	135,481	59,298	101,046	69,793	31,253	93,733	65,688	28,045
65 to 69.....	141,590	98,900	42,690	72,472	49,976	22,496	69,118	48,924	20,194
70 to 74.....	94,060	68,222	25,838	47,686	34,262	13,424	46,374	33,960	12,414
75 and over.	97,871	72,971	24,900	47,650	35,218	12,432	50,221	37,753	12,468
Unknown...	17,528	16,251	1,277	10,973	10,254	719	6,555	5,997	558
BROAD AGE PERIODS									
Under 15...	2,201,925	2,129,597	72,328	1,109,571	1,073,703	35,868	1,092,354	1,055,894	36,460
15 to 24.....	1,226,637	1,068,446	158,191	611,036	537,275	73,761	615,601	531,171	84,430
25 to 44.....	1,912,454	1,401,575	510,879	970,040	716,378	253,662	942,414	685,197	257,217
45 to 64.....	1,123,687	763,720	359,967	581,847	392,376	189,471	541,840	371,344	170,496
65 and over.	333,521	240,093	93,428	167,808	119,456	48,352	165,713	120,637	45,076
Per cent.	100.0	100.0	100.0	100.0	100.0	100.0	100.0	100.0	100.0
Under 15...	32.3	37.9	6.0	32.1	37.7	6.0	32.5	38.1	6.1
15 to 19.....	9.0	9.9	4.8	8.9	9.8	4.5	9.1	10.0	5.1
20 to 24.....	9.0	9.1	8.4	8.8	9.0	7.8	9.2	9.2	9.1
25 to 29.....	8.1	7.7	10.2	8.0	7.7	9.6	8.2	7.7	10.8
30 to 34.....	7.4	6.6	11.1	7.4	6.6	10.8	7.3	6.5	11.4
35 to 39.....	6.7	5.8	11.0	6.7	5.8	11.0	6.6	5.7	10.9
40 to 44.....	5.9	4.9	10.5	6.0	5.0	10.8	5.8	4.9	10.3
45 to 49.....	5.4	4.4	10.4	5.5	4.4	10.8	5.3	4.4	9.9
50 to 54.....	4.7	3.9	8.5	4.8	3.9	9.0	4.6	3.8	8.1
55 to 59.....	3.5	2.9	6.2	3.6	3.0	6.5	3.4	2.9	5.9
60 to 64.....	2.9	2.4	5.0	2.9	2.4	5.2	2.8	2.4	4.7
65 to 69.....	2.1	1.8	3.6	2.1	1.8	3.7	2.1	1.8	3.4
70 to 74.....	1.4	1.2	2.2	1.4	1.2	2.2	1.4	1.2	2.1
75 and over.	1.4	1.3	2.1	1.4	1.2	2.1	1.5	1.4	2.1
Unknown...	0.3	0.3	0.1	0.3	0.4	0.1	0.2	0.2	0.1
BROAD AGE PERIODS									
Under 15...	32.3	37.9	6.0	32.1	37.7	6.0	32.5	38.1	6.1
15 to 24.....	18.0	19.0	13.2	17.7	18.9	12.3	18.3	19.2	14.2
25 to 44.....	28.1	24.9	42.7	28.1	25.1	42.1	28.0	24.7	43.3
45 to 64.....	16.5	13.6	30.1	16.9	13.8	31.5	16.1	13.4	28.7
65 and over.	4.9	4.3	7.8	4.9	4.2	8.0	4.9	4.4	7.6

In general, there are relatively little differences as between males and females in the 1931 age distribution of the Canadian born in Canada or in the 1930 distribution of the Canadian born in the United States, though in the latter group somewhat larger percentages of females are found in some of the younger ages—7.7 per cent of the females in the age period 20 to 24 years, as compared with 6.7 per cent of the males ; and in some of the periods representing persons 55 years old or over, the figures for males are appreciably larger. In 1910 the situation was somewhat different, the percentages of females among the Canadian born in the United States being appreciably higher in all the age periods up to 35 years, and appreciably smaller in all the later age periods.

FIGURE **27**. AGE DISTRIBUTION OF CANADIAN BORN IN CANADA AND IN THE UNITED STATES: 1930/31

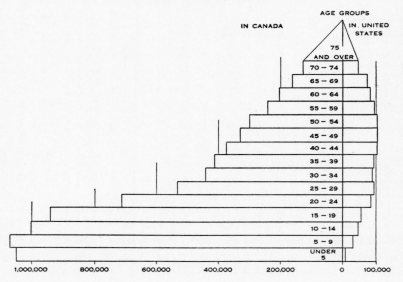

Table 54 gives the number of males per 100 females among the Canadian born, both in Canada and in the United States, in 1910/11 and 1930/31, by age.

The number of males per 100 females in the whole number of Canadian-born white persons in the United States decreased from 101.3 in 1910 to 93.3 in 1930, there being, in 1910, 7,596 more males than females, while in 1930 there were 44,241 more females than males. The decrease in the sex ratio, which represents an increase in the relative number of females, was most marked in the ages from 35 years upwards, there being relatively little change in the sex distribution of persons under 35. The maximum change was from the ratio of 109.9 males to 100 females in the age period 45 to 49 in 1910, to a ratio of 88.9 males per 100 females in 1930. By contrast, the sex ratios for the Canadian born in Canada show relatively little change between 1911 and 1931.

TABLE **54**. SEX RATIOS FOR THE CANADIAN-BORN POPULATION RESIDENT BOTH IN CANADA AND IN THE UNITED STATES, BY AGE AND PLACE OF RESIDENCE: 1930/31 AND 1910/11

AGE	ALL CANADIAN BORN, 1930/31			ALL CANADIAN BORN, 1910/11		
	Total	In Canada, 1931	In United States, 1930	Total	In Canada, 1911	In United States, 1910
All ages.....................	**100.8**	**102.1**	**93.3**	**102.6**	**102.9**	**101.3**
Under 15 years................	102.0	102.1	99.1	101.6	101.7	98.4
15 to 19 years................	100.4	100.7	95.3	99.9	101.2	88.8
20 to 24 years................	98.4	100.9	81.1	98.6	101.1	86.6
25 to 29 years................	98.2	99.5	91.6	100.3	103.3	90.3
30 to 34 years................	97.9	99.2	92.3	102.9	105.5	95.9
35 to 39 years................	98.0	100.4	88.8	104.4	105.2	102.5
40 to 44 years................	100.3	103.1	91.2	105.1	104.5	106.3
45 to 49 years................	102.0	106.8	88.9	106.5	104.8	109.9
50 to 54 years................	104.1	108.6	93.5	107.9	105.8	112.4
55 to 59 years................	106.3	108.6	101.1	107.8	106.3	111.1
60 to 64 years................	103.7	105.3	100.1	107.8	106.2	111.4
65 to 69 years................	102.1	103.0	100.3	104.9	102.2	111.4
70 to 74 years................	101.8	103.1	98.7	102.8	100.9	108.1
75 and over..................	92.9	94.1	90.1	94.9	93.3	99.7
Unknown.....................	207.4	249.6	99.4	167.4	171.0	128.9
BROAD AGE PERIODS						
Under 15 years...............	102.0	102.1	99.1	101.6	101.7	98.4
15 to 24 years................	99.5	100.8	86.5	99.3	101.1	87.4
25 to 44 years................	98.6	100.4	91.0	102.9	104.6	98.6
45 to 64 years................	103.9	107.4	95.4	107.4	105.7	111.1
65 and over..................	99.2	100.2	96.9	101.3	99.0	107.3

Table 55 gives the percentage of all Canadian born in Canada and the United States who were in the United States, by 5-year age periods, for 1930 and 1910.

In 1930 the Canadian born in the United States represented 13.7 per cent of the whole number of Canadian born in both countries, as compared with 17.5 per cent in 1910. One would expect, then, appreciable decreases as between 1910 and 1930 in the percentages shown for the several age groups making up the total. These decreases are most in evidence in the ages under 55, while from age 60 upwards the percentage in the United States was larger in 1930 than for the same age group in 1910. The percentage of Canadian-born persons under 15 years of age who were in the United States, while it was somewhat smaller in 1930 than in 1910, was only a little over 3 per cent even in 1910. Of the whole number of Canadian-born persons 15 to 19 years of age in 1930, 6.1 per cent were in the United States, as compared with 9.4 per cent of the corresponding age group in 1910. Similar ratios obtain for the several

5-year age periods up to age 44, the percentage in the United States in 1930 being in each case roughly two-thirds of that shown in 1910 for the corresponding age group. Of Canadian-born persons aged 45 to 49 in 1930, 25.1 per cent were in the United States, as compared with 33.4 per cent of the corresponding group in 1910. For the age period 50 to 54, the corresponding figures were 28.7 in 1930 and 32.0 in 1910. For the next period the difference is only that between 30.0 and 31.2; and for the group comprising persons aged 60 to 64 as already indicated, the percentage in the United States in 1930 was slightly greater than that in 1910, 30.9 as compared with 30.4. The succeeding periods show scattered differences in the same direction.

TABLE **55**. PERCENTAGE OF ALL CANADIAN BORN RESIDING IN THE UNITED STATES, BY AGE AND SEX: 1930 AND 1910

(Based on Canadian-born population resident both in Canada and in the United States, as shown in Tables 52 and 53)

AGE	TOTAL		MALE		FEMALE	
	1930	1910	1930	1910	1930	1910
All ages.................................	13.7	17.5	13.1	17.4	14.2	17.7
Under 15 years............................	3.0	3.3	2.9	3.2	3.0	3.3
15 to 19 years............................	6.1	9.4	6.0	8.8	6.3	9.9
20 to 24 years............................	11.4	16.4	10.3	15.4	12.4	17.5
25 to 29 years............................	16.3	21.9	15.7	20.8	16.9	23.1
30 to 34 years............................	18.2	26.4	17.6	25.5	18.7	27.3
35 to 39 years............................	19.7	28.9	18.7	28.6	20.7	29.2
40 to 44 years............................	22.7	31.2	21.6	31.4	23.7	31.0
45 to 49 years............................	25.1	33.4	23.4	33.9	26.8	32.9
50 to 54 years............................	28.7	32.0	27.2	32.6	30.3	31.3
55 to 59 years............................	30.0	31.2	29.3	31.7	30.8	30.7
60 to 64 years............................	30.9	30.4	30.4	30.9	31.5	29.9
65 to 69 years............................	32.8	30.2	32.5	31.0	33.0	29.2
70 to 74 years............................	29.1	27.5	28.7	28.2	29.6	26.8
75 and over..............................	28.9	25.4	28.4	26.1	29.3	24.8
Unknown.................................	18.2	7.3	13.5	6.5	28.1	8.5
BROAD AGE PERIODS						
Under 15................................	3.0	3.3	2.9	3.2	3.0	3.3
15 to 24 years............................	8.5	12.9	7.9	12.1	9.1	13.7
25 to 44 years............................	19.0	26.7	18.2	26.1	19.7	27.3
45 to 64 years............................	28.3	32.0	27.2	32.6	29.6	31.5
65 and over..............................	30.5	28.0	30.2	28.8	30.9	27.2

Of the whole number of male Canadian born in the United States and Canada in 1930, 13.1 per cent were in the United States, while of the female Canadian born, 14.2 per cent were in the United States. This larger percentage of females in the United States is well distributed over the entire age scale, the percentage shown for females in every age period being at least a little in excess of the corresponding age percentage for males, and the differences for the older age periods being about as great as for the younger. The maximum difference is shown for the age group comprising Canadian-born persons 50 to 54 years, in which 30.3

per cent of the females, as compared with 27.2 per cent of the males, were in the United States.

Data showing the relation between the estimated survivors of the Canadian born enumerated in 1910, classified by age, and those enumerated in 1930, are presented in Table 56. In preparing these estimates two sets of survival rates were used. Survival rates for the period 1910 to 1920 were derived by taking the mean of the 1909–11 rates for whites in the original registration States and the 1919–21 rates for whites in the registration States of 1920 for each 5-year age group. These were then applied to the number of Canadian born in each 5-year age group enumerated in 1910 in order to find the estimated number of survivors in 1920. In the same manner the 1920–29 survival rates for whites in the registration States of 1920 were applied to the survivors to 1920 in order to find the estimated number of survivors to 1930, by 5-year age periods.

TABLE **56**. RELATION BETWEEN SURVIVORS OF CANADIAN BORN WHO WERE IN THE UNITED STATES IN 1910 AND NUMBER ENUMERATED IN 1930, BY AGE

(A minus sign (—) denotes excess of "survivors" over enumerated)

AGE IN 1910 (YEARS)	POPULATION, 1910		Age in 1930 (years)	SURVIVORS FROM 1910 TO 1930		ENUMERATED IN 1930		GAIN OVER SURVIVORS	
	Male	Female		Male	Female	Male	Female	Male	Female
Under 5............	7,073	7,009	20 to 24	6,612	6,596	41,140	50,737	34,528	44,141
5 to 9.............	12,083	12,171	25 to 29	11,338	11,464	49,411	53,941	38,073	42,477
10 to 14............	16,712	17,280	30 to 34	15,450	16,024	47,633	51,592	32,183	35,568
15 to 19............	27,065	30,486	35 to 39	24,540	27,750	48,352	54,454	23,812	26,704
20 to 24..... ...	46,696	53,944	40 to 44	41,455	48,257	52,728	57,847	11,273	9,590
25 to 29	57,704	63,912	45 to 49	49,773	56,107	53,264	59,928	3,491	3,821
30 to 34............	64,716	67,496	50 to 54	53,643	57,619	58,221	62,250	4,578	4,631
35 to 39............	66,484	64,868	55 to 59	52,088	52,973	51,966	51,386	—122	—1,587
40 to 44............	64,758	60,941	60 to 64	46,479	46,235	45,066	45,014	—1,413	—1,221
45 to 49............	64,948	59,080	65 to 69	40,450	39,519	40,293	40,178	—157	659
50 to 54............	54,097	48,112	70 to 74	26,893	26,241	25,960	26,311	—933	70
55 to 59............	39,173	35,259	75 to 79	13,687	13,904				
60 to 64............	31,253	28,045	80 to 84	6,397	6,644	24,848	27,565	—2,982	4,182
65 to 69............	22,496	20,194	85 to 89	2,093	2,209				
70 to 74............	13,424	12,414	90 to 94	5,653	626				

When the estimated number of survivors is compared with the number of persons in the corresponding age groups, as enumerated in 1930, it becomes apparent that there had been a large net immigration of persons who were below the age of 55 in 1930, especially of those below 35 or 40, since at each age below 55 the number of persons enumerated exceeded the expected number of survivors. However, among males aged 55 years and over in 1930 the expected number of survivors exceeded the number actually enumerated, indicating a net loss of population in these ages through the return of some of the older male immigrants to Canada. Among the female Canadian born aged 55 to 64 there appears, also, to have been a net loss through return to Canada, but in the ages 65 and over there was a net gain, indicating that the tendency of the older females to return to Canada was less pronounced than the movement of the older males. It should be borne in mind that the figures in Table 56 do not represent actual recorded migration, but only indicate the general tendency insofar as it can be inferred from the censuses of 1910 and 1930 and the mortality rates for the period.

Urban and Rural Areas

In Table 57 are summarized the statistics of the Canadian stock in the United States classified by age for urban and rural areas, with certain percentages for the United States as a whole for comparison. The age distribution of the Canadian stock and its various elements is presented in greater detail by sex in Table 58. The main purpose of these two tables is to show the differences in age distribution as between urban and rural areas.

TABLE **57**. White Population of Canadian Stock in Urban and Rural Areas by Age, with Data for Total Population, etc.: 1930

[For United States total see Table 49]

| AREA AND AGE | CANADIAN STOCK | | | | | | POPULATION OF THE UNITED STATES, PER CENT | | |
| | Number | | | Per cent | | | | | |
	Total	Cana-dian born	Canadian parentage	Total	Cana-dian born	Cana-dian-par-entage	Total	For-eign-born white	Native white
Urban	2,450,541	988,738	1,461,803	100.0	100.0	100.0	100.0	100.0	100.0
Under 15 years	459,812	73,932	385,880	18.8	7.5	26.4	25.8	2.3	30.5
15 to 24 years	418,742	124,770	293,972	17.1	12.6	20.1	18.0	8.0	19.9
25 to 44 years	865,706	340,899	524,807	35.3	34.5	35.9	32.8	44.1	30.1
45 to 64 years	541,050	322,136	218,914	22.1	32.6	15.0	18.1	34.8	15.1
65 and over	164,171	126,480	37,691	6.7	12.8	2.6	5.1	10.7	4.3
Unknown	1,060	521	539	...	0.1	...	0.1	0.1	0.1
Rural-nonfarm	555,867	189,946	365,921	100.0	100.0	100.0	100.0	100.0	100.0
Under 15 years	108,195	14,057	94,138	19.5	7.4	25.7	31.3	2.1	33.4
15 to 24 years	84,705	18,516	66,189	15.2	9.7	18.1	17.5	5.3	18.0
25 to 44 years	178,125	55,178	122,947	32.0	29.0	33.6	27.8	36.4	27.0
45 to 64 years	131,428	66,032	65,396	23.6	34.8	17.9	16.8	37.8	15.5
65 and over	53,170	36,051	17,119	9.6	19.0	4.7	6.6	18.3	6.0
Unknown	244	112	132	...	0.1	...	0.1	0.1	0.1
Rural-farm	330,937	99,737	231,200	100.0	100.0	100.0	100.0	100.0	100.0
Under 15 years	61,943	7,811	54,132	18.7	7.8	23.4	36.0	1.4	36.5
15 to 24 years	51,892	10,459	41,433	15.7	10.5	17.9	19.4	4.3	19.6
25 to 44 years	92,830	19,881	72,949	28.1	19.9	31.6	23.0	27.9	23.1
45 to 64 years	90,333	38,927	51,406	27.3	39.0	22.2	16.4	45.8	15.8
65 and over	33,848	22,624	11,224	10.2	22.7	4.9	5.1	20.5	4.9
Unknown	91	35	56	...	...	...	...	...	...

By way of comment on the figures presented in these tables for the entire Canadian stock, it may be said in general that there were proportionately fewer old people in the urban areas than in the rural-nonfarm or in the rural-farm; and that, contrary to what might have been expected, the percentage of children under 15 was about the same. The most consistent variations are perhaps those which appear in the percentage of the Canadian stock between the ages of 25 and 44, which was 35.3 for the urban areas, 32.0 for the rural-nonfarm, and 28.1 for the rural-farm. These figures show distinctly the effect of the migration to the cities of persons in the earlier working ages. The general relation of these percentages as between urban and rural areas is about the same for males and females.

TABLE **58**. WHITE POPULATION OF CANADIAN BIRTH AND PARENTAGE, FRENCH AND ENGLISH, BY AGE AND SEX, FOR URBAN AND RURAL AREAS: 1930

[For United States total see Table 50]

AREA AND AGE	TOTAL			FRENCH			ENGLISH		
	Total	Male	Female	Total	Male	Female	Total	Male	Female
CAN. BORN									
Urban........	**988,738**	**464,065**	**524,673**	**292,564**	**144,357**	**148,207**	**696,174**	**319,708**	**376,466**
Under 15 years......	73,932	36,529	37,403	16,870	8,148	8,722	57,062	28,381	28,681
15 to 24 years......	124,770	56,342	68,428	32,092	14,712	17,380	92,678	41,630	51,048
25 to 44 years......	340,899	160,852	180,047	103,438	51,310	52,128	237,461	109,542	127,919
45 to 64 years......	322,136	152,298	169,838	100,361	50,189	50,172	221,775	102,109	119,666
65 and over........	126,480	57,791	68,689	39,696	19,937	19,759	86,784	37,854	48,930
Unknown..........	521	253	268	107	61	46	414	192	222
Per cent........	**100.0**	**100.0**	**100.0**	**100.0**	**100.0**	**100.0**	**100.0**	**100.0**	**100.0**
Under 15 years......	7.5	7.9	7.1	5.8	5.6	5.9	8.2	8.9	7.6
15 to 24 years......	12.6	12.1	13.0	11.0	10.2	11.7	13.3	13.0	13.6
25 to 44 years......	34.5	34.7	34.3	35.4	35.5	35.2	34.1	34.3	34.0
45 to 64 years......	32.6	32.8	32.4	34.3	34.8	33.9	31.9	31.9	31.8
65 and over........	12.8	12.5	13.1	13.6	13.8	13.3	12.5	11.8	13.0
Unknown..........	0.1	0.1	0.1	...	...	...	0.1	0.1	0.1
Rural-nonfarm..	**189,946**	**97,927**	**92,019**	**55,620**	**30,018**	**25,602**	**134,326**	**67,909**	**66,417**
Under 15 years......	14,057	7,104	6,953	3,288	1,640	1,648	10,769	5,464	5,305
15 to 24 years......	18,516	9,109	9,407	5,588	2,824	2,764	12,928	6,285	6,643
25 to 44 years......	55,178	27,464	27,714	18,032	9,476	8,556	37,146	17,988	19,158
45 to 64 years......	66,032	34,774	31,258	19,019	10,487	8,532	47,013	24,287	22,726
65 and over........	36,051	19,419	16,632	9,670	5,580	4,090	26,381	13,839	12,542
Unknown..........	112	57	55	23	11	12	89	46	43
Per cent........	**100.0**	**100.0**	**100.0**	**100.0**	**100.0**	**100.0**	**100.0**	**100.0**	**100.0**
Under 15 years......	7.4	7.3	7.6	5.9	5.5	6.4	8.0	8.0	8.0
15 to 24 years......	9.7	9.3	10.2	10.0	9.4	10.8	9.6	9.3	10.0
25 to 44 years......	29.0	28.0	30.0	32.4	31.6	33.4	27.7	26.5	28.8
45 to 64 years......	34.8	35.5	34.0	34.2	34.9	33.3	35.0	35.8	34.2
65 and over........	19.0	19.8	18.1	17.4	18.6	16.0	19.6	20.4	18.9
Unknown..........	0.1	0.1	0.1	...	...	...	0.1	0.1	0.1
Rural-farm......	**99,737**	**55,098**	**44,639**	**22,668**	**13,148**	**9,520**	**77,069**	**41,950**	**35,119**
Under 15 years......	7,811	4,057	3,754	1,845	955	890	5,966	3,102	2,864
15 to 24 years......	10,459	5,874	4,585	2,606	1,505	1,101	7,853	4,369	3,484
25 to 44 years......	19,881	9,808	10,073	5,404	2,870	2,534	14,477	6,938	7,539
45 to 64 years......	38,927	21,445	17,482	8,185	4,791	3,394	30,742	16,654	14,088
65 and over........	22,624	13,891	8,733	4,622	3,021	1,601	18,002	10,870	7,132
Unknown..........	35	23	12	6	6	...	29	17	12
Per cent........	**100.0**	**100.0**	**100.0**	**100.0**	**100.0**	**100.0**	**100.0**	**100.0**	**100.0**
Under 15 years......	7.8	7.4	8.4	8.1	7.3	9.3	7.7	7.4	8.2
15 to 24 years......	10.5	10.7	10.3	11.5	11.4	11.6	10.2	10.4	9.9
25 to 44 years......	19.9	17.8	22.6	23.8	21.8	26.6	18.8	16.5	21.5
45 to 64 years......	39.0	38.9	39.2	36.1	36.4	35.7	39.9	39.7	40.1
65 and over........	22.7	25.2	19.6	20.4	23.0	16.8	23.4	25.9	20.3
Unknown..........	...	...	...	...	...	...	...	...	...

TABLE **58**. WHITE POPULATION OF CANADIAN BIRTH AND PARENTAGE, FRENCH AND ENGLISH, BY AGE AND SEX, FOR URBAN AND RURAL AREAS: 1930—Continued

[For United States total see Table 50]

AREA AND AGE	TOTAL			FRENCH			ENGLISH		
	Total	Male	Female	Total	Male	Female	Total	Male	Female
CAN. PARENTAGE									
Urban..........	1,461,803	701,772	760,031	554,954	270,695	284,259	906,849	431,077	475,772
Under 15 years......	385,880	194,926	190,954	160,886	81,012	79,874	224,994	113,914	111,080
15 to 24 years.......	293,972	141,000	152,972	117,831	56,654	61,177	176,141	84,346	91,795
25 to 44 years.......	524,807	245,149	279,658	190,617	91,285	99,332	334,190	153,864	180,326
45 to 64 years.......	218,914	103,322	115,592	73,683	36,020	37,663	145,231	67,302	77,929
65 and over.........	37,691	17,129	20,562	11,785	5,664	6,121	25,906	11,465	14,441
Unknown..........	539	246	293	152	60	92	387	186	201
Per cent........	100.0	100.0	100.0	100.0	100.0	100.0	100.0	100.0	100.0
Under 15 years......	26.4	27.8	25.1	29.0	29.9	28.1	24.8	26.4	23.3
15 to 24 years......	20.1	20.1	20.1	21.2	20.9	21.5	19.4	19.6	19.3
25 to 44 years......	35.9	34.9	36.8	34.3	33.7	34.9	36.9	35.7	37.9
45 to 64 years......	15.0	14.7	15.2	13.3	13.3	13.2	16.0	15.6	16.4
65 and over........	2.6	2.4	2.7	2.1	2.1	2.2	2.9	2.7	3.0
Unknown..........	...	...	...	...	...	...	...	...	...
Rural-nonfarm..	365,921	184,422	181,499	123,288	63,561	59,727	242,633	120,861	121,772
Under 15 years......	94,138	48,045	46,093	34,499	17,560	16,939	59,639	30,485	29,154
15 to 24 years......	66,189	33,358	32,831	23,040	11,792	11,248	43,149	21,566	21,583
25 to 44 years......	122,947	60,652	62,295	39,831	20,428	19,403	83,116	40,224	42,892
45 to 64 years......	65,396	33,433	31,963	20,488	10,870	9,618	44,908	22,563	22,345
65 and over........	17,119	8,877	8,242	5,403	2,901	2,502	11,716	5,976	5,740
Unknown..........	132	57	75	27	10	17	105	47	58
Per cent........	100.0	100.0	100.0	100.0	100.0	100.0	100.0	100.0	100.0
Under 15 years......	25.7	26.1	25.4	28.0	27.6	28.4	24.6	25.2	23.9
15 to 24 years......	18.1	18.1	18.1	18.7	18.6	18.8	17.8	17.8	17.7
25 to 44 years......	33.6	32.9	34.3	32.3	32.1	32.5	34.3	33.3	35.2
45 to 64 years......	17.9	18.1	17.6	16.6	17.1	16.1	18.5	18.7	18.3
65 and over........	4.7	4.8	4.5	4.4	4.6	4.2	4.8	4.9	4.7
Unknown..........	...	...	...	...	...	...	...	...	...
Rural-farm......	231,200	124,596	106,604	57,065	31,566	25,499	174,135	93,030	81,105
Under 15 years......	54,132	27,791	26,341	15,004	7,700	7,304	39,128	20,091	19,037
15 to 24 years......	41,433	23,586	17,847	9,961	5,815	4,146	31,472	17,771	13,701
25 to 44 years......	72,949	38,280	34,669	16,245	8,873	7,372	56,704	29,407	27,297
45 to 64 years......	51,406	28,032	23,374	12,664	7,216	5,448	38,742	20,816	17,926
65 and over........	11,224	6,876	4,348	3,180	1,957	1,223	8,044	4,919	3,125
Unknown..........	56	31	25	11	5	6	45	26	19
Per cent........	100.0	100.0	100.0	100.0	100.0	100.0	100.0	100.0	100.0
Under 15 years......	23.4	22.3	24.7	26.3	24.4	28.6	22.5	21.6	23.5
15 to 24 years......	17.9	18.9	16.7	17.5	18.4	16.3	18.1	19.1	16.9
25 to 44 years......	31.6	30.7	32.5	28.5	28.1	28.9	32.6	31.6	33.7
45 to 64 years......	22.2	22.5	21.9	22.2	22.9	21.4	22.2	22.4	22.1
65 and over........	4.9	5.5	4.1	5.6	6.2	4.8	4.6	5.3	3.9
Unknown..........	...	...	...	...	...	...	...	...	...

Among the Canadian born the percentage of children under 15 shows little variation between the cities and the farms, being 7.5 for the urban areas, 7.4 for the rural-nonfarm, and 7.8 for the rural-farm. The percentage of persons 65 years old and over, however, was only 12.8 in the urban area as compared with 22.7 in the rural-farm, and 19.0, or about half way between, in the rural-nonfarm. There is likewise a marked difference in the relation between the two age groups covering persons in the working period. In the urban population, 34.5 per cent were from 25 to 44; and 32.6 per cent from 45 to 64. In the rural-farm population, on the other hand, only 19.9 per cent were between 25 and 44 years of age, and 39.0 per cent were from 45 to 64. This would indicate that recent immigrants from Canada to the United States had gone much more largely to the cities than to the farms, and that the farm population was more definitely growing older with the passage of time, while the urban population was being recruited from time to time by new additions of young immigrants.

The urban-rural relationships do not differ very greatly as between the French and the English stock. The French stock as a whole has slightly higher percentages of children in all three of the urban-rural areas, but this is the natural result of the fact that a larger fraction of the French stock than of the English is made up of persons in the second generation.

Among the French Canadian born taken alone, the general characteristics of the age distribution are similar to those already discussed, though the differences are less marked than for the English or for the total Canadian born. The percentage of children under 15 in this group, for example, was higher on the farms than in the cities, being 8.1 in the rural-farm areas, as compared with 5.8 in the urban; and the differences in the percentages in the two major age groups, while tending in the same direction, were appreciably less than in the case of the English Canadian born.

Among the English Canadian born the percentage of children under 15 was highest in urban areas and lowest on the farms, being 8.2 for the urban group and only 7.7 for the rural-farm. This difference is perhaps the result of the fact that the females in the rural-farm areas are considerably older than those in the cities, and that they have been in the United States so long that whatever children may have come from Canada with them have passed the age of 15. As regards the two major age groups, namely, those comprising persons 25 to 44 years of age and persons 45 to 64 years of age, the relations shown by the statistics of the English Canadian born are about the same as those already commented on for the total Canadian born, except that the differences are somewhat greater.

Among the persons born in the United States of Canadian parentage, the relation of the percentage of children under 15 in the urban and rural areas again runs counter to general expectation, in that there are relatively fewer children on the farms than in the cities. The percentage of children under 15 in urban areas was 26.4; in rural-nonfarm, 25.7; and in rural-farm, only 23.4. The relations in the next age group are similar; 20.1 per cent of those in urban areas were from 15 to 24 years of age, as compared with 17.9 per cent on the farms; and 35.9 per cent were 25 to 44 years old in urban areas, as compared with 31.6 per cent on farms. On the other hand, the percentages in the older age groups were much higher on the farms than in the cities.[2]

The higher percentages of children in the cities than on the farms obtain both for the French stock and for the English; and the relations between the urban and the rural areas are generally similar for the older age groups.

Sex Ratios by Age

THE number of males per 100 females in the Canadian stock, by age, is presented, for urban and rural areas, in Table 59.

TABLE **59**. SEX RATIOS FOR THE WHITE CANADIAN STOCK, FRENCH AND ENGLISH, BY AGE, FOR URBAN AND RURAL AREAS: 1930

AREA AND AGE	ALL CANADIAN STOCK			CANADIAN BORN			CANADIAN PARENTAGE		
	Total	French	English	Total	French	English	Total	French	English
United States.......	**95.2**	**100.1**	**92.9**	**93.3**	**102.3**	**89.9**	**96.4**	**99.0**	**95.0**
Under 15 years.........	102.2	101.4	102.7	99.1	95.4	100.3	102.8	102.1	103.3
15 to 24 years..........	94.1	95.4	93.5	86.5	89.6	85.5	97.2	97.0	97.3
25 to 44 years..........	91.2	97.3	88.4	91.0	100.7	87.0	91.4	95.6	89.2
45 to 64 years..........	95.8	104.1	92.4	95.4	105.4	91.4	96.4	102.6	93.6
65 and over............	97.5	110.7	92.4	96.9	112.1	91.2	99.2	106.9	95.9
Urban..............	**90.7**	**96.0**	**88.1**	**88.4**	**97.4**	**84.9**	**92.3**	**95.2**	**90.6**
Under 15 years.........	101.4	100.6	101.8	97.7	93.4	99.0	102.1	101.4	102.6
15 to 24 years..........	89.1	90.8	88.2	82.3	84.6	81.6	92.2	92.6	91.9
25 to 44 years..........	88.3	94.1	85.5	89.3	98.4	85.6	87.7	91.9	85.3
45 to 64 years..........	89.6	98.1	85.7	89.7	100.0	85.3	89.4	95.6	86.4
65 and over............	83.9	98.9	77.8	84.1	100.9	77.4	83.3	92.5	79.4
Rural-nonfarm.....	**103.2**	**109.7**	**100.3**	**106.4**	**117.2**	**102.2**	**101.6**	**106.4**	**99.3**
Under 15 years.........	104.0	103.3	104.3	102.2	99.5	103.0	104.2	103.7	104.6
15 to 24 years..........	100.5	104.3	98.7	96.8	102.2	94.6	101.6	104.8	99.9
25 to 44 years..........	97.9	107.0	93.8	99.1	110.8	93.9	97.4	105.3	93.8
45 to 64 years..........	107.9	117.7	103.9	111.2	122.9	106.9	104.6	113.0	101.0
65 and over............	113.8	128.7	108.4	116.8	136.4	110.3	107.7	115.9	104.1
Rural-farm.........	**118.8**	**127.7**	**116.1**	**123.4**	**138.1**	**119.5**	**116.9**	**123.8**	**114.7**
Under 15 years.........	105.8	105.6	105.9	108.1	107.3	108.3	105.5	105.4	105.5
15 to 24 years..........	131.3	139.5	128.8	128.1	136.7	125.4	132.2	140.3	129.7
25 to 44 years..........	107.5	118.5	104.3	97.4	113.3	92.0	110.4	120.4	107.7
45 to 64 years..........	121.1	135.8	117.0	122.7	141.2	118.2	119.9	132.5	116.1
65 and over............	158.8	176.3	153.9	159.1	188.7	152.4	158.1	160.0	157.4

2. Strictly, perhaps, one should not put too much emphasis on comparisons between children born in the United States of Canadian parentage and adults of Canadian parentage, since many of the second-generation children are in the families of the Canadian born; and in many of the families whose adult members are natives of Canadian parentage, the children are of the third generation and classified in the United States census as natives of native parentage and thus omitted altogether from the figures representing the Canadian stock. Since one of these factors in part offsets the other, however, it seems worth while to make the comparisons set forth here, as indicating at least general tendencies and relationships.

The variations in the sex distribution of the several elements of the Canadian stock in the United States, especially when classified by age, present one of the most difficult problems for interpretation that is found in the whole field of available statistical data. In the entire Canadian stock in 1930 there were 95.2 males for every 100 females, the excess of females being practically all in the English stock, since the sex ratio (the number of males per 100 females) for the French alone was 100.1, and for the English, 92.9. Among the French Canadian born taken alone, we find a slight excess of males, the sex ratio being 102.3, which may be compared with a ratio of 89.9 for the English Canadian born. Among the French Canadians of the second generation the sex distribution was nearly even, there being 99.0 males per 100 females, while among the English of the second generation, there were only 95.0 males per 100 females.

Among the English Canadian born there were, as already noted, only 89.9 males per 100 females. This excess of females was not, as would normally be the case with a stable resident population, concentrated in the higher ages; on the contrary, the lowest sex ratio—that is, the highest excess of females—was in the age group 15 to 24, where there were only 85.5 males per 100 females. There was, however, relatively little increase with advancing age, the sex ratio for age 25 to 44 being 87.0, and even that for age 65 and over, only 91.2. The maximum excess of females —that is, the lowest sex ratio—was likewise found among the French Canadian born in the age period 15 to 24, the ratio being 89.6. In the next age period, 25 to 44 years, the ratio for the French Canadian born had increased to 100.7; and in the last period, comprising persons 65 years old and over, to 112.1.

Among the second generation of Canadian stock in the United States the highest excess of females—that is, the lowest sex ratio—was found in the age period 25 to 44 years, being 91.4 for the group as a whole; 95.6 for the French, and 89.2 for the English, the latter again showing relatively little increase with increasing age.

The excess of females was confined almost entirely to the population resident in urban areas. The number of males per 100 females in the entire Canadian stock of all ages in urban areas was 90.7, as compared with 103.2 in rural-nonfarm areas, and 118.8 in rural-farm areas. Among the Canadian born of all ages there were 88.4 males per 100 females in urban areas, as compared with 123.4 on the farms; and even in the second generation of Canadian stock there were similar differences, the urban sex ratio being 92.3, as compared with a rural-farm ratio of 116.9. The greatest difference in sex ratios between urban and farm areas is shown for the French Canadian born, the ratios being 97.4 for urban and 138.1 for rural-farm areas.

The lowest sex ratios—that is, the greatest excesses of females—are shown for the English Canadian born, the ratio for all ages combined being 84.9, and for the group 15 to 24, 81.6. The sex ratio for the English Canadians 25 to 44 and 45 to 64 in urban areas was between 85 and 86, both for the Canadian born and for the second generation.

The general explanation for the relatively larger numbers of females in urban as compared with rural or farm populations is that the cities offer employment in offices and factories to female workers whose services are not needed on the farms; and that the farms, conversely, require mainly male workers. This, however, does not explain the excess of females in the entire Canadian-born population in the United States, unless one assumes that young women have left Canada in larger numbers than young men to seek occupations in the cities of the United States. One must assume, also, that this condition obtains with the English Canadian population and not with the French, since the sex distribution of all French Canadians in the United States, both Canadian born and of Canadian parentage, is nearly even.

It is difficult, however, to draw satisfactory conclusions with respect to the reasons for many of the variations shown by the statistical tables solely on the basis of figures for the United States as a whole, since these are aggregates, including data from a wide variety of areas with widely different conditions both with respect to employment opportunities and with respect to other social and economic conditions which might appeal in different fashion to different classes of immigrants or prospective immigrants. The situation is further complicated by the undoubted existence of a very considerable amount of back-and-forth movement of persons of Canadian birth or parentage between Canada and the United States; in fact, there are certain relations in the statistics representing the population of Canadian origin in the United States from decade to decade which can only be explained on the assumption that considerable numbers of Canadians in the United States at the time of one census had actually returned to Canada during the decade between that census and the next. Similar return movements on the part of the children of the Canadian born in the United States must likewise be assumed; and in this case the existence of such movement can be statistically demonstrated, since the Canadian census shows the numbers of American-born persons in Canada whose parents were Canadian born.[3]

3. Out of 344,574 American born in Canada in 1931, nearly one-third, or 110,128, had one or both parents born in Canada. This total comprised 66,953 with both parents Canadian born and 43,175 with either father or mother born in Canada—the other in most cases being presumably born in the United States.

MEDIAN AGES

THE median may be defined in a general way as that item which stands at the midpoint of a series arranged in order of size or value. The median age of a group of persons would be, therefore, the age of the person standing in the middle of the series if the whole number of persons were arranged in order of age. For the computation of median ages it is highly desirable to have a tabulation of age by single years, since one or two assumptions not certain to be true have to be made in computing medians from tabulations in groups of ages. Especially with such broad age groups as those used in the tabulation of the 1930 Canadian stock in the United States, a considerable element of approximation in the medians is inevitable. The differences in the computed medians as between one class and another are so great, however, that the figures are significant in spite of this element of approximation. The median ages are presented for the various elements of the Canadian stock by sex, and for urban and rural areas in Table 60.

TABLE **60**. MEDIAN AGES FOR THE WHITE CANADIAN STOCK, FRENCH AND ENGLISH, BY SEX, FOR URBAN AND RURAL AREAS, 1930, AND FOR THE CANADIAN BORN, 1910

AREA AND CLASS	TOTAL			FRENCH			ENGLISH		
	Total	Male	Female	Total	Male	Female	Total	Male	Female
All Canadian stock, 1930......	33.5	33.3	33.6	31.9	32.2	31.7	34.3	33.9	34.6
Urban.....................	33.0	32.6	33.4	31.5	31.6	31.5	33.8	33.1	34.3
Rural-nonfarm..............	34.5	34.9	34.2	33.0	33.7	32.2	35.3	35.5	35.1
Rural-farm.................	36.1	36.9	35.3	34.6	35.9	33.2	36.6	37.2	35.9
Canadian born, 1930.........	43.7	44.1	43.4	44.4	45.1	43.7	43.4	43.7	43.2
Urban.....................	42.3	42.3	42.4	43.8	44.2	43.4	41.7	41.4	41.9
Rural-nonfarm..............	47.2	48.0	46.2	45.9	47.0	44.6	47.7	48.5	46.8
Rural-farm.................	51.0	52.3	49.5	48.6	50.2	46.4	51.7	52.9	50.2
Canadian parentage, 1930.....	27.6	27.1	28.0	25.5	25.4	25.6	28.7	28.1	29.2
Urban.....................	26.9	26.2	27.6	24.9	24.6	25.2	28.1	27.2	28.9
Rural-nonfarm..............	28.7	28.6	28.8	27.1	27.4	26.7	29.4	29.2	29.7
Rural-farm.................	30.5	30.7	30.3	29.4	30.1	28.5	30.8	30.9	30.7
Canadian born, 1910...........	39.3	40.2	38.4	....	....	....	....	....	....

There is a great difference in age, of course, between the Canadian born in the United States and the native population of Canadian parentage, the median ages in 1930 being 43.7 years for the former, and 27.6 years for the latter, with a median age of 33.5 years for the whole Canadian stock in the United States, which was made up of 1,278,421 Canadian born and 2,058,924 American-born persons of Canadian parentage.

The median age of the French Canadian born was 44.4, as compared with 43.4 for the English. The median age of the French Canadian-born males was 45.1, as compared with 43.7 for the females; while among the English Canadian born there was much less difference between males and females, the figures being, respectively, 43.7 and 43.2.

Attention has already been called to the fact that the population of Canadian stock (especially the Canadian born) in rural areas, and particularly the population on farms, was older than the corresponding classes in urban areas. The median ages shown in Table 60 furnish a more definite measure of the extent of this difference than any of the data previously discussed. The median age of the total Canadian born in urban areas was 42.3, as compared with 47.2 in rural-nonfarm areas and 51.0 in rural-farm areas. The differences for the English Canadian born were even greater, the medians being 41.7, 47.7, and 51.7, respectively, while the corresponding differences for the French Canadian born were, of course, slightly less.

The median age of all native persons of Canadian parentage in urban areas in 1930 was 26.9, as compared with 28.7 in rural-nonfarm areas, and 30.5 in rural-farm. It may be noted that not only are the ages very much lower than those of the Canadian born, but that the difference between the median age for urban areas and that for rural-farm areas is very much less, and that, consequently, the difference in the median age shown for the two generations is appreciably less in urban areas than in rural-farm. The median age of the second generation of French Canadian stock was materially lower than the corresponding figures for the English, 25.5, as compared with 28.7; and unlike the situation with the Canadian born, the difference between the medians for urban areas and rural-farm areas was somewhat greater among persons of French Canadian parentage than among those of English Canadian parentage. The median age of females was slightly higher than the median age of males in the group of French Canadian parentage, and appreciably higher in the corresponding group of English parentage, the figures for the latter being 28.1 for males and 29.2 for females.

AGE DISTRIBUTION BY STATES

In Table 61 are presented the 1930 data for the Canadian-born white classified by age in 5-year periods for the 12 selected States to which reference was made on page 120, with 1910 figures for comparison. These 12 States include a number in which the Canadian born are of considerable importance and some representation for the more important of the broad areas into which the country might be divided on the basis of the general relation of the Canadian-born population to the total, namely, New England, where the Canadian born are and have been especially important; the Middle West, where their numbers are materially smaller than a generation ago; and the Pacific Coast, where the Canadian born are largely of recent arrival. Tables 62 and 63 present similar age data for the French and English Canadian born for the 12 States for 1930 only.

These figures are presented in detail primarily to make available important data not to be found elsewhere in its entirety. The 12-State total is not exactly representative of the total Canadian-born population of the United States, since it is somewhat overweighted with urban territory (through the inclusion of Massachusetts), as may be noted by comparing its percentage distribution with that shown for the country as a whole in Table 51. The figures for individual States, however, represent actual tabulated age distributions for both 1930 and 1910 and the data in Tables 62 and 63 constitute the only available detailed age distribution of the French and English Canadian born. These figures should therefore prove of considerable value in any analysis of the Canadian-born population of the States represented.

The age data for the Canadian stock and its various elements, in broad age periods as tabulated for 1930, are presented by States in a series of tables as follows: In Table 64, the entire Canadian stock in the United States; in Table 65, the Canadian born as a whole; in Table 66, the Canadian born by sex; in Table 67, the Canadian born, French and English; in Table 68, the French Canadian born by sex; in Table 69, the English Canadian born by sex; in Table 70, all native white persons of Canadian parentage; in Table 71, the second generation of the Canadian stock, French and English; in Table 72, persons of French Canadian parentage by sex; and in Table 73, persons of English Canadian parentage by sex. In Tables 66, 67, 68, 69, 71, 72, and 73 figures are presented only for the 29 States in which the Canadian born formed one per cent or more of the population.

In Table 74 are presented, for the Canadian stock and its major elements, data for persons under 15 years of age by 5-year periods, for all States. These figures are presented in a separate table by way of supplement to the broad age groups given in Tables 64 to 73.

These detailed State tables are presented, like many of the other State tables, primarily for two reasons—first, to meet the direct demand for information about the Canadian born in specific areas and, second, as a source of material for those who may be interested in making for individual States or groups of States comparisons and analyses similar to those suggested by the discussion of the figures for larger areas in the earlier pages of this chapter.[4]

4. See footnote, p. 149.

TABLE **61**. CANADIAN-BORN WHITE POPULATION BY AGE (5-YEAR PERIODS) AND SEX, FOR 12 SELECTED STATES: 1930 AND 1910

(Per cent not shown where less than 0.1)

SEX AND AGE (YEARS)	TOTAL FOR 12 STATES		NEW HAMPSHIRE		MASSACHUSETTS		NEW YORK		OHIO		MINNESOTA	
	1930	1910	1930	1910	1930	1910	1930	1910	1930	1910	1930	1910
Male	291,073	312,236	24,775	28,725	127,586	134,878	68,332	57,050	12,952	11,376	14,295	23,819
Under 15	19,837	19,356	1,113	2,611	6,788	8,670	6,546	3,874	1,099	577	759	775
15 to 19	13,259	14,924	839	2,150	4,354	7,553	3,806	2,681	736	426	660	530
20 to 24	18,071	26,212	1,288	3,058	7,544	13,169	5,774	4,847	771	771	517	1,253
25 to 29	23,340	31,965	1,846	3,145	10,670	15,381	7,219	5,861	1,056	1,065	415	1,910
30 to 34	22,500	35,372	2,069	3,094	10,473	16,328	6,361	6,392	1,075	1,268	448	2,518
35 to 39	22,840	36,070	2,112	3,177	10,889	16,516	5,746	6,532	1,103	1,326	663	2,608
40 to 44	24,907	33,701	2,383	2,839	12,060	14,374	5,750	6,042	1,153	1,358	843	2,745
45 to 49	26,540	32,631	2,517	2,512	12,797	13,159	5,516	5,597	1,143	1,351	1,155	3,095
50 to 54	29,010	26,026	2,596	2,040	13,644	9,524	5,775	4,575	1,214	1,091	1,593	2,730
55 to 59	25,893	18,598	2,448	1,427	12,110	7,000	4,704	3,243	1,044	705	1,554	1,886
60 to 64	22,455	14,816	2,069	1,090	9,975	5,414	3,884	2,755	922	563	1,587	1,458
65 to 69	18,700	10,253	1,554	694	7,646	3,728	3,193	1,993	722	435	1,655	1,002
70 to 74	12,048	6,186	1,020	428	4,429	2,088	2,041	1,286	722 / 493	221	1,224	636
75 and over	11,532	5,799	909	431	4,159	1,883	1,974	1,308	408	207	1,220	647
Unknown	141	327	12	29	48	91	43	64	13	12	2	26
Per cent	100.0	100.0	100.0	100.0	100.0	100.0	100.0	100.0	100.0	100.0	100.0	100.0
Under 15	6.8	6.2	4.5	9.1	5.3	6.4	9.6	6.8	8.5	5.1	5.3	3.3
15 to 19	4.6	4.8	3.4	7.5	3.4	5.6	5.6	4.7	5.7	3.7	4.6	2.2
20 to 24	6.2	8.4	5.2	10.6	5.9	9.8	8.4	8.5	6.0	6.8	3.6	5.3
25 to 29	8.0	10.2	7.5	10.9	8.4	11.4	10.6	10.3	8.2	9.4	2.9	8.0
30 to 34	7.7	11.3	8.4	10.8	8.2	12.1	9.3	11.2	8.3	11.1	3.1	10.6
35 to 39	7.8	11.6	8.5	11.1	8.5	12.3	8.4	11.4	8.5	11.7	4.6	10.9
40 to 44	8.6	10.8	9.6	9.9	9.5	10.7	8.4	10.6	8.9	11.9	5.9	11.5
45 to 49	9.1	10.5	10.2	8.7	10.0	9.8	8.1	9.8	8.8	11.9	8.1	13.0
50 to 54	10.0	8.3	10.5	7.1	10.7	7.1	8.5	8.0	9.4	9.6	11.1	11.5
55 to 59	8.9	6.0	9.9	5.0	9.5	5.2	6.9	5.7	8.1	6.2	10.9	7.9
60 to 64	7.7	4.7	8.4	3.8	7.8	4.0	5.7	4.8	7.1	4.9	11.1	6.1
65 to 69	6.4	3.3	6.3	2.4	6.0	2.8	4.7	3.5	5.6	3.8	11.6	4.2
70 to 74	4.1	2.0	4.1	1.5	3.5	1.5	3.0	2.3	3.8	1.9	8.6	2.7
75 and over	4.0	1.9	3.7	1.5	3.3	1.4	2.9	2.3	3.2	1.8	8.5	2.7
Unknown	...	0.1	...	0.1	...	0.1	0.1	0.1	0.1	0.1	...	0.1
Female	333,576	328,312	26,184	29,121	160,465	160,753	79,542	65,592	13,895	11,815	12,807	17,099
Under 15	20,347	19,754	1,223	2,786	7,161	8,869	6,515	3,864	1,071	616	755	792
15 to 19	15,310	17,358	972	2,494	5,690	9,291	4,282	3,055	734	470	707	521
20 to 24	24,517	32,153	1,544	3,259	11,716	18,153	7,312	6,227	902	968	591	1,051
25 to 29	27,690	37,733	1,942	3,249	13,706	20,163	8,076	7,769	1,103	1,264	542	1,465
30 to 34	26,484	38,754	2,120	3,124	13,035	19,858	7,163	7,791	1,160	1,356	546	1,891
35 to 39	27,953	36,585	2,351	3,160	14,185	18,401	7,011	7,270	1,258	1,320	672	1,889
40 to 44	29,695	33,573	2,611	2,772	15,167	16,480	7,007	6,387	1,332	1,266	875	1,838
45 to 49	31,458	31,398	2,696	2,490	16,242	14,571	6,949	6,195	1,266	1,322	1,087	1,891
50 to 54	32,677	24,987	2,720	1,914	16,754	10,968	6,676	4,941	1,253	1,119	1,459	1,693
55 to 59	26,974	18,158	2,451	1,363	13,818	8,059	5,224	3,620	929	704	1,250	1,270
60 to 64	23,630	14,401	2,007	1,010	11,810	6,176	4,351	3,105	888	547	1,183	1,030
65 to 69	19,945	10,323	1,553	678	9,521	4,385	3,775	2,194	851	379	1,197	789
70 to 74	13,061	6,401	1,023	406	5,692	2,629	2,483	1,498	594	222	908	468
75 and over	13,684	6,471	961	400	5,916	2,665	2,657	1,609	543	249	1,033	493
Unknown	151	263	10	16	52	85	61	67	11	13	2	18
Per cent	100.0	100.0	100.0	100.0	100.0	100.0	100.0	100.0	100.0	100.0	100.0	100.0
Under 15	6.1	6.0	4.7	9.6	4.5	5.5	8.2	5.9	7.7	5.2	5.9	4.6
15 to 19	4.6	5.3	3.7	8.6	3.6	5.8	5.4	4.7	5.3	4.0	5.5	3.0
20 to 24	7.3	9.8	5.9	11.2	7.3	11.3	9.2	9.5	6.5	8.2	4.6	6.1
25 to 29	8.3	11.5	7.4	11.2	8.5	12.5	10.2	11.8	7.9	10.7	4.2	8.6
30 to 34	7.9	11.8	8.1	10.7	8.1	12.4	9.0	11.9	8.3	11.5	4.3	8.6
35 to 39	8.4	11.1	9.0	10.9	8.8	11.4	8.8	11.1	9.1	11.2	5.2	11.1
40 to 44	8.9	10.2	10.0	9.5	9.5	10.3	8.8	9.7	9.6	10.7	6.8	10.7
45 to 49	9.4	9.6	10.3	8.6	10.1	9.1	8.7	9.4	9.1	11.2	8.5	11.1
50 to 54	9.8	7.6	10.4	6.6	10.4	6.8	8.4	7.5	9.0	9.5	11.4	9.9
55 to 59	8.1	5.5	9.4	4.7	8.6	5.0	6.6	5.5	6.7	6.0	9.8	7.4
60 to 64	7.1	4.4	7.7	3.5	7.4	3.8	5.5	4.7	6.4	4.6	9.2	6.0
65 to 69	6.0	3.1	5.9	2.3	5.9	2.7	4.7	3.3	6.1	3.2	9.3	4.6
70 to 74	3.9	1.9	3.9	1.4	3.5	1.6	3.1	2.3	4.3	1.9	7.1	2.7
75 and over	4.1	2.0	3.7	1.4	3.7	1.7	3.3	2.5	3.9	2.1	8.1	2.9
Unknown	...	0.1	...	0.1	...	0.1	0.1	0.1	0.1	0.1	...	0.1

TABLE **61**. CANADIAN-BORN WHITE POPULATION BY AGE (5-YEAR PERIODS) AND SEX, FOR 12 SELECTED STATES: 1930 AND 1910—Continued

[Per cent not shown where less than 0.1]

SEX AND AGE (YEARS)	IOWA 1930	IOWA 1910	MISSOURI 1930	MISSOURI 1910	NORTH DAKOTA 1930	NORTH DAKOTA 1910	SOUTH DAKOTA 1930	SOUTH DAKOTA 1910	NEBRASKA 1930	NEBRASKA 1910	KANSAS 1930	KANSAS 1910	WASHINGTON 1930	WASHINGTON 1910
Male........	3,174	6,031	2,783	4,279	6,441	11,797	1,808	3,475	2,190	3,853	2,071	3,827	24,666	23,126
Under 15....	115	108	125	93	318	676	55	94	90	76	88	67	2,741	1,735
15 to 19......	86	91	108	93	307	439	88	63	106	39	64	40	2,105	819
20 to 24.......	84	171	114	157	188	789	44	144	74	110	62	113	1,611	1,630
25 to 29.......	79	252	127	280	173	1,067	45	239	53	213	64	152	1,593	2,400
30 to 34.......	99	377	119	398	188	1,452	48	330	57	300	72	252	1,491	2,663
35 to 39.......	128	455	163	415	269	1,507	75	334	55	387	83	290	1,554	2,523
40 to 44.......	167	618	204	542	360	1,389	75	369	97	489	89	388	1,726	2,548
45 to 49.......	189	765	236	572	566	1,368	141	421	135	532	123	523	2,022	2,736
50 to 54.......	267	775	260	505	851	1,262	216	462	232	482	153	437	2,209	2,143
55 to 59.......	324	627	277	368	874	739	198	353	255	369	200	395	1,905	1,486
60 to 64.......	396	612	294	335	766	484	215	274	304	356	245	416	1,798	1,059
65 to 69.......	424	484	306	236	670	286	218	187	277	222	292	336	1,743	650
70 to 74.......	354	341	224	161	530	156	199	98	206	156	238	221	1,090	394
75 and over....	461	342	225	119	377	155	189	103	248	117	298	191	1,064	296
Unknown......	1	13	1	5	4	28	2	4	1	5	..	6	14	44
Per cent.....	100.0	100.0	100.0	100.0	100.0	100.0	100.0	100.0	100.0	100.0	100.0	100.0	100.0	100.0
Under 15.......	3.6	1.8	4.5	2.2	4.9	5.7	3.0	2.7	4.1	2.0	4.2	1.8	11.1	7.5
15 to 19........	2.7	1.5	3.9	2.2	4.8	3.7	4.9	1.8	4.8	1.0	3.1	1.0	8.5	3.5
20 to 24........	2.6	2.8	4.1	3.7	2.9	6.7	2.4	4.1	3.4	2.9	3.0	3.0	6.5	7.0
25 to 29........	2.5	4.2	4.6	6.5	2.7	9.0	2.5	6.9	2.4	5.5	3.1	4.0	6.5	10.4
30 to 34........	3.1	6.3	4.3	9.3	2.9	12.3	2.7	9.5	2.6	7.8	3.5	6.6	6.0	11.5
35 to 39........	4.0	7.5	5.9	9.7	4.2	12.8	4.1	9.6	2.5	10.0	4.0	7.6	6.3	10.9
40 to 44........	5.3	10.2	7.3	12.7	5.6	11.8	4.1	10.6	4.4	12.7	4.3	10.1	7.0	11.0
45 to 49........	6.0	12.7	8.5	13.4	8.8	11.6	7.8	12.1	6.2	13.8	5.9	13.7	8.2	11.8
50 to 54........	8.4	12.9	9.3	11.8	13.2	10.7	11.9	13.3	10.6	12.5	7.4	11.4	9.0	9.3
55 to 59........	10.2	10.4	10.0	8.6	13.6	6.3	11.0	10.2	11.6	9.6	9.7	10.3	7.7	6.4
60 to 64........	12.5	10.1	10.6	7.8	11.9	4.1	11.9	7.9	13.9	9.2	11.8	10.9	7.3	4.6
65 to 69........	13.4	8.0	11.0	5.5	10.4	2.4	12.1	5.4	12.6	5.8	14.1	8.8	7.1	2.8
70 to 74........	11.2	5.7	8.0	3.8	8.2	1.3	11.0	2.8	9.4	4.0	11.5	5.8	4.4	1.7
75 and over.....	14.5	5.7	8.1	2.8	5.9	1.3	10.5	3.0	11.3	3.0	14.4	5.0	4.3	1.3
Unknown......	...	0.2	...	0.1	0.1	0.2	0.1	0.1	...	0.1	...	0.2	0.1	0.2
Female.....	3,159	5,565	2,629	3,682	5,800	9,300	1,543	2,517	2,188	3,418	1,966	3,313	23,398	16,137
Under 15.......	123	128	129	106	333	588	97	81	102	81	68	79	2,770	1,764
15 to 19........	103	90	99	105	322	390	85	69	109	40	77	39	2,130	794
20 to 24........	85	155	101	161	256	622	53	108	70	114	55	86	1,832	1,249
25 to 29........	97	271	112	325	229	994	37	198	52	211	52	159	1,742	1,665
30 to 34........	96	362	157	345	215	1,337	41	257	64	330	58	233	1,829	1,870
35 to 39........	135	396	168	325	291	1,232	71	262	62	306	68	292	1,681	1,732
40 to 44........	164	549	194	424	360	1,065	77	293	113	414	99	383	1,696	1,702
45 to 49........	206	684	247	430	576	974	121	307	157	472	130	433	1,781	1,629
50 to 54........	284	721	263	411	841	800	157	270	232	404	154	416	1,884	1,330
55 to 59........	274	582	223	309	684	514	161	225	236	318	186	356	1,538	838
60 to 64........	337	564	249	276	601	337	176	165	259	269	268	313	1,501	609
65 to 69........	419	459	236	211	457	200	163	145	271	204	241	243	1,261	436
70 to 74........	354	286	211	140	326	116	144	76	232	133	220	147	874	280
75 and over.....	481	313	239	105	308	116	158	55	228	122	290	130	870	214
Unknown......	1	5	1	9	1	15	2	6	1	..	...	4	9	25
Per cent.....	100.0	100.0	100.0	100.0	100.0	100.0	100.0	100.0	100.0	100.0	100.0	100.0	100.0	100.0
Under 15.......	3.9	2.3	4.9	2.9	5.7	6.3	6.3	3.2	4.7	2.4	3.5	2.4	11.8	10.9
15 to 19........	3.3	1.6	3.8	2.9	5.6	4.2	5.5	2.7	5.0	1.2	3.9	1.2	9.1	4.9
20 to 24........	2.7	2.8	3.8	4.4	4.4	6.7	3.4	4.3	3.2	3.3	2.8	2.6	7.8	7.7
25 to 29........	3.1	4.9	4.3	8.8	3.9	10.7	2.4	7.9	2.4	6.2	2.6	4.8	7.4	10.3
30 to 34........	3.0	6.5	6.0	9.4	3.7	14.4	2.7	10.2	2.9	9.7	3.0	7.0	7.8	11.6
35 to 39........	4.3	7.1	6.4	8.8	5.0	13.2	4.6	10.4	2.8	9.0	3.5	8.8	7.2	10.7
40 to 44........	5.2	9.9	7.4	11.5	6.2	11.5	5.0	11.6	5.2	12.1	5.0	11.6	7.2	10.5
45 to 49........	6.5	12.3	9.4	11.7	9.9	10.5	7.8	12.2	7.2	13.8	6.6	13.1	7.6	10.1
50 to 54........	9.0	13.0	10.0	11.2	14.5	8.6	10.2	10.7	10.6	11.8	7.8	12.6	8.1	8.2
55 to 59........	8.7	10.5	8.5	8.4	11.8	5.5	10.4	8.9	10.8	9.3	9.5	10.7	6.6	5.2
60 to 64........	10.7	10.1	9.5	7.5	10.4	3.6	11.4	6.6	11.8	7.9	13.6	9.4	6.4	3.8
65 to 69........	13.3	8.2	9.0	5.7	7.9	2.2	10.6	5.8	12.4	6.0	12.3	7.3	5.4	2.7
70 to 74........	11.2	5.1	8.0	3.8	5.6	1.2	9.3	3.0	10.6	3.9	11.2	4.4	3.7	1.7
75 and over.....	15.2	5.6	9.1	2.9	5.3	1.2	10.2	2.2	10.4	3.6	14.8	3.9	3.7	1.3
Unknown......	...	0.1	...	0.2	...	0.2	0.1	0.2	...	...	...	0.1	...	0.2

TABLE **62.** FRENCH CANADIAN BORN BY AGE (5-YEAR PERIODS) AND SEX, FOR 12 SELECTED STATES 1930

[Per cent not shown where less than 0.1]

SEX AND AGE (YEARS)	Total for 12 states	New Hampshire	Massachusetts	New York	Ohio	Minnesota	Iowa	Missouri	North Dakota	South Dakota	Nebraska	Kansas	Washington
Male....	**99,113**	**18,724**	**56,192**	**14,780**	**1,297**	**3,591**	**304**	**317**	**745**	**273**	**228**	**299**	**2,3(**
Under 15...	4,693	836	2,405	1,184	59	55	4	9	11	2	2	11	11
15 to 19....	3,350	671	1,737	709	51	51	4	9	9	2	9	5	9
20 to 24....	5,517	1,041	2,797	1,396	71	49	5	16	24	6	6	7	9
25 to 29....	7,924	1,516	4,241	1,770	103	78	9	25	30	4	9	7	13
30 to 34....	7,986	1,728	4,401	1,426	123	95	15	21	27	12	5	12	12
35 to 39....	8,385	1,705	4,960	1,255	93	132	11	29	33	10	5	10	14
40 to 44....	9,435	1,883	5,666	1,263	142	169	14	30	62	16	17	17	15
45 to 49....	9,608	1,843	5,834	1,134	122	297	15	23	73	28	12	19	20
50 to 54....	10,279	1,863	6,243	1,148	120	441	30	24	79	30	26	25	22
55 to 59....	9,012	1,762	5,378	876	91	422	27	27	91	27	30	31	25
60 to 64....	7,660	1,454	4,462	735	107	454	36	19	88	29	25	23	22
65 to 69....	6,520	1,059	3,641	737	89	501	38	32	83	32	24	45	23
70 to 74....	4,313	714	2,216	529	68	401	39	19	77	38	22	31	19
75 and over.	4,394	639	2,196	609	58	445	57	34	58	37	35	56	17
Unknown..	37	10	15	9	..	1	..	..	..	..	..	1	..
Per cent.	**100.0**	**100.0**	**100.0**	**100.0**	**100.0**	**100.0**	**100.0**	**100.0**	**100.0**	**100.0**	**100.0**	**100.0**	**100.**
Under 15...	4.7	4.5	4.3	8.0	4.5	1.5	1.3	2.8	1.5	0.7	0.9	3.7	4.
15 to 19....	3.4	3.6	3.1	4.8	3.9	1.4	1.3	2.8	1.2	0.7	3.9	1.7	3.
20 to 24....	5.6	5.6	5.0	9.4	5.5	1.4	1.6	5.0	3.2	2.2	2.6	2.3	4.
25 to 29....	8.0	8.1	7.5	12.0	7.9	2.2	3.0	7.9	4.0	1.5	3.9	2.3	5.
30 to 34....	8.1	9.2	7.8	9.6	9.5	2.6	4.9	6.6	3.6	4.4	2.2	4.0	5.
35 to 39....	8.5	9.1	8.8	8.5	7.2	3.7	3.6	9.1	4.4	3.7	2.2	3.3	6.
40 to 44....	9.5	10.1	10.1	8.5	10.9	4.7	4.6	9.5	8.3	5.9	7.5	5.7	6.
45 to 49....	9.7	9.8	10.4	7.7	9.4	8.3	4.9	7.3	9.8	10.3	5.3	6.4	8.
50 to 54....	10.4	9.9	11.1	7.8	9.3	12.3	9.9	7.6	10.6	11.0	11.4	8.4	10.
55 to 59....	9.1	9.4	9.6	5.9	7.0	11.8	8.9	8.5	12.2	9.9	13.2	10.4	10.
60 to 64....	7.7	7.8	7.9	5.0	8.2	12.6	11.8	6.0	11.8	10.6	11.0	7.7	9.
65 to 69....	6.6	5.7	6.5	5.0	6.9	14.0	12.5	10.1	11.1	11.7	10.5	15.1	10.
70 to 74....	4.4	3.8	3.9	3.6	5.2	11.2	12.8	6.0	10.3	13.9	9.6	10.4	6.
75 and over.	4.4	3.4	3.9	4.1	4.5	12.4	18.8	10.7	7.8	13.6	15.4	18.7	7.
Unknown..	...	0.1	0.1	..	...	...	...	...	...	...	...	...	
Female..	**100,242**	**18,958**	**59,049**	**14,175**	**1,309**	**2,893**	**304**	**271**	**609**	**219**	**208**	**270**	**1,97**
Under 15...	5,113	988	2,661	1,172	75	57	3	8	19	8	7	4	11
15 to 19....	3,838	784	2,029	737	62	80	6	6	17	3	5	5	10
20 to 24....	6,573	1,211	3,630	1,382	89	81	6	18	15	6	5	3	12
25 to 29....	7,986	1,542	4,477	1,553	114	93	15	17	28	3	8	6	13
30 to 34....	8,207	1,669	4,684	1,384	115	116	9	18	25	9	5	5	16
35 to 39....	8,705	1,762	5,289	1,213	107	120	15	22	27	10	4	10	12
40 to 44....	9,639	1,904	5,967	1,164	129	184	13	20	50	15	12	14	16
45 to 49....	9,812	1,877	6,169	1,094	111	244	17	22	69	9	15	23	16
50 to 54....	10,335	1,897	6,366	1,083	121	395	37	26	94	34	38	25	21
55 to 59....	8,460	1,675	5,186	832	75	353	19	20	60	19	21	23	17
60 to 64....	7,240	1,327	4,437	724	96	288	36	21	70	31	22	33	15
65 to 69....	6,142	1,040	3,645	743	86	312	33	23	50	22	19	31	13
70 to 74....	3,979	683	2,245	478	57	254	40	19	40	18	21	32	9
75 and over.	4,186	593	2,253	607	72	316	55	31	45	32	26	56	10
Unknown..	27	6	11	9	..	..	..	..	..	..	..	..	
Per cent.	**100.0**	**100.0**	**100.0**	**100.0**	**100.0**	**100.0**	**100.0**	**100.0**	**100.0**	**100.0**	**100.0**	**100.0**	**100.**
Under 15...	5.1	5.2	4.5	8.3	5.7	2.0	1.0	3.0	3.1	3.7	3.4	1.5	5.
15 to 19....	3.8	4.1	3.4	5.2	4.7	2.8	2.0	2.2	2.8	1.4	2.4	1.9	5.
20 to 24....	6.6	6.4	6.1	9.7	6.8	2.8	2.0	6.6	2.5	2.7	2.4	1.1	6.
25 to 29....	8.0	8.1	7.6	11.0	8.7	3.2	4.9	6.3	4.6	1.4	3.8	2.2	6.
30 to 34....	8.2	8.8	7.9	9.8	8.8	4.0	3.0	6.6	4.1	4.1	2.4	1.9	8.
35 to 39....	8.7	9.3	9.0	8.6	8.2	4.1	4.9	8.1	4.4	4.6	1.9	3.7	6.
40 to 44....	9.6	10.0	10.1	8.2	9.9	6.4	4.3	7.4	8.2	6.8	5.8	5.2	8.
45 to 49....	9.8	9.9	10.4	7.7	8.5	8.4	5.6	8.1	11.3	4.1	7.2	8.5	8.
50 to 54....	10.3	10.0	10.8	7.6	9.2	13.7	12.2	9.6	15.4	15.5	18.3	9.3	11.
55 to 59....	8.4	8.8	8.8	5.9	5.7	12.2	6.3	7.4	9.9	8.7	10.1	8.5	9.
60 to 64....	7.2	7.0	7.5	5.1	7.3	10.0	11.8	7.7	11.5	14.2	10.6	12.2	7.
65 to 69....	6.1	5.5	6.2	5.2	6.6	10.8	10.9	8.5	8.2	10.0	9.1	11.5	7.
70 to 74....	4.0	3.6	3.8	3.4	4.4	8.8	13.2	7.0	6.6	8.2	10.1	11.9	4.
75 and over.	4.2	3.1	3.8	4.3	5.5	10.9	18.1	11.4	7.4	14.6	12.5	20.7	5.
Unknown..	...	...	...	0.1	...	...	...	...	...	...	...	...	0.

TABLE **63**. ENGLISH CANADIAN BORN BY AGE (5-YEAR PERIODS) AND SEX, FOR 12 SELECTED STATES: 1930

[Per cent not shown where less than 0.1]

SEX AND AGE (YEARS)	Total for 12 States	New Hampshire	Massachusetts	New York	Ohio	Minnesota	Iowa	Missouri	North Dakota	South Dakota	Nebraska	Kansas	Washington
Male....	**191,960**	**6,051**	**71,394**	**53,552**	**11,655**	**10,704**	**2,870**	**2,466**	**5,696**	**1,535**	**1,962**	**1,772**	**22,303**
Under 15....	15,144	277	4,383	5,362	1,040	704	111	116	307	53	88	77	2,626
15 to 19....	9,909	168	2,617	3,097	685	609	82	99	298	86	97	59	2,012
20 to 24....	12,554	247	4,747	4,378	700	468	79	98	164	38	68	55	1,512
25 to 29....	15,416	330	6,429	5,449	953	337	70	102	143	41	44	57	1,461
30 to 34....	14,514	341	6,072	4,935	952	353	84	98	161	36	52	60	1,370
35 to 39....	14,455	407	5,929	4,491	1,010	531	117	134	236	65	50	73	1,412
40 to 44....	15,472	500	6,394	4,487	1,011	674	153	174	298	59	80	72	1,570
45 to 49....	16,932	674	6,963	4,382	1,021	858	174	213	493	113	123	104	1,814
50 to 54....	18,731	733	7,401	4,627	1,094	1,152	237	236	772	186	206	128	1,959
55 to 59....	16,881	686	6,732	3,828	953	1,132	297	250	783	171	225	169	1,655
60 to 64....	14,795	615	5,513	3,149	815	1,133	360	275	678	186	279	222	1,570
65 to 69....	12,180	495	4,005	2,456	633	1,154	386	274	587	186	253	247	1,504
70 to 74....	7,735	306	2,213	1,512	425	823	315	205	453	161	184	207	931
75 and over.	7,138	270	1,963	1,365	350	775	404	191	319	152	213	242	894
Unknown..	104	2	33	34	13	1	1	1	4	2	..	...	13
Per cent.	**100.0**	**100.0**	**100.0**	**100.0**	**100.0**	**100.0**	**100.0**	**100.0**	**100.0**	**100.0**	**100.0**	**100.0**	**100.0**
Under 15....	7.9	4.6	6.1	10.0	8.9	6.6	3.9	4.7	5.4	3.5	4.5	4.3	11.8
15 to 19....	5.2	2.8	3.7	5.8	5.9	5.7	2.9	4.0	5.2	5.6	4.9	3.3	9.0
20 to 24....	6.5	4.1	6.6	8.2	6.0	4.4	2.8	4.0	2.9	2.5	3.5	3.1	6.8
25 to 29....	8.0	5.5	9.0	10.2	8.2	3.1	2.4	4.1	2.5	2.7	2.2	3.2	6.6
30 to 34....	7.6	5.6	8.5	9.2	8.2	3.3	2.9	4.0	2.8	2.3	2.7	3.4	6.1
35 to 39....	7.5	6.7	8.3	8.4	8.7	5.0	4.1	5.4	4.1	4.2	2.5	4.1	6.3
40 to 44....	8.1	8.3	9.0	8.4	8.7	6.3	5.3	7.1	5.2	3.8	4.1	4.1	7.0
45 to 49....	8.8	11.1	9.8	8.2	8.8	8.0	6.1	8.6	8.7	7.4	6.3	5.9	8.1
50 to 54....	9.8	12.1	10.4	8.6	9.4	10.8	8.3	9.6	13.6	12.1	10.5	7.2	8.8
55 to 59....	8.8	11.3	9.4	7.1	8.2	10.6	10.3	10.1	13.7	11.1	11.5	9.5	7.4
60 to 64....	7.7	10.2	7.7	5.9	7.0	10.6	12.5	11.2	11.9	12.1	14.2	12.5	7.0
65 to 69....	6.3	8.2	5.6	4.6	5.4	10.8	13.4	11.1	10.3	12.1	12.9	13.9	6.7
70 to 74....	4.0	5.1	3.1	2.8	3.6	7.7	11.0	8.3	8.0	10.5	9.4	11.7	4.2
75 and over.	3.7	4.5	2.7	2.5	3.0	7.2	14.1	7.7	5.6	9.9	10.9	13.7	4.0
Unknown..	0.1	...	...	0.1	0.1	...	...	...	0.1	0.1	...	...	0.1
Female..	**233,334**	**7,226**	**101,416**	**65,367**	**12,586**	**9,914**	**2,855**	**2,358**	**5,191**	**1,324**	**1,980**	**1,696**	**21,421**
Under 15...	15,234	235	4,500	5,343	996	698	120	121	314	89	95	64	2,659
15 to 19....	11,472	188	3,661	3,545	672	627	97	93	305	82	104	72	2,026
20 to 24....	17,944	333	8,086	5,930	813	510	79	83	241	47	65	52	1,705
25 to 29....	19,704	400	9,229	6,523	989	449	82	95	201	34	44	46	1,612
30 to 34....	18,277	451	8,351	5,779	1,045	430	87	139	190	32	59	53	1,661
35 to 39....	19,248	589	8,896	5,798	1,151	552	120	146	264	61	58	58	1,555
40 to 44....	20,056	707	9,200	5,843	1,203	691	151	174	310	62	101	85	1,529
45 to 49....	21,646	819	10,073	5,855	1,155	843	189	225	507	112	142	107	1,619
50 to 54....	22,342	823	10,388	5,593	1,132	1,064	247	237	747	123	194	129	1,665
55 to 59....	18,514	776	8,632	4,392	854	897	255	203	624	142	215	163	1,361
60 to 64....	16,390	680	7,373	3,627	792	895	301	228	531	145	237	235	1,346
65 to 69....	13,803	513	5,876	3,032	765	885	386	213	407	141	252	210	1,123
70 to 74....	9,082	340	3,447	2,005	537	654	314	192	286	126	211	188	782
75 and over.	9,498	368	3,663	2,050	471	717	426	208	263	126	202	234	770
Unknown..	124	4	41	52	11	2	1	1	1	2	1	...	8
Per cent.	**100.0**	**100.0**	**100.0**	**100.0**	**100.0**	**100.0**	**100.0**	**100.0**	**100.0**	**100.0**	**100.0**	**100.0**	**100.0**
Under 15...	6.5	3.3	4.4	8.2	7.9	7.0	4.2	5.1	6.0	6.7	4.8	3.8	12.4
15 to 19....	4.9	2.6	3.6	5.4	5.3	6.3	3.4	3.9	5.9	6.2	5.3	4.2	9.5
20 to 24....	7.7	4.6	8.0	9.1	6.5	5.1	2.8	3.5	4.6	3.5	3.3	3.1	8.0
25 to 29....	8.4	5.5	9.1	10.0	7.9	4.5	2.9	4.0	3.9	2.6	2.2	2.7	7.5
30 to 34....	7.8	6.2	8.2	8.8	8.3	4.3	3.0	5.9	3.7	2.4	3.0	3.1	7.8
35 to 39....	8.2	8.2	8.8	8.9	9.1	5.6	4.2	6.2	5.1	4.6	2.9	3.4	7.3
40 to 44....	8.6	9.8	9.1	8.9	9.6	7.0	5.3	7.4	6.0	4.7	5.1	5.0	7.1
45 to 49....	9.3	11.3	9.9	9.0	9.2	8.5	6.6	9.5	9.8	8.5	7.2	6.3	7.6
50 to 54....	9.6	11.4	10.2	8.6	9.0	10.7	8.7	10.1	14.4	9.3	9.8	7.6	7.8
55 to 59....	7.9	10.7	8.5	6.7	6.8	9.0	8.9	8.6	12.0	10.7	10.9	9.6	6.4
60 to 64....	7.0	9.4	7.3	5.5	6.3	9.0	10.5	9.7	10.2	11.0	12.0	13.9	6.3
65 to 69....	5.9	7.1	5.8	4.6	6.1	8.9	13.5	9.0	7.8	10.6	12.7	12.4	5.2
70 to 74....	3.9	4.7	3.4	3.1	4.3	6.6	11.0	8.1	5.5	9.5	10.7	11.1	3.7
75 and over.	4.1	5.1	3.6	3.1	3.7	7.2	14.9	8.8	5.1	9.5	10.2	13.8	3.6
Unknown..	0.1	0.1	...	0.1	0.1	...	...	...	...	0.2	0.1	...	...

The median age of the Canadian stock and its various elements is presented for 1930, in Table 75, together with the median age of the Canadian born for 1910. The median age provides a convenient means of comparing the population in one State with that in another and affords a numerical measure of differences too small to be conveniently evaluated on the basis of the more complex figures representing the age distribution. The highest median age for the total Canadian born, namely, 59.1 years, is shown for Iowa; and all the States in the West North Central Division show medians above 50 years. The lowest median age for the Canadian born, namely, 38.8, is shown for New Jersey, a State already referred to as one in which a considerable proportion of the Canadian born had arrived in the United States in recent years. For the French Canadian born alone the lowest median age, 37.1, is shown for Vermont, another State into which there has been extensive recent immigration from Canada, and the highest median age for any State with as many as 1,000 French Canadian born is 59.4, for Wisconsin. For the English Canadian born taken alone the lowest median age, 38.8, is shown for New Jersey, and the highest, 58.9, for Iowa.

The median ages of the second generation of the Canadian stock are of course very much lower than those of the Canadian born, since this group contains far larger percentages of children. The spread between the median age of the Canadian born and that of the second generation is much greater in some of the States, however, than in others. In New Hampshire, for example, the median age of the native population of Canadian parentage was only 21.4, as compared with 46.1 for the Canadian born, a difference of 24.7 years, while the difference between the two medians for the country as a whole was only 16.1, these medians being 27.6 and 43.7, respectively. In California, on the other hand, the median age of the second generation of the Canadian stock was 33.0, as compared with 42.0 for the Canadian born, a difference of only 9 years.

While in general the median age of the Canadian-born population in 1930 was 3 or 4 years higher than the median age in 1910, there are considerable variations from this differential in individual States. In North Dakota, for example, the median age was 39.0 in 1910 and 53.0 in 1930, an increase of 14 years, and in a number of other States in the Middle West and also in Maine and New Hampshire the increase was 6 or 8 years or more. In California, on the other hand, the median age of the Canadian-born population in 1930 was actually lower than in 1910—42.0 years in 1930 as compared with 43.5 in 1910.

In Tables 76 and 77 are presented the 1910 age distributions by 5-year periods for males and females in all States. These figures have already been referred to in the discussion of the age data for larger areas (see page 120) and are presented here as representing source material heretofore unpublished. The broad age groups corresponding to those shown in the 1930 tabulation are shown at the bottom of each section of these tables to facilitate comparison of the 1910 figures with those presented for 1930 (for 29 States) in Table 66. The variety of the interrelations is so great as to preclude their discussion in the brief space here available.

4. The figures presented in Tables 64 to 74 represent (except for the States omitted from the selected State tables) practically all of the age data tabulated for the Canadian born in connection with the 1930 census, except that there are available on the tabulation sheets similar age distributions for the population of each State classified as urban, rural-farm, and rural-nonfarm, and for individual cities of 25,000 or more.

TABLE **64**. WHITE POPULATION OF CANADIAN STOCK, BY AGE, BY STATES: 1930

DIVISION AND STATE	All ages	Under 15 years	15 to 24 years	25 to 44 years	45 to 64 years	65 years and over	PER CENT OF TOTAL				
							Under 15	15 to 24	25 to 44	45 to 64	65 and over
United States..	3,337,345	629,950	555,339	1,136,661	762,811	251,189	18.9	16.6	34.1	22.9	7.5
NEW ENGLAND:											
Maine...........	201,748	53,867	36,911	59,973	38,794	12,135	26.7	18.3	29.7	19.2	6.0
New Hampshire...	137,418	32,520	25,135	43,400	27,890	8,429	23.7	18.3	31.6	20.3	6.1
Vermont.........	74,023	17,804	12,143	21,173	16,595	6,290	24.1	16.4	28.6	22.4	8.5
Massachusetts....	724,800	151,752	129,018	244,375	154,869	44,589	20.9	17.8	33.7	21.4	6.2
Rhode Island.....	110,551	24,107	21,191	37,413	22,112	5,698	21.8	19.2	33.8	20.0	5.2
Connecticut......	97,015	20,986	18,458	34,326	18,481	4,741	21.6	19.0	35.4	19.0	4.9
MIDDLE ATLANTIC:											
New York........	340,644	63,410	57,629	118,686	76,684	24,031	18.6	16.9	34.8	22.5	7.1
New Jersey.......	40,348	7,506	7,011	15,212	8,511	2,089	18.6	17.4	37.7	21.1	5.2
Pennsylvania.....	43,903	8,044	7,065	15,570	10,316	2,882	18.3	16.1	35.5	23.5	6.6
E. NORTH CENTRAL:											
Ohio............	70,006	11,734	10,369	25,143	17,360	5,365	16.8	14.8	35.9	24.8	7.7
Indiana.........	19,254	3,022	2,637	6,647	5,088	1,850	15.7	13.7	34.5	26.4	9.6
Illinois.........	121,777	15,852	18,084	45,125	32,031	10,595	13.0	14.9	37.1	26.3	8.7
Michigan........	499,002	94,887	79,109	177,179	108,924	38,742	19.0	15.9	35.5	21.8	7.8
Wisconsin.......	64,718	7,338	9,037	22,291	18,301	7,726	11.3	14.0	34.4	28.3	11.9
W. NORTH CENTRAL:											
Minnesota........	95,935	12,494	15,162	32,998	25,163	10,097	13.0	15.8	34.4	26.2	10.5
Iowa...........	30,622	2,263	3,028	10,150	10,619	4,548	7.4	9.9	33.1	34.7	14.9
Missouri.........	20,259	1,998	2,201	7,174	6,461	2,413	9.9	10.9	35.4	31.9	11.9
North Dakota.....	40,177	7,759	8,362	12,556	8,430	3,056	19.3	20.8	31.3	21.0	7.6
South Dakota.....	14,736	1,444	2,007	5,256	4,276	1,739	9.8	13.6	35.7	29.0	11.8
Nebraska.........	19,068	1,616	2,467	6,941	5,731	2,305	8.5	12.9	36.4	30.1	12.1
Kansas..........	19,229	1,359	2,062	6,717	6,414	2,670	7.1	10.7	34.9	33.4	13.9
SOUTH ATLANTIC:											
Delaware........	1,146	206	213	397	252	77	18.0	18.6	34.6	22.0	6.7
Maryland........	6,067	1,080	1,046	2,230	1,345	357	17.8	17.2	36.8	22.2	5.9
Dist. of Columbia..	4,864	473	678	2,020	1,334	348	9.7	13.9	41.5	27.4	7.2
Virginia.........	4,671	795	777	1,719	1,061	316	17.0	16.6	36.8	22.7	6.8
West Virginia.....	2,658	569	439	891	574	183	21.4	16.5	33.5	21.6	6.9
North Carolina....	2,491	515	325	913	574	158	20.7	13.0	36.7	23.0	6.3
South Carolina....	896	169	151	321	213	41	18.9	16.9	35.8	23.8	4.6
Georgia..........	2,901	460	412	1,070	740	216	15.9	14.2	36.9	25.5	7.4
Florida..........	17,194	2,821	2,296	5,295	4,834	1,938	16.4	13.4	30.8	28.1	11.3
E. SOUTH CENTRAL:											
Kentucky........	2,962	441	390	1,081	778	268	14.9	13.2	36.5	26.3	9.0
Tennessee........	2,957	434	385	1,071	835	229	14.7	13.0	36.2	28.2	7.7
Alabama.........	2,667	472	405	901	646	243	17.7	15.2	33.8	24.2	9.1
Mississippi.......	1,222	156	183	373	373	133	12.8	15.0	30.5	30.5	10.9
W. SOUTH CENTRAL:											
Arkansas........	2,582	339	337	779	821	306	13.1	13.1	30.2	31.8	11.9
Louisiana........	3,583	437	452	1,216	1,134	343	12.2	12.6	33.9	31.6	9.6
Oklahoma...	9,757	1,039	1,145	3,584	2,921	1,066	10.6	11.7	36.7	29.9	10.9
Texas...........	14,766	1,885	2,090	5,626	3,912	1,242	12.8	14.2	38.1	26.5	8.4
MOUNTAIN:											
Montana.........	31,585	5,907	5,705	10,044	7,433	2,486	18.7	18.1	31.8	23.5	7.9
Idaho...........	13,715	2,443	2,168	4,216	3,649	1,234	17.8	15.8	30.7	26.6	9.0
Wyoming........	4,271	551	605	1,669	1,086	358	12.9	14.2	39.1	25.4	8.4
Colorado........	19,256	2,036	2,589	6,618	5,670	2,336	10.6	13.4	34.4	29.4	12.1
New Mexico......	2,117	243	281	764	630	199	11.5	13.3	36.1	29.8	9.4
Arizona.........	5,872	825	785	2,216	1,578	464	14.0	13.4	37.7	26.9	7.9
Utah...........	4,851	793	639	1,376	1,397	645	16.3	13.2	28.4	28.8	13.3
Nevada..........	2,869	298	307	1,098	879	286	10.4	10.7	38.3	30.6	10.0
PACIFIC:											
Washington......	113,206	21,608	19,847	36,846	25,790	9,040	19.1	17.5	32.5	22.8	8.0
Oregon..........	45,659	7,736	7,584	15,088	11,275	3,959	16.9	16.6	33.0	24.7	8.7
California........	225,327	33,457	34,019	78,934	58,027	20,728	14.8	15.1	35.0	25.8	9.2

TABLE **65**. CANADIAN-BORN WHITE POPULATION, BY AGE, BY STATES: 1930

DIVISION AND STATE	All ages	Under 15 years	15 to 24 years	25 to 44 years	45 to 64 years	65 years and over	PER CENT OF TOTAL				
							Under 15	15 to 24	25 to 44	45 to 64	65 and over
United States...	1,278,421	95,800	153,745	415,958	427,095	185,155	7.5	12.0	32.5	33.4	14.5
NEW ENGLAND:											
Maine............	73,743	4,423	7,995	26,203	25,969	9,122	6.0	10.8	35.5	35.2	12.4
New Hampshire....	50,959	2,336	4,643	17,434	19,504	7,020	4.6	9.1	34.2	38.3	13.8
Vermont..........	27,182	2,792	4,050	8,738	7,930	3,665	10.3	14.9	32.1	29.2	13.5
Massachusetts.....	288,051	13,949	29,304	100,185	107,150	37,363	4.8	10.2	34.8	37.2	13.0
Rhode Island......	39,278	2,048	4,263	13,377	14,636	4,936	5.2	10.9	34.1	37.3	12.6
Connecticut.......	37,808	3,109	5,669	13,745	11,451	3,819	8.2	15.0	36.4	30.3	10.1
MIDDLE ATLANTIC:											
New York........	147,874	13,061	21,174	54,333	43,079	16,123	8.8	14.3	36.7	29.1	10.9
New Jersey........	16,521	1,649	2,391	6,133	4,909	1,432	10.0	14.5	37.1	29.7	8.7
Pennsylvania.......	16,352	1,554	2,136	5,521	5,094	2,036	9.5	13.1	33.8	31.2	12.5
E. NORTH CENTRAL:											
Ohio..............	26,847	2,170	3,143	9,240	8,659	3,611	8.1	11.7	34.4	32.3	13.5
Indiana...........	6,201	640	766	2,020	1,815	954	10.3	12.4	32.6	29.3	15.4
Illinois...........	43,589	3,427	5,453	13,249	14,397	7,017	7.9	12.5	30.4	33.0	16.1
Michigan..........	202,316	19,050	24,738	68,829	59,303	30,312	9.4	12.2	34.0	29.3	15.0
Wisconsin.........	15,572	920	1,234	2,865	5,799	4,747	5.9	7.9	18.4	37.2	30.5
W. NORTH CENTRAL:											
Minnesota.........	27,102	1,514	2,475	5,004	10,868	7,237	5.6	9.1	18.5	40.1	26.7
Iowa.............	6,333	238	358	965	2,277	2,493	3.8	5.7	15.2	36.0	39.4
Missouri..........	5,412	254	422	1,244	2,049	1,441	4.7	7.8	23.0	37.9	26.6
North Dakota......	12,241	651	1,073	2,085	5,759	2,668	5.3	8.8	17.0	47.0	21.8
South Dakota.....	3,351	152	270	469	1,385	1,071	4.5	8.1	14.0	41.3	32.0
Nebraska..........	4,378	192	359	553	1,810	1,462	4.4	8.2	12.6	41.3	33.4
Kansas............	4,037	156	258	585	1,459	1,579	3.9	6.4	14.5	36.1	39.1
SOUTH ATLANTIC:											
Delaware..........	460	23	64	165	151	57	5.0	13.9	35.9	32.8	12.4
Maryland..........	2,266	201	303	831	692	236	8.9	13.4	36.7	30.5	10.4
Dist. of Columbia...	1,681	68	180	597	594	240	4.0	10.7	35.5	35.3	14.3
Virginia..........	1,617	91	165	575	556	228	5.6	10.2	35.6	34.4	14.1
West Virginia......	957	110	145	303	278	119	11.5	15.2	31.7	29.0	12.4
North Carolina.....	930	53	74	343	342	113	5.7	8.0	36.9	36.8	12.2
South Carolina.....	278	11	27	112	105	23	4.0	9.7	40.3	37.8	8.3
Georgia...........	1,094	69	125	389	360	149	6.3	11.4	35.6	32.9	13.6
Florida...........	8,156	716	955	2,183	2,868	1,427	8.8	11.7	26.8	35.2	17.5
E. SOUTH CENTRAL:											
Kentucky..........	918	60	91	297	292	177	6.5	9.9	32.4	31.8	19.3
Tennessee.........	939	57	80	300	345	157	6.1	8.5	31.9	36.7	16.7
Alabama..........	902	57	100	272	309	164	6.3	11.1	30.2	34.3	18.2
Mississippi........	351	3	28	86	146	85	0.9	8.0	24.5	41.6	24.2
W. SOUTH CENTRAL:											
Arkansas..........	695	34	43	154	297	167	4.9	6.2	22.2	42.7	24.0
Louisiana.........	981	24	79	299	399	179	2.4	8.1	30.5	40.7	18.2
Oklahoma.........	2,119	72	169	535	766	576	3.4	8.0	25.2	36.1	27.2
Texas.............	4,525	278	494	1,349	1,622	778	6.1	10.9	29.8	35.8	17.2
MOUNTAIN:											
Montana..........	10,753	699	1,452	2,521	4,125	1,951	6.5	13.5	23.4	38.4	18.1
Idaho.............	4,502	378	545	1,041	1,738	799	8.4	12.1	23.1	38.6	17.7
Wyoming..........	1,136	67	153	286	405	225	5.9	13.5	25.2	35.7	19.8
Colorado..........	5,816	195	389	1,127	2,478	1,624	3.4	6.7	19.4	42.6	27.9
New Mexico.......	613	18	48	156	261	130	2.9	7.8	25.4	42.6	21.2
Arizona...........	2,018	89	166	664	795	303	4.4	8.2	32.9	39.4	15.0
Utah.............	1,190	125	179	331	371	183	10.5	15.0	27.8	31.2	15.4
Nevada...........	952	48	63	290	336	215	5.0	6.6	30.5	35.3	22.6
PACIFIC:											
Washington........	48,064	5,511	7,678	13,312	14,638	6,902	11.5	16.0	27.7	30.5	14.4
Oregon...........	17,916	2,178	2,828	4,652	5,526	2,727	12.2	15.8	26.0	30.8	15.2
California.........	101,445	10,280	14,948	30,011	30,998	15,113	10.1	14.7	29.6	30.6	14.9

TABLE **66**. CANADIAN-BORN WHITE POPULATION, BY SEX AND AGE, FOR 29 SELECTED STATES: 1930

STATE AND SEX	All ages	Under 15 years	15 to 24 years	25 to 44 years	45 to 64 years	65 years and over	PER CENT OF TOTAL				
							Under 15	15 to 24	25 to 44	45 to 64	65 and over
MALE											
United States	**617,090**	**47,690**	**71,325**	**198,124**	**208,517**	**91,101**	**7.7**	**11.6**	**32.1**	**33.8**	**14.8**
Maine	35,990	2,217	3,589	12,516	13,139	4,514	6.2	10.0	34.8	36.5	12.5
New Hampshire	24,775	1,113	2,127	8,410	9,630	3,483	4.5	8.6	33.9	38.9	14.1
Vermont	14,174	1,407	2,215	4,505	4,126	1,917	9.9	15.6	31.8	29.1	13.5
Massachusetts	127,586	6,788	11,898	44,092	48,526	16,234	5.3	9.3	34.6	38.0	12.7
Rhode Island	18,337	1,022	1,828	6,188	7,009	2,283	5.6	10.0	33.7	38.2	12.5
Connecticut	18,782	1,514	2,767	6,931	5,740	1,820	8.1	14.7	36.9	30.6	9.7
New York	68,332	6,546	9,580	25,076	19,879	7,208	9.6	14.0	36.7	29.1	10.5
New Jersey	7,624	817	1,054	2,818	2,326	607	10.7	13.8	37.0	30.5	8.0
Pennsylvania	7,826	799	984	2,650	2,485	904	10.2	12.6	33.9	31.8	11.6
Ohio	12,952	1,099	1,507	4,387	4,323	1,623	8.5	11.6	33.9	33.4	12.5
Indiana	3,285	330	390	1,071	996	495	10.0	11.9	32.6	30.3	15.1
Illinois	21,844	1,756	2,720	6,877	7,167	3,300	8.0	12.5	31.5	32.8	15.1
Michigan	101,756	9,557	12,183	35,611	29,080	15,274	9.4	12.0	35.0	28.6	15.0
Wisconsin	8,572	459	631	1,531	3,205	2,742	5.4	7.4	17.9	37.4	32.0
Minnesota	14,295	759	1,177	2,369	5,889	4,099	5.3	8.2	16.6	41.2	28.7
Iowa	3,174	115	170	473	1,176	1,239	3.6	5.4	14.9	37.1	39.0
Missouri	2,783	125	222	613	1,067	755	4.5	8.0	22.0	38.3	27.1
North Dakota	6,441	318	495	990	3,057	1,577	4.9	7.7	15.4	47.5	24.5
South Dakota	1,808	55	132	243	770	606	3.0	7.3	13.4	42.6	33.5
Nebraska	2,190	90	180	262	926	731	4.1	8.2	12.0	42.3	33.4
Kansas	2,071	88	126	308	721	828	4.2	6.1	14.9	34.8	40.0
Florida	3,796	349	437	931	1,292	783	9.2	11.5	24.5	34.0	20.6
Texas	2,497	137	260	714	908	476	5.5	10.4	28.6	36.4	19.1
Montana	6,153	345	721	1,274	2,542	1,267	5.6	11.7	20.7	41.3	20.6
Idaho	2,689	185	273	605	1,098	527	6.9	10.2	22.5	40.8	19.6
Colorado	2,926	100	188	539	1,263	834	3.4	6.4	18.4	43.2	28.5
Washington	24,666	2,741	3,716	6,364	7,934	3,897	11.1	15.1	25.8	32.2	15.8
Oregon	9,192	1,045	1,347	2,249	2,994	1,554	11.4	14.7	24.5	32.6	16.9
California	48,942	5,155	7,263	14,137	14,960	7,387	10.5	14.8	28.9	30.6	15.1
FEMALE											
United States	**661,331**	**48,110**	**82,420**	**217,834**	**218,578**	**94,054**	**7.3**	**12.5**	**32.9**	**33.1**	**14.2**
Maine	37,753	2,206	4,406	13,687	12,830	4,608	5.8	11.7	36.3	34.0	12.2
New Hampshire	26,184	1,223	2,516	9,024	9,874	3,537	4.7	9.6	34.5	37.7	13.5
Vermont	13,008	1,385	1,835	4,233	3,804	1,748	10.6	14.1	32.5	29.2	13.4
Massachusetts	160,465	7,161	17,406	56,093	58,624	21,129	4.5	10.8	35.0	36.5	13.2
Rhode Island	20,941	1,026	2,435	7,189	7,627	2,653	4.9	11.6	34.3	36.4	12.7
Connecticut	19,026	1,595	2,902	6,814	5,711	1,999	8.4	15.3	35.8	30.0	10.5
New York	79,542	6,515	11,594	29,257	23,200	8,915	8.2	14.6	36.8	29.2	11.2
New Jersey	8,897	832	1,337	3,315	2,583	825	9.4	15.0	37.3	29.0	9.3
Pennsylvania	8,526	755	1,152	2,871	2,609	1,132	8.9	13.5	33.7	30.6	13.3
Ohio	13,895	1,071	1,636	4,853	4,336	1,988	7.7	11.8	34.9	31.2	14.3
Indiana	2,916	310	376	949	819	459	10.6	12.9	32.5	28.1	15.7
Illinois	21,745	1,671	2,733	6,372	7,230	3,717	7.7	12.6	29.3	33.2	17.1
Michigan	100,560	9,493	12,555	33,218	30,223	15,038	9.4	12.5	33.0	30.1	15.0
Wisconsin	7,000	461	603	1,334	2,594	2,005	6.6	8.6	19.1	37.1	28.6
Minnesota	12,807	755	1,298	2,635	4,979	3,138	5.9	10.1	20.6	38.9	24.5
Iowa	3,159	123	188	492	1,101	1,254	3.9	6.0	15.6	34.9	39.7
Missouri	2,629	129	200	631	982	686	4.9	7.6	24.0	37.4	26.1
North Dakota	5,800	333	578	1,095	2,702	1,091	5.7	10.0	18.9	46.6	18.8
South Dakota	1,543	97	138	226	615	465	6.3	8.9	14.6	39.9	30.1
Nebraska	2,188	102	179	291	884	731	4.7	8.2	13.3	40.4	33.4
Kansas	1,966	68	132	277	738	751	3.5	6.7	14.1	37.5	38.2
Florida	4,360	367	518	1,252	1,576	644	8.4	11.9	28.7	36.1	14.8
Texas	2,028	141	234	635	714	302	7.0	11.5	31.3	35.2	14.9
Montana	4,600	354	731	1,247	1,583	684	7.7	15.9	27.1	34.4	14.9
Idaho	1,813	193	272	436	640	272	10.6	15.0	24.0	35.3	15.0
Colorado	2,890	95	201	588	1,215	790	3.3	7.0	20.3	42.0	27.3
Washington	23,398	2,770	3,962	6,948	6,704	3,005	11.8	16.9	29.7	28.7	12.8
Oregon	8,724	1,133	1,481	2,403	2,532	1,173	13.0	17.0	27.5	29.0	13.4
California	52,503	5,125	7,685	15,874	16,038	7,726	9.8	14.6	30.2	30.5	14.7

TABLE **67**. CANADIAN-BORN WHITE POPULATION, FRENCH AND ENGLISH, BY AGE, FOR 29 SELECTED STATES: 1930

STATE	All ages	Under 15 years	15 to 24 years	25 to 44 years	45 to 64 years	65 years and over	PER CENT OF TOTAL				
							Under 15	15 to 24	25 to 44	45 to 64	65 and over
FRENCH											
United States	370,852	22,003	40,286	126,874	127,565	53,988	5.9	10.9	34.2	34.4	14.6
Maine	36,947	2,386	4,531	13,867	12,000	4,146	6.5	12.3	37.5	32.5	11.2
New Hampshire	37,682	1,824	3,707	13,709	13,698	4,728	4.8	9.8	36.4	36.4	12.5
Vermont	17,320	2,178	3,006	5,729	4,339	2,064	12.6	17.4	33.1	25.1	11.9
Massachusetts	115,241	5,066	10,193	39,685	44,075	16,196	4.4	8.8	34.4	38.2	14.1
Rhode Island	31,501	1,627	3,417	10,800	11,687	3,955	5.2	10.8	34.3	37.1	12.6
Connecticut	25,570	2,126	4,059	9,239	7,571	2,570	8.3	15.9	36.1	29.6	10.1
New York	28,955	2,356	4,224	11,028	7,626	3,703	8.1	14.6	38.1	26.3	12.8
New Jersey	2,470	195	356	1,031	693	195	7.9	14.4	41.7	28.1	7.9
Pennsylvania	1,911	160	230	711	561	249	8.4	12.0	37.2	29.4	13.0
Ohio	2,606	134	273	926	843	430	5.1	10.5	35.5	32.3	16.5
Indiana	682	45	66	215	198	158	6.6	9.7	31.5	29.0	23.2
Illinois	6,189	313	522	1,796	2,136	1,418	5.1	8.4	29.0	34.5	22.9
Michigan	28,539	2,313	3,059	9,537	8,525	5,095	8.1	10.7	33.4	29.9	17.9
Wisconsin	4,292	47	117	649	1,844	1,633	1.1	2.7	15.1	43.0	38.0
Minnesota	6,484	112	261	987	2,894	2,229	1.7	4.0	15.2	44.6	34.4
Iowa	608	7	21	101	217	262	1.2	3.5	16.6	35.7	43.1
Missouri	588	17	49	182	182	158	2.9	8.3	31.0	31.0	26.9
North Dakota	1,354	30	65	282	624	353	2.2	4.8	20.8	46.1	26.1
South Dakota	492	10	17	79	207	179	2.0	3.5	16.1	42.1	36.4
Nebraska	436	9	25	65	189	147	2.1	5.7	14.9	43.3	33.7
Kansas	569	15	20	81	202	251	2.6	3.5	14.2	35.5	44.1
Florida	985	85	111	284	347	158	8.6	11.3	28.8	35.2	16.0
Texas	452	14	36	168	156	76	3.1	8.0	37.2	34.5	16.8
Montana	1,966	35	124	479	844	481	1.8	6.3	24.4	42.9	24.5
Idaho	571	16	39	144	254	118	2.8	6.8	25.2	44.5	20.7
Colorado	572	9	31	121	228	183	1.6	5.4	21.2	39.9	32.0
Washington	4,340	226	423	1,142	1,649	898	5.2	9.7	26.3	38.0	20.7
Oregon	1,345	71	112	413	471	277	5.3	8.3	30.7	35.0	20.6
California	7,657	470	942	2,554	2,445	1,240	6.1	12.3	33.4	31.9	16.2
ENGLISH											
United States	907,569	73,797	113,459	289,084	299,530	131,167	8.1	12.5	31.9	33.0	14.5
Maine	36,796	2,037	3,464	12,336	13,969	4,976	5.5	9.4	33.5	38.0	13.5
New Hampshire	13,277	512	936	3,725	5,806	2,292	3.9	7.0	28.1	43.7	17.3
Vermont	9,862	614	1,044	3,009	3,591	1,601	6.2	10.6	30.5	36.4	16.2
Massachusetts	172,810	8,883	19,111	60,500	63,075	21,167	5.1	11.1	35.0	36.5	12.2
Rhode Island	7,777	421	846	2,577	2,949	981	5.4	10.9	33.1	37.9	12.6
Connecticut	12,238	983	1,610	4,506	3,880	1,249	8.0	13.2	36.8	31.7	10.2
New York	118,919	10,705	16,950	43,305	35,453	12,420	9.0	14.3	36.4	29.8	10.4
New Jersey	14,051	1,454	2,035	5,102	4,216	1,237	10.3	14.5	36.3	30.0	8.8
Pennsylvania	14,441	1,394	1,906	4,810	4,533	1,787	9.7	13.2	33.3	31.4	12.4
Ohio	24,241	2,036	2,870	8,314	7,816	3,181	8.4	11.8	34.3	32.2	13.1
Indiana	5,519	595	700	1,805	1,617	796	10.8	12.7	32.7	29.3	14.4
Illinois	37,400	3,114	4,931	11,453	12,261	5,599	8.3	13.2	30.6	32.8	15.0
Michigan	173,777	16,737	21,679	59,292	50,778	25,217	9.6	12.5	34.1	29.2	14.5
Wisconsin	11,280	873	1,117	2,216	3,955	3,114	7.7	9.9	19.6	35.1	27.6
Minnesota	20,618	1,402	2,214	4,017	7,974	5,008	6.8	10.7	19.5	38.7	24.3
Iowa	5,725	231	337	864	2,060	2,231	4.0	5.9	15.1	36.0	39.0
Missouri	4,824	237	373	1,062	1,867	1,283	4.9	7.7	22.0	38.7	26.6
North Dakota	10,887	621	1,008	1,803	5,135	2,315	5.7	9.3	16.6	47.2	21.3
South Dakota	2,859	142	253	390	1,178	892	5.0	8.8	13.6	41.2	31.2
Nebraska	3,942	183	334	488	1,621	1,315	4.6	8.5	12.4	41.1	33.4
Kansas	3,468	141	238	504	1,257	1,328	4.1	6.9	14.5	36.2	38.3
Florida	7,171	631	844	1,899	2,521	1,269	8.8	11.8	26.5	35.2	17.7
Texas	4,073	264	458	1,181	1,466	702	6.5	11.2	29.0	36.0	17.2
Montana	8,787	664	1,328	2,042	3,281	1,470	7.6	15.1	23.2	37.3	16.7
Idaho	3,931	362	506	897	1,484	681	9.2	12.9	22.8	37.8	17.3
Colorado	5,244	186	358	1,006	2,250	1,441	3.5	6.8	19.2	42.9	27.5
Washington	43,724	5,285	7,255	12,170	12,989	6,004	12.1	16.6	27.8	29.7	13.7
Oregon	16,571	2,107	2,716	4,239	5,055	2,450	12.7	16.4	25.6	30.5	14.8
California	93,788	9,810	14,006	27,457	28,553	13,873	10.5	14.9	29.3	30.4	14.8

TABLE **68.** FRENCH CANADIAN BORN, BY SEX AND AGE, FOR 29 SELECTED STATES: 1930

STATE AND SEX	All ages	Under 15 years	15 to 24 years	25 to 44 years	45 to 64 years	65 years and over	PER CENT OF TOTAL				
							Under 15	15 to 24	25 to 44	45 to 64	65 and over
MALE											
United States	187,523	10,743	19,041	63,656	65,467	28,538	5.7	10.2	33.9	34.9	15.2
Maine	18,413	1,196	2,089	6,797	6,199	2,124	6.5	11.3	36.9	33.7	11.5
New Hampshire	18,724	836	1,712	6,832	6,922	2,412	4.5	9.1	36.5	37.0	12.9
Vermont	9,367	1,096	1,650	3,092	2,379	1,148	11.7	17.6	33.0	25.4	12.3
Massachusetts	56,192	2,405	4,534	19,268	21,917	8,053	4.3	8.1	34.3	39.0	14.3
Rhode Island	15,173	802	1,518	5,156	5,782	1,909	5.3	10.0	34.0	38.1	12.6
Connecticut	13,070	1,023	2,006	4,834	3,934	1,270	7.8	15.3	37.0	30.1	9.7
New York	14,780	1,184	2,105	5,714	3,893	1,875	8.0	14.2	38.7	26.3	12.7
New Jersey	1,193	97	148	503	353	92	8.1	12.4	42.2	29.6	7.7
Pennsylvania	965	82	96	371	288	128	8.5	9.9	38.4	29.8	13.3
Ohio	1,297	59	122	461	440	215	4.5	9.4	35.5	33.9	16.6
Indiana	366	25	31	119	104	87	6.8	8.5	32.5	28.4	23.8
Illinois	3,142	164	245	921	1,070	739	5.2	7.8	29.3	34.1	23.5
Michigan	15,434	1,148	1,543	5,206	4,563	2,966	7.4	10.0	33.7	29.6	19.2
Wisconsin	2,455	23	55	328	1,023	1,025	0.9	2.2	13.4	41.7	41.8
Minnesota	3,591	55	100	474	1,614	1,347	1.5	2.8	13.2	44.9	37.5
Iowa	304	4	9	49	108	134	1.3	3.0	16.1	35.5	44.1
Missouri	317	9	25	105	93	85	2.8	7.9	33.1	29.3	26.8
North Dakota	745	11	33	152	331	218	1.5	4.4	20.4	44.4	29.3
South Dakota	273	2	8	42	114	107	0.7	2.9	15.4	41.8	39.2
Nebraska	228	2	15	36	93	81	0.9	6.6	15.8	40.8	35.5
Kansas	299	11	12	46	98	132	3.7	4.0	15.4	32.8	44.1
Florida	508	39	52	140	183	94	7.7	10.2	27.6	36.0	18.5
Texas	263	6	22	103	88	43	2.3	8.4	39.2	33.5	16.3
Montana	1,165	17	61	222	530	332	1.5	5.2	19.1	45.5	28.5
Idaho	366	6	20	87	172	81	1.6	5.5	23.8	47.0	22.1
Colorado	310	5	17	64	112	112	1.6	5.5	20.6	36.1	36.1
Washington	2,363	115	192	551	936	568	4.9	8.1	23.3	39.6	24.0
Oregon	727	36	51	202	260	178	5.0	7.0	27.8	35.8	24.5
California	4,048	246	439	1,309	1,348	703	6.1	10.8	32.3	33.3	17.4
FEMALE											
United States	183,329	11,260	21,245	63,218	62,098	25,450	6.1	11.6	34.5	33.9	13.9
Maine	18,534	1,190	2,442	7,070	5,801	2,022	6.4	13.2	38.1	31.3	10.9
New Hampshire	18,958	988	1,995	6,877	6,776	2,316	5.2	10.5	36.3	35.7	12.2
Vermont	7,953	1,082	1,356	2,637	1,960	916	13.6	17.1	33.2	24.6	11.5
Massachusetts	59,049	2,661	5,659	20,417	22,158	8,143	4.5	9.6	34.6	37.5	13.8
Rhode Island	16,328	825	1,899	5,644	5,905	2,046	5.1	11.6	34.6	36.2	12.5
Connecticut	12,500	1,103	2,053	4,405	3,637	1,300	8.8	16.4	35.2	29.1	10.4
New York	14,175	1,172	2,119	5,314	3,733	1,828	8.3	14.9	37.5	26.3	12.9
New Jersey	1,277	98	208	528	340	103	7.7	16.3	41.3	26.6	8.1
Pennsylvania	946	78	134	340	273	121	8.2	14.2	35.9	28.9	12.8
Ohio	1,309	75	151	465	403	215	5.7	11.5	35.5	30.8	16.4
Indiana	316	20	35	96	94	71	6.3	11.1	30.4	29.7	22.5
Illinois	3,047	149	277	875	1,066	679	4.9	9.1	28.7	35.0	22.3
Michigan	13,105	1,165	1,516	4,331	3,962	2,129	8.9	11.6	33.0	30.2	16.2
Wisconsin	1,837	24	62	321	821	608	1.3	3.4	17.5	44.7	33.1
Minnesota	2,893	57	161	513	1,280	882	2.0	5.6	17.7	44.2	30.5
Iowa	304	3	12	52	109	128	1.0	3.9	17.1	35.9	42.1
Missouri	271	8	24	77	89	73	3.0	8.9	28.4	32.8	26.9
North Dakota	609	19	32	130	293	135	3.1	5.3	21.3	48.1	22.2
South Dakota	219	8	9	37	93	72	3.7	4.1	16.9	42.5	32.9
Nebraska	208	7	10	29	96	66	3.4	4.8	13.9	46.2	31.7
Kansas	270	4	8	35	104	119	1.5	3.0	13.0	38.5	44.1
Florida	477	46	59	144	164	64	9.6	12.4	30.2	34.4	13.4
Texas	189	8	14	65	68	33	4.2	7.4	34.4	36.0	17.5
Montana	801	18	63	257	314	149	2.2	7.9	32.1	39.2	18.6
Idaho	205	10	19	57	82	37	4.9	9.3	27.8	40.0	18.0
Colorado	262	4	14	57	116	71	1.5	5.3	21.8	44.3	27.1
Washington	1,977	111	231	591	713	330	5.6	11.7	29.9	36.1	16.7
Oregon	618	35	61	211	211	99	5.7	9.9	34.1	34.1	16.0
California	3,609	224	503	1,245	1,097	537	6.2	13.9	34.5	30.4	14.9

TABLE **69.** ENGLISH CANADIAN BORN, BY SEX AND AGE, FOR 29 SELECTED STATES: 1930

STATE AND SEX	All ages	Under 15 years	15 to 24 years	25 to 44 years	45 to 64 years	65 years and over	PER CENT OF TOTAL				
							Under 15	15 to 24	25 to 44	45 to 64	65 and over
MALE											
United States	**429,567**	**36,947**	**52,284**	**134,468**	**143,050**	**62,563**	**8.6**	**12.2**	**31.3**	**33.3**	**14.6**
Maine	17,577	1,021	1,500	5,719	6,940	2,390	5.8	8.5	32.5	39.5	13.6
New Hampshire	6,051	277	415	1,578	2,708	1,071	4.6	6.9	26.1	44.8	17.7
Vermont	4,807	311	565	1,413	1,747	769	6.5	11.8	29.4	36.3	16.0
Massachusetts	71,394	4,383	7,364	24,824	26,609	8,181	6.1	10.3	34.8	37.3	11.5
Rhode Island	3,164	220	310	1,032	1,227	374	7.0	9.8	32.6	38.8	11.8
Connecticut	5,712	491	761	2,097	1,806	550	8.6	13.3	36.7	31.6	9.6
New York	53,552	5,362	7,475	19,362	15,986	5,333	10.0	14.0	36.2	29.9	10.0
New Jersey	6,431	720	906	2,315	1,973	515	11.2	14.1	36.0	30.7	8.0
Pennsylvania	6,861	717	888	2,279	2,197	776	10.5	12.9	33.2	32.0	11.3
Ohio	11,655	1,040	1,385	3,926	3,883	1,408	8.9	11.9	33.7	33.3	12.1
Indiana	2,919	305	359	952	892	408	10.4	12.3	32.6	30.6	14.0
Illinois	18,702	1,592	2,475	5,956	6,097	2,561	8.5	13.2	31.8	32.6	13.7
Michigan	86,322	8,409	10,640	30,405	24,517	12,308	9.7	12.3	35.2	28.4	14.3
Wisconsin	6,117	436	576	1,203	2,182	1,717	7.1	9.4	19.7	35.7	28.1
Minnesota	10,704	704	1,077	1,895	4,275	2,752	6.6	10.1	17.7	39.9	25.7
Iowa	2,870	111	161	424	1,068	1,105	3.9	5.6	14.8	37.2	38.5
Missouri	2,466	116	197	508	974	670	4.7	8.0	20.6	39.5	27.2
North Dakota	5,696	307	462	838	2,726	1,359	5.4	8.1	14.7	47.9	23.9
South Dakota	1,535	53	124	201	656	499	3.5	8.1	13.1	42.7	32.5
Nebraska	1,962	88	165	226	833	650	4.5	8.4	11.5	42.5	33.1
Kansas	1,772	77	114	262	623	696	4.3	6.4	14.8	35.2	39.3
Florida	3,288	310	385	791	1,109	689	9.4	11.7	24.1	33.7	21.0
Texas	2,234	131	238	611	820	433	5.9	10.7	27.4	36.7	19.4
Montana	4,988	328	660	1,052	2,012	935	6.6	13.2	21.1	40.3	18.7
Idaho	2,323	179	253	518	926	446	7.7	10.9	22.3	39.9	19.2
Colorado	2,616	95	171	475	1,151	722	3.6	6.5	18.2	44.0	27.6
Washington	22,303	2,626	3,524	5,813	6,998	3,329	11.8	15.8	26.1	31.4	14.9
Oregon	8,465	1,009	1,296	2,047	2,734	1,376	11.9	15.3	24.2	32.3	16.3
California	44,894	4,909	6,824	12,828	13,612	6,684	10.9	15.2	28.6	30.3	14.9
FEMALE											
United States	**478,002**	**36,850**	**61,175**	**154,616**	**156,480**	**68,604**	**7.7**	**12.8**	**32.3**	**32.7**	**14.4**
Maine	19,219	1,016	1,964	6,617	7,029	2,586	5.3	10.2	34.4	36.6	13.5
New Hampshire	7,226	235	521	2,147	3,098	1,221	3.3	7.2	29.7	42.9	16.9
Vermont	5,055	303	479	1,596	1,844	832	6.0	9.5	31.6	36.5	16.5
Massachusetts	101,416	4,500	11,747	35,676	36,466	12,986	4.4	11.6	35.2	36.0	12.8
Rhode Island	4,613	201	536	1,545	1,722	607	4.4	11.6	33.5	37.3	13.2
Connecticut	6,526	492	849	2,409	2,074	699	7.5	13.0	36.9	31.8	10.7
New York	65,367	5,343	9,475	23,943	19,467	7,087	8.2	14.5	36.6	29.8	10.8
New Jersey	7,620	734	1,129	2,787	2,243	722	9.6	14.8	36.6	29.4	9.5
Pennsylvania	7,580	677	1,018	2,531	2,336	1,011	8.9	13.4	33.4	30.8	13.3
Ohio	12,586	996	1,485	4,388	3,933	1,773	7.9	11.8	34.9	31.2	14.1
Indiana	2,600	290	341	853	725	388	11.2	13.1	32.8	27.9	14.9
Illinois	18,698	1,522	2,456	5,497	6,164	3,038	8.1	13.1	29.4	33.0	16.2
Michigan	87,455	8,328	11,039	28,887	26,261	12,909	9.5	12.6	33.0	30.0	14.8
Wisconsin	5,163	437	541	1,013	1,773	1,397	8.5	10.5	19.6	34.3	27.1
Minnesota	9,914	698	1,137	2,122	3,699	2,256	7.0	11.5	21.4	37.3	22.8
Iowa	2,855	120	176	440	992	1,126	4.2	6.2	15.4	34.7	39.4
Missouri	2,358	121	176	554	893	613	5.1	7.5	23.5	37.9	26.0
North Dakota	5,191	314	546	965	2,409	956	6.0	10.5	18.6	46.4	18.4
South Dakota	1,324	89	129	189	522	393	6.7	9.7	14.3	39.4	29.7
Nebraska	1,980	95	169	262	788	665	4.8	8.5	13.2	39.8	33.6
Kansas	1,696	64	124	242	634	632	3.8	7.3	14.3	37.4	37.3
Florida	3,883	321	459	1,108	1,412	580	8.3	11.8	28.5	36.4	14.9
Texas	1,839	133	220	570	646	269	7.2	12.0	31.0	35.1	14.6
Montana	3,799	336	668	990	1,269	535	8.8	17.6	26.1	33.4	14.1
Idaho	1,608	183	253	379	558	235	11.4	15.7	23.6	34.7	14.6
Colorado	2,628	91	187	531	1,099	719	3.5	7.1	20.2	41.8	27.4
Washington	21,421	2,659	3,731	6,357	5,991	2,675	12.4	17.4	29.7	28.0	12.5
Oregon	8,106	1,098	1,420	2,192	2,321	1,074	13.5	17.5	27.0	28.6	13.2
California	48,894	4,901	7,182	14,629	14,941	7,189	10.0	14.7	29.9	30.6	14.7

TABLE **70**. NATIVE WHITE POPULATION OF CANADIAN PARENTAGE, BY AGE, BY STATES: 1930

DIVISION AND STATE	All ages	Under 15 years	15 to 24 years	25 to 44 years	45 to 64 years	65 years and over	PER CENT OF TOTAL				
							Under 15	15 to 24	25 to 44	45 to 64	65 and over
United States...	2,058,924	534,150	401,594	720,703	335,716	66,034	25.9	19.5	35.0	16.3	3.2
NEW ENGLAND:											
Maine............	128,005	49,444	28,916	33,770	12,825	3,013	38.6	22.6	26.4	10.0	2.4
New Hampshire....	86,459	30,184	20,492	25,966	8,386	1,409	34.9	23.7	30.0	9.7	1.6
Vermont..........	46,841	15,012	8,093	12,435	8,665	2,625	32.0	17.3	26.5	18.5	5.6
Massachusetts......	436,749	137,803	99,714	144,190	47,719	7,226	31.6	22.8	33.0	10.9	1.7
Rhode Island......	71,273	22,059	16,928	24,036	7,476	762	31.0	23.8	33.7	10.5	1.1
Connecticut.......	59,207	17,877	12,789	20,581	7,030	922	30.2	21.6	34.8	11.9	1.6
MIDDLE ATLANTIC:											
New York.........	192,770	50,349	36,455	64,353	33,605	7,908	26.1	18.9	33.4	17.4	4.1
New Jersey........	23,827	5,857	4,620	9,079	3,602	657	24.6	19.4	38.1	15.1	2.8
Pennsylvania......	27,551	6,490	4,929	10,049	5,222	846	23.6	17.9	36.5	19.0	3.1
E. NORTH CENTRAL:											
Ohio..............	43,159	9,564	7,226	15,903	8,701	1,754	22.2	16.7	36.8	20.2	4.1
Indiana...........	13,053	2,382	1,871	4,627	3,273	896	18.2	14.3	35.4	25.1	6.9
Illinois...........	78,188	12,425	12,631	31,876	17,634	3,578	15.9	16.2	40.8	22.6	4.6
Michigan..........	296,686	75,837	54,371	108,350	49,621	8,430	25.6	18.3	36.5	16.7	2.8
Wisconsin.........	49,146	6,418	7,803	19,426	12,502	2,979	13.1	15.9	39.5	25.4	6.1
W. NORTH CENTRAL:											
Minnesota.........	68,833	10,980	12,687	27,994	14,295	2,860	16.0	18.4	40.7	20.8	4.2
Iowa..............	24,289	2,025	2,670	9,185	8,342	2,055	8.3	11.0	37.8	34.3	8.5
Missouri..........	14,847	1,744	1,779	5,930	4,412	972	11.7	12.0	39.9	29.7	6.5
North Dakota......	27,936	7,108	7,289	10,471	2,671	388	25.4	26.1	37.5	9.6	1.4
South Dakota......	11,385	1,292	1,737	4,787	2,891	668	11.3	15.3	42.0	25.4	5.9
Nebraska..........	14,690	1,424	2,108	6,388	3,921	843	9.7	14.3	43.5	26.7	5.8
Kansas............	15,192	1,203	1,804	6,132	4,955	1,091	7.9	11.9	40.4	32.6	7.2
SOUTH ATLANTIC:											
Delaware..........	686	183	149	232	101	20	26.7	21.7	33.8	14.7	2.9
Maryland..........	3,801	879	743	1,399	653	121	23.1	19.5	36.8	17.2	3.2
Dist. of Columbia...	3,183	405	498	1,423	740	108	12.7	15.6	44.7	23.2	3.4
Virginia...........	3,054	704	612	1,144	505	88	23.1	20.0	37.5	16.5	2.9
West Virginia......	1,701	459	294	588	296	64	27.0	17.3	34.6	17.4	3.8
North Carolina.....	1,561	462	251	570	232	45	29.6	16.1	36.5	14.9	2.9
South Carolina.....	618	158	124	209	108	18	25.6	20.1	33.8	17.5	2.9
Georgia...........	1,807	391	287	681	380	67	21.6	15.9	37.7	21.0	3.7
Florida............	9,038	2,105	1,341	3,112	1,966	511	23.3	14.8	34.4	21.8	5.7
E. SOUTH CENTRAL:											
Kentucky..........	2,044	381	299	784	486	91	18.6	14.6	38.4	23.8	4.5
Tennessee.........	2,018	377	305	771	490	72	18.7	15.1	38.2	24.3	3.6
Alabama..........	1,765	415	305	629	337	79	23.5	17.3	35.6	19.1	4.5
Mississippi........	871	153	155	287	227	48	17.6	17.8	33.0	26.1	5.5
W. SOUTH CENTRAL:											
Arkansas..........	1,887	305	294	625	524	139	16.2	15.6	33.1	27.8	7.4
Louisiana..........	2,602	413	373	917	735	164	15.9	14.3	35.2	28.2	6.3
Oklahoma.........	7,638	967	976	3,049	2,155	490	12.7	12.8	39.9	28.2	6.4
Texas.............	10,241	1,607	1,596	4,277	2,290	464	15.7	15.6	41.8	22.4	4.5
MOUNTAIN:											
Montana..........	20,832	5,208	4,253	7,523	3,308	535	25.0	20.4	36.1	15.9	2.6
Idaho.............	9,213	2,065	1,623	3,175	1,911	435	22.4	17.6	34.5	20.7	4.7
Wyoming..........	3,135	484	452	1,383	681	133	15.4	14.4	44.1	21.7	4.2
Colorado..........	13,440	1,841	2,200	5,491	3,192	712	13.7	16.4	40.9	23.8	5.3
New Mexico.......	1,504	225	233	608	369	69	15.0	15.5	40.4	24.5	4.6
Arizona...........	3,854	736	619	1,552	783	161	19.1	16.1	40.3	20.3	4.2
Utah..............	3,661	668	460	1,045	1,026	462	18.2	12.6	28.5	28.0	12.6
Nevada............	1,917	250	244	808	543	71	13.0	12.7	42.1	28.3	3.7
PACIFIC:											
Washington........	65,142	16,097	12,169	23,534	11,152	2,138	24.7	18.7	36.1	17.1	3.3
Oregon............	27,743	5,558	4,756	10,436	5,749	1,232	20.0	17.1	37.6	20.7	4.4
California..........	123,882	23,177	19,071	48,923	27,029	5,615	18.7	15.4	39.5	21.8	4.5

TABLE **71**. NATIVE WHITE POPULATION OF CANADIAN PARENTAGE, FRENCH AND ENGLISH, BY AGE, FOR 29 SELECTED STATES: 1930

STATE	All ages	Under 15 years	15 to 24 years	25 to 44 years	45 to 64 years	65 years and over	PER CENT OF TOTAL				
							Under 15	15 to 24	25 to 44	45 to 64	65 and over
FRENCH											
United States....	**735,307**	**210,389**	**150,832**	**246,693**	**106,835**	**20,368**	**28.6**	**20.5**	**33.5**	**14.5**	**2.8**
Maine..............	62,818	26,599	14,304	16,248	4,806	847	42.3	22.8	25.9	7.7	1.3
New Hampshire......	63,642	23,913	15,424	18,428	5,190	673	37.6	24.2	29.0	8.2	1.1
Vermont...........	29,636	10,110	4,824	7,467	5,502	1,724	34.1	16.3	25.2	18.6	5.8
Massachusetts......	221,630	70,892	50,578	72,844	24,248	3,029	32.0	22.8	32.9	10.9	1.4
Rhode Island.......	59,672	19,065	14,427	19,804	5,867	499	31.9	24.2	33.2	9.8	0.8
Connecticut........	41,560	13,027	9,220	14,050	4,702	556	31.3	22.2	33.8	11.3	1.3
New York..........	54,102	12,728	9,251	17,897	10,996	3,197	23.5	17.1	33.1	20.3	5.9
New Jersey........	4,953	1,082	915	2,026	791	137	21.8	18.5	40.9	16.0	2.8
Pennsylvania.......	4,230	818	702	1,715	853	140	19.3	16.6	40.5	20.2	3.3
Ohio..............	6,822	1,150	952	2,626	1,696	397	16.9	14.0	38.5	24.9	5.8
Indiana...........	2,438	298	264	896	790	190	12.2	10.8	36.8	32.4	7.8
Illinois...........	18,061	2,098	2,535	7,340	4,986	1,097	11.6	14.0	40.6	27.6	6.1
Michigan..........	59,372	13,650	10,828	22,632	10,396	1,857	23.0	18.2	38.1	17.5	3.1
Wisconsin..........	17,751	2,120	3,015	7,215	4,333	1,060	11.9	17.0	40.6	24.4	6.0
Minnesota.........	22,900	3,121	4,038	9,493	5,121	1,119	13.6	17.6	41.5	22.4	4.9
Iowa.............	3,625	243	370	1,301	1,327	383	6.7	10.2	35.9	36.6	10.6
Missouri...........	2,113	215	175	796	741	185	10.2	8.3	37.7	35.1	8.8
North Dakota.......	4,730	1,099	1,087	1,821	620	102	23.2	23.0	38.5	13.1	2.2
South Dakota.......	2,281	199	283	977	642	178	8.7	12.4	42.8	28.1	7.8
Nebraska...........	2,155	177	285	885	645	162	8.2	13.2	41.1	29.9	7.5
Kansas............	3,019	244	301	1,080	1,092	301	8.1	10.0	35.8	36.2	10.0
Florida...........	1,373	261	195	512	326	79	19.0	14.2	37.3	23.7	5.8
Texas.............	1,345	177	182	556	358	72	13.2	13.5	41.3	26.6	5.4
Montana...........	4,822	1,010	992	1,844	823	153	20.9	20.6	38.2	17.1	3.2
Idaho.............	1,504	239	256	580	359	70	15.9	17.0	38.6	23.9	4.7
Colorado..........	1,996	226	268	769	577	156	11.3	13.4	38.5	28.9	7.8
Washington........	9,797	1,829	1,658	3,871	2,024	406	18.7	16.9	39.5	20.7	4.1
Oregon...........	3,585	493	480	1,417	954	239	13.8	13.4	39.5	26.6	6.7
California.........	15,986	2,144	1,981	6,732	4,204	915	13.4	12.4	42.1	26.3	5.7
ENGLISH											
United States.....	**1,323,617**	**323,761**	**250,762**	**474,010**	**228,881**	**45,666**	**24.5**	**18.9**	**35.8**	**17.3**	**3.5**
Maine..............	65,187	22,845	14,612	17,522	8,019	2,166	35.0	22.4	26.9	12.3	3.3
New Hampshire......	22,817	6,271	5,068	7,538	3,196	736	27.5	22.2	33.0	14.0	3.2
Vermont...........	17,205	4,902	3,269	4,968	3,163	901	28.5	19.0	28.9	18.4	5.2
Massachusetts.......	215,119	66,911	49,136	71,346	23,471	4,197	31.1	22.8	33.2	10.9	2.0
Rhode Island.......	11,601	2,994	2,501	4,232	1,609	263	25.8	21.6	36.5	13.9	2.3
Connecticut........	17,647	4,850	3,569	6,531	2,328	366	27.5	20.2	37.0	13.2	2.1
New York..........	138,668	37,621	27,204	46,456	22,609	4,711	27.1	19.6	33.5	16.3	3.4
New Jersey........	18,874	4,775	3,705	7,053	2,811	520	25.3	19.6	37.4	14.9	2.8
Pennsylvania.......	23,321	5,672	4,227	8,334	4,369	706	24.3	18.1	35.7	18.7	3.0
Ohio..............	36,337	8,414	6,274	13,277	7,005	1,357	23.2	17.3	36.5	19.3	3.7
Indiana...........	10,615	2,084	1,607	3,731	2,483	706	19.6	15.1	35.1	23.4	6.7
Illinois...........	60,127	10,327	10,096	24,536	12,648	2,481	17.2	16.8	40.8	21.0	4.1
Michigan..........	237,314	62,187	43,543	85,718	39,225	6,573	26.2	18.3	36.1	16.5	2.8
Wisconsin..........	31,395	4,298	4,788	12,211	8,169	1,919	13.7	15.3	38.9	26.0	6.1
Minnesota.........	45,933	7,859	8,649	18,501	9,174	1,741	17.1	18.8	40.3	20.0	3.8
Iowa.............	20,664	1,782	2,300	7,884	7,015	1,672	8.6	11.1	38.2	33.9	8.1
Missouri...........	12,734	1,529	1,604	5,134	3,671	787	12.0	12.6	40.3	28.8	6.2
North Dakota.......	23,206	6,009	6,202	8,650	2,051	286	25.9	26.7	37.3	8.8	1.2
South Dakota.......	9,104	1,093	1,454	3,810	2,249	490	12.0	16.0	41.8	24.7	5.4
Nebraska...........	12,535	1,247	1,823	5,503	3,276	681	9.9	14.5	43.9	26.1	5.4
Kansas............	12,173	959	1,503	5,052	3,863	790	7.9	12.3	41.5	31.7	6.5
Florida...........	7,665	1,844	1,146	2,600	1,640	432	24.1	15.0	33.9	21.4	5.6
Texas.............	8,896	1,430	1,414	3,721	1,932	392	16.1	15.9	41.8	21.7	4.4
Montana...........	16,010	4,198	3,261	5,679	2,485	382	26.2	20.4	35.5	15.5	2.4
Idaho.............	7,709	1,826	1,367	2,595	1,552	365	23.7	17.7	33.7	20.1	4.7
Colorado..........	11,444	1,615	1,932	4,722	2,615	556	14.1	16.9	41.3	22.9	4.9
Washington........	55,345	14,268	10,511	19,663	9,128	1,732	25.8	19.0	35.5	16.5	3.1
Oregon...........	24,158	5,065	4,276	9,019	4,795	993	21.0	17.7	37.3	19.8	4.1
California.........	107,896	21,033	17,090	42,191	22,825	4,700	19.5	15.8	39.1	21.2	4.4

TABLE **72**. NATIVE WHITE POPULATION OF FRENCH CANADIAN PARENTAGE, BY SEX AND AGE, FOR 29 SELECTED STATES: 1930

STATE AND SEX	All ages	Under 15 years	15 to 24 years	25 to 44 years	45 to 64 years	65 years and over	PER CENT OF TOTAL				
							Under 15	15 to 24	25 to 44	45 to 64	65 and over
MALE											
United States......	365,822	106,272	74,261	120,586	54,106	10,522	29.1	20.3	33.0	14.8	2.9
Maine................	31,554	13,527	6,995	7,968	2,582	481	42.9	22.2	25.3	8.2	1.5
New Hampshire........	31,658	12,073	7,543	8,944	2,724	365	38.1	23.8	28.3	8.6	1.2
Vermont.............	15,171	5,128	2,507	3,734	2,912	887	33.8	16.5	24.6	19.2	5.8
Massachusetts........	108,899	35,850	24,623	34,847	12,006	1,561	32.9	22.6	32.0	11.0	1.4
Rhode Island.........	28,983	9,437	6,975	9,414	2,892	259	32.6	24.1	32.5	10.0	0.9
Connecticut..........	20,691	6,420	4,508	7,060	2,416	284	31.0	21.8	34.1	11.7	1.4
New York............	27,222	6,402	4,679	9,089	5,455	1,589	23.5	17.2	33.4	20.0	5.8
New Jersey...........	2,511	559	450	1,051	393	57	22.3	17.9	41.9	15.7	2.3
Pennsylvania.........	2,148	439	352	858	435	64	20.4	16.4	39.9	20.3	3.0
Ohio................	3,306	564	466	1,254	833	188	17.1	14.1	37.9	25.2	5.7
Indiana.............	1,210	151	136	440	386	97	12.5	11.2	36.4	31.9	8.0
Illinois.............	8,835	1,069	1,241	3,531	2,459	531	12.1	14.0	40.0	27.8	6.0
Michigan............	30,298	6,977	5,558	11,476	5,306	976	23.0	18.3	37.9	17.5	3.2
Wisconsin...........	9,094	1,071	1,472	3,749	2,228	572	11.8	16.2	41.2	24.5	6.3
Minnesota...........	11,200	1,545	1,962	4,540	2,556	593	13.8	17.5	40.5	22.8	5.3
Iowa...............	1,736	135	173	604	626	198	7.8	10.0	34.8	36.1	11.4
Missouri............	1,030	113	84	390	357	85	11.0	8.2	37.9	34.7	8.3
North Dakota........	2,495	558	585	938	357	56	22.4	23.4	37.6	14.3	2.2
South Dakota........	1,174	113	135	481	344	101	9.6	11.5	41.0	29.3	8.6
Nebraska............	1,046	95	148	398	323	81	9.1	14.1	38.0	30.9	7.7
Kansas.............	1,537	128	158	504	578	169	8.3	10.3	32.8	37.6	11.0
Florida.............	643	136	93	224	148	42	21.2	14.5	34.8	23.0	6.5
Texas..............	711	84	104	295	186	42	11.8	14.6	41.5	26.2	5.9
Montana............	2,515	518	517	923	461	96	20.6	20.6	36.7	18.3	3.8
Idaho..............	802	129	132	301	199	41	16.1	16.5	37.5	24.8	5.1
Colorado............	984	114	124	378	288	80	11.6	12.6	38.4	29.3	8.1
Washington..........	4,989	951	824	1,894	1,093	223	19.1	16.5	38.0	21.9	4.5
Oregon.............	1,830	268	234	707	490	130	14.6	12.8	38.6	26.8	7.1
California...........	7,656	1,106	940	3,118	2,049	437	14.4	12.3	40.7	26.8	5.7
FEMALE											
United States......	369,485	104,117	76,571	126,107	52,729	9,846	28.2	20.7	34.1	14.3	2.7
Maine................	31,264	13,072	7,309	8,280	2,224	366	41.8	23.4	26.5	7.1	1.2
New Hampshire........	31,984	11,840	7,881	9,484	2,466	308	37.0	24.6	29.7	7.7	1.0
Vermont.............	14,465	4,982	2,317	3,733	2,590	837	34.4	16.0	25.8	17.9	5.8
Massachusetts........	112,731	35,042	25,955	37,997	12,242	1,468	31.1	23.0	33.7	10.9	1.3
Rhode Island.........	30,689	9,628	7,452	10,390	2,975	240	31.4	24.3	33.9	9.7	0.8
Connecticut..........	20,869	6,607	4,712	6,990	2,286	272	31.7	22.6	33.5	11.0	1.3
New York............	26,880	6,326	4,572	8,808	5,541	1,608	23.5	17.0	32.8	20.6	6.0
New Jersey...........	2,442	523	465	975	398	80	21.4	19.0	39.9	16.3	3.3
Pennsylvania.........	2,082	379	350	857	418	76	18.2	16.8	41.2	20.1	3.7
Ohio................	3,516	586	486	1,372	863	209	16.7	13.8	39.0	24.5	5.9
Indiana.............	1,228	147	128	456	404	93	12.0	10.4	37.1	32.9	7.6
Illinois.............	9,226	1,029	1,294	3,809	2,527	566	11.2	14.0	41.3	27.4	6.1
Michigan............	29,074	6,673	5,270	11,156	5,090	881	23.0	18.1	38.4	17.5	3.0
Wisconsin...........	8,657	1,049	1,543	3,466	2,105	488	12.1	17.8	40.0	24.3	5.6
Minnesota...........	11,700	1,576	2,076	4,953	2,565	526	13.5	17.7	42.3	21.9	4.5
Iowa...............	1,889	108	197	697	701	185	5.7	10.4	36.9	37.1	9.8
Missouri............	1,083	102	91	406	384	100	9.4	8.4	37.5	35.5	9.2
North Dakota........	2,235	541	502	883	263	46	24.2	22.5	39.5	11.8	2.1
South Dakota........	1,107	86	148	496	298	77	7.8	13.4	44.8	26.9	7.0
Nebraska............	1,109	82	137	487	322	81	7.4	12.4	43.9	29.0	7.3
Kansas.............	1,482	116	143	576	514	132	7.8	9.6	38.9	34.7	8.9
Florida.............	730	125	102	288	178	37	17.1	14.0	39.5	24.4	5.1
Texas..............	634	93	78	261	172	30	14.7	12.3	41.2	27.1	4.7
Montana............	2,307	492	475	921	362	57	21.3	20.6	39.9	15.7	2.5
Idaho..............	702	110	124	279	160	29	15.7	17.7	39.7	22.8	4.1
Colorado............	1,012	112	144	391	289	76	11.1	14.2	38.6	28.6	7.5
Washington..........	4,808	878	834	1,977	931	183	18.3	17.3	41.1	19.4	3.8
Oregon.............	1,755	225	246	710	464	109	12.8	14.0	40.5	26.4	6.2
California...........	8,330	1,038	1,041	3,614	2,155	478	12.5	12.5	43.4	25.9	5.7

TABLE 73. NATIVE WHITE POPULATION OF ENGLISH CANADIAN PARENTAGE, BY SEX AND AGE, FOR 29 SELECTED STATES: 1930

STATE AND SEX	All ages	Under 15 years	15 to 24 years	25 to 44 years	45 to 64 years	65 years and over	Under 15	15 to 24	25 to 44	45 to 64	65 and over
							PER CENT OF TOTAL				
MALE											
United States......	644,968	164,490	123,683	223,495	110,681	22,360	25.5	19.2	34.7	17.2	3.5
Maine...............	32,544	11,581	7,354	8,407	4,038	1,154	35.6	22.6	25.8	12.4	3.5
New Hampshire.......	11,040	3,171	2,461	3,474	1,570	360	28.7	22.3	31.5	14.2	3.3
Vermont.............	8,493	2,524	1,676	2,328	1,520	444	29.7	19.7	27.4	17.9	5.2
Massachusetts........	103,138	33,903	23,566	32,949	10,879	1,820	32.9	22.8	31.9	10.5	1.8
Rhode Island.........	5,466	1,526	1,212	1,896	718	112	27.9	22.2	34.7	13.1	2.0
Connecticut..........	8,401	2,388	1,722	3,012	1,106	170	28.4	20.5	35.9	13.2	2.0
New York............	67,338	19,197	13,387	21,957	10,611	2,155	28.5	19.9	32.6	15.8	3.2
New Jersey...........	9,142	2,397	1,813	3,393	1,318	213	26.2	19.8	37.1	14.4	2.3
Pennsylvania.........	11,255	2,839	2,144	3,877	2,057	331	25.2	19.0	34.4	18.3	2.9
Ohio................	17,335	4,275	3,084	6,143	3,229	598	24.7	17.8	35.4	18.6	3.4
Indiana.............	5,082	1,060	767	1,734	1,192	327	20.9	15.1	34.1	23.5	6.4
Illinois.............	28,730	5,256	4,871	11,404	6,014	1,167	18.3	17.0	39.7	20.9	4.1
Michigan............	117,175	31,599	21,730	41,366	19,126	3,315	27.0	18.5	35.3	16.3	2.8
Wisconsin...........	15,214	2,227	2,370	5,673	3,939	1,001	14.6	15.6	37.3	25.9	6.6
Minnesota...........	22,147	4,077	4,194	8,423	4,550	900	18.4	18.9	38.0	20.5	4.1
Iowa................	9,930	922	1,149	3,672	3,390	790	9.3	11.6	37.0	34.1	8.0
Missouri............	6,029	791	790	2,336	1,708	401	13.1	13.1	38.7	28.3	6.7
North Dakota........	11,864	2,990	3,222	4,328	1,150	168	25.2	27.2	36.5	9.7	1.4
South Dakota........	4,656	556	749	1,901	1,164	281	11.9	16.1	40.8	25.0	6.0
Nebraska............	6,046	626	913	2,570	1,592	343	10.4	15.1	42.5	26.3	5.7
Kansas..............	5,948	489	740	2,397	1,891	429	8.2	12.4	40.3	31.8	7.2
Florida.............	3,518	908	519	1,119	757	214	25.8	14.8	31.8	21.5	6.1
Texas...............	4,555	756	742	1,867	991	196	16.6	16.3	41.0	21.8	4.3
Montana............	8,189	2,120	1,657	2,784	1,403	223	25.9	20.2	34.0	17.1	2.7
Idaho...............	4,013	919	712	1,299	871	209	22.9	17.7	32.4	21.7	5.2
Colorado............	5,473	838	959	2,152	1,215	306	15.3	17.5	39.3	22.2	5.6
Washington..........	27,351	7,163	5,201	9,353	4,671	938	26.2	19.0	34.2	17.1	3.4
Oregon.............	11,924	2,599	2,179	4,220	2,418	504	21.8	18.3	35.4	20.3	4.2
California...........	52,209	10,763	8,360	20,055	10,807	2,202	20.6	16.0	38.4	20.7	4.2
FEMALE											
United States......	678,649	159,271	127,079	250,515	118,200	23,306	23.5	18.7	36.9	17.4	3.4
Maine...............	32,643	11,264	7,258	9,115	3,981	1,012	34.5	22.2	27.9	12.2	3.1
New Hampshire.......	11,777	3,100	2,607	4,064	1,626	376	26.3	22.1	34.5	13.8	3.2
Vermont.............	8,712	2,378	1,593	2,640	1,643	457	27.3	18.3	30.3	18.9	5.2
Massachusetts........	111,981	33,008	25,570	38,397	12,592	2,377	29.5	22.8	34.3	11.2	2.1
Rhode Island.........	6,135	1,468	1,289	2,336	891	151	23.9	21.0	38.1	14.5	2.5
Connecticut..........	9,246	2,462	1,847	3,519	1,222	196	26.6	20.0	38.1	13.2	2.1
New York............	71,330	18,424	13,817	24,499	11,998	2,556	25.8	19.4	34.3	16.8	3.6
New Jersey...........	9,732	2,378	1,892	3,660	1,493	307	24.4	19.4	37.6	15.3	3.2
Pennsylvania.........	12,066	2,833	2,083	4,457	2,312	375	23.5	17.3	36.9	19.2	3.1
Ohio................	19,002	4,139	3,190	7,134	3,776	759	21.8	16.8	37.5	19.9	4.0
Indiana.............	5,533	1,024	840	1,997	1,291	379	18.5	15.2	36.1	23.3	6.8
Illinois.............	31,397	5,071	5,225	13,132	6,634	1,314	16.2	16.6	41.8	21.1	4.2
Michigan............	120,139	30,588	21,813	44,352	20,099	3,258	25.5	18.2	36.9	16.7	2.7
Wisconsin...........	16,181	2,071	2,418	6,538	4,230	918	12.8	14.9	40.4	26.1	5.7
Minnesota...........	23,786	3,782	4,455	10,078	4,624	841	15.9	18.7	42.4	19.4	3.5
Iowa................	10,734	860	1,151	4,212	3,625	882	8.0	10.7	39.2	33.8	8.2
Missouri............	6,705	738	814	2,798	1,963	386	11.0	12.1	41.7	29.3	5.8
North Dakota........	11,342	3,019	2,980	4,322	901	118	26.6	26.3	38.1	7.9	1.0
South Dakota........	4,448	537	705	1,909	1,085	209	12.1	15.8	42.9	24.4	4.7
Nebraska............	6,489	621	910	2,933	1,684	338	9.6	14.0	45.2	26.0	5.2
Kansas..............	6,225	470	763	2,655	1,972	361	7.6	12.3	42.7	31.7	5.8
Florida.............	4,147	936	627	1,481	883	218	22.6	15.1	35.7	21.3	5.3
Texas...............	4,341	674	672	1,854	941	196	15.5	15.5	42.7	21.7	4.5
Montana............	7,821	2,078	1,604	2,895	1,082	159	26.6	20.5	37.0	13.8	2.0
Idaho...............	3,696	907	655	1,296	681	156	24.5	17.5	35.1	18.4	4.2
Colorado............	5,971	777	973	2,570	1,400	250	13.0	16.3	43.0	23.4	4.2
Washington..........	27,994	7,105	5,310	10,310	4,457	794	25.4	19.0	36.8	15.9	2.8
Oregon.............	12,234	2,466	2,097	4,799	2,377	489	20.2	17.1	39.2	19.4	4.0
California...........	55,687	10,270	8,730	22,136	12,018	2,498	18.4	15.7	39.8	21.6	4.5

TABLE **74**. WHITE POPULATION OF CANADIAN STOCK UNDER 15 YEARS OF AGE, BY 5-YEAR PERIOD BY STATES: 1930

DIVISION AND STATE	ALL CANADIAN STOCK				CANADIAN BORN				CANADIAN PARENTAGE			
	Under 15 years	Under 5 years	5 to 9 years	10 to 14 years	Under 15 years	Under 5 years	5 to 9 years	10 to 14 years	Under 15 years	Under 5 years	5 to 9 years	10 to 14 years
United States.	629,950	183,489	211,962	234,499	95,800	8,823	35,887	51,090	534,150	174,666	176,075	183,4(
NEW ENGLAND:												
Maine...........	53,867	16,255	18,817	18,795	4,423	369	1,540	2,514	49,444	15,886	17,277	16,28
New Hampshire..	32,520	9,433	11,298	11,789	2,336	170	860	1,306	30,184	9,263	10,438	10,4
Vermont........	17,804	5,662	6,005	6,137	2,792	315	952	1,525	15,012	5,347	5,053	4,6
Massachusetts....	151,752	45,856	51,075	54,821	13,949	1,014	5,659	7,276	137,803	44,842	45,416	47,5
Rhode Island.....	24,107	6,704	8,354	9,049	2,048	112	710	1,226	22,059	6,592	7,644	7,8
Connecticut......	20,986	6,671	6,976	7,339	3,109	308	1,227	1,574	17,877	6,363	5,749	5,7(
MIDDLE ATLANTIC:												
New York.......	63,410	19,856	21,090	22,464	13,061	1,593	5,082	6,386	50,349	18,263	16,008	16,0
New Jersey......	7,506	2,240	2,468	2,798	1,649	187	607	855	5,857	2,053	1,861	1,9
Pennsylvania.....	8,044	2,278	2,676	3,090	1,554	155	550	849	6,490	2,123	2,126	2,2
E. N. CENTRAL:												
Ohio...........	11,734	3,376	4,018	4,340	2,170	195	781	1,194	9,564	3,181	3,237	3,1
Indiana........	3,022	846	1,016	1,160	640	48	257	335	2,382	798	759	8
Illinois	15,852	4,288	5,154	6,410	3,427	305	1,290	1,832	12,425	3,983	3,864	4,5
Michigan........	94,887	29,316	31,801	33,770	19,050	2,449	7,781	8,820	75,837	26,867	24,020	24,9
Wisconsin.......	7,338	1,596	2,330	3,412	920	70	298	552	6,418	1,526	2,032	2,8(
W. N. CENTRAL:												
Minnesota.......	12,494	2,731	4,093	5,670	1,514	95	503	916	10,980	2,636	3,590	4,7
Iowa...........	2,263	497	753	1,013	238	11	82	145	2,025	486	671	8(
Missouri........	1,998	536	648	814	254	17	84	153	1,744	519	564	6(
North Dakota....	7,759	1,814	2,495	3,450	651	62	208	381	7,108	1,752	2,287	3,0(
South Dakota....	1,444	327	413	704	152	14	41	97	1,292	313	372	6(
Nebraska........	1,616	361	496	759	192	10	52	130	1,424	351	444	6
Kansas..........	1,359	325	447	587	156	14	47	95	1,203	311	400	4
SOUTH ATLANTIC:												
Delaware........	206	60	65	81	23	3	9	11	183	57	56	
Maryland.......	1,080	307	367	406	201	18	75	108	879	289	292	2
Dist. of Columbia.	473	140	150	183	68	9	21	38	405	131	129	1
Virginia........	795	225	296	274	91	7	34	50	704	218	262	2
West Virginia....	569	158	193	218	110	12	28	70	459	146	165	1
North Carolina...	515	159	172	184	53	2	22	29	462	157	150	1
South Carolina...	169	41	58	70	11	1	3	7	158	40	55	
Georgia.........	460	157	143	160	69	11	21	37	391	146	122	1
Florida..........	2,821	806	928	1,087	716	33	268	415	2,105	773	660	6
E. S. CENTRAL:												
Kentucky.......	441	119	163	159	60	2	22	36	381	117	141	1
Tennessee.......	434	133	139	162	57	10	17	30	377	123	122	1
Alabama........	472	124	167	181	57	2	15	40	415	122	152	1
Mississippi......	156	42	48	66	3	..	..	3	153	42	48	(
W. S. CENTRAL:												
Arkansas........	339	82	114	143	34	1	15	18	305	81	99	1
Louisiana.......	437	111	170	156	24	3	10	11	413	108	160	1
Oklahoma.......	1,039	245	374	420	72	7	25	40	967	238	349	3
Texas...........	1,885	492	641	752	278	23	90	165	1,607	469	551	5
MOUNTAIN:												
Montana........	5,907	1,527	1,850	2,530	699	66	214	419	5,208	1,461	1,636	2,1
Idaho..........	2,443	695	773	975	378	31	136	211	2,065	664	637	7
Wyoming........	551	143	212	196	67	6	21	40	484	137	191	1
Colorado........	2,036	469	663	904	195	5	66	124	1,841	464	597	78
New Mexico.....	243	58	78	107	18	..	6	12	225	58	72	
Arizona.........	825	214	308	303	89	8	32	49	736	206	276	2
Utah...........	793	239	252	302	125	16	45	64	668	223	207	2
Nevada.........	298	74	102	122	48	6	20	22	250	68	82	1
PACIFIC:												
Washington......	21,608	5,532	7,244	8,832	5,511	411	1,871	3,229	16,097	5,121	5,373	5,6(
Oregon..........	7,736	1,904	2,539	3,293	2,178	111	712	1,355	5,558	1,793	1,827	1,9
California.......	33,457	8,265	11,330	13,862	10,280	506	3,478	6,296	23,177	7,759	7,852	7,5(

TABLE **75**. MEDIAN AGE OF CANADIAN STOCK, FRENCH AND ENGLISH, 1930, AND OF CANADIAN BORN, 1910, BY STATES

[Median age not shown where total population is less than 100]

DIVISION AND STATE	All Canadian stock, 1930	CANADIAN BORN, 1930			CANADIAN PARENTAGE, 1930			Canadian born, 1910
		Total	French	English	Total	French	English	
United States	33.5	43.7	44.4	43.4	27.6	25.5	28.7	39.3
NEW ENGLAND:								
Maine	28.4	43.7	41.7	45.8	20.0	18.4	21.7	35.1
New Hampshire	30.1	46.1	44.4	50.0	21.4	20.1	25.2	34.9
Vermont	31.7	40.4	37.1	46.5	25.5	24.8	26.7	39.5
Massachusetts	31.7	45.1	46.3	44.3	23.1	22.9	23.3	36.5
Rhode Island	30.3	44.9	44.8	45.3	23.0	22.5	26.4	35.0
Connecticut	30.3	39.7	39.3	40.6	24.2	23.4	26.2	36.9
MIDDLE ATLANTIC:								
New York	33.3	39.6	39.3	39.7	28.0	30.6	26.9	38.2
New Jersey	32.4	38.8	38.3	38.8	28.2	29.7	27.7	37.9
Pennsylvania	33.8	41.2	40.9	41.3	29.7	31.9	29.2	39.8
EAST NORTH CENTRAL:								
Ohio	35.2	42.5	44.4	42.3	31.0	35.0	30.2	40.3
Indiana	36.9	41.7	46.5	41.2	34.8	39.7	33.7	44.2
Illinois	36.9	44.5	49.3	43.6	33.8	37.0	32.8	42.6
Michigan	33.5	41.7	43.6	41.3	28.3	29.6	28.0	42.5
Wisconsin	39.3	54.5	59.4	52.2	35.6	35.4	35.8	48.0
WEST NORTH CENTRAL:								
Minnesota	37.3	53.4	58.0	51.7	32.7	34.0	32.0	43.5
Iowa	44.7	59.1	61.1	58.9	41.2	43.4	40.8	51.1
Missouri	41.5	52.7	50.1	52.9	38.1	41.7	37.6	46.0
North Dakota	31.3	53.0	54.6	52.8	24.4	27.0	24.0	39.0
South Dakota	39.9	56.3	58.5	55.9	36.1	38.5	35.5	46.0
Nebraska	40.7	57.0	57.5	56.9	36.9	38.9	36.6	47.6
Kansas	43.4	59.0	61.7	58.5	40.0	42.9	39.3	50.2
SOUTH ATLANTIC:								
Delaware	32.7	42.3	....	42.5	25.9	23.8	26.5	37.1
Maryland	33.1	40.1	38.6	40.4	28.9	29.2	28.9	38.8
Dist. of Columbia	37.6	44.8	45.4	44.7	34.6	34.9	34.5	40.1
Virginia	33.9	44.2	42.0	44.5	28.7	31.5	28.2	39.6
West Virginia	32.2	39.7	39.7	39.7	28.3	26.7	28.6	42.0
North Carolina	33.8	44.6	....	44.9	27.4	24.8	27.6	40.8
South Carolina	32.9	43.0	....	43.1	27.5	27.4	27.6	40.2
Georgia	35.8	43.1	41.1	43.3	31.6	34.5	31.1	40.9
Florida	38.1	46.5	45.7	46.7	31.9	34.0	31.5	43.4
EAST SOUTH CENTRAL:								
Kentucky	37.0	45.7	....	45.7	33.7	36.1	33.3	44.8
Tennessee	37.3	46.9	....	47.4	33.4	32.1	33.6	44.1
Alabama	35.1	46.4	40.8	47.2	30.2	30.9	30.0	41.7
Mississippi	39.5	52.8	....	53.1	33.9	35.5	33.4	43.3
WEST SOUTH CENTRAL:								
Arkansas	40.8	52.8	....	53.0	36.0	38.6	35.6	45.2
Louisiana	39.8	49.4	49.8	49.3	36.2	40.3	35.1	43.8
Oklahoma	40.0	52.4	54.8	52.0	37.3	41.1	36.7	46.1
Texas	37.1	46.7	45.9	46.8	34.0	36.3	33.6	43.7
MOUNTAIN:								
Montana	33.3	48.4	53.1	47.2	27.5	29.4	26.9	38.6
Idaho	35.6	48.3	51.8	47.7	30.8	33.9	30.1	41.0
Wyoming	36.7	48.1	50.1	47.8	34.1	36.2	33.8	40.5
Colorado	40.1	54.6	56.0	54.5	34.8	38.1	34.2	43.6
New Mexico	39.0	51.5	....	51.2	34.7	38.5	34.0	42.0
Arizona	36.9	47.3	44.4	47.5	32.4	35.1	31.9	39.7
Utah	39.4	42.6	....	42.4	38.4	39.5	38.3	41.4
Nevada	40.1	49.5	54.2	48.6	36.5	37.3	36.3	44.7
PACIFIC:								
Washington	33.2	41.3	49.6	40.3	28.6	32.3	27.9	38.5
Oregon	34.9	42.0	48.2	41.3	31.8	36.6	31.1	41.2
California	36.4	42.0	43.9	41.8	33.0	36.5	32.5	43.5

TABLE **76**. CANADIAN-BORN MALES BY AGE (5-YEAR PERIODS), BY STATES: 1910

SEX AND AGE	United States	Maine	New Hampshire	Vermont	Massachusetts	Rhode Island	Connecticut	New York	New Jersey	Pennsylvania	Ohio	Indiana
All ages.........	601,833	37,954	28,725	13,566	134,878	20,185	13,153	57,050	4,358	7,625	11,376	3,129
Under 5 years......	7,073	628	440	239	1,558	304	193	829	62	101	138	36
5 to 9 years......	12,083	1,300	890	445	2,808	646	340	1,331	90	152	175	55
10 to 14 years......	16,712	1,668	1,281	557	4,304	987	481	1,714	111	190	264	55
15 to 19 years......	27,065	2,688	2,150	787	7,553	1,618	814	2,681	181	275	426	79
20 to 24 years......	46,696	3,888	3,058	1,073	13,169	2,075	1,191	4,847	297	528	771	160
25 to 29 years......	57,704	4,227	3,145	1,191	15,381	2,141	1,357	5,861	433	681	1,065	228
30 to 34 years......	64,716	4,008	3,094	1,131	16,328	2,129	1,443	6,392	535	897	1,268	294
35 to 39 years......	66,484	4,081	3,177	1,277	16,516	2,076	1,456	6,532	601	905	1,326	334
40 to 44 years......	64,758	3,586	2,839	1,256	14,374	2,023	1,302	6,042	523	851	1,358	320
45 to 49 years......	64,948	3,215	2,512	1,184	13,159	1,907	1,257	5,597	468	892	1,351	341
50 to 54 years......	54,097	2,554	2,040	1,030	9,524	1,433	1,032	4,575	391	625	1,091	349
55 to 59 years......	39,173	1,847	1,427	916	7,000	1,073	769	3,243	219	440	705	237
60 to 64 years......	31,253	1,489	1,090	767	5,414	740	624	2,755	178	432	563	228
65 to 69 years......	22,496	1,152	694	612	3,728	488	423	1,993	141	355	435	190
70 to 74 years......	13,424	766	428	485	2,088	287	260	1,286	64	167	221	109
75 to 79 years......	7,751	447	260	338	1,184	141	115	761	38	81	130	62
80 to 84 years......	3,106	199	105	166	467	68	54	362	13	21	57	32
85 years and over...	1,575	136	66	96	232	28	30	185	10	13	20	11
Unknown..........	719	75	29	16	91	21	12	64	3	19	12	9
BROAD AGE GROUPS												
Under 15 years......	35,868	3,596	2,611	1,241	8,670	1,937	1,014	3,874	263	443	577	146
15 to 24 years......	73,761	6,576	5,208	1,860	20,722	3,693	2,005	7,528	478	803	1,197	239
25 to 44 years......	253,662	15,902	12,255	4,855	62,599	8,369	5,558	24,827	2,092	3,334	5,017	1,176
45 to 64 years......	189,471	9,105	7,069	3,897	35,097	5,153	3,682	16,170	1,256	2,389	3,710	1,155
65 years and over...	48,352	2,700	1,553	1,697	7,699	1,012	882	4,587	266	637	863	404

born 1865-1885
"   1845-1865

SEX AND AGE	Illinois	Michigan	Wisconsin	Minnesota	Iowa	Missouri	North Dakota	South Dakota	Nebraska	Kansas	Delaware	Maryland
All ages.........	22,637	87,225	14,431	23,819	6,031	4,279	11,797	3,475	3,853	3,827	256	692
Under 5 years......	180	762	77	213	28	20	166	16	24	13	7	9
5 to 9 years......	224	1,207	100	250	35	33	229	50	28	29	20	20
10 to 14 years......	313	1,958	173	312	45	40	281	28	24	25	19	10
15 to 19 years......	632	3,183	228	530	91	93	439	63	39	40	15	28
20 to 24 years......	1,358	5,732	519	1,253	171	157	789	144	110	113	16	46
25 to 29 years......	1,956	7,186	793	1,910	252	280	1,067	239	213	152	19	65
30 to 34 years......	2,452	8,621	1,033	2,518	377	398	1,452	330	300	252	22	87
35 to 39 years......	2,507	8,823	1,401	2,608	455	415	1,507	334	387	290	19	92
40 to 44 years......	2,792	9,208	1,563	2,745	618	542	1,389	369	489	388	28	80
45 to 49 years......	2,856	10,301	1,889	3,095	765	572	1,368	421	532	523	19	78
50 to 54 years......	2,392	9,563	1,803	2,730	775	505	1,262	462	482	437	18	38
55 to 59 years......	1,555	7,138	1,431	1,886	627	368	739	353	369	395	22	39
60 to 64 years......	1,234	5,365	1,190	1,458	612	335	484	274	356	416	10	41
65 to 69 years......	982	3,966	973	1,002	484	236	286	187	222	336	8	23
70 to 74 years......	619	2,179	579	636	341	161	156	98	156	221	4	23
75 to 79 years......	345	1,250	396	395	224	85	102	66	70	130	5	6
80 to 84 years......	149	461	159	176	78	26	36	30	34	47	..	6
85 years and over...	54	241	107	76	40	8	17	7	13	14	3	1
Unknown..........	37	81	17	26	13	5	28	4	5	6	2	..
BROAD AGE GROUPS												
Under 15 years......	717	3,927	350	775	108	93	676	94	76	67	46	39
15 to 24 years......	1,990	8,915	747	1,783	262	250	1,228	207	149	153	31	74
25 to 44 years......	9,707	33,838	4,790	9,781	1,702	1,635	5,415	1,272	1,389	1,082	88	324
45 to 64 years......	8,037	32,367	6,313	9,169	2,779	1,780	3,853	1,510	1,739	1,771	69	196
65 years and over...	2,149	8,097	2,214	2,285	1,167	516	597	388	495	748	20	59

TABLE **76**. CANADIAN-BORN MALES BY AGE (5-YEAR PERIODS), BY STATES: 1910—Continued

SEX AND AGE	District of Columbia	Virginia	West Virginia	North Carolina	South Carolina	Georgia	Florida	Kentucky	Tennessee	Alabama	Mississippi	Arkansas	Louisiana
All ages.........	509	734	499	266	154	435	847	588	660	459	277	676	741
Under 5 years......	10	7	9	2	2	..	7	5	3	2	..	6	3
5 to 9 years......	14	22	9	3	2	5	12	5	3	9	3	5	8
10 to 14 years......	9	22	5	5	2	7	16	11	11	6	4	6	11
15 to 19 years......	11	24	10	7	1	12	21	14	13	21	3	13	13
20 to 24 years......	24	44	32	11	10	30	41	30	34	21	7	22	22
25 to 29 years......	46	62	31	22	14	34	65	36	48	28	25	46	61
30 to 34 years......	72	82	48	22	18	43	75	57	55	46	29	67	74
35 to 39 years......	51	88	57	34	17	53	96	59	71	52	33	79	80
40 to 44 years......	79	64	63	42	18	54	94	72	69	59	37	66	85
45 to 49 years......	43	80	71	38	29	56	90	68	79	59	24	77	97
50 to 54 years......	38	60	48	29	11	37	77	73	77	44	34	77	87
55 to 59 years......	24	51	31	17	10	35	70	36	46	39	14	57	54
60 to 64 years......	28	36	38	9	8	34	58	48	58	27	27	55	64
65 to 69 years......	38	49	26	7	5	14	67	35	47	22	16	40	36
70 to 74 years......	11	28	11	13	4	13	26	21	29	13	9	38	24
75 to 79 years......	7	14	7	5	1	7	25	11	11	8	4	14	17
80 to 84 years......	4	1	1	..	..	..	5	1	4	1	4	4	3
85 years and over...	..	..	..	..	1	1	..	2	2	2	1	2	2
Unknown..........	..	..	2	..	1	..	2	4	..	..	3	2	..
BROAD AGE GROUPS													
Under 15 years.....	33	51	23	10	6	12	35	21	17	17	7	17	22
15 to 24 years......	35	68	42	18	11	42	62	44	47	42	10	35	35
25 to 44 years......	248	296	199	120	67	184	330	224	243	185	124	258	300
45 to 64 years......	133	227	188	93	58	162	295	225	260	169	99	266	302
65 years and over...	60	92	45	25	11	35	123	70	93	46	34	98	82

SEX AND AGE	Oklahoma	Texas	Montana	Idaho	Wyoming	Colorado	New Mexico	Arizona	Utah	Nevada	Washington	Oregon	California
All ages.........	1,684	2,115	8,607	3,497	899	5,230	603	1,164	1,006	1,273	23,126	7,236	24,227
Under 5 years......	12	18	109	51	10	40	1	6	15	4	380	110	218
5 to 9 years......	24	21	130	76	10	48	9	10	22	11	626	132	407
10 to 14 years......	22	23	138	72	11	88	7	12	13	10	729	142	490
15 to 19 years......	27	48	220	74	21	107	9	15	29	13	819	187	700
20 to 24 years......	62	86	655	179	70	263	33	66	57	49	1,630	439	1,314
25 to 29 years......	96	141	905	306	101	408	51	102	106	94	2,400	707	1,927
30 to 34 years......	134	210	1,108	406	118	541	54	140	104	139	2,663	739	2,311
35 to 39 years......	175	228	1,020	412	89	535	82	193	117	141	2,523	768	2,312
40 to 44 years......	206	232	1,081	445	88	659	70	165	119	148	2,548	878	2,632
45 to 49 years......	222	281	1,140	452	97	699	69	137	104	170	2,736	843	2,885
50 to 54 years......	214	251	821	385	115	699	68	100	103	160	2,143	765	2,470
55 to 59 years......	144	185	487	236	56	404	50	93	49	128	1,486	550	2,023
60 to 64 years......	155	160	358	158	42	341	44	64	57	80	1,059	395	1,795
65 to 69 years......	97	118	211	114	31	205	26	36	42	71	650	246	1,331
70 to 74 years......	45	58	103	78	23	108	18	11	36	28	394	168	780
75 to 79 years......	28	41	72	32	9	54	9	10	20	19	198	109	388
80 to 84 years......	9	6	28	9	5	16	1	2	9	3	61	32	151
85 years and over...	8	4	10	8	1	6	1	1	1	..	37	13	64
Unknown..........	4	4	11	4	2	9	1	1	3	5	44	13	29
BROAD AGE GROUPS													
Under 15 years.....	58	62	377	199	31	176	17	28	50	25	1,735	384	1,115
15 to 24 years......	89	134	875	253	91	370	42	81	86	62	2,449	626	2,014
25 to 44 years......	611	811	4,114	1,569	396	2,143	257	600	446	522	10,134	3,092	9,182
45 to 64 years......	735	877	2,806	1,231	310	2,143	231	394	313	538	7,424	2,553	9,173
65 years and over...	187	227	424	241	69	389	55	60	108	121	1,340	568	2,714

TABLE 77. CANADIAN-BORN FEMALES BY AGE (5-YEAR PERIODS), BY STATES: 1910

SEX AND AGE	United States	Maine	New Hampshire	Vermont	Massachusetts	Rhode Island	Connecticut	New York	New Jersey	Pennsylvania	Ohio	Indiana
All ages	594,237	37,964	29,121	12,474	160,753	21,709	13,533	65,592	4,693	7,653	11,815	2,655
Under 5 years	7,009	630	466	249	1,565	335	182	819	71	81	115	25
5 to 9 years	12,171	1,269	985	473	2,838	673	357	1,297	102	129	183	40
10 to 14 years	17,280	1,766	1,335	530	4,466	1,003	503	1,748	123	206	318	39
15 to 19 years	30,486	3,071	2,494	777	9,291	1,910	1,001	3,055	201	295	470	87
20 to 24 years	53,944	4,215	3,259	1,081	18,153	2,364	1,465	6,227	442	608	968	167
25 to 29 years	63,912	4,292	3,249	1,098	20,163	2,413	1,413	7,769	577	897	1,264	250
30 to 34 years	67,496	4,038	3,124	1,192	19,858	2,289	1,483	7,791	625	886	1,356	275
35 to 39 years	64,868	3,931	3,160	1,136	18,401	2,246	1,422	7,270	558	854	1,320	259
40 to 44 years	60,941	3,488	2,772	1,045	16,480	2,129	1,348	6,387	478	812	1,266	276
45 to 49 years	59,080	3,159	2,490	1,043	14,571	1,905	1,253	6,195	439	861	1,322	296
50 to 54 years	48,112	2,352	1,914	950	10,968	1,473	1,002	4,941	348	662	1,119	265
55 to 59 years	35,259	1,696	1,363	798	8,059	1,079	761	3,620	209	433	704	184
60 to 64 years	28,045	1,425	1,010	684	6,176	727	544	3,105	203	378	547	175
65 to 69 years	20,194	1,107	678	572	4,385	566	376	2,194	133	269	379	125
70 to 74 years	12,414	694	406	365	2,629	297	208	1,498	83	155	222	88
75 to 79 years	7,569	450	222	252	1,607	170	119	971	56	83	155	74
80 to 84 years	3,209	251	104	137	715	74	44	389	23	24	63	22
85 and over	1,690	95	74	80	343	35	40	249	16	12	31	6
Unknown	558	35	16	12	85	21	12	67	6	8	13	2
BROAD AGE GROUPS												
Under 15 years	36,460	3,665	2,786	1,252	8,869	2,011	1,042	3,864	296	416	616	104
15 to 24 years	84,430	7,286	5,753	1,858	27,444	4,274	2,466	9,282	643	903	1,438	254
25 to 44 years	257,217	15,749	12,305	4,471	74,902	9,077	5,666	29,217	2,238	3,449	5,206	1,060
45 to 64 years	170,496	8,632	6,777	3,475	39,774	5,184	3,560	17,861	1,199	2,334	3,692	920
65 and over	45,076	2,597	1,484	1,406	9,679	1,142	787	5,301	311	543	850	315

SEX AND AGE	Illinois	Michigan	Wisconsin	Minnesota	Iowa	Missouri	North Dakota	South Dakota	Nebraska	Kansas	Delaware	Maryland
All ages	22,596	83,932	10,490	17,099	5,565	3,682	9,300	2,517	3,418	3,313	239	701
Under 5 years	178	769	70	212	36	23	136	23	20	16	4	12
5 to 9 years	247	1,229	79	278	40	26	192	31	30	30	5	17
10 to 14 years	369	1,951	144	302	52	57	260	27	31	33	20	8
15 to 19 years	675	3,177	234	521	90	105	390	69	29	39	14	28
20 to 24 years	1,583	6,131	491	1,051	155	161	622	108	114	86	18	65
25 to 29 years	2,160	7,700	726	1,465	271	325	994	198	211	159	23	84
30 to 34 years	2,536	9,144	896	1,891	362	345	1,337	257	330	233	25	74
35 to 39 years	2,536	8,962	975	1,889	396	325	1,232	262	306	292	27	94
40 to 44 years	2,398	8,960	1,081	1,838	549	424	1,065	293	414	383	18	75
45 to 49 years	2,612	9,633	1,182	1,891	684	430	974	307	472	433	20	62
50 to 54 years	2,128	8,448	1,146	1,693	721	411	800	270	404	416	25	42
55 to 59 years	1,548	6,240	1,038	1,270	582	309	514	225	318	356	9	29
60 to 64 years	1,344	4,573	874	1,030	564	276	337	165	269	313	15	49
65 to 69 years	1,007	3,204	658	789	459	211	200	145	204	243	8	28
70 to 74 years	614	1,929	415	468	286	140	116	76	133	147	3	15
75 to 79 years	371	1,106	297	287	199	67	80	31	77	89	2	11
80 to 84 years	160	448	129	134	75	26	28	13	24	28	3	3
85 and over	88	263	43	72	39	12	8	11	21	13	..	2
Unknown	42	65	12	18	5	9	15	6	11	4	..	3
BROAD AGE GROUPS												
Under 15 years	794	3,949	293	792	128	106	588	81	81	79	29	37
15 to 24 years	2,258	9,308	725	1,572	245	266	1,012	177	143	125	32	93
25 to 44 years	9,630	34,766	3,678	7,083	1,578	1,419	4,628	1,010	1,261	1,067	93	327
45 to 64 years	7,632	28,894	4,240	5,884	2,551	1,426	2,625	967	1,463	1,518	69	182
65 and over	2,240	6,950	1,542	1,750	1,058	456	432	276	459	520	16	59

TABLE **77**. CANADIAN-BORN FEMALES BY AGE (5-YEAR PERIODS), BY STATES: 1910—Continued

SEX AND AGE	District of Columbia	Virginia	West Virginia	North Carolina	South Carolina	Georgia	Florida	Kentucky	Tennessee	Alabama	Mississippi	Arkansas	Louisiana
All ages	**614**	**603**	**355**	**268**	**119**	**346**	**851**	**449**	**481**	**355**	**158**	**390**	**418**
Under 5 years	7	14	3	1	2	2	8	5	5	11	1	3	3
5 to 9 years	8	25	4	5	3	4	14	4	5	2	2	5	5
10 to 14 years	20	22	14	9	3	5	14	5	11	8	2	8	5
15 to 19 years	9	20	13	10	7	19	36	16	16	16	6	9	8
20 to 24 years	45	52	28	23	6	26	43	24	29	23	8	24	26
25 to 29 years	77	64	42	23	14	42	70	32	58	38	18	22	49
30 to 34 years	76	71	39	27	18	48	113	55	53	50	20	53	55
35 to 39 years	79	63	40	52	15	45	90	46	62	41	16	43	53
40 to 44 years	68	62	44	31	14	36	93	45	45	34	22	48	51
45 to 49 years	61	52	26	27	10	32	93	56	54	33	23	50	41
50 to 54 years	49	51	29	16	6	25	57	57	42	29	13	39	33
55 to 59 years	33	37	30	12	7	19	72	30	30	31	7	31	19
60 to 64 years	32	28	24	16	6	16	61	27	31	18	7	23	21
65 to 69 years	27	25	8	9	2	9	43	22	15	9	6	12	20
70 to 74 years	11	7	5	5	..	8	24	17	13	4	3	6	15
75 to 79 years	7	6	2	1	3	7	15	6	8	4	..	10	6
80 to 84 years	1	4	3	1	1	3	3	1	1	1	3	2	4
85 and over	2	..	1	..	1	..	2	..	1	1	1	..	2
Unknown	2	..	..	..	1	..	..	1	2	2	..	2	2
BROAD AGE GROUPS													
Under 15 years	35	61	21	15	8	11	36	14	21	21	5	16	13
15 to 24 years	54	72	41	33	13	45	79	40	45	39	14	33	34
25 to 44 years	300	260	165	133	61	171	366	178	218	163	76	166	208
45 to 64 years	175	168	109	71	29	92	283	170	157	111	50	143	114
65 and over	48	42	19	16	7	27	87	46	38	19	13	30	47

SEX AND AGE	Oklahoma	Texas	Montana	Idaho	Wyoming	Colorado	New Mexico	Arizona	Utah	Nevada	Washington	Oregon	California
All ages	**1,147**	**1,383**	**4,894**	**1,864**	**520**	**4,303**	**406**	**654**	**681**	**571**	**16,137**	**5,129**	**20,327**
Under 5 years	14	14	124	36	6	23	5	10	17	..	352	102	204
5 to 9 years	22	21	157	81	10	68	9	20	24	7	636	147	342
10 to 14 years	27	28	144	54	12	73	11	18	20	5	776	132	554
15 to 19 years	23	39	217	72	22	108	11	22	25	14	794	199	721
20 to 24 years	51	92	427	122	40	230	23	46	45	26	1,249	384	1,318
25 to 29 years	77	141	605	178	54	395	47	75	69	51	1,665	484	1,821
30 to 34 years	91	178	637	210	53	475	57	96	59	63	1,870	602	2,080
35 to 39 years	106	165	588	221	67	505	50	95	66	76	1,732	571	2,128
40 to 44 years	161	161	535	206	57	531	42	80	69	81	1,702	534	2,210
45 to 49 years	139	150	524	207	57	554	42	64	66	53	1,629	556	2,247
50 to 54 years	122	115	353	164	57	482	31	44	53	70	1,330	456	1,891
55 to 59 years	93	93	220	104	31	294	25	27	42	44	838	350	1,396
60 to 64 years	90	76	150	69	24	257	24	22	32	36	609	249	1,314
65 to 69 years	64	46	94	63	12	152	19	14	40	21	436	165	921
70 to 74 years	37	35	64	36	10	66	4	13	30	16	280	100	618
75 to 79 years	21	13	26	24	5	57	4	4	15	7	120	60	362
80 to 84 years	4	9	20	7	1	17	1	2	6	1	65	21	110
85 and over	3	4	3	3	1	7	1	..	3	..	29	13	59
Unknown	2	3	6	7	1	9	..	2	..	..	25	4	31
BROAD AGE GROUPS													
Under 15 years	63	63	425	171	28	164	25	48	61	12	1,764	381	1,100
15 to 24 years	74	131	644	194	62	338	34	68	70	40	2,043	583	2,039
25 to 44 years	435	645	2,365	815	231	1,906	196	346	263	271	6,969	2,191	8,239
45 to 64 years	444	434	1,247	544	169	1,587	122	157	193	203	4,406	1,611	6,848
65 and over	129	107	207	133	29	299	29	33	94	45	930	359	2,070

CHAPTER IX

MARITAL STATUS OF THE CANADIAN STOCK

UNDER the heading "marital status" (or "conjugal condition") the census, both in Canada and in the United States, classifies the population as "single," "married," "widowed," or "divorced," with a small residual group made up of those for whom no information with regard to marital status was obtained. A person separated or living apart from husband or wife, but not actually divorced, is counted as married. It is probable that appreciable numbers of divorced persons are returned as single, married, or widowed, and that for this reason the census returns somewhat understate the actual number of divorced persons who have not remarried.

The data with respect to persons of Canadian stock in the United States relate to the whole number in each of the various classes who were 15 years old and over at the time of the 1930 census, without further classification by age. The lack of age classification very seriously limits the possibilities of detailed interpretation of these statistics, since the composition of a given group of persons with respect to marital status changes rapidly with increasing age, and the percentages single, married, or widowed in a series of population groups are affected profoundly by the age composition of the groups.

It should be noted also that the distribution percentages shown for males and females for an identical age group, for example, 15 to 19, or 15 years old and over, do not give an identical representation of the marital status because of the fact that very few males are married before age 17, while the percentage of females married at 15 and 16 is considerable. For many purposes the comparison would be better if the general statistics were presented for males 17 years old and over, and females 15 years old and over. Because of the complications which this double set of age limits would bring into the statistics, however, it has so far not been adopted.

Where statistics of marital status are available in combination with age, it may be noted that the percentage married increases rapidly to a maximum somewhere in the neighborhood of age 40, and then declines rather slowly—much more slowly for males than for females—as the percentage widowed increases. The percentage widowed increases slowly at the beginning of the age series and more rapidly toward the end, finding its maximum always in the highest age period. In considering two population groups with appreciably different age distributions, therefore, one may expect that the group containing the smaller percentage of persons just over 15 will, other things being equal, have a larger proportion single and a smaller proportion married; and that the group having the larger proportion of old people will almost certainly have a larger percentage widowed.

Table 78 shows the 1930 population of Canadian stock in the United States classified by sex and marital status. In this table, and likewise in all the tables relating to marital status, figures are presented only for males and females separately, since conditions affecting marital status apply in many respects differently to males and females, so that there is little significance in figures for the two classes combined. The classification of the Canadian stock by marital status is also shown graphically in Figure 28.

TABLE **78**. WHITE PERSONS OF CANADIAN STOCK 15 YEARS OLD AND OVER, FRENCH AND ENGLISH, BY SEX AND MARITAL STATUS: 1930

SEX AND MARITAL STATUS	ALL CANADIAN STOCK			CANADIAN BORN			CANADIAN PARENTAGE		
	Total	French	English	Total	French	English	Total	French	English
Male..........	1,309,428	436,330	873,098	569,400	176,780	392,620	740,028	259,550	480,478
Single..........	421,024	140,600	280,424	136,654	38,716	97,938	284,370	101,884	182,486
Married.........	804,045	267,654	536,391	382,997	121,303	261,694	421,048	146,351	274,697
Widowed........	65,581	23,351	42,230	41,997	14,953	27,044	23,584	8,398	15,186
Divorced........	17,197	4,242	12,955	7,013	1,587	5,426	10,184	2,655	7,529
Unknown........	1,581	483	1,098	739	221	518	842	262	580
Per cent.......	100.0	100.0	100.0	100.0	100.0	100.0	100.0	100.0	100.0
Single..........	32.2	32.2	32.1	24.0	21.9	24.9	38.4	39.3	38.0
Married.........	61.4	61.3	61.4	67.3	68.6	66.7	56.9	56.4	57.2
Widowed........	5.0	5.4	4.8	7.4	8.5	6.9	3.2	3.2	3.2
Divorced........	1.3	1.0	1.5	1.2	0.9	1.4	1.4	1.0	1.6
Unknown........	0.1	0.1	0.1	0.1	0.1	0.1	0.1	0.1	0.1
Female........	1,397,967	437,437	960,530	613,221	172,069	441,152	784,746	265,368	519,378
Single..........	367,700	117,868	249,832	124,158	30,890	93,268	243,542	86,978	156,564
Married.........	852,067	271,114	580,953	380,034	113,146	266,888	472,033	157,968	314,065
Widowed........	156,701	43,477	113,224	100,642	26,423	74,219	56,059	17,054	39,005
Divorced........	20,264	4,645	15,619	7,800	1,471	6,329	12,464	3,174	9,290
Unknown........	1,235	333	902	587	139	448	648	194	454
Per cent.......	100.0	100.0	100.0	100.0	100.0	100.0	100.0	100.0	100.0
Single..........	26.3	26.9	26.0	20.2	18.0	21.1	31.0	32.8	30.1
Married.........	61.0	62.0	60.5	62.0	65.8	60.5	60.2	59.5	60.5
Widowed........	11.2	9.9	11.8	16.4	15.4	16.8	7.1	6.4	7.5
Divorced........	1.4	1.1	1.6	1.3	0.9	1.4	1.6	1.2	1.8
Unknown........	0.1	0.1	0.1	0.1	0.1	0.1	0.1	0.1	0.1

The distribution of the whole Canadian stock in the United States by marital status differs very little from the corresponding distribution of the entire population of the United States, in spite of the fact that the Canadian element contains a considerably larger proportion of foreign born than the total population and is considerably older, its median age (see Table 60) being 33.5, as compared with 26.4 for the total population.

The whole number of males 15 years old and over in the United States in 1930 who were either Canadian born or of Canadian parentage was 1,309,428, of whom 421,024, or 32.2 per cent, were single; 804,045, or 61.4 per cent, were married; 65,581, or 5.0 per cent, were widowed; and 17,197, or 1.3 per cent, were reported as divorced. The corresponding proportions for the total population of the United States were 34.1 per cent single; 60.0 per cent married; 4.6 per cent widowed; and 1.1 per cent divorced.

FIGURE **28**. CANADIAN STOCK IN THE UNITED STATES BY MARITAL STATUS: 1930

(Persons 15 years old and over)

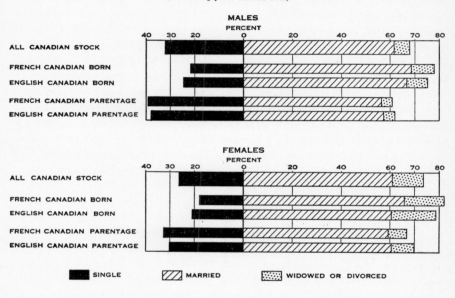

The whole number of females 15 years old and over was 1,397,967, of whom 367,700, or 26.3 per cent, were single; 852,067, or 61.0 per cent, were married; 156,701, or 11.2 per cent, were widowed; and 20,264, or 1.4 per cent, were reported as divorced. The corresponding percentages for the female population of the United States as a whole were 26.4 single; 61.1 married; 11.1 widowed; and 1.3 divorced.

In comparing the percentages for males and females, it may be noted that the percentage single shown for males is materially higher than that for females, this being mainly the result of the fact referred to above, that relatively few males are married at ages 15 or 16. The percentages married, however, are very nearly the same for males and females, while the proportion of females widowed is more than twice that shown for males, this higher percentage widowed making up for the lower percentage single.

In actual numbers there were in the Canadian stock in 1930, 156,701 widows as compared with 65,581 widowers. This excess of widows over widowers is primarily due to the greater longevity of women as compared with men, and to the fact that men usually marry at a later age than women; as a result of these factors, marriage is much more often broken by the death of the husband than by the death of the wife.

There are, of course, radical differences in the distribution by marital status of the Canadian born in the United States and the natives of Canadian parentage, resulting mainly from the differing age composition of these two groups. Since there are relatively few Canadian born in the younger ages, the percentage single in this group is materially less than in the second generation, since the latter at the present time includes somewhat more than a normal percentage of persons 15 to 44 years old, and somewhat fewer persons of advanced age. Thus, only 24.0 per cent of the Canadian-born males 15 years old and over were single, as compared with 38.4 per cent in the second generation of Canadian stock, and 34.1 per cent in the total population of the United States. Likewise, only 20.2 per cent of the Canadian-born females 15 years old and over were single, as compared with 31.0 per cent of the females of the second generation, and 26.4 per cent of those in the total population of the United States.

The percentages married were of course correspondingly higher for the Canadian born, being 67.3, as compared with 56.9 for males of the second generation and 62.0 for the Canadian-born females, as compared with 60.2 for the second generation. The extreme differences, however, were in the percentages widowed, these being in each case more than twice as high for the Canadian born as for the second generation, 7.4 as compared with 3.2 for males, and 16.4 as compared with 7.1 for females. The very high percentage widowed among the Canadian-born females in great measure explains the relatively low percentage married—relatively low, that is, as compared either with the corresponding percentage for males, or (in view of the age differential) with the percentage for the second generation.

The French Canadian-born males show considerably higher percentages married and widowed than the English Canadian born, and a correspondingly lower percentage single. They also show a much smaller percentage divorced than do the English, this relation running consistently through all of the tables showing French and English separately, and representing presumably the effect of the church affiliation of the French stock.

Of the French Canadian-born females 15 years old and over, 65.8 per cent were married, as compared with 60.5 per cent of the English Canadian born, but only 18.0 per cent were single, as compared with 21.1 per cent of the English. The percentage widowed was slightly lower among the French Canadian-born females than among the English.

As between the French and the English stock in the second generation of Canadians in the United States, the differences in distribution by marital status were relatively small, the French, both males and females, showing a slightly higher percentage single and a slightly lower percentage married. These differences are at least in part the result of differences in the age composition of the two groups, the median age of the French of the second generation being only 25.5 as compared with 28.7 for the English. Further, the difference in median age, like the difference in the percentages single and married, is somewhat greater for the females than for the males. The excess in the number of married females over the number of married males need not give rise to the sort of questions that would come up if we were dealing with the total population, since there are many mixed marriages as between persons of Canadian stock and others in the population of the United States. It may be noted, however, that in the French Canadian stock the numbers of married males and females are nearly equal, and that the excess of married females in the English stock is much less than the excess of all females as compared with all males in the English stock.

Urban and Rural Areas

Statistics of the marital status of the Canadian stock and its two main elements are presented for urban and rural areas in Table 79.

In general, there were relatively small variations in the percentages single or the percentages married for males of the Canadian stock as between urban, rural-nonfarm, and rural-farm areas, the percentage single being 32.4 for urban areas, 30.3 for rural-nonfarm, and 33.3 for rural-farm. Among the females, however, there were very appreciable differences, the proportion single being largest in the cities and smallest on farms. The percentages of females single in the several areas were as follows: Urban, 28.3; rural-nonfarm, 20.9; and rural-farm, 18.5.

As between the French and the English stock there were practically no differences in the percentage single for urban and rural-farm areas, but the percentage for the French was appreciably higher than that for the English in rural-nonfarm areas.

Among the Canadian-born males taken alone, the percentages single again showed relatively little variation as between urban and rural areas, being, respectively, 24.3, 22.6, and 23.6, for urban, rural-nonfarm, and rural-farm areas. The Canadian-born females, however, showed a much higher percentage single in urban areas than in rural, namely, 22.1 per cent, as compared with 14.1 per cent in rural-nonfarm areas and 11.2 in rural-farm. In urban areas the percentage single among the French Canadian born, both male and female, was appreciably lower than that shown for the English, but in the other two areas the differences were rela-

TABLE **79**. WHITE PERSONS OF CANADIAN STOCK 15 YEARS OLD AND OVER, FRENCH AND ENGLISH, BY SEX AND MARITAL STATUS, FOR URBAN AND RURAL AREAS: 1930

(For United States totals see Table 78)

CLASS AND SEX	Total	SINGLE		MARRIED		WIDOWED		Di-vorced	Un-known
		Number	Per cent	Number	Per cent	Number	Per cent		
ALL CANADIAN STOCK									
Urban:									
Male, total.........	934,382	303,006	32.4	575,374	61.6	42,610	4.6	12,208	1,184
French..........	325,892	105,354	32.3	200,968	61.7	16,217	5.0	2,959	394
English..........	608,490	197,652	32.5	374,406	61.5	26,393	4.3	9,249	790
Female, total.......	1,056,347	299,095	28.3	618,737	58.6	120,498	11.4	17,023	994
French..........	343,870	97,946	28.5	207,292	60.3	34,448	10.0	3,911	273
English........	712,477	201,149	28.2	411,445	57.7	86,050	12.1	13,112	721
Rural-nonfarm:									
Male, total.......	227,200	68,845	30.3	141,068	62.1	13,748	6.1	3,298	241
French..........	74,379	23,361	31.4	45,385	61.0	4,681	6.3	903	49
English..........	152,821	45,484	29.8	95,683	62.6	9,067	5.9	2,395	192
Female, total.......	220,472	46,175	20.9	145,963	66.2	25,677	11.6	2,478	179
French..........	66,742	14,939	22.4	44,311	66.4	6,855	10.3	596	41
English..........	153,730	31,236	20.3	101,652	66.1	18,822	12.2	1,882	138
Rural-farm:									
Male, total.......	147,846	49,173	33.3	87,603	59.3	9,223	6.2	1,691	156
French..........	36,059	11,885	33.0	21,301	59.1	2,453	6.8	380	40
English..........	111,787	37,288	33.4	66,302	59.3	6,770	6.1	1,311	116
Female, total.......	121,148	22,430	18.5	87,367	72.1	10,526	8.7	763	62
French..........	26,825	4,983	18.6	19,511	72.7	2,174	8.1	138	19
English..........	94,323	17,447	18.5	67,856	71.9	8,352	8.9	625	43
CANADIAN BORN									
Urban:									
Male, total.........	427,536	104,102	24.3	289,296	67.7	28,516	6.7	5,045	577
French..........	136,209	29,169	21.4	94,860	69.6	10,873	8.0	1,122	185
English..........	291,327	74,933	25.7	194,436	66.7	17,643	6.1	3,923	392
Female, total.......	487,270	107,611	22.1	292,757	60.1	79,685	16.4	6,732	485
French..........	139,485	26,465	19.0	89,937	64.5	21,699	15.6	1,268	116
English..........	347,785	81,146	23.3	202,820	58.3	57,986	16.7	5,464	369
Rural-nonfarm:									
Male, total.......	90,823	20,501	22.6	60,665	66.8	8,227	9.1	1,313	117
French..........	28,378	6,569	23.1	18,685	65.8	2,769	9.8	330	25
English..........	62,445	13,932	22.3	41,980	67.2	5,458	8.7	983	92
Female, total.......	85,066	11,985	14.1	57,234	67.3	14,945	17.6	821	81
French..........	23,954	3,429	14.3	16,679	69.6	3,658	15.3	173	15
English..........	61,112	8,556	14.0	40,555	66.4	11,287	18.5	648	66
Rural-farm:									
Male, total.......	51,041	12,051	23.6	33,036	64.7	5,254	10.3	655	45
French..........	12,193	2,978	24.4	7,758	63.6	1,311	10.8	135	11
English..........	38,848	9,073	23.4	25,278	65.1	3,943	10.1	520	34
Female, total.......	40,885	4,562	11.2	30,043	73.5	6,012	14.7	247	21
French..........	8,630	996	11.5	6,530	75.7	1,066	12.4	30	8
English..........	32,255	3,566	11.1	23,513	72.9	4,946	15.3	217	13

TABLE **79**. WHITE PERSONS OF CANADIAN STOCK 15 YEARS OLD AND OVER, FRENCH
AND ENGLISH, BY SEX AND MARITAL STATUS, FOR URBAN AND RURAL AREAS:
1930—Continued

(For United States totals see Table 78)

CLASS AND SEX	Total	SINGLE		MARRIED		WIDOWED		Di-vorced	Un-known
		Number	Per cent	Number	Per cent	Number	Per cent		
CANADIAN PARENTAGE									
Urban:									
Male, total........	506,846	198,904	39.2	286,078	56.4	14,094	2.8	7,163	607
French..........	189,683	76,185	40.2	106,108	55.9	5,344	2.8	1,837	209
English..........	317,163	122,719	38.7	179,970	56.7	8,750	2.8	5,326	398
Female, total.......	569,077	191,484	33.6	325,980	57.3	40,813	7.2	10,291	509
French..........	204,385	71,481	35.0	117,355	57.4	12,749	6.2	2,643	157
English..........	364,692	120,003	32.9	208,625	57.2	28,064	7.7	7,648	352
Rural-nonfarm:									
Male, total........	136,377	48,344	35.4	80,403	59.0	5,521	4.0	1,985	124
French..........	46,001	16,792	36.5	26,700	58.0	1,912	4.2	573	24
English..........	90,376	31,552	34.9	53,703	59.4	3,609	4.0	1,412	100
Female, total.......	135,406	34,190	25.2	88,729	65.5	10,732	7.9	1,657	98
French..........	42,788	11,510	26.9	27,632	64.6	3,197	7.5	423	26
English..........	92,618	22,680	24.5	61,097	66.0	7,535	8.1	1,234	72
Rural-farm:									
Male, total........	96,805	37,122	38.3	54,567	56.4	3,969	4.1	1,036	111
French..........	23,866	8,907	37.3	13,543	56.7	1,142	4.8	245	29
English..........	72,939	28,215	38.7	41,024	56.2	2,827	3.9	791	82
Female, total.......	80,263	17,868	22.3	57,324	71.4	4,514	5.6	516	41
French..........	18,195	3,987	21.9	12,981	71.3	1,108	6.1	108	11
English..........	62,068	13,881	22.4	44,343	71.4	3,406	5.5	408	30

tively small. For males the percentages widowed were lowest in urban
areas, higher in rural-nonfarm, and highest in rural-farm; while for females the highest percentage widowed was in the rural-nonfarm areas,
with the urban slightly lower, and the rural-farm considerably lower.

The pattern of the distribution by marital status of the second generation of Canadians in the United States was in general similar to that
shown for the Canadian born. There was relatively little difference as between urban and rural for the males, but a decidedly higher percentage
single for females in the cities than in the rural areas. Thus, of the French
Canadian females in urban areas, 35.0 per cent were single, as compared
with 26.9 per cent in rural-nonfarm areas and 21.9 per cent in rural-
farm areas. The figures for the English females in the same areas were
32.9, 24.5, and 22.4, respectively.

DATA FOR STATES

STATISTICS of the Canadian born and of the native white population of
Canadian parentage are presented by States in four tables as follows:
In Table 80 for the Canadian born as a whole; in Table 81 for the Cana-

dian born, French and English; in Table 82 for all native persons of Canadian parentage; and in Table 83 for the French and English in the Canadian-parentage group. For economy of space it was found necessary to combine the figures for widowed and divorced in these four tables. Table 84, however, presents the numbers of divorced for the several elements in the Canadian stock and is designed to serve two purposes: First, to provide separate figures for persons returned as divorced, for whatever value they may have in themselves, and second, to make it possible to obtain by subtraction from the combined figures presented in Tables 80–83 the exact numbers of persons returned as widowed.

These State tables are presented primarily for reference purposes, in order that persons interested in studying the statistics of the Canadian stock for any given State or group of States may find the figures conveniently available. The factors which contribute to the variations in the distribution by marital status are so complex that it is not practicable to undertake any extensive discussion of the State figures within the limits of these pages. One very important factor affecting the percentage single or married for any population group is the age of the group. If a comparison is made, however, between the percentages married as shown in Tables 80 to 83 and the age distribution or the median age as shown in the corresponding table in Chapter VIII, it appears that while in general the State in which the Canadian born are older shows a higher percentage married, there are a number of exceptions to this general relation. In California, for example, a State in which the percentage of the male Canadian born who were 45 years old or over was rather low—45.7 as compared with a United States average of 48.6—the percentage of males married was also low, being 61.1 as compared with an average of 67.3 for the United States as a whole; but in Connecticut, where the percentage of the male Canadian born 45 or over was still lower, being only 40.3, the percentage married was much higher, being 67.0, or almost as much as the United States average. The percentage widowed and divorced shows a closer relation with age, but even here there are individual variations which indicate the existence of important factors other than age.

Most of the other factors affecting marital status are factors for which no statistical indexes are available, or at least not conveniently available by States. These include, on the one hand, factors like urban-rural residence, for which statistical measures could be had, if the numbers concerned were large enough to make them valid, and, on the other hand, matters like recency of arrival in the United States, the extent and frequency of movements back and forth between Canada and the United States, and such more general factors as the dominant occupations of the Canadian stock.

TABLE **80**. CANADIAN-BORN WHITE PERSONS 15 YEARS OLD AND OVER, BY SEX AND MARITAL STATUS BY STATES: 1930

DIVISION AND STATE	MALES 15 YEARS OLD AND OVER						FEMALES 15 YEARS OLD AND OVER					
	Total	Single	Married Number	Married Per cent	Widowed or divorced Number	Widowed or divorced Per cent	Total	Single	Married Number	Married Per cent	Widowed or divorced Number	Widowed or divorced Per cent
United States	569,400	136,654	382,997	67.3	49,010	8.6	613,221	124,158	380,034	62.0	108,442	17.
NEW ENGLAND:												
Maine	33,773	6,913	23,957	70.9	2,871	8.5	35,547	5,641	24,676	69.4	5,193	14.
New Hampshire	23,662	4,532	16,919	71.5	2,195	9.3	24,961	4,193	16,882	67.6	3,869	15.
Vermont	12,767	3,389	8,248	64.6	1,116	8.7	11,623	1,956	7,960	68.5	1,695	14.
Massachusetts	120,798	25,006	85,630	70.9	9,985	8.3	153,304	33,969	92,901	60.6	26,319	17.
Rhode Island	17,315	3,377	12,395	71.6	1,531	8.8	19,915	4,207	12,414	62.3	3,281	16.
Connecticut	17,268	4,485	11,575	67.0	1,196	6.9	17,431	3,609	11,421	65.5	2,391	13.
MIDDLE ATLANTIC:												
New York	61,786	17,482	39,973	64.7	4,211	6.8	73,027	18,700	43,150	59.1	11,061	15.
New Jersey	6,807	1,837	4,577	67.2	392	5.8	8,065	2,045	4,816	59.7	1,200	14.
Pennsylvania	7,027	1,782	4,746	67.5	493	7.0	7,771	1,743	4,726	60.8	1,295	16.
EAST N. CENTRAL:												
Ohio	11,853	2,637	8,244	69.6	960	8.1	12,824	2,405	8,109	63.2	2,304	18.
Indiana	2,955	675	2,024	68.5	252	8.5	2,606	435	1,691	64.9	478	18.
Illinois	20,088	5,308	13,004	64.7	1,749	8.7	20,074	4,416	11,180	55.7	4,445	22.
Michigan	92,199	22,372	61,965	67.2	7,803	8.5	91,067	14,442	60,513	66.4	16,059	17.
Wisconsin	8,113	1,619	5,445	67.1	1,030	12.7	6,539	924	3,855	59.0	1,751	26.
WEST N. CENTRAL:												
Minnesota	13,536	2,881	8,991	66.4	1,651	12.2	12,052	2,124	7,006	58.1	2,915	24.
Iowa	3,059	474	2,174	71.1	407	13.3	3,036	387	1,694	55.8	951	31.
Missouri	2,658	495	1,857	69.9	298	11.2	2,500	442	1,399	56.0	657	26.
North Dakota	6,123	1,300	4,177	68.2	636	10.4	5,467	759	3,604	65.9	1,099	20.
South Dakota	1,753	344	1,201	68.5	205	11.7	1,446	185	912	63.1	349	24.
Nebraska	2,100	368	1,436	68.4	296	14.1	2,086	284	1,215	58.2	584	28.
Kansas	1,983	350	1,345	67.8	284	14.3	1,898	258	1,067	56.2	573	30.
SOUTH ATLANTIC:												
Delaware	227	81	130	57.3	16	7.0	210	33	142	67.6	35	16.
Maryland	1,023	304	662	64.7	55	5.4	1,042	219	675	64.8	143	13.
Dist. of Columbia	687	218	406	59.1	63	9.2	926	267	491	53.0	167	18.
Virginia	757	203	484	63.9	69	9.1	769	140	483	62.8	146	19.
West Virginia	457	122	293	64.1	41	9.0	390	76	253	64.9	61	15.
North Carolina	387	61	293	75.7	32	8.3	490	93	302	61.6	95	19.
South Carolina	127	29	90	70.9	8	6.3	140	32	92	65.7	16	11.
Georgia	520	122	362	69.6	35	6.7	505	100	316	62.6	89	17.
Florida	3,447	742	2,387	69.2	308	8.9	3,993	781	2,465	61.7	740	18.
EAST S. CENTRAL:												
Kentucky	452	95	308	68.1	49	10.8	406	100	229	56.4	77	19.
Tennessee	453	82	323	71.3	48	10.6	429	66	275	64.1	88	20.
Alabama	456	91	324	71.1	41	9.0	389	56	250	64.3	83	21.
Mississippi	200	38	134	67.0	27	13.5	148	19	106	71.6	23	15.
WEST S. CENTRAL:												
Arkansas	361	52	265	73.4	43	11.9	300	45	173	57.7	82	27.
Louisiana	583	146	380	65.2	56	9.6	374	77	229	61.2	67	17.
Oklahoma	1,152	187	812	70.5	152	13.2	895	95	562	62.8	237	26.
Texas	2,360	553	1,565	66.3	236	10.0	1,887	326	1,207	64.0	351	18.
MOUNTAIN:												
Montana	5,808	1,823	3,365	57.9	605	10.4	4,246	711	2,752	64.8	778	18.
Idaho	2,504	788	1,455	58.1	258	10.3	1,620	224	1,086	67.0	309	19.
Wyoming	573	151	350	61.1	70	12.2	496	81	321	64.7	92	18.
Colorado	2,826	571	1,918	67.9	333	11.8	2,795	391	1,583	56.6	817	29.
New Mexico	331	75	204	61.6	52	15.7	264	40	171	64.8	53	20.
Arizona	1,072	274	683	63.7	113	10.5	857	132	563	65.7	161	18.
Utah	601	146	395	65.7	60	10.0	464	105	271	58.4	87	18.
Nevada	554	198	269	48.6	87	15.7	350	40	210	60.0	100	28.
PACIFIC:												
Washington	21,925	6,491	13,423	61.2	1,967	9.0	20,628	4,245	12,694	61.5	3,652	17.
Oregon	8,147	2,300	5,087	62.4	755	9.3	7,591	1,679	4,574	60.3	1,334	17.
California	43,787	13,085	26,747	61.1	3,870	8.8	47,378	10,861	26,368	55.7	10,090	21.

TABLE **81**. CANADIAN-BORN WHITE PERSONS 15 YEARS OLD AND OVER, FRENCH AND ENGLISH, BY SEX AND MARITAL STATUS, FOR 29 SELECTED STATES: 1930

CLASS AND STATE	MALES 15 YEARS OLD AND OVER						FEMALES 15 YEARS OLD AND OVER					
	Total	Single	Married		Widowed or divorced		Total	Single	Married		Widowed or divorced	
			Number	Per cent	Number	Per cent			Number	Per cent	Number	Per cent
FRENCH												
United States	**176,780**	**38,716**	**121,303**	**68.6**	**16,540**	**9.4**	**172,069**	**30,890**	**113,146**	**65.8**	**27,894**	**16.2**
Maine	17,217	3,791	12,128	70.4	1,284	7.5	17,344	3,244	11,924	68.8	2,165	12.5
New Hampshire	17,888	3,464	12,824	71.7	1,589	8.9	17,970	3,231	12,212	68.0	2,518	14.0
Vermont	8,271	2,393	5,172	62.5	697	8.4	6,871	1,336	4,686	68.2	840	12.2
Massachusetts	53,787	9,958	38,773	72.1	4,983	9.3	56,388	10,112	36,954	65.5	9,296	16.5
Rhode Island	14,371	2,766	10,301	71.7	1,292	9.0	15,503	3,091	9,921	64.0	2,479	16.0
Connecticut	12,047	3,186	7,980	66.2	874	7.3	11,397	2,279	7,658	67.2	1,458	12.8
New York	13,596	4,046	8,460	62.2	1,057	7.8	13,003	2,749	8,263	63.5	1,961	15.1
New Jersey	1,096	304	720	65.7	72	6.6	1,179	279	734	62.3	166	14.1
Pennsylvania	883	223	575	65.1	84	9.5	868	176	533	61.4	158	18.2
Ohio	1,238	270	841	67.9	123	9.9	1,234	198	768	62.2	268	21.7
Indiana	341	68	231	67.7	42	12.3	296	42	181	61.1	72	24.3
Illinois	2,978	654	1,933	64.9	387	13.0	2,898	503	1,626	56.1	764	26.4
Michigan	14,286	3,424	9,345	65.4	1,509	10.6	11,940	1,401	8,426	70.6	2,109	17.7
Wisconsin	2,432	340	1,687	69.4	400	16.4	1,813	131	1,149	63.4	532	29.3
Minnesota	3,536	531	2,450	69.3	549	15.5	2,836	310	1,775	62.6	749	26.4
Iowa	300	49	198	66.0	51	17.0	301	28	161	53.5	111	36.9
Missouri	308	60	206	66.9	42	13.6	263	53	142	54.0	68	25.9
North Dakota	734	120	508	69.2	105	14.3	590	52	397	67.3	138	23.4
South Dakota	271	40	193	71.2	38	14.0	211	15	143	67.8	53	25.1
Nebraska	226	28	155	68.6	43	19.0	201	18	126	62.7	57	28.4
Kansas	288	38	202	70.1	48	16.7	266	32	143	53.8	91	34.2
Florida	469	112	305	65.0	50	10.7	431	113	242	56.1	76	17.6
Texas	257	84	145	56.4	27	10.5	181	31	110	60.8	39	21.5
Montana	1,148	327	670	58.4	147	12.8	783	125	507	64.8	151	19.3
Idaho	360	108	207	57.5	45	12.5	195	34	118	60.5	43	22.1
Colorado	305	76	189	62.0	39	12.8	258	29	145	56.2	84	32.6
Washington	2,248	569	1,415	62.9	257	11.4	1,866	358	1,138	61.0	358	19.2*
Oregon	691	157	439	63.5	94	13.6	583	115	361	61.9	107	18.4
California	3,802	1,157	2,190	57.6	442	11.6	3,385	623	1,968	58.1	787	23.2
ENGLISH												
United States	**392,620**	**97,938**	**261,694**	**66.7**	**32,470**	**8.3**	**441,152**	**93,268**	**266,888**	**60.5**	**80,548**	**18.3**
Maine	16,556	3,122	11,829	71.4	1,587	9.6	18,203	2,397	12,752	70.1	3,028	16.6
New Hampshire	5,774	1,068	4,095	70.9	606	10.5	6,991	962	4,670	66.8	1,351	19.3
Vermont	4,496	996	3,076	68.4	419	9.3	4,752	620	3,274	68.9	855	18.0
Massachusetts	67,011	15,048	46,857	69.9	5,002	7.5	96,916	23,857	55,947	57.7	17,023	17.6
Rhode Island	2,944	611	2,094	71.1	239	8.1	4,412	1,116	2,493	56.5	802	18.2
Connecticut	5,221	1,299	3,595	68.9	322	6.2	6,034	1,330	3,763	62.4	933	15.5
New York	48,190	13,436	31,513	65.4	3,154	6.5	60,024	15,951	34,887	58.1	9,100	15.2
New Jersey	5,711	1,533	3,857	67.5	320	5.6	6,886	1,766	4,082	59.3	1,034	15.0
Pennsylvania	6,144	1,559	4,171	67.9	409	6.7	6,903	1,567	4,193	60.7	1,137	16.5
Ohio	10,615	2,367	7,403	69.7	837	7.9	11,590	2,207	7,341	63.3	2,036	17.6
Indiana	2,654	607	1,793	68.6	210	8.0	2,310	393	1,510	65.4	406	17.6
Illinois	17,110	4,654	11,071	64.7	1,362	8.0	17,176	3,913	9,554	55.6	3,681	21.4
Michigan	77,913	18,948	52,620	67.5	6,294	8.1	79,127	13,041	52,087	65.8	13,950	17.6
Wisconsin	5,681	1,279	3,758	66.2	630	11.1	4,726	793	2,706	57.3	1,219	25.8
Minnesota	10,000	2,350	6,541	65.4	1,102	11.0	9,216	1,814	5,231	56.8	2,166	23.5
Iowa	2,759	425	1,976	71.6	356	12.9	2,735	359	1,533	56.1	840	30.7
Missouri	2,350	435	1,651	70.3	256	10.9	2,237	389	1,257	56.2	589	26.3
North Dakota	5,389	1,180	3,669	68.1	531	9.9	4,877	707	3,207	65.8	961	19.7
South Dakota	1,482	304	1,008	68.0	167	11.3	1,235	170	769	62.3	296	24.0
Nebraska	1,874	340	1,281	68.4	253	13.5	1,885	266	1,089	57.8	527	28.0
Kansas	1,695	312	1,143	67.4	236	13.9	1,632	226	924	56.6	482	29.5
Florida	2,978	630	2,082	69.9	258	8.7	3,562	668	2,223	62.4	664	18.6
Texas	2,103	469	1,420	67.5	209	9.9	1,706	295	1,097	64.3	312	18.3
Montana	4,660	1,496	2,695	57.8	458	9.8	3,463	586	2,245	64.8	627	18.1
Idaho	2,144	680	1,248	58.2	213	9.9	1,425	190	968	67.9	266	18.7
Colorado	2,521	495	1,729	68.6	294	11.7	2,533	362	1,438	56.7	733	28.9
Washington	19,677	5,922	12,008	61.0	1,710	8.7	18,762	3,887	11,556	61.6	3,294	17.6
Oregon	7,456	2,143	4,648	62.3	661	8.9	7,008	1,564	4,213	60.1	1,227	17.5
California	39,985	11,928	24,557	61.4	3,428	8.6	43,993	10,238	24,400	55.5	9,303	21.1

TABLE **82**. NATIVE WHITE PERSONS OF CANADIAN PARENTAGE 15 YEARS OLD AND OVER, BY SEX AN*
MARITAL STATUS, BY STATES: 1930

DIVISION AND STATE	MALES 15 YEARS OLD AND OVER						FEMALES 15 YEARS OLD AND OVER					
	Total	Single	Married Number	Married Per cent	Widowed or divorced Number	Widowed or divorced Per cent	Total	Single	Married Number	Married Per cent	Widowed or divorced Number	Per ce*
United States......	740,028	284,370	421,048	56.9	33,768	4.6	784,746	243,542	472,033	60.2	68,523	8
NEW ENGLAND:												
Maine.............	38,990	17,385	20,047	51.4	1,489	3.8	39,571	14,998	22,014	55.6	2,520	6
New Hampshire.....	27,454	12,455	13,963	50.9	1,013	3.7	28,821	11,329	15,911	55.2	1,565	5
Vermont...........	16,012	5,770	9,193	57.4	1,041	6.5	15,817	4,150	10,001	63.2	1,656	10
Massachusetts.....	142,284	64,948	72,791	51.2	4,380	3.1	156,662	63,720	83,216	53.1	9,582	6
Rhode Island.......	23,486	10,549	12,220	52.0	706	3.0	25,728	10,535	13,773	53.5	1,414	5
Connecticut........	20,284	8,228	11,359	56.0	675	3.3	21,046	7,219	12,621	60.0	1,197	5
MIDDLE ATLANTIC:												
New York.........	68,961	26,811	38,936	56.5	3,103	4.5	73,460	23,599	42,726	58.2	7,029	9
New Jersey........	8,697	3,208	5,214	60.0	269	3.1	9,273	2,929	5,574	60.1	760	8
Pennsylvania......	10,125	3,740	5,980	59.1	395	3.9	10,936	3,271	6,678	61.1	978	8
EAST N. CENTRAL:												
Ohio.............	15,802	5,265	9,726	61.5	803	5.1	17,793	4,872	11,049	62.1	1,864	10
Indiana...........	5,081	1,406	3,345	65.8	326	6.4	5,590	1,215	3,734	66.8	636	11
Illinois...........	31,240	10,173	19,416	62.2	1,623	5.2	34,523	9,460	21,227	61.5	3,804	11
Michigan..........	108,897	38,832	64,820	59.5	5,162	4.7	111,952	27,922	74,744	66.8	9,240	8
Wisconsin.........	21,010	6,711	13,148	62.6	1,118	5.3	21,718	5,298	14,112	65.0	2,278	10
WEST N. CENTRAL:												
Minnesota.........	27,725	10,030	16,435	59.3	1,235	4.5	30,128	8,935	18,570	61.6	2,602	8
Iowa.............	10,609	2,614	7,273	68.6	720	6.8	11,655	2,326	7,874	67.6	1,449	12
Missouri..........	6,155	1,611	4,125	67.0	418	6.8	6,948	1,469	4,534	65.3	940	13
North Dakota......	10,811	5,389	5,114	47.3	291	2.7	10,017	3,754	5,828	58.2	422	4
South Dakota......	5,161	1,620	3,217	62.3	309	6.0	4,932	1,041	3,387	68.7	503	10
Nebraska..........	6,371	1,809	4,209	66.1	342	5.4	6,895	1,489	4,714	68.4	684	9
Kansas...........	6,868	1,590	4,847	70.6	430	6.3	7,121	1,384	4,909	68.9	822	11
SOUTH ATLANTIC:												
Delaware..........	262	133	123	46.9	6	2.3	241	71	151	62.7	19	7
Maryland..........	1,515	634	844	55.7	37	2.4	1,407	430	851	60.5	121	8
Dist. of Columbia....	1,277	491	729	57.1	56	4.4	1,501	532	787	52.4	179	11
Virginia..........	1,198	509	649	54.2	40	3.3	1,152	304	761	66.1	87	7
West Virginia......	591	204	367	62.1	20	3.4	651	179	410	63.0	62	9
North Carolina.....	519	175	329	63.4	14	2.7	580	173	344	59.3	63	10
South Carolina.....	234	100	125	53.4	9	3.8	226	65	127	56.2	34	15
Georgia...........	695	234	438	63.0	23	3.3	721	179	450	62.4	91	12
Florida............	3,117	885	2,055	65.9	176	5.6	3,816	880	2,400	62.9	533	14
EAST S. CENTRAL:												
Kentucky..........	759	229	492	64.8	37	4.9	904	289	514	56.9	101	11
Tennessee.........	762	222	504	66.1	36	4.7	879	221	540	61.4	118	13
Alabama..........	633	201	401	63.3	31	4.9	717	192	445	62.1	80	11
Mississippi........	376	93	262	69.7	21	5.6	342	96	201	58.8	45	13
WEST S. CENTRAL:												
Arkansas..........	794	187	550	69.3	56	7.1	788	154	516	65.5	117	14
Louisiana..........	1,065	325	671	63.0	69	6.5	1,124	274	674	60.0	176	15
Oklahoma.........	3,339	804	2,289	68.6	244	7.3	3,332	562	2,350	70.5	419	12
Texas.............	4,426	1,381	2,754	62.2	287	6.5	4,208	909	2,765	65.7	534	12
MOUNTAIN:												
Montana..........	8,066	3,485	4,147	51.4	422	5.2	7,558	2,089	4,888	64.7	577	7
Idaho............	3,767	1,389	2,137	56.7	229	6.1	3,381	744	2,305	68.2	328	9
Wyoming..........	1,402	453	860	61.3	89	6.3	1,249	234	896	71.7	119	9
Colorado..........	5,505	1,751	3,382	61.4	363	6.6	6,094	1,400	3,952	64.9	742	12
New Mexico........	616	210	362	58.8	44	7.1	663	165	423	63.8	74	11
Arizona...........	1,621	532	989	61.0	99	6.1	1,497	332	1,002	66.9	159	10
Utah.............	1,455	320	1,028	70.7	106	7.3	1,538	271	1,004	65.3	263	17
Nevada...........	902	334	484	53.7	84	9.3	765	135	530	69.3	99	12
PACIFIC:												
Washington........	24,226	9,127	13,618	56.2	1,423	5.7	24,819	6,344	15,893	64.0	2,550	10
Oregon............	10,887	3,749	6,387	58.7	744	6.8	11,298	2,601	7,391	65.4	1,305	11
California.........	47,996	16,069	28,694	59.8	3,155	6.6	52,709	12,802	32,267	61.2	7,583	14

TABLE **83**. WHITE PERSONS OF CANADIAN PARENTAGE 15 YEARS OLD AND OVER, FRENCH AND ENGLISH, BY SEX AND MARITAL STATUS, FOR 29 SELECTED STATES: 1930

| | MALES 15 YEARS OLD AND OVER | | | | | | FEMALES 15 YEARS OLD AND OVER | | | | | |
| | | | Married | | Widowed or divorced | | | | Married | | Widowed or divorced | |
CLASS AND STATE	Total	Single	Number	Per cent	Number	Per cent	Total	Single	Number	Per cent	Number	Per cent
FRENCH												
United States	**259,550**	**101,884**	**146,351**	**56.4**	**11,053**	**4.3**	**265,368**	**86,978**	**157,968**	**59.5**	**20,228**	**7.6**
Maine	18,027	8,540	8,895	49.3	564	3.1	18,192	7,858	9,461	52.0	856	4.7
New Hampshire	19,585	9,262	9,683	49.4	619	3.2	20,144	8,487	10,753	53.4	889	4.4
Vermont	10,043	3,548	5,795	57.7	697	6.9	9,483	2,448	5,996	63.2	1,033	10.9
Massachusetts	73,049	32,224	38,520	52.7	2,229	3.1	77,689	30,402	43,052	55.4	4,176	5.4
Rhode Island	19,546	8,843	10,135	51.9	557	2.8	21,061	8,789	11,225	53.3	1,041	4.9
Connecticut	14,271	5,853	7,947	55.7	456	3.2	14,262	4,973	8,527	59.8	756	5.3
New York	20,820	7,153	12,486	60.0	1,158	5.6	20,554	5,500	12,732	61.9	2,301	11.2
New Jersey	1,952	624	1,265	64.8	61	3.1	1,919	514	1,228	64.0	175	9.1
Pennsylvania	1,709	566	1,067	62.4	73	4.3	1,703	429	1,125	66.1	149	8.7
Ohio	2,742	711	1,871	68.2	159	5.8	2,930	598	1,960	66.9	372	12.7
Indiana	1,059	214	760	71.8	83	7.8	1,081	162	783	72.4	135	12.5
Illinois	7,766	2,128	5,183	66.7	453	5.8	8,197	1,853	5,321	64.9	1,018	12.4
Michigan	23,321	8,242	13,895	59.6	1,168	5.0	22,401	5,176	15,239	68.0	1,979	8.8
Wisconsin	8,023	2,470	5,113	63.7	420	5.2	7,608	1,762	5,044	66.3	785	10.3
Minnesota	9,655	3,139	6,021	62.4	481	5.0	10,124	2,562	6,614	65.3	939	9.3
Iowa	1,601	342	1,117	69.8	141	8.8	1,781	269	1,253	70.4	257	14.4
Missouri	917	189	654	71.3	74	8.1	981	175	626	63.8	180	18.3
North Dakota	1,937	846	1,027	53.0	63	3.3	1,694	525	1,056	62.3	110	6.5
South Dakota	1,061	286	702	66.2	67	6.3	1,021	172	723	70.8	125	12.2
Nebraska	951	242	655	68.9	54	5.7	1,027	183	717	69.8	127	12.4
Kansas	1,409	277	1,034	73.4	98	7.0	1,366	224	972	71.2	169	12.4
Florida	507	139	337	66.5	31	6.1	605	122	400	66.1	83	13.7
Texas	627	180	402	64.1	44	7.0	541	84	384	71.0	73	13.5
Montana	1,997	831	1,039	52.0	125	6.3	1,815	446	1,211	66.7	158	8.7
Idaho	673	229	409	60.8	35	5.2	592	119	410	69.3	63	10.6
Colorado	870	217	580	66.7	72	8.3	900	160	609	67.7	131	14.6
Washington	4,038	1,301	2,484	61.5	245	6.1	3,930	770	2,740	69.7	414	10.5
Oregon	1,562	449	983	62.9	130	8.3	1,530	267	1,058	69.2	205	13.4
California	6,550	1,878	4,192	64.0	475	7.3	7,292	1,332	4,817	66.1	1,139	15.6
ENGLISH												
United States	**480,478**	**182,486**	**274,697**	**57.2**	**22,715**	**4.7**	**519,378**	**156,564**	**314,065**	**60.5**	**48,295**	**9.3**
Maine	20,963	8,845	11,152	53.2	925	4.4	21,379	7,140	12,553	58.7	1,664	7.8
New Hampshire	7,869	3,193	4,280	54.4	394	5.0	8,677	2,842	5,158	59.4	676	7.8
Vermont	5,969	2,222	3,398	56.9	344	5.8	6,334	1,702	4,005	63.2	623	9.8
Massachusetts	69,235	32,724	34,271	49.5	2,151	3.1	78,973	33,318	40,164	50.9	5,406	6.8
Rhode Island	3,940	1,706	2,085	52.9	149	3.8	4,667	1,746	2,548	54.6	373	8.0
Connecticut	6,013	2,375	3,412	56.7	219	3.6	6,784	2,246	4,094	60.3	441	6.5
New York	48,141	19,658	26,450	54.9	1,945	4.0	52,906	18,099	29,994	56.7	4,728	8.9
New Jersey	6,745	2,584	3,949	58.5	208	3.1	7,354	2,415	4,346	59.1	585	8.0
Pennsylvania	8,416	3,174	4,913	58.4	322	3.8	9,233	2,842	5,553	60.1	829	9.0
Ohio	13,060	4,554	7,855	60.1	644	4.9	14,863	4,274	9,089	61.2	1,492	10.0
Indiana	4,022	1,192	2,585	64.3	243	6.0	4,509	1,053	2,951	65.4	501	11.1
Illinois	23,474	8,045	14,233	60.6	1,170	5.0	26,326	7,607	15,906	60.4	2,786	10.6
Michigan	85,576	30,590	50,925	59.5	3,994	4.7	89,551	22,746	59,505	66.4	7,261	8.1
Wisconsin	12,987	4,241	8,035	61.9	698	5.4	14,110	3,536	9,068	64.3	1,493	10.6
Minnesota	18,070	6,891	10,414	57.6	754	4.2	20,004	6,373	11,956	59.8	1,663	8.3
Iowa	9,008	2,272	6,156	68.3	579	6.4	9,874	2,057	6,621	67.1	1,192	12.1
Missouri	5,238	1,422	3,471	66.3	344	6.6	5,967	1,294	3,908	65.5	760	12.7
North Dakota	8,874	4,543	4,087	46.1	228	2.6	8,323	3,229	4,772	57.3	312	3.7
South Dakota	4,100	1,334	2,515	61.3	242	5.9	3,911	869	2,664	68.1	378	9.7
Nebraska	5,420	1,567	3,554	65.6	288	5.3	5,868	1,306	3,997	68.1	557	9.5
Kansas	5,459	1,313	3,813	69.8	332	6.1	5,755	1,160	3,937	68.4	653	11.3
Florida	2,610	746	1,718	65.8	145	5.6	3,211	758	2,000	62.3	450	14.0
Texas	3,799	1,201	2,352	61.9	243	6.4	3,667	825	2,381	64.9	461	12.6
Montana	6,069	2,654	3,108	51.2	297	4.9	5,743	1,643	3,677	64.0	419	7.3
Idaho	3,094	1,160	1,728	55.9	194	6.3	2,789	625	1,895	67.9	265	9.5
Colorado	4,635	1,534	2,802	60.5	291	6.3	5,194	1,240	3,343	64.4	611	11.8
Washington	20,188	7,826	11,134	55.2	1,178	5.8	20,889	5,574	13,153	63.0	2,136	10.2
Oregon	9,325	3,300	5,404	58.0	614	6.6	9,768	2,334	6,333	64.8	1,100	11.3
California	41,446	14,191	24,502	59.1	2,680	6.5	45,417	11,470	27,450	60.4	6,444	14.2

TABLE **84**. DIVORCED PERSONS IN THE CANADIAN STOCK, FRENCH AND ENGLISH, BY STATES: 1930

[This table is presented by way of supplement to Tables 81 to 83, in which widowed and divorced persons are combined, first to present the divorce figures for their own significance, and second to make it possible to obtain, by subtraction, figures for widowed alone]

DIVISION AND STATE	CANADIAN BORN						CANADIAN PARENTAGE					
	Total		French		English		Total		French		English	
	Male	Female	Male	Female	Male	Female	Male	Female	Male	Female	Male	Female
United States	7,013	7,800	1,587	1,471	5,426	6,329	10,184	12,464	2,655	3,174	7,529	9,290
NEW ENGLAND:												
Maine	363	323	123	84	240	239	376	474	143	154	233	320
New Hampshire	250	241	148	141	102	100	290	330	163	188	127	142
Vermont	127	93	71	37	56	56	212	176	132	94	80	82
Massachusetts	889	1,468	320	365	569	1,103	999	1,682	418	638	581	1,044
Rhode Island	126	191	94	135	32	56	171	324	121	224	50	100
Connecticut	83	115	44	53	39	62	139	174	92	99	47	75
MIDDLE ATLANTIC:												
New York	369	484	79	80	290	404	509	628	144	165	365	463
New Jersey	53	55	8	8	45	47	42	85	10	26	32	59
Pennsylvania	49	67	12	8	37	59	89	119	18	23	71	96
EAST NORTH CENTRAL:												
Ohio	196	231	26	22	170	209	265	377	54	77	211	300
Indiana	41	28	4	4	37	24	108	91	29	27	79	64
Illinois	251	331	47	56	204	275	476	668	109	153	367	515
Michigan	1,305	1,374	214	147	1,091	1,227	1,804	1,835	367	344	1,437	1,491
Wisconsin	95	79	31	30	64	49	268	350	99	114	169	236
WEST NORTH CENTRAL:												
Minnesota	185	151	51	38	134	113	345	421	119	145	226	276
Iowa	39	44	4	7	35	37	186	209	42	36	144	173
Missouri	50	35	10	7	40	28	128	142	15	20	113	122
North Dakota	64	46	8	8	56	38	74	83	11	20	63	63
South Dakota	22	17	3	..	19	17	72	60	12	8	60	52
Nebraska	38	15	5	..	33	15	95	130	17	21	78	109
Kansas	38	15	7	2	31	13	117	117	21	24	96	93
SOUTH ATLANTIC:												
Delaware	1	3	1	1	..	2	..	1	..	..	..	1
Maryland	7	15	2	1	5	14	11	14	1	..	10	14
Dist. of Columbia	10	14	3	3	7	11	16	33	3	4	13	29
Virginia	12	4	3	..	9	4	16	9	2	..	14	9
West Virginia	7	5	..	1	7	4	5	10	1	1	4	9
North Carolina	2	2	..	..	2	2	3	6	1	..	2	6
South Carolina	2	..	..	..	2	..	1	2	1	..	..	2
Georgia	5	6	..	..	5	6	5	9	3	..	2	9
Florida	55	54	12	6	43	48	57	82	6	11	51	71
EAST SOUTH CENTRAL:												
Kentucky	4	2	2	..	2	2	11	13	1	1	10	12
Tennessee	7	11	..	..	7	11	15	12	4	1	11	11
Alabama	3	7	1	..	2	7	7	8	1	1	6	7
Mississippi	1	1	1	..	..	1	4	6	..	2	4	4
WEST SOUTH CENTRAL:												
Arkansas	10	4	..	..	10	4	14	12	3	1	11	11
Louisiana	2	7	..	2	2	5	18	11	4	1	14	10
Oklahoma	29	18	3	5	26	13	90	65	21	12	69	53
Texas	44	25	4	5	40	20	104	98	13	10	91	88
MOUNTAIN:												
Montana	141	77	34	15	107	62	168	134	40	42	128	92
Idaho	80	26	14	4	66	22	95	49	14	8	81	41
Wyoming	17	5	2	1	15	4	35	26	8	4	27	22
Colorado	62	47	5	7	57	40	130	136	21	15	109	121
New Mexico	7	4	..	..	7	4	17	8	5	1	12	7
Arizona	25	13	2	1	23	12	40	17	8	4	32	13
Utah	18	7	1	..	17	7	28	26	2	4	26	22
Nevada	37	15	6	4	31	11	38	25	7	5	31	20
PACIFIC:												
Washington	522	495	56	44	466	451	642	690	108	105	534	585
Oregon	209	162	19	5	190	157	333	338	48	40	285	298
California	1,061	1,368	107	134	954	1,234	1,516	2,149	193	301	1,323	1,848

CHAPTER X

ILLITERACY IN THE CANADIAN STOCK

In the reports of the United States census a person who is able to read and write, either in English or in any other language, is classified as literate, and one who is not able both to read and to write is classified as illiterate. This classification is based on the answers given to the census enumerator in response to the question "Whether able to read and write." These replies represent simply the opinion of the person giving the information to the enumerator, since no specific test of ability to read and write has been prescribed—except that in 1930 it was specifically stated that a person was not to be returned as literate merely because he could write his own name. There is doubtless, therefore, a rather wide range in the actual extent of ability to read and write which has been accepted as qualifying a person for the literate classification. The general behavior of the statistics, however, over a period of six decades and as between different areas and various population classes, is highly consistent and leads one to believe that they represent fairly well the minimum educational qualifications indicated.

The definition of illiteracy employed in the Canadian census is slightly narrower, comprising persons not able either to read or to write, thus omitting a class reported as able to read but not to write. This class was returned separately in the United States censuses up to and including 1920, but included as a part of the illiterate, forming, in 1920, 9.1 per cent of the whole number of illiterates.

The statistics of illiteracy are usually presented for the population 10 years old and over.

The data on illiteracy for the Canadian stock in the United States in 1930 are summarized in Table 85.

Among the 2,941,894 persons 10 years old and over in the entire Canadian stock in the United States in 1930, there were 57,247 persons, forming 1.9 per cent of the total, who were illiterate, that is, unable to read and write. Of the males, 2.2 per cent were illiterate, and of the females, 1.7.

The percentage of illiteracy was considerably higher among the Canadian born than among those persons born in the United States of Canadian parentage—3.3 as compared with 1.0. This difference is due in considerable part, however, to differences in the age distribution, since the percentage of illiteracy is always higher among older persons, and the average age of the Canadian born is much higher than that of the native population of Canadian parentage.

TABLE **85**. ILLITERACY AMONG PERSONS OF WHITE CANADIAN STOCK 10 YEARS OLD
AND OVER, FRENCH AND ENGLISH, BY SEX: 1930

CLASS AND SEX	TOTAL			FRENCH			ENGLISH		
	Number	Illiterate		Number	Illiterate		Number	Illiterate	
		Num-ber	Per cent		Num-ber	Per cent		Num-ber	Per cent
All Canadian stock.........	2,941,894	57,247	1.9	957,650	48,303	5.0	1,984,244	8,944	0.5
Male....................	1,427,190	31,461	2.2	478,306	26,147	5.5	948,884	5,314	0.6
Female..................	1,514,704	25,786	1.7	479,344	22,156	4.6	1,035,360	3,630	0.4
Canadian born............	1,233,711	40,668	3.3	360,724	35,760	9.9	872,987	4,908	0.6
Male....................	594,661	21,549	3.6	182,590	18,698	10.2	412,071	2,851	0.7
Female..................	639,050	19,119	3.0	178,134	17,062	9.6	460,916	2,057	0.4
Canadian parentage.......	1,708,183	16,579	1.0	596,926	12,543	2.1	1,111,257	4,036	0.4
Male....................	832,529	9,912	1.2	295,716	7,449	2.5	536,813	2,463	0.5
Female..................	875,654	6,667	0.8	301,210	5,094	1.7	574,444	1,573	0.3

The difference in the percentage of illiteracy between the French and
the English stock was much greater, however, than the difference between the first and the second generations of either the French or the
English. Of the French Canadian born, 9.9 per cent were returned as illiterate, as compared with 0.6 per cent of the English. Of the second generation of French parentage, 2.1 per cent were illiterate, as compared
with 0.4 per cent for the second generation of English Canadian parentage. The percentage of illiteracy for the English Canadians—even the
Canadian born—compares very favorably with the percentage of illiteracy among the natives of native parentage in the United States; in fact,
if we make the comparison with the average for the entire United States,
we find the percentage for the English Canadian born very much the
lower, being 0.6 as compared with 1.8 for the native whites of native parentage in the entire United States. If we should base this comparison,
however, on the data for those Northern and Western States in which
most of the Canadian born live, we should find the percentages about the
same, with the percentage of illiteracy for the native population of English Canadian parentage even lower.

In general, the percentage of illiteracy among the males in the Canadian stock in 1930 was appreciably higher than among the females. Of
the whole number of males, 2.2 per cent were illiterate, as compared with
1.7 per cent of the females. For the French Canadian born, 10.2 per cent
of the males were illiterate, as compared with 9.6 per cent of the females;
for the English Canadian born, 0.7 per cent of the males, as compared
with 0.4 per cent of the females; for the French of the second generation,
2.5 per cent, as compared with 1.7 per cent; and for the English of the
second generation, 0.5 per cent, as compared with 0.3 per cent.

The relation between age and illiteracy is clearly shown by the figures
in Table 86, in which the available data with respect to illiteracy in the
Canadian stock are presented for five specific age groups. The percentages of illiteracy in the several age groups are also shown graphically
in Figure 29.

FIGURE 29. ILLITERACY IN THE CANADIAN STOCK, BY AGE: 1930

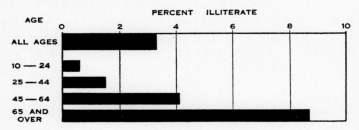

For the group falling within the range of elementary school ages, that
is, for persons 10 to 14 years old, the highest percentage of illiteracy
shown in the table for any class is 0.2. From this point the percentage of
illiteracy increases rather rapidly with increasing age, being, for the entire Canadian stock, 0.4 for persons 15 to 24 years old; 0.9 for those 25
to 44; 3.1 for those 45 to 64; and 7.9 for those 65 years old and over.

For the French Canadian born the percentages ranged from 0.2 for
those 10 to 14 years of age to 25.7 for those 65 years old and over; and
for the English Canadian born, from 0.1 to 1.7. For persons of French
Canadian parentage, the percentages of illiteracy ranged from 0.2 for
those 10 to 14 years old to 5.0 for those 45 to 64, and 14.7 for the small
number (about 20,000) 65 years old and over. For the second generation
of English Canadians the percentage of illiteracy for all persons under 45
years of age was less than 0.3, and for those 65 years old and over, only
1.6.

When the illiteracy figures as presented for males and females separately in Table 86 are compared, we find that in practically every age
group for every one of the constituent elements making up the Canadian
stock the percentage of illiteracy for the females is appreciably lower
than that for the males, though in many cases the percentage for both
males and females is so low that the difference does not appear in the computation of the percentage to the nearest tenth.

TABLE **86**. ILLITERACY AMONG PERSONS OF WHITE CANADIAN STOCK 10 YEARS OLD AND OVER, FRENCH AND ENGLISH, BY AGE AND SEX: 1930

CLASS, SEX, AND AGE	TOTAL			FRENCH			ENGLISH		
	Number	Illiterate		Number	Illiterate		Number	Illiterate	
		Number	Per cent		Number	Per cent		Number	Per cent
ALL CANADIAN STOCK									
Total...............	2,941,894	57,247	1.9	957,650	48,303	5.0	1,984,244	8,944	0.5
10 to 14 years........	234,499	424	0.2	83,883	168	0.2	150,616	256	0.2
15 to 24 years........	555,339	2,457	0.4	191,118	1,705	0.9	364,221	752	0.2
25 to 44 years........	1,136,661	10,592	0.9	373,567	8,707	2.3	763,094	1,885	0.2
45 to 64 years........	762,811	23,908	3.1	234,400	20,820	8.9	528,411	3,088	0.6
65 and over..........	251,189	19,814	7.9	74,356	16,877	22.7	176,833	2,937	1.7
Unknown............	1,395	52	3.7	326	26	8.0	1,069	26	2.4
**Male............... **	1,427,190	31,461	2.2	478,306	26,147	5.5	948,884	5,314	0.6
10 to 14 years........	117,762	224	0.2	41,976	87	0.2	75,786	137	0.2
15 to 24 years........	269,269	1,395	0.5	93,302	960	1.0	175,967	435	0.2
25 to 44 years........	542,205	5,730	1.1	184,242	4,618	2.5	357,963	1,112	0.3
45 to 64 years........	373,304	13,298	3.6	119,573	11,377	9.5	253,731	1,921	0.8
65 and over..........	123,983	10,791	8.7	39,060	9,093	23.3	84,923	1,698	2.0
Unknown............	667	23	3.4	153	12	7.8	514	11	2.1
**Female.............. **	1,514,704	25,786	1.7	479,344	22,156	4.6	1,035,360	3,630	0.4
10 to 14 years........	116,737	200	0.2	41,907	81	0.2	74,830	119	0.2
15 to 24 years........	286,070	1,062	0.4	97,816	745	0.8	188,254	317	0.2
25 to 44 years........	594,456	4,862	0.8	189,325	4,089	2.2	405,131	773	0.2
45 to 64 years........	389,507	10,610	2.7	114,827	9,443	8.2	274,680	1,167	0.4
65 and over..........	127,206	9,023	7.1	35,296	7,784	22.1	91,910	1,239	1.3
Unknown............	728	29	4.0	173	14	8.1	555	15	2.7
CANADIAN BORN									
Total................	1,233,711	40,668	3.3	360,724	35,760	9.9	872,987	4,908	0.6
10 to 14 years........	51,090	70	0.1	11,875	19	0.2	39,215	51	0.1
15 to 24 years........	153,745	1,086	0.7	40,286	904	2.2	113,459	182	0.2
25 to 44 years........	415,958	6,059	1.5	126,874	5,443	4.3	289,084	616	0.2
45 to 64 years........	427,095	17,315	4.1	127,565	15,497	12.1	299,530	1,818	0.6
65 and over..........	185,155	16,106	8.7	53,988	13,880	25.7	131,167	2,226	1.7
Unknown............	668	32	4.8	136	17	12.5	532	15	2.8
**Male................ **	594,661	21,549	3.6	182,590	18,698	10.2	412,071	2,851	0.7
10 to 14 years........	25,261	37	0.1	5,810	8	0.1	19,451	29	0.1
15 to 24 years........	71,325	532	0.7	19,041	440	2.3	52,284	92	0.2
25 to 44 years........	198,124	2,978	1.5	63,656	2,629	4.1	134,468	349	0.3
45 to 64 years........	208,517	9,328	4.5	65,467	8,197	12.5	143,050	1,131	0.8
65 and over..........	91,101	8,661	9.5	28,538	7,415	26.0	62,563	1,246	2.0
Unknown............	333	13	3.9	78	9	11.5	255	4	1.6
**Female.............. **	639,050	19,119	3.0	178,134	17,062	9.6	460,916	2,057	0.4
10 to 14 years........	25,829	33	0.1	6,065	11	0.2	19,764	22	0.1
15 to 24 years........	82,420	554	0.7	21,245	464	2.2	61,175	90	0.1
25 to 44 years........	217,834	3,081	1.4	63,218	2,814	4.5	154,616	267	0.2
45 to 64 years........	218,578	7,987	3.7	62,098	7,300	11.8	156,480	687	0.4
65 and over..........	94,054	7,445	7.9	25,450	6,465	25.4	68,604	980	1.4
Unknown............	335	19	5.7	58	8	13.8	277	11	4.0
CANADIAN PARENTAGE									
Total	1,708,183	16,579	1.0	596,926	12,543	2.1	1,111,257	4,036	0.4
10 to 14 years........	183,409	354	0.2	72,008	149	0.2	111,401	205	0.2
15 to 24 years........	401,594	1,371	0.3	150,832	801	0.5	250,762	570	0.2
25 to 44 years........	720,703	4,533	0.6	246,693	3,264	1.3	474,010	1,269	0.3
45 to 64 years........	335,716	6,593	2.0	106,835	5,323	5.0	228,881	1,270	0.6
65 and over..........	66,034	3,708	5.6	20,368	2,997	14.7	45,666	711	1.6
Unknown............	727	20	2.8	190	9	4.7	537	11	2.0
**Male................ **	832,529	9,912	1.2	295,716	7,449	2.5	536,813	2,463	0.5
10 to 14 years........	92,501	187	0.2	36,166	79	0.2	56,335	108	0.2
15 to 24 years........	197,944	863	0.4	74,261	520	0.7	123,683	343	0.3
25 to 44 years........	344,081	2,752	0.8	120,586	1,989	1.6	223,495	763	0.3
45 to 64 years........	164,787	3,970	2.4	54,106	3,180	5.9	110,681	790	0.7
65 and over..........	32,882	2,130	6.5	10,522	1,678	15.9	22,360	452	2.0
Unknown............	334	10	3.0	75	3	4.0	259	7	2.7
**Female.............. **	875,654	6,667	0.8	301,210	5,094	1.7	574,444	1,573	0.3
10 to 14 years........	90,908	167	0.2	35,842	70	0.2	55,066	97	0.2
15 to 24 years........	203,650	508	0.2	76,571	281	0.4	127,079	227	0.2
25 to 44 years........	376,622	1,781	0.5	126,107	1,275	1.0	250,515	506	0.2
45 to 64 years........	170,929	2,623	1.5	52,729	2,143	4.1	118,200	480	0.4
65 and over..........	33,152	1,578	4.8	9,846	1,319	13.4	23,306	259	1.1
Unknown............	393	10	2.5	115	6	5.2	278	4	1.4

Comparison with Other Countries

In Table 87 are presented data on illiteracy for the foreign-born white population in the United States from selected European countries for comparison with the Canadian figures already discussed.

Table **87**. Illiteracy Among the Foreign-Born White from Selected Countries, by Age: 1930

(Per cent not shown when less than 0.1)

Country of birth	Total 10 Years Old and Over			Per cent illiterate in specified age groups				
	Number	Illiterate		10 to 14 years	15 to 24 years	25 to 44 years	45 to 64 years	65 and over
		Number	Per cent					
Canada	1,233,711	40,668	3.3	0.1	0.7	1.5	4.1	8.7
French	360,724	35,760	9.9	0.2	2.2	4.3	12.1	25.7
English	872,987	4,908	0.6	0.1	0.2	0.2	0.6	1.7
England	800,657	4,870	0.6	0.1	0.2	0.2	0.4	2.1
Scotland	344,182	1,161	0.3	...	0.1	0.1	0.3	1.4
Ireland	918,532	13,038	1.4	0.1	0.2	0.3	1.3	4.4
Northern Ireland	177,319	2,188	1.2	...	0.2	0.3	1.1	3.5
Irish Free State	741,213	10,850	1.5	0.1	0.2	0.3	1.3	4.6
Norway	345,231	6,743	2.0	0.3	3.5	1.2	1.1	4.4
Sweden	592,291	9,011	1.5	0.2	2.3	0.9	0.9	3.6
Denmark	178,212	1,766	1.0	...	1.4	0.6	0.7	2.3
Germany	1,589,249	50,197	3.2	0.2	3.6	2.4	2.2	5.4
Poland	1,262,892	239,651	19.0	0.4	1.9	15.7	25.3	34.2
Italy	1,769,705	447,831	25.3	0.7	4.7	19.7	35.5	53.3
Greece	173,531	23,630	13.6	0.2	7.1	11.9	19.8	43.7

Among those persons in the United States in 1930 who were born in Scotland, only 0.3 per cent were returned as illiterate, Scotland being the only country on the list to show a percentage of illiteracy lower than that of the English Canadian born. Persons born in England had the same percentage of illiteracy as the English Canadian born, namely, 0.6, while all the other countries, even those northern European countries which contributed to the so-called old immigration to the United States, show illiteracy percentages appreciably higher, ranging from 1.0 for Denmark to 3.2 for Germany. Those countries given in the table as representing the "new" immigration, namely, Poland, Italy, and Greece, show, respectively, 19.0, 25.3, and 13.6 per cent of illiteracy.

The relation between age and illiteracy already referred to appears very clearly in the figures presented for the selected countries, the percentages for the first two age periods being relatively low, even for those countries having a rather high figure for all ages combined.

Urban and Rural Areas

In Table 88 statistics of illiteracy in the Canadian stock in the United States are presented for urban and rural areas.

TABLE **88**. Illiteracy Among Persons of White Canadian Stock 10 Years Old and Over, French and English, by Sex, for Urban and Rural Areas: 1930

(For United States total see Table 85)

CLASS, AREA, AND SEX	TOTAL			FRENCH			ENGLISH		
	Number	Illiterate		Number	Illiterate		Number	Illiterate	
		Number	Per cent		Number	Per cent		Number	Per cent
ALL CANADIAN STOCK									
Urban..............	2,159,002	36,140	1.7	733,513	31,980	4.4	1,425,489	4,160	0.3
Male..............	1,018,299	18,091	1.8	357,595	15,967	4.5	660,704	2,124	0.3
Female............	1,140,703	18,049	1.6	375,918	16,013	4.3	764,785	2,036	0.3
Rural-nonfarm.......	487,740	13,846	2.8	154,643	10,932	7.1	333,097	2,914	0.9
Male..............	247,528	8,297	3.4	81,224	6,495	8.0	166,304	1,802	1.1
Female............	240,212	5,549	2.3	73,419	4,437	6.0	166,793	1,112	0.7
Rural-farm.........	295,152	7,261	2.5	69,494	5,391	7.8	225,658	1,870	0.8
Male..............	161,363	5,073	3.1	39,487	3,685	9.3	121,876	1,388	1.1
Female............	133,789	2,188	1.6	30,007	1,706	5.7	103,782	482	0.5
CANADIAN BORN									
Urban..............	953,829	27,972	2.9	284,804	25,441	8.9	669,025	2,531	0.4
Male..............	446,589	13,709	3.1	140,567	12,475	8.9	306,022	1,234	0.4
Female............	507,240	14,263	2.8	144,237	12,966	9.0	363,003	1,297	0.4
Rural-nonfarm.......	183,287	8,712	4.8	54,052	7,296	13.5	129,235	1,416	1.1
Male..............	94,595	5,141	5.4	29,276	4,251	14.5	65,319	890	1.4
Female............	88,692	3,571	4.0	24,776	3,045	12.3	63,916	526	0.8
Rural-farm.........	96,595	3,984	4.1	21,868	3,023	13.8	74,727	961	1.3
Male..............	53,477	2,699	5.0	12,747	1,972	15.5	40,730	727	1.8
Female............	43,118	1,285	3.0	9,121	1,051	11.5	33,997	234	0.7
CANADIAN PARENTAGE									
Urban..............	1,205,173	8,168	0.7	448,709	6,539	1.5	756,464	1,629	0.2
Male..............	571,710	4,382	0.8	217,028	3,492	1.6	354,682	890	0.3
Female............	633,463	3,786	0.6	231,681	3,047	1.3	401,782	739	0.2
Rural-nonfarm.......	304,453	5,134	1.7	100,591	3,636	3.6	203,862	1,498	0.7
Male..............	152,933	3,156	2.1	51,948	2,244	4.3	100,985	912	0.9
Female............	151,520	1,978	1.3	48,643	1,392	2.9	102,877	586	0.6
Rural-farm.........	198,557	3,277	1.7	47,626	2,368	5.0	150,931	909	0.6
Male..............	107,886	2,374	2.2	26,740	1,713	6.4	81,146	661	0.8
Female............	90,671	903	1.0	20,886	655	3.1	69,785	248	0.4

The percentage of illiteracy in the population of Canadian stock was uniformly lower in urban areas than in either rural-nonfarm or rural-farm areas. For the Canadian stock as a whole, the percentage of illiteracy was 1.7 in urban areas, 2.8 in rural-nonfarm, and 2.5 in rural-farm.

Of the French Canadian born in urban areas, 8.9 per cent were illiterate, as compared with 13.5 per cent in rural-nonfarm areas and 13.8 per cent in rural-farm. Of the English Canadian born in urban areas only 0.4 per cent were illiterate, as compared with 1.1 per cent in rural-nonfarm areas and 1.3 per cent in rural-farm. The figures for the second generation, that is, for persons born in the United States of Canadian parentage, show similar relations, though at a lower level—1.5, 3.6, and 5.0, respectively, for persons of French Canadian parentage in the three areas, and 0.2, 0.7, and 0.6, respectively, for persons of English Canadian parentage.

In each of the three areas, as in the figures already discussed for the United States as a whole, the percentage of illiteracy among the females was uniformly lower, often much lower, than that shown for the males; in fact, in the rural-farm area in particular, the percentage of illiteracy among the females was in many cases less than one-half of that among the males.

DATA FOR STATES

STATISTICS of illiteracy among the Canadian born are presented by States, with separate figures for males and females, in Table 89. In Table 90 are presented similar data for native white persons of Canadian parentage. In Tables 91 and 92 are given illiteracy data for 29 selected States (the States with 10,000 or more of Canadian stock) for the Canadian born and for persons of Canadian parentage, respectively, further classified as French and English and by age, this cross-classification being of great importance in the interpretation of the illiteracy figures for different areas.

By reason of the generally higher percentages of illiteracy returned for the French elements in the Canadian stock, the percentages shown for all Canadian born or all natives of Canadian parentage are higher for those States where the Canadian stock is dominantly or largely French than for States where it is mainly English. This is especially true with respect to the figures for the Canadian born, since the figures for the second generation of the Canadian stock are so low in almost all the States that the differences are of little significance. In the individual States, as in the larger areas commented on above, the percentage of illiteracy was appreciably lower for females than for males.

The tables presenting data on illiteracy by age (Tables 91 and 92) offer some explanation for the variations in the general percentages for the several States, in that they show to what extent the high rate in a State which has a high rate results from the presence of a considerable number of older persons, with their generally higher rates of illiteracy. Among the French Canadian born in Massachusetts, to take a State which has a rather high percentage illiterate for all ages combined (10.4), only 1.4 per cent of the French Canadian born 10 to 24 years old were illiterate, but the high over-all figure grows out of percentages of 12.4 and 28.5 for persons 45 to 64 years of age and 65 and over, respectively. Similarly, among the English Canadian born the highest figure for persons 10 years old and over was 1.6 in Maine. Of the English Canadian born 10 to 24 years of age in this State, only 0.3 per cent were illiterate, but among persons 65 years old and over the percentage was 4.0.

The differences among the various States in the percentage of illiteracy among the native white population of Canadian parentage as presented in Table 92, are similar to those just referred to, with much smaller variations in general between one State and another, but in some cases with an even wider range between the percentages for the youngest and oldest age groups.

TABLE **89**. ILLITERACY AMONG CANADIAN-BORN WHITE PERSONS 10 YEARS OLD AND OVER, BY SEX, BY STATES: 1930

DIVISION AND STATE	TOTAL			MALE			FEMALE		
	Number	Illiterate		Number	Illiterate		Number	Illiterate	
		Number	Per cent		Number	Per cent		Number	Per cent
United States	**1,233,711**	**40,668**	**3.3**	**594,661**	**21,549**	**3.6**	**639,050**	**19,119**	**3.0**
NEW ENGLAND:									
Maine	71,834	5,654	7.9	35,031	3,047	8.7	36,803	2,607	7.1
New Hampshire	49,929	4,410	8.8	24,265	2,508	10.3	25,664	1,902	7.4
Vermont	25,915	1,630	6.3	13,528	950	7.0	12,387	680	5.5
Massachusetts	281,378	12,639	4.5	124,307	5,974	4.8	157,071	6,665	4.2
Rhode Island	38,456	3,472	9.0	17,931	1,720	9.6	20,525	1,752	8.5
Connecticut	36,273	2,996	8.3	18,071	1,517	8.4	18,202	1,479	8.1
MIDDLE ATLANTIC:									
New York	141,199	2,243	1.6	64,984	1,158	1.8	76,215	1,085	1.4
New Jersey	15,727	98	0.6	7,242	43	0.6	8,485	55	0.6
Pennsylvania	15,647	90	0.6	7,460	39	0.5	8,187	51	0.6
EAST NORTH CENTRAL:									
Ohio	25,871	161	0.6	12,443	73	0.6	13,428	88	0.7
Indiana	5,896	45	0.8	3,123	27	0.9	2,773	18	0.6
Illinois	41,994	350	0.8	21,001	175	0.8	20,993	175	0.8
Michigan	192,086	3,628	1.9	96,524	2,236	2.3	95,562	1,392	1.5
Wisconsin	15,204	766	5.0	8,399	502	6.0	6,805	264	3.9
WEST NORTH CENTRAL:									
Minnesota	26,504	885	3.3	13,999	586	4.2	12,505	299	2.4
Iowa	6,240	44	0.7	3,130	28	0.9	3,110	16	0.5
Missouri	5,311	35	0.7	2,731	18	0.7	2,580	17	0.7
North Dakota	11,971	208	1.7	6,302	129	2.0	5,669	79	1.4
South Dakota	3,296	43	1.3	1,788	28	1.6	1,508	15	1.0
Nebraska	4,316	35	0.8	2,161	20	0.9	2,155	15	0.7
Kansas	3,976	74	1.9	2,035	38	1.9	1,941	36	1.9
SOUTH ATLANTIC:									
Delaware	448	4	0.9	233	3	1.3	215	1	0.5
Maryland	2,173	12	0.6	1,077	8	0.7	1,096	4	0.4
Dist. of Columbia	1,651	5	0.3	710	2	0.3	941	3	0.3
Virginia	1,576	15	1.0	784	13	1.7	792	2	0.3
West Virginia	917	10	1.1	485	7	1.4	432	3	0.7
North Carolina	906	3	0.3	403	2	0.5	503	1	0.2
South Carolina	274	2	0.7	130	1	0.8	144	1	0.7
Georgia	1,062	6	0.6	539	3	0.6	523	3	0.6
Florida	7,855	36	0.5	3,647	17	0.5	4,208	19	0.5
EAST SOUTH CENTRAL:									
Kentucky	894	6	0.7	466	3	0.6	428	3	0.7
Tennessee	912	8	0.9	470	6	1.3	442	2	0.5
Alabama	885	7	0.8	479	6	1.3	406	1	0.2
Mississippi	351	2	0.6	202	1	0.5	149	1	0.7
WEST SOUTH CENTRAL:									
Arkansas	679	8	1.2	371	5	1.3	308	3	1.0
Louisiana	968	13	1.3	588	9	1.5	380	4	1.1
Oklahoma	2,087	23	1.1	1,172	18	1.5	915	5	0.5
Texas	4,412	16	0.4	2,439	10	0.4	1,973	6	0.3
MOUNTAIN:									
Montana	10,473	177	1.7	6,019	133	2.2	4,454	44	1.0
Idaho	4,335	45	1.0	2,609	37	1.4	1,726	8	0.5
Wyoming	1,109	2	0.2	588	..	...	521	2	0.4
Colorado	5,745	39	0.7	2,890	23	0.8	2,855	16	0.6
New Mexico	607	4	0.7	336	3	0.9	271	1	0.4
Arizona	1,978	4	0.2	1,098	4	0.4	880	..	...
Utah	1,129	..	...	642	..	...	487	..	...
Nevada	926	7	0.8	565	6	1.1	361	1	0.3
PACIFIC:									
Washington	45,782	332	0.7	23,532	199	0.8	22,250	133	0.6
Oregon	17,093	90	0.5	8,811	52	0.6	8,282	38	0.5
California	97,461	286	0.3	46,921	162	0.3	50,540	124	0.2

TABLE **90**. ILLITERACY AMONG NATIVE WHITE PERSONS OF CANADIAN PARENTAGE 10 YEARS OLD AND OVER, BY SEX, BY STATES: 1930

STATE	TOTAL			MALE			FEMALE		
	Number	Illiterate		Number	Illiterate		Number	Illiterate	
		Number	Per cent		Number	Per cent		Number	Per cent
United States.......	1,708,183	16,579	1.0	832,529	9,912	1.2	875,654	6,667	0.8
NEW ENGLAND:									
Maine...............	94,842	2,655	2.8	47,220	1,766	3.7	47,622	889	1.9
New Hampshire........	66,758	1,029	1.5	32,755	582	1.8	34,003	447	1.3
Vermont.............	36,441	1,171	3.2	18,310	754	4.1	18,131	417	2.3
Massachusetts........	346,491	2,911	0.8	166,198	1,530	0.9	180,293	1,381	0.8
Rhode Island.........	57,037	1,038	1.8	27,379	523	1.9	29,658	515	1.7
Connecticut..........	47,095	686	1.5	23,097	353	1.5	23,998	333	1.4
MIDDLE ATLANTIC:									
New York............	158,499	2,140	1.4	77,151	1,294	1.7	81,348	846	1.0
New Jersey..........	19,913	49	0.2	9,669	22	0.2	10,244	27	0.3
Pennsylvania.........	23,302	55	0.2	11,247	31	0.3	12,055	24	0.2
EAST NORTH CENTRAL:									
Ohio................	36,741	127	0.3	17,393	69	0.4	19,348	58	0.3
Indiana.............	11,496	60	0.5	5,497	35	0.6	5,999	25	0.4
Illinois............	70,341	295	0.4	33,573	163	0.5	36,768	132	0.4
Michigan............	245,799	1,965	0.8	121,536	1,293	1.1	124,263	672	0.5
Wisconsin...........	45,588	480	1.1	22,496	324	1.4	23,092	156	0.7
WEST NORTH CENTRAL:									
Minnesota...........	62,607	643	1.0	30,115	405	1.3	32,492	238	0.7
Iowa................	23,132	79	0.3	11,064	40	0.4	12,068	39	0.3
Missouri............	13,764	73	0.5	6,495	41	0.6	7,269	32	0.4
North Dakota........	23,897	126	0.5	12,341	71	0.6	11,556	55	0.5
South Dakota........	10,700	48	0.4	5,479	32	0.6	5,221	16	0.3
Nebraska............	13,895	40	0.3	6,699	27	0.4	7,196	13	0.2
Kansas..............	14,481	117	0.8	7,133	65	0.9	7,348	52	0.7
SOUTH ATLANTIC:									
Delaware............	573	2	0.3	299	1	0.3	274	1	0.4
Maryland............	3,220	11	0.3	1,680	7	0.4	1,540	4	0.3
Dist. of Columbia......	2,923	3	0.1	1,360	1	0.1	1,563	2	0.1
Virginia............	2,574	8	0.3	1,308	4	0.3	1,266	4	0.3
West Virginia........	1,390	7	0.5	669	5	0.7	721	2	0.3
North Carolina.......	1,254	4	0.3	601	2	0.3	653	2	0.3
South Carolina.......	523	2	0.4	270	..	...	253	2	0.8
Georgia.............	1,539	8	0.5	768	6	0.8	771	2	0.3
Florida.............	7,605	25	0.3	3,442	17	0.5	4,163	8	0.2
EAST SOUTH CENTRAL:									
Kentucky............	1,786	6	0.3	816	4	0.5	970	2	0.2
Tennessee...........	1,773	13	0.7	833	10	1.2	940	3	0.3
Alabama.............	1,491	14	0.9	708	11	1.6	783	3	0.4
Mississippi..........	781	3	0.4	400	1	0.3	381	2	0.5
WEST SOUTH CENTRAL:									
Arkansas............	1,707	24	1.4	858	19	2.2	849	5	0.6
Louisiana...........	2,334	34	1.5	1,139	22	1.9	1,195	12	1.0
Oklahoma............	7,051	30	0.4	3,516	18	0.5	3,535	12	0.3
Texas...............	9,221	28	0.3	4,730	18	0.4	4,491	10	0.2
MOUNTAIN:									
Montana.............	17,735	71	0.4	9,123	49	0.5	8,612	22	0.3
Idaho...............	7,912	26	0.3	4,151	16	0.4	3,761	10	0.3
Wyoming.............	2,807	4	0.1	1,483	1	0.1	1,324	3	0.2
Colorado............	12,379	31	0.3	5,903	13	0.2	6,476	18	0.3
New Mexico..........	1,374	9	0.7	657	6	0.9	717	3	0.4
Arizona.............	3,372	4	0.1	1,743	4	0.2	1,629	..	...
Utah................	3,231	6	0.2	1,577	2	0.1	1,654	4	0.2
Nevada..............	1,767	2	0.1	958	...	...	809	2	0.2
PACIFIC:									
Washington..........	54,648	183	0.3	27,055	111	0.4	27,593	72	0.3
Oregon..............	24,123	67	0.3	11,912	49	0.4	12,211	18	0.1
California..........	108,271	167	0.2	51,723	95	0.2	56,548	72	0.1

TABLE **91**. ILLITERACY AMONG CANADIAN-BORN WHITE PERSONS 10 YEARS OLD AND OVER, FRENCH AND ENGLISH, BY AGE, FOR 29 SELECTED STATES: 1930

CLASS AND STATE	TOTAL 10 YEARS OLD AND OVER			ILLITERATE, BY AGE							
	Number	Illiterate		10 to 24 years		25 to 44 years		45 to 64 years		65 years and over	
		Number	Per cent	Number	Per cent	Number	Per cent	Number	Per cent	Number	Per cent
FRENCH											
United States....	360,724	35,760	9.9	923	1.8	5,443	4.3	15,497	12.1	13,880	25.7
Maine............	35,993	5,072	14.1	173	2.9	1,121	8.1	2,241	18.7	1,533	37.0
New Hampshire.....	36,888	4,247	11.5	89	1.9	743	5.4	2,001	14.6	1,410	29.8
Vermont..........	16,331	1,519	9.3	70	1.7	262	4.6	538	12.4	649	31.4
Massachusetts......	113,043	11,795	10.4	182	1.4	1,527	3.8	5,475	12.4	4,609	28.5
Rhode Island......	30,855	3,409	11.0	66	1.5	480	4.4	1,710	14.6	1,151	29.1
Connecticut.......	24,525	2,928	11.9	238	4.6	696	7.5	1,186	15.7	807	31.4
New York.........	27,690	1,733	6.3	59	1.1	290	2.6	591	7.7	791	21.4
New Jersey........	2,380	67	2.8	4	0.9	16	1.6	30	4.3	17	8.7
Pennsylvania......	1,842	34	1.8	1	0.3	10	1.4	10	1.8	13	5.2
Ohio.............	2,545	77	3.0	1	0.3	17	1.8	21	2.5	38	8.8
Indiana...........	663	20	3.0	..	....	..	....	8	4.0	12	7.6
Illinois...........	6,044	234	3.9	..	....	17	0.9	62	2.9	155	10.9
Michigan..........	27,212	2,434	8.9	26	0.6	174	1.8	888	10.4	1,345	26.4
Wisconsin.........	4,271	613	14.4	..	....	14	2.2	170	9.2	429	26.3
Minnesota........	6,447	705	10.9	1	0.3	12	1.2	262	9.1	430	19.3
Iowa.............	605	20	3.3	..	....	2	2.0	5	2.3	13	5.0
Missouri..........	579	16	2.8	..	....	..	....	2	1.1	14	8.9
North Dakota......	1,340	123	9.2	..	....	9	3.2	46	7.4	68	19.3
South Dakota......	488	25	5.1	..	....	..	....	7	3.4	18	10.1
Nebraska..........	434	13	3.0	..	....	..	....	6	3.2	7	4.8
Kansas............	560	49	8.8	..	....	..	....	5	2.5	44	17.5
Florida...........	944	18	1.9	..	....	1	0.4	6	1.7	11	7.0
Texas............	448	5	1.1	..	....	1	0.6	1	0.6	3	....
Montana..........	1,947	136	7.0	3	2.1	9	1.9	55	6.5	68	14.1
Idaho............	564	23	4.1	..	....	1	0.7	8	3.1	14	11.9
Colorado..........	568	13	2.3	..	....	..	....	3	1.3	10	5.5
Washington........	4,253	197	4.6	4	0.7	11	1.0	76	4.6	106	11.8
Oregon...........	1,319	44	3.3	1	0.6	2	0.5	16	3.4	25	9.0
California.........	7,469	129	1.7	4	0.3	21	0.8	46	1.9	58	4.7
ENGLISH											
United States....	872,987	4,908	0.6	233	0.2	616	0.2	1,818	0.6	2,226	1.7
Maine............	35,841	582	1.6	15	0.3	95	0.8	271	1.9	200	4.0
New Hampshire.....	13,041	163	1.2	3	0.2	26	0.7	62	1.1	71	3.1
Vermont..........	9,584	111	1.2	3	0.2	13	0.4	37	1.0	58	3.6
Massachusetts......	168,335	844	0.5	33	0.1	112	0.2	368	0.6	330	1.6
Rhode Island......	7,601	63	0.8	4	0.4	8	0.3	25	0.8	26	2.7
Connecticut.......	11,748	68	0.6	2	0.1	11	0.2	28	0.7	27	2.2
New York.........	113,509	510	0.4	37	0.2	67	0.2	196	0.6	209	1.7
New Jersey........	13,347	31	0.2	3	0.1	11	0.2	8	0.2	9	0.7
Pennsylvania......	13,805	56	0.4	4	0.2	13	0.3	17	0.4	21	1.2
Ohio.............	23,326	84	0.4	6	0.2	13	0.2	30	0.4	35	1.1
Indiana...........	5,233	25	0.5	1	0.1	1	0.1	7	0.4	15	1.9
Illinois...........	35,950	116	0.3	11	0.2	11	0.1	30	0.2	59	1.1
Michigan..........	164,874	1,194	0.7	39	0.1	112	0.2	413	0.8	628	2.5
Wisconsin.........	10,933	153	1.4	4	0.2	4	0.2	42	1.1	103	3.3
Minnesota........	20,057	180	0.9	8	0.3	13	0.3	68	0.9	90	1.8
Iowa.............	5,635	24	0.4	..	....	..	....	4	0.2	20	0.9
Missouri..........	4,732	19	0.4	..	....	3	0.3	5	0.3	11	0.9
North Dakota......	10,631	85	0.8	3	0.2	13	0.7	34	0.7	35	1.5
South Dakota......	2,808	18	0.6	..	....	1	0.3	3	0.3	13	1.5
Nebraska..........	3,882	22	0.6	1	0.2	3	0.6	7	0.4	11	0.8
Kansas............	3,416	25	0.7	..	....	2	0.4	7	0.6	16	1.2
Florida...........	6,911	18	0.3	..	....	4	0.2	7	0.3	7	0.6
Texas............	3,964	11	0.3	1	0.2	2	0.2	3	0.2	5	0.7
Montana..........	8,526	41	0.5	2	0.1	2	0.1	15	0.5	22	1.5
Idaho............	3,771	22	0.6	..	....	3	0.3	11	0.7	8	1.2
Colorado..........	5,177	26	0.5	2	0.4	3	0.3	2	0.1	19	1.3
Washington........	41,529	135	0.3	15	0.1	17	0.1	41	0.3	62	1.0
Oregon...........	15,774	46	0.3	6	0.1	7	0.2	8	0.2	25	1.0
California.........	89,992	157	0.2	24	0.1	38	0.1	37	0.1	58	0.4

TABLE **92**. ILLITERACY AMONG NATIVE WHITE PERSONS OF CANADIAN PARENTAGE 10 YEARS OLD AND OVER, FRENCH AND ENGLISH, BY AGE, FOR 29 SELECTED STATES: 1930

CLASS AND STATE	TOTAL 10 YEARS OLD AND OVER			ILLITERATE, BY AGE							
	Number	Illiterate		10 to 24 years		25 to 44 years		45 to 64 years		65 years and over	
		Number	Per cent	Number	Per cent	Number	Per cent	Number	Per cent	Number	Per cent
FRENCH											
United States	596,926	12,543	2.1	950	0.4	3,264	1.3	5,323	5.0	2,997	14.7
Maine	44,545	2,273	5.1	265	1.2	744	4.6	875	18.2	389	45.9
New Hampshire	47,884	915	1.9	118	0.5	317	1.7	360	6.9	117	17.4
Vermont	22,473	1,048	4.7	36	0.5	174	2.3	495	9.0	343	19.9
Massachusetts	175,639	2,440	1.4	217	0.3	703	1.0	1,028	4.2	488	16.1
Rhode Island	47,407	985	2.1	89	0.4	332	1.7	461	7.9	103	20.6
Connecticut	32,719	638	1.9	45	0.3	215	1.5	287	6.1	91	16.4
New York	45,350	1,600	3.5	46	0.3	207	1.2	698	6.3	649	20.3
New Jersey	4,206	25	0.6	7	0.6	7	0.3	7	0.9	4	2.9
Pennsylvania	3,697	14	0.4	2	0.2	4	0.2	6	0.7	2	1.4
Ohio	6,077	53	0.9	3	0.2	3	0.1	25	1.5	21	5.3
Indiana	2,242	23	1.0	...	...	5	0.6	7	0.9	11	5.8
Illinois	16,786	185	1.1	4	0.1	17	0.2	63	1.3	101	9.2
Michigan	50,352	1,000	2.0	58	0.4	270	1.2	409	3.9	263	14.2
Wisconsin	16,682	344	2.1	14	0.3	71	1.0	142	3.3	117	11.0
Minnesota	21,217	507	2.4	18	0.3	107	1.1	241	4.7	140	12.5
Iowa	3,494	15	0.4	...	...	4	0.3	5	0.4	6	1.6
Missouri	1,966	23	1.2	...	...	1	0.1	14	1.9	8	4.3
North Dakota	4,104	66	1.6	8	0.5	15	0.8	26	4.2	17	16.7
South Dakota	2,170	24	1.1	1	0.3	10	1.0	7	1.1	6	3.4
Nebraska	2,066	10	0.5	1	0.3	4	0.5	3	0.5	2	1.2
Kansas	2,883	80	2.8	...	...	3	0.3	42	3.8	35	11.6
Florida	1,190	7	0.6	...	...	2	0.4	2	0.6	3	...
Texas	1,224	6	0.5	1	0.4	1	0.2	3	0.8	1	...
Montana	4,265	45	1.1	5	0.3	9	0.5	17	2.1	14	9.2
Idaho	1,367	8	0.6	1	0.3	2	0.3	1	0.3	4	...
Colorado	1,866	11	0.6	...	...	2	0.3	5	0.9	4	2.6
Washington	8,643	79	0.9	4	0.2	16	0.4	36	1.8	23	5.7
Oregon	3,244	24	0.7	1	0.2	4	0.3	12	1.3	7	2.9
California	14,537	40	0.3	2	0.1	9	0.1	17	0.4	12	1.3
ENGLISH											
United States	1,111,257	4,036	0.4	775	0.2	1,269	0.3	1,270	0.6	711	1.6
Maine	50,297	382	0.8	77	0.3	105	0.6	139	1.7	60	2.8
New Hampshire	18,874	114	0.6	30	0.4	44	0.6	18	0.6	22	3.0
Vermont	13,968	123	0.9	14	0.3	26	0.5	46	1.5	37	4.1
Massachusetts	170,852	471	0.3	148	0.2	170	0.2	116	0.5	35	0.8
Rhode Island	9,630	53	0.6	13	0.4	16	0.4	18	1.1	6	2.3
Connecticut	14,376	48	0.3	11	0.2	16	0.2	14	0.6	7	1.9
New York	113,149	540	0.5	75	0.2	116	0.2	181	0.8	168	3.6
New Jersey	15,707	24	0.2	10	0.2	7	0.1	3	0.1	4	0.8
Pennsylvania	19,605	41	0.2	11	0.2	12	0.1	14	0.3	4	0.6
Ohio	30,664	74	0.2	13	0.1	21	0.2	19	0.3	21	1.5
Indiana	9,254	37	0.4	2	0.1	5	0.1	16	0.6	14	2.0
Illinois	53,555	110	0.2	16	0.1	31	0.1	35	0.3	27	1.1
Michigan	195,447	965	0.5	145	0.2	346	0.4	333	0.8	139	2.1
Wisconsin	28,906	136	0.5	14	0.2	40	0.3	49	0.6	33	1.7
Minnesota	41,390	136	0.3	30	0.3	52	0.3	36	0.4	17	1.0
Iowa	19,638	64	0.3	7	0.2	23	0.3	22	0.3	12	0.7
Missouri	11,798	50	0.4	5	0.2	10	0.2	23	0.6	12	1.5
North Dakota	19,793	60	0.3	29	0.3	21	0.2	8	0.4	2	0.7
South Dakota	8,530	24	0.3	5	0.3	11	0.3	8	0.4	...	...
Nebraska	11,829	30	0.3	6	0.3	15	0.3	6	0.2	3	0.4
Kansas	11,598	37	0.3	2	0.1	10	0.2	16	0.4	9	1.1
Florida	6,415	18	0.3	4	0.2	5	0.2	3	0.2	6	1.4
Texas	7,997	22	0.3	1	0.1	11	0.3	9	0.5	1	0.3
Montana	13,470	26	0.2	5	0.1	7	0.1	9	0.4	5	1.3
Idaho	6,545	18	0.3	5	0.2	6	0.2	5	0.3	2	0.5
Colorado	10,513	20	0.2	3	0.1	7	0.1	6	0.2	4	0.7
Washington	46,005	104	0.2	35	0.2	33	0.2	25	0.3	11	0.6
Oregon	20,879	43	0.2	11	0.2	11	0.1	17	0.4	4	0.4
California	93,734	127	0.1	29	0.1	57	0.1	28	0.1	11	0.2

CHAPTER XI

ABILITY TO SPEAK ENGLISH AMONG FRENCH CANADIANS IN THE UNITED STATES

THE classification in accordance with ability to speak English, which is one of the standard classifications in the statistics presented for the foreign born in the reports of the United States census, is of significance, of course, only with respect to the French element in the Canadian stock. As in the case of illiteracy, no specific test is provided whereby the census enumerator may determine ability to speak English. He simply accepts the statement of his informant on this point. The basis of the classification is practically the same, however, as that used in the Canadian census for the statistics of ability to speak either of the official languages, that is, either English or French; and in both instances the consistent behavior of the statistics seems to indicate that the basis is reasonably satisfactory. In the published reports of the United States census the classification in accordance with ability to speak English is given only for the foreign born, and not for the second generation of the foreign white stock. From unpublished sources, however, some data have been supplied for the second generation of French Canadian origin. The statistics with respect to ability to speak English are presented, as in the case of illiteracy, for the population 10 years old and over.

The statistics for the French Canadian stock in the United States classified by ability to speak English are summarized in Table 93.

TABLE **93**. WHITE PERSONS 10 YEARS OLD AND OVER OF FRENCH CANADIAN STOCK, BY SEX AND ABILITY TO SPEAK ENGLISH: 1930

CLASS AND ABILITY TO SPEAK ENGLISH	TOTAL		MALE		FEMALE	
	Number	Per cent	Number	Per cent	Number	Per cent
All French Canadian stock	**957,650**	**100.0**	**478,306**	**100.0**	**479,344**	**100.0**
Able to speak English	922,881	96.4	469,146	98.1	453,735	94.7
Not able to speak English	34,769	3.6	9,160	1.9	25,609	5.3
French Canadian born	**360,724**	**100.0**	**182,590**	**100.0**	**178,134**	**100.0**
Able to speak English	329,023	91.2	174,547	95.6	154,476	86.7
Not able to speak English	31,701	8.8	8,043	4.4	23,658	13.3
French Canadian parentage	**596,926**	**100.0**	**295,716**	**100.0**	**301,210**	**100.0**
Able to speak English	593,858	99.5	294,599	99.6	299,259	99.4
Not able to speak English	3,068	0.5	1,117	0.4	1,951	0.6

The whole number of persons 10 years old and over of French Canadian stock in the United States in 1930 was 957,650, of whom 922,881, or 96.4 per cent, were returned as able to speak English, and 34,769, or 3.6 per cent, as not able to speak English. While the numbers of males and females in the French Canadian stock were approximately equal, the major part of those unable to speak English were females, such persons representing 5.3 per cent of the whole number of females, as compared with 1.9 per cent of the males.

The inability to speak English was very largely confined to the Canadian born, of whom 8.8 per cent were so classified—4.4 per cent of the males and 13.3 per cent of the females. Of the second generation, that is, persons born in the United States of French Canadian parentage, practically all were able to speak English, that is, all except 0.5 per cent of the total number, made up of 0.4 per cent of the males and 0.6 per cent of the females. It is apparent, then, that the French Canadians in the United States make rapid progress in learning the English language, in spite of the fact that in many localities, especially in New England, there are considerable areas in which the population is rather largely French.

French and English Languages in Canada

By way of background it may be worth while to note briefly the relation between the French and English languages in Canada itself. The data, based on the tabulations by mother tongue in combination with official language spoken, are summarized in Table 94, separate figures being shown for the Province of Quebec and for the remainder of Canada.

Of the 2,088,615 persons 10 years old and over of French mother tongue in Canada in 1931, 986,615, or 47.2 per cent, had learned to speak English (as compared with 91.2 per cent of the French Canadian born in the United States). Taking by itself the Province of Quebec, which is predominantly French, we find that here only 39.0 per cent of the French population had learned to speak English, while of the French outside Quebec, 81.8 per cent had learned to speak English. Conditions in the provinces outside Quebec are presumably much more like the conditions under which the French Canadians in the United States live, for the most part scattered through a larger English-speaking population, than are the conditions in Quebec.

Of the entire Canadian population of English mother tongue, only 3.7 per cent had learned to speak French. In the Province of Quebec, however, 28.7 per cent of the English population had learned to speak French, this figure at least approaching the percentage of French in Quebec who had learned English.

In all cases it may be noted that the percentage of males who had learned the second language, whether French or English, was in every case considerably higher than the corresponding percentage of females. This is in accordance with the findings in connection with ability to speak English on the part of French Canadians in the United States.

TABLE **94**. POPULATION OF CANADA 10 YEARS OLD AND OVER, BY MOTHER TONGUE AND OFFICIAL LANGUAGE SPOKEN: 1931

MOTHER TONGUE AND LANGUAGE SPOKEN	Canada, total	PROVINCE OF QUEBEC			OUTSIDE QUEBEC		
		Total	Male	Female	Total	Male	Female
Total...............	8,169,620	2,167,517	1,091,418	1,076,099	6,002,103	3,167,443	2,834,660
Mother tongue English or French...............	**6,867,998**	**2,041,532**	**1,018,683**	**1,022,849**	**4,826,466**	**2,478,481**	**2,347,985**
Speaking—							
English only.............	4,604,676	253,328	119,345	133,983	4,351,348	2,228,288	2,123,060
French only.............	1,102,000	1,028,803	458,176	570,627	73,197	29,914	43,283
Both English and French..	1,161,322	759,401	441,162	318,239	401,921	220,279	181,642
Mother tongue other than English or French.....	**1,301,622**	**125,985**	**72,735**	**53,250**	**1,175,637**	**688,962**	**486,675**
Speaking—							
English................	1,078,284	65,522	38,333	27,189	1,012,762	606,968	405,794
French................	6,039	4,922	2,174	2,748	1,117	486	631
English and French.......	69,147	43,735	26,578	17,157	25,412	16,121	9,291
Neither English nor French	148,152	11,806	5,650	6,156	136,346	65,387	70,959
Mother tongue English......	**4,779,383**	**355,484**	**177,379**	**178,105**	**4,423,899**	**2,266,807**	**2,157,092**
English who have learned French................	174,707	102,156	58,034	44,122	72,551	38,519	34,032
Per cent................	3.7	28.7	32.7	24.8	1.6	1.7	1.6
Mother tongue French.....	**2,088,615**	**1,686,048**	**841,304**	**844,744**	**402,567**	**211,674**	**190,893**
French who have learned English................	986,615	657,245	383,128	274,117	329,370	181,760	147,610
Per cent................	47.2	39.0	45.5	32.4	81.8	85.9	77.3

There were in Canada in 1931, 1,301,622 persons of mother tongue other than English or French. Of these, 69,147, or 5.3 per cent, had learned to speak both French and English; 6,039, or 0.5 per cent, had learned to speak French only; and 1,078,284, or 82.8 per cent, had learned to speak English only, leaving 148,152, or 11.4 per cent, unable to speak either of the official languages of Canada. This last percentage, it may be noted, is very much higher than the percentage of the French Canadian born in the United States who had not learned to speak English.

LITERACY AND ABILITY TO SPEAK ENGLISH

IN Table 95 the data for persons of French Canadian birth and parentage are classified by literacy in combination with ability to speak English.

Of the whole number of French Canadian born returned as able to speak English, 7.3 per cent were illiterate, as compared with 37.6 per cent of those returned as not able to speak English. Conversely, of the French Canadian born who were literate, only 6.1 per cent were unable to speak

English, while of the illiterate, 33.3 per cent were unable to speak English. There appears to be, therefore, very close correlation between ability to read and write and ability to speak English.

TABLE **95**. FRENCH CANADIANS IN THE UNITED STATES 10 YEARS OLD AND OVER, BY SEX, LITERACY, AND ABILITY TO SPEAK ENGLISH: 1930

CLASS	TOTAL		MALE		FEMALE	
	Number	Per cent	Number	Per cent	Number	Per cent
French Canadian born..................	360,724	....	182,590	....	178,134	....
Able to speak English.....................	329,023	100.0	174,547	100.0	154,476	100.0
Literate...................................	305,167	92.7	159,532	91.4	145,635	94.3
Illiterate..................................	23,856	7.3	15,015	8.6	8,841	5.7
Not able to speak English...............	31,701	100.0	8,043	100.0	23,658	100.0
Literate...................................	19,797	62.4	4,360	54.2	15,437	65.3
Illiterate..................................	11,904	37.6	3,683	45.8	8,221	34.7
Literate....................................	324,964	100.0	163,892	100.0	161,072	100.0
Able to speak English.....................	305,167	93.9	159,532	97.3	145,635	90.4
Not able to speak English.................	19,797	6.1	4,360	2.7	15,437	9.6
Illiterate...................................	35,760	100.0	18,698	100.0	17,062	100.0
Able to speak English.....................	23,856	66.7	15,015	80.3	8,841	51.8
Not able to speak English.................	11,904	33.3	3,683	19.7	8,221	48.2
Per cent not able to speak English...........	....	8.8	....	4.4	....	13.3
Per cent illiterate...........................	....	9.9	....	10.2	....	9.6
French Canadian parentage..............	596,926	....	295,716	....	301,210	....
Able to speak English.....................	593,858	100.0	294,599	100.0	299,259	100.0
Literate...................................	582,687	98.1	287,737	97.7	294,950	98.6
Illiterate..................................	11,171	1.9	6,862	2.3	4,309	1.4
Not able to speak English...............	3,068	100.0	1,117	100.0	1,951	100.0
Literate...................................	1,696	55.3	530	47.4	1,166	59.8
Illiterate..................................	1,372	44.7	587	52.6	785	40.2
Literate....................................	584,383	100.0	288,267	100.0	296,116	100.0
Able to speak English.....................	582,687	99.7	287,737	99.8	294,950	99.6
Not able to speak English.................	1,696	0.3	530	0.2	1,166	0.4
Illiterate...................................	12,543	100.0	7,449	100.0	5,094	100.0
Able to speak English.....................	11,171	89.1	6,862	92.1	4,309	84.6
Not able to speak English.................	1,372	10.9	587	7.9	785	15.4
Per cent not able to speak English...........	....	0.5	....	0.4	....	0.6
Per cent illiterate...........................	....	2.1	....	2.5	....	1.7

Similar relations appear in the statistics for the second generation of French Canadian stock. The percentage of illiteracy is very low among those able to speak English, and very high (44.7 per cent) among those not able to speak English. Of those classified as literate, all but 0.3 per cent were able to speak English, while of those classified as illiterate, 10.9 per cent were unable to speak English.

In Table 96 the statistics of ability to speak English are presented by age, with a section showing also the percentage of illiteracy, for comparison.

TABLE **96**. WHITE PERSONS OF FRENCH CANADIAN BIRTH AND PARENTAGE 10 YEARS OLD AND OVER, BY AGE, SEX, AND ABILITY TO SPEAK ENGLISH, WITH PERCENTAGE OF ILLITERACY FOR COMPARISON: 1930

AGE	BOTH SEXES			MALE			FEMALE			PER CENT ILLITERATE		
	Total	Not able to speak English		Total	Not able to speak English		Total	Not able to speak English		Both sexes	Male	Female
		Number	Per cent		Number	Per cent		Number	Per cent			
French Canadian born........	360,724	31,701	8.8	182,590	8,043	4.4	178,134	23,658	13.3	9.9	10.2	9.6
10 to 14 years.....	11,875	442	3.7	5,810	198	3.4	6,065	244	4.0	0.2	0.1	0.2
15 to 24 years.....	40,286	2,625	6.5	19,041	892	4.7	21,245	1,733	8.2	2.2	2.3	2.2
25 to 44 years.....	126,874	8,256	6.5	63,656	1,931	3.0	63,218	6,325	10.0	4.3	4.1	4.5
45 to 64 years.....	127,565	11,789	9.2	65,467	2,672	4.1	62,098	9,117	14.7	12.1	12.5	11.8
65 and over.......	53,988	8,576	15.9	28,538	2,342	8.2	25,450	6,234	24.5	25.7	26.0	25.4
Unknown.........	136	13	9.6	78	8	...	58	5	...	12.5	...	...
French Canadian parentage.....	596,926	3,068	0.5	295,716	1,117	0.4	301,210	1,951	0.6	2.1	2.5	1.7
10 to 14 years.....	72,008	529	0.7	36,166	280	0.8	35,842	249	0.7	0.2	0.2	0.2
15 to 24 years.....	150,832	375	0.2	74,261	170	0.2	76,571	205	0.3	0.5	0.7	0.4
25 to 44 years.....	246,693	903	0.4	120,586	255	0.2	126,107	648	0.5	1.3	1.6	1.0
45 to 64 years.....	106,835	865	0.8	54,106	266	0.5	52,729	599	1.1	5.0	5.9	4.1
65 and over........	20,368	392	1.9	10,522	145	1.4	9,846	247	2.5	14.7	15.9	13.4
Unknown.........	190	4	2.1	75	1	...	115	3	2.6	4.7	...	5.2

While there is a definite relation between age and ability to speak English, especially for the females, the increase in the percentage of those unable to speak English with increasing age is by no means as marked as in the case of illiteracy. Of the whole number of French Canadian born 10 to 14 years of age, all but 3.7 per cent were able to speak English, while among those 65 years old and over there were 15.9 per cent who could not speak English. The corresponding range in the percentage of illiteracy was from 0.2 to 25.7. Taking the males alone, the range in the percentage unable to speak English is only from 3.4 in the youngest group to 8.2 in the oldest, with the minimum percentage in an intermediate group, that comprising persons from 25 to 44 years of age. For the females taken alone, the range in the percentage unable to speak English is from 4.0 in the youngest group to 24.5 in the group comprising persons 65 years old and over.

In the second generation of the French Canadian stock there are relatively few persons not able to speak English; and while the maximum percentages are in every case shown for the oldest age group, the minimum percentage is not by any means always shown for the youngest.

In Table 97 the statistics of ability to speak English are presented for the French Canadian born in combination with both age and illiteracy. In Figure 30 are shown in graphic form both the percentage unable to speak English and the percentage illiterate, by age.

TABLE **97**. FRENCH CANADIAN BORN 10 YEARS OLD AND OVER, BY ABILITY TO SPEAK
ENGLISH IN COMBINATION WITH LITERACY, BY AGE AND SEX: 1930

[Per cent not shown where base is less than 100]

SEX AND CLASS	Total (age 10 and over)	10 to 14 years	15 to 24 years	25 to 44 years	45 to 64 years	65 years and over	Un-known
Total	**360,724**	**11,875**	**40,286**	**126,874**	**127,565**	**53,988**	**136**
Able to speak English	329,023	11,433	37,661	118,618	115,776	45,412	123
Per cent of total	91.2	96.3	93.5	93.5	90.8	84.1	90.4
Literate	305,167	11,422	37,219	115,140	104,900	36,375	111
Illiterate	23,856	11	442	3,478	10,876	9,037	12
Per cent of those able to speak English	7.3	0.1	1.2	2.9	9.4	19.9	9.8
Not able to speak English	31,701	442	2,625	8,256	11,789	8,576	13
Per cent of total	8.8	3.7	6.5	6.5	9.2	15.9	9.6
Literate	19,797	434	2,163	6,291	7,168	3,733	8
Illiterate	11,904	8	462	1,965	4,621	4,843	5
Per cent of those not able to speak English	37.6	1.8	17.6	23.8	39.2	56.5	...
Male	**182,590**	**5,810**	**19,041**	**63,656**	**65,467**	**28,538**	**78**
Able to speak English	174,547	5,612	18,149	61,725	62,795	26,196	70
Per cent of total	95.6	96.6	95.3	97.0	95.9	91.8	...
Literate	159,532	5,606	17,895	59,640	55,956	20,371	64
Illiterate	15,015	6	254	2,085	6,839	5,825	6
Per cent of those able to speak English	8.6	0.1	1.4	3.4	10.9	22.2	...
Not able to speak English	8,043	198	892	1,931	2,672	2,342	8
Per cent of total	4.4	3.4	4.7	3.0	4.1	8.2	...
Literate	4,360	196	706	1,387	1,314	752	5
Illiterate	3,683	2	186	544	1,358	1,590	3
Per cent of those not able to speak English	45.8	1.0	20.9	28.2	50.8	67.9	...
Female	**178,134**	**6,065**	**21,245**	**63,218**	**62,098**	**25,450**	**58**
Able to speak English	154,476	5,821	19,512	56,893	52,981	19,216	53
Per cent of total	86.7	96.0	91.8	90.0	85.3	75.5	...
Literate	145,635	5,816	19,324	55,500	48,944	16,004	47
Illiterate	8,841	5	188	1,393	4,037	3,212	6
Per cent of those able to speak English	5.7	0.1	1.0	2.4	7.6	16.7	...
Not able to speak English	23,658	244	1,733	6,325	9,117	6,234	5
Per cent of total	13.3	4.0	8.2	10.0	14.7	24.5	...
Literate	15,437	238	1,457	4,904	5,854	2,981	3
Illiterate	8,221	6	276	1,421	3,263	3,253	2
Per cent of those not able to speak English	34.7	2.5	15.9	22.5	35.8	52.2	...

FIGURE **30**. ABILITY TO SPEAK ENGLISH AND ILLITERACY AMONG THE FRENCH CANADIAN
BORN, BY AGE: 1930

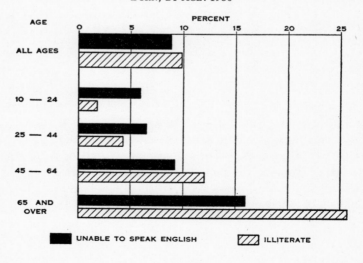

Of the French Canadian born aged 10 to 14 who were not able to speak English, only 1.8 per cent were illiterate. Of those 15 to 24 years old, 17.6 per cent; of those 25 to 44 years old, 23.8 per cent; of those 45 to 64 years old, 39.2 per cent; and of those 65 years old and over, 56.5 per cent. These figures show the results of combining two sets of characteristics both of which tend to increase with increasing age.

Urban and Rural Areas

Data for the French Canadian born classified by ability to speak English in combination with literacy are presented in Table 98 for urban and rural areas.

Table **98**. French Canadian Born 10 Years Old and Over, by Ability to Speak English in Combination with Literacy, by Sex, for Urban and Rural Areas: 1930

[For United States totals see Table 95]

CLASS	TOTAL			MALE			FEMALE		
	Urban	Rural-non-farm	Rural-farm	Urban	Rural-non-farm	Rural-farm	Urban	Rural-non-farm	Rural-farm
Total..................	284,804	54,052	21,868	140,567	29,276	12,747	144,237	24,776	9,121
Able to speak English..........	260,110	48,925	19,988	134,470	27,883	12,194	125,640	21,042	7,794
Literate....................	243,885	43,648	17,634	124,812	24,281	10,439	119,073	19,367	7,195
Illiterate...................	16,225	5,277	2,354	9,658	3,602	1,755	6,567	1,675	599
Per cent of those able to speak English..........	6.2	10.8	11.8	7.2	12.9	14.4	5.2	8.0	7.7
Not able to speak English......	24,694	5,127	1,880	6,097	1,393	553	18,597	3,734	1,327
Per cent of total..............	8.7	9.5	8.6	4.3	4.8	4.3	12.9	15.1	14.5
Literate....................	15,478	3,108	1,211	3,280	744	336	12,198	2,364	875
Illiterate...................	9,216	2,019	669	2,817	649	217	6,399	1,370	452
Per cent of those not able to speak English..........	37.3	39.4	35.6	46.2	46.6	39.2	34.4	36.7	34.1
Literate.....................	259,363	46,756	18,845	128,092	25,025	10,775	131,271	21,731	8,070
Able to speak English........	243,885	43,648	17,634	124,812	24,281	10,439	119,073	19,367	7,195
Not able to speak English......	15,478	3,108	1,211	3,280	744	336	12,198	2,364	875
Per cent of literate..........	6.0	6.6	6.6	2.6	3.0	3.1	9.3	10.9	10.8
Illiterate....................	25,441	7,296	3,023	12,475	4,251	1,972	12,966	3,045	1,051
Per cent of total..	8.9	13.5	13.8	8.9	14.5	15.5	9.0	12.3	11.5
Able to speak English	16,225	5,277	2,354	9,658	3,602	1,755	6,567	1,675	599
Not able to speak English	9,216	2,019	669	2,817	649	217	6,399	1,370	452
Per cent of illiterate	36.2	27.7	22.1	22.6	15.3	11.0	49.4	45.0	43.0

While the percentage of illiteracy was appreciably lower in urban areas than in rural, there was relatively little difference between one area and another in the percentage of the French Canadian-born population unable to speak English, the figures being 8.7 for urban areas, 9.5 for rural-nonfarm, and 8.6 for rural-farm. Of those in urban areas unable to speak English, 37.3 per cent were also illiterate; in rural-nonfarm, 39.4

per cent; and in rural-farm, 35.6 per cent. Conversely, of those returned as illiterate, 36.2 per cent in urban areas were also unable to speak English, as compared with 27.7 per cent in the rural-nonfarm areas, and 22.1 per cent in rural-farm.

Data for States

Data for the French Canadian born classified by sex and ability to speak English are presented by States in Table 99. The States in which the highest proportion of the French Canadian born were unable to speak English were Maine, with 17.0 per cent, New Hampshire, with 14.5 per cent, and Rhode Island, with 13.1 per cent, these being States in which the French Canadian born were highly concentrated in certain counties and cities, forming more than 5 per cent of the total population in several counties. The percentages were also high in Connecticut, Vermont, and Massachusetts, where somewhat similar conditions obtain with respect to the existence of the solid groups of French Canadians in the population. Outside these six New England States the percentage of the French Canadian born who could not speak English was much smaller. In Michigan and New York, for example, States in which the total number of French Canadian born exceeded that in Connecticut or Vermont and almost equaled that in Rhode Island, all but 2.8 per cent of their numbers were able to speak English, this being obviously the result of a wider distribution among the English-speaking population and less concentration in French-speaking groups or areas.

TABLE **99**. FRENCH CANADIAN BORN 10 YEARS OLD AND OVER, BY SEX AND ABILITY TO SPEAK ENGLISH, BY STATES: 1930

[Per cent not shown where base is less than 100]

DIVISION AND STATE	TOTAL			MALE			FEMALE		
	Number	Unable to speak English		Number	Unable to speak English		Number	Unable to speak English	
		Number	Per cent		Number	Per cent		Number	Per cent
United States........	**360,724**	**31,701**	**8.8**	**182,590**	**8,043**	**4.4**	**178,134**	**23,658**	**13.3**
NEW ENGLAND:									
Maine.................	35,993	6,123	17.0	17,943	1,428	8.0	18,050	4,695	26.0
New Hampshire..........	36,888	5,352	14.5	18,339	1,311	7.1	18,549	4,041	21.8
Vermont...............	16,331	1,726	10.6	8,860	533	6.0	7,471	1,193	16.0
Massachusetts..........	113,043	9,443	8.4	55,168	2,381	4.3	57,875	7,062	12.2
Rhode Island...........	30,855	4,039	13.1	14,858	1,045	7.0	15,997	2,994	18.7
Connecticut............	24,525	2,643	10.8	12,590	768	6.1	11,935	1,875	15.7
MIDDLE ATLANTIC:									
New York.............	27,690	767	2.8	14,145	234	1.7	13,545	533	3.9
New Jersey............	2,380	37	1.6	1,148	11	1.0	1,232	26	2.1
Pennsylvania...........	1,842	16	0.9	931	7	0.8	911	9	1.0
EAST NORTH CENTRAL:									
Ohio..................	2,545	26	1.0	1,272	7	0.6	1,273	19	1.5
Indiana...............	663	4	0.6	355	1	0.3	308	3	1.0
Illinois................	6,044	75	1.2	3,054	15	0.5	2,990	60	2.0
Michigan..............	27,212	764	2.8	14,760	154	1.0	12,452	610	4.9
Wisconsin..............	4,271	111	2.6	2,447	23	0.9	1,824	88	4.8
WEST NORTH CENTRAL:									
Minnesota.............	6,447	234	3.6	3,576	53	1.5	2,871	181	6.3
Iowa.................	605	8	1.3	303	2	0.7	302	6	2.0
Missouri..............	579	4	0.7	313	..	...	266	4	1.5
North Dakota..........	1,340	60	4.5	741	4	0.5	599	56	9.3
South Dakota..........	488	7	1.4	272	2	0.7	216	5	2.3
Nebraska..............	434	5	1.2	227	..	...	207	5	2.4
Kansas................	560	37	6.6	293	7	2.4	267	30	11.2
SOUTH ATLANTIC:									
Delaware..............	60	..	...	33			27	..	...
Maryland..............	280	4	1.4	158	1	0.6	122	3	2.5
Dist. of Columbia.......	221	1	0.5	113	..	...	108	1	0.9
Virginia..............	154	..	...	81	..	...	73	..	...
West Virginia..........	115	..	...	61	..	...	54	..	...
North Carolina.........	75	1	...	38	..	...	37	1	...
South Carolina.........	30	..	...	17	..	...	13	..	...
Georgia...............	106	..	...	53	..	...	53	..	...
Florida...............	944	18	1.9	488	7	1.4	456	11	2.4
EAST SOUTH CENTRAL:									
Kentucky..............	92	2	...	52	1	...	40	1	...
Tennessee.............	89	..	...	47	..	...	42	..	...
Alabama..............	113	2	1.8	64	1	...	49	1	...
Mississippi............	42	..	...	21	..	...	21	..	...
WEST SOUTH CENTRAL:									
Arkansas..............	77	1	...	37	1	...	40	..	...
Louisiana.............	222	5	2.3	138	1	0.7	84	4	...
Oklahoma.............	241	..	...	151	..	...	90	..	...
Texas................	448	3	0.7	262	..	...	186	3	1.6
MOUNTAIN:									
Montana..............	1,947	30	1.5	1,160	8	0.7	787	22	2.8
Idaho................	564	5	0.9	364	1	0.3	200	4	2.0
Wyoming..............	117	..	...	69	..	...	48	..	...
Colorado..............	568	4	0.7	308	1	0.3	260	3	1.2
New Mexico............	62	..	...	46	..	...	16	..	...
Arizona...............	156	1	0.6	100	..	...	56	1	...
Utah.................	91	1	...	59	..	...	32	1	...
Nevada...............	134	2	1.5	84	2	...	50	..	...
PACIFIC:									
Washington............	4,253	66	1.6	2,322	20	0.9	1,931	46	2.4
Oregon...............	1,319	12	0.9	715	1	0.1	604	11	1.8
California..............	7,469	62	0.8	3,954	12	0.3	3,515	50	1.4

CHAPTER XII

CANADIAN-BORN WORKERS IN THE UNITED STATES IN 1910 BY OCCUPATION

In connection with the census of 1910 a tabulation of foreign-born white workers by occupation in combination with country of birth was made. Because of lack of funds, however, this tabulation was carried no further than the completion of the machine sheets; that is, not only were the results not published, but they were not even made up into tables ready for publication. This material is significant for the present study as representing the most recent tabulation of data for the Canadian born in the United States by occupation; and since economic conditions—or at least conditions affecting choice of occupation—were not radically different in 1910 from those obtaining in 1930, these occupational data may well be considered in connection with the other tabulations, most of which are for 1930.

To meet the need for a brief classification of broader social and economic significance than one composed either of broad occupational groups or broad industrial groups, the classification into 12 categories designated social-economic groups has been designed.[1]

The occupational data for Canadian-born gainful workers in the United States in 1910 have been assembled into these 12 social-economic groups in Table 100, in the last column of which is shown for comparison the percentage distribution of all workers in the 16 States in which one per cent or more of the 1930 population was Canadian born. These States, which are listed in the footnote to Table 100, were selected for comparative purposes because it seemed more significant to compare the occupational distribution of the Canadian born with that of the total population in the States in which they were most numerous (instead of making the comparisons with any United States total), since differences which would arise because of the small number of Canadian born in the predominantly agricultural Southern States were thereby eliminated.

1. See *A Social-Economic Grouping of the Gainful Workers of the United States: 1930,* by Alba M. Edwards, published by the United States Bureau of the Census in 1938. This publication lists the specific occupations making up each of the social-economic groups. A list alone, with a brief explanation of the classification, is contained in an article entitled "A Social-economic Grouping of the Gainful Workers of the United States," published in the *Journal of the American Statistical Association,* Vol. 28, Dec., 1933, a reprint of which can be obtained on request from the Bureau of the Census, Washington, D. C.

TABLE **100**. CANADIAN-BORN GAINFUL WORKERS 16 YEARS OLD AND OVER IN THE UNITED STATES, BY SOCIAL-ECONOMIC GROUPS AND SEX, WITH COMPARATIVE DATA FOR ALL WORKERS 10 YEARS OLD AND OVER IN 16 SELECTED STATES: 1910

SEX AND SOCIAL-ECONOMIC GROUP	CANADIAN-BORN WORKERS 16 YEARS OLD AND OVER						All workers in 16 selected States,* per cent
	Number			Per cent			
	Total	French	English	Total	French	English	
Total.....................	636,667	215,759	420,908	100.0	100.0	100.0	100.0
1. Professional persons................	33,515	4,514	29,001	5.3	2.1	6.9	5.2
2. Proprietors, managers, and officials....	105,606	22,378	83,228	16.6	10.4	19.8	17.0
2-a. Farmers (owners and tenants)...	54,946	12,227	42,719	8.6	5.7	10.1	9.1
2-b. Wholesale and retail dealers....	20,521	5,384	15,137	3.2	2.5	3.6	3.9
2-c. Other proprietors, managers, and officials.................	30,139	4,767	25,372	4.7	2.2	6.0	4.0
3. Clerks and kindred workers..........	62,740	9,613	53,127	9.9	4.5	12.6	13.0
4. Skilled workers and foremen..........	116,856	34,133	82,723	18.4	15.8	19.7	14.6
5. Semiskilled workers.................	170,124	89,158	80,966	26.7	41.3	19.2	23.3
5-a. Semiskilled workers in manu- facturing...................	122,704	76,479	46,225	19.3	35.4	11.0	14.9
5-b. Other semiskilled workers......	47,420	12,679	34,741	7.4	5.9	8.2	6.4
6. Unskilled workers...................	147,826	55,963	91,863	23.2	25.9	21.8	28.8
6-a. Farm laborers..............	24,435	7,053	17,382	3.8	3.3	4.1	7.4
6-b. Factory and building construc- tion laborers..............	44,058	24,247	19,811	6.9	11.2	4.7	6.9
6-c. Other laborers..............	42,779	16,778	26,001	6.7	7.8	6.2	7.4
6-d. Servant classes..............	36,554	7,885	28,669	5.7	3.7	6.8	7.1
Male.......................	491,125	164,578	326,547	100.0	100.0	100.0	100.0
1. Professional persons................	18,713	2,357	16,356	3.8	1.4	5.0	3.6
2. Proprietors, managers, and officials....	100,585	21,446	79,139	20.5	13.0	24.2	20.8
2-a. Farmers (owners and tenants)...	52,844	11,894	40,950	10.8	7.2	12.5	11.1
2-b. Wholesale and retail dealers....	18,987	4,988	13,999	3.9	3.0	4.3	4.7
2-c. Other proprietors, managers, and officials	28,754	4,564	24,190	5.9	2.8	7.4	4.9
3. Clerks and kindred workers..........	45,750	7,579	38,171	9.3	4.6	11.7	11.5
4. Skilled workers and foremen..........	114,727	33,678	81,049	23.4	20.5	24.8	18.2
5. Semiskilled workers.................	94,438	50,248	44,190	19.2	30.5	13.5	16.3
5-a. Semiskilled workers in manu- facturing...................	65,314	40,748	24,566	13.3	24.8	7.5	10.5
5-b. Other semiskilled workers.....	29,124	9,500	19,624	5.9	5.8	6.0	5.7
6. Unskilled workers...................	116,912	49,270	67,642	23.8	29.9	20.7	29.7
6-a. Farm laborers................	23,782	6,898	16,884	4.8	4.2	5.2	9.1
6-b. Factory and building construc- tion laborers................	42,374	23,123	19,251	8.6	14.0	5.9	8.4
6-c. Other laborers..............	42,574	16,712	25,862	8.7	10.2	7.9	9.4
6-d. Servant classes..............	8,182	2,537	5,645	1.7	1.5	1.7	2.7
Female.....................	145,542	51,181	94,361	100.0	100.0	100.0	100.0
1. Professional persons................	14,802	2,157	12,645	10.2	4.2	13.4	10.8
2. Proprietors, managers, and officials....	5,021	932	4,089	3.4	1.8	4.3	3.4
2-a. Farmers (owners and tenants)...	2,102	333	1,769	1.4	0.7	1.9	1.6
2-b. Wholesale and retail dealers....	1,534	396	1,138	1.1	0.8	1.2	1.0
2-c. Other proprietors, managers, and officials.................	1,385	203	1,182	1.0	0.4	1.3	0.8
3. Clerks and kindred workers..........	16,990	2,034	14,956	11.7	4.0	15.8	18.4
4. Skilled workers and foremen..........	2,129	455	1,674	1.5	0.9	1.8	1.7
5. Semiskilled workers	75,686	38,910	36,776	52.0	76.0	39.0	40.0
5-a. Semiskilled workers in manu- facturing...................	57,390	35,731	21,659	39.4	69.8	23.0	31.1
5-b. Other semiskilled workers......	18,296	3,179	15,117	12.6	6.2	16.0	8.9
6. Unskilled workers...................	30,914	6,693	24,221	21.2	13.1	25.7	25.7
6-a. Farm laborers..............	653	155	498	0.4	0.3	0.5	1.2
6-b. Factory and building construc- tion laborers..............	1,684	1,124	560	1.2	2.2	0.6	1.2
6-c. Other laborers..............	205	66	139	0.1	0.1	0.1	0.3
6-d. Servant classes..............	28,372	5,348	23,024	19.5	10.4	24.4	23.0

*The 16 States in which 1 per cent or more of the 1930 population was Canadian born are as follows: Maine, New Hampshire, Vermont, Massachusetts, Rhode Island, Connecticut, New York, Michigan, Minnesota, North Dakota, Montana, Idaho, Nevada, Washington, Oregon, and California.

Figures are shown separately for French and English Canadian born, and the differences between these two classes are in some cases very considerable. The 1910 tabulation of Canadian-born workers was made for those 16 years old and over, while the available figures for all workers in the 16 States represent those 10 years old and over. The difference in the percentage distribution as between one age group and the other, however, is immaterial. The percentages of the French Canadian born, the English Canadian born, and all workers in the 16 States in each of the social-economic groups are shown in graphic form in Figure 31.

In the professional group were found 5.3 per cent of the Canadian-born workers, as compared with 5.2 per cent of all workers in the 16 States. Of the French Canadians, 2.1 per cent were in the professional group, and of the English Canadians, 6.9 per cent. For males alone the percentages professional were as follows: French Canadian born, 1.4; English Canadian born, 5.0; and all workers in the 16 States, 3.6. For females alone the percentages professional were: French Canadian born, 4.2; English Canadian born, 13.4; and all workers in the 16 States, 10.8.

Only 8.6 per cent of the Canadian-born workers in the United States in 1910 (5.7 per cent of the French and 10.1 per cent of the English) were farmers, as compared with 15.9 per cent of all white workers in the United States. This is in harmony with the fact already referred to a number of times, that the Canadian born in the United States are found mainly in urban areas, with very few in any part of the South, where relatively large proportions of all workers are engaged in agriculture. The difference in the percentage of farmers is not so great, therefore, when comparison is made between the Canadian born and the total number of workers in the 16 selected States, that is, in those Northern and Western States where most of the Canadian born are living. In these States 9.1 per cent of all gainful workers were farmers—a percentage only a little higher than the 8.6 shown for the Canadian born.

In the group designated "Wholesale and retail dealers" were found 3.2 per cent of the Canadian born, as compared with 3.9 per cent of all workers in the 16 States; and in the group designated "Other proprietors, managers, and officials," 4.7 per cent, as compared with 4.0 per cent of all workers in the 16 States.

In the clerical group, which includes salespeople, agents, etc., as well as clerks and stenographers, were found 9.9 per cent of the Canadian-born workers, as compared with 13.0 per cent of all workers in the 16 States in 1910. For the French Canadians alone the percentage was 4.5, and for the English, 12.6. This group included 9.3 per cent of the Canadian-born males and 11.7 per cent of the females, the corresponding figures for all workers in the 16 States being 11.5 per cent of the males and

FIGURE **31**. CANADIAN-BORN WORKERS, FRENCH AND ENGLISH, AND ALL WORKERS IN 16 SELECTED STATES, BY SOCIAL-ECONOMIC GROUPS: 1910

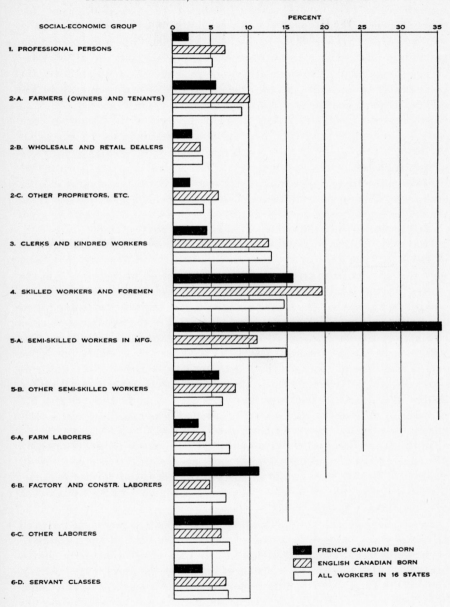

18.4 per cent of the females. In the group designated "Skilled workers and foremen" were found 18.4 per cent of the Canadian-born workers, as compared with 14.6 per cent of all workers in the 16 States. For male workers alone the difference was even more in favor of the Canadian workers, 23.4 per cent of the Canadian male workers being in this group, as compared with 18.2 per cent of all male workers in the 16 States. In this case the difference as between French and English Canadians was relatively small, the percentage for the former being 20.5, and for the latter, 24.8.

The greatest differences between the Canadian born and the total population of the 16 selected States with respect to occupational distribution appear in the group designated "Semiskilled workers in manufacturing," which is made up mainly of factory operatives. In this group were found 19.3 per cent of all Canadian-born workers, as compared with 14.9 per cent of all workers in the 16 States. This group shows a wider divergence than any other between the French and English Canadians, including 35.4 per cent of the French Canadian workers and only 11.0 per cent of the English. Of the male Canadian workers, 13.3 per cent were in this group, as compared with 10.5 per cent of all male workers in the 16 States. For the French Canadian males alone, however, the percentage was 24.8, as compared with 7.5 for the English Canadians. Of the female workers, 39.4 per cent were in this factory-operative group, as compared with 31.1 per cent for all female workers in the 16 States. By far the greatest concentration shown anywhere in the table is represented by the 69.8 per cent of the French female workers found in this group, the corresponding percentage for English female workers being 23.0, or materially less than the percentage for all white female workers in the 16 States, which was 31.1.

Of the whole number of Canadian-born workers, 23.2 per cent were classified as unskilled, as compared with 28.8 per cent of all workers in the 16 States. This difference in the group total results primarily from the fact, however, that only 3.8 per cent of the Canadian workers were farm laborers, as compared with 7.4 per cent of the 16-State total. The percentage unskilled among the French Canadian workers was 25.9, as compared with 21.8 among the English Canadian workers.

Within the unskilled group, factory and construction workers represented 6.9 per cent of the Canadian-born workers (11.2 per cent of the French and 4.7 per cent of the English) which was exactly the same as the proportion among all workers in the 16 States. In the group designated "Other laborers," the percentages differed by only a small amount. In the servant classes were found 5.7 per cent of the Canadian-born workers, as compared with 7.1 per cent of all workers in the 16 States, the

Canadian figure comprising 3.7 per cent of the French and 6.8 per cent of the English workers. Of the males alone, 1.7 per cent of the Canadian born were in the servant classes, as compared with 2.7 per cent of all workers in the 16 States; and of the females, 19.5 per cent of the Canadian born, as compared with 23.0 per cent for the 16-State group. Of the female French Canadian workers alone, however, only 10.4 per cent were in the servant class, as compared with 24.4 per cent of the English.

The detailed occupational classification of the Canadian born in the United States in 1910, arranged under broad industrial headings and specific occupational headings, is presented in Table 101.

The largest industrial-occupational group is that designated "Manufacturing and mechanical industries," in which 286,487 persons were employed. The second largest group was agriculture and forestry, with 92,834 persons, followed by domestic and personal service, with 69,383 persons, and trade, with 64,743 persons. Among both males and females, manufacturing and mechanical industries employed the largest number, with 225,310 males and 61,177 females. The second largest group among males was agriculture and forestry, with 89,989, while among females the second largest group was domestic and personal service, with 47,416. The largest single specific occupational group outside of agriculture was that comprising the carpenters, with 31,072 persons, of whom 10,046 were French and 21,026 were English. Space does not permit further analysis of the figures presented in Table 101, but the data, hitherto unpublished, are presented in full detail for the use of those interested in specific occupations.

TABLE **101**. CANADIAN-BORN GAINFUL WORKERS 16 YEARS OLD AND OVER IN THE UNITED STATES, BY OCCUPATION AND SEX: 1910

OCCUPATION	MALE			FEMALE		
	Total	French	English	Total	French	English
All occupations....................	491,125	164,578	326,547	145,542	51,181	94,361
Agriculture, forestry, etc.................	89,989	24,000	65,989	2,845	498	2,347
Dairy farmers.............................	1,099	281	818	43	9	34
Dairy farm laborers.......................	475	130	345	23	5	18
Farmers.................................	49,247	11,207	38,040	1,888	306	1,582
Farm laborers............................	20,825	6,189	14,636	573	134	439
Home farm...........................	2,686	672	2,014	397	88	309
Working out..........................	18,136	5,517	12,619	176	46	130
Turpentine farm laborers.................	3	..	3	..	..	..
Dairy farm foremen.......................	16	4	12	2	1	1
Farm foremen............................	579	87	492	83	6	77
Garden and greenhouse foremen.............	11	1	10	..	..	..
Orchard, nursery, etc., foremen.............	55	5	50	1	1	..
Fishermen and oystermen...................	2,456	673	1,783	4	2	2
Foresters................................	306	34	272	..	..	..
Florists.................................	80	13	67	11	1	10
Fruit growers and nurserymen..............	610	69	541	57	..	57
Gardeners...............................	789	174	615	32	11	21
Landscape gardeners......................	98	22	76	..	..	..
Cranberry bog laborers....................	57	49	8	11	8	3
Garden laborers..........................	1,162	318	844	18	5	13
Greenhouse laborers......................	179	43	136	10	1	9
Orchard and nursery laborers...............	312	45	267	8	..	8
Lumbermen, raftsmen, and woodchoppers.........	9,327	4,230	5,097	..	..	..
Foremen and overseers.................	668	164	504	..	..	..
Lumbermen and raftsmen...................	7,352	3,280	4,072	..	..	..
Teamsters and haulers....................	587	239	348	..	..	..
Woodchoppers and tie cutters.............	720	547	173	..	..	..
Owners and managers, log and timber camps......	610	174	436	..	..	..
Stock herders, drovers, and feeders..............	514	84	430	..	..	..
Stock raisers.............................	701	99	602	30	2	28
Apiarists................................	37	3	34	3	..	3
Corn shellers, hay balers, grain threshers, etc.......	50	4	46	..	..	..
Ditchers (farm)...........................	76	16	60	..	..	..
Poultry raisers and poultry yard laborers..........	242	34	208	43	5	38
Other and not specified pursuits.................	76	12	64	5	1	4
Extraction of minerals..................	6,736	1,923	4,813	11	6	5
Foremen and overseers......................	390	97	293	..	..	..
Inspectors...............................	12	1	11	..	..	..
Managers................................	210	16	194	..	..	..
Officials.................................	29	2	27	..	..	..
Operators...............................	323	38	285	1	..	1
Coal mine operatives......................	703	100	603	..	..	..
Copper mine operatives....................	909	343	566	2	1	1
Gold and silver mine operatives..............	1,575	277	1,298	..	..	..
Iron mine operatives......................	515	365	150	..	..	..
Lead and zinc mine operatives...............	127	23	104	..	..	..
All other mine operatives..................	579	86	493	2	2	..
Quarry operatives........................	1,054	524	530	..	..	..
Oil and gas well operatives..................	216	15	201	..	..	..
Salt well and works operatives.................	94	36	58	6	3	3

TABLE **101**. CANADIAN-BORN GAINFUL WORKERS 16 YEARS OLD AND OVER IN THE UNITED STATES, BY OCCUPATION AND SEX: 1910—Continued

OCCUPATION	MALE			FEMALE		
	Total	French	English	Total	French	English
Manufacturing and mechanical industries	**225,310**	**98,075**	**127,235**	**61,177**	**37,313**	**23,864**
Apprentices to building and hand trades	273	96	177	..	..	..
Apprentices to dressmakers and milliners	..	..	..	104	45	59
Other apprentices	632	217	415	32	8	24
Bakers	1,656	832	824	131	20	111
Blacksmiths	7,437	2,399	5,038	..	..	..
Forgemen, hammermen, and welders	132	57	75	..	..	..
Boilermakers	806	200	606	..	..	..
Brick and stone masons	3,928	1,141	2,787	..	..	..
Builders and building contractors	6,458	1,321	5,137	18	3	15
Butchers and dressers (slaughterhouse)	127	32	95	..	..	..
Cabinetmakers	777	210	567	..	..	..
Carpenters	31,072	10,046	21,026	..	..	..
Compositors, linotypers, and typesetters	2,419	345	2,074	230	20	210
Coopers	552	112	440	..	..	..
Dressmakers and seamstresses (not in factory)	9	4	5	11,186	3,066	8,120
Dyers	462	350	112	23	14	9
Electricians and electrical engineers	3,095	478	2,617	3	2	1
Electrotypers and stereotypers	93	9	84	5	1	4
Lithographers	128	10	118	5	..	5
Engineers (mechanical)	349	32	317	..	..	..
Engineers (stationary)	6,529	1,347	5,182	..	..	..
Engravers	239	41	198	11	..	11
Buffers and polishers (metal)	1,064	585	479	94	26	68
Filers (metal)	580	192	388	6	3	3
Grinders (metal)	207	111	96	15	1	14
Firemen (except locomotive and fire department)	2,862	1,269	1,593	..	..	..
Foremen and overseers (mfg.)	5,405	1,739	3,666	406	74	332
Furnace men and smelter men	172	60	112	..	..	..
Heaters	66	20	46	1	..	1
Ladlers and pourers	26	14	12	..	..	..
Puddlers	30	5	25	..	..	..
Glass blowers	120	13	107	1	..	1
Goldsmiths and silversmiths	106	50	56	8	3	5
Jewelers and lapidaries (factory)	108	54	54	93	46	47
Jewelers and watchmakers (not in factory)	262	40	222	8	3	5
Laborers in manufacturing and mechanical industries (not otherwise specified)	39,245	21,760	17,485	1,683	1,124	559
Building and hand trades	16,285	7,752	8,533	171	56	115
General and not specified	15,311	7,232	8,079	171	56	115
Helpers	974	520	454	..	..	..
Chemical industries	430	155	275	24	5	19
Fertilizer factories	17	4	13	..	..	..
Paint factories	28	10	18	..	..	..
Powder, cartridge, fireworks, etc., factories	61	36	25	4	1	3
Other chemical factories	324	105	219	20	4	16
Clay, glass, and stone industries	1,427	1,020	407	13	11	2
Brick, tile, and terra cotta factories	940	766	174	..	..	..
Glass factories	76	37	39	12	11	1
Lime, cement, and gypsum factories	228	110	118	..	..	..
Marble and stone yards	160	102	58	..	..	..
Potteries	23	5	18	1	..	1
Iron and steel industries	3,582	1,717	1,865	60	31	29
Automobile factories	552	111	441	5	1	4
Blast furnaces and rolling mills	384	142	242	8	3	5
Car and railroad shops	333	197	136	2	..	2
Wagon and carriage factories	111	44	67	1	..	1
Other iron and steel works	2,202	1,223	979	44	27	17

TABLE **101**. CANADIAN-BORN GAINFUL WORKERS 16 YEARS OLD AND OVER IN THE UNITED STATES, BY OCCUPATION AND SEX: 1910—Continued

OCCUPATION	MALE			FEMALE		
	Total	French	English	Total	French	English
Manufacturing and mech. ind.—Con.						
Laborers, mfg. and mech. (n.o.s.)—Con.						
Other metal industries......................	489	271	218	39	20	19
Brass mills..............................	108	66	42	7	6	1
Copper factories........................	186	124	62	..	..	..
Lead and zinc factories..................	20	9	11	..	..	..
Tinware and enamelware factories...........	39	10	29	2	..	2
Other metal factories....................	136	62	74	30	14	16
Lumber and furniture industries...............	6,103	3,214	2,889	51	25	26
Furniture, piano, and organ factories.........	292	147	145	10	4	6
Saw and planing mills....................	5,097	2,645	2,452	23	12	11
Other woodworking factories...............	714	422	292	18	9	9
Textile industries...........................	4,104	3,810	294	711	635	76
Cotton mills............................	2,550	2,463	87	386	363	23
Silk mills..............................	64	61	3	13	11	2
Woolen and worsted mills.................	711	620	91	191	173	18
Other textile mills......................	779	666	113	121	88	33
Other industries...........................	6,825	3,821	3,004	614	341	273
Charcoal and coke works.................	22	4	18	..	..	..
Cigar and tobacco factories................	8	3	5	8	3	5
Clothing industries.....................	68	45	23	86	62	24
Electric light and power plants.............	82	21	61	1	1	..
Electrical supply factories.................	146	59	87	37	13	24
Bakeries...............................	46	22	24	6	3	3
Butter and cheese factories................	48	13	35	1	..	1
Fish curing and packing..................	148	2	146	32	..	32
Flour and grain mills....................	116	53	63	3	..	3
Fruit and vegetable canning, etc.............	23	8	15	4	1	3
Slaughter and packing houses..............	110	26	84	2	..	2
Sugar factories and refineries..............	34	6	28	..	..	..
Other food factories.....................	65	13	52	13	3	10
Gas works.............................	209	102	107	..	..	..
Liquor and beverage industries.............	104	43	61	..	..	..
Oil refineries..........................	56	6	50	..	..	..
Paper and pulp mills....................	2,450	1,605	845	48	19	29
Printing and publishing..................	131	64	67	24	8	16
Rubber factories........................	208	103	105	20	9	11
Shoe factories..........................	333	257	76	76	54	22
Tanneries..............................	180	87	93	1	1	..
Turpentine distillers.....................	2	1	1	..	..	..
Other factories.........................	2,236	1,278	958	252	164	88
Loom fixers................................	2,423	2,279	144	..	..	..
Machinists and millwrights..................	14,148	4,803	9,345	2	1	1
Toolmakers and die setters and sinkers............	339	123	216	2	..	2
Managers and superintendents (mfg.)............	2,793	271	2,522	31	4	27
Manufacturers and officials..................	5,172	840	4,332	139	16	123
Manufacturers..........................	4,756	819	3,937	130	13	117
Officials...............................	416	21	395	9	3	6
Mechanics (not otherwise specified).............	957	317	640	..	..	..
Gunsmiths, locksmiths, and bellhangers.........	35	9	26	..	..	..
Wheelwrights...........................	152	58	94	..	..	..
Other mechanics........................	770	250	520	..	..	..
Millers (grain, flour, feed, etc.)................	394	50	344	..	..	..
Milliners and millinery dealers................	90	25	65	2,649	784	1,865
Molders, founders, and casters, metal............	2,718	950	1,768	1	..	1
Brass molders, founders, and casters.........	200	78	122	..	..	..
Iron molders, founders, and casters............	2,462	855	1,607	1	..	1
Other molders, founders, and casters..........	56	17	39	..	..	..
Oilers of machinery........................	457	239	218	1	..	1
Enamelers, lacquerers, and japanners............	43	12	31	50	21	29
Painters, glaziers, and varnishers (building)........	4,688	247	4,441	10	3	7

TABLE **101**. CANADIAN-BORN GAINFUL WORKERS 16 YEARS OLD AND OVER IN THE
UNITED STATES, BY OCCUPATION AND SEX: 1910—Continued

OCCUPATION	MALE			FEMALE		
	Total	French	English	Total	French	English
Manufacturing and mech. ind.—Con.						
Painters, glaziers, and varnishers (factory)........	1,690	617	1,073	29	16	13
Paper hangers.............................	359	90	269	19	7	12
Pattern and model makers.....................	571	106	465	10	3	7
Plasterers.................................	852	247	605	..	..	..
Plumbers and gas and steam fitters.............	3,354	775	2,579	..	..	..
Pressmen (printing).........................	356	53	303	6	1	5
Rollers and roll hands (metal).................	79	23	56	..	..	..
Roofers and slaters..........................	365	151	214	..	..	..
Sawyers...................................	1,736	846	890	..	..	..
Semiskilled operatives (not otherwise specified)....	57,752	37,314	20,438	38,491	29,406	9,085
Chemical industries..........................	384	87	297	161	35	126
Paint factories..........................	71	5	66	8	..	8
Powder, cartridge, fireworks, etc., factories....	53	23	30	19	9	10
Other chemical factories..................	260	59	201	134	26	108
Cigar and tobacco factories...................	601	240	361	147	58	89
Brick, tile, and terra cotta factories............	496	413	83	1	1	..
Glass factories.............................	197	27	170	14	3	11
Lime, cement, and gypsum factories.............	85	26	59	..	..	..
Marble and stone yards......................	262	106	156	..	..	..
Potteries.................................	76	28	48	21	2	19
Clothing industries..........................	872	379	493	709	288	421
Hat factories (felt)......................	183	85	98	57	23	34
Suit, coat, cloak, and overall factories.......	243	38	205	141	34	107
Other clothing factories..................	446	256	190	511	231	280
Food industries............................	882	172	710	527	67	460
Bakeries...............................	36	19	17	61	15	46
Butter and cheese factories................	222	36	186	9	1	8
Candy factories.........................	175	35	140	222	36	186
Flour and grain mills.....................	84	18	66	4	..	4
Fruit and vegetable canning, etc............	31	4	27	21	3	18
Slaughter and packing houses, etc...........	85	25	60	13	1	12
Other food factories.....................	249	35	214	197	11	186
Harness and saddle industries.................	747	240	507	18	8	10
Iron and steel industries.....................	7,602	2,656	4,946	467	185	282
Automobile factories.....................	1,308	289	1,019	32	1	31
Blast furnaces and rolling mills............	520	147	373	39	19	20
Car and railroad shops...................	706	266	440	..	..	..
Wagon and carriage factories..............	627	211	416	19	7	12
Other iron and steel works................	4,441	1,743	2,698	377	158	219
Other metal industries.......................	1,453	695	758	957	357	600
Brass mills.............................	348	144	204	63	51	12
Clock and watch factories.................	248	103	145	430	102	328
Gold and silver and jewelry factories.........	585	355	230	413	189	224
Lead and zinc factories...................	18	1	17	3	1	2
Tinware and enamelware factories...........	75	14	61	22	3	19
Other metal factories....................	179	78	101	26	11	15
Liquor and beverage industries.................	165	66	99	4	1	3
Breweries..............................	79	31	48	..	..	..
Distilleries.............................	30	8	22	..	..	..
Other liquor and beverage factories..........	56	27	29	4	1	3
Lumber and furniture industries................	4,800	2,130	2,670	223	126	97
Furniture and organ and piano factories.......	1,698	804	894	117	63	54
Saw and planing mills....................	1,984	813	1,171	24	9	15
Other woodworking factories...............	1,118	513	605	82	54	28
Paper and pulp mills.........................	2,213	1,235	978	495	334	161
Printing and publishing......................	516	154	362	558	189	369
Shoe factories..............................	7,519	4,662	2,857	3,780	1,718	2,062
Tanneries.................................	837	398	439	11	4	7

TABLE **101**. CANADIAN-BORN GAINFUL WORKERS 16 YEARS OLD AND OVER IN THE UNITED STATES, BY OCCUPATION AND SEX: 1910—Continued

OCCUPATION	MALE			FEMALE		
	Total	French	English	Total	French	English
Manufacturing and mech. ind.—Con.						
Semiskilled operatives—Con.						
Textile industries........................	23,613	21,685	1,928	27,911	25,209	2,702
Beamers, warpers, and slashers..............	729	630	99	643	598	45
Cotton mills.........................	535	488	47	478	450	28
Silk mills...........................	16	12	4	93	88	5
Woolen and worsted mills.................	131	92	39	35	34	1
Other textile mills......................	47	38	9	37	26	11
Bobbin boys, doffers, and carriers...........	415	358	57	642	602	40
Cotton mills.........................	153	128	25	464	439	25
Silk mills...........................	4	3	1	8	8	..
Woolen and worsted mills.................	176	154	22	127	120	7
Other textile mills......................	82	73	9	43	35	8
Carders, combers, and lappers...............	1,381	1,275	106	752	688	64
Cotton mills.........................	903	862	41	641	588	53
Silk mills...........................	4	4	..	3	2	1
Woolen and worsted mills.................	355	299	56	69	65	4
Other textile mills......................	119	110	9	39	33	6
Drawers, rovers, and twisters...............	741	716	25	1,615	1,518	97
Cotton mills.........................	624	609	15	1,236	1,186	50
Silk mills...........................	24	24	..	30	22	8
Woolen and worsted mills.................	54	46	8	275	246	29
Other textile mills......................	39	37	2	74	64	10
Spinners................................	2,783	2,599	184	5,169	5,009	160
Cotton mills.........................	2,054	1,969	85	4,449	4,357	92
Silk mills...........................	19	17	2	42	35	7
Woolen and worsted mills.................	519	450	69	472	427	45
Other textile mills......................	191	163	28	206	190	16
Weavers................................	11,335	10,780	555	9,692	8,831	861
Cotton mills.........................	8,283	8,044	239	7,307	6,947	360
Silk mills...........................	403	385	18	499	424	75
Woolen and worsted mills.................	2,063	1,882	181	1,343	1,129	214
Other textile mills......................	586	469	117	543	331	212
Winders, reelers, and spoolers..............	436	364	72	4,659	4,287	372
Cotton mills.........................	301	280	21	3,225	3,078	147
Silk mills...........................	10	9	1	260	208	52
Woolen and worsted mills.................	55	45	10	545	470	75
Other textile mills......................	70	30	40	629	531	98
Other occupations........................	5,793	4,963	830	4,739	3,676	1,063
Cotton mills.........................	3,162	2,947	215	1,804	1,591	213
Silk mills...........................	79	60	19	241	171	70
Woolen and worsted mills.................	1,036	791	245	717	549	168
Other textile mills......................	1,516	1,165	351	1,977	1,365	612
Electrical supply factories..................	417	129	288	409	136	273
Paper box factories........................	112	56	56	183	81	102
Rubber factories..........................	601	214	387	499	114	385
Other factories...........................	3,302	1,516	1,786	1,396	490	906
Sewers and sewing machine operators (factory).....	272	122	150	4,579	2,321	2,258
Shoemakers and cobblers (not in factory)...........	1,620	931	689	24	9	15
Skilled occupations (not otherwise specified).......	366	89	277	8	2	6
Annealers and temperers (metal)..............	66	32	34	..	..	..
Piano and organ tuners....................	135	18	117	5	2	3
Wood carvers............................	110	33	77	1	..	1
Other skilled occupations...................	55	6	49	2	..	2
Stonecutters.............................	1,057	501	556	..	..	..
Structural iron workers (building).............	421	43	378	..	..	..
Tailors and tailoresses.....................	1,444	504	940	1,031	244	787
Tinsmiths and coppersmiths.................	1,044	267	777	..	..	..
Coppersmiths.........................	41	14	27	..	..	..
Tinsmiths............................	1,003	253	750	..	..	..
Upholsterers.............................	324	49	275	32	16	16

TABLE **101**. CANADIAN-BORN GAINFUL WORKERS 16 YEARS OLD AND OVER IN THE UNITED STATES, BY OCCUPATION AND SEX: 1910—Continued

OCCUPATION	MALE			FEMALE		
	Total	French	English	Total	French	English
Transportation.................	**45,853**	**12,091**	**33,762**	**1,189**	**116**	**1,073**
Water transportation (selected occupations)......	3,906	717	3,189	2	..	2
Boatmen, canalmen, and lock keepers..........	118	37	81	1	..	1
Captains, masters, mates, and pilots............	1,235	112	1,123	..	..	..
Longshoremen and stevedores.................	1,335	361	974	1	..	1
Sailors and deck hands......................	1,218	207	1,011	..	..	..
Road and street transportation (selected occupations)......	14,606	4,725	9,881	17	2	15
Carriage and hack drivers...................	582	171	411	1	..	1
Foremen of livery and transfer companies.......	246	49	197	..	..	..
Garage keepers and managers.................	137	20	117	..	..	..
Hostlers and stable hands...................	1,213	380	833	..	..	..
Livery stable keepers and managers............	852	150	702	7	2	5
Proprietors and managers of transfer companies..	490	92	398	8	..	8
Draymen, teamsters, and expressmen...........	10,021	3,609	6,412	..	..	..
Chauffeurs.................................	1,065	254	811	1	..	1
Railroad transportation (selected occupations).....	19,718	4,869	14,849	77	18	59
Baggagemen and freight agents................	386	56	330	..	..	..
Baggagemen............................	278	51	227	..	..	..
Freight agents..........................	108	5	103	..	..	..
Boiler washers and engine hostlers.............	106	44	62	..	..	..
Brakemen.................................	1,728	492	1,236	..	..	..
Conductors................................	2,876	401	2,475	..	..	..
Steam railroad..........................	1,561	177	1,384	..	..	..
Street railroad..........................	1,315	224	1,091	..	..	..
Foremen and overseers......................	1,546	337	1,209	4	..	4
Laborers..................................	4,876	2,300	2,576	35	15	20
Steam railroad..........................	4,454	2,070	2,384	30	12	18
Street railroad..........................	422	230	192	5	3	2
Locomotive engineers.......................	2,280	237	2,043	..	..	..
Locomotive firemen.........................	1,055	178	877	..	..	..
Motormen.................................	1,840	333	1,507	..	..	..
Officials and superintendents................	695	37	658	..	..	..
Steam railroad..........................	603	31	572	..	..	..
Street railroad..........................	92	6	86	..	..	..
Switchmen, flagmen, and yardmen.............	1,816	393	1,423	1	..	1
Switchmen and flagmen..................	1,570	357	1,213	1	..	1
Steam railroad.......................	1,527	349	1,178	1	..	1
Street railroad.......................	43	8	35	..	..	..
Yardmen (steam railroad).................	246	36	210	..	..	..
Ticket and station agents....................	514	61	453	37	3	34
Express, post, telegraph, and telephone (selected occupations).........................	3,015	438	2,577	1,049	91	958
Agents, express companies....................	85	11	74	..	..	..
Express messengers and railway mail clerks......	209	18	191	..	..	..
Express messengers......................	109	7	102	..	..	..
Railway mail clerks......................	100	11	89	..	..	..
Mail carriers..............................	679	95	584	3	2	1
Telegraph and telephone linemen..............	765	154	611	..	..	..
Telegraph messengers.......................	53	10	43	..	..	..
Telegraph operators........................	1,101	133	968	158	13	145
Telephone operators........................	123	17	106	888	76	812

TABLE **101**. CANADIAN-BORN GAINFUL WORKERS 16 YEARS OLD AND OVER IN THE UNITED STATES, BY OCCUPATION AND SEX: 1910—Continued

OCCUPATION	MALE			FEMALE		
	Total	French	English	Total	French	English
Transportation—Con.						
Other transportation pursuits.................	4,608	1,342	3,266	44	5	39
Foremen and overseers (not otherwise specified)..	456	47	409	6	..	6
Road and street building and repairing........	158	18	140	..	..	..
Telegraph and telephone companies.........	139	8	131	6	..	6
Water transportation......................	132	20	112	..	..	..
Other transportation.....................	27	1	26	..	..	..
Inspectors...............................	713	107	606	3	1	2
Steam railroad...........................	556	91	465	2	1	1
Street railroad..........................	62	8	54	..	..	..
Other transportation.....................	95	8	87	1	..	1
Laborers (n.o.s.)...........................	2,418	963	1,455	..	..	..
Road and street building and repairing........	1,849	781	1,068	..	..	..
Street cleaning..........................	76	39	37	..	..	..
Other transportation.....................	493	143	350	..	..	..
Proprietors, officials, and managers (n.o.s.)......	279	19	260	28	3	25
Telegraph and telephone companies..........	136	10	126	27	2	25
Other transportation.....................	143	9	134	1	1	..
Other occupations (semiskilled)................	742	206	536	7	1	6
Steam railroad...........................	409	123	286	3	1	2
Street railroad..........................	168	38	130	1	..	1
Other transportation.....................	165	45	120	3	..	3
Trade.................................	**56,939**	**13,923**	**43,016**	**7,804**	**1,526**	**6,278**
Bankers, brokers, and money lenders.............	1,620	108	1,512	33	1	32
Bankers and bank officials..................	640	42	598	15	..	15
Commercial brokers and commission men.......	427	25	402	5	..	5
Loan brokers and loan company officials........	16	2	14	..	..	..
Pawnbrokers............................	12	3	9	..	..	..
Stockbrokers............................	295	18	277	3	..	3
Brokers not specified and promoters...........	230	18	212	10	1	9
Clerks in stores............................	4,264	1,323	2,941	1,604	314	1,290
Commercial travelers........................	3,452	329	3,123	59	7	52
Decorators, drapers, and window dressers.........	85	12	73	5	..	5
Delivery men...............................	6,019	2,093	3,926	..	..	..
Bakeries and laundries......................	630	210	420	..	..	..
Stores...................................	5,389	1,883	3,506	..	..	..
Floorwalkers, foremen, and overseers............	633	109	524	83	5	78
Floorwalkers and foremen in stores.............	557	98	459	83	5	78
Foremen, warehouses, stockyards, etc...........	76	11	65	..	..	..
Inspectors, gaugers, and samplers................	250	42	208	14	1	13
Insurance agents and officials....................	2,095	428	1,667	44	4	40
Insurance agents..........................	1,845	400	1,445	42	3	39
Officials of insurance companies..............	250	28	222	2	1	1
Laborers in coal and lumber yards, etc............	1,877	961	916	1	..	1
Coal yards...............................	373	236	137	..	..	..
Elevators................................	91	16	75	..	..	..
Lumber yards............................	1,273	688	585	..	..	..
Stockyards..............................	32	8	24	..	..	..
Warehouses..............................	108	13	95	1	..	1
Laborers, porters, and helpers in stores............	906	299	607	38	15	23
Newsboys..................................	140	21	119	..	..	..
Proprietors, officials, and managers (n.o.s.)........	473	35	438	14	1	13
Employment office keepers..................	53	6	47	12	1	11
Proprietors, etc., elevators..................	111	7	104	..	..	..
Proprietors, etc., warehouses................	85	5	80	..	..	..
Other proprietors, officials, and managers........	224	17	207	2	..	2
Real estate agents and officials....................	2,692	291	2,401	70	5	65
Retail dealers..............................	18,106	4,851	13,255	1,517	392	1,125

TABLE **101**. CANADIAN-BORN GAINFUL WORKERS 16 YEARS OLD AND OVER IN THE UNITED STATES, BY OCCUPATION AND SEX: 1910—Continued

OCCUPATION	MALE			FEMALE		
	Total	French	English	Total	French	English
Trade—Con.						
Salesmen and saleswomen	12,315	2,563	9,752	4,232	768	3,464
Auctioneers	57	3	54	..	..	..
Demonstrators	22	3	19	102	4	98
Sales agents	710	150	560	93	9	84
Salesmen, stores	11,526	2,407	9,119	4,037	755	3,282
Undertakers	334	84	250	13	2	11
Wholesale dealers, importers and exporters	881	137	744	17	4	13
Other pursuits (semiskilled)	797	237	560	60	7	53
Fruit graders and packers	33	3	30	3	..	3
Meat cutters	525	190	335	1	..	1
Other occupations	239	44	195	56	7	49
Public service, not elsewhere classified	**8,100**	**2,252**	**5,848**	**179**	**16**	**163**
Firemen (fire department)	672	98	574	..	..	..
Guards, watchmen, and doorkeepers	2,288	846	1,442	2	..	2
Laborers (public service)	1,292	715	577	8	3	5
Garbage men and scavengers	37	7	30	..	..	..
Other laborers	1,255	708	547	8	3	5
Marshals, sheriffs, detectives, etc.	354	41	313	8	0	8
Detectives	100	4	96	3	..	3
Marshals and constables	121	18	103	..	..	..
Probation and truant officers	17	5	12	5	..	5
Sheriffs	116	14	102	..	..	..
Officials and inspectors	1,386	155	1,231	160	12	148
City	558	82	476	21	1	20
County	215	20	195	23	3	20
State	138	9	129	27	3	24
Federal	475	44	431	89	5	84
Policemen	1,197	197	1,000	..	..	..
Soldiers, sailors, and marines	703	145	558	..	..	..
Lifesavers	53	16	37	..	..	..
Lighthouse keepers	30	7	23	..	..	..
Other occupations	125	32	93	1	1	..
Professional service	**18,874**	**2,399**	**16,475**	**15,227**	**2,215**	**13,012**
Actors	322	42	280	263	44	219
Architects	365	39	326	4	..	4
Artists, sculptors, and teachers of art	335	47	288	306	19	287
Authors, editors, and reporters	549	50	499	114	10	104
Authors	54	2	52	39	3	36
Editors and reporters	495	48	447	75	7	68
Chemists, assayers, and metallurgists	332	30	302	6	..	6
Civil and mining engineers and surveyors	865	59	806	..	..	..
Civil engineers and surveyors	708	51	657	..	..	..
Mining engineers	157	8	149	..	..	..
Clergymen	2,908	476	2,432	16	1	15
College presidents and professors	326	25	301	102	23	79
Dentists	1,477	91	1,386	27	2	25
Designers, draftsmen, and inventors	762	93	669	59	12	47
Designers	151	30	121	51	10	41
Draftsmen	538	53	485	4	1	3
Inventors	73	10	63	4	1	3
Lawyers, judges, and justices	1,186	92	1,094	7	2	5
Musicians and teachers of music	719	200	519	1,097	184	913
Photographers	654	124	530	113	15	98
Physicians and surgeons	4,562	590	3,972	280	21	259
Showmen	330	78	252	20	6	14

TABLE **101**. CANADIAN-BORN GAINFUL WORKERS 16 YEARS OLD AND OVER IN THE
UNITED STATES, BY OCCUPATION AND SEX: 1910—Continued

OCCUPATION	MALE			FEMALE		
	Total	French	English	Total	French	English
Professional service—Con.						
Teachers....................................	1,101	146	955	5,505	1,334	4,171
Teachers, athletics, dancing, etc............	93	15	78	17	2	15
Teachers, school..........................	1,008	131	877	5,488	1,332	4,156
Trained nurses..............................	195	13	182	6,297	413	5,884
Veterinary surgeons........................	581	38	543	..	..	..
Other professional pursuits..................	148	12	136	110	2	108
Semiprofessional pursuits....................	1,000	114	886	785	115	670
Abstractors, notaries, and justices of peace......	88	7	81	11	3	8
Fortune tellers, hypnotists, spiritualists, etc......	16	4	12	30	5	25
Healers (except physicians and surgeons)........	50	7	43	156	11	145
Keepers of charitable and penal institutions......	98	14	84	184	29	155
Officials of lodges, societies, etc...............	159	18	141	67	8	59
Religious and charity workers.................	248	19	229	320	58	262
Theatrical owners, managers, and officials.....	195	25	170	7	1	6
Other occupations........................	146	20	126	10	..	10
Attendants and helpers (professional service).......	157	40	117	116	12	104
Domestic and personal service...........	**21,967**	**7,741**	**14,226**	**47,416**	**8,671**	**38,745**
Barbers, hairdressers, and manicurists............	3,776	2,004	1,772	499	85	414
Bartenders..................................	1,924	751	1,173	4	..	4
Billiard room, dance hall, skating rink, etc., keepers.	317	118	199	15	4	11
Billiard and pool room keepers.................	280	112	168	3	..	3
Dance hall, skating rink, etc., keepers.........	37	6	31	12	4	8
Boarding and lodging house keepers..............	757	284	473	5,456	1,262	4,194
Bootblacks.................................	22	10	12	..	..	..
Charwomen and cleaners......................	66	17	49	439	110	329
Elevator tenders............................	505	254	251	..	..	..
Hotel keepers and managers....................	1,534	369	1,165	397	72	325
Housekeepers and stewards....................	441	87	354	5,197	1,059	4,138
Janitors and sextons.........................	1,943	604	1,339	298	40	258
Laborers (domestic and professional service)......	981	388	593	45	11	34
Launderers and laundresses (not in laundry).......	102	38	64	3,271	1,186	2,085
Laundry operatives..........................	505	191	314	1,237	305	932
Laundry owners, officials, and managers..........	324	66	258	26	6	20
Midwives..................................	..	..	..	34	11	23
Nurses (not trained).........................	460	54	406	5,748	452	5,296
Porters (except in stores).....................	430	123	307	..	..	..
Restaurant, cafe, and lunch room keepers.........	969	241	728	297	46	251
Saloon keepers..............................	1,381	526	855	20	4	16
Servants...................................	3,895	1,184	2,711	21,251	3,548	17,703
Bell boys, chore boys, etc....................	193	54	139	7	1	6
Coachmen and footmen......................	594	172	422	..	..	..
Chambermaids.............................	..	..	..	815	128	687
Cooks....................................	2,325	746	1,579	3,233	454	2,779
Other servants............................	783	212	571	17,196	2,965	14,231
Waiters....................................	1,219	307	912	3,113	464	2,649
Other pursuits..............................	416	125	291	69	6	63
Bathhouse keepers and attendants..............	52	6	46	23	1	22
Cemetery keepers..........................	92	25	67	..	..	..
Cleaners and renovators (clothing, etc.).........	127	35	92	39	5	34
Umbrella menders and scissors grinders.........	8	4	4	1	..	1
Other occupations..........................	137	55	82	6	..	6

TABLE **101**. CANADIAN-BORN GAINFUL WORKERS 16 YEARS OLD AND OVER IN THE UNITED STATES, BY OCCUPATION AND SEX: 1910—Continued

OCCUPATION	MALE			FEMALE		
	Total	French	English	Total	French	English
Clerical occupations.....................	**17,357**	**2,174**	**15,183**	**9,694**	**820**	**8,874**
Agents, canvassers, and collectors................	1,923	247	1,676	175	28	147
Agents..	1,070	93	977	37	3	34
Canvassers...................................	283	49	234	112	20	92
Collectors...................................	570	105	465	26	5	21
Bookkeepers, cashiers, and accountants..........	5,415	547	4,868	3,604	388	3,216
Clerks (except clerks in stores)...................	8,895	1,215	7,680	1,999	199	1,800
Shipping clerks..............................	1,700	320	1,380	35	3	32
Other clerks.................................	7,195	895	6,300	1,964	196	1,768
Messenger, bundle, and office boys..............	530	117	413	99	24	75
Bundle and cash boys and girls................	19	4	15	57	9	48
Messenger, errand, and office boys.............	511	113	398	42	15	27
Stenographers and typists......................	594	48	546	3,817	181	3,636

CHAPTER XIII

CANADIAN FAMILIES BY TENURE AND VALUE OR RENT OF HOME

THE term "family," as it is used in this discussion, is limited to what might be called private families, excluding the institutions and hotel or boarding house groups which have sometimes been counted as families in the census reports. A family may therefore be defined as a group of persons related either by blood or by marriage or adoption, who live together as one household, usually sharing the same table. Single persons living alone are counted as families, however, as are a few small groups of unrelated persons sharing the same living accommodations as "partners." Households reporting more than 10 lodgers are classified as boarding or lodging houses rather than as families.

A Canadian family, as the term is here used, is a family whose head is a Canadian-born person.[1] These Canadian families, like all families having a foreign-born white person as head, are to a large extent composite with respect to membership, since most of the children, having been born since the parents arrived in the United States, are native. Indeed, in a considerable number of cases, the wife as well as the children may be natives of the United States. This situation explains the relatively large number of foreign-born white families in proportion to the foreign-born white population, or, conversely, the small number of foreign-born white persons per foreign-born white family. Because of this situation, the following tables do not show either the average population per family or any other figures based on the relation between the number of Canadian families in the United States and the number of Canadian-born persons.

The whole number of Canadian families in the United States in 1930 was 460,731, comprising 141,118 French Canadian, and 319,613 English Canadian.

FAMILIES BY TENURE

THE classification by tenure of home is one of the most significant of the various possible classifications of families. Since a home is defined in the United States census reports as the living quarters occupied by a family, the number of homes is always the same as the number of families. In the

1. The tabulations in the 1930 census of the United States relating to families classified by country of birth of head were limited to those made up of white persons. It may be noted, therefore, that Canadian born in this connection means Canadian-born white.

classification by tenure, a home is counted as owned if it is owned wholly or in part by any related member of the family. A home owned by a lodger, however, is counted as rented; in fact, a home is counted as rented if it is not owned by any member of the family, even though no specific cash rental is paid. Living accommodations received as a part of a man's salary or wages, for example, or occupied rent free under any other conditions, are thus counted as rented.

The Canadian families, French and English, in the United States in 1930 are classified by tenure in Table 102, which gives parallel figures for all families in the United States for comparison, and also shows the number and percentage of each class living in urban and rural areas.

TABLE **102**. WHITE CANADIAN FAMILIES IN THE UNITED STATES, FRENCH AND ENGLISH, BY TENURE OF HOME AND BY RESIDENCE (URBAN OR RURAL), WITH DATA FOR ALL FAMILIES, ETC.: 1930

(A Canadian family is a family having a Canadian-born person as its head)

TENURE AND RESIDENCE	ALL CANADIAN FAMILIES		FRENCH CANA-DIAN FAMILIES		ENGLISH CANA-DIAN FAMILIES		ALL FAMILIES IN UNITED STATES		ALL FOREIGN-BORN WHITE FAMILIES IN UNITED STATES	
	Num-ber	Per cent	Num-ber	Per cent	Num-ber	Per cent	Num-ber	Per cent	Num-ber	Per cent
All families..........	460,731	100.0	141,118	100.0	319,613	100.0	29,904,663	100.0	5,736,491	100.0
Owners.............	222,265	48.2	61,227	43.4	161,038	50.4	14,002,074	46.8	2,968,707	51.8
Tenants............	232,169	50.4	78,215	55.4	153,954	48.2	15,319,817	51.2	2,690,300	46.9
Tenure unknown.....	6,297	1.4	1,676	1.2	4,621	1.4	582,772	1.9	77,484	1.4
Families living in—										
Urban areas.........	348,169	75.6	110,721	78.5	237,448	74.3	17,372,524	58.1	4,535,603	79.1
Rural-nonfarm.......	74,031	16.1	21,883	15.5	52,148	16.3	5,927,502	19.8	689,999	12.0
Rural-farm..........	38,531	8.4	8,514	6.0	30,017	9.4	6,604,637	22.1	510,889	8.9

Of the 460,731 Canadian families in the United States in 1930, 222,265, or 48.2 per cent, were living in their own homes, and 232,169, or 50.4 per cent, were living in rented homes, while for 6,297 families, no report was received with respect to tenure of home. The 48.2 per cent which represents the proportion of Canadian families owning their own homes may be compared with 46.8 per cent of all families in the United States, and with 51.8 per cent of all foreign-born white families in the United States—that is, of all families having a foreign-born white person of any nationality as head.

Of the 141,118 French Canadian families in the United States in 1930, 61,227, or 43.4 per cent, owned the homes in which they were living; and of the 319,613 English Canadian families, 161,038, or 50.4 per cent, were living in their own homes. The lower percentage of ownership among the French Canadian families may be in part the result of the fact that a larger fraction of the whole number of these families were living in cities, there being, as will be noted presently, a general tendency toward lower percentages of ownership in cities and much higher percentages of ownership in rural areas and especially on farms.

URBAN AND RURAL AREAS

OF the whole number of Canadian families (French and English together) 348,169, or 75.6 per cent, were living in urban areas, that is, in cities and other incorporated places having 2,500 inhabitants or more; 74,031, or 16.1 per cent, were living in rural-nonfarm areas (that is, outside urban places but still not on farms); and 38,531, or 8.4 per cent, were living in rural-farm areas. For all of the families in the United States, the corresponding percentages were: 58.1 in urban areas; 19.8 in rural-nonfarm; and 22.1 in rural-farm. These figures, however, are rather heavily weighted with families living in Southern States which are primarily agricultural, and which, incidentally, have practically no Canadians living in them. Comparison may also be made with the urban-rural distribution of all foreign-born white families, these being distributed as follows: 79.1 per cent urban; 12.0 per cent rural-nonfarm; and 8.9 per cent rural-farm. Except for the somewhat lower percentage urban and appreciably higher percentage rural-nonfarm, the distribution of the Canadian families follows very closely that of all foreign-born white families.

In Table 103 Canadian families are shown by tenure for urban and rural areas, and in Figure 32 the proportions of homes owned and rented by the families occupying them are presented in graphic form.

TABLE **103**. WHITE CANADIAN FAMILIES IN THE UNITED STATES, FRENCH AND ENGLISH, BY TENURE OF HOME, FOR URBAN AND RURAL AREAS: 1930

[For United States total, see Table 102]

CLASS AND TENURE	URBAN		RURAL-NONFARM		RURAL-FARM		PER CENT OF TOTAL		
	Number	Per cent	Number	Per cent	Number	Per cent	Urban	Rural-nonfarm	Rural-farm
All Canadian families.........	348,169	100.0	74,031	100.0	38,531	100.0	75.6	16.1	8.4
Owners......................	147,252	42.3	44,530	60.2	30,483	79.1	66.3	20.0	13.7
Tenants...	196,879	56.5	28,408	38.4	6,882	17.9	84.8	12.2	3.0
Tenure unknown.	4,038	1.2	1,093	1.5	1,166	3.0	64.1	17.4	18.5
French......................	110,721	100.0	21,883	100.0	8,514	100.0	78.5	15.5	6.0
Owners......................	42,779	38.6	11,556	52.8	6,892	80.9	69.9	18.9	11.3
Tenants.....................	66,778	60.3	10,043	45.9	1,394	16.4	85.4	12.8	1.8
Tenure unknown.............	1,164	1.2	284	1.3	228	2.7	69.5	16.9	13.6
English......................	237,448	100.0	52,148	100.0	30,017	100.0	74.3	16.3	9.4
Owners......................	104,473	44.0	32,974	63.2	23,591	78.6	64.9	20.5	14.6
Tenants.....................	130,101	54.8	18,365	35.2	5,488	18.3	84.5	11.9	3.6
Tenure unknown..............	2,874	1.2	809	1.6	938	3.1	62.2	17.5	20.3

FIGURE 32. CANADIAN FAMILIES, FRENCH AND ENGLISH, BY TENURE OF HOME: 1930

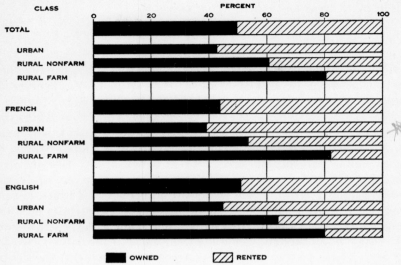

Of the 348,169 Canadian families living in urban areas in the United States in 1930, 147,252, or 42.3 per cent, were living in their own homes; 196,879, or 56.5 per cent, were living in rented homes; and for 4,038 there was no report with respect to home tenure. In rural-nonfarm areas, by way of contrast, 60.2 per cent of the homes were owned, and only 38.4 per cent were rented; and in rural-farm areas, 79.1 per cent, or almost four-fifths of the whole number, were owned by the families living in them, and only 17.9 per cent were returned as rented. The percentages of home ownership among the whole number of foreign-born white families in the United States show similar, though not quite so marked, differences as between urban and rural areas, the percentages of home ownership being 47.0 in urban areas, 64.5 in rural-nonfarm, and 76.6 in rural-farm. For all families in the United States, while the difference between urban and rural areas was considerable, the difference between rural-farm areas and rural-nonfarm was very slight.

The range in the percentages of home ownership as between urban and rural-farm areas among the French Canadian families was far greater than among the English Canadian families. For the former, the range was from 38.6 in urban areas to 80.9 in rural-farm areas; for the latter, from 44.0 in urban areas to 78.6 in rural-farm areas.

While the distribution of the families in the several urban-rural areas by tenure is the fundamental distribution, there may be some interest in a distribution running, so to speak, at right angles with the tenure distribution and showing the percentage of families in each tenure group living in each one of the three areas. Thus, of the tenant families, 84.8 lived in urban areas, while only 3.0 lived in rural-farm areas; while of the owner families, only 66.3 lived in urban areas and 13.7 on farms in rural areas. The general relationship of these figures is similar for the French and the English Canadian families, except that the French families show an even more extreme distribution of tenants, 85.4 per cent being in the urban areas, and only 1.8 per cent on farms.

FARM AND NONFARM FAMILIES

STATISTICS have already been presented both for rural population and for rural families subdivided into two groups designated, respectively, rural-nonfarm and rural-farm. The classification as farm and nonfarm could likewise be made for urban families as well as for rural, though the percentage of farm families in urban areas would be so small as to make the classification ordinarily not worth while. It is needed, however, in order to make a complete explanation of the data on value and monthly rental of homes which are presented in the next section.

The classification of families or population as farm or nonfarm is made on the basis of replies to a question on the population schedule which reads: "Does this family live on a farm?" The classification is therefore based entirely on residence without regard to occupation or any other characteristic of the population. The data for Canadian families in the United States in 1930, classified by tenure, with both urban and rural families further classified as farm and nonfarm, appear in Table 104.

TABLE **104**. WHITE CANADIAN FAMILIES IN THE UNITED STATES, NONFARM AND FARM, URBAN AND RURAL, BY TENURE: 1930

TENURE	TOTAL				URBAN			RURAL		
	Total	Non-farm	Farm	Per cent farm	Total	Non-farm	Farm	Total	Non-farm	Farm
All Canadian families.............	**460,731**	**419,974**	**40,757**	**8.8**	**348,169**	**345,943**	**2,226**	**112,562**	**74,031**	**38,531**
Owners..............	222,265	189,963	32,302	14.5	147,252	145,433	1,819	75,013	44,530	30,483
Tenants.............	232,169	224,919	7,250	3.1	196,879	196,511	368	35,290	28,408	6,882
Tenure unknown......	6,297	5,092	1,205	19.1	4,038	3,999	39	2,259	1,093	1,166
Per cent...........	**100.0**	**100.0**	**100.0**	....	**100.0**	**100.0**	**100.0**	**100.0**	**100.0**	**100.0**
Owners..............	48.2	45.2	79.3	....	42.3	42.0	81.7	66.6	60.2	79.1
Tenants.............	50.4	53.6	17.8	....	56.5	56.8	16.5	31.5	38.4	17.9
Tenure unknown......	1.4	1.2	3.0	....	1.2	1.2	1.8	2.0	1.5	3.0

Of the 348,169 urban Canadian families, only 2,226, or six-tenths of 1 per cent, were living on farms; while of the 112,562 rural Canadian families, 38,531, or 34.2 per cent, were living on farms. Of the whole number of Canadian families, urban and rural together, 8.8 per cent were living on farms; of the owner families, 14.5 per cent; and of the tenant families, 3.1 per cent.

The tenure classification of all Canadian farm families was practically identical with the classification of the rural-farm families already discussed. Of all the nonfarm families taken together, 45.2 per cent were living in homes which they owned, as contrasted with 79.3 per cent of all the farm families.

FAMILIES BY VALUE OR RENT OF HOME

IN the 1930 census of the United States the enumerator was instructed to report on the population schedule for each nonfarm family owning its home the approximate current market value of the home and for each nonfarm family occupying rented quarters, the monthly rental; or if rental was not paid by the month, then the equivalent monthly rental or the approximate rental value per month. The value of the farm homes was obtained on the farm schedule rather than on the population schedule, in order that it might be correlated with other farm census items. Since the farm schedule does not show country of birth, these values cannot be tabulated separately for Canadian farm families.

In the tabulation of the data for foreign-born white families by country of birth from which the figures for Canadian families come, the values have been assembled into six groups and the rentals into five. The figures presented in Tables 105 and 106 represent the number of homes in each of these groups. In Table 105 are presented the figures for Canadian families in the United States occupying owned nonfarm homes, classified by value of home; and in Table 106, corresponding data for Canadian families occupying rented nonfarm homes.

Of the whole number of nonfarm homes occupied by Canadian families in the United States in 1930, 8.3 per cent were valued at less than $1,500; 14.8 per cent at from $1,500 to $2,999; 23.0 per cent at from $3,000 to $4,999; 24.2 per cent at from $5,000 to $7,499; 11.0 per cent at from $7,500 to $9,999; and 17.2 per cent at $10,000 and over. In the classification of homes occupied by French and English Canadian families, respectively, the French families show larger percentages for the three value groups under $5,000, and smaller percentages for the three groups above this figure.

TABLE **105**. WHITE CANADIAN FAMILIES, FRENCH AND ENGLISH, OCCUPYING OWNED NONFARM HOMES, BY VALUE OF HOME, FOR URBAN AND RURAL AREAS: 1930

VALUE	ALL NONFARM FAMILIES			URBAN-NONFARM FAMILIES			RURAL-NONFARM FAMILIES		
	Total	French	English	Total	French	English	Total	French	English
Owned homes*.......	189,963	53,532	136,431	145,433	41,976	103,457	44,530	11,556	32,974
Value of home:									
Under $1,500.........	15,856	5,247	10,609	5,670	2,269	3,401	10,186	2,978	7,208
$1,500 to $2,999.....	28,112	9,717	18,395	16,298	6,421	9,877	11,814	3,296	8,518
$3,000 to $4,999.....	43,689	14,558	29,131	32,864	11,654	21,210	10,825	2,904	7,921
$5,000 to $7,499.....	45,915	12,515	33,400	39,556	11,048	28,508	6,359	1,467	4,892
$7,500 to $9,999.....	20,961	4,756	16,205	19,363	4,446	14,917	1,598	310	1,288
$10,000 and over......	32,669	5,998	26,671	30,120	5,649	24,471	2,549	349	2,200
Not reported.........	2,761	741	2,020	1,562	489	1,073	1,199	252	947
Per cent.............	100.0	100.0	100.0	100.0	100.0	100.0	100.0	100.0	100.0
Under $1,500.........	8.3	9.8	7.8	3.9	5.4	3.3	22.9	25.8	21.9
$1,500 to $2,999.....	14.8	18.2	13.5	11.2	15.3	9.5	26.5	28.5	25.8
$3,000 to $4,999.....	23.0	27.2	21.4	22.6	27.8	20.5	24.3	25.1	24.0
$5,000 to $7,499.....	24.2	23.4	24.5	27.2	26.3	27.6	14.3	12.7	14.8
$7,500 to $9,999.....	11.0	8.9	11.9	13.3	10.6	14.4	3.6	2.7	3.9
$10,000 and over......	17.2	11.2	19.5	20.7	13.5	23.7	5.7	3.0	6.7
Not reported.........	1.5	1.4	1.5	1.1	1.2	1.0	2.7	2.2	2.9
Median value..........	$5,324	$4,570	$5,679	$6,081	$5,090	$6,465	$2,958	$2,717	$3,070

*Omitting the 1,819 urban owner families living on farms. See Table 104.

TABLE **106**. WHITE CANADIAN FAMILIES, FRENCH AND ENGLISH, OCCUPYING RENTED NONFARM HOMES, BY MONTHLY RENTAL OF HOME, FOR URBAN AND RURAL AREAS: 1930

MONTHLY RENTAL	ALL NONFARM FAMILIES			URBAN-NONFARM FAMILIES*			RURAL-NONFARM FAMILIES		
	Total	French	English	Total	French	English	Total	French	English
Rented homes........	224,919	76,707	148,212	196,511	66,664	129,847	28,408	10,043	18,365
Monthly rental:									
Under $15...........	28,847	16,160	12,687	15,938	10,412	5,526	12,909	5,748	7,161
$15 to $29...........	76,914	38,268	38,646	66,223	34,812	31,411	10,691	3,456	7,235
$30 to $49...........	69,603	16,307	53,296	66,712	15,820	50,892	2,891	487	2,404
$50 to $99...........	40,745	4,644	36,101	39,966	4,537	35,429	779	107	672
$100 and over........	4,919	464	4,455	4,768	450	4,318	151	14	137
Not reported.........	3,891	864	3,027	2,904	633	2,271	987	231	756
Per cent.............	100.0	100.0	100.0	100.0	100.0	100.0	100.0	100.0	100.0
Under $15...........	12.8	21.1	8.6	8.1	15.6	4.3	45.4	57.2	39.0
$15 to $29...........	34.2	49.9	26.1	33.7	52.2	24.2	37.6	34.4	39.4
$30 to $49...........	30.9	21.3	36.0	33.9	23.7	39.2	10.2	4.8	13.1
$50 to $99...........	18.1	6.1	24.4	20.3	6.8	27.3	2.7	1.1	3.7
$100 and over........	2.2	0.6	3.0	2.4	0.7	3.3	0.5	0.1	0.7
Not reported.........	1.7	1.1	2.0	1.5	0.9	1.7	3.5	2.3	4.1
Median rental..........	$31.37	$23.53	$37.98	$34.39	$24.74	$40.55	$16.12	(†)	$18.41

*Omitting the 368 urban tenant families living on farms. See Table 104.
†Median rental less than $15.00.

Because of the very considerable difference in home values as between cities and rural areas, the figures for urban areas or for rural areas taken alone are perhaps more significant than those representing all the Canadian families in the United States. The whole number of urban nonfarm Canadian families in the United States in 1930 was 145,433, of which 5,670, or 3.9 per cent, occupied homes valued at less than $1,500; 16,298, or 11.2 per cent of the homes were valued at from $1,500 to $2,999;

32,864, or 22.6 per cent, from $3,000 to $4,999; 39,556, or 27.2 per cent, at from $5,000 to $7,499 (this being the largest of the six groups); 19,363, or 13.3 per cent, at $7,500 to $9,999; and 30,120, or 20.7 per cent, at $10,000 or over. In this classification again, materially larger percentages of the homes occupied by French Canadian families than of the English were found in the lower value groups, and correspondingly smaller percentages in the higher value groups. For example, 5.4 per cent of the homes occupied by French Canadian families were valued at less than $1,500, as compared with 3.3 per cent of the homes of the English Canadian families; and at the other end of the scale, only 13.5 per cent of the French Canadian homes were valued at $10,000 and over, as compared with 23.7 per cent of the English Canadian homes.

Since the value of homes in the small villages and in the open country is in general very much lower, even for physically identical accommodations, the distribution of the rural-nonfarm homes by value, both for the English Canadian families and the French, was radically different from that of the urban homes, and incidentally, the differences as between the French and the English were very much less marked. There were in all 44,530 rural-nonfarm homes occupied by Canadian families in the United States, of which 10,186, or 22.9 per cent, were valued at less than $1,500; 11,814, or 26.5 per cent, at from $1,500 to $2,999 (this being the largest single group in the classification); 10,825, or 24.3 per cent, were valued at from $3,000 to $4,999; 6,359, or 14.3 per cent, at from $5,000 to $7,499; and much smaller numbers in the higher value groups.

While there are no statistics available with respect to the values of the farm homes, it may be stated in general that the values of farm homes in the United States run very much lower than the values of nonfarm homes in the same rural areas.

Of the nonfarm Canadian families in the United States occupying rented homes, 12.8 per cent reported a monthly rental under $15; 34.2 per cent reported a rental of from $15 to $29; 30.9 per cent, from $30 to $49; 18.1 per cent, from $50 to $99; and 2.2 per cent paid $100 and over. The percentages of the French Canadian families reporting rentals under $30 were very much higher than the corresponding percentages for the English Canadian families, while of the latter, much larger percentages reported monthly rentals of from $30 to $99, the number of either French or English families reporting rentals of more than $100 being very small.

As in the case of values, the current monthly rentals of urban homes are much higher than the rentals of rural homes. The more significant figures relating to home rentals are, therefore, those presenting the classifications of urban and rural homes separately. The whole number of urban Canadian families occupying rented nonfarm homes was 196,511;

of this number, 15,938, or 8.1 per cent, paid a monthly rental of less than $15; 66,223, or 33.7 per cent, paid from $15 to $29; 66,712, or practically the same number, paid from $30 to $49; 39,966, or 20.3 per cent, paid from $50 to $99; and only 4,768, or 2.4 per cent, paid $100 or over. Comparing the urban French Canadian families with the urban English Canadian families, it may be noted that 15.6 per cent of the former, as compared with 4.3 per cent of the latter, paid rentals under $15; 52.2 per cent of the French, as compared with 24.2 per cent of the English, paid rentals between $15 and $29; while only 23.7 per cent of the French families, as compared with 39.2 per cent of the English, paid rentals from $30 to $49; and only 6.8 per cent of the French, as compared with 27.3 per cent of the English, paid from $50 to $99.

Of the 28,408 rural Canadian families occupying rented nonfarm homes in the United States, 45.4 per cent paid a monthly rental of less than $15; 37.6 per cent paid from $15 to $29; 10.2 per cent paid from $30 to $49; and only 3.3 per cent paid $50 or more.

Of the French Canadian families in rural-nonfarm areas, 57.2 per cent occupied homes for which they paid less than $15 a month rent, as compared with 39.0 per cent of the English, while in all the rental groups above $15 the percentage shown for the English Canadian families was higher than that shown for the French—in most cases two or three times as high.

In addition to the classification of nonfarm homes into various groups based on value or rental, there are presented in Tables 105 and 106, for the various population classes, the median value of owned homes and the median rental of rented homes. The median value is the value of the home which would stand in the middle of the series if all of the homes were arranged according to value, beginning with the lowest and ending with the highest.[2] To compute the median exactly, it would be necessary to have

2. Medians are computed in accordance with the following formula:

$$M = L + \frac{\left(\frac{N}{2} - k\right)c}{f}$$

in which
 M = the median.
 L = the lowest value in the median group—the group in which the median or middle item (family) falls.
 N = the whole number of items (families).
 k = the number of items (families) in the groups preceding the median group.
 c = the group interval. (In the computations for median size of family, $c = 1$.)
 f = the number of items (families) in the median group.

In computing the median value (or rental), families not reporting value (or rental) are excluded from the computation; that is, N = number of families reporting value (or rental).

In computing the median size of family, since the families grouped according to size the data in much smaller groups than those available from the existing tabulations. It would be desirable, that is, to know at least the numbers of homes reporting rental of $20, $21, $22, etc., instead of only the numbers reporting rent between $15 and $19, $20 and $29, etc. There is, therefore, some degree of approximation in the medians presented in the accompanying tables. It is believed, however, that this is not great enough to interfere with the significance of the figures.

It is not possible from the data available to compute the arithmetical average of the value, since no definite total value can be assigned to the first value group (under $1,500), or of the last ($10,000 and over); and likewise with the monthly rental. The median is therefore the most practicable and useful of the summary figures that could be computed, and gives a definite idea of the relation between home values in urban and rural areas, for example, much more quickly than such an idea can be obtained from comparing either the figures themselves or the percentage distributions.

The median value of all owned nonfarm homes occupied by Canadian families in 1930 was $5,324; for the urban homes included in this total the median was $6,081, and for the rural homes, $2,958. The median value of all nonfarm homes occupied by French Canadian owner families was $4,570, as compared with $5,679 for English Canadian owners. The corresponding figures for urban homes alone were $5,090 for French families and $6,465 for English; and for rural homes alone, $2,717 for French and $3,070 for English, the difference between the French and English being, as already noted, materially less in rural areas than in urban.

The median monthly rental of all rented nonfarm homes occupied by Canadian families in the United States in 1930 was $31.37, the median rental of the urban homes alone being $34.39 and of the rural homes alone, $16.12. For all rented homes occupied by French Canadian families the median rental was $23.53, as compared with $37.98 for English Canadian families. The corresponding figures for Canadian families in urban areas were $24.74 for the French and $40.55 for the English; and in rural areas, "less than $15.00" for the French and $18.41 for the English.

The median values of homes occupied by Canadian families, French and English, in urban and rural-nonfarm areas are shown in graphic form in Figure 33. In this graph the extent of the difference in home values between urban and rural-nonfarm areas, to which reference has been made above, is brought out very effectively. The bar outlined with broken lines represents a rough estimate of the median value of homes in the rural-

constitute a discrete series, it is necessary to assume that the group value stands in the middle of the group. This means that when the median is in the 3-family group, for example, the lower and upper limits of the group are assumed to be 2½ and 3½, respectively, whence $L = 2\frac{1}{2}$.

farm area. No statistics are available to show directly the value of rural-farm homes occupied by Canadian families, and the length of this bar represents an approximation derived from values available for all farm homes in the United States, considered in combination with the relation between values for Canadian families and values for all families in areas for which both sets of figures are available.

FIGURE **33**. MEDIAN VALUE OF OWNED HOMES OCCUPIED BY CANADIAN FAMILIES, FRENCH AND ENGLISH: 1930

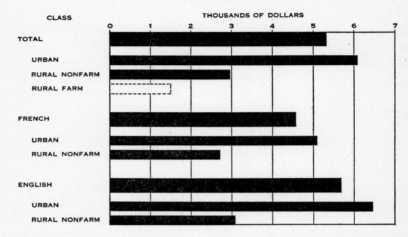

In Figure 34 are presented in corresponding form the median rentals of rented farm homes occupied by Canadian families, French and English, in urban and rural-nonfarm areas.

FIGURE **34**. MEDIAN MONTHLY RENT OF RENTED HOMES OCCUPIED BY CANADIAN FAMILIES, FRENCH AND ENGLISH: 1930

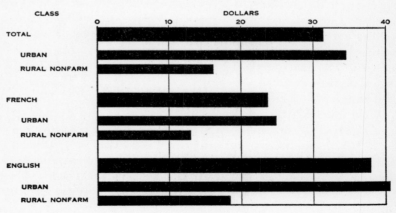

DATA on the number of white Canadian families, with classification by tenure and value or rent of home, are presented by States in five tables as follows, with separate figures for French and English families in all cases: In Table 107, the number of families, with number and percentage French and English and number and percentage home owners and tenants; in Table 108, families classified as living in urban, rural-nonfarm, or rural-farm areas in each State; in Table 109 (29 States only), families classified by tenure in combination with urban or rural residence; and in Tables 110 and 111 (29 States only), home-owner families classified by value of home and tenant families classified by monthly rental, with median value or rental not only for all families in each State but also for those in urban and rural-nonfarm areas. The last two tables are limited to nonfarm families, since no separate tabulation of value or rental of homes was made in the 1930 census for farm families.

When the relative proportions of French and English Canadian families in the various States are compared it will be noticed that the relationship is almost the same as that observed in the total Canadian-born population as shown in Table 29. There are a few striking differences, however, as in the case of Massachusetts where 44.0 per cent of all Canadian families were French, while only 40.0 per cent of the Canadian born were French. In most of the States, however, the proportion French among all Canadian families is slightly lower than the proportion French among all Canadian-born persons.

Considerable variation appears in the relative proportions of Canadian families living in owned homes and in rented homes in the various States. This variation appears to be due principally to differences in the proportions living in urban and rural areas, as shown in Table 108. In this respect, Maine, where 51.2 per cent of the families were home owners, may be compared with Massachusetts, where only 38.6 per cent of the families were home owners. The respective proportions of the Canadian families living in urban areas in these States were 53.6 per cent and 91.9 per cent. The same relationship obtains in the cases of other pairs of States, as for example, Michigan and Illinois, and Washington and California.

While there is little difference in the proportions of French and English Canadian families living in urban areas for the country as a whole, Table 108 shows striking variations in the pattern of settlement in the different States. In Maine, New Hampshire, and Vermont, for example, a far greater proportion of the French than of the English Canadian families live in urban areas, while in other areas of heavy settlement, such as Massachusetts, Rhode Island, Illinois, Ohio, and Michigan, the proportions of the two groups living in urban areas are about the same. In Connecticut, Minnesota, Washington, and California, on the other hand, a larger proportion of the English Canadian families live in urban areas.

The data presented in Table 109 make possible the comparison of the relative proportions of home owners among French and English Canadian families in the three residence areas in each State. In the majority of the cases where the numbers are large enough to make comparisons valid, the proportion of home owners is higher among English than among French Canadian families in urban and rural-nonfarm areas, and higher among French than among English Canadian families in rural-farm areas.

Tables 110 and 111, which give the median value of owned homes and the median rental of rented homes in urban and rural-nonfarm areas, show higher figures in almost every State for English Canadian families than for French Canadian families in corresponding areas. The only important exception is the State of Maine, where the median value of homes owned by French Canadian families is greater than that shown for the English Canadians. Although the differences between the French and English Canadian families in this respect are consistently in the same direction (except in Maine), there are large variations between States in the value of homes owned or the rental paid, resulting from variations in local conditions.

TABLE **107**. WHITE CANADIAN FAMILIES, FRENCH AND ENGLISH, BY TENURE OF HOME, BY STATES: 1930

STATE	All Cana-dian families	FRENCH		ENGLISH		BY TENURE OF HOME					
						Owners		Tenants		Tenure unknown	
		Number	Per cent	Number	Per cent	Number	Per cent	Number	Per cent	Number	Per cent
United States	460,731	141,118	30.6	319,613	69.4	222,265	48.2	232,169	50.4	6,297	1.4
NEW ENGLAND:											
Maine	27,271	13,545	49.7	13,726	50.3	13,964	51.2	12,886	47.3	421	1.5
New Hampshire	19,864	14,795	74.5	5,069	25.5	9,578	48.2	10,092	50.8	194	1.0
Vermont	9,209	5,599	60.8	3,610	39.2	5,320	57.8	3,808	41.4	81	0.9
Massachusetts	103,097	45,394	44.0	57,703	56.0	39,805	38.6	62,234	60.4	1,058	1.0
Rhode Island	14,833	12,161	82.0	2,672	18.0	5,306	35.8	9,407	63.4	120	0.8
Connecticut	13,054	8,913	68.3	4,141	31.7	3,700	28.3	9,213	70.6	141	1.1
MIDDLE ATLANTIC:											
New York	47,261	9,479	20.1	37,782	79.9	19,329	40.9	27,366	57.9	566	1.2
New Jersey	5,186	789	15.2	4,397	84.8	2,238	43.2	2,879	55.5	69	1.3
Pennsylvania	5,536	642	11.6	4,894	88.4	2,668	48.2	2,785	50.3	83	1.5
E. N. CENTRAL:											
Ohio	9,604	999	10.4	8,605	89.6	4,626	48.2	4,881	50.8	97	1.0
Indiana	2,267	275	12.1	1,992	87.9	1,232	54.3	1,000	44.1	35	1.5
Illinois	15,613	2,362	15.1	13,251	84.9	6,277	40.2	9,175	58.8	161	1.0
Michigan	72,637	10,795	14.9	61,842	85.1	41,781	57.5	29,845	41.1	1,011	1.4
Wisconsin	6,802	2,111	31.0	4,691	69.0	4,468	65.7	2,237	32.9	97	1.4
W. N. CENTRAL:											
Minnesota	11,326	3,039	26.8	8,287	73.2	7,293	64.4	3,866	34.1	167	1.5
Iowa	2,925	287	9.8	2,638	90.2	2,032	69.5	852	29.1	41	1.4
Missouri	2,281	253	11.1	2,028	88.9	1,266	55.5	964	42.3	51	2.2
North Dakota	5,366	655	12.2	4,711	87.8	3,633	67.7	1,521	28.3	212	4.0
South Dakota	1,544	249	16.1	1,295	83.9	1,038	67.2	479	31.0	27	1.7
Nebraska	1,941	199	10.3	1,742	89.7	1,371	70.6	520	26.8	50	2.6
Kansas	1,857	285	15.3	1,572	84.7	1,379	74.3	454	24.4	24	1.3
SOUTH ATLANTIC:											
Delaware	153	19	12.4	134	87.6	76	49.7	72	47.1	5	3.3
Maryland	698	85	12.2	613	87.8	363	52.0	326	46.7	9	1.3
Dist. Columbia	526	72	13.7	454	86.3	191	36.3	324	61.6	11	2.1
Virginia	543	58	10.7	485	89.3	280	51.6	259	47.7	4	0.7
West Virginia	320	36	11.3	284	88.8	131	40.9	181	56.6	8	2.5
North Carolina	321	28	8.7	293	91.3	155	48.3	157	48.9	9	2.8
South Carolina	96	11	11.5	85	88.5	38	39.6	52	54.2	6	6.3
Georgia	363	40	11.0	323	89.0	142	39.1	211	58.1	10	2.8
Florida	3,079	388	12.6	2,691	87.4	1,719	55.8	1,279	41.5	81	2.6
E. S. CENTRAL:											
Kentucky	373	42	11.3	331	88.7	196	52.5	172	46.1	5	1.3
Tennessee	384	36	9.4	348	90.6	208	54.2	162	42.2	14	3.6
Alabama	354	40	11.3	314	88.7	181	51.1	167	47.2	6	1.7
Mississippi	156	21	13.5	135	86.5	85	54.5	61	39.1	10	6.4
W. S. CENTRAL:											
Arkansas	318	34	10.7	284	89.3	185	58.2	131	41.2	2	0.6
Louisiana	416	98	23.6	318	76.4	180	43.3	227	54.6	9	2.2
Oklahoma	964	114	11.8	850	88.2	592	61.4	352	36.5	20	2.1
Texas	1,810	180	9.9	1,630	90.1	997	55.1	766	42.3	47	2.6
MOUNTAIN:											
Montana	4,456	901	20.2	3,555	79.8	2,676	60.1	1,647	37.0	133	3.0
Idaho	1,853	275	14.8	1,578	85.2	1,153	62.2	657	35.5	43	2.3
Wyoming	458	65	14.2	393	85.8	251	54.8	192	41.9	15	3.3
Colorado	2,634	270	10.3	2,364	89.7	1,659	63.0	920	34.9	55	2.1
New Mexico	272	32	11.8	240	88.2	158	58.1	111	40.8	3	1.1
Arizona	840	81	9.6	759	90.4	432	51.4	386	46.0	22	2.6
Utah	469	49	10.4	420	89.6	270	57.6	193	41.2	6	1.3
Nevada	416	68	16.3	348	83.7	226	54.3	181	43.5	9	2.2
PACIFIC:											
Washington	16,709	1,731	10.4	14,978	89.6	10,075	60.3	6,273	37.5	361	2.2
Oregon	6,295	555	8.8	5,740	91.2	3,773	59.9	2,410	38.3	112	1.8
California	35,981	2,963	8.2	33,018	91.8	17,569	48.8	17,836	49.6	576	1.6

TABLE **108**. WHITE CANADIAN FAMILIES, FRENCH AND ENGLISH, IN URBAN AND RURAL AREAS, BY STATES: 1930

[Per cent not shown where base is less than 100]

DIVISION AND STATE	TOTAL			FRENCH			ENGLISH			PER CENT URBAN		
	Urban	Rural-non-farm	Rural-farm	Urban	Rural-non-farm	Rural-farm	Urban	Rural-non-farm	Rural-farm	Total	Fr.	Eng.
United States.	348,169	74,031	38,531	110,721	21,883	8,514	237,448	52,148	30,017	75.6	78.5	74.3
NEW ENGLAND:												
Maine.........	14,627	9,531	3,113	8,949	3,886	710	5,678	5,645	2,403	53.6	66.1	41.4
New Hampshire..	14,218	4,477	1,169	11,668	2,651	476	2,550	1,826	693	71.6	78.9	50.3
Vermont........	3,358	3,003	2,848	2,217	1,524	1,858	1,141	1,479	990	36.5	39.6	31.6
Massachusetts...	94,700	7,242	1,155	41,668	3,204	522	53,032	4,038	633	91.9	91.8	91.9
Rhode Island....	14,018	727	88	11,498	597	66	2,520	130	22	94.5	94.5	94.3
Connecticut.....	9,149	3,558	347	6,168	2,526	219	2,981	1,032	128	70.1	69.2	72.0
MIDDLE ATLANTIC:												
New York......	37,046	6,919	3,296	6,948	1,771	760	30,098	5,148	2,536	78.4	73.3	79.7
New Jersey......	4,458	643	85	692	88	9	3,766	555	76	86.0	87.7	85.6
Pennsylvania....	4,459	846	231	523	105	14	3,936	741	217	80.5	81.5	80.4
E.N. CENTRAL:												
Ohio...........	8,331	993	280	854	118	27	7,477	875	253	86.7	85.5	86.9
Indiana........	1,822	304	141	201	59	15	1,621	245	126	80.4	73.1	81.4
Illinois........	14,398	954	261	2,136	184	42	12,262	770	219	92.2	90.4	92.5
Michigan.......	52,531	10,847	9,259	7,917	1,709	1,169	44,614	9,138	8,090	72.3	73.3	72.1
Wisconsin......	4,263	1,454	1,085	1,326	428	357	2,937	1,026	728	62.7	62.8	62.6
W.N. CENTRAL:												
Minnesota.......	7,564	1,960	1,802	1,913	541	585	5,651	1,419	1,217	66.8	62.9	68.2
Iowa...........	1,577	862	486	172	69	46	1,405	793	440	53.9	59.9	53.3
Missouri........	1,641	380	260	174	53	26	1,467	327	234	71.9	68.8	72.3
North Dakota...	1,068	2,012	2,286	122	223	310	946	1,789	1,976	19.9	18.6	20.1
South Dakota....	507	571	466	48	110	91	459	461	375	32.8	19.3	35.4
Nebraska........	859	654	428	80	66	53	779	588	375	44.3	40.2	44.7
Kansas.........	749	577	531	104	95	86	645	482	445	40.3	36.5	41.0
SOUTH ATLANTIC:												
Delaware.......	75	52	26	10	7	2	65	45	24	49.0	....	48.5
Maryland.......	449	188	61	58	25	2	391	163	59	64.3	....	63.8
Dist. Columbia...	526	...	...	72	...	...	454	...	...	100.0	....	100.0
Virginia........	313	160	70	32	19	7	281	141	63	57.6	....	57.9
West Virginia....	201	96	23	18	15	3	183	81	20	62.8	....	64.4
North Carolina..	196	101	24	14	12	2	182	89	22	61.1	....	62.1
South Carolina...	61	24	11	10	...	1	51	24	10	....	....	....
Georgia.........	262	74	27	29	10	1	233	64	26	72.2	....	72.1
Florida.........	2,115	741	223	259	90	39	1,856	651	184	68.7	66.8	69.0
E.S. CENTRAL:												
Kentucky.......	288	67	18	33	7	2	255	60	16	77.2	....	77.0
Tennessee.......	304	46	34	32	3	1	272	43	33	79.2	....	78.2
Alabama........	223	84	47	25	5	10	198	79	37	63.0	....	63.1
Mississippi......	95	39	22	11	7	3	84	32	19	60.9	....	62.2
W.S. CENTRAL:												
Arkansas........	164	77	77	22	9	3	142	68	74	51.6	....	50.0
Louisiana.......	292	84	40	57	31	10	235	53	30	70.2	....	73.9
Oklahoma.......	567	200	197	65	26	23	502	174	174	58.8	57.0	59.1
Texas...........	1,313	283	214	130	36	14	1,183	247	200	72.5	72.2	72.6
MOUNTAIN:												
Montana........	1,785	1,364	1,307	367	277	257	1,418	1,087	1,050	40.1	40.7	39.9
Idaho..........	698	707	448	111	95	69	587	612	379	37.7	40.4	37.2
Wyoming.......	177	172	109	27	20	18	150	152	91	38.6	....	38.2
Colorado........	1,691	540	403	156	69	45	1,535	471	358	64.2	57.8	64.9
New Mexico.....	143	88	41	17	11	4	126	77	37	52.6	....	52.5
Arizona.........	427	341	72	41	32	8	386	309	64	50.8	....	50.9
Utah...........	366	68	35	39	6	4	327	62	31	78.0	....	77.9
Nevada.........	171	210	35	28	34	6	143	176	29	41.1	....	41.1
PACIFIC:												
Washington.....	10,856	3,567	2,286	1,027	409	295	9,829	3,158	1,991	65.0	59.3	65.6
Oregon.........	3,948	1,392	955	319	142	94	3,629	1,250	861	62.7	57.5	63.2
California.......	29,120	4,752	2,109	2,334	479	150	26,786	4,273	1,959	80.9	78.8	81.1

TABLE **109**. WHITE CANADIAN FAMILIES, FRENCH AND ENGLISH, IN URBAN AND RURAL AREAS, BY TENURE, FOR 29 SELECTED STATES: 1930

(Per cent not shown where base is less than 100)

STATE AND CLASS	URBAN				RURAL-NONFARM				RURAL-FARM			
	Total	Owners Number	Owners Per cent	Tenants	Total	Owners Number	Owners Per cent	Tenants	Total	Owners Number	Owners Per cent	Tenants
United States..	**348,169**	**147,252**	**42.3**	**196,879**	**74,031**	**44,530**	**60.2**	**28,408**	**38,531**	**30,483**	**79.1**	**6,882**
French......	110,721	42,779	38.6	66,778	21,883	11,556	52.8	10,043	8,514	6,892	80.9	1,394
English......	237,448	104,473	44.0	130,101	52,148	32,974	63.2	18,365	30,017	23,591	78.6	5,488
Maine.........	**14,627**	**6,243**	**42.7**	**8,202**	**9,531**	**5,203**	**54.6**	**4,205**	**3,113**	**2,518**	**80.9**	**479**
French.......	8,949	3,597	40.2	5,251	3,886	2,032	52.3	1,799	710	587	82.7	103
English.......	5,678	2,646	46.6	2,951	5,645	3,171	56.2	2,406	2,403	1,931	80.4	376
New Hampshire.	**14,218**	**6,113**	**43.0**	**7,972**	**4,477**	**2,441**	**54.5**	**1,988**	**1,169**	**1,024**	**87.6**	**132**
French.......	11,668	4,902	42.0	6,661	2,651	1,403	52.9	1,222	476	433	91.0	40
English.......	2,550	1,211	47.5	1,311	1,826	1,038	56.8	766	693	591	85.3	92
Vermont........	**3,358**	**1,445**	**43.0**	**1,884**	**3,003**	**1,469**	**48.9**	**1,511**	**2,848**	**2,406**	**84.5**	**413**
French.......	2,217	944	42.6	1,254	1,524	699	45.9	812	1,858	1,550	83.4	289
English.......	1,141	501	43.9	630	1,479	770	52.1	699	990	856	86.5	124
Massachusetts...	**94,700**	**34,572**	**36.5**	**59,179**	**7,242**	**4,282**	**59.1**	**2,876**	**1,155**	**951**	**82.3**	**179**
French.......	41,668	14,955	35.9	26,298	3,204	1,759	54.9	1,413	522	465	89.1	48
English.......	53,032	19,617	37.0	32,881	4,038	2,523	62.5	1,463	633	486	76.8	131
Rhode Island....	**14,018**	**4,942**	**35.3**	**8,958**	**727**	**294**	**40.4**	**432**	**88**	**70**	**....**	**17**
French.......	11,498	4,002	34.8	7,404	597	234	39.2	362	66	55	....	11
English.......	2,520	940	37.3	1,554	130	60	46.2	70	22	15	....	6
Connecticut.....	**9,149**	**2,169**	**23.7**	**6,868**	**3,558**	**1,269**	**35.7**	**2,264**	**347**	**262**	**75.5**	**81**
French.......	6,168	1,360	22.0	4,733	2,526	764	30.2	1,748	219	176	80.4	39
English.......	2,981	809	27.1	2,135	1,032	505	48.9	516	128	86	67.2	42
New York......	**37,046**	**13,119**	**35.4**	**23,507**	**6,919**	**3,992**	**57.7**	**2,835**	**3,296**	**2,218**	**67.3**	**1,024**
French.......	6,948	2,292	33.0	4,585	1,771	882	49.8	863	760	515	67.8	231
English.......	30,098	10,827	36.0	18,922	5,148	3,110	60.4	1,972	2,536	1,703	67.2	793
New Jersey.....	**4,458**	**1,789**	**40.1**	**2,615**	**643**	**388**	**60.3**	**242**	**85**	**61**	**....**	**22**
French.......	692	210	30.3	468	88	52	....	35	9	6	....	2
English.......	3,766	1,579	41.9	2,147	555	336	60.5	207	76	55	....	20
Pennsylvania....	**4,459**	**2,041**	**45.8**	**2,355**	**846**	**462**	**54.6**	**372**	**231**	**165**	**71.4**	**58**
French.......	523	203	38.8	310	105	48	45.7	55	14	11	....	2
English.......	3,936	1,838	46.7	2,045	741	414	55.9	317	217	154	71.0	56
Ohio..........	**8,331**	**3,775**	**45.3**	**4,473**	**993**	**631**	**63.5**	**353**	**280**	**220**	**78.6**	**55**
French.......	854	388	45.4	458	118	78	66.1	37	27	21	....	4
English.......	7,477	3,387	45.3	4,015	875	553	63.2	316	253	199	78.7	51
Indiana........	**1,822**	**924**	**50.7**	**873**	**304**	**203**	**66.8**	**97**	**141**	**105**	**74.5**	**30**
French.......	201	111	55.2	87	59	43	....	14	15	9	....	5
English.......	1,621	813	50.2	786	245	160	65.3	83	126	96	76.2	25
Illinois........	**14,398**	**5,414**	**37.6**	**8,844**	**954**	**701**	**73.5**	**238**	**261**	**162**	**62.1**	**93**
French.......	2,136	838	39.2	1,273	184	138	75.0	43	42	26	....	15
English.......	12,262	4,576	37.3	7,571	770	563	73.1	195	219	136	62.1	78
Michigan.......	**52,531**	**25,802**	**49.1**	**26,104**	**10,847**	**8,037**	**74.1**	**2,677**	**9,259**	**7,942**	**85.8**	**1,064**
French.......	7,917	3,949	49.9	3,873	1,709	1,210	70.8	473	1,169	1,007	86.1	121
English.......	44,614	21,853	49.0	22,231	9,138	6,827	74.7	2,204	8,090	6,935	85.7	943
Wisconsin......	**4,263**	**2,479**	**58.2**	**1,737**	**1,454**	**1,024**	**70.4**	**402**	**1,085**	**965**	**88.9**	**98**
French.......	1,326	828	62.4	484	428	289	67.5	129	357	329	92.2	21
English.......	2,937	1,651	56.2	1,253	1,026	735	71.6	273	728	636	87.4	77
Minnesota......	**7,564**	**4,496**	**59.4**	**3,002**	**1,960**	**1,387**	**70.8**	**545**	**1,802**	**1,410**	**78.2**	**319**
French.......	1,913	1,189	62.2	709	541	394	72.8	139	585	464	79.3	86
English.......	5,651	3,307	58.5	2,293	1,419	993	70.0	406	1,217	946	77.7	233
Iowa..........	**1,577**	**1,019**	**64.6**	**540**	**862**	**678**	**78.7**	**175**	**486**	**335**	**68.9**	**137**
French.......	172	97	56.4	70	69	53	....	15	46	19	....	26
English.......	1,405	922	65.6	470	793	625	78.8	160	440	316	71.8	111
Missouri........	**1,641**	**797**	**48.6**	**808**	**380**	**260**	**68.4**	**111**	**260**	**209**	**80.4**	**45**
French.......	174	74	42.5	96	53	33	....	20	26	22	....	3
English.......	1,467	723	49.3	712	327	227	69.4	91	234	187	79.9	42
North Dakota....	**1,068**	**648**	**60.7**	**402**	**2,012**	**1,407**	**69.9**	**556**	**2,286**	**1,578**	**69.0**	**563**
French.......	122	68	55.7	50	223	150	67.3	69	310	213	68.7	83
English.......	946	580	61.3	352	1,789	1,257	70.3	487	1,976	1,365	69.1	480

TABLE **109**. WHITE CANADIAN FAMILIES, FRENCH AND ENGLISH, IN URBAN AND RURAL AREAS, BY TENURE, FOR 29 SELECTED STATES: 1930—Continued

(Per cent not shown where base is less than 100)

STATE AND CLASS	URBAN				RURAL-NONFARM				RURAL-FARM			
	Total	Owners		Tenants	Total	Owners		Tenants	Total	Owners		Tenants
		Number	Per cent			Number	Per cent			Number	Per cent	
South Dakota...	507	325	64.1	178	571	402	70.4	159	466	311	66.7	142
French.........	48	27	....	21	110	86	78.2	21	91	61	....	27
English........	459	298	64.9	157	461	316	68.5	138	375	250	66.7	115
Nebraska.......	859	567	66.0	277	654	503	76.9	136	428	301	70.3	107
French.........	80	43	....	35	66	49	....	14	53	25	....	24
English........	779	524	67.3	242	588	454	77.2	122	375	276	73.6	83
Kansas.........	749	520	69.4	223	577	444	76.9	125	531	415	78.2	106
French.........	104	70	67.3	32	95	81	....	13	86	63	....	22
English........	645	450	69.8	191	482	363	75.3	112	445	352	79.1	84
Florida.........	2,115	1,058	50.0	1,005	741	473	63.8	246	223	188	84.3	28
French.........	259	120	46.3	134	90	53	....	33	39	33	....	5
English........	1,856	938	50.5	871	651	420	64.5	213	184	155	84.2	23
Texas...........	1,313	675	51.4	612	283	153	54.1	114	214	169	79.0	40
French.........	130	55	42.3	71	36	15	....	18	14	11	....	2
English........	1,183	620	52.4	541	247	138	55.9	96	200	158	79.0	38
Montana........	1,785	1,022	57.3	748	1,364	754	55.3	575	1,307	900	68.9	324
French.........	367	226	61.6	136	277	168	60.6	101	257	192	74.7	52
English........	1,418	796	56.1	612	1,087	586	53.9	474	1,050	708	67.4	272
Idaho..........	698	417	59.7	272	707	381	53.9	307	448	355	79.2	78
French.........	111	79	71.2	32	95	59	....	35	69	55	....	13
English........	587	338	57.6	240	612	322	52.6	272	379	300	79.2	65
Colorado.......	1,691	999	59.1	664	540	363	67.2	168	403	297	73.7	88
French.........	156	85	54.5	66	69	39	....	27	45	34	....	8
English........	1,535	914	59.5	598	471	324	68.8	141	358	263	73.5	80
Washington.....	10,856	5,992	55.2	4,669	3,567	2,236	62.7	1,246	2,286	1,847	80.8	358
French.........	1,027	598	58.2	413	409	254	62.1	148	295	238	80.7	45
English........	9,829	5,394	54.9	4,256	3,158	1,982	62.8	1,098	1,991	1,609	80.8	313
Oregon........	3,948	2,146	54.4	1,737	1,392	854	61.4	509	955	773	80.9	164
French.........	319	168	52.7	143	142	83	58.5	55	94	81	....	10
English........	3,629	1,978	54.5	1,594	1,250	771	61.7	454	861	692	80.4	154
California......	29,120	13,215	45.4	15,491	4,752	2,752	57.9	1,924	2,109	1,602	76.0	421
French.........	2,334	1,039	44.5	1,266	479	261	54.5	210	150	106	70.7	40
English........	26,786	12,176	45.5	14,225	4,273	2,491	58.3	1,714	1,959	1,496	76.4	381

TABLE **110**. WHITE CANADIAN FAMILIES, FRENCH AND ENGLISH, OCCUPYING OWNED NONFARM HOMES, BY VALUE OF HOME, WITH MEDIAN VALUES FOR URBAN AND RURAL AREAS, FOR 29 SELECTED STATES: 1930

[Median not shown where number of families reporting value is less than 100 or where median falls in first or last rent class]

STATE AND CLASS	OWNED NONFARM HOMES, BY VALUE								MEDIAN VALUE OF HOMES		
	Total	Under $1500	$1500 to $2999	$3000 to $4999	$5000 to $7499	$7500 to $9999	$10000 and over	Not reported	All non-farm homes	Urban	Rural-non-farm
United States..	**189,963**	**15,856**	**28,112**	**43,689**	**45,915**	**20,961**	**32,669**	**2,761**	**$5,324**	**$6,081**	**$2,958**
French..........	53,532	5,247	9,717	14,558	12,515	4,756	5,998	741	4,570	5,090	2,717
English..........	136,431	10,609	18,395	29,131	33,400	16,205	26,671	2,020	5,679	6,465	3,073
Maine............	**11,115**	**1,983**	**2,765**	**3,034**	**1,924**	**476**	**693**	**240**	**3,455**	**4,203**	**2,677**
French..........	5,410	730	1,348	1,599	978	247	421	87	3,730	4,326	2,785
English..........	5,705	1,253	1,417	1,435	946	229	272	153	3,148	4,016	2,597
New Hampshire....	**8,329**	**1,051**	**2,140**	**2,710**	**1,581**	**364**	**363**	**120**	**3,674**	**4,200**	**2,376**
French..........	6,166	727	1,611	2,034	1,192	260	258	84	3,691	4,117	2,244
English..........	2,163	324	529	676	389	104	105	36	3,623	4,562	2,570
Vermont..........	**2,880**	**326**	**683**	**938**	**593**	**151**	**151**	**38**	**3,878**	**4,890**	**2,790**
French..........	1,626	191	416	543	326	64	71	15	3,731	4,636	2,488
English..........	1,254	135	267	395	267	87	80	23	4,081	5,629	3,205
Massachusetts.....	**38,197**	**1,199**	**4,077**	**9,542**	**11,692**	**5,113**	**6,159**	**415**	**5,871**	**6,100**	**4,085**
French..........	16,391	688	2,247	4,784	4,618	1,766	2,083	205	5,202	5,455	3,577
English..........	21,806	511	1,830	4,758	7,074	3,347	4,076	210	6,307	6,532	4,440
Rhode Island......	**5,172**	**101**	**376**	**1,111**	**1,658**	**851**	**1,049**	**26**	**6,485**	**6,614**	**4,126**
French..........	4,186	86	309	928	1,317	684	838	24	6,439	6,577	4,080
English..........	986	15	67	183	341	167	211	2	6,664	6,759	...
Connecticut........	**3,424**	**111**	**299**	**729**	**941**	**475**	**818**	**51**	**6,455**	**7,172**	**5,089**
French..........	2,116	88	233	540	589	264	369	33	5,766	6,682	4,345
English..........	1,308	23	66	189	352	211	449	18	7,678	8,333	6,865
New York.........	**17,078**	**881**	**1,855**	**2,893**	**4,353**	**2,400**	**4,475**	**221**	**6,608**	**7,241**	**4,120**
French..........	3,171	364	657	699	687	309	422	33	4,568	5,162	2,908
English..........	13,907	517	1,198	2,194	3,666	2,091	4,053	188	7,012	7,681	4,436
New Jersey........	**2,173**	**24**	**72**	**153**	**420**	**390**	**1,086**	**28**	*****	*****	**7,216**
French..........	260	1	21	33	65	48	85	7	7,839	8,388	...
English..........	1,913	23	51	120	355	342	1,001	21	*	*	7,377
Pennsylvania......	**2,502**	**93**	**177**	**461**	**602**	**347**	**794**	**28**	**7,101**	**7,495**	**4,694**
French..........	251	17	25	60	70	28	50	1	5,821	6,230	...
English..........	2,251	76	152	401	532	319	744	27	7,270	7,776	4,820
Ohio..............	**4,399**	**115**	**278**	**705**	**1,295**	**727**	**1,232**	**47**	**7,081**	**7,420**	**4,624**
French..........	463	22	43	104	152	54	85	3	6,003	6,352	...
English..........	3,936	93	235	601	1,143	673	1,147	44	7,224	7,600	4,741
Indiana...........	**1,124**	**72**	**139**	**259**	**314**	**130**	**200**	**10**	**5,693**	**6,214**	**3,293**
French..........	154	17	20	37	52	15	12	1	5,120	5,814	...
English..........	970	55	119	222	262	115	188	9	5,806	6,287	3,383
Illinois...........	**6,109**	**135**	**371**	**755**	**1,363**	**1,026**	**2,370**	**89**	**8,441**	**9,083**	**4,067**
French..........	976	32	84	159	247	168	271	15	7,080	7,704	3,553
English..........	5,133	103	287	596	1,116	858	2,099	74	8,746	9,346	4,204
Michigan..........	**33,768**	**3,943**	**5,300**	**6,525**	**6,864**	**4,426**	**6,206**	**504**	**5,315**	**6,454**	**2,336**
French..........	5,152	1,048	1,040	1,096	891	494	511	72	3,825	4,648	1,594
English..........	28,616	2,895	4,260	5,429	5,973	3,932	5,695	432	5,631	6,754	2,444
Wisconsin.........	**3,479**	**532**	**846**	**865**	**617**	**262**	**272**	**85**	**3,738**	**4,385**	**2,384**
French..........	1,109	233	319	289	154	48	37	29	2,944	3,322	2,010
English..........	2,370	299	527	576	463	214	235	56	4,149	4,983	2,501
Minnesota.........	**5,855**	**615**	**1,026**	**1,581**	**1,545**	**439**	**556**	**93**	**4,569**	**5,239**	**2,545**
French..........	1,576	245	365	453	331	64	83	35	3,709	4,270	2,053
English..........	4,279	370	661	1,128	1,214	375	473	58	4,914	5,616	2,746
Iowa.............	**1,687**	**186**	**356**	**452**	**436**	**112**	**101**	**44**	**4,237**	**5,147**	**2,894**
French..........	150	19	33	32	40	12	6	8	4,188	...	...
English..........	1,537	167	323	420	396	100	95	36	4,240	5,171	2,888
Missouri..........	**1,056**	**94**	**143**	**207**	**245**	**122**	**230**	**15**	**5,781**	**6,559**	**2,956**
French..........	107	9	14	29	25	12	16	2	5,050	...	...
English..........	949	85	129	178	220	110	214	13	5,864	6,647	2,889
North Dakota......	**2,052**	**459**	**562**	**474**	**334**	**88**	**78**	**57**	**2,937**	**5,365**	**2,325**
French..........	217	65	63	41	27	11	4	6	2,464	...	2,040
English..........	1,835	394	499	433	307	77	74	51	2,997	5,509	2,358

*Median value over $10,000.

TABLE **110**. WHITE CANADIAN FAMILIES, FRENCH AND ENGLISH, OCCUPYING OWNED
NONFARM HOMES, BY VALUE OF HOME, WITH MEDIAN VALUES FOR URBAN AND
RURAL AREAS, FOR 29 SELECTED STATES: 1930—Continued

[Median not shown where number of families reporting value is less than 100 or where median falls
in first or last rent class]

STATE AND CLASS	OWNED NONFARM HOMES, BY VALUE								MEDIAN VALUE OF HOMES		
	Total	Under $1500	$1500 to $2999	$3000 to $4999	$5000 to $7499	$7500 to $9999	$10000 and over	Not reported	All nonfarm homes	Urban	Rural-nonfarm
South Dakota......	723	108	189	191	138	46	26	25	$3,545	$4,644	$2,765
French...........	113	27	32	26	12	3	4	9	2,672	...	...
English..........	610	81	157	165	126	43	22	16	3,715	4,759	2,849
Nebraska.........	1,065	100	216	327	253	66	80	23	4,254	5,221	3,288
French...........	91	11	24	28	17	5	5	1	...	...	...
English..........	974	89	192	299	236	61	75	22	4,304	5,252	3,345
Kansas...........	962	183	239	279	144	50	48	19	3,355	4,139	2,436
French...........	151	49	47	30	14	3	4	4	2,282	...	...
English..........	811	134	192	249	130	47	44	15	3,578	4,256	2,618
Florida..........	1,520	215	323	319	264	84	283	32	4,292	5,058	2,532
French...........	173	30	58	40	18	5	17	5	2,897	3,393	...
English..........	1,347	185	265	279	246	79	266	27	4,505	5,349	2,572
Texas............	823	69	102	219	175	68	171	19	5,171	5,801	2,859
French...........	69	6	6	28	14	5	8	2	...	...	...
English..........	754	63	96	191	161	63	163	17	5,287	5,909	2,831
Montana..........	1,775	500	429	380	239	66	122	39	2,787	3,986	†
French...........	393	147	94	79	39	8	20	6	2,242	3,153	†
English..........	1,382	353	335	301	200	58	102	33	2,940	4,211	1,592
Idaho............	794	252	194	190	83	22	31	22	2,536	3,393	†
French...........	138	57	40	25	9	1	2	4	1,875	...	...
English..........	656	195	154	165	74	21	29	18	2,708	3,641	1,568
Colorado.........	1,361	227	231	346	298	101	129	29	4,202	4,890	2,145
French...........	124	31	20	28	25	8	10	2	3,714	...	...
English..........	1,237	196	211	318	273	93	119	27	4,245	4,920	2,151
Washington........	8,191	1,036	2,131	2,561	1,499	314	513	137	3,672	4,030	2,577
French...........	848	142	265	257	122	19	30	13	3,082	3,507	2,162
English..........	7,343	894	1,866	2,304	1,377	295	483	124	3,737	4,090	2,630
Oregon...........	2,991	338	624	996	620	163	222	28	4,043	4,506	2,496
French...........	250	40	61	92	36	8	12	1	3,511	4,105	...
English..........	2,741	298	563	904	584	155	210	27	4,097	4,547	2,546
California........	15,753	515	1,523	3,733	4,621	1,713	3,450	198	6,086	6,431	4,271
French...........	1,292	63	159	377	358	104	208	23	5,248	5,633	3,976
English..........	14,461	452	1,364	3,356	4,263	1,609	3,242	175	6,156	6,497	4,306

† Median value less than $1,500.

TABLE **111**. WHITE CANADIAN FAMILIES, FRENCH AND ENGLISH, OCCUPYING RENTED
NONFARM HOMES, BY MONTHLY RENTAL OF HOME, WITH MEDIAN RENTALS FOR
URBAN AND RURAL AREAS, FOR 29 SELECTED STATES: 1930

(Median not shown where number of families reporting rental is less than 100)

STATE AND CLASS	RENTED NONFARM HOMES, BY MONTHLY RENTAL							MEDIAN RENTAL		
	Total	Under $15	$15 to $29	$30 to $49	$50 to $99	$100 and over	Not re-ported	All non-farm homes	Urban non-farm	Rural-non-farm
United States........	224,919	28,847	76,914	69,603	40,745	4,919	3,891	$31.37	$34.39	$16.12
French............	76,707	16,160	38,268	16,307	4,644	464	864	23.53	24.74	*
English...........	148,212	12,687	38,646	53,296	36,101	4,455	3,027	37.98	40.55	18.41
Maine.................	12,387	3,827	6,578	1,573	194	17	198	20.17	22.20	*
French.............	7,041	2,138	4,029	728	59	9	78	20.00	21.31	*
English............	5,346	1,689	2,549	845	135	8	120	20.44	24.02	*
New Hampshire........	9,929	3,245	5,578	839	87	8	172	19.39	20.61	*
French.............	7,865	2,650	4,525	507	50	4	129	19.04	20.07	*
English............	2,064	595	1,053	332	37	4	43	20.92	23.56	*
Vermont.............	3,390	1,285	1,643	377	49	3	33	18.59	21.99	*
French.............	2,062	852	997	179	14	1	19	17.55	20.69	*
English............	1,328	433	646	198	35	2	14	20.20	24.65	*
Massachusetts.........	61,866	6,452	26,591	22,076	5,818	393	536	28.66	29.19	18.67
French.............	27,655	4,673	15,721	6,268	770	43	180	23.65	24.01	*
English............	34,211	1,779	10,870	15,808	5,048	350	356	35.41	36.03	22.13
Rhode Island..........	9,382	1,639	5,409	1,956	296	45	37	23.41	23.80	*
French.............	7,761	1,483	4,716	1,375	134	26	27	22.58	22.97	*
English............	1,621	156	693	581	162	19	10	29.06	29.54	...
Connecticut...........	9,123	1,855	3,854	2,663	601	68	82	25.37	28.39	*
French.............	6,475	1,656	2,925	1,632	186	23	53	22.97	26.30	*
English............	2,648	199	929	1,031	415	45	29	33.52	35.75	24.49
New York.............	26,321	1,933	6,117	9,085	6,871	1,648	667	40.52	42.66	19.41
French.............	5,438	908	1,952	1,430	902	141	105	28.51	31.89	*
English............	20,883	1,025	4,165	7,655	5,969	1,507	562	42.99	44.67	21.86
New Jersey...........	2,857	66	401	1,043	1,103	172	72	47.75	48.81	32.75
French.............	503	17	102	221	127	22	14	41.36	42.36	...
English............	2,354	49	299	822	976	150	58	49.46	51.24	35.00
Pennsylvania..........	2,726	216	612	973	732	144	49	40.49	43.11	19.37
French.............	365	44	93	151	62	4	11	35.30	37.83	...
English............	2,361	172	519	822	670	140	38	41.45	44.09	20.35
Ohio.................	4,823	175	904	1,999	1,535	134	76	42.95	44.07	24.43
French.............	495	28	114	244	94	8	7	38.36	39.22	...
English............	4,328	147	790	1,755	1,441	126	69	43.59	44.74	24.53
Indiana..............	970	76	220	403	247	14	10	39.13	40.83	...
French.............	101	13	21	48	16	2	1	36.67	...	...
English............	869	63	199	355	231	12	9	39.46	41.12	...
Illinois..............	9,080	240	1,075	2,049	4,712	806	198	61.43	62.51	21.30
French.............	1,316	48	258	386	542	61	21	47.69	48.65	...
English............	7,764	192	817	1,663	4,170	745	177	63.45	64.45	21.61
Michigan.............	28,768	2,040	4,440	9,833	11,397	626	432	45.64	48.03	15.66
French.............	4,345	603	853	1,659	1,119	55	56	38.30	40.78	*
English............	24,423	1,437	3,587	8,174	10,278	571	376	47.13	49.54	17.42
Wisconsin............	2,135	382	669	605	390	47	42	29.90	35.10	*
French.............	613	149	237	127	75	8	17	24.43	27.56	*
English............	1,522	233	432	478	315	39	25	33.49	37.97	*
Minnesota............	3,544	580	1,167	1,076	625	41	55	29.97	34.17	*
French.............	847	194	363	210	68	2	10	24.48	26.31	*
English............	2,697	386	804	866	557	39	45	33.14	37.04	*
Iowa.................	713	108	248	232	104	4	17	29.52	34.81	17.64
French.............	85	11	40	23	9	1	1	...	...	...
English............	628	97	208	209	95	3	16	30.10	35.77	18.20
Missouri.............	919	105	195	250	286	61	22	41.88	45.42	15.81
French.............	116	25	25	35	23	4	4	33.43	...	...
English............	803	80	170	215	263	57	18	43.26	46.62	...
North Dakota.........	958	275	319	213	111	2	38	23.70	39.03	16.10
French.............	119	35	42	28	9	..	5	22.86	...	...
English............	839	240	277	185	102	2	33	23.83	39.51	16.00

*Median rental less than $15.

TABLE **111**. WHITE CANADIAN FAMILIES, FRENCH AND ENGLISH, OCCUPYING RENTED NONFARM HOMES, BY MONTHLY RENTAL OF HOME, WITH MEDIAN RENTALS FOR URBAN AND RURAL AREAS, FOR 29 SELECTED STATES: 1930—Continued

(Median not shown where number of families reporting rental is less than 100)

STATE AND CLASS	RENTED NONFARM HOMES, BY MONTHLY RENTAL							MEDIAN RENTAL		
	Total	Under $15	$15 to $29	$30 to $49	$50 to $99	$100 and over	Not reported	All nonfarm homes	Urban nonfarm	Rural nonfarm
South Dakota	337	92	127	75	29	2	12	$23.33	$31.77	$16.52
French	42	15	21	5	..	..	1	...	...	...
English	295	77	106	70	29	2	11	24.20	34.86	16.55
Nebraska	413	75	145	118	49	7	19	27.62	34.62	18.69
French	49	9	17	13	8	..	2	...	...	...
English	364	66	128	105	41	7	17	27.60	34.89	18.75
Kansas	347	93	125	74	32	4	19	23.52	28.63	*
French	44	21	10	6	5	..	2	...	...	...
English	303	72	115	68	27	4	17	24.26	29.27	...
Florida	1,249	239	498	297	149	26	40	26.01	27.96	17.17
French	167	40	72	34	13	3	5	23.54	25.33	...
English	1,082	199	426	263	136	23	35	26.43	28.42	17.66
Texas	726	81	209	241	148	17	30	34.81	38.03	18.83
French	89	13	27	30	9	4	6	...	...	...
English	637	68	182	211	139	13	24	35.36	38.49	...
Montana	1,320	372	494	284	115	5	50	22.99	29.04	*
French	236	96	76	34	14	..	16	17.76	23.44	...
English	1,084	276	418	250	101	5	34	23.94	30.62	16.29
Idaho	579	226	234	74	24	2	19	18.46	25.07	*
French	67	27	28	8	3	..	1	...	...	...
English	512	199	206	66	21	2	18	18.50	25.19	*
Colorado	832	152	259	230	136	15	40	29.13	34.39	*
French	93	29	29	18	10	3	4	...	...	...
English	739	123	230	212	126	12	36	29.90	34.90	15.59
Washington	5,912	1,062	2,286	1,635	659	51	219	26.71	29.89	*
French	561	122	251	122	43	3	20	23.87	26.63	*
English	5,351	940	2,035	1,513	616	48	199	27.06	30.43	*
Oregon	2,241	440	963	590	177	10	61	25.12	27.93	*
French	198	54	89	43	9	..	3	22.33	25.74	...
English	2,043	386	874	547	168	10	58	25.41	28.16	*
California	17,375	924	4,545	7,709	3,257	429	511	37.69	39.12	23.24
French	1,474	115	479	605	199	30	46	33.97	36.08	20.69
English	15,901	809	4,066	7,104	3,058	399	465	38.00	39.38	23.55

*Median rental less than $15.

CHAPTER XIV

CANADIAN FAMILIES BY SIZE, NUMBER OF CHILDREN, NUMBER OF GAINFUL WORKERS, AND NUMBER OF LODGERS

FAMILIES BY SIZE

IN the classification of families according to size in 1930, only related persons were counted. Lodgers, resident servants, etc., were omitted, though a separate count was made of the number of lodgers. Persons related in any way to the head of the family, by blood, marriage, or adoption, were counted as members of the family. Most of the 1-person families shown in the classification represent persons living alone, though a small number of so-called "partnership" families are included in this group. In such families one person was selected, sometimes more or less arbitrarily, as the head, and the others were counted as lodgers.

The data for Canadian families in the United States classified by size are presented in Table 112. In this classification, as in the classification by tenure presented in Table 102, all Canadian families, that is, all white families with a Canadian-born person as head, are included, farm as well as nonfarm.

The whole number of Canadian families in the United States in 1930 was 460,731, of which 43,899, or 9.5 per cent, were 1-person families; 120,738, or 26.2 per cent, were 2-person families; 96,226, or 20.9 per cent, were 3-person families; 74,305, or 16.1 per cent, were 4-person families; and the remainder, 125,563, or 27.3 per cent, comprised five or more related persons each.

Of the French Canadian families, 6.9 per cent were composed of one person only; 20.5 per cent of two persons; 18.3 per cent of three persons; 15.7 per cent of four persons; and 38.6 per cent of five persons or more.

The English Canadian families were materially smaller, as indicated by the classification, which shows larger percentages for the smaller sizes and smaller percentages for the larger sizes, as follows: 1-person families, 10.7; 2-person families, 28.7; 3-person families, 22.0; 4-person families, 16.3; and families of five persons or more, only 22.2.

When the Canadian families are classified in accordance with their residence in urban or rural areas, it appears that the families in rural-nonfarm areas are somewhat smaller than those in urban areas, mainly because they contain relatively large numbers of 1-person and 2-person families; and that the rural-farm families are slightly larger than the urban because they contain relatively larger numbers of families comprising five persons or more, in spite of the fact that they also contain a relatively high percentage of 1-person families. These differences, which appear in the figures for both the French Canadian families and the English Canadian families taken separately, follow the same general pattern as the figures for all families in the United States, at least to the extent that the percentage of 1-person families is highest in the rural-nonfarm areas.

TABLE **112**. WHITE CANADIAN FAMILIES IN THE UNITED STATES, FRENCH AND ENGLISH, BY SIZE, FOR URBAN AND RURAL AREAS: 1930

SIZE OF FAMILY AND CLASS	TOTAL		URBAN		RURAL-NONFARM		RURAL-FARM	
	Number	Per cent	Number	Per cent	Number	Per cent	Number	Per cent
All Canadian families............	**460,731**	**100.0**	**348,169**	**100.0**	**74,031**	**100.0**	**38,531**	**100.0**
Families comprising—								
1 person........................	43,899	9.5	30,237	8.7	9,808	13.2	3,854	10.0
2 persons.......................	120,738	26.2	91,423	26.3	20,057	27.1	9,258	24.0
3 persons.......................	96,226	20.9	75,089	21.6	14,036	19.0	7,101	18.4
4 persons.......................	74,305	16.1	57,982	16.7	10,801	14.6	5,522	14.3
5 persons.......................	49,078	10.7	37,412	10.7	7,384	10.0	4,282	11.1
6 persons.......................	31,020	6.7	23,316	6.7	4,725	6.4	2,979	7.7
7 persons.......................	18,910	4.1	13,913	4.0	2,912	3.9	2,085	5.4
8 persons.......................	11,456	2.5	8,249	2.4	1,838	2.5	1,369	3.6
9 or more......................	15,099	3.3	10,548	3.0	2,470	3.3	2,081	5.4
French......................	**141,118**	**100.0**	**110,721**	**100.0**	**21,883**	**100.0**	**8,514**	**100.0**
Families comprising—								
1 person........................	9,741	6.9	6,758	6.1	2,292	10.5	691	8.1
2 persons.......................	28,892	20.5	22,619	20.4	4,748	21.7	1,525	17.9
3 persons.......................	25,852	18.3	20,784	18.8	3,738	17.1	1,330	15.6
4 persons.......................	22,118	15.7	17,877	16.1	3,115	14.2	1,126	13.2
5 persons.......................	17,384	12.3	13,851	12.5	2,517	11.5	1,016	11.9
6 persons.......................	12,741	9.0	10,114	9.1	1,839	8.4	788	9.3
7 persons.......................	9,006	6.4	7,066	6.4	1,300	5.9	640	7.5
8 persons.......................	6,014	4.3	4,667	4.2	899	4.1	448	5.3
9 or more......................	9,370	6.6	6,985	6.3	1,435	6.6	950	11.2
English......................	**319,613**	**100.0**	**237,448**	**100.0**	**52,148**	**100.0**	**30,017**	**100.0**
Families comprising—								
1 person........................	34,158	10.7	23,479	9.9	7,516	14.4	3,163	10.5
2 persons.......................	91,846	28.7	68,804	29.0	15,309	29.4	7,733	25.8
3 persons.......................	70,374	22.0	54,305	22.9	10,298	19.7	5,771	19.2
4 persons.......................	52,187	16.3	40,105	16.9	7,686	14.7	4,396	14.6
5 persons.......................	31,694	9.9	23,561	9.9	4,867	9.3	3,266	10.9
6 persons.......................	18,279	5.7	13,202	5.6	2,886	5.5	2,191	7.3
7 persons.......................	9,904	3.1	6,847	2.9	1,612	3.1	1,445	4.8
8 persons.......................	5,442	1.7	3,582	1.5	939	1.8	921	3.1
9 or more......................	5,729	1.8	3,563	1.5	1,035	2.0	1,131	3.8

The distribution of French and English Canadian families by size is shown graphically in Figure 35.

In connection with the median size of family, the general definition of the median as that item which stands at the midpoint of the series arranged according to size must be qualified somewhat, since this figure (in common with the average size of family) is presented with a fraction or decimal which must be interpreted in an abstract or theoretical sense rather than literally. When the median size of all Canadian families in the United States is shown as 3.18, this does not mean that there are 3.18 persons in any family, any more than the average size, 3.63, means that there are 3.63 persons in any actual family. In the tabulation on which the computation of the median is based, the families are arranged in groups having, respectively, one person, two persons, three persons, four persons, etc., per family. If the midpoint in the series of families thus arranged is located exactly in the middle of the 3-person group, then the median will be exactly 3. In this case it will be necessary to pass over all of the 1-person and 2-person families and one-half of the 3-person families, in order to reach the midpoint. If, however, it is necessary to take, say, three-fourths of the 3-person families in order to reach the midpoint, the median would be one-fourth of a unit higher, or 3.25. Similarly, if only

FIGURE 35. SIZE OF FAMILIES IN THE CANADIAN STOCK, FRENCH AND ENGLISH: 1930

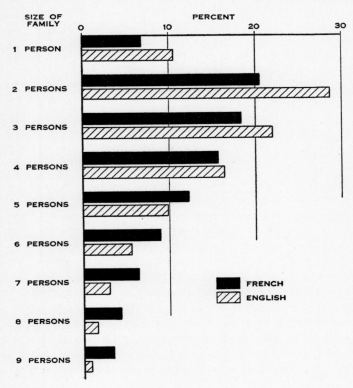

four-tenths of the 3-person families are needed to reach the midpoint, the median will be one-tenth of a unit lower, or 2.90.

In actual use, however, it is not necessary to keep in mind the process of obtaining the median; it may simply be accepted as a convenient summary figure representing the size of family in the various areas and the various classes. Medians of 3.18 for Canadian families in the United States and 3.75 for all foreign-born white families, for example, indicate that the Canadian families are somewhat the smaller, and give a definite measure of the difference in size.

The median size of Canadian families in the United States in 1930 is presented in Table 113, with corresponding figures for all families in the United States, and for all foreign-born white families.

TABLE **113**. MEDIAN SIZE OF CANADIAN FAMILIES, FRENCH AND ENGLISH, WITH COMPARATIVE DATA FOR ALL FAMILIES, ETC., FOR URBAN AND RURAL AREAS: 1930

CLASS	MEDIAN SIZE OF FAMILY				AVERAGE SIZE OF FAMILY
	Total	Urban	Rural-nonfarm	Rural-farm	
All Canadian families...................	3.18	3.20	3.01	3.37	3.63
French.............................	3.77	3.79	3.55	4.13	4.25
English............................	2.98	2.99	2.82	3.21	3.36
All families in United States..............	3.40	3.26	3.28	4.02	3.81
All foreign-born white families............	3.75	3.77	3.37	4.08	4.09

The median size of all Canadian families in the United States, as already noted, was 3.18. The median size of French Canadian families was 3.77, as compared with 2.98 for English Canadian families. The median size of all Canadian families in urban areas was 3.20; in rural-nonfarm areas, 3.01; and in rural-farm areas, 3.37. The French Canadian families taken alone show similar differences as between one area and another, though at a somewhat higher level, the medians being 3.79 in urban areas, 3.55 in rural-nonfarm, and 4.13 in rural-farm. For the English Canadian families the corresponding figures were 2.99 in urban areas, 2.82 in rural-nonfarm, and 3.21 in rural-farm.

The median size of Canadian families in both urban and rural areas was slightly lower than the median size of all families in the United States, and in urban areas very much lower than the median size of all foreign-born white families (there being little difference in rural areas between the median size of all Canadian families and of all foreign-born white families).

The median size of Canadian families, French and English, in urban, rural-nonfarm, and rural-farm areas, is shown in graphic form in Figure 36.

FIGURE **36**. MEDIAN SIZE OF CANADIAN FAMILIES, FRENCH AND ENGLISH, IN URBAN AND RURAL AREAS: 1930

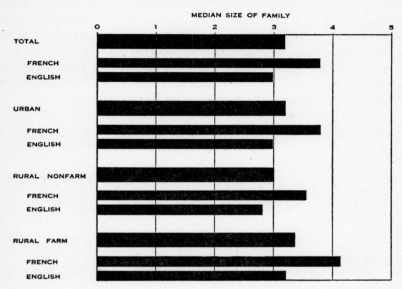

The average size of family (3.63 for all Canadian families, as compared with the median of 3.18) is likely to be always appreciably higher than the median because the very large families have a greater effect on the average than on the median. The addition of 100 10-person families, for example, to an area having originally 1,000 3-person families, would increase the average much more than the addition of 100 1-person families would decrease it, while the effect of these two additions on the median would be identical, that is, one would exactly balance or cancel the other, leaving the median unchanged.

FAMILIES BY NUMBER OF CHILDREN

IN making a classification of families by number of children, the age limit of 10 years was selected as affording a better measure of fertility than higher or lower age limits. At ages under 10 all of the living children are likely to be enumerated with their parents, giving a complete record of the children of those ages; and there is less likelihood of the inclusion of grandchildren, nephews, nieces, etc., with this age limit than with a higher one. In the tabulation of children under 10, however, all children within this age period were counted who were related in any way to the head of the family, either by blood or by adoption, as it was impracticable to restrict the count to the children of the head of the family. In the aggregate, though, the number of grandchildren, nephews, nieces, and others not sons or daughters of the head of the family who were thus included is relatively small.

In making comparisons between the various population groups on the basis of number of children in the family, it should be borne in mind that, other things being equal, the population group having the highest average age will tend to show the highest percentage of families with no children, since in any population group the no-children families are made up to a considerable extent of those whose children have all passed the age of 10 years.

In Table 114 the Canadian families in the United States in 1930 are classified in accordance with the number of children under 10 years of age, while in Table 115 are presented some of the more significant percentages in compact form for convenient comparison.

TABLE **114**. WHITE CANADIAN FAMILIES, FRENCH AND ENGLISH, BY NUMBER OF CHILDREN UNDER 10 YEARS OLD, FOR URBAN AND RURAL AREAS: 1930

NUMBER OF CHILDREN AND CLASS	TOTAL		URBAN		RURAL-NONFARM		RURAL-FARM	
	Number	Per cent	Number	Per cent	Number	Per cent	Number	Per cent
All Canadian families.........	**460,731**	**100.0**	**348,169**	**100.0**	**74,031**	**100.0**	**38,531**	**100.0**
Families having—								
No children......................	318,507	69.1	240,642	69.1	51,028	68.9	26,837	69.7
1 child.........................	70,346	15.3	54,610	15.7	10,618	14.3	5,118	13.3
2 children......................	38,542	8.4	29,229	8.4	6,214	8.4	3,099	8.0
3 children......................	18,777	4.1	13,693	3.9	3,342	4.5	1,742	4.5
4 children......................	8,868	1.9	6,156	1.8	1,704	2.3	1,008	2.6
5 children......................	3,906	0.8	2,669	0.8	763	1.0	474	1.2
6 or more......................	1,785	0.4	1,170	0.3	362	0.5	253	0.7
French......................	**141,118**	**100.0**	**110,721**	**100.0**	**21,883**	**100.0**	**8,514**	**100.0**
Families having—								
No children......................	88,486	62.7	69,635	62.9	13,708	62.6	5,143	60.4
1 child.........................	22,537	16.0	17,980	16.2	3,292	15.0	1,265	14.9
2 children......................	13,787	9.8	10,872	9.8	2,114	9.7	801	9.4
3 children......................	8,157	5.8	6,264	5.7	1,342	6.1	551	6.5
4 children......................	4,616	3.3	3,410	3.1	812	3.7	394	4.6
5 children......................	2,355	1.7	1,740	1.6	402	1.8	213	2.5
6 or more......................	1,180	0.8	820	0.7	213	1.0	147	1.7
English......................	**319,613**	**100.0**	**237,448**	**100.0**	**52,148**	**100.0**	**30,017**	**100.0**
Families having—								
No children......................	230,021	72.0	171,007	72.0	37,320	71.6	21,694	72.3
1 child.........................	47,809	15.0	36,630	15.4	7,326	14.0	3,853	12.8
2 children......................	24,755	7.7	18,357	7.7	4,100	7.9	2,298	7.7
3 children......................	10,620	3.3	7,429	3.1	2,000	3.8	1,191	4.0
4 children......................	4,252	1.3	2,746	1.2	892	1.7	614	2.0
5 children......................	1,551	0.5	929	0.4	361	0.7	261	0.9
6 or more......................	605	0.2	350	0.1	149	0.3	106	0.4

TABLE **115**. PERCENTAGE OF CANADIAN FAMILIES, FRENCH AND ENGLISH, HAVING SPECIFIED NUMBERS OF CHILDREN, FOR URBAN AND RURAL AREAS: 1930

(Classification based on number of children under 10 years of age in family at time of census)

CLASS	PER CENT OF FAMILIES HAVING NO CHILDREN				PER CENT OF FAMILIES HAVING THREE OR MORE CHILDREN			
	Total	Urban	Rural-non-farm	Rural-farm	Total	Urban	Rural-non-farm	Rural-farm
All Canadian families...........	69.1	69.1	68.9	69.7	7.2	6.8	8.3	9.0
French.....................	62.7	62.9	62.6	60.4	11.6	11.0	12.7	15.3
English....................	72.0	72.0	71.6	72.3	5.3	4.8	6.5	7.2
All families in the United States....	58.8	62.4	57.4	50.7	10.2	7.3	11.5	16.5
All foreign-born white families....	61.1	60.8	62.8	61.7	9.5	8.7	11.9	13.0

Of the whole number of Canadian families in the United States (460,731), 318,507, or 69.1 per cent, had no children under 10 in the family at the time the 1930 census was taken; 70,346, or 15.3 per cent, had one child; 38,542, or 8.4 per cent, had two children; and 33,336, or 7.2 per cent, had three children or more. Of the French Canadian families taken alone, an appreciably smaller percentage, 62.7, were without any children, and a considerably larger percentage, 11.6, had three or more. Of the English Canadian families, 72.0 per cent had no children, and only 5.3 per cent had three or more.

The percentage of Canadian families having no children, namely, 69.1, was very much higher than the corresponding percentage for all families in the United States, which was 58.8, this being perhaps mainly the result of the fact that the average age of any immigrant population tends to be considerably higher than that of the total resident population. The Canadian figure was also appreciably higher, however, than the percentage of all foreign-born white families in the United States having no children, which was 61.1. The percentage of Canadian families having three or more children, 7.2, may likewise be compared with the corresponding figures for all families in the United States, which was 10.2; and with the percentage for all foreign-born white families, which was 9.5, the relations on the basis of this percentage being in each case consistent with those shown by the percentage of families having no children.

As between the urban and rural areas the differences in the percentages of the families having no children were not very great; the percentage having three or more children, however, was 6.8 in urban areas as compared with 8.3 in rural-nonfarm, and 9.0 in rural-farm, with similar relations obtaining on a considerably higher level for the French Canadian families alone, and on a somewhat lower level for the English Canadian families alone.

Families by Number of Gainful Workers

In the classification of families according to the number of gainful workers, all related members of the family who were returned as usually working at a gainful occupation were counted, including some who were temporarily unemployed at the time of the census. Gainfully employed lodgers or boarders were not counted. In general, it may be said that the number of gainful workers includes those persons who are presumably contributing to the family income. The families reporting no gainful workers were mainly those of widows and of elderly men who had retired from active employment. The gainful workers on the farms, it may be noted, included in some cases members of the family working on the farm but not receiving wages.

The data for Canadian families classified in accordance with the number of gainful workers are presented in Table 116.

TABLE **116**. White Canadian Families, French and English, by Number of Gainful Workers, for Urban and Rural Areas: 1930

NUMBER OF GAINFUL WORKERS AND CLASS	TOTAL		URBAN		RURAL-NONFARM		RURAL-FARM	
	Number	Per cent	Number	Per cent	Number	Per cent	Number	Per cent
All Canadian families..........	**460,731**	**100.0**	**348,169**	**100.0**	**74,031**	**100.0**	**38,531**	**100.0**
Families having—								
No gainful workers................	36,764	8.0	25,624	7.4	9,844	13.3	1,296	3.4
1 gainful worker..................	256,078	55.6	189,678	54.5	43,331	58.5	23,069	59.9
2 gainful workers.................	103,168	22.4	80,360	23.1	13,605	18.4	9,203	23.9
3 gainful workers.................	40,248	8.7	32,070	9.2	4,801	6.5	3,377	8.8
4 or more.......................	24,473	5.3	20,437	5.9	2,450	3.3	1,586	4.1
French........................	**141,118**	**100.0**	**110,721**	**100.0**	**21,883**	**100.0**	**8,514**	**100.0**
Families having—								
No gainful workers................	8,187	5.8	5,952	5.4	2,044	9.3	191	2.2
1 gainful worker..................	67,172	47.6	51,096	46.1	11,455	52.3	4,621	54.3
2 gainful workers.................	33,987	24.1	27,278	24.6	4,591	21.0	2,118	24.9
3 gainful workers.................	17,375	12.3	14,173	12.8	2,201	10.1	1,001	11.8
4 or more.......................	14,397	10.2	12,222	11.0	1,592	7.3	583	6.8
English.......................	**319,613**	**100.0**	**237,448**	**100.0**	**52,148**	**100.0**	**30,017**	**100.0**
Families having—								
No gainful workers................	28,577	8.9	19,672	8.3	7,800	15.0	1,105	3.7
1 gainful worker..................	188,906	59.1	138,582	58.4	31,876	61.1	18,448	61.5
2 gainful workers.................	69,181	21.6	53,082	22.4	9,014	17.3	7,085	23.6
3 gainful workers.................	22,873	7.2	17,897	7.5	2,600	5.0	2,376	7.9
4 or more.......................	10,076	3.2	8,215	3.5	858	1.6	1,003	3.3

Of the whole number of Canadian families in the United States, 8.0 per cent returned no gainful workers; 55.6 per cent returned one gainful worker; 22.4 per cent, two gainful workers; 8.7 per cent, three gainful workers; and 5.3 per cent, four or more. The corresponding figures for all families in the United States were as follows: No gainful workers, 6.0 per cent; one gainful worker, 62.1 per cent; two gainful workers, 21.1 per cent; three gainful workers, 7.2 per cent; and four or more gainful workers, 3.6 per cent. The main differences are, therefore, that the Canadian families show a little larger percentage with no gainful workers, and appreciably larger percentages with two, three, and four gainful workers. Of all foreign-born white families in the United States, 6.5 per cent had no gainful workers; 54.3 per cent had one; 22.5 per cent had two; 10.5 per cent had three; and 6.3 per cent had four or more.

Of the French Canadian families, 5.8 per cent had no gainful workers as compared with 8.9 per cent of the English Canadian families; 47.6 per cent of the French families had one gainful worker, as compared with 59.1 per cent of the English; 24.1 per cent had two gainful workers, as compared with 21.6 per cent of the English families; 12.3 per cent had three gainful workers, as compared with 7.2 per cent of the English; and 10.2 per cent had four or more gainful workers, as compared with 3.2 per cent of the English families.

As between the various urban and rural areas, the rural-nonfarm area showed much the highest percentage of Canadian families having no gainful workers, namely, 13.3, as compared with 7.4 in urban areas and 3.4 in rural-farm. On the other hand, the urban areas showed considerably higher percentages of families having three or more gainful workers in the family, 15.1 as compared with 12.9 in rural-farm areas and 9.8 in rural-nonfarm. The French Canadian families and the English, taken separately, show similar relations as between one and another of the urban and rural areas, though on somewhat different levels corresponding to the generally larger families of the French Canadians.

FAMILIES BY NUMBER OF LODGERS

IN the classification of families according to the number of lodgers, certain other persons besides those specifically returned as lodgers or boarders were included. The more important of these were farm laborers living in the farm family, foster children or wards, and guests, that is, guests having no other usual place of abode. On the other hand, it should be noted that no household having more than 10 lodgers was included in the classification of private families.

Canadian families in the United States in 1930 are classified in accordance with the number of lodgers in Table 117.

Of the whole number of Canadian families in the United States, 87.6 per cent reported no lodgers; 7.7 per cent reported one; 2.4 per cent reported two; and 2.2 per cent reported three or more. These figures indicate that there was a slightly higher percentage of families with lodgers among the Canadian families than in the whole number of families in the United States—12.4, as compared with 9.8. The percentages of Canadian families, not only for those having lodgers, but for those having one, two, and three lodgers, are practically identical, however, with those for all foreign-born white families in the United States.

TABLE **117**. WHITE CANADIAN FAMILIES, FRENCH AND ENGLISH, BY NUMBER OF LODGERS, FOR URBAN AND RURAL AREAS: 1930

NUMBER OF LODGERS AND CLASS	TOTAL		URBAN		RURAL-NONFARM		RURAL-FARM	
	Number	Per cent	Number	Per cent	Number	Per cent	Number	Per cent
All Canadian families........	**460,731**	**100.0**	**348,169**	**100.0**	**74,031**	**100.0**	**38,531**	**100.0**
Families having—								
No lodgers......................	403,828	87.6	302,797	87.0	67,335	91.0	33,696	87.5
1 lodger........................	35,345	7.7	27,133	7.8	4,426	6.0	3,786	9.8
2 lodgers.......................	11,209	2.4	9,305	2.7	1,231	1.7	673	1.7
3 lodgers.......................	4,623	1.0	3,888	1.1	517	0.7	218	0.6
4 or 5 lodgers..................	3,453	0.7	2,991	0.9	348	0.5	114	0.3
6 or more.......................	2,273	0.5	2,055	0.6	174	0.2	44	0.1
French......................	**141,118**	**100.0**	**110,721**	**100.0**	**21,883**	**100.0**	**8,514**	**100.0**
Families having—								
No lodgers......................	126,035	89.3	98,721	89.2	19,882	90.9	7,432	87.3
1 lodger........................	9,536	6.8	7,369	6.7	1,320	6.0	847	9.9
2 lodgers.......................	2,952	2.1	2,421	2.2	373	1.7	158	1.9
3 lodgers.......................	1,188	0.8	996	0.9	151	0.7	41	0.5
4 or 5 lodgers..................	837	0.6	714	0.6	98	0.4	25	0.3
6 or more.......................	570	0.4	500	0.5	59	0.3	11	0.1
English.....................	**319,613**	**100.0**	**237,448**	**100.0**	**52,148**	**100.0**	**30,017**	**100.0**
Families having—								
No lodgers......................	277,793	86.9	204,076	85.9	47,453	91.0	26,264	87.5
1 lodger........................	25,809	8.1	19,764	8.3	3,106	6.0	2,939	9.8
2 lodgers.......................	8,257	2.6	6,884	2.9	858	1.6	515	1.7
3 lodgers.......................	3,435	1.1	2,892	1.2	366	0.7	177	0.6
4 or 5 lodgers..................	2,616	0.8	2,277	1.0	250	0.5	89	0.3
6 or more.......................	1,703	0.5	1,555	0.7	115	0.2	33	0.1

A slightly smaller percentage of the French Canadian families than of English reported lodgers, though the differences were not very great.

For all Canadian families taken together, the percentage having lodgers was largest in urban areas, with rural-farm areas only slightly lower; and smallest in rural-nonfarm areas. For the French Canadian families taken alone, the percentage of families having lodgers was highest in rural-farm areas and lowest in rural-nonfarm. For the English Canadian families taken alone, the percentage was highest in urban areas, considerably lower in rural-farm areas, and lowest in rural-nonfarm.

DATA FOR STATES

IN Tables 118 to 121 are presented, for 29 States, figures for Canadian families classified according to size, number of children under 10 years old, number of gainful workers, and number of lodgers, respectively. In each case data are presented separately for French Canadian and English Canadian families, together with medians for size of family and percentage distributions for the other classifications. Limitations of space do not allow an extensive analysis of the data, but a few points of special interest may be noted, in the hope that these may suggest further examination and comparison of the State figures.

It has been pointed out above that for the United States as a whole the median French Canadian family was larger in 1930 than the English Canadian. Table 118 shows that this is true for every State in which there was a large number of Canadian families. There were, however, great differences in the median size of family in different parts of the country which, in general, follow the differences in the pattern of family size found in the native population. For example, the median size of French Canadian families is found to range from 4.35 in Maine to 2.95 in Ohio (to take only States with at least approximately 1,000 French Canadian families), while in the case of the English Canadian families, the range was from 3.48 in Maine to 2.37 in Florida. Thus in family size Canadian families (both French and English) tend to resemble the native families in the same area more closely than Canadian families of the same ethnic stock in other areas. A similar conclusion results from inspection of Table 119, which shows, by States, the number of families having a specified number of children under 10 years old. It is apparent that in almost every State there were fewer no-child families and more families with three or more children among the French Canadian families than among the English Canadian. The difference between the two groups in any one State, however, was not so marked as the differences between families of the same ethnic group residing in different States. The largest proportion of French Canadian families with three or more children was found in Vermont (18.8 per cent), while the smallest proportion was found in California (3.1 per cent)—again considering only States with at least 1,000 French Canadian families. The largest proportion of English Canadian families with three or more children was found in Maine (11.1 per cent) and the smallest proportion in California (2.0 per cent).

It will be noted from Table 120 that the distribution of families by number of gainful workers in the various States is similar to the distribution of families by size, as shown in Table 118. The extremes in this case are found in Rhode Island, where 15.1 per cent of the French Canadian families had four or more gainful workers in 1930, and in Florida, where only 1.0 per cent of either French or English Canadian families had four or more gainful workers.

TABLE **118**. WHITE CANADIAN FAMILIES, FRENCH AND ENGLISH, BY SIZE, FOR 29 SELECTED STATES: 1930

STATE AND CLASS	Total	FAMILIES COMPRISING—									Median size of family
		1 person	2 persons	3 persons	4 persons	5 persons	6 persons	7 persons	8 persons	9 or more	
United States...	460,731	43,899	120,738	96,226	74,305	49,078	31,020	18,910	11,456	15,099	3.18
French........	141,118	9,741	28,892	25,852	22,118	17,384	12,741	9,006	6,014	9,370	3.77
English........	319,613	34,158	91,846	70,374	52,187	31,694	18,279	9,904	5,442	5,729	2.98
Maine........	27,271	1,745	5,204	4,903	4,357	3,432	2,644	1,799	1,223	1,964	3.91
French........	13,545	624	2,108	2,216	2,146	1,790	1,508	1,063	769	1,321	4.35
English........	13,726	1,121	3,096	2,687	2,211	1,642	1,136	736	454	643	3.48
New Hampshire...	19,864	1,551	4,201	3,600	3,035	2,418	1,722	1,235	846	1,256	3.69
French...	14,795	985	2,784	2,555	2,273	1,908	1,387	1,044	726	1,133	3.97
English........	5,069	566	1,417	1,045	762	510	335	191	120	123	3.03
Vermont........	9,209	627	1,949	1,731	1,427	1,103	768	577	361	666	3.71
French........	5,599	285	1,012	978	799	697	543	427	282	576	4.16
English........	3,610	342	937	753	628	406	225	150	79	90	3.20
Massachusetts....	103,097	7,454	22,764	20,649	17,201	12,551	8,612	5,633	3,537	4,696	3.54
French........	45,394	2,540	8,657	8,171	7,214	5,870	4,407	3,181	2,136	3,218	3.96
English........	57,703	4,914	14,107	12,478	9,987	6,681	4,205	2,452	1,401	1,478	3.29
Rhode Island.....	14,833	853	2,953	2,747	2,490	1,839	1,366	974	620	991	3.85
French...	12,161	592	2,246	2,158	2,004	1,566	1,200	878	569	948	4.04
English........	2,672	261	707	589	486	273	166	96	51	43	3.12
Connecticut......	13,054	682	2,785	2,669	2,264	1,688	1,111	752	443	660	3.67
French........	8,913	378	1,705	1,726	1,510	1,199	845	594	374	582	3.93
English........	4,141	304	1,080	943	754	489	266	158	69	78	3.23
New York........	47,261	4,831	13,122	10,418	7,826	4,793	2,781	1,559	931	1,000	3.04
French........	9,479	795	2,250	1,897	1,497	1,104	720	468	306	442	3.39
English........	37,782	4,036	10,872	8,521	6,329	3,689	2,061	1,091	625	558	2.97
New Jersey.......	5,186	407	1,322	1,241	993	602	315	148	83	75	3.20
French........	789	63	177	176	135	111	51	32	17	27	3.38
English........	4,397	344	1,145	1,065	858	491	264	116	66	48	3.17
Pennsylvania.....	5,536	471	1,554	1,264	957	604	311	183	96	96	3.09
French........	642	62	163	137	117	60	35	33	21	14	3.20
English........	4,894	409	1,391	1,127	840	544	276	150	75	82	3.07
Ohio...........	9,604	799	2,984	2,319	1,636	948	505	215	116	82	2.94
French........	999	104	293	226	153	97	63	26	20	17	2.95
English........	8,605	695	2,691	2,093	1,483	851	442	189	96	65	2.94
Indiana........	2,267	166	724	518	392	227	123	57	30	30	2.97
French........	275	30	84	56	47	27	15	6	4	6	2.92
English........	1,992	136	640	462	345	200	108	51	26	24	2.98
Illinois...........	15,613	1,367	4,972	3,638	2,616	1,504	730	387	210	189	2.90
French........	2,362	215	666	527	356	242	137	108	60	51	3.07
English........	13,251	1,152	4,306	3,111	2,260	1,262	593	279	150	138	2.88
Michigan........	72,637	6,376	20,429	16,100	12,013	7,518	4,579	2,558	1,461	1,603	3.09
French........	10,795	850	2,512	2,082	1,671	1,252	930	595	388	515	3.48
English........	61,842	5,526	17,917	14,018	10,342	6,266	3,649	1,963	1,073	1,088	3.03
Wisconsin.......	6,802	736	1,872	1,406	1,062	664	440	269	161	192	3.06
French........	2,111	215	527	387	330	219	164	106	70	93	3.31
English........	4,691	521	1,345	1,019	732	445	276	163	91	99	2.97
Minnesota.......	11,326	1,219	3,080	2,319	1,815	1,169	747	399	247	331	3.09
French........	3,039	307	764	574	454	328	235	137	99	141	3.28
English........	8,287	912	2,316	1,745	1,361	841	512	262	148	190	3.02
Iowa...........	2,925	375	1,037	628	376	234	134	65	33	43	2.58
French........	287	44	83	63	42	20	14	11	5	5	2.76
English........	2,638	331	954	565	334	214	120	54	28	38	2.56
Missouri........	2,281	250	791	513	357	173	99	53	23	22	2.69
French........	253	30	83	54	43	15	12	11	3	2	2.75
English........	2,028	220	708	459	314	158	87	42	20	20	2.69
North Dakota.....	5,366	605	1,147	1,039	802	582	416	308	186	281	3.40
French........	655	73	120	105	89	79	51	39	24	75	3.83
English........	4,711	532	1,027	934	713	503	365	269	162	206	3.35

TABLE **118**. WHITE CANADIAN FAMILIES, FRENCH AND ENGLISH, BY SIZE, FOR 29 SELECTED STATES: 1930—Continued

STATE AND CLASS	Total	FAMILIES COMPRISING—									Median size of family
		1 person	2 persons	3 persons	4 persons	5 persons	6 persons	7 persons	8 persons	9 or more	
South Dakota.....	1,544	218	479	301	211	149	79	48	31	28	2.75
French...........	249	34	63	36	36	33	22	8	6	11	3.26
English..........	1,295	184	416	265	175	116	57	40	25	17	2.68
Nebraska.........	1,941	275	625	377	256	187	100	56	29	36	2.69
French...........	199	27	60	38	28	17	9	9	3	8	2.83
English..........	1,742	248	565	339	228	170	91	47	26	28	2.67
Kansas...........	1,857	297	643	386	217	129	81	45	26	33	2.48
French...........	285	47	105	42	26	23	13	14	4	11	2.41
English..........	1,572	250	538	344	191	106	68	31	22	22	2.50
Florida...........	3,079	551	1,135	620	343	209	118	52	20	31	2.37
French...........	388	74	131	74	38	34	16	11	5	5	2.42
English..........	2,691	477	1,004	546	305	175	102	41	15	26	2.37
Texas............	1,810	189	554	405	311	179	90	40	22	20	2.90
French...........	180	28	59	33	22	19	7	4	2	6	2.59
English..........	1,630	161	495	372	289	160	83	36	20	14	2.93
Montana.........	4,456	847	1,121	811	621	420	272	152	89	123	2.82
French...........	901	198	215	154	109	89	50	34	21	31	2.74
English..........	3,555	649	906	657	512	331	222	118	68	92	2.84
Idaho............	1,853	336	496	362	264	185	85	66	31	28	2.76
French...........	275	59	67	53	42	25	11	6	7	5	2.72
English..........	1,578	277	429	309	222	160	74	60	24	23	2.77
Colorado.........	2,634	445	859	540	372	203	103	55	37	20	2.52
French...........	270	55	74	53	30	25	15	9	6	3	2.61
English..........	2,364	390	785	487	342	178	88	46	31	17	2.51
Washington......	16,709	2,222	5,096	3,629	2,663	1,463	856	381	199	200	2.79
French...........	1,731	238	491	333	270	153	95	62	41	48	2.91
English..........	14,978	1,984	4,605	3,296	2,393	1,310	761	319	158	152	2.77
Oregon...........	6,295	877	1,997	1,375	973	533	270	149	60	61	2.70
French...........	555	92	166	119	87	48	20	7	8	8	2.66
English..........	5,740	785	1,831	1,256	886	485	250	142	52	53	2.70
California........	35,981	5,969	12,352	7,923	5,142	2,555	1,159	478	201	202	2.47
French...........	2,963	534	932	636	403	225	117	56	26	34	2.52
English..........	33,018	5,435	11,420	7,287	4,739	2,330	1,042	422	175	168	2.47

Table 121 shows that there was only a slight variation among the States in the number of lodgers per family. In the majority of the States there was a greater proportion of families with no lodgers among the French Canadian families than among the English Canadian. The extremes among the French Canadian families in this respect were found in South Dakota, where 16.5 per cent of the families had one or more lodgers (probably in many cases hired farm hands), and in Rhode Island, where only 8.1 per cent of the families had lodgers. Among the English Canadian families the extremes were found in North Dakota, where 20.3 per cent had one or more lodgers, and in Washington, where only 9.2 per cent had lodgers.

In many cases there are definite relationships between the dominance of urban or rural area in the population of a State and its showing in respect to one or another of the various classifications of Canadian families presented in the preceding paragraphs, and likewise fairly consistent relationships with the dominant industries of the several States—especially as between agriculture, on the one hand, and manufacturing, on the other.

TABLE **119**. WHITE CANADIAN FAMILIES, FRENCH AND ENGLISH, BY NUMBER OF CHILDREN UNDER 10 YEARS OLD, FOR 29 SELECTED STATES: 1930

STATE AND CLASS	Total	FAMILIES HAVING SPECIFIED NUMBER OF CHILDREN UNDER 10 YEARS OLD							PER CENT OF ALL FAMILIES HAVING—			
		None	1	2	3	4	5	6 or more	None	1	2	3 or more
United States....	460,731	318,507	70,346	38,542	18,777	8,868	3,906	1,785	69.1	15.3	8.4	7.2
French........	141,118	88,486	22,537	13,787	8,157	4,616	2,355	1,180	62.7	16.0	9.8	11.6
English........	319,613	230,021	47,809	24,755	10,620	4,252	1,551	605	72.0	15.0	7.7	5.3
Maine..........	27,271	15,917	4,582	2,900	1,843	1,118	587	324	58.4	16.8	10.6	14.2
French..........	13,545	7,405	2,283	1,505	1,039	693	395	225	54.7	16.9	11.1	17.4
English........	13,726	8,512	2,299	1,395	804	425	192	99	62.0	16.7	10.2	11.1
New Hampshire....	19,864	12,619	3,126	1,826	1,119	663	330	181	63.5	15.7	9.2	11.5
French..........	14,795	9,018	2,353	1,459	951	557	294	163	61.0	15.9	9.9	13.3
English........	5,069	3,601	773	367	168	106	36	18	71.0	15.2	7.2	6.5
Vermont.........	9,209	5,385	1,500	984	630	370	217	123	58.5	16.3	10.7	14.6
French..........	5,599	2,915	959	671	458	310	182	104	52.1	17.1	12.0	18.8
English........	3,610	2,470	541	313	172	60	35	19	68.4	15.0	8.7	7.9
Massachusetts.....	103,097	68,200	16,092	9,415	5,039	2,594	1,175	582	66.2	15.6	9.1	9.1
French..........	45,394	28,309	7,275	4,462	2,634	1,524	781	409	62.4	16.0	9.8	11.8
English.........	57,703	39,891	8,817	4,953	2,405	1,070	394	173	69.1	15.3	8.6	7.0
Rhode Island.......	14,833	9,619	2,306	1,422	771	418	211	86	64.8	15.5	9.6	10.0
French..........	12,161	7,655	1,949	1,201	689	384	198	85	62.9	16.0	9.9	11.2
English.........	2,672	1,964	357	221	82	34	13	1	73.5	13.4	8.3	4.9
Connecticut.......	13,054	7,921	2,356	1,425	748	383	160	61	60.7	18.0	10.9	10.4
French..........	8,913	5,221	1,602	1,027	564	315	129	55	58.6	18.0	11.5	11.9
English.........	4,141	2,700	754	398	184	68	31	6	65.2	18.2	9.6	7.0
New York........	47,261	32,911	7,498	3,909	1,758	764	308	113	69.6	15.9	8.3	6.2
French..........	9,479	5,970	1,589	959	514	262	133	52	63.0	16.8	10.1	10.1
English.........	37,782	26,941	5,909	2,950	1,244	502	175	61	71.3	15.6	7.8	5.2
New Jersey........	5,186	3,545	939	437	182	56	16	11	68.4	18.1	8.4	5.1
French..........	789	498	152	74	44	15	3	3	63.1	19.3	9.4	8.2
English.........	4,397	3,047	787	363	138	41	13	8	69.3	17.9	8.3	4.5
Pennsylvania......	5,536	3,899	890	426	197	88	26	10	70.4	16.1	7.7	5.8
French..........	642	440	112	52	20	10	7	1	68.5	17.4	8.1	5.9
English.........	4,894	3,459	778	374	177	78	19	9	70.7	15.9	7.6	5.8
Ohio............	9,604	6,977	1,482	734	298	76	28	9	72.6	15.4	7.6	4.3
French..........	999	725	136	80	38	11	7	2	72.6	13.6	8.0	5.8
English.........	8,605	6,252	1,346	654	260	65	21	7	72.7	15.6	7.6	4.1
Indiana.........	2,267	1,622	346	182	73	32	10	2	71.5	15.3	8.0	5.2
French..........	275	206	35	16	12	3	2	1	74.9	12.7	5.8	6.5
English.........	1,992	1,416	311	166	61	29	8	1	71.1	15.6	8.3	5.0
Illinois.........	15,613	11,842	2,195	1,041	384	101	38	12	75.8	14.1	6.7	3.4
French..........	2,362	1,769	314	165	73	28	10	3	74.9	13.3	7.0	4.8
English.........	13,251	10,073	1,881	876	311	73	28	9	76.0	14.2	6.6	3.2
Michigan.........	72,637	49,026	12,114	6,577	3,069	1,244	462	145	67.5	16.7	9.1	6.8
French..........	10,795	6,777	1,800	1,103	646	295	136	38	62.8	16.7	10.2	10.3
English.........	61,842	42,249	10,314	5,474	2,423	949	326	107	68.3	16.7	8.9	6.2
Wisconsin........	6,802	5,207	839	435	205	69	38	9	76.6	12.3	6.4	4.7
French..........	2,111	1,619	254	125	74	27	7	5	76.6	12.0	5.9	5.4
English.........	4,691	3,588	585	310	131	42	31	4	76.5	12.5	6.6	4.4
Minnesota........	11,326	8,694	1,373	714	325	148	54	18	76.8	12.1	6.3	4.8
French..........	3,039	2,302	363	195	90	56	26	7	75.7	11.9	6.4	5.9
English.........	8,287	6,392	1,010	519	235	92	28	11	77.1	12.2	6.3	4.4
Iowa............	2,925	2,460	271	121	45	19	8	1	84.1	9.3	4.1	2.5
French..........	287	234	36	10	3	2	2	..	81.5	12.5	3.5	2.4
English.........	2,638	2,226	235	111	42	17	6	1	84.4	8.9	4.2	2.5
Missouri.........	2,281	1,841	250	123	41	21	3	2	80.7	11.0	5.4	2.9
French..........	253	196	29	18	4	6	..	..	77.5	11.5	7.1	4.0
English.........	2,028	1,645	221	105	37	15	3	2	81.1	10.9	5.2	2.8
North Dakota......	5,366	3,839	726	411	210	105	50	25	71.5	13.5	7.7	7.3
French..........	655	440	93	40	35	23	10	14	67.2	14.2	6.1	12.5
English.........	4,711	3,399	633	371	175	82	40	11	72.2	13.4	7.9	6.5
South Dakota......	1,544	1,252	167	62	39	15	8	1	81.1	10.8	4.0	4.1
French..........	249	183	35	12	10	7	1	1	73.5	14.1	4.8	7.6
English.........	1,295	1,069	132	50	29	8	7	..	82.5	10.2	3.9	3.4
Nebraska.........	1,941	1,601	190	97	33	14	2	4	82.5	9.8	5.0	2.7
French..........	199	164	18	11	4	1	..	1	82.4	9.0	5.5	3.0
English.........	1,742	1,437	172	86	29	13	2	3	82.5	9.9	4.9	2.7

TABLE **119**. WHITE CANADIAN FAMILIES, FRENCH AND ENGLISH, BY NUMBER OF CHILDREN UNDER 10 YEARS OLD, FOR 29 SELECTED STATES: 1930—Continued

STATE AND CLASS	Total	FAMILIES HAVING SPECIFIED NUMBER OF CHILDREN UNDER 10 YEARS OLD							PER CENT OF ALL FAMILIES HAVING—			
		None	1	2	3	4	5	6 or more	None	1	2	3 or more
Kansas	**1,857**	**1,571**	**168**	**57**	**32**	**18**	**9**	**2**	**84.6**	**9.0**	**3.1**	**3.3**
French	285	231	24	15	9	4	2	..	81.1	8.4	5.3	5.3
English	1,572	1,340	144	42	23	14	7	2	85.2	9.2	2.7	2.9
Florida	**3,079**	**2,418**	**383**	**178**	**66**	**28**	**4**	**2**	**78.5**	**12.4**	**5.8**	**3.2**
French	388	291	56	18	16	4	3	..	75.0	14.4	4.6	5.9
English	2,691	2,127	327	160	50	24	1	2	79.0	12.2	5.9	2.9
Texas	**1,810**	**1,344**	**277**	**129**	**46**	**9**	**3**	..	**74.3**	**15.3**	**7.1**	**3.3**
French	180	121	29	19	10	..	..	1	67.2	16.1	10.6	6.1
English	1,630	1,223	248	110	36	9	3	1	75.0	15.2	6.7	3.0
Montana	**4,456**	**3,271**	**639**	**306**	**145**	**66**	**20**	**9**	**73.4**	**14.3**	**6.9**	**5.4**
French	901	672	126	57	29	14	2	1	74.6	14.0	6.3	5.1
English	3,555	2,599	513	249	116	52	18	8	73.1	14.4	7.0	5.5
Idaho	**1,853**	**1,379**	**257**	**122**	**63**	**19**	**10**	**3**	**74.4**	**13.9**	**6.6**	**5.1**
French	275	214	36	14	7	2	2	..	77.8	13.1	5.1	4.0
English	1,578	1,165	221	108	56	17	8	3	73.8	14.0	6.8	5.3
Colorado	**2,634**	**2,172**	**259**	**139**	**45**	**14**	**4**	**1**	**82.5**	**9.8**	**5.3**	**2.4**
French	270	218	20	17	12	2	1	..	80.7	7.4	6.3	5.6
English	2,364	1,954	239	122	33	12	3	1	82.7	10.1	5.2	2.1
Washington	**16,709**	**12,363**	**2,482**	**1,236**	**432**	**128**	**50**	**18**	**74.0**	**14.9**	**7.4**	**3.8**
French	1,731	1,255	247	137	59	22	9	2	72.5	14.3	7.9	5.3
English	14,978	11,108	2,235	1,099	373	106	41	16	74.2	14.9	7.3	3.6
Oregon	**6,295**	**4,813**	**827**	**455**	**128**	**46**	**18**	**8**	**76.5**	**13.1**	**7.2**	**3.2**
French	555	417	79	37	14	5	1	2	75.1	14.2	6.7	4.0
English	5,740	4,396	748	418	114	41	17	6	76.6	13.0	7.3	3.1
California	**35,981**	**28,611**	**4,562**	**2,042**	**566**	**155**	**32**	**13**	**79.5**	**12.7**	**5.7**	**2.1**
French	2,963	2,295	385	190	63	21	6	3	77.5	13.0	6.4	3.1
English	33,018	26,316	4,177	1,852	503	134	26	10	79.7	12.7	5.6	2.0

TABLE **120**. White Canadian Families, French and English, by Number of Gainful Workers, for 29 Selected States: 1930

STATE AND CLASS	Total	FAMILIES HAVING SPECIFIED NUMBER OF GAINFUL WORKERS					PER CENT OF ALL FAMILIES HAVING—				
		None	1	2	3	4 or more	None	1	2	3	4 or more
United States...	460,731	36,764	256,078	103,168	40,248	24,473	8.0	55.6	22.4	8.7	5.3
French	141,118	8,187	67,172	33,987	17,375	14,397	5.8	47.6	24.1	12.3	10.2
English	319,613	28,577	188,906	69,181	22,873	10,076	8.9	59.1	21.6	7.2	3.2
Maine	27,271	1,376	14,467	6,541	2,911	1,976	5.0	53.0	24.0	10.7	7.2
French	13,545	539	6,269	3,397	1,829	1,511	4.0	46.3	25.1	13.5	11.2
English	13,726	837	8,198	3,144	1,082	465	6.1	59.7	22.9	7.9	3.4
New Hampshire...	19,864	1,125	9,747	4,815	2,266	1,911	5.7	49.1	24.2	11.4	9.6
French	14,795	683	6,795	3,672	1,875	1,770	4.6	45.9	24.8	12.7	12.0
English	5,069	442	2,952	1,143	391	141	8.7	58.2	22.5	7.7	2.8
Vermont	9,209	594	5,394	2,009	776	436	6.5	58.6	21.8	8.4	4.7
French	5,599	290	3,121	1,275	552	361	5.2	55.7	22.8	9.9	6.4
English	3,610	304	2,273	734	224	75	8.4	63.0	20.3	6.2	2.1
Massachusetts....	103,097	5,728	50,823	25,263	12,232	9,051	5.6	49.3	24.5	11.9	8.8
French	45,394	2,162	19,643	11,457	6,402	5,730	4.8	43.3	25.2	14.1	12.6
English	57,703	3,566	31,180	13,806	5,830	3,321	6.2	54.0	23.9	10.1	5.8
Rhode Island.....	14,833	707	6,302	3,689	2,161	1,974	4.8	42.5	24.9	14.6	13.3
French	12,161	523	4,875	3,040	1,887	1,836	4.3	40.1	25.0	15.5	15.1
English	2,672	184	1,427	649	274	138	6.9	53.4	24.3	10.3	5.2
Connecticut......	13,054	537	6,483	3,137	1,597	1,300	4.1	49.7	24.0	12.2	10.0
French	8,913	302	4,027	2,213	1,230	1,141	3.4	45.2	24.8	13.8	12.8
English	4,141	235	2,456	924	367	159	5.7	59.3	22.3	8.9	3.8
New York........	47,261	3,089	28,079	10,590	3,659	1,844	6.5	59.4	22.4	7.7	3.9
French	9,479	512	5,303	2,144	882	638	5.4	55.9	22.6	9.3	6.7
English	37,782	2,577	22,776	8,446	2,777	1,206	6.8	60.3	22.4	7.4	3.2
New Jersey.......	5,186	285	3,156	1,078	446	221	5.5	60.9	20.8	8.6	4.3
French	789	28	450	169	91	51	3.5	57.0	21.4	11.5	6.5
English	4,397	257	2,706	909	355	170	5.8	61.5	20.7	8.1	3.9
Pennsylvania.....	5,536	417	3,397	1,146	400	176	7.5	61.4	20.7	7.2	3.2
French	642	41	377	138	58	28	6.4	58.7	21.5	9.0	4.4
English	4,894	376	3,020	1,008	342	148	7.7	61.7	20.6	7.0	3.0
Ohio............	9,604	678	6,016	2,070	596	244	7.1	62.6	21.6	6.2	2.5
French	999	89	592	214	74	30	8.9	59.3	21.4	7.4	3.0
English	8,605	589	5,424	1,856	522	214	6.8	63.0	21.6	6.1	2.5
Indiana.........	2,267	201	1,430	453	131	52	8.9	63.1	20.0	5.8	2.3
French	275	33	156	56	21	9	12.0	56.7	20.4	7.6	3.3
English	1,992	168	1,274	397	110	43	8.4	64.0	19.9	5.5	2.2
Illinois.........	15,613	1,262	9,103	3,499	1,195	554	8.1	58.3	22.4	7.7	3.5
French	2,362	220	1,215	564	223	140	9.3	51.4	23.9	9.4	5.9
English	13,251	1,042	7,888	2,935	972	414	7.9	59.5	22.1	7.3	3.1
Michigan........	72,637	5,980	43,115	16,198	5,210	2,134	8.2	59.4	22.3	7.2	2.9
French	10,795	862	5,823	2,483	1,078	549	8.0	53.9	23.0	10.0	5.1
English	61,842	5,118	37,292	13,715	4,132	1,585	8.3	60.3	22.2	6.7	2.6
Wisconsin........	6,802	873	3,625	1,479	557	268	12.8	53.3	21.7	8.2	3.9
French	2,111	275	1,016	476	217	127	13.0	48.1	22.5	10.3	6.0
English	4,691	598	2,609	1,003	340	141	12.7	55.6	21.4	7.2	3.0
Minnesota........	11,326	1,350	6,068	2,442	1,046	420	11.9	53.6	21.6	9.2	3.7
French	3,039	400	1,421	704	330	184	13.2	46.8	23.2	10.9	6.1
English	8,287	950	4,647	1,738	716	236	11.5	56.1	21.0	8.6	2.8
Iowa............	2,925	693	1,469	514	171	78	23.7	50.2	17.6	5.8	2.7
French	287	63	133	60	22	9	22.0	46.3	20.9	7.7	3.1
English	2,638	630	1,336	454	149	69	23.9	50.6	17.2	5.6	2.6
Missouri.........	2,281	235	1,397	452	144	53	10.3	61.2	19.8	6.3	2.3
French	253	22	155	58	13	5	8.7	61.3	22.9	5.1	2.0
English	2,028	213	1,242	394	131	48	10.5	61.2	19.4	6.5	2.4
North Dakota.....	5,366	577	2,898	1,171	490	230	10.8	54.0	21.8	9.1	4.3
French	655	55	342	133	84	41	8.4	52.2	20.3	12.8	6.3
English	4,711	522	2,556	1,038	406	189	11.1	54.3	22.0	8.6	4.0

TABLE **120**. WHITE CANADIAN FAMILIES, FRENCH AND ENGLISH, BY NUMBER OF
GAINFUL WORKERS, FOR 29 SELECTED STATES: 1930—Continued

STATE AND CLASS	Total	FAMILIES HAVING SPECIFIED NUMBER OF GAINFUL WORKERS					PER CENT OF ALL FAMILIES HAVING—				
		None	1	2	3	4 or more	None	1	2	3	4 or more
South Dakota.....	1,544	267	854	288	96	39	17.3	55.3	18.7	6.2	2.5
French..........	249	47	132	50	13	7	18.9	53.0	20.1	5.2	2.8
English.........	1,295	220	722	238	83	32	17.0	55.8	18.4	6.4	2.5
Nebraska.........	1,941	399	988	365	136	53	20.6	50.9	18.8	7.0	2.7
French..........	199	43	95	38	15	8	21.6	47.7	19.1	7.5	4.0
English.........	1,742	356	893	327	121	45	20.4	51.3	18.8	6.9	2.6
Kansas...........	1,857	400	989	327	93	48	21.5	53.3	17.6	5.0	2.6
French..........	285	75	135	56	11	8	26.3	47.4	19.6	3.9	2.8
English.........	1,572	325	854	271	82	40	20.7	54.3	17.2	5.2	2.5
Florida..........	3,079	677	1,819	449	103	31	22.0	59.1	14.6	3.3	1.0
French..........	388	71	236	55	22	4	18.3	60.8	14.2	5.7	1.0
English.........	2,691	606	1,583	394	81	27	22.5	58.8	14.6	3.0	1.0
Texas............	1,810	161	1,157	345	103	44	8.9	63.9	19.1	5.7	2.4
French..........	180	17	121	31	7	4	9.4	67.2	17.2	3.9	2.2
English.........	1,630	144	1,036	314	96	40	8.8	63.6	19.3	5.9	2.5
Montana.........	4,456	382	2,886	823	246	119	8.6	64.8	18.5	5.5	2.7
French..........	901	89	561	166	49	36	9.9	62.3	18.4	5.4	4.0
English.........	3,555	293	2,325	657	197	83	8.2	65.4	18.5	5.5	2.3
Idaho............	1,853	160	1,232	353	75	33	8.6	66.5	19.1	4.0	1.8
French..........	275	29	177	49	15	5	10.5	64.4	17.8	5.5	1.8
English.........	1,578	131	1,055	304	60	28	8.3	66.9	19.3	3.8	1.8
Colorado.........	2,634	363	1,568	511	142	50	13.8	59.5	19.4	5.4	1.9
French..........	270	42	161	52	10	5	15.6	59.6	19.3	3.7	1.9
English.........	2,364	321	1,407	459	132	45	13.6	59.5	19.4	5.6	1.9
Washington......	16,709	1,507	10,661	3,327	890	324	9.0	63.8	19.9	5.3	1.9
French..........	1,731	161	1,032	363	112	63	9.3	59.6	21.0	6.5	3.6
English.........	14,978	1,346	9,629	2,964	778	261	9.0	64.3	19.8	5.2	1.7
Oregon...........	6,295	608	3,878	1,344	342	123	9.7	61.6	21.4	5.4	2.0
French..........	555	62	341	109	29	14	11.2	61.4	19.6	5.2	2.5
English.........	5,740	546	3,537	1,235	313	109	9.5	61.6	21.5	5.5	1.9
California........	35,981	5,303	21,640	6,932	1,588	518	14.7	60.1	19.3	4.4	1.4
French..........	2,963	361	1,802	582	160	58	12.2	60.8	19.6	5.4	2.0
English.........	33,018	4,942	19,838	6,350	1,428	460	15.0	60.1	19.2	4.3	1.4

TABLE **121**. WHITE CANADIAN FAMILIES, FRENCH AND ENGLISH, BY NUMBER OF LODGERS, FOR 29 SELECTED STATES: 1930

(For total number of families, French and English, in each State, see Table 120)

STATE	CANADIAN FAMILIES HAVING SPECIFIED NUMBER OF LODGERS				FRENCH CANADIAN FAMILIES HAVING SPECIFIED NUMBER OF LODGERS				ENGLISH CANADIAN FAMILIES HAVING SPECIFIED NUMBER OF LODGERS			
	None	1	2	3 or more	None	1	2	3 or more	None	1	2	3 or more
United States..	403,828	35,345	11,209	10,349	126,035	9,536	2,952	2,595	277,793	25,809	8,257	7,754
Maine............	24,229	1,996	564	482	12,182	900	248	215	12,047	1,096	316	267
New Hampshire....	17,804	1,360	377	323	13,372	923	275	225	4,432	437	102	98
Vermont..........	7,950	882	212	165	4,851	533	131	84	3,099	349	81	81
Massachusetts.....	90,271	7,753	2,480	2,593	41,166	2,730	832	666	49,105	5,023	1,648	1,927
Rhode Island......	13,538	831	223	241	11,174	639	173	175	2,364	192	50	66
Connecticut.......	11,391	1,001	338	324	7,745	690	250	228	3,646	311	88	96
New York.........	40,886	3,882	1,272	1,221	8,265	732	243	239	32,621	3,150	1,029	982
New Jersey........	4,590	357	125	114	678	62	27	22	3,912	295	98	92
Pennsylvania......	4,920	373	136	107	556	39	28	19	4,364	334	108	88
Ohio.............	8,503	675	239	187	882	69	26	22	7,621	606	213	165
Indiana...........	2,012	158	51	46	251	15	4	5	1,761	143	47	41
Illinois...........	13,502	1,263	446	402	2,044	184	66	68	11,458	1,079	380	334
Michigan.........	61,983	6,398	2,325	1,931	9,155	960	353	327	52,828	5,438	1,972	1,604
Wisconsin.........	6,020	499	152	131	1,894	144	35	38	4,126	355	117	93
Minnesota........	9,945	846	284	251	2,735	191	49	64	7,210	655	235	187
Iowa.............	2,611	206	56	52	253	26	5	3	2,358	180	51	49
Missouri..........	2,052	136	52	41	227	10	11	5	1,825	126	41	36
North Dakota.....	4,316	715	187	148	560	63	18	14	3,756	652	169	134
South Dakota......	1,288	162	57	37	208	27	6	8	1,080	135	51	29
Nebraska.........	1,718	133	44	46	179	10	4	6	1,539	123	40	40
Kansas...........	1,666	133	32	26	256	19	4	6	1,410	114	28	20
Florida...........	2,792	199	42	46	351	26	5	6	2,441	173	37	40
Texas............	1,610	112	40	48	155	17	4	4	1,455	95	36	44
Montana..........	3,848	381	111	116	780	78	24	19	3,068	303	87	97
Idaho............	1,635	145	34	39	242	23	6	4	1,393	122	28	35
Colorado..........	2,386	146	51	51	245	13	6	6	2,141	133	45	45
Washington.......	15,177	1,003	254	275	1,577	106	25	23	13,600	897	229	252
Oregon...........	5,715	376	113	91	506	27	13	9	5,209	349	100	82
California........	32,010	2,650	701	620	2,634	216	53	60	29,376	2,434	648	560
Per cent of total												
United States..	87.6	7.7	2.4	2.2	89.3	6.8	2.1	1.8	86.9	8.1	2.6	2.4
Maine............	88.8	7.3	2.1	1.8	89.9	6.6	1.8	1.6	87.8	8.0	2.3	1.9
New Hampshire....	89.6	6.8	1.9	1.6	90.4	6.2	1.9	1.5	87.4	8.6	2.0	1.9
Vermont..........	86.3	9.6	2.3	1.8	86.6	9.5	2.3	1.5	85.8	9.7	2.2	2.2
Massachusetts.....	87.6	7.5	2.4	2.5	90.7	6.0	1.8	1.5	85.1	8.7	2.9	3.3
Rhode Island......	91.3	5.6	1.5	1.6	91.9	5.3	1.4	1.4	88.5	7.2	1.9	2.5
Connecticut.......	87.3	7.7	2.6	2.5	86.9	7.7	2.8	2.6	88.0	7.5	2.1	2.3
New York.........	86.5	8.2	2.7	2.6	87.2	7.7	2.6	2.5	86.3	8.3	2.7	2.6
New Jersey........	88.5	6.9	2.4	2.2	85.9	7.9	3.4	2.8	89.0	6.7	2.2	2.1
Pennsylvania......	88.9	6.7	2.5	1.9	86.6	6.1	4.4	3.0	89.2	6.8	2.2	1.8
Ohio.............	88.5	7.0	2.5	1.9	88.3	6.9	2.6	2.2	88.6	7.0	2.5	1.9
Indiana...........	88.8	7.0	2.2	2.0	91.3	5.5	1.5	1.8	88.4	7.2	2.4	2.1
Illinois...........	86.5	8.1	2.9	2.6	86.5	7.8	2.8	2.9	86.5	8.1	2.9	2.5
Michigan.........	85.3	8.8	3.2	2.7	84.8	8.9	3.3	3.0	85.4	8.8	3.2	2.6
Wisconsin.........	88.5	7.3	2.2	1.9	89.7	6.8	1.7	1.8	88.0	7.6	2.5	2.0
Minnesota........	87.8	7.5	2.5	2.2	90.0	6.3	1.6	2.1	87.0	7.9	2.8	2.3
Iowa.............	89.3	7.0	1.9	1.8	88.2	9.1	1.7	1.0	89.4	6.8	1.9	1.9
Missouri..........	90.0	6.0	2.3	1.8	89.7	4.0	4.3	2.0	90.0	6.2	2.0	1.8
North Dakota.....	80.4	13.3	3.5	2.8	85.5	9.6	2.7	2.1	79.7	13.8	3.6	2.8
South Dakota......	83.4	10.5	3.7	2.4	83.5	10.8	2.4	3.2	83.4	10.4	3.9	2.2
Nebraska.........	88.5	6.9	2.3	2.4	89.9	5.0	2.0	3.0	88.3	7.1	2.3	2.3
Kansas...........	89.7	7.2	1.7	1.4	89.8	6.7	1.4	2.1	89.7	7.3	1.8	1.3
Florida...........	90.7	6.5	1.4	1.5	90.5	6.7	1.3	1.5	90.7	6.4	1.4	1.5
Texas............	89.0	6.2	2.2	2.7	86.1	9.4	2.2	2.2	89.3	5.8	2.2	2.7
Montana..........	86.4	8.6	2.5	2.6	86.6	8.7	2.7	2.1	86.3	8.5	2.4	2.7
Idaho............	88.2	7.8	1.8	2.1	88.0	8.4	2.2	1.5	88.3	7.7	1.8	2.2
Colorado..........	90.6	5.5	1.9	1.9	90.7	4.8	2.2	2.2	90.6	5.6	1.9	1.9
Washington.......	90.8	6.0	1.5	1.6	91.1	6.1	1.4	1.3	90.8	6.0	1.5	1.7
Oregon...........	90.8	6.0	1.8	1.4	91.2	4.9	2.3	1.6	90.7	6.1	1.7	1.4
California........	89.0	7.4	1.9	1.7	88.9	7.3	1.8	2.0	89.0	7.4	2.0	1.7

APPENDIX

UNITED STATES CENSUS STATISTICS ON POPULATION OF CANADIAN BIRTH OR PARENTAGE IN THE UNITED STATES: 1850 TO 1930

STATISTICS PUBLISHED IN THE CENSUS REPORTS

THERE are listed below, either by chapter or by table number or page, those sections of the reports of the United States Census Bureau from 1850 to 1930 which contain statistics for persons of Canadian birth or parentage. In the reports of the censuses for 1930 back to 1890, figures are presented both for the Canadian born and, to some extent, for persons born in the United States of Canadian parentage. For the censuses prior to 1890, the data are limited to the Canadian born.

The references are in all cases to tables giving population by country of birth or country of birth of parents, in which persons of Canadian origin appear as one of a considerable number of categories.

1930—POPULATION, VOLUME II (figures given in general for the United States, urban and rural areas, States, and the larger cities):

Chapter 5. Country of birth of the foreign born.

Chapter 6. Country of origin of the foreign white stock.

Chapter 7. Mother tongue of the foreign-born white population.

Chapter 8. Citizenship of the foreign born: Data by country of birth— Tables 2, 5, 6, 8, 9, 16, 17, 20, 23, 24, and 25.

Chapter 9. Year of immigration of the foreign born: Data by country of birth—Tables 2, 7, 8, 9, 14, 15, 18, and 19.

Chapter 10. Age distribution: Data by country of birth—Tables 40–43.

Chapter 11. Marital condition: Data by country of birth—Tables 31– 34.

Chapter 13. Illiteracy: Data by country of birth—Tables 26–31.

Chapter 14. Inability to speak English: Data by country of birth— Tables 2, 6, 7, 8, 14, 15, 16, and 18.

1930—POPULATION, VOLUME III:

United States Summary:

Tables 14, 27, 52, and 67. Foreign-born white, by country of birth, for the United States, States, and cities of 100,000 or more.

Tables 26, 28, and 29. Foreign white stock, by country of origin, for the United States and for urban and rural areas.

Tables 53 and 68. Native white population of foreign or mixed parentage, by country of birth of parents, for States and for cities of 100,000 or more.

State sections:

Table 9. Foreign white stock by country of origin, for the State and urban and rural areas.

Table 18. Foreign-born white by country of birth, for counties and for cities of 10,000 or more.

Table 19. Native white of foreign or mixed parentage, by country of birth of parents, for counties and for cities of 10,000 or more.

1930—SPECIAL REPORTS:

Age of the foreign-born white population by country of birth.

Foreign-born white families by country of birth of head.

1930—ABSTRACT OF THE FIFTEENTH CENSUS—POPULATION (figures given in general for the United States, urban and rural areas, States, and the larger cities):

Country of birth—Tables 59–64.

Country of origin—Tables 65–71.

Mother tongue of the foreign-born white population—Tables 72–76.

Citizenship of the foreign born—Tables 78 and 79.

Year of immigration of the foreign born—Tables 89–91.

Age distribution of the foreign-born white, by country of birth—Tables 105 and 106.

Illiteracy in the foreign-born white population, by country of birth, for the United States—Table 141.

Inability to speak English in the foreign-born white population, by literacy and country of birth, for the United States—Table 149.

1920—POPULATION, VOLUME II (figures given in general for the United States, urban and rural areas, States, and the larger cities):

Chapter VI. Country of birth of the foreign-born population.

Chapter VIII. Citizenship of the foreign-born population: Data by country of birth—Tables 3, 4, 8, 9, 10, 14, 15, 16, and 19.

Chapter IX. Country of origin of the foreign white stock.

Chapter X. Mother tongue of the foreign white stock.

1920—POPULATION, VOLUME III:

Summary tables:

Tables 6, 12, and 13. Country of birth of the foreign-born white, by States and for cities of 100,000 or more.

State sections (under each State):

Table 12. Country of birth of the foreign-born white, by counties and for cities of 100,000 or more.

1920—IMMIGRANTS AND THEIR CHILDREN (Monograph VII).

1920—ABSTRACT OF THE FOURTEENTH CENSUS—POPULATION (figures given in general for the United States, urban and rural areas, States, and the larger cities):

Country of birth of the foreign born—Tables 69–77.

Citizenship of the foreign born—Tables 89, 90, and 99.

Country of origin of the foreign white stock—Tables 101–108.

Mother tongue of the foreign white stock—Tables 109–115.

1910—POPULATION, VOLUME I (figures given in general for the United States, urban and rural areas, States, and the larger cities):

Chapter VII. Country of birth of the foreign born.

Chapter VIII. Country of origin of the foreign white stock.

Chapter IX. Mother tongue of the foreign white stock.

Chapter XI. Voting age, militia age, and naturalization: Data by country of birth—Tables 28, 32, 33, 34, and 35.

1910—POPULATION, VOLUMES II AND III, STATE REPORTS:

Tables 5 and 12. Foreign white stock by nationality for the State and for its cities of 100,000 or more.

Tables I, II, and III. Foreign-born white, by country of birth, and native white with both parents foreign born, by country of birth of parents, for counties and for cities of 10,000 or more.

Table V. Foreign-born white, by country of birth, for cities of 50,000 or more, by wards.

1910—ABSTRACT OF THE CENSUS:

Chapter 5. Population of foreign birth and foreign parentage, by country of origin (figures given in general for the United States, urban and rural areas, States, and the larger cities).

1900—POPULATION, PART I:

Tables LXXIX–LXXXIII. Foreign-born population by country of birth, for States and for principal cities.

Tables LXXXVIII and LXXXIX. Persons of foreign parentage by country of birth of parents, by States.

Foreign-born males of voting age and number of aliens, by country of birth, for the United States, page ccxvii.

Males of voting age, of foreign parentage, by country of birth of parents, for the United States, page ccxvii.

Tables 33, 34, and 35. Foreign born, by country of birth, for States, counties, and for cities of 25,000 or more.

Tables 38–56; 59–66. Persons of foreign parentage, by country of birth of parents, for States and for cities of 25,000 or more.

Tables 71 and 83. Foreign-born males 21 years of age and over, by country of birth, for States and for cities of 25,000 or more.

Tables 72 and 84. Alien population (males), by country of birth, for States and for cities of 25,000 or more.

Tables 73 and 85. Total males 21 years of age and over, by parentage, for States and for cities of 25,000 or more.

1900—ABSTRACT OF THE TWELFTH CENSUS:

Table 8. Foreign born, by country of birth: 1850 to 1900, for the United States.

Table 9. Parentage, by country of birth of parents, for the total and native, and foreign-born white, for the United States.

Table 22. Foreign-born males of voting age and aliens by country of birth, for the United States.

Tables 49 and 82. Foreign born by country of birth, for States and for cities of 25,000 or more.

1900—SPECIAL REPORT, OCCUPATIONS:

Tables 22, 23, and 24. Total persons, males and females, by occupation, by country of birth of parents, for the United States.

Tables 38 and 39. Males and females, by general division of occupations, by country of birth of parents, by States.

Tables 41 and 43. Males and females in selected groups of occupations, by country of birth of parents, for States and for cities of 50,000 or more.

1890—POPULATION, PART I:

Country of birth of the foreign born: Text and tables, pp. cxxxiv–cliii.

White persons of foreign parentage: Text and tables, pp. cliv–clxxv.

Tables 32, 33, and 34: Foreign born by country of birth for States, counties, and for cities of 25,000 or more.

Tables 37–49 and 52–62. White persons of foreign parentage, by country of birth of parents, for States and for cities of 25,000 or more.

1890—POPULATION, PART II:

Citizenship of foreign-born males, by country of birth, text and tables, pages lxxii and lxxv.

Tables 73 and 74. Alien population (males), by country of birth, for States and for cities of 25,000 or more.

Table 108. Foreign born, by general division of occupations and country of birth, by States.

Table 109. Foreign born, by occupations and country of birth, for the United States.

Table 110. White population by general division of occupations, by birthplace of mother, by States.

Tables 111, 112, and 113. White population, native and foreign born, in each occupation, by birthplace of mother, for the United States.

Tables 116 and 118. Males and females in selected occupations, by country of birth, for States and for cities of 50,000 or more.

1890—ABSTRACT OF THE ELEVENTH CENSUS:

Table 14. Foreign-born population, by country of birth, by States.

1880—POPULATION, VOLUME I:

Summary of immigration into the United States, by decades, from 1821 to 1850, text pp. 459–472.

Tables XIII, XIV, and XVI. Nativity of the foreign born, by States, counties, and for fifty principal cities.

Persons of foreign parentage, text and summary tables, pp. 674–677.

Table XXVI. Parentage of persons having one or both parents foreign born, by States.

Table XXVII. Population classified by country of birth of father in combination with country of birth of mother, for selected States.

Tables XXX and XXXV. Persons, by general division of occupations, by nativity, by States, and for fifty principal cities.

Table XXXI. Persons in each of 20 selected occupations, by nativity, by States.

Table XXXII. Persons by occupations, by nativity, for the United States.

Tables XXXIV and XXXVI. Persons in 70 selected occupations, by nativity, by States, and for fifty principal cities.

1880—COMPENDIUM OF THE TENTH CENSUS:

Table XXX. Nativity of the foreign-born population, by States.

Table XXXI. Foreign born for selected countries of birth, for counties.

Table XXXIII. Foreign born by country of birth, for fifty principal cities.

Table CVII. Parentage of persons having one or both parents foreign born, for 35 States.

1870—VOLUME I, POPULATION AND SOCIAL STATISTICS:

Tables VI, VII, and VIII. Nativity of the population, by States, counties, and for fifty principal cities.

Tables XXVIII and XXXI. Persons in each class of occupations, for selected nationalities, by States and for fifty principal cities.

Table XXIX. Persons in each occupation, for selected nationalities, for the United States.

Tables XXX and XXXII. Persons in selected occupations, for selected nationalities, by States and for thirty principal cities.

1870—VOLUME III, INDUSTRY AND WEALTH:

Table XIX. Same as Table XXVIII of Volume I.

Table XX. Same as Table XXIX of Volume I.

1860—POPULATION OF THE UNITED STATES:

Immigration—Text tables, pp. XXI and XXII.

Nativity of the population—Text tables, pp. XXVIII, XXIX, XXXI, and XXXII.

Table 5. Nativity of the population, by States.

Nativity of the population for largest cities and for States, pp. 608–615 and 620.

Nativity of defective classes, pp. 628, 636, 644, and 652.

1850—SEVENTH CENSUS OF THE UNITED STATES:
Table XV. Nativity of the population of the United States.
Table LXXI. Nativity of passengers arriving in the United States.

UNPUBLISHED DATA AVAILABLE

MOST of the data for 1920 and 1930 contained in the tables presented in this volume, either for the United States or for States and cities, were tabulated for smaller areas. The count of Canadian-born white persons and of native white persons of Canadian parentage was made for counties and for incorporated places of 2,500 or more (and for 1920 only, for all towns in the New England States). Most of the other data were tabulated in 1930 for cities of 25,000 or more and for the remainder of each State classified as urban, rural-farm, and rural-nonfarm. The 1920 tabulation areas were the same except that the rural area was not subdivided into farm and nonfarm. The 1910 classification of Canadian-born workers by occupation, which is presented for the United States as a whole in Table 101, was made by States. Unpublished figures can be obtained from the Bureau of the Census, Washington, D. C., upon payment of the cost of transcription.

INDEX

Age, of Canadian population, 119; by single years, for 12 States, 120; of components of Canadian stock, 121–124; and sex, 124; and marital status, 166, 173; and illiteracy, 181, 183; and ability to speak English, 195; changes in age distribution of Canadian born, 127, 131; median age, 141, 142, 148

Agriculture, Canadian workers in, 23, 202, 205

American born in Canada, children of Canadian immigrants, 6; proportion to other foreign born, 12, 13

Americanization, *see* Citizenship

Birth rates, use of, for estimates of survival, 99, 100, 133

Border counties, Canadian born concentrated in, 30–32

Border States, concentration of Canadian born in, 25; French and English in, 52; French Canadian stock in, 74; return migration from, 103

British Isles, immigration to Canada from, 13, 15, 45; *see also* England

California, 173, 228, 247

Canadian born: The major part of the entire volume is devoted to the Canadian born in the United States; for specific references, see Contents (p. ix) and list of tables (pp. xii–xvi) or descriptive items in this Index.

Canadian Northwest, opening up of, 15; effect on Canadian immigration, 61; *see also* Prairie Provinces

Canadian parentage: A considerable part of Chapters V, VIII, IX, and X is devoted to native persons in the United States of Canadian parentage; for specific references, see Contents (p. ix) and list of tables (pp. xii–xvi) or descriptive items in this Index.

Canadian stock, definition, 56; elements of, 56, 64; proportions French and English, 59, 63; first and second generations, 63, 65; concentration in certain States, 74, 75; in the principal cities, 86. Data for Canadian stock appear throughout Chapters V, VIII, IX, X; for specific references, see Contents (p. ix) and list of tables (pp. xii–xvi).

Canadian workers, in broad social-economic groups, 200; proportion of skilled workers, 204

Censuses, United States and Canada, 2, 8

Children of Canadians, migration back to Canada, 140

Children under 10, families classified by number of, 241

Cities of the United States, Canadian born in, 1860 to 1930, 34; percentage of Canadian born in, 36; all cities having 1,000 or more Canadian born, 51

Citizenship of Canadian born in the United States, 108; proportion naturalized, 108; lower percentage for French Canadian, 109; naturalization of women, 112; compared with other foreign born, 113; lowest proportions naturalized, in urban areas, 116; variations among States, 117

Color or race of Canadian born, 38

Commerce, early, between Canada and New England, 28

Concentration of Canadian born, in 16 States, 25; in certain counties, 5, 30, 32; in individual cities, 34–36; convenience of access a factor, 25, 30, 74; pioneer settlements in Western States, 28; French element, in border States, 44, 52

Connecticut, 29, 116, 173, 198, 228

Counties, French and English Canadians in, 32, 51; distribution of all Canadian born by, 54

Denmark, 21, 95, 113, 183

Density of Canadian born population, in border States, 30; county maps, 31, 33; in principal cities, 35

Divorce, *see* Marital status

Dominion Bureau of Statistics, 2, 9

Employment, *see* Occupations

England (or British Isles), 15, 20, 21, 183

English, ability to speak, significant only for French Canadian stock, 191; in relation to sex, 192; in relation to nativity, 192; among French in Canada, 192; in Province of Quebec, 192; in relation to literacy, 193; in relation to age, 196

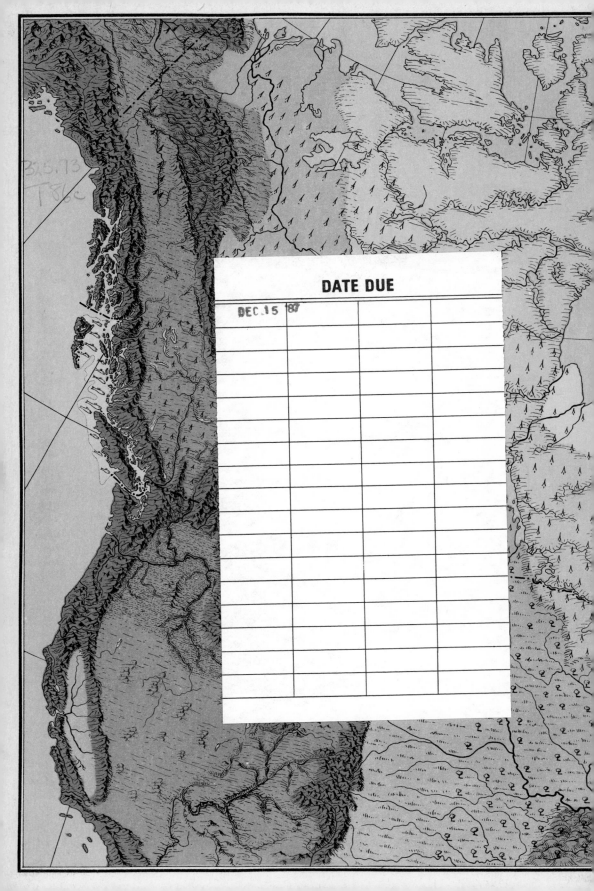